PRINCIPLES OF BEHAVIORAL ANALYSIS

PRINCIPLES

of

BEHAVIORAL ANALYSIS

J. R. Millenson

THE MACMILLAN COMPANY, NEW YORK
COLLIER-MACMILLAN LIMITED, LONDON

Fourth Printing, 1970

Library of Congress catalog card number: 67–15540

THE MACMILLAN COMPANY
866 THIRD AVENUE, NEW YORK, NEW YORK 10022
COLLIER-MACMILLAN CANADA, LTD., TORONTO, ONTARIO

PRINTED IN THE UNITED STATES OF AMERICA

ACKNOWLEDGMENTS

We wish to thank the following for permission to reproduce copyrighted material:

American Association for the Advancement of Science. *Science:* Figure 7–5, from Human vigilance, by J. G. Holland, *128* (1958), pp. 61–67. Figure 13–6, from Concept formation in chimpanzees, by R. Kelleher, *128* (1958), pp. 777–778. Figure 15–2, from Progressive ratio as a measure of reward strength, by W. Hodos, *134* (1961), pp. 943–944. Figures 16–15 and 16–16, from Imprinting, by E. H. Hess, *130* (1959), pp. 133–141. Figure 17–8, from Behavioral method for study of pain in the monkey, by Elliott Weitzman, *133* (1961), pp. 37–38. Copyright 1958, 1959, 1961 by the American Association for the Advancement of Science.

American Institute of Biological Sciences. *Quarterly Review of Biology:* Figure 16–2, from Animal behavior and internal drives, by Curt P. Richter, *2* (1927), p. 321.

American Journal of Psychology: Figure 5–4, from A statistical description of operant conditioning, by F. C. Frick and G. A. Miller, *64* (1951), p. 20. Figure 12–11, from The electrophysiology of mental activities, by Edmund Jacobson, *44* (1932), pp. 682–683. Figure 17–10, from The role of incentive in conditioning and extinction, by W. J. Brogden, E. A. Lipman, and Elmer Culler, *51* (1938), p. 110.

iv

American Orthopsychiatric Association. *American Journal of Orthopsychiatry:* Figures 16–12, 16–13, and 16–14, from Primary affectional patterns in primates, by Harry F. Harlow, *30* (1960), pp. 678, 679, 680.

American Philosophical Society. *Proceedings of the American Philosophical Society:* Figure 11–5, from Will, by R. J. Herrnstein, *108* (1964), p. 455.

American Physiological Society. *Journal of Applied Physiology:* Figure 15–1, from Operant conditioning techniques for studying fasting patterns in normal and obese mice, by J. Anliker and J. Mayer, *8* (1956), p. 669.

American Psychological Association. *American Psychologist:* Figure 10–7, from Pigeons in a pelican, by B. F. Skinner, *15* (1960), p. 35. Figure 14–10, from On the growth of intelligence, by Nancy Bayley, *10* (1955), p. 814. *Journal of Abnormal and Social Psychology:* Figure 5–16 and excerpt on pp. 105–106, entire article, The elimination of tantrum behavior by extinction procedures, by C. D. Williams, *59* (1959), p. 269. *Journal of Comparative and Physiological Psychology:* Figure 5–6, from The effect of effort upon extinction by J. Capehart, W. Viney, and I. M. Hulicka, *51* (1958), p. 506. Figure 8–11, from On the selective reinforcement of spaced responses, by M. P. Wilson and F. S. Keller, *46* (1953), p. 191. Figures 10–1 and 10–2, from Changes in S^D and S^Δ rates during the development of an operant discrimination, by R. M. Herrick, J. L. Myers, and A. L. Korotkin, *52* (1959), pp. 361, 362. Figure 11–2 from Sustained performance in rats based on secondary reinforcement, by D. W. Zimmerman, *52* (1959), p. 356. Figure 15–5, from The relationship between voluntary water intake, body weight loss, and number of hours of water privation in the rat, by P. S. Siegel, *40* (1947), pp. 231–238. Figure 15–12, from Diurnal drinking patterns in the rat, by P. T. Young and H. W. Richey, *45* (1952), p. 84. Figure 17–5c, from The effects of noxious stimulus intensity and duration during intermittent reinforcement of escape behavior, by M. Kaplan, *45* (1952), pp. 545, 547. Figure 17–6 from Training rats to press a bar to turn off shock, by J. A. Dinsmoor and L. H. Hughes, *49* (1956), p. 236. Figure 18–4, from Some effects of electro-convulsive shock on a conditioned emotional response ("anxiety"), by H. F. Hunt and J. V. Brady, *44* (1951), p. 90. Figure 18–7, from Some effects of response-independent positive reinforcement on maintained operant behavior, by R. J. Herrnstein and W. H. Morse, *50* (1957), p. 465. *Journal of Experimental Psychology:* Figure 3–3, from Eyelid conditioning as influenced by the presence of sensitized Beta-responses, by D. A. Grant and E. B. Norris, *37* (1947), p. 425. Figure 5–8, from An effect of repeated conditioning-extinction upon operant strength, by D. H. Bullock and W. C. Smith, *46* (1953), p. 350. Figure 5–18, from Behavior potentiality as a joint function of the amount of training and the degree of hunger at the time of extinction, by C. T. Perin, *30* (1942), p. 101. Figure 9–8, from The pigeon and the spectrum and other complexities, by N. Guttman, *2* (1956), p. 451. Figure 9–10, from Effect of discrimination training on auditory generalization, by H. M. Jenkins and R. H. Harrison, *59* (1960), p. 247. Figure 9–12, from Stimulus generalization after equal training on two stimuli, by H. I. Kalish and N. Guttman, *53* (1957), p. 140. *Psychological Monographs: General and Applied:* Figure 13–4, from Quantitative aspects of the evolution of concepts, by C. L. Hull, *28* (1920), p. 10. *Psychological Review:* Figure 7–9, from Are theories of learning necessary? by B. F. Skinner, *57* (1950), p. 207. Figures 10–5 and 13–1, from The formation of learning sets, by H. F. Harlow, *56* (1949), pp. 52, 53.

American Speech and Hearing Association. *Journal of Speech and Hearing Disorders:* Figure 4–6, from Infant speech: development of vowel sounds, by O. C. Irwin, *13* (1948), p. 32.

Appleton-Century-Crofts, Inc., New York: Figures 4–2, 5–1, 11–1, 12–3, 15–6, and 17–3 from *Behavior of Organisms,* by B. F. Skinner. Copyright 1938 by D. Appleton-Century Company, Inc.; Table on pp. 67–70 from *Cumulative Record,* Enlarged Edition, by B. F. Skinner. Copyright © 1959, 1961 by Appleton-Century-Crofts, Inc.; Figure 1–1, from *Great Experiments in Psychology,* by Henry E. Garrett. Copyright 1941 (Second Edition) by D. Appleton-Century Company, Inc.; Figure 8–2, from *Principles of Behavior,* by C. L. Hull. Copyright 1943 by D. Appleton-Century Company, Inc.; excerpts on pp. 38–39, 51, 228–29, and 251, from *Principles of Psychology,* by Fred S. Keller and William N. Schoenfeld. Copyright 1950, Appleton-Century-Crofts, Inc.; Figures 7–2 and 8–7, from *Schedules of Reinforcement,* by C. B. Ferster and B. F. Skinner. Copyright © 1957 by Appleton-Century-Crofts, Inc.; all reprinted by permission of Appleton-Century-Crofts.

Clarendon Press: Excerpts on pp. 37, 40, and 52–53, from *Conditioned Reflexes* (1927), by I. P. Pavlov. Used by permission of the Clarendon Press, Oxford.

Columbia University Press: Figure 15–11, from C. J. Warden, *Animal Motivation Studies,* 1931.

Harcourt, Brace and World, Inc.: Figure 14–11, from *Educational Psychology,* by L. J. Cronbach, copyright, 1954, © 1962, 1963, by Harcourt, Brace & World, Inc., and reproduced with their permission.

Holt, Rinehart and Winston: Figure 18–3, from *The Startle Pattern,* by C. Landis and W. A. Hunt, copyright 1939 by Carney Landis and William A. Hunt. Used by permission of Holt, Rinehart and Winston, Inc.

Houghton Mifflin Company: Figures 13–18 and 13–20, from J. J. Gibson, *The Perception of the Visual World,* 1950.

International Publishers: Figure 3–1, from p. 271 of *Lectures on Conditioned Reflexes,* I. P. Pavlov. New York: International Publishers, 1928. By permission of International Publishers Co. Inc.

The Jester Humor Magazine: Figure 4–7, from *The Jester.*

Journal of Experimental Analysis of Behavior: Figure 7–3, from Behavior under extended exposure to a high-valued FI reinforcement schedule, by W. W. Cumming and W. N. Schoenfeld, *1* (1958), p. 250. Figure 7–7, from Behavior stability and response rate as functions of reinforcement probability on "random ratio" schedules, by N. A. Sidley and W. N. Schoenfeld, *7* (1964), p. 282. Figure 8–5, from The successive differentiation of a lever displacement response, by R. M. Herrick, *7* (1964), p. 213. Figure 8–8, from Amplitude induction gradient of a small scale (covert) operant, by R. F. Hefferline and B. Keenan, *6* (1963), p. 311. Figure 9–11, from The shape of some wavelength generalization gradients, by D. Blough, *4* (1961), p. 37. Figure 15–4, from Food satiation in the pigeon, by T. W. Reese and M. J. Hogenson, *5* (1962), p. 241. Figure 15–7, from The effect of deprivation and frequency of reinforcement on variable interval responding, by F. C. Clark, *1* (1958), p. 224. Figures 17–4 and 17–5a, from Shock intensity in VI escape schedules, by J. A. Dinsmoor and E. Winograd, *1* (1958), p. 146. Figure 17–12, from Avoidance responding as a function of simultaneous and equal changes in two temporal parameters, by

T. Verhave, *2* (1959), p. 185. Figure 18–5, from Stimulus factors in aversive controls: the generalization of conditioned suppression, by H. S. Hoffman and M. Fleshler, *4* (1961), p. 374. Figure 18–6, from Extinction-induced aggression, by N. H. Azrin, R. R. Hutchinson, and D. F. Hake, *9* (1966), p. 192. Figure 18–10, from Avoidance behavior and the development of gastroduodenal ulcers, by J. V. Brady, R. W. Porter, D. G. Conrad, and J. W. Mason, *1* (1958), pp. 70, 71.

The Journal Press. *Journal of Genetic Psychology:* Figure 3–6, from Conditioning as a function of the interval between the conditioned stimulus and the original stimulus, by H. M. Wolfle, *7* (1932), p. 90. Figure 10–3, from The mechanism of vision XV preliminary studies of the rat's capacity for detail vision, by K. S. Lashley, *18* (1938), p. 126.

McGraw-Hill Book Company, Inc. Figure 12–1, from Jack Michael, *Laboratory Studies in Operant Behavior,* 1963.

The New Yorker: Figure 5–17, from *The New Yorker.*

Oxford University Press: Excerpt on pp. 204–205 from C. E. Osgood, *Method and Theory in Experimental Psychology,* 1953.

Prentice-Hall, Inc.: Figure 8–10. By permission from S. A. Mednick, *Learning.* © 1964. Prentice-Hall, Inc. Figure 13–19. By permission from J. E. Hochberg, *Perception.* © 1964. Prentice-Hall, Inc. Figure 9–6. By permission from D. J. Lewis, *Scientific Principles of Psychology.* © 1963. Prentice-Hall, Inc.

The Psychological Corporation: Figure 14–12. Reproduced by permission. Copyright © 1951, The Psychological Corporation, New York, N.Y. All rights reserved.

Psychological Monographs: Table 14–1 from Mechanization in problem solving, by A. S. Luchins, *54*, No. 248.

Psychological Record: Figure 9–14, from Generalization of extinction on the spectral continuum, by W. K. Honig, *11* (1961), p. 273.

Psychological Reports: Figure 15–8, from Drive level and response strength in the bar pressing apparatus, by C. P. Crocetti, *10* (1962), pp. 563–575. Figure 17–5b, from Relations between stimulus intensity and strength of escape responding, by J. J. Barry and J. M. Harrison, *3* (1957), pp. 3–8.

Quarterly Journal of Experimental Psychology and W. Heffer and Sons. *Quarterly Journal of Experimental Psychology:* Figure 5–2, from Periodicity of response in operant extinction, by H. M. B. Hurwitz, *9* (1957), p. 181.

Random House, Inc., Alfred A. Knopf, Inc. Figures 16–6 and 16–7, reprinted with permission of the publisher from *Psychology in the Making,* by Leo Postman. Copyright, © 1962 by Alfred A. Knopf, Inc.

The Ronald Press Company: Figures 13–5, 14–9, and 18–11, from Gregory A. Kimble and Norman Garmezy—*Principles of General Psychology,* Second Edition. Copyright © 1963 The Ronald Press Company.

Society of the Sigma Xi. *American Scientist:* Figure 8–12, from The experimental analysis of behavior, by B. F. Skinner, *45* (1957), p. 350.

University of Chicago Press: Figure 15–3, from N. Kleitman, *Sleep and Wakefulness* (revised and enlarged edition), 1963.

University of Texas Press: Figure 18–8, from D. E. Sheer (ed.), *Electrical Stimulation of the Brain,* 1961.

University of Wisconsin and H. F. Harlow: Illustration for Part Four, p. 287.

D. Van Nostrand Company, Inc.: Figure 5–14, from J. P. Guilford, *General Psychology*, 1939.

Wadsworth Press: Figure 16–5, from F. H. Sanford, *Psychology: A Scientific Study of Man*, Second Edition, 1965.

John Wiley and Sons, Inc.: Figure 3–11, from H. Cramér, *The Elements of Probability Theory*, 1955. Figures 13–8 and 13–9, from B. Kleinmuntz (ed.), *First Annual Symposium on Cognition*, in press. Figure 9–4, from E. G. Boring, H. S. Langfeld, and H. P. Weld, *Foundations of Psychology*, 1948. Figure 17–9, from S. S. Stevens (ed.), *Handbook of Experimental Psychology*, 1951. Table on p. 277 from L. Carmichael, *Manual of Child Psychology*, 1954. Figures 10–4, 15–10, and 16–3 from T. G. Andrews (ed.), *Methods of Psychology*, 1948. Table on p. 460 from P. T. Young, *Motivation and Emotion*, 1961. Figure 13–16, from J. P. Lysaught and C. M. Williams, *Programmed Instruction*, 1963. Figure 14–8, from J. S. Bruner, J. J. Goodnow, and G. A. Austin, *A Study of Thinking*, 1956.

Williams and Wilkins Company, Inc. *Journal of Comparative Psychology:* Figure 3–7, from Salivary, cardiac, and motor indices of conditioning in two sows, by A. U. Moore and F. L. Marcuse, *38* (1945), p. 7. Figure 17–1 from Motivation in learning, VI. Escape from electric shock compared with hunger-food tension in the visual discrimination habit, by K. I. Muenzinger and F. M. Fletcher, *22* (1936), p. 83. Figure 17–14 from Habit progression and regression—a laboratory investigation of some factors relevant to human socialization, by J. W. Whiting and O. H. Mowrer, *36* (1943), p. 231.

Yale University Press: Figure 11–4, from N. E. Miller and J. Dollard, *Social Learning and Imitation*, 1941.

to *Vivienne*

PREFACE

THE AIM OF THIS TEXT IS TO PROVIDE A RIGOROUS, data-oriented introduction to behavioral psychology. It addresses itself principally to the student in the first course on psychology and comprises material suitable for two contiguous semesters or a one-year term. Although the text attempts an unusual degree of systematization for the introductory level, the material contained is not necessarily more difficult than that of most survey texts in the field. With a limited set of general concepts I have tried to build a sound framework so that the student, whether this be his first, only, or last course in the science, will be provided the means to interpret and order a wide variety of psychological phenomena.

I have made no attempt to review all the multifarious activities of psychologists-at-large in the mid-twentieth century. For the most part, I have kept to the straight and narrow path of experimental psychology. Within those limits, I have concentrated on what, in traditional terms, would be called learning and conditioning, motivation and emotion, and to a lesser extent, psychophysics, perception, and problem solving. Physiological correlates of behavior are embedded in discussions of motivation and emotion. Behavior disorders are framed as pathological emotional phenomena. Perception and psychophysics find no chapter headings as such, but their basic concepts, and some representative data, are woven into the fabric of the text in the chapters on stimulus control, discrimination, and concept acquisition, and elsewhere. The treatment of the field is in terms of functional behavior analysis, a point of view long associated with B. F. Skinner. While the majority of the "principles" described have their origins in the animal laboratory, their relevance to human affairs is repeatedly emphasized.

A few primitive statistical ideas are presented, principally to provide some flavor for variability in data and to point out the usefulness of statistical tools for summarizing and interpreting results. My method has been to append a number of chapters with sections on data analysis, many of which describe simple statistical concepts. Although these are so arranged as to incorporate empirical data of the chapter which they trail, they provide an independent sequence set apart from the body of the text.

A system of R and S notation for describing behavioral procedures is an integral part of the text. The procedures of the field are becoming more and more complex, and some formal scheme for reducing them to their elements seems desirable if the student is to appreciate procedural similarities and differences. Whether the particular notation elaborated here will find a permanent place in the science remains to be seen. But by its inclusion I mean to emphasize that some such symbolic representation of the logic of our procedures is becoming mandatory for efficient exposition and communication.

I expect the instructor will find it difficult to modify the sequence of chapters, or completely omit any. (*Sections* which can be omitted without destroying continuity are set in small type.) The concepts build one upon another, and the book is a unit. The level of difficulty seems to me to be a direct function of chapter number. In using the material with various levels of students, the principal degree of freedom seems to be the rate at which the instructor may progress. In keeping with Bruner's[1] principle that "any subject can be taught effectively in some intellectually honest form to any [individual] at any stage of development," I would hope the book to find use at diverse levels: as an adjunct text for the undergraduate learning course, perhaps, or even as a source book for graduate courses in the experimental analysis of behavior.

A concurrent laboratory is a valuable complement to a course such as this one, and the sequential order of the text is such as to expedite a logical order of experimental topics for the laboratory.

My thanks go to my many former students at Columbia University, Birkbeck College (University of London), and Carnegie Institute of Technology who, over the years, set the conditions for writing and who largely shaped the structure of the book. To Susan Alcott, Nancy Innis, Mary Carol Perrott, and particularly Isabelle Alter, I owe a debt for critically reading, re-reading, and editing preliminary drafts. Suggestions by my colleagues, Daryl Bem, John Boren, Derek Hendry, Dennis Kelly, Bernard Migler, and the editor of this series, Melvin Marx, who between them read every chapter in the book, clarified the final version

[1] J. S. Bruner, *The process of education*, Cambridge: Harvard Univer. Press, 1963, p. 33.

appreciably. Evalyn Segal generously undertook the arduous task of reading the entire manuscript during a summer's leave of absence, and her detailed comments helped improve the book in many ways. To W. N. Schoenfeld and Francis Mechner must go credit for whatever of original value is to be found within; it should go without saying that they are in no way responsible for the defects and deficiencies, and I hope they will forgive whatever distortions of their ideas I may have inadvertently created.

J. R. M.

CONTENTS

REMARKS TO STUDENTS   xxi

**PART ONE: THE LAWFULNESS OF
BEHAVIOR**   **1**

CHAPTER 1: A BACKGROUND TO THE
SCIENTIFIC APPROACH TO BEHAVIOR   3

1.1   *Early attempts to explain and classify human behavior*   3
1.2   *Reflex action*   5
1.3   *Conditioned or acquired reflexes*   6
1.4   *The theory of evolution and adaptive behavior*   7
1.5   *The earliest experiments on "voluntary" behavior*   9
1.6   *The* Zeitgeist   10
1.7   *Psychology loses its mind*   11
1.8   *The firm establishment of an experimental analysis of
      behavior*   14
1.9   *In review*   17

CHAPTER 2: REFLEX (ELICITED) BEHAVIOR   19

2.1   *The S-R formula*   19
2.2   *Primary reflex laws*   22
2.3   *Secondary laws of the reflex*   24
2.4   *Reflex strength: a hypothetical construct*   26

2.5 *Common examples of reflexes*   27
2.6 *Variability in measurements; summarizing data in frequency distributions; some simple statistics; the normal curve*   29

CHAPTER 3: PAVLOVIAN CONDITIONING   37

3.1 *Conditioned reflexes and the nature of an experiment*   38
3.2 *The Pavlovian paradigm: a schematic method of representing conditioning*   40
3.3 *Time relations in conditioning paradigms*   47
3.4 *The extension of classical conditioning*   50
3.5 *The experimental method*   52
3.6 *Introduction to elementary probability concepts*   56

CHAPTER 4: OPERANT STRENGTHENING   61

4.1 *Introduction to purposive behavior*   62
4.2 *A prototype experiment*   64
4.3 *Absolute rate changes*   66
4.4 *Relative rate changes*   71
4.5 *Sequential changes in the order of responding*   72
4.6 *Variability changes*   73
4.7 *Operants and reinforcing stimuli*   74
4.8 *The operant-strengthening paradigm*   77
4.9 *Vocal operants*   78
4.10 *The extension of operant strengthening*   80
4.11 *Superstition*   83
4.12 *Operant conditioning*   84

CHAPTER 5: OPERANT EXTINCTION AND RECONDITIONING   89

5.1 *Changes in response rate during extinction*   90
5.2 *Topographical and structural changes in extinction*   91
5.3 *Resistance to extinction*   93
5.4 *Spontaneous recovery*   97
5.5 *Successive conditioning and extinction*   98
5.6 *Forgetting and extinction*   100
5.7 *A comprehensive definition of operant extinction*   104
5.8 *The extension of extinction concepts*   105
5.9 *Graphical representations of results of experiments in which several independent variables are studied jointly*   109

PART TWO: THE FUNDAMENTAL UNITS OF ANALYSIS   **115**

CHAPTER 6: RESPONSE AND STIMULUS CONTINGENCY NOTATION   117

6.1	*Behavioral events and responses*	118
6.2	*Environmental events and situations*	120
6.3	*The idea of a behavioral contingency*	122
6.4	*The initial situation* (S_A)	124
6.5	*Multiple contingencies in the same situation*	125
6.6	*The null contingency*	127
6.7	*The duration of situations and contingencies*	128
6.8	*More than a single response required for the S consequence*	129
6.9	*Repetitive contingencies*	130
6.10	*Facilitation*	132
6.11	*Negative contingencies*	133
6.12	*Probabilistic contingencies*	134
6.13	*Discriminations*	135
6.14	*R and S functionally dependent*	135
6.15	*Nested contingencies*	136

CHAPTER 7: INTERMITTENT REINFORCEMENT   139

7.1	*Interval contingencies*	140
7.2	*Probability of reinforcement*	147
7.3	*Theoretical rates on reinforcement schedules*	149
7.4	*The effects of intermittent reinforcement on resistance to extinction*	151
7.5	*Other behavioral effects of intermittent reinforcement*	153
7.6	*Behavioral steady states*	154

CHAPTER 8: RESPONSE SPECIFICATION   157

8.1	*The definition of response classes*	157
8.2	*A set theory definition of operant response*	162
8.3	*The differentiation paradigm*	163
8.4	*Successive approximation*	168
8.5	*Extension of the concept of the operant*	170
8.6	*Rate differentiation*	175
8.7	*Reinforcement of continuous responding*	178
8.8	*Summary*	180
8.9	*The language and logic of sets*	181

CHAPTER 9: ENVIRONMENTAL CONTROL 187

9.1 *Stimulus dimensions* 188
9.2 *Stimulus generalization* 194
9.3 *Generalization of extinction* 201
9.4 *Some implications of generalization* 203
9.5 *Notes on design for experiments in psychology using animal subjects* 205

PART THREE: COMPOUNDING BEHAVIORAL UNITS **209**

CHAPTER 10: DISCRIMINATION 211

10.1 *Two stimulus conditions, one response class* 212
10.2 *The discrimination paradigm* 217
10.3 *Two stimulus conditions, two response classes* 218
10.4 m *stimulus conditions,* n *response classes* 221
10.5 *Continuous changes in behavior as a function of continuous changes in a stimulus dimension* 223
10.6 *Discrimination without* S^{Δ} *responding* 226
10.7 *Discriminative reaction times* 228
10.8 *The implications of operant stimulus control* 229
10.9 *Significance of differences between two means* 231

CHAPTER 11: ACQUIRED REINFORCERS 237

11.1 *The reinforcing properties of positive discriminative stimuli* 238
11.2 *Amplifying the durability of conditioned reinforcers* 239
11.3 *Token rewards* 244
11.4 *Generalized reinforcers* 245
11.5 *Observing responses* 246
11.6 *The necessary and sufficient conditions for creating conditioned reinforcers* 248
11.7 *Secondary reinforcement in social behavior* 251

CHAPTER 12: CHAINING 257

12.1 *The elements of behavioral chains* 257
12.2 *The development of a complex chain* 259
12.3 *Maze learning as chaining* 264
12.4 *The effects of selective extinction at different points in the chain* 265

12.5   Chained schedules   268
12.6   Everyday human behavior as chaining   271
12.7   Vocal chains   274
12.8   Branching chains and flow-diagram representation   278
12.9   Covert behavior chains   282

PART FOUR: COMPLEX
CONTINGENCIES   287

CHAPTER 13:   CONCEPT ACQUISITION   289

13.1   Simple learning sets   290
13.2   Some variables affecting L-set acquisition   294
13.3   More complex L-sets   295
13.4   Simple human concept-formation experiments   297
13.5   Animal studies in concept formation   301
13.6   Arbitrary S^D classes: disjunctive concepts   307
13.7   Meaning and understanding considered as the interrela-
       tions between concepts   310
13.8   The acquisition of concepts through programmed in-
       struction   318
13.9   The perceptual constancies   326

CHAPTER 14:   PROBLEM SOLVING AND
INTELLIGENCE   331

14.1   The structure of a problem and the nature of a solution   331
14.2   Puzzles   335
14.3   Heuristic search strategies   339
14.4   Concept identification   343
14.5   The measurement of problem-solving abilities: intelli-
       gence tests   345
14.6   Correlation, test reliability, and validity   350

PART FIVE: REINFORCEMENT
DYNAMICS   357

CHAPTER 15:   MOTIVATION I   359

15.1   Cause and effect and the idea of scientific law   359
15.2   Fictional causes of behavior   362
15.3   Past histories with conditioning and extinction contin-
       gencies as causes of behavior   363

15.4 *Motives and reinforcers*   364
15.5 *Drive operations*   365
15.6 *Periodicities in reinforcement value*   367
15.7 *Deprivation and satiation paradigms*   369
15.8 *The measurement of drives*   372

CHAPTER 16: MOTIVATION II   385

16.1 *Activation and directional aspects of motivation*   385
16.2 *Incentive*   390
16.3 *Physiological factors in motivation*   391
16.4 *Additional primary reinforcers*   396
16.5 *Acquired drives*   402

CHAPTER 17: AVERSIVE CONTINGENCIES   409

17.1 *Negative reinforcers*   409
17.2 *Escape conditioning*   410
17.3 *Parameters of* S^- 412
17.4 *Conditioned aversive stimuli*   417
17.5 *Avoidance conditioning*   419
17.6 *Punishment*   426
17.7 *Masochism*   430

CHAPTER 18: EMOTIONAL BEHAVIOR   433

18.1 *Is emotion a cause of behavior or a behavioral effect?*   433
18.2 *Three concepts of emotion*   436
18.3 *The anxiety paradigm*   441
18.4 *Anger*   445
18.5 *Elation*   447
18.6 *A model for representing and interrelating emotional phenomena*   451
18.7 *Psychosomatic medicine*   455
18.8 *The autonomic nervous system*   458
18.9 *Emotional control, emotional maturity, and pathological emotional behavior*   462
18.10 *An index of emotional change*   466

INDEX TO REFERENCES   469
SUBJECT INDEX   481

REMARKS TO STUDENTS

INTRODUCTORY PSYCHOLOGY MAY BE CONSTRUED AS an introduction to the methods and principles of the scientific analysis of behavior. Although older definitions of psychology emphasized the "mental processes," for reasons that will be made clear throughout this text a modern approach to psychology takes the *behavior* of humans as well as lower animals as its subject matter. Holding fast to the canon that only what can be observed can be studied scientifically, this modern viewpoint attacks traditional psychological problems through the medium of behavioral analysis. In the course of the text we shall find ourselves studying and representing in the language of behavior such topics as learning and memory, problem solving and intelligence, sensation and perception, and emotion and motivation.

The organization of this book will permit you to arrive at a preliminary understanding of the basic principles of human behavior. Although many of the fundamental concepts and paradigms that are treated in detail were originally derived from laboratory experiments with animal subjects, they are by no means limited to animals. We employ animal subjects in psychological research for pragmatic reasons: a twentieth-century human being would be unlikely to submit freely to the long-range environmental control necessary for a scientific study; and even if he would, society would not permit him.

In order to acquire an understanding of the causes of human and animal behavior, you will first have to acquire a technical vocabulary and a thorough familiarity with the basic concepts of psychology. There is no known short-cut to this vocabulary. You must learn it in much the same way that, in preparation for playing winning chess, you must learn the names and permissible moves of the pieces, the most common openings, and the basic principles of attack and defense.

When approaching psychology, you may suffer a peculiar handicap that is absent in your initial learning of chess. Certain preconceived opinions and views about the causes of behavior that are a standard part of the everyday common-sense interpretation of the world may first have to be unlearned. Unfortunately, this common-sense view of human nature is not always the most useful for formulating a systematic science of the relations between behavior and its controlling variables. You will do well, therefore, to try to put aside your preconceptions about people's actions, and in particular your representational system of their so-called inner mental processes. Try rather to approach the subject matter with a fresh point of view, contenting yourself initially with merely asking simple-minded questions such as "What was the organism observed to do?" and "What is related consistently to its doing that?" Your progress may seem slow at first, but it will always be sure.

J. R. M.

PART ONE

The Lawfulness of Behavior

1. A BACKGROUND TO THE SCIENTIFIC APPROACH TO BEHAVIOR

2. REFLEX (ELICITED) BEHAVIOR

3. PAVLOVIAN CONDITIONING

4. OPERANT STRENGTHENING

5. OPERANT EXTINCTION AND RECONDITIONING

Chapter 1   A BACKGROUND TO THE SCIENTIFIC APPROACH TO BEHAVIOR

WHEN SOCRATES HEARD ABOUT THE NEW discoveries in anatomy which purported to prove that the causes of bodily movement were due to an ingenious mechanical arrangement of muscle, bone, and joints, he remarked: "That hardly explains why I am sitting here in a curved position . . . talking to you" (Kantor, 1963). It is 2300 years since Socrates' complaint, and in the intervening centuries the causes of human behavior have been attributed to the tides, the divine soul, the position of the stars, and frequently simply to caprice. The last hundred years have seen the rise of a *science* of behavior bringing with it a fresh conceptual framework with new attitudes toward the causes of behavior. A brief history of the events which led to the development of this science makes an apt prelude to its study. For just as there is no better way to understand the present activities of a person than through an acquaintance with his past history, so too there is no better way to understand the present activities of a science than through an acquaintance with its past.

1.1 EARLY ATTEMPTS TO EXPLAIN AND CLASSIFY HUMAN BEHAVIOR

The precise origins of behavior science, like those of all bodies of knowledge, are lost in the obscurity of time. Still, we do know that by 325 B.C. in ancient Greece, Aristotle had combined observation and interpretation into a naturalistic, if primitive, system of behavior. Aristotle sought the causes of (1) body movements, and (2) the discrimina-

3

tions made by organisms. He described many categories of behavior, such as sense perception, sight, smell, hearing, common sense, simple and complex thinking, appetite, memory, sleep, and dreaming. His topics ring familiar to us today, and they are still to be found in some form or other in nearly every comprehensive text of psychology. Aristotle was less interested in prediction and control of nature than we are today, and consequently his explanations of behavior have a less modern flavor. Aristotle was concerned to explain the various activities of an individual by showing them to be specific instances of general "qualities," such as appetite, passion, reason, will, and sense-ability (Toulmin and Goodfield, 1962).

The observations and classifications of Aristotle and the Greek investigators who followed him were a substantial beginning in a naturalistic attempt to understand the causes of human and animal behavior. But the new science declined with the demise of Hellenic civilization. The early Christian era and the Middle Ages produced an intellectual climate poorly suited to observation and investigation: man turned his attention to metaphysical matters. The Church Fathers began, and the medieval theologians completed, a conceptual transformation of one of Aristotle's purely abstract "qualities" into a supernatural soul to which the causes of man's behavior were assigned. In regarding this soul as *non*-material, *in*-substantial, and *super*-natural, a sharp *dualistic* division was established between it and the body. By locating the causes of behavior in the unobservable realm of the spirit, this dualism inhibited a naturalistic study of behavior. Thus for a very long time behavior science lay dormant. We have to jump forward to the seventeenth century, the time of Galileo and the rise of modern physics, to pick up the threads that were eventually to be rewoven into a scientific fabric.

The theories of the philosopher and mathematician René Descartes (1596–1650), Galileo's French contemporary, represent a partial break from the metaphysical explanations of behavior. Taking as his model the mechanical figures of the royal gardens of Versailles which moved and produced sounds, Descartes suggested that bodily movement was the result of similar mechanical causes.

The machines in the royal gardens worked on hydraulic principles. Water was pumped through concealed tubes to inflate the limbs of the figures, producing movement, or was conducted through devices that emitted words or music as the water flowed by. Descartes imagined that animals and man were in effect a kind of complex machine, analogously constructed. He substituted animal spirits, a kind of intangible, invisible elastic substance, for the water of the Royal Figures; and supposed the spirits to flow in the nerves in such a way as to enter the muscles, thereby causing them to expand and contract, and in turn making the limbs move.

Some of the Royal Figures were so arranged that if onlookers chanced to tread on hidden tiles, hydraulic actuating mechanisms caused the figures to approach or withdraw. Descartes took this mechanical responsiveness as a model for explaining how an external environmental *stimulus* might cause a bodily movement. An illustration (see Part One, p. 1) in one of his works shows a withdrawal of a human limb from a flame. According to Descartes, the "machine of our body is so formed" that the heat of the flame excites a nerve which conducts that excitation to the brain. From the brain, animal spirits are then passed out, or *reflected* back via that nerve to the limb, enlarging the muscle, and so causing a contraction and withdrawal (Fearing, 1930).

Descartes' willingness to view human behavior as determined by natural forces was only partial. He confined his mechanical hypotheses to certain "involuntary" behaviors and supposed the rest were governed by the soul, located in the brain. The soul guided even the mechanisms of the "involuntary" behaviors much in the way an engineer might have directed the workings of the Royal Figures. In spite of this dualism, and in spite of his choice of a hydraulic principle, Descartes' formulation represented an advance over earlier thinking about behavior. The theory of the body as a specific kind of machine was one that was testable by observation and experiment. That was the property so conspicuously lacking in medieval explanations. In re-establishing the idea that at least some of the causes of animal and human behavior might be found in the observable environment, Descartes laid the philosophical foundations that would eventually justify an experimental approach to behavior.

1.2 REFLEX ACTION

Descartes' views symbolize the new interest in mechanism that was to lead to experimentation on "reflected" animal action. In 1750 a Scottish physiologist, Robert Whytt, experimentally rediscovered and extended Descartes' principle of the stimulus. By observing systematic contraction of the pupil of the eye to light, salivation to irritants, and various other *reflexes,* Whytt was able to state a necessary relationship between two separate events: an external stimulus (for example, a light) and a bodily response (for example, a pupil contraction). Moreover, Whytt's demonstration that a number of reflex behaviors could be elicited in the decapitated frog weakened the attractiveness of a soul explanation. Yet the eighteenth century was not quite able to regard the stimulus alone as a sufficient cause of behavior. The soul, thought Whytt, probably diffused itself throughout the spinal cord and the brain, thereby retaining master control of reflexes.

In the ensuing 150 years more and more reflex relationships were discovered and elaborated, and the concept of the stimulus grew increasingly powerful. At the same time, nerve action became understood as an electrical rather than a hydraulic system. By the turn of the nineteenth century spiritual direction had become superfluous for "involuntary action," and Sir Charles Sherrington, the celebrated English physiologist, could summarize the causes of reflex behavior in quantitative stimulus-response laws. These laws relate the speed, magnitude, and probability of the reflex response to the intensity, frequency, and other measurable properties of the stimulus. Science had entirely annexed the reflex. Still, a vast proportion of the behavior of human beings and higher animals remained to be freed from supernatural forces.

1.3 CONDITIONED OR ACQUIRED REFLEXES

Just before the beginning of the twentieth century, Ivan Pavlov, the Russian physiologist, was investigating the digestive secretions of dogs. In the course of these experiments, he noticed that while the introduction of food or acid into the mouth resulted in a flow of saliva, the mere appearance of the experimenter bringing food would also elicit a similar flow. Pavlov was by no means the first man to make observations of this sort; but he seems to have been the first to suspect that their detailed study might provide a clue to the understanding of adjustive and adaptive behaviors of organisms. It was this insight that led him to a systematic study of these reflexes, which he called *conditional reflexes*—because they depended or were conditional upon some previous events in the life of the organism. The appearance of the experimenter had not originally elicited saliva. It was only after his appearance had been frequently associated with food or acid that it had this effect. Pavlov's unique contribution was to show experimentally how conditional reflexes came to be acquired, how they could be removed (extinguished), and what range of environmental energies was effective in their production. In time, Pavlov was to lay down a general law of conditioning: after repeated temporal association of two stimuli, the one that occurs first comes eventually to elicit the response that is normally elicited by the second stimulus. Slightly modified, this law is with us today.

Three general aspects of Pavlov's work deserve our close attention. First, he was not satisfied merely to observe the gross aspects of conditioning, as many others had done before him (c.f. Hall and Hodge, 1890). Instead he proceeded to verify the generality of the phenomenon using many stimuli and many dogs. It was only after numerous demonstrations that he encoded what he had discovered in a law—applicable, he thought, to *all* stimuli and *all* higher organisms. Second, Pavlov concerned himself with the measurable, or *quantitative* aspects of the phenomenon. His measurable quantities, such as amount of salivation and number of reflex pairings, were useful in providing a detailed analysis of conditioning. A third aspect of Pavlov's work was its systematic nature. By confining his studies to the effects of numerous conditions on a single quantity (amount of salivation), Pavlov assured that his experimental findings would be interrelated, and therefore more meaningful.

Pavlov saw clearly how explanation of behavior must proceed.

> The naturalist must consider only one thing: what is the relation of this or that external reaction of the animal to the phenomena of the external world? This response may be extremely complicated in comparison with the reaction of any inanimate object, but the principle involved remains the same.
>
> Strictly speaking, natural science is under obligation to determine only the precise connection which exists between a given natural phenomenon and the response of the living organism to that phenomenon . . . (Pavlov, 1928, p. 82).

And yet, in spite of his own stated interest in the relation of environment and response, Pavlov increasingly came to regard conditioning as a study of brain function. His explanations tended to be in terms of hypothetical brain processes. But in fact Pavlov rarely measured any actual relationships between brain and behavior, so that these explanations were as fictional as the earlier soul explanations. In trying to explain away behavior by appealing to unknown brain functions, he was avoiding a direct description of behavior itself, thus violating one of his own dicta: that a behavior science need determine only "the precise connection which exists between a given natural phenomenon and the response of the living organism to that phenomenon."

1.4 THE THEORY OF EVOLUTION AND ADAPTIVE BEHAVIOR

Pavlov's work represents, in a way, the culmination of Descartes' mechanistic doctrine of reflex behavior. With regard to behavior that traditionally fell under the control of will, or volition, Descartes had followed the prejudices of his time, assigning it to the control of an unobservable soul. Such a "solution," however, only postponed a scientific enquiry, since the original problem of accounting for the behavior was merely shifted to the more difficult one of accounting for the behavior of the postulated soul. In 1859, a major scientific event occurred which was to alter the intellectual climate favorably for a naturalistic study of voluntary behavior. In that year, Charles Darwin proposed his theory of evolution, holding that man was a member of the animal kingdom, and that differences between man and other animals were quantitative and matters of degree. As a distinguished historian of psychology put it:

> The theory of evolution raised the problem of animal psychology because it demands continuity between different animal forms and between man and the animals. In a vague way the Cartesian [Descartes'] notion still prevailed. Man possessed a soul and the animals were believed to be soulless; and there was, moreover, little distinction then made between a soul and a mind. Opposition to the theory of evolution was based primarily upon its assumption of continuity between man and the brutes, and the obvious reply to criticism was to demonstrate the continuity. The exhibition of mind in animals and of the continuity between the animal and the human mind thus became crucial to the life of the new theory (Boring, 1929, pp. 462–463).

Darwin's theory derived support from the many careful observations that he had made of fossils and the structure of flora and fauna living in isolated areas of the earth. In addition, he had investigated the behavior by which animals adapted to their environments. Darwin's behavioral observations were so comprehensive and detailed as to mark the first systematic attempt at a comparative animal psychology (see Darwin, 1873).

Darwin's interest in behavior was, as Professor Boring noted, based on what it could reveal about mind. Thus the demonstration of complexity and variety in adaptive behaviors of animals in relation to their changing environments seemed to prove that they, like men, must also think, have ideas, and feel desires. Eventually Darwin was to be criticized for his *anthropomorphism,* that is, for trying to explain animal behavior in terms of mentalistic concepts. But few thought at the time to raise the far more radical methodological question: whether the traditional mentalistic concepts (thoughts, ideas, desires) have explanatory value even for human behavior.

Darwin's friend, George John Romanes, an English writer and popularizer of science, wrote a book on animal intelligence (Romanes, 1886) in which he compared the behavior of various species of animals. Romanes gathered material from careful observation of animals, but he also took evidence from popular accounts of pets and circus animals. For this reason, his method has come to be called *anecdotal*. The anthropomorphic and anecdotal methods of Darwin and Romanes, respectively, marked the renewal of interest in adaptive animal behavior and its relation to human behavior, and therefore represent important historical precursors of a true experimental analysis of behavior.

1.5 THE EARLIEST EXPERIMENTS ON "VOLUNTARY" BEHAVIOR

In 1898, Edward L. Thorndike of Columbia University published the results of a number of laboratory studies on kittens, dogs, and chicks. His methods departed radically from those of the casual observers who had preceded him. Thorndike's apparatus is shown in Fig. 1–1. The behavior studied was escape from a confining enclosure, and the acts, such as pulling a string, moving a latch, pressing a lever, or prying open a lock, were chosen for their convenience and reliability of observation. Since any of these behaviors could be arranged to be instrumental in producing escape from the box, Thorndike called them *instrumental behaviors*.

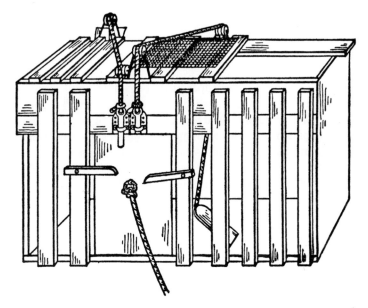

Figure 1–1. Thorndike's puzzle box for studying instrumental learning of animals (Garrett, 1951).

Four elements of Thorndike's work with instrumental behavior impart to it a modern quality not seen in behavioral investigations before his time. (1) He recognized the importance of making observations of animals whose *past histories were known* and were more or less uniform. Thus he raised his animals in the laboratory where they would obtain similar environmental conditions prior to experimentation. (2) Thorndike understood the necessity for making *repeated observations* on individual animals, and making observations on more than one animal in more than one species. In only this way could he be sure the results he obtained were applicable to animals in general. (3) Thorndike saw that unless he considered more than one particular act of behavior, his conclusions would hold only for the single bit of behavior he chose. Thus he employed *diverse behaviors* in several different apparatus. (4) Still another quality of Thorndike's work, and one which we have come to recognize as characteristic of science, was his attempt to make a *quantitative presentation* of his findings.

From his work with animals in puzzle boxes, Thorndike set forth a number of principles or general laws of behavior which he believed held for many species and for many kinds of behavior. One of these, in a somewhat modified form, has come down to us today. Thorndike noticed that when animals were first put into the puzzle box, they made many diffuse struggling responses. Eventually, one of these diffuse behaviors would chance to trip the escape mechanism and the door would then open, permitting the animal to escape from the box and to obtain a small quantity of food. Thorndike observed that the behavior which first let the animal out was only one of many that the animal made in the situation. Yet as the animal was repeatedly exposed to the situation, it came to make fewer and fewer superfluous behaviors, until eventually it made practically none save the successful ones. Thorndike concluded from this that the successful past results or *effects* of behavior must be an important influence in determining the animal's present behavioral tendencies. Thorndike called this—the ability of the past effects of behavior to modify the behavior patterns of the animal—the *law of effect*. It survives today as a fundamental principle in the analysis and control of adaptive behavior.

1.6 THE *ZEITGEIST*

Thorndike had provided a new experimental method, and with its help he had formulated what was soon to be accepted as a basic law of adaptive behavior. But just as Whytt had left the reflex concept 150 years earlier partly in the state of observed fact and partly in the state of superfluous interpretation, so Thorndike left the law of effect. In his statement of the principle, Thorndike was not content to regard the "effect" as mere escape from confinement, or mere access to food. Rather, he felt it necessary to infer that success led to pleasure and satisfaction, and *these* were the real causes of the observed behavioral changes. In this way he threw the burden of explanation on hypothetical mental states, pleasure and satisfaction, which were no more real than Descartes' souls. For Thorndike, as for his contemporaries, the behavior of the cat in escaping from the puzzle box was not important as behavior, but only as a means of shedding light on the mental processes and associations of ideas of the animal.

Thorndike thus went along with his times and traditions in viewing behavior as interesting principally for what it revealed about some other system. The constraints by which the times and traditions bind even the most original of thinkers are often referred to as the *Zeitgeist*. The great men of an era will rise above their *Zeitgeist* in some ways, yet be bound by it in others. Descartes rose above it when he propounded an original mechanistic theory of bodily movement. That he was bound by the *Zeitgeist* is evident in his retention of the earlier "soul-body" dualism. We see the *Zeitgeist* in Whytt, who rediscovered the principle of the stimulus, but was unable to relinquish the soul as the final cause of the reflexes he observed. Pavlov studied conditioned reflexes, a phenomenon whose importance had been neglected for centuries. Yet we see that Pavlov was bound by the *Zeitgeist;* he held the view that conditioned reflexes, though manifestly a behavioral phenomenon, were of interest for the understanding of the brain rather than behavior. Now we see the *Zeitgeist* in Thorndike, who performed some of the earliest experiments on "voluntary" behavior, but explained away his findings by appeal to the association of ideas. In fact, the *Zeitgeist* principle is so pervasive in all of science that we may take as a general rule that every man's work will be colored by the accepted theories and viewpoints of his time. Thus, while a particular man's greatness is that he frees himself from certain established modes of thinking and sees what no one before him has seen as clearly or in the same way, he will not completely escape the social, philosophical, and cultural climate in which he works.

1.7 PSYCHOLOGY LOSES ITS MIND

Thorndike introduced adaptive behavior into the laboratory and in so doing discovered the significance of the law of effect. Thorndike's interest in behavior arose from his interest, as a psychologist, in mental processes. It will be instructive at this point to examine the discipline of psychology, which, in the first half of the twentieth century, was to merge with other historical tributaries of behavior science. Experimental psychological research began in the middle of the nineteenth century as a discipline growing out of the physiology of the sense organs. In fact, its early pioneers, Hermann Helmholtz, Johannes Müller, and Wilhelm Wundt, were all physicists and physiologists. These early experimental psychologists adopted the categories of behavior described by Aristotle, but, unlike Aristotle, they were interested in behavior only as it threw light on mental processes. Thus the work of the early psychologists represents an attempt to make the naturalistic experimental methods introduced by Galileo compatible with the metaphysical doctrines of the Middle Ages.

It was Wundt who, in 1879, founded the first psychological laboratory in Leipzig. We may take his system as representative of the activities of this new discipline, which was less than twenty years old when Thorndike was performing his experiments with cats and chicks at Columbia. Wundt held that psychology was the science of *experience*; and, as such, its subject matter comprised feelings, thoughts, and sensations. He laid down the doctrine that the method of psychology was introspective, an examination of the conscious processes of the experiencing organism. Thus Wundt outlined the problem of psychology as "(1) the analysis of conscious processes into elements, (2) the determination of the manner of connection of these elements and (3) the determination of the laws of connection" (Boring, 1929, p. 328, ital. omitted.) The experiments that Wundt and his followers performed give a better picture of the content of this psychology than do Wundt's definitions. Much of the work was classified under human sensation and concerned the visual sense in particular. Numerous experiments measured the minimum intensities of light that an observer could detect under various conditions. Others concerned themselves with the smallest environmental changes needed for an observer to report just noticeable changes in brightness, color, and distance of objects. Such investigations came to be called threshold experiments in *psychophysics*. Psycho—because sensations were considered to be under study; physics—because physical changes in the environment were manipulated and measured in the experiments. Hearing, touch, taste, smell, and the sense of time, were also investigated, as were reaction time, attention, and feeling. The memorization of nonsense syllables of various sorts was a method used for treating the association of ideas and deducing the properties of memory.

Though psychology asserted that it was a science of mental contents, mental processes, and mental acts, what in fact it investigated was behavior. Associations of ideas were inferred from the learning of nonsense syllables; identical sensations were inferred from observations of behavior when a human subject matched two different environmental objects in different contexts (for example, two samples of gray paper under different conditions of illumination); speed of the mental process was inferred from an individual's reaction time. So it was no paradox that when Thorndike came to make a closer investigation of the association of ideas, he was at liberty to choose animal subjects. If the behavior of human organisms could lead to inferences about mental processes, why not the behavior of animals? Thus it happened that Thorndike's work helped to bring animal research methods into psychology. There they have remained, side by side with methodological descendants of the classical sensory and introspective psychology of the nineteenth century.

But perhaps the man who did the most to clarify the relationship between behavior and psychology was John B. Watson. The earliest work of this American psychologist was concerned with the sense-modalities that the rat uses in learning a maze. As Watson carried on his animal studies, he came to be more and more disturbed by the prevailing view that behavior possessed significance only as it shed light on mental or conscious processes. It occurred to Watson that the data of behavior were valuable in their own right and that the traditional problems of psychology—imagery, sensation, feeling, association of ideas—could all be studied by strictly behavioral methods.

In 1913 Watson published a now classic paper defining psychology as the science of behavior and naming this new psychology "behaviorism." Watson argued in that paper that the study of behavior could achieve an independent status within science. The goal of such a science could be the prediction and control of the behavior of *all* animals, and no special preference need be given human beings. The behaviorist, claimed Watson, need relate his studies of rats and cats to human behavior no more (nor less) than the zoologist need relate his dissections on frogs and earthworms to human anatomy. By his doctrine Watson was destroying the homocentric theory of man's importance in the behavior world just as effectively as Copernicus, four hundred years earlier, had destroyed the geocentric (earth-centered) theory of the universe.

Watson's critical point was that psychology must be objective—that is, it must have a subject matter which, like that of the other sciences, is independent of the observer. Classical psychology, in attempting to take as its subject matter *self-observation,* lacked an independent observer located outside of the system being considered. The adoption of behavior as the subject matter being observed gave the new psychology the necessary independent observer.

Watson's program was far-reaching and, for its time, remarkably sophisticated. In its insistence on behavior as an independent subject matter of a science aimed at prediction and control of behavior, and in its stress on a microscopic analysis of the environment and behavior into stimulus and response as the way to eventual understanding of complex patterns of behavior, Watson's program laid the base for our modern viewpoints.

1.8 THE FIRM ESTABLISHMENT OF AN EXPERIMENTAL ANALYSIS OF BEHAVIOR

Thorndike's early experiments on animal behavior and Watson's definition of psychology as a science of behavior established animal research in psychology. Even so, the scientific status of the new psychology was precarious. In Pavlov's principle of conditioned reflexes Watson thought he saw an explanatory mechanism for the many complex and subtle adjustments adult organisms, including man, make to their environments. But the attempt to force *all* behavior into the reflex mold was to prove a failure. Watson failed to appreciate the significance of Thorndike's law of effect, largely one might guess, because of the excess conceptual baggage with which Thorndike had encumbered it. Watson's view that the task of a predictive behavior science is the compilation of all the hereditary and acquired stimulus-response correlations that a given organism exhibits, distracted attention from the search for general laws of behavior. In this theoretical vacuum, traditional mentalistic concepts continued to survive. The experimental rigor of behaviorism was unquestioned, but its methodology was in danger of proving barren.

> Twenty years of the 'natural science method' heralded by Behaviorism had failed to provide a consistent and useful systematic formulation. The . . . experimental data reflected many arbitrary properties of the apparatus. Acceptable conclusions of any degree of generality referred to aspects, characteristics, or limiting capacities. While many of these were valid enough, few were logically compelling, and individual preferences had led to many individual 'sciences' of behavior (Skinner, 1944, p. 276).

In a series of papers beginning in 1930, B. F. Skinner proposed a formulation of behavior which arose out of observations made on single organisms responding in a carefully controlled and highly standardized artificial experimental situation. Skinner's organism was the white rat, and his apparatus consisted of a box containing a small lever, which if depressed by the rat resulted in the delivery of a small pellet of food to a cup located directly under the lever. Under these experimental condi-

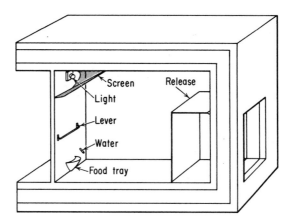

Figure 1–2. Skinner's box for studying oper- ant behaviors of small animals (Skinner, 1938).

tions, a hungry rat left alone in the box would soon come to press the lever at a sustained moderate rate until the number of food pellets delivered had begun to satiate the animal. Skinner's experimental situa- tion and his approach to the problems of behavior were unique in many respects. Skinner saw the necessity for making available a sensitive and reliable dependent variable; that is, some quantitative aspect of behavior which could vary over a wide range and enter into lawful and orderly relationships with past and present environmental variables. His dis- covery that the frequency of occurrence of the lever-press response dur- ing a given interval of time (its rate) satisfied these conditions was a major step towards a sophisticated analysis of individual behavior.

Skinner's approach to the problems of behavior differed in certain ways from those of his predecessors as well as his contemporaries work- ing in animal psychology. As a fundamental proposition, he held that a science of behavior could be what he called descriptive or functional; that is, it could limit itself to the discovery of relationships or correlations between measurable variables. Skinner also argued that the investiga- tions must be systematic, in that the relationships obtained be linked by a common thread. By confining his observations to the ways that a single dependent variable (the frequency per unit time of an arbitrary, yet representative act) changed with varied environmental conditions, Skin- ner kept his own work highly systematic.

A subject matter often awaits instruments to bring the observer into better contact with it. Skinner invented a recording device which made a visual record of successive responses by a slight vertical displacement of a pen moving horizontally in time. As the actual experiment progressed, a graph was thus drawn of cumulative responses against time. This cumulative-response recorder makes available a fine-grained qualitative record of behavioral processes for immediate inspection and has functioned for the behaviorist in a way not unlike the way the microscope has functioned for the biologist.

Skinner's actual methodological contributions to modern behavior science are numerous, and we can only sketch some of the more important here. He recognized the age-old dichotomy between *reflex* and voluntary actions, or as he called the latter, *operants*. But by showing that Pavlov's principle applied to the strengthening of reflexes, whereas Thorndike's law of effect described the strengthening of operants, he placed both types into harmonious perspective. He formulated a precise vocabulary whose terms were defined by reference to the observables that he measured and manipulated. It is this terminology which stands at the base of our modern conceptual framework.

From the very first, Skinner emphasized the importance of detailed prediction and control of individual behavior rather than gross differences between groups of animals. His own researches were invariably characterized by a great many measurements on very few organisms, with the reproduceability of the process under study as the test for reliability. Skinner's focus on the rate of a representative operant response has avoided many of the problems associated with more indirect measures of behavior. Thorndike had observed the number of errors made and the time taken to achieve success in his puzzle box, but neither of these was an actual property of the instrumental behavior that was being acquired. If we wish to train a dog to jump through a hoop, for instance, we are not interested in the errors he makes, but in the hoop-jumping behavior itself. Errors are a measure of behaviors other than those we are in the process of investigating. Interesting questions about whether or not a given act will occur, or how often it will occur, could never be answered in terms of errors or time scores. Skinner's basic datum, rate of response, is closely related to the probability of occurrence of behavior, and has been especially useful in providing answers to questions of response probability.

As time has gone on, Skinner has broadened his empirical base. Response and organism combinations other than the lever pressing of rats have been studied. The original hope that this act would be characteristic of operant behavior generally has apparently been confirmed. Furthermore, the relationships that Skinner has obtained warrant in many cases the label of behavioral principles; they appear to hold for a great number of organisms, including man, and for all responses that can be classified as operants.

The work of B. F. Skinner brings us to a point close to our modern conception of behavior science. We are still too close in historical time, too much in our own *Zeitgeist,* to have the necessary perspective to determine the weakest points in Skinner's system. In the chapters that follow, however, we shall see that behavior science, now firmly re-established as a natural science, is expanding on many research frontiers. Perhaps the most convincing proof that this science has at last come of age is to be found in the recent rise of a behavioral technology drawing directly from it. As we shall discover, applications of behavioral techniques are being made increasingly to drug research, animal training, warfare, treatment of abnormal human behavior, and education.

1.9 IN REVIEW

The history of behavior science begins with Aristotle's naturalistic classification of behavior. Soon superseded by a theological philosophy, behavior analysis remains dormant for nearly 2000 years. But in the seventeenth century it arises anew with Descartes' conception that the animal body is a machine, some of whose movements are lawful and regular. These automatic-like movements presently are shown by Robert Whytt and several generations of subsequent physiologists to be related in precise ways to particular events in the animal's environment. This relation between an environmental event and a particular movement becomes the first lawful unit of analysis for behavior science. It is the reflex. Eventually Pavlov extends the reflex concept to include environment-behavior relations which are conditional upon prior operations in the animal's history. These conditional reflexes make possible an analysis of some of the behavior that an organism acquires during its lifetime. Behavior that has a spontaneity not seen in reflexes is shown first by Thorndike to obey certain qualitative laws that differ from the laws of reflexes. At about this time John Watson begins his campaign to convince psychology, the study of mind, that mind is mostly behavior. With the discovery by B. F. Skinner of a reliable subject matter in operant response rate, spontaneously emitted behavior begins to yield up laws of its own, every bit as general and predictable as those of the reflex. The history of behavior analysis reveals that men are remarkably inclined to adopt superfluous interpretations about behavior, rather than accept the adequacy of descriptions of behavior itself. Nearly every contributor to the science has shared some of the superstitions of his times about the behavior which he is investigating.

References for Chapter 1

Boring, E. G. *A history of experimental psychology.* New York: The Century Company, 1929.

Darwin, C. R. *The expression of the emotions in man and animals.* London: Murray, 1873.

Dennis, W. *Readings in the history of psychology.* New York: Appleton-Century, 1948. (Chapters 3, 45, 48, and 50.)

Fearing, F. *Reflex action: a study in the history of physiological psychology.* Baltimore: Williams and Wilkins, 1930.

Garrett, H. *Great experiments in psychology.* New York: Appleton-Century-Crofts, 1951.

Hall, G. S., and Hodge, C. F. A sketch of the history of reflex action. *Amer. J. Psychol.,* 1890, **3,** 71–86; 149–173; 343–363.

Kantor, J. R. *The scientific evolution of psychology.* Vol. 1. Chicago: Principia Press, 1963.

Pavlov, I. P. *Lectures on conditioned reflexes.* New York: International Publishers, 1928.

Romanes, G. J. *Animal intelligence.* (4th ed.) London: Kegan Paul, 1886.

Skinner, B. F. A review of C. L. Hull's Principles of behavior. *Amer. J. Psychol.,* 1944, **57,** 276–281.

Skinner, B. F. The concept of the reflex in the description of behavior. *J. gen. Psychol.,* 1931, **5,** 427–458.

Thorndike, E. L. Animal intelligence. *Psychol. Rev. Monogr. Suppl.* 1898, No. 8.

Toulmin, S., and Goodfield, June. *The architecture of matter.* New York: Harper and Row, 1962.

Watson, J. B. Psychology as the behaviorist views it. *Psychol. Rev.,* 1913, **20,** 158–177.

Chapter 2 **REFLEX (ELICITED) BEHAVIOR**

██T WOULD BE CONSISTENT WITH OUR HISTORICAL account of behavior science to assert that psychology is the science concerned with the way an organism's behavior is related to its environment. Perhaps the simplest of these environment-behavior relationships is the reflex.

For the physiologist, the reflex is a phenomenon to be explained. That is, the physiologist will be interested in the anatomical structures underlying the reflex and the bodily events that occur between the eliciting stimulus and the response. His interest lies in the composition or *analysis* of the reflex. For the psychologist, on the other hand, the reflex is a phenomenon to be used in explaining other behaviors. That is, the psychologist will be interested in showing that complex behavior patterns are composed of, or can be *synthesized* from, reflexes. The analysis-synthesis distinction shows at once the common meeting ground and point of departure of the two sciences. From the reflex, the two disciplines move off in different directions. As psychologists, we wish to use the reflex as an explanatory principle or as a unit of analysis of more complex behavior. Accordingly, we must understand some of the quantitative and conceptual properties of reflexes.

2.1 THE S-R FORMULA

As we have seen in considering reflexive behavior in Chapter 1, both Descartes and Whytt represented the environment with the concept of the *stimulus*. And they represented behavior in terms of the organism's movements or *response to* that stimulus. These concepts have continued to be useful for the description of lawful relationships between the environment and behavior. In this chapter, we shall designate the stimulus in the reflex relationship by the symbol S, and the response by the symbol R. The lawfulness exhibited in the relationship between environmental events and reflex actions may thus be summarized in the formula

$$R_2 = f(S_2)$$

This formula states that a certain reflex response, R_2 (called a *respondent*), is a function of (that is, depends upon) a stimulus event, S_2 (called an *elicitor*).[1] This formula expresses an important relationship or correlation between two events. In the rest of this chapter we examine this correlation in detail.

One of Sherrington's experiments suffices as an illustration. He connected one of the leg muscles of a cat to a device for measuring the contraction of that muscle. Earlier, under anesthesia, the cat's brain had been severed from the spinal cord. (In the study of reflexes, influences that are not directly under the control of the experimenter are often surgically removed. In this case, severing brain from cord removes any possible effects the brain might have on the muscle being studied.) Brief electric shocks of various strengths were then applied to a sensory nerve known to be involved in a reflex arc to that muscle.

Figure 2–1 illustrates hypothetical results of the kind that Sherrington might have obtained as he gradually stepped up the shock intensity over seven successive trials. Some of the properties of a typical reflex are represented: for example, if we observe in Fig. 2–1 that the time line moves from left to right, we can see first of all that the weakest shock (the shortest and leftmost shock) does not elicit a respondent at all. Values of shock too low to elicit respondents are said to be *subliminals*. The next value of shock still seems too weak to elicit a reflex response. But to be certain, we present the same value of shock again on trial 3. This time we get a response. This value of shock lies in what we shall call the penumbra or threshold region: it is strong enough so that sometimes it elicits a respondent and sometimes it does not. Continuing our shock presentations at yet greater strengths, we observe a number of interesting effects: (1) Each shock presentation is followed by (elicits) a respondent, (2) stronger shock elicitors are followed by stronger respondents, (3) respondents occur more rapidly following the stronger elicitors; that is, the time between elicitor and respondent, called the *latency,* is shorter when the elicitor is stronger.

---

[1] The numerical subscripts will be clarified in Chapter 3.

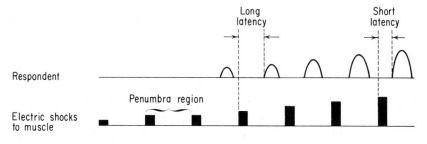

Figure 2–1. Schematic temporal sequence of repeated presentations of an elicitor and the occurrence of associated respondents. The height of the respondents indicates their magnitude. The height of the elicitors indicates their intensity. The distance between the onset of the elicitor and the onset of the respondent represents the latency. The time line is made by a periodic marker which marks off arbitrary equal intervals of time.

The discovery of relations and properties like those illustrated in Fig. 2–1 is one of the persistent goals of science. When relationships that hold between the values of one event (such as shock intensities) and the values of another event (such as the magnitude or rapidity of muscle movement) can be isolated and reproduced day after day, experiment after experiment, we often speak of the lawfulness of nature. Figuratively we are saying that nature appears to be bound by certain laws whose discovery is a prime aim of scientific research.

We must carefully qualify this latter statement, however, for it seems certain that nature's relationships or laws are not like sea shells on a beach, waiting for us to come along and gather them into a scientific basket. Before we can establish laws relating our concepts, we must have formulated, at least to a first approximation, our concepts. The discovery of the reflex laws was preceded by nearly three hundred years of a gradual evolution of the concept of the stimulus, beginning with Descartes. Thus, science is a bootstrap operation. In pre-scientific stages, our intuitions and crude experience lead us to suspect that a certain order exists in nature, and we speculate as to the nature of that order. (For example, consider Descartes' guess that involuntary behavior was machine-like.) Then we begin to perturb nature a bit, that is, to do experiments and thereby change the natural course of events so that we can get a better idea of what can happen with a particular phenomenon.

But to do even a first, exploratory, experiment, we usually need to define our phenomenon more precisely, so as to decide just what to alter, and just where to look for the effects of our experimental alteration. The results of our first experiment will enable us to define our terms even more accurately. In this way we continually modify our concepts. At the same time we enrich them by relating them to other things that are known. Moreover, having refined our concepts on the basis of experiment, we are led to new experiments. A good experiment is sometimes said to answer one old question and raise two new ones. There is no endpoint to this process (which is science) since we are continually refining and redefining our concepts, and continually relating one to another.

2.2 PRIMARY REFLEX LAWS

The order or lawfulness illustrated by Fig. 2–1 is at the level of one of the simplest units of behavior, the reflex. Because this lawfulness involves the *behavior* of organisms as the property that is subject to, or sensitive to, changes in the eliciting stimulus, we call these laws behavior laws.

Scientists attempt to formulate their laws as generally as possible. They would not be satisfied to have one law for the effect of electric shocks on leg muscle, another for the effect of acids in the mouth on salivation, and yet another for the pupillary reflex. They prefer to express their laws in terms of certain properties common to all these relations, so that they encompass as wide a range of phenomena as possible. So, when Sherrington studied reflexes he made a study of many reflexes involving different elicitors and respondents. From experiments of this sort he formulated three laws which we may call the three primary laws of the reflex. These laws are not stated in terms of any particular elicitor such as electric shock, or any particular respondent such as a given muscle movement. They are, rather, stated *generally* in terms of eliciting stimuli (*any* elicitor) and responses (*any* respondent). In so stating them we obtain a pleasing generality, but at a sacrifice of particular details. For instance, the exact relation between stimulus intensity and respondent magnitude varies from reflex to reflex. Sometimes the relationship is very nearly directly proportional, so that over a wide range of stimulus intensities doubling the stimulus intensity will double the respondent magnitude, and so on. In other reflexes, a tenfold increase in stimulus intensity may be required to produce a doubling of respondent magnitude. Our primary reflex laws are written in such a way that these differences are hidden.

Elicitors may always be specified on an intensity dimension. Thus shock elicitors may be weak, moderate, or strong in intensity. Light elicitors for pupillary responses may vary from faint intensities that we can just see to intensities so high that the light is painful. As we have noted, energies below a certain level on the intensity dimension are insufficient to elicit any response. As the intensity is gradually raised, a region is found about which values of intensity *may or may not* elicit a movement. This region of indeterminacy where the intensity may or may not be strong enough to elicit a respondent is the threshold penumbra region. We may state this information more specifically in a law:

1. *Law of the Threshold.* There is a range of intensities below which no response will occur and above which a response will always occur. Within this range itself responses will occur with some uncertainty. An arbitrary point within this uncertainty region (say, that intensity which elicits the response 50 per cent of the time) is called the threshold, and intensities above that point are called *eliciting stimuli.*

As the stimulus is raised further in intensity, the response now occurs each time and appears graded in relation to the stimulus. Thus, strong elicitors rapidly elicit strong and long-lasting respondents. Weak elicitors are followed more slowly by weak and shorter-lasting responses. Most of this information may be represented by two reflex laws:

2. *Law of Intensity-Magnitude.* As the eliciting stimulus intensity is increased, the magnitude of the elicited respondent also increases.
3. *Law of Latency.* As the eliciting stimulus intensity is increased, the time (latency) between the onset of the eliciting stimulus and the onset of the respondent decreases.

The laws of the reflex are important in defining the reflex concept. A reflex may be said to be a correlation between a change in part of the environment and a behavioral property such that the three very special laws we described above hold. Schematically, a reflex may be represented as

$$S_2 \rightarrow R_2$$

where S_2 represents an elicitor, $\rightarrow$ represents "causes by the laws of the reflex," and R_2 represents the behavioral change produced. In this bare formula nothing is said about *how* R_2 depends on S_2. Such a formula may be said to be maximally general (it describes every reflex action) and minimally precise (it specifies the details of no particular reflex action). The arrow $\rightarrow$ may be read *elicits,* where elicit is defined as "leads to, by the laws of the reflex." The term elicit is of some importance in the science of behavior for it denotes a very specific set of causal laws between environment and behavior, namely these laws of the reflex. Thus, S_2 may be spoken of as an eliciting stimulus, a change in the environment that is correlated with behavior by the laws of the reflex. Similarly, R_2, the respondent, is defined as an elicited response. It is useful to reserve the word elicit for the precise definition stated above. In later chapters we shall employ the term stimulus repeatedly in conjunction with a different sort of control over behavior, but we shall distinguish that control by carefully omitting the qualifier "elicit" in that context.

2.3 SECONDARY LAWS OF THE REFLEX

Certain so-called secondary laws of the reflex encode additional information. One of these is the *Law of Reflex Fatigue*. When a respondent is repeatedly elicited many times per second by a constant stimulus intensity, the respondent magnitude gradually declines, and eventually the response may cease altogether. This phenomenon is called reflex fatigue and is shown schematically in Fig. 2–2.

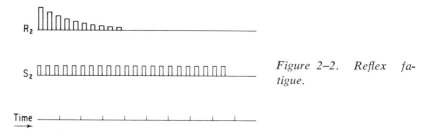

Figure 2–2. Reflex fatigue.

A common error is made in saying that the respondent's decline to zero is *due* to fatigue. This is an example of an entirely empty explanation and should be avoided. A phenomenon, (y), is partially explained when it can be related to another phenomenon, (x), occurring earlier in time. Rain, (y), is partially explained when it can be related to condensation of water vapor that occurs when a warm cloud is rapidly cooled, (x). Typhoid fever, (y), is partially explained when it can be related to the activities, (x), of a small microorganism, *Salmonella typhosa*. But in explaining the respondent decline, (y), of Fig. 2–2 as being due to fatigue, to what (x) are we relating it? Fatigue, used in this sense, is an unobservable entity without any independent properties to relate to the observable phenomenon. This decline of the respondent *is* fatigue, not *due* to fatigue.

Another secondary reflex law is the *Law of Temporal Summation of Subliminals*. We recall from the Law of the Threshold that very weak presentations of appropriate energies do not elicit respondents. These low energy values are said to be below the threshold, and are called subliminals. Nevertheless, if we present two or more of these subliminals in quick succession we can, under certain conditions, produce a respondent. This phenomenon is shown schematically in Fig. 2–3. It is as though the two subliminal intensities added up to make a single elicitor. The temporal summation seen in Fig. 2–3 further defines just exactly what we mean by these concepts we call reflexes, eliciting stimuli, and elicited responses.

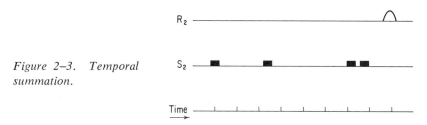

Figure 2–3. Temporal summation.

We may note in this connection that the word elicit is often uncritically taken to be identical to "cause." (For example, a light stimulus may be said to "cause" a pupillary respondent.) The term "cause" is an old word used at times in the history of philosophy and science to denote a necessary and sufficient relationship between events. The word appears to have been used to describe an event X whenever X is related to an event Y such that *if* event X, *then* event Y will happen; and *if not Y, then not X*. Try this formula. Let Y be a respondent, say a muscle contraction, "caused" by a shock stimulus we shall call X. Clearly it is true that *if* the shock *then* the contraction. And it is also true that if we do not observe the contraction (*not Y*) then there must not have been a shock stimulus given (*not X*). It is thus evident that, logically, an eliciting stimulus may be said to "cause" a response in reflex action, but it is also clear that such a statement offers little information about the exact nature of the causal relation. In general we shall demand a more detailed description of the relation between behavior and its causes than is afforded by the mere statement of their logical succession in the X and Y formula. Therefore, the term *elicit* is preferable to "cause" in the present context—not because it is any more objective or logical than the word "cause"—but because "elicit" carries with it the tremendous weight of all the primary and secondary laws of the reflex. Evidently, when we kick a football we "cause" it to "respond" by flying through the air. But the laws governing that "response" are Galileo's laws of motion, not Sherrington's laws of the reflex.

2.4 REFLEX STRENGTH: A HYPOTHETICAL CONSTRUCT

Consider a given reflex, say the knee jerk to a tap on the knee. At any given moment this reflex will have a given threshold, indexed by the least intense tap necessary to elicit *some* movement of the leg. Furthermore, at any given moment, a tap of a fixed intensity will elicit a movement of a given magnitude, with a given latency between S_2 and R_2. Also, at that same moment we may conceive that a given number of taps would be necessary to fatigue the reflex. An important characteristic of reflexes is found in the observation that at those times when the threshold is low (a very weak tap is effective), the R_2 magnitude to a given (standard) value of S_2 will be high, the latency will be short, and the number of successive S_2's needed to fatigue the reflex will be large. Conversely, at those times when the threshold is high (a strong tap is needed for *any* movement), the R_2 magnitude to a standard value of S_2 will be low, the latency will be long, and only a few successive S_2's will be needed to fatigue the reflex. This systematic "hanging together" or *covariance* of reflex properties (threshold, magnitude, latency, etc.) gives rise to an interesting logical construction. We are led to name this covariance and to infer that a hypothetical entity exists which intervenes between the stimulus and the respondent. It is argued that this entity, to be designated as *reflex strength,* determines the systematic variation, or the covariance, of each respondent property. In the case of the reflex, the construct of reflex strength is defined by this covariance in such a way that large magnitudes, short latencies, low thresholds, slowly fatigued R_2's, etc., represent strong reflexes. Conversely, small magnitudes, long latencies, high thresholds, rapidly fatigued R_2's etc., constitute weak reflexes. Note that the construct is not defined exclusively in terms of the values of the respondent. It incorporates (in the threshold) the value of the elicitor as well. Hence, a large-magnitude R_2 need not necessarily represent a strong reflex. It might well result from a weak reflex being tested with an intense S_2. The construct of reflex strength is represented in Fig. 2–4.

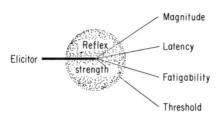

Figure 2–4. The construct of reflex strength.

The construct of Fig. 2–4 is said to be hypothetical simply because it is not directly observed. Nobody ever saw the strength of a reflex; what we see are merely the changes in the behavior. But the fact that the behavioral changes are correlated one with another is an inducement to group them as reflections of an underlying single entity. Forming constructs like reflex strength has certain dangers, particularly in ascribing properties to the hypothetical construct that go far beyond the observations that give rise to it. Still hypothetical construction is an important and persistent kind of concept formation in all sciences and its justification is seen in its usefulness. In the particular case of reflex strength, it enters as a useful concept into the formation of other laws in a behavior system. (Remember, *first* we must have our concepts, *then* we arrive at our laws.) For example, drugs, diseases of the central nervous system, and simultaneous elicitation of other reflexes all cause concurrent changes in the quantities that define reflex strength. Hence it is convenient to represent these related laws by a single term, reflex strength. We shall see other examples of this kind of summarization and compounding of relations in later chapters.

2.5 COMMON EXAMPLES OF REFLEXES

The observations that are summarized as the laws of the reflex are most easily made on muscles isolated surgically from influences other than those of the elicitor under study. Although we study reflexes in surgically prepared muscles to obtain precision of control, reflexes are easily seen in qualitative form in the intact behavior of all animals, from man to the lowliest of species. Descartes' illustration of the withdrawal of a human limb from a flame (see p. 1) is one such intact human reflex. Others are the elicitation of tears by onion juice, of sneezing by pepper in the nose, of jerking of the knee by a tap on the patellar tendon, of discharge of saliva by food placed in the mouth, of change in heart beat by a loud sound, and so on. All of these reflexes conform to our fundamental model, or *paradigm*

$$S_2 \rightarrow R_2$$

where some S_2 elicits some respondent R_2; and if the reflex could be properly isolated, a relation like that in Fig. 2–1 would be obtained. Some examples of elicitor-respondent sequences are shown in Table 2–1. All of the correlations in Table 2–1 are reflexes. Some involve skeletal muscles (sneezes, knee jerks, shivering), some involve cardiac muscles (heart-rate changes), some involve glands (salivation, tears), and some involve smooth muscles (blanching of skin, pupillary changes). All have

Table 2–1
COMMON REFLEX SEQUENCES

NAME OF REFLEX	ELICITOR S_2	BY THE LAWS OF THE REFLEX LEADS TO	RESPONDENT R_2
Tearing	Onion juice in the eye	$\longrightarrow$	Tearing of the eye
Sneeze	Feather in the nose	$\longrightarrow$	Sneeze
Patellar	Tap to knee	$\longrightarrow$	Knee jerk
Salivary	Food in mouth	$\longrightarrow$	Salivation
Startle	Loud sound	$\longrightarrow$	Heart rate speeds up, skeletal muscles contract, pupils dilate, etc.
Shiver	Cold	$\longrightarrow$	Shivering, blanching of skin
Pupillary	Light in eye	$\longrightarrow$	Pupil contraction

been called involuntary reflexes at one time or another. The term involuntary is a historical term used to express crudely the automatic, elicited nature of certain behaviors. Since Sherrington's quantitative analysis of the reflex, the original conception of elicitation has been very greatly refined. It seems judicious, therefore, to replace the older and vaguer term "involuntary" with the more exact "elicited," which encompasses all the reflex laws in its definition. This eventual replacement of a poorly specified term, which was often associated with a pre-scientific frame of reference, is a common and typical occurrence in science. On the other hand, sometimes a scientific analysis will retain the old word but rededicate it with a new and precise meaning. Science has retained the words *force* in physics, *element* in chemistry, and *motive* in psychology from the vernacular, but has greatly changed and expanded their meaning. But it is not always easy to slough off the connotations of pre-scientific concepts, and sometimes a new word aids the conceptual shift. The old word will then be left to die the slow death of disuse. Such is the fate of the word "involuntary" in psychology.

2.6 VARIABILITY IN MEASUREMENTS; SUMMARIZING DATA IN FREQUENCY DISTRIBUTIONS; SOME SIMPLE STATISTICS; THE NORMAL CURVE

An important step towards the analysis of any natural phenomenon occurs when certain of its aspects can be *measured*. Measurements imply numbers, and numbers that are recorded by investigators under various conditions of observation make up what are called raw quantitative *data* (the plural form of the word *datum*). A prodigious number of measurements, or data, are often collected in the course of a single experiment. Even a very casual demonstration of one of the laws of the reflex could easily require as many as 250 measurements of respondent magnitude. The numerous measurements which constitute the raw data of an experiment are inconvenient. Their very bulk makes them difficult to comprehend, even by the investigator who collected them. Certainly, they could hardly be communicated in their raw form to the scientific community at large. Under such pressures, methods of summarizing data and characterizing them by certain of their prominent features have evolved. Such summaries and descriptive characterizations constitute what are called *descriptive statistics*. In the remainder of this section we will briefly consider certain simple statistical ideas which experimentalists have found useful in describing and summarizing their data.

Suppose we have been given the task of determining the magnitude of the patellar respondent, elicited by a tap of 3-oz force applied to the knee. We begin by seating our subject comfortably, positioning his limbs in a standard way, and then applying our 3-oz tap to a particular place as precisely as we can. We proceed to measure the extent of the resulting knee jerk by noting the maximum height (excursion) that the leg travels, say at the ankle, before returning to its original position. Let us imagine that our leg excursion measures are made with an ordinary ruler and that we observe in this case that the leg traveled a distance of 1¾ in. At this point we may be inclined to announce that the knee-jerk magnitude to an elicitor of 3-oz force is 1.75 in.

Now science is generally never content with unrepeatable observations, so we may be challenged to repeat our simple operations. We may thus find ourselves eliciting the reflex and measuring the respondent magnitude over again several times, each time recording the numerical results of our measurement operations. Though we have been careful to tap in the same spot each time, to check the original position of the limb, and to give the subject a brief rest between taps, we observe nevertheless that our answer for the respondent magnitude is 1¾ in. on one trial, 1⅝ in. on another, and 1¹³⁄₁₆ in. on still a third. We find ourselves somewhat at a loss as to which particular measurement to report as the *true* value of the respondent magnitude to a 3-oz tap. What started out as a simple task has become more complicated than we had originally suspected.

Suppose now that we decide to make some sort of an average of our measurements and call this average *the* respondent magnitude to a 3-oz tap. We add up our values

$$
\begin{array}{r}
1\tfrac{3}{4} \\
1\tfrac{5}{8} \\
1\tfrac{13}{16} \\
\hline
5\tfrac{3}{16}
\end{array}
$$

and then—to give each measurement equal representation in the average—divide by the number of measurements we have, in this case, 3. We obtain a decimal number 1.7291. . . . Since we were unable originally to read our ruler to better than $\frac{1}{16}$ we shall be inclined to round our answer to two decimal places, and report that the knee-jerk magnitude is 1.73 inches.

But consider now what we have actually done by such a simple thing as taking an average of our measurements in this way. On what grounds are we permitted to add up our measurements and divide by the number of measurements and call this the "true" value? We discover that the question is not easily answered. Why, for example, did we not choose the result that lay midway between all the measures as the "true" measure, in this case, $1\frac{3}{4}$?

An even more important difficulty presents itself when we attempt to measure the knee jerk again the next day and discover that, while our measures are again close to each other (say $1\frac{1}{2}$, $1\frac{3}{4}$, $1\frac{11}{16}$), they are not exactly the same as yesterday's values. What number do we now assign as the true value of the respondent to 3 oz? Not only are errors of measurement present, but uncontrolled conditions such as temperature, humidity, and how much sleep our subject obtained overnight may be affecting our measures. It is unlikely that we could ever completely control all the influences that have a disturbing effect on our measurements. We are forced in the end to conclude that the "true" value of the respondent is only a fictional concept and that no operations exist for us to discover it.

In practice, of course, the situation is not nearly so bad as we have made it out to be. In fact our measurements are all reasonably close to each other, and we are often in a position to compute just such an average, or *arithmetic mean*. Having once computed this arithmetic mean, we can let it stand as our best *estimate* of the respondent magnitude and abandon as unrealistic our search for the one and only one true value.

The average or arithmetic mean is one of the most primitive though common statistical concepts in all of science. This concept makes possible the abstraction, from a number of repeated measurements, of one value which is taken to represent the whole lot of measurements. Thus we may measure the boiling point of ethyl alcohol many times and conclude that its average boiling point equals 78.1°F. Or, we may observe the frequency of cars crossing a bridge in successive 5-min intervals for an hour and conclude that the average 5-min rate is 31 cars per 5 min. We justify such averaging by appeal to certain general properties of the measurements, which we now examine.

The rationale for the use of an average is best seen by looking closely at some of the properties of repeated R_2 measurements. Suppose we have obtained 20 values for R_2 magnitude in inches, recorded in Table 2–2 as

Table 2–2

MAGNITUDE OF KNEE-JERK RESPONDENTS IN INCHES ON 20 SUCCESSIVE APPLICATIONS OF A TAP TO THE KNEE

TRIAL	R_2 EXCURSION IN INCHES
1	1.75
2	1.62
3	1.81
4	1.50
5	1.75
6	1.69
7	1.46
8	1.55
9	1.62
10	1.69
11	1.38
12	1.75
13	1.69
14	1.69
15	1.62
16	1.55
17	1.81
18	1.94
19	1.70
20	1.42

decimal numbers for simplicity. We wish now to display or represent these raw data in a form that will reveal some of their properties at a glance. For this purpose one of the first manipulations that will often prove useful is to group the measurements into somewhat broader classes than those in which they are originally given. Suppose we group the results of Table 2–2 in categories of tenths of an inch. Thus we might usefully establish the set of categories shown in the left-hand column of Table 2–3. These categories are tenths of an inch wide. In Table 2–3 the trial numbers on which the respondent happened to fall into a given category are depicted in the right-hand column.

Table 2–3 successfully boils down our data into the 7 categories from 1.30 to 1.99. Where we began with 20 individual measurements, we now have 7 categories of measurements. We have lost some precision (1.50 can no

Table 2–3
REGROUPING OF THE MEASUREMENTS OF
TABLE 2–2 INTO BROADER (1/10-IN.) CATEGORIES

CATEGORY	THE TRIALS ON WHICH THE RESPONDENT FELL INTO THE PARTICULAR CATEGORY
1.00–1.09	
1.10–1.19	
1.20–1.29	
1.30–1.39	11
1.40–1.49	7, 20
1.50–1.59	4, 8, 16
1.60–1.69	2, 6, 9, 10, 13, 14, 15
1.70–1.79	1, 5, 12, 19
1.80–1.89	3, 17
1.90–1.99	18
2.00–2.09	
2.10–2.19	

longer be distinguished from 1.55 in Table 2–3), but we have gained some economy in representation. The gain is not large with only 20 original measurements, but it would be very large had we begun with 20,000.

A useful further summary could be made if our data were to be pictured graphically. A number of pictorial schemes have been suggested as aids to representing data of the sort we have here. We consider one class of these. It is possible first to space out regularly the various values of our measurement groups on a horizontal line, called the *x* axis, or *abscissa*. Second, we may let a vertical intersecting line (called the *y* axis, or *ordinate*) represent the number or frequency of measurements. In this way if we place a × for each of our measurements in such a framework (called a rectangular or Cartesian coordinate system) we shall obtain the pictorial representation of the *distribution* of values shown in Fig. 2–5.

Some features of Fig. 2–5 are of particular interest. First note that there are exactly 20 ×'s. Thus each measurement appears as a unique × in Fig. 2–5, and the total number of ×'s is the total number of measurements taken.

A second feature of Fig. 2–5 is its shape. It appears to pile up around a central value, and to be roughly symmetrical. These characteristics of many repeated measurements justify the use of a single average to summarize the entire lot of measurements. Behind that one "average" number tacitly hides a picture more or less like Fig. 2–5. The average of a frequency distribution, such as Fig. 2–5, is said to represent an index of the so-called *central tendency* of the distribution. But we may note that there are several possible choices for central tendency indices. A simple one would be to choose the category containing the largest frequency (the most ×'s). Choosing the

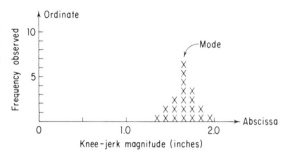

Figure 2–5. Hypothetical knee-jerk measurements (categorized in tenths of inches) represented as a frequency distribution in a rectangular coordinate system.

central tendency value in this manner is called finding the *mode* of a distribution. In the present case the mode is the 1.60–1.69 category, for it contains 7 measurements, the most of any category (see Fig. 2–5).

A second type of average is found by isolating the particular measurement category that has the same number of measurements below it as it has above it. Such a statistic of central tendency is called the *median* value of a distribution. The median category of the present data lies within the 1.60–1.69 category because a value can be found within the category which would be greater than the lower 10 and less than the higher 10 values.

The third type of average, known as the *mean,* is the kind we calculated previously by adding up the measurements and dividing by the total number of measurements. In the present case, this average, or *arithmetic mean,* turns out to be about 1.71.

Which of these three "averages" represents the closest to the actual respondent magnitude? No general answer is possible to this question, because "actual respondent magnitude" is a fictional quantity. The only way we have of assessing respondent magnitude is to obtain repeated measurements of it under as nearly constant conditions as we can arrange. These measurements would be like those represented by Fig. 2–5. If pressed for a single number to summarize them, the best we could do would be to calculate one or more indices of central tendency. In the present case the symmetrical shape insures that any of the three indices will agree closely, but in some distributions containing a few measurements very far from the mode (such as in the distribution of incomes in the United States where a *few* people are *very* rich but most people cluster around a central point) the arithmetic mean is dragged out towards the few, whereas the median is less affected and the mode is undisturbed.

The distribution of Fig. 2–5 is more conventionally represented by either (A) or (B) of Fig. 2–6. In (A) the ×'s have been replaced by bars whose height is proportional to the actual frequency, *f.* Part (A) is called a *histogram* and will find frequent use in describing behavioral data in subsequent chapters. In (B), the ×'s have been replaced by straight lines drawn connecting the height of each category. Part (B) is called a *frequency polygon.* Both representations shown in Fig. 2–6 are merely alternate ways of picturing frequency distributions.

In all frequency distributions the indices of central tendency assume great

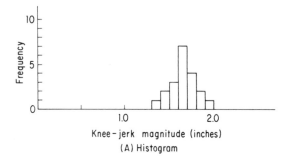

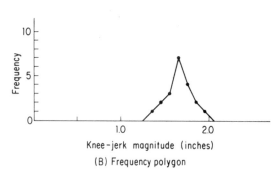

Figure 2–6. Two more representations of frequency distributions (A) as histogram and (B) as frequency polygon. The data are derived from Figure 2–5.

importance. But another important property of frequency distributions is the spread of measurements, technically called their *dispersion*. Consider the two respondent magnitude distributions of Fig. 2–7 taken, let us say, from two different subjects. Both distributions have identical central tendency measures (means, medians, and modes) yet they differ in such an obvious way that we should like to have a summary index to characterize this kind of difference. Let us note first of all that the difference between the two curves of Fig. 2–7 is grossly one of "spread." But clearly the spread of a distribution is related to the *variability* of the measures it contains. The more variable our

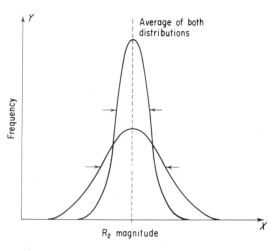

Figure 2–7. Two frequency distributions with identical central tendencies and different spreads, or dispersions.

measurements and the more they differ one from another, the greater will be the spread. A simple though crude statistic for summarizing the spread or dispersion of measurements can be calculated by finding the largest measurement (in our original reflex data 1.94) and subtracting from it the lowest obtained score, 1.38. In the data at hand such an operation yields a value $1.94 - 1.38 = 0.56$. Such a statistic is called the *range* of the distribution. The range is easy to calculate but not as useful as we would wish. Its difficulty is that a single very extreme measurement changes it drastically. For this reason we are likely to say that the range is a statistic that lacks stability.

Another more sophisticated measure of the dispersion of a distribution is provided by first approximating the data summarized by Figs. 2–5 and 2–6 with the kind of mathematically smooth bell-shaped curves shown in Fig. 2–7. These smooth curves are symmetrical and are called *normal* curves. The inquiring student may well be interested in how these smooth curves of Fig. 2–7 were discovered, but unfortunately their mathematical derivation cannot be treated here. We must be content to say that they do seem to approximate reasonably well many sorts of repeated measurements, of which our respondent magnitude is one. A useful index for dispersion or variability can be found by examining closely the shape of the two curves of Fig. 2–7. If we begin at the extreme leftmost of either curve we shall observe that at first the curve is concave upward in shape. Then for both distributions the curve passes through a region in which the curve is almost a straight line. Finally, continuing rightward, the curve assumes a concave downward shape, eventually reaching a maximum at the point labeled average. Since these normal curves are symmetrical, a corresponding analysis can be made beginning from the right tail and moving to the left. The two symmetrical points at which the curves change from concave upward to concave downward are called the *points of inflection* and they are located at the horizontal arrows in Fig. 2–7. These localized points make good landmarks to characterize the spread of the distributions (compare the distance between the two sets of arrows of Fig. 2–7 placed at these points). And, although they are difficult to judge exactly by eye, they are not difficult to calculate from actual measurements.

It should be noted that the points of inflection are related to the average or mean of the distribution such that *the greater the spread of a normal curve, the further away from the mean these points lie.* In other words, the greater the dispersion, the greater will the points of inflection deviate from the mean. This idea of deviation is embodied in the name usually given to the points of inflection of a normal curve, the *standard deviation* points. The standard deviation (abbreviated σ, or sigma) is the distance from the mean to either one of the inflection points. The great advantage of these points as indices to the spread of a distribution over other measures (for example, the range) is that they partition the normal distribution in an extremely useful way, as is shown by Fig. 2–8. In particular, it turns out that for data which can be approximated by a normal curve, about 34 per cent of the measurements will lie in the region between -1σ and the mean; and about 34 per cent will lie in the region between $+1\sigma$ and the mean. Hence about 68 per

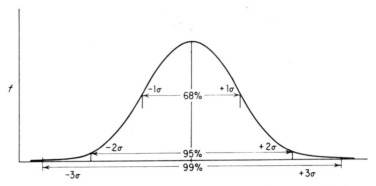

Figure 2–8. Normal curve, partitioned by its standard deviation, showing the percentage of measurements lying in each region.

cent of the measurements will be contained within the mean $\pm 1\sigma$. Similarly, about 95 per cent will be contained within $\pm 2\sigma$; over 99 per cent within $\pm 3\sigma$. Thus, there exists a very exact relationship between the standard deviation and the percentage of measurements to be found in different regions of the curve, a fact not true for the range or other common measures of variability. Computational methods for estimating σ for any given set of measurements are to be found in numerous elementary statistics texts and will not be described here.

Transformation to Relative-Frequency Distributions. A very useful and simple change is often made in the original measurements in dealing with distributions. Rather than graphing the actual number of events in a given category directly, we often divide the number observed in a given category by the total number of measurements we took. The result of this operation is always a number less than or equal to 1, which is called the *relative* frequency of that category. For example, referring to Table 2–3, we might divide the total number of measurements in the 1.70–1.79 category (4) by the total number of measurements (20) to obtain $\frac{4}{20} = 0.2$, the relative frequency in that particular category. A useful way to think of relative frequency is to consider it as the proportion of the total measurements that occur in a given category. If we multiply this number by 100 we get that percentage of all the measurements that falls into the particular category. A set of such percentages, or relative frequencies, provides us with a convenient way of comparing two distributions when the total number of measurements in each is not necessarily the same. Notice that a relative-frequency distribution or per cent distribution curve has exactly the same shape, or *form,* as the distribution curve of the actual observed frequencies from which it was derived.

EXERCISE 1.

Transform the distribution of Fig. 2–5 into a relative-frequency distribution.

Chapter 3   **PAVLOVIAN CONDITIONING**

AROUND 1903, PAVLOV, THE RUSSIAN PHYSIOLOGIST, became interested in the phenomenon that he at first called "psychic secretions." Pavlov describes the point of departure of his investigations in the following quotation:

> If food or some rejectable substance finds its way into the mouth, a secretion of saliva is produced. The purpose of this secretion is in the case of food to alter it chemically, in the case of a rejectable substance to dilute and wash it out of the mouth. This is an example of a reflex due to the physical and chemical properties of a substance when it comes into contact with the mucous membrane of the mouth and tongue. But, in addition to this, a similar reflex secretion is evoked when these substances are placed at a distance from the dog and the receptor organs affected are only those of smell and sight. Even the vessel from which the food has been given is sufficient to evoke an alimentary reflex complete in all its details; and, further, the secretion may be provoked even by the sight of the person who brought the vessel, or by the sound of his footsteps (Pavlov, 1927, p. 13).

It was clear to Pavlov from the beginning that some kind of *association* between the salivary reflex $S_2 \rightarrow R_2$ and such arbitrary events as food containers and footsteps was responsible for the ability of the latter to evoke "psychic secretions." Pavlov's first major contribution to behavior science was his description and elaboration of the necessary and sufficient conditions for this association. Through systematic study of the salivary respondent of dogs, Pavlov discovered that if any arbitrary environmental

37

change (say, S_1) directly and reliably preceded the reflex elicitor for salivation, S_1 could itself come to produce salivation.

3.1 CONDITIONED REFLEXES AND THE NATURE OF AN EXPERIMENT

We examine in detail an experiment by one of Pavlov's students (Anrep, 1920) as an example of the Pavlovian method and results which led to this important conclusion. Figure 3–1 depicts the experimental situation used by Pavlov and his colleagues at the Institute of

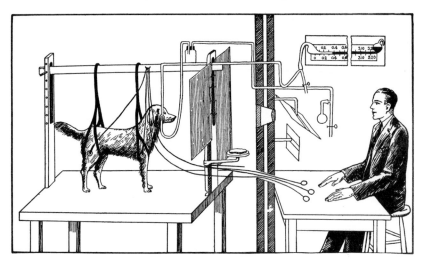

Figure 3–1. Representation of a Pavlovian situation for conditioning the salivary response in a dog (Pavlov, 1928).

Experimental Medicine in Petrograd (later Leningrad). It is well described by Keller and Schoenfeld:

> First, a normal dog is familiarized with the experimental situation until he shows no disturbance when placed in harness and left alone in a room especially designed to cut off unwanted outside stimuli. A small opening or fistula is made in the dog's cheek near the duct of one of the salivary glands. When the fistula is healed, a glass funnel is carefully cemented to the outside of the cheek so that it will draw off the saliva whenever the gland is activated. From the funnel, the saliva then flows into a glass container or falls, drop by drop, upon a lightly balanced recording platform. The magnitude of responses to various stimuli can be measured by the total vol-

ume or the number of drops secreted in a given unit of time. The experimenter, who sits in an adjoining room, can make his measurements, apply what stimuli he desires (including food), and observe the dog's behavior through a window (Keller and Schoenfeld, 1950, pp. 16–17).

The experimenter is thus in a position to measure the salivary reflex precisely. He is also able to control carefully the presentations of various stimulus events to the organism.

In an experiment by Anrep (1920), a tone was sounded in the animal's room for 5 sec. Then, 2 or 3 sec later, a bit of food was given to the dog. This *pairing* of tone with food was repeated after intervals ranging from 5 to 35 min. In order to observe the effect of the tone alone, the experimenter occasionally presented it for 30 sec unpaired with food. Over the course of 16 days, 50 tone-food associations and 6 tone-alone tests were made. The principal data of Anrep's experiment were obtained during the 6 tone-alone tests. During these tests he carefully measured both the total drops of saliva and the time between the onset of the 30-sec test tone and the first drop of saliva. Table 3–1 presents the data.

Table 3–1

ACQUISITION OF A SALIVARY RESPONDENT TO A TONE
(DATA FROM ANREP, 1920)

NUMBER OF PREVIOUS TONE-FOOD PAIRINGS X	DROPS OF SALIVA Y	TIME ELAPSING BETWEEN ONSET OF TONE AND ENSUING SALIVATION (SECONDS) Z
1	0	—
10	6	18
20	20	9
30	60	2
40	62	1
50	59	2

It is seen in the table that after 1 tone-food pairing, presentation of the tone alone produced no salivation at all. After 10 such pairings, however, 6 drops appeared in the tone-alone test, and the first of these 6 drops came 18 sec after the onset of the test tone. After 20 such pairings, 20 drops were produced, the first drop coming now at only 9 sec. From 30 pairings onward, approximately 60 drops of saliva were obtained during each test, and they began to appear in the first second or two after the onset of the test tone. The results of the experiment are clear-cut. Salivation occurs reliably to an arbitrarily selected tone after the tone is paired with food 30 times.

The process by which a tone comes to *acquire* the ability to produce a salivary response of its own, as pairings with food are increased, is called "conditioning." Pavlov saw the close resemblance between this new correlation of tone with salivation and ordinary reflex action, and was led therefore to call the new correlation a conditional reflex (poorly translated as a "conditioned reflex"). Why he did so is apparent from these words:

> I have termed these new reflexes *conditioned reflexes* to distinguish them from the inborn or *unconditioned reflexes*. The term 'conditioned' is becoming more and more generally employed, and I think its use is fully justified in that, compared with the inborn reflexes, these new reflexes actually do *depend on very many conditions* [ital. added] both in their formation and in the maintenance of their physiological activity. Of course, the terms 'conditioned' and 'unconditioned' could be replaced by others of arguably equal merit. Thus, for example, we might retain the term 'inborn reflexes', and call the new type 'acquired reflexes'; or call the former 'species reflexes' since they are characteristic of the species, and the latter 'individual reflexes' since they vary from animal to animal in a species, and even in the same animal at different times and under different conditions (Pavlov, 1927, p. 25).

3.2 THE PAVLOVIAN PARADIGM: A SCHEMATIC METHOD OF REPRESENTING CONDITIONING

The principle of the conditioned reflex is conveniently summarized by a simple stimulus-response model, or paradigm. The elements of the paradigm are two initial reflexes and a newly developed conditioned "reflex."

Let us represent the reflexes on which conditioning is based as $S_1 \rightarrow R_1$ and $S_2 \rightarrow R_2$. In Pavlov's procedure S_1 precedes S_2. If we ignore the respondent to S_1 this pairing might be represented as

$$S_1$$

$$S_2 \rightarrow R_2$$

According to Pavlov's principle, after a number of such pairings

$(S_1, S_2; S_1, S_2; S_1, S_2; \ldots)$ S_1 comes to evoke a new response, the conditioned response (CR) in diagram [3.1]:

$$S_1 \searrow \\ CR \qquad\qquad [3.1] \\ S_2 \rightarrow R_2.$$

Diagram [3.1] is known as the Pavlovian Paradigm, and represents schematically the procedure and the results of Pavlovian or *classical* conditioning.

Diagram [3.1] gives a schematic or symbolic description of certain aspects of the paradigm, but we may desire a more complete specification. As a useful guide for summarizing the Pavlovian, as well as the many other behavioral paradigms that will occur in subsequent chapters, we introduce a four-part structural representation of such paradigms. In general, every behavioral paradigm will consist of a *Given,* a *Procedure,* a *Process,* and a *Result.* In that framework the Pavlovian paradigm works out as follows.

GIVEN: Two elicitors, S_1 and S_2.

PROCEDURE: Repeatedly pair S_1 with S_2, always in the order S_1, S_2; S_1, S_2; ....

PROCESS: S_1 comes gradually to control a new response (CR), which may resemble the R_2 to S_2.

RESULT: S_1 reliably evokes a CR.

Note certain characteristics of such a paradigm. The *Given* often contains a description of the behavioral state prior to performing the *Procedure.* Here we have to have two elicitors, or two intact reflexes, before we can begin. The *Procedure* is a succinct description of what experimenters do. (We shall often find it useful to represent the procedural aspect of our behavioral paradigms by symbols.) The *Process* tells briefly what happens over time to significant aspects of behavior as we keep applying our procedure. A description of a behavioral process typically takes the form of a graph, with time on the horizontal (X) axis and some property of the organism's behavior on the vertical (Y) axis. We discuss this more completely in a later section. Finally, the *Result* is the end state of the process. When the behavior has ceased changing significantly under the given procedure, the result has been reached. In the following subsections we elaborate some of the more important aspects of the Pavlovian paradigm.

The Relation of CR to R_2. We may regard it an historical accident that Pavlov began his investigation of conditioning with a reflex that yielded CR's very similar in nature to the unconditioned R_2. Both CR and R_2 involve secretory production from the salivary glands. Indeed, the casual observer is unlikely even to detect any difference between conditioned and unconditioned salivation. The similarity between CR and R_2 in the salivary reflex is probably responsible for the general belief, perpetrated until modern times, that CR *is* R_2. But Pavlov himself knew this to be untrue. Not only was the magnitude of the CR different from R_2, but the actual chemical composition of the saliva differed between CR and R_2. Pavlov, however, chose to ignore the differences between CR and R_2 and concentrate on the similarities. This is often sound strategy in preliminary scientific investigation. It was Galileo's genius that enabled him to ignore the slight differences in speed of fall of heavy and light objects in favor of a theory that idealized them as falling at the same speed. He did this in the face of a well-established theory of nature that demanded exactly the opposite conclusion. In formulating a theoretical principle which asserted that $CR = R_2$, Pavlov was employing Galileo's strategy of ignoring small differences. S_1, he supposed, comes to elicit S_2's respondent, as a result of its pairing with S_2.

This principle, known as the principle of *stimulus substitution* (S_1 substitutes for S_2), had a great appeal in terms of its apparent (1) generality, (2) simplicity, and (3) ability to explain other phenomena. Since these three aspects are characteristic of our best concepts in science, it is not surprising that the principle of stimulus substitution was adopted by John Watson and other early behaviorists as the basis for explaining all behavior. In stimulus substitution they thought they saw the mechanism underlying complex patterns of learned behaviors and compound habits. Consider Watson's bold program for an experimental analysis of behavior: "given the stimulus we can predict the response; given the response we can predict the stimulus." In this framework it was natural to view the attaching of new stimuli to old responses (stimulus substitution) as a powerful principle for creating new behavior sequences. Watson believed that complicated human and animal behavior represented the pyramiding and compounding of conditioned reflexes. Because of the theoretical importance of stimulus substitution in the theories of Pavlov and Watson, later investigators ignored the differences between CR's and R_2's for some time. Nevertheless, for two reasons, Pavlov's substitution principle has not withstood the test of time.

(1) Though Watson proposed that all behavior could be viewed as an interaction and compounding of conditioned reflexes, the proposal did not lead to powerful new ways of predicting and controlling behavior. The test of all scientific concepts is their use in predicting, controlling, and ordering the raw materials of nature. At first, stimulus substitution seemed to be helpful in ordering behavior, but as the years went by it remained sterile in predicting and controlling. Even the men who had employed it most enthusiastically began to doubt its fundamental nature.

Eventually, with a renewed exploitation of Thorndike's law of effect, it became apparent that much behavior was not to fit the Pavlovian mold at all. But that is a story to be postponed until the next chapter.

(2) As more and more information on conditioning became available, cases were discovered in which the *CR* was not only slightly different from R_2 but in some instances exactly the opposite. An experiment by Notterman, Schoenfeld, and Bersh (1952) employing human subjects is illustrative. In their study, S_1 was an audible tone and S_2 was a mild electric shock delivered to the subjects' left hand. These investigators measured the heart-rate respondent with a variation of the machine known as an electrocardiograph, familiar in many physicians' offices. Instead of constraining their subjects in a Pavlovian frame (Fig. 3–1), they sat them in an ordinary chair, instructing them to remain as quiet as possible for about 90 min. During this time, the experimenters recorded the heart rate of their subjects during presentation of tones and shocks. Notterman, Schoenfeld, and Bersh found clear-cut evidence for a heart-rate *CR* after 11 pairings of shock and tone. However, whereas the unconditioned response to shock (R_2) was a heart-rate acceleration, the conditioned response (*CR*) involved a deceleration. Although later work (Zeaman and Smith, 1965) indicates that differences between heart-rate *CR*'s and R_2's are closely related to corresponding respiration differences, the disparity between the forms of conditioned and unconditioned behaviors remains.

Extreme examples such as this one have led us to take a new look at Pavlovian or classical conditioning. In nearly all cases of supposed stimulus substitution, marked differences between the *CR* and R_2 exist. In many cases, they were hidden by the crude measures taken when investigators were only interested in conditioning as a substitution phenomenon.

The brief history of stimulus substitution is an interesting example of the continual ferment of science. A concept may hold sway for a few years or decades because it seems to provide intellectual comfort and promise ordering of nature. But unless it lives up to its promises, it will eventually give way to the weight of experimental evidence. During its heyday, however, such a concept may direct research in ways which effectually put blinders on scientists as regards the weaknesses of the concept. It is almost as though, to give the concept a "chance," we ignore for a time certain discrepancies, certain fuzzinesses in its definition. This temporary permissiveness at the early stage of exploration is justified over the long run because many of our well-established concepts went through just such an initiation and emerged stronger and clearer for it. The reflex itself is a good example of this, and so are many concepts of physical science which have survived the test of time.

The Importance of the $S_1 \to R_1$ *Reflex.* Pavlov suggested that $S_1 \to R_1$ ought to be a "biologically weaker" reflex than $S_2 \to R_2$ for classical conditioning to occur. The notion of "biological weakness" is not entirely clear. Presumably it is a way of saying that if the energies of S_1 and S_2 were somehow equated, then R_1 would always be smaller or would occur less frequently than R_2. A related fact that Pavlov emphasized was that conditioning is easiest to observe (though not necessarily easiest to obtain) when S_1 does not initially elicit R_2. It should be apparent that if S_1 elicits R_2 before conditioning, then the effect of the pairing of S_1 and S_2 may be obscured. Thus, in most conditioning experiments, care is taken to select an S_1 that has no original capacity to elicit R_2. Such an S_1 is said to be *neutral* with respect to R_2. A neutral S_1 is especially desirable if, during conditioning, we are going to look for *CR* in the same place where we observe R_2. Nevertheless, the initial neutrality of S_1 with respect to R_2 is *not* a necessary feature for the occurrence of classical conditioning, as Long (1941) showed some time ago. In one of Long's experiments, a ½-sec-duration tone was used as S_1 and a brief flash of light as S_2; in both cases an eyelid respondent in human subjects was measured. Both the light and the tone elicited lid blinks from the start; but after pairings the S_1, tone-alone, came to elicit two blinks in succession. Figure 3–2 gives an instance of one of Long's records when just S_1 was presented.

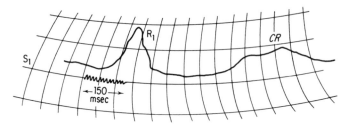

Figure 3–2. Eyelid responses to a ½-sec tone after 30 tone-light pairings (after Long, 1941).

Even more impressive was an experiment by Long in which S_1 and S_2 were *identical tones*. In that experiment, a similar result was obtained: the first tone came to produce two lid movements after pairings. Thus the special case of the Pavlovian paradigm with $S_1 = S_2$ yields results in keeping with the general paradigm.

Long's results have an added significance. If, prior to conditioning, a stimulus elicits R_1 and after conditioning it evokes R_1 *and CR,* we can generalize this to cases in which a single stimulus could come to control a variety of different behaviors, depending on various past histories of pairing with different S_2's. This result can be represented diagramatically as

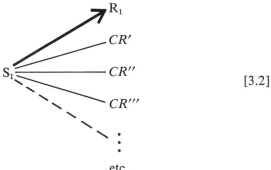

$$[3.2]$$

etc.

Thus a tone, paired independently with a shock, a light, and food, might eventually evoke simultaneous *CR*'s of heart-rate change, eye blink, and salivation, respectively. This entire constellation of behaviors evoked by a single stimulus may have importance for our study of emotion, as we shall see in a later chapter. Of course it should be emphasized that, in diagram [3.2], R_1 is a summary for all the behaviors initially elicited by S_1. Though we often confine our discussions of conditioning to one or two responses, conditioning is a phenomenon that pervades the complete behavioral system of an individual. When we examine a single response in detail, we do so because we hope it is *representative* of what is taking place generally in the response system, not because it is *all* that is happening. To try to investigate the total system at once would overwhelm us with unmanageable detail. We take a representative sample and attempt to explore it in depth. This is another research strategy that has paid off well in scientific investigation, though its success evidently depends on how lucky we are in picking a sample that is indeed representative of the phenomenon in general. The fact that the salivary *CR* and R_2 are so similar and so dominant in Pavlov's case suggests possibly that his sample was not as representative as he might have hoped.

Is S_1 — CR a "New Reflex"? In the old substitution principle, $S_1 \rightarrow R_2$ was viewed as the new "conditioned" reflex. Even though we may prefer to represent the effects of classical conditioning as the formation of a *CR* to S_1, we still have to face the systematic question of whether S_1 — *CR* is a reflex, or some other kind of stimulus-response correlation. There is very little experimental evidence we can bring to bear on the matter, but what little we have indicates that it is not in fact a true reflex.

In the first place, increases in the intensity of S_1 do not result in increases in the magnitude of the *CR,* or in decreases in its latency.

Rather, the maximum *CR* magnitude and minimum *CR* latency are obtained at the precise value of S_1 used in conditioning (Mostofsky, 1965). Values both more or less intense result in weaker *CR*'s. On the other hand, recall from Chapter 2 that the laws of reflex magnitude and latency specify a simple proportionality between S_2 intensity and R_2 strength.

Second, the latency of the *CR* acquired to S_1 is generally longer than the latency of reflexive respondents (R_1's) associated with that same S_1. This may be demonstrated by pairing a light (S_1) with an air puff to the eyelid (S_2). Originally, both S_1 *and* S_2 elicit eye blinks. As a result of pairing, S_1 comes to evoke two distinct eye blinks, an R_1 followed by a *CR*. Using this procedure with human subjects, Grant and Norris (1947) identified several modal latency regions, as the histogram of Fig. 3–3 shows. The investigators called the region between 50 and 110

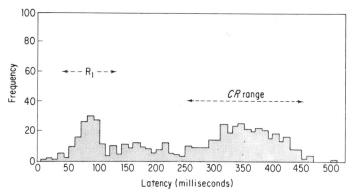

Figure 3–3. Latency distribution of all eyelid responses elicited by a strong light during the course of a conditioning experiment on human subjects (after Grant and Norris, 1947).

milliseconds ($1 \text{ msec} = 10^{-3} \text{ sec} = \frac{1}{1000} \text{ sec}$) the true reflex range; the region between 250 and 450 msec represents the *CR* range.

Third, if S_1 — *CR* is a true reflex, it should be possible to build more conditioned reflexes on top of it. Pavlov himself saw the possibilities of this pyramiding of conditioning, as well as the implications for human behavior. For instance, in an experiment by Frolov (cited by Pavlov, 1927, pp. 33–34), a ticking metronome was first used as an S_1 in the paradigm, with *Food → Saliva* as the unconditioned reflex. After some pairings, the usual result was obtained in that the metronome alone evoked a salivary *CR*. Frolov then attempted to use the new correlation S_1 — *CR* as the basis for a *second-order* conditioned reflex. He held a black square in the dog's line of vision for 10 sec, then waited a further

15 sec, and finally sounded the metronome for 30 sec. This is a variation from the "simultaneous" pairing discussed above and, according to Pavlov, was necessary to achieve second-order conditioning. After 10 such trials, the black square came to evoke some salivation although it had never been paired with food. We represent this example of higher-order conditioning as a two-step operation in Fig. 3–4.

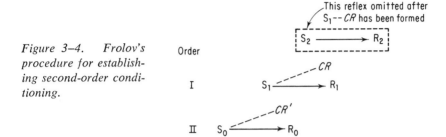

Figure 3–4. Frolov's procedure for establishing second-order conditioning.

Typically, the higher-order CR' was small in magnitude, long in latency, variable in occurrence, and short in life span. Attempts to go beyond the second order of conditioning without the use of the original $S_2 \rightarrow R_2$ were unsuccessful with salivary respondents. The importance of higher-order conditioning of this sort is still in dispute among psychologists. Its transient character (if the S_2 is omitted for very many trials it disappears altogether), its difficulty in establishment, and its inability to extend to very many orders have led some writers to remark that "the influence of higher order conditioning could hardly be expected to play much of a part in the everyday behavior of organisms" (Keller and Schoenfeld, 1950, p. 32). On the other hand, its theoretical possibilities as an explanatory principle have favorably impressed others, such as C. E. Osgood (1953), who considers that "this process is certainly greatly extended in human learning, especially in the area of language behavior" (Osgood, 1953, p. 316).

In summary, it appears that the $S_1 — CR$ relations established by conditioning are probably different enough from true reflexes to group them separately.

3.3 TIME RELATIONS IN CONDITIONING PARADIGMS

Pavlovian or classical conditioning may conveniently be regarded as the characteristic effect of presenting stimuli in certain temporal relations, that is, in a certain order in time. Up until now we have been content to state the fundamental operation of Pavlovian conditioning as a "pairing" of two eliciting stimuli. It is now time to consider in more detail the nature of that pairing operation. In Fig. 3–5, four different ways in which S_1 may be paired in time with S_2 are shown and labeled.

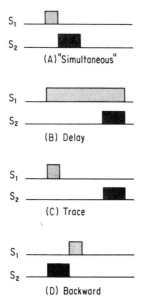

S_1

S_2

(A) "Simultaneous"

S_1

S_2

(B) Delay

S_1

S_2

(C) Trace

S_1

S_2

(D) Backward

Figure 3–5. Some possible time relations between S_1 and S_2 in classical conditioning.

The first case (A) is perhaps the most common type and is referred to in the literature of conditioning as "simultaneous" conditioning. The S_1 is short and its onset occurs about ½ sec before S_2. In Fig. 3–5A, S_1 is shown terminating before S_2; however, S_1 can overlap S_2 without altering the results. Another temporal procedure employed in classical conditioning is shown in Fig. 3–5B. The S_1 is allowed to come on well before S_2 and to remain on for a considerable time interval. Toward the end of S_1, the S_2 is presented. This is called the *delay* procedure. It too gives successful *CR*'s with delays up to several minutes under Pavlov's conditions. The case illustrated in Fig. 3–5C is similar to "simultaneous" conditioning except that S_1 is presented earlier, and terminates before S_2 is presented. This is the procedure that Frolov used in his second-order experiment. This case is referred to as the *trace* procedure on the assumption that a "trace" of S_1 is left in the nervous system of the organism after S_1 has terminated. As long as the time between S_1 and S_2 is not too great (a few minutes) *CR*'s will be formed to S_1 by the trace procedure.

How long can the time between S_1 and S_2 be before conditioning becomes impossible? No general answer is possible, for it depends on the particular $S_2 \to R_2$ reflex, on the intensities of S_1 and S_2, and on many other factors. A related question is easier to answer: What is the optimum interval between S_1 onset and S_2 onset? That is to say, what interval gives the most reliable CR's? A study by Wolfle (1932) using finger retraction to an electric shock as $S_2 \to R_2$ yielded the curve shown in Fig. 3–6. Note that the maximum percentage of CR's occurred at

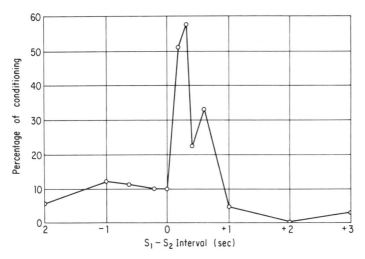

Figure 3–6. *Relative conditionability as a function of* S_1—S_2 *interval (after Wolfle, 1932).*

about ½ sec and this value is often taken to be the *optimum* S_1 — S_2 interval. Very few CR's were recorded at 0 sec (true simultaneity). Negative values of S_1 — S_2 interval (those to the left of 0 in Fig. 3–6) hold some theoretical interest. They represent the case (shown as Fig. 3–5D) in which S_1 comes *after* (!) S_2. This is the procedure of so-called *backward conditioning*. It is now generally agreed that the backward-conditioning procedure does not result in S_1 taking on a new CR, and Fig. 3–6 supports that view. From our analysis of the previous section, we might expect S_2 (now the first stimulus) to take on a CR, however. Though such a result would not be consistent with Pavlov's notion that the prior stimulus should belong to a "biologically weaker" reflex, it would be compatible with an analysis of classical conditioning purely in terms of the temporal relations between stimuli.

A final procedure, not shown in Fig. 3–5, occurs when S_2 is presented alone periodically *without any* S_1 at all. In one experiment, Pavlov fed a dog regularly every 30 min. No stimulus change preceded feeding. When this feeding routine had been well established, food was withheld altogether and the effects measured. Under these conditions salivation was observed to commence at approximately the end of the 30-min period, the time when food would ordinarily have come. Pavlov called this procedure *time* conditioning on the analogy that the time interval since the previous feeding comes to act in some way like an S_1.

3.4 THE EXTENSION OF CLASSICAL CONDITIONING

The reader should emerge from this introduction to classical conditioning with a clear understanding of the invariant nature of one aspect of the phenomenon. Whenever two elicitors are associated in time by the rules laid down in our discussion of "pairing," an inevitable result is obtained. The first elicitor will come eventually to evoke some new set of behaviors in the organism. This holds whether the pairing is performed by a human experimenter in a carefully constructed laboratory or by the action of nature in the jungle. Often some of the new behavior so evoked or "conditioned" will resemble some of the respondents of the second elicitor, but this does not need to be so.

This phenomenon appears to be a rather general one extending throughout the animal kingdom. *CR*'s have been formed in worms, crabs, fish, reptiles, pigeons, chickens, sheep, dogs, monkeys, and 7-month-old human fetuses still in the mother's womb (Hilgard and Marquis, 1940).

In the early history of classical conditioning research, when the paradigm was taken to be $S_1 \rightarrow R_2$, it was supposed that any reflex could be "conditioned." That is, any respondent (R_2) could be transferred by stimulus substitution to new S_1's. With the fall of stimulus substitution and the general acceptance that *CR* may not duplicate R_2, this position was weakened. Some failures to obtain conditioning are illuminating. In a series of careful experiments using different S_1's and S_2's, and various $S_1 - S_2$ intervals, F. A. Young (1958) was unable to obtain a transference of the pupillary respondent to S_1. Young summarizes the literature over the past thirty years of supposed conditioning of this respondent and concludes that the evidence indicates that no investigator has ever unequivocally shown conditioning of this respondent. Schlosberg (1928) indicates that knee-jerk conditioning may be artifactual and due to the processes that we shall take up in Chapter 4. Reinwald (cited in Keller and Schoenfeld, 1950) was unable to obtain a knee-jerk *CR* in over 1000 pairings of a light and a tap to the patellar tendon. It is possible that these investigators were looking for a *CR* too closely resembling the original R_2. Classical conditioning may have been distorted somewhat for many years by looking for CR's only along the most obvious R_2 dimensions. The fact is that CR's may show up on different behavioral dimensions from R_2 altogether. Actually, it is well known that classical conditioning is a phenomenon that pervades many aspects of the organism's behavioral response system. Moore and Marcuse (1945) showed that when several behavioral systems are examined, CR's are seen more conspicuously in some (like respiration, salivation, and heart rate) than in others (motor or general activity). Figure 3–7, one of

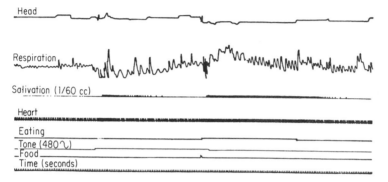

Figure 3–7. *Piglet responses in a number of behavioral systems to a tone signal that had been previously paired with food (after Moore and Marcuse, 1945).*

Moore and Marcuse's records, taken from a pig restrained in a Pavlovian harness and previously subjected to tones (S_1) paired with biscuits (S_2), is instructive. CR's seem most convincingly formed in respondents which depend on the function of the autonomic nervous system. As Keller and Schoenfeld (1950) point out:

> These involve the actions of glands and smooth muscles (e.g., the secretion of sweat and the contraction of blood vessels). Since the action of such effectors is often associated with states of emotion (in 'fear' the saliva dries up, the sweat pours out, the skin cools, the pupils of the eyes dilate, etc.) it will come as no surprise . . . to learn, that these states may be conditioned in Pavlovian fashion (Keller and Schoenfeld, 1950, pp. 27–28).

With the demise of Watson's hope that stimulus substitution would be the basic building block from which to construct a general theory of all learned behavior, fundamental research in classical conditioning has until recently lagged in this country (Prokasy, 1965). The Russians, on the other hand, were never so committed to conditioning as a tool for psychological analysis; for that reason, perhaps, research on conditioned reflexes never declined there. Although classical conditioning may never play the role that its enthusiastic supporters hoped for thirty or forty years ago, it seems likely that it may yet emerge, albeit in a different costume, as an important concept for understanding behavior. The fact that our emotions seem to follow Pavlov's laws rather than Thorndike's law of effect gives a clue as to the possible importance of classical conditioning. Rather than being the units of learned behavior as Watson conceived them, it may be that classically conditioned states of emotion accompany and are even essential for the maintenance of many of our ongoing behavior patterns. But this is mere speculation at the moment, and even a more detailed presentation must await a later chapter.

3.5 THE EXPERIMENTAL METHOD

In the sequel we shall make recurrent use of certain basic concepts of experimental science. In the present section we are about to introduce some simple principles of the experimental method as they are used in psychology, motivating the discussion by reference to the experiments of Pavlov and his co-workers.

In every experiment, the scientist attempts to study certain aspects of the natural world as they relate to certain other aspects. One of the first tasks of the scientist is to attempt to constrain the influences on the object of his study in which he is not at the moment of his experiment directly interested. Thus, in the study of how respondent magnitude varied with changes in stimulus intensity, Sherrington severed the brain from the spinal cord to *eliminate* the unknown influences the brain would have on respondent magnitude. Similarly, Pavlov routinely confined his dogs to a special room in which they were isolated from the outside world. He says:

> It was thought at the beginning of our research that it would be sufficient simply to isolate the experimenter in the research chamber with the dog on its stand, and to refuse admission to anyone else during the course of an experiment. But this precaution was found to be wholly inadequate, since the experimenter, however still he might try to be, was himself a constant source of a large number of stimuli. His slightest movements— blinking of the eyelids or movement of the eyes, posture, respiration and so on—all acted as stimuli which, falling upon the dog, were sufficient to vitiate the experiments by making exact interpretation of the results extremely difficult. In order to exclude this undue influence on the part of the experimenter as far as possible, he had to be stationed outside the room in which the dog was placed, and even this precaution proved unsuccessful in laboratories not specially designed for the study of these particular reflexes. The environment of the animal, even when shut up by itself in a room, is perpetually changing. Footfalls of a passer-by, chance conversations in neighbouring rooms, slamming of a

door or vibration from a passing van, street-cries, even shadows cast through the windows into the room, any of these casual uncontrolled stimuli falling upon the receptors of the dog . . . vitiate the experiments (Pavlov, 1927, p. 20).

It is clear from Pavlov's account that scientists go to great lengths to attempt to *control* unwanted influences on their experiments. When we speak of a controlled experiment, this is one of the meanings we intend. Sometimes, however, it is impossible to eliminate an undesired influence. The best we can do is try to keep it from varying. The temperature and humidity of the dog's room cannot be removed. If they change drastically, they alter reflex properties. The age of the animal, its health, and its degree of food deprivation are similar influences. The best we can do is to try to keep them as constant as possible during the course of an experiment. This then, is a second meaning of a controlled experiment: we hold many influences on our phenomenon *constant*.

Having controlled our unwanted influences by removing them or keeping them constant, we proceed to perform an experiment. But what does that entail? In every experiment, regardless of the science, there are certain basic ingredients that go into its makeup. In the first place, since every experiment is an attempt to relate two or more things to each other, it deals with at least two quantities that can take on different values. (In Pavlov's experiments, two such quantities were often number of pairings and response magnitude.) Quantities that can take on different values have been assigned the name of *variables* by mathematicians, and we shall adopt that name, using it frequently throughout the remainder of the text. Both variables in an experiment must be measurable, and one of them must be controllable or manipulable by the experimenter. That is, he must be able to change one of them, at least, as desired.

In Anrep's experiment (see section 3.1) there are three variables, three quantities that took on different values: number of previous tone-food pairings, drops of saliva, and time elapsing between onset of tone and ensuing salivation (Table 3–1). Let us for purposes of simplicity confine our attention to only two of these: number of pairings and drops of saliva. Both of these variables were measured by Dr. Anrep. However, only one variable was manipulated by him. That is to say, he directly determined the value of only one of these. That one was number of pairings. A variable that is measured and manipulated in an experiment is called the *independent variable*. Any other variable which is concurrently measured in that experiment but not manipulated is called a *dependent variable*. Anrep, therefore, had two dependent variables: drops of saliva and time for the first drop to appear. We consider for the moment only the first of these.

Suppose we attempt to represent our variables and our results in a two-dimensional rectangular coordinate system, as shown in Fig. 3–8. We assign the independent variable to the horizontal axis (the X axis) and the dependent variable to the vertical axis (the Y axis). (This location of the dependent variable is exactly opposite to that of a histogram. See Fig. 2–6.) Several

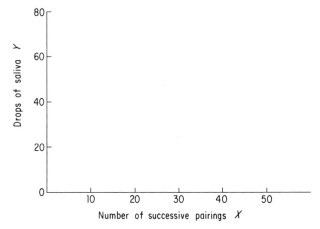

Figure 3–8. Representation of Anrep's (1920) independent variable and one of his dependent variables on a rectangular coordinate system.

properties of Fig. 3–8 are worth noting. (1) We always give our axes informative labels describing our variables. (2) We mark off equal distances along the axes and let these distances represent equal increments of our variables. (3) The scales of the X and Y axes do not have to be the same. (4) Zero coincides for both axes where the coordinate lines meet at the point called their *origin*.

We now proceed to represent Anrep's data in the rectangular coordinate frame. We use columns 1 and 2 of Table 3–1 to place points at appropriate locations within the framework. Let each point represent a pair of numbers: The number of drops of saliva associated with a given pairing number. If we do this we get Fig. 3–9.

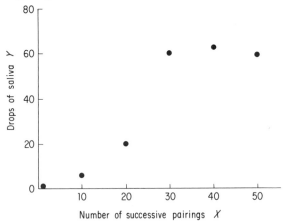

Figure 3–9. Anrep's (1920) data on drops of saliva and number of pairings plotted as two-dimensional points in a rectangular coordinate system.

The last step is to connect the points with straight lines. From this operation we obtain Fig. 3–10, which we call the curve or *function* relating the number of drops of salivation to the number of previous tone-food pairings over the range of the independent variable from 0 to 60 pairings. The shape of such curves or functions is of some interest. In the present case we see that beyond the 30-pairing point not much change occurs in the dependent variable. When a function reaches a limiting value around which it hovers thereafter, we say that it has reached its asymptote. Presumably, even if we went on giving thousands of additional pairings we would still get only approximately 60 drops of saliva at each test.

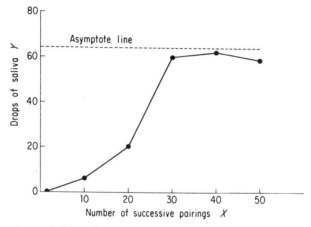

Figure 3–10. Anrep's (1920) function between drops of saliva and number of pairings showing its asymptote.

We are now in a position to define an experiment as *the measurement and manipulation of one variable and the concurrent measurement and non-manipulation* of another. Strictly speaking, this definition holds for only the simplest of experiments, those with one independent variable and one dependent variable. More complicated experiments may have many independent and dependent variables, but it suffices for the present merely to understand that an increase in variables entails no new principles.

Anrep's experiment serves further to illustrate a special characteristic of psychological experiments. In a psychological experiment, the dependent variable(s) is inevitably some aspect of the behavior of the organism; the independent variable(s) is inevitably some aspect of the organism's immediate or previous environment. Here, for instance, drops of saliva is a behavioral quantity; number of pairings refers to the frequency of some previous state of the animal's environment. Note carefully that neither saliva nor tones are variables as we have defined them. *Drops* of saliva and *number* of tones presented are variables. Thus a variable is the quantity that can take on different (variable) values; it is what we measure and record.

Now that we possess the tools to understand and represent experiments and their results we are in a much better position to understand Anrep's data and similar results. The function of Fig. 3–10 represents our first example of a *behavioral process*. A behavioral process may be defined as a change in behavior over time (or trials in time) in which a constant procedure is kept in effect. You can verify that Anrep's experiment meets these conditions. He followed the same procedure—pairing tone with food—trial after trial, occasionally testing for the effect of tone alone. At no point in his 50 trials did he deviate and institute a new and different procedure. Always it was the same: tone-food, wait a while, tone-food, . . . and so forth. Thus the changing curve that we see in Fig. 3–10 up until the asymptote is reached is the process in which a tone comes gradually, as pairings are increased, to acquire the ability to produce a salivary response of its own.

3.6 INTRODUCTION TO ELEMENTARY PROBABILITY CONCEPTS

Many of the things that psychologists undertake to observe and record occur with far less than perfect certainty, even when all conditions of experimentation and observation are as carefully controlled as possible. For example, on any given test trial prior to reaching the asymptote of acquisition, the presentation of S_1 in Anrep's experiment (see Fig. 3–4) might not have yielded any *CR* at all. If we imagine any test trial given prior to the asymptote, we would have to admit that there was a very real uncertainty attached to the prediction of whether or not any *CR* would occur to S_1. Of course, as the number of trials progresses, the uncertainty decreases. A conditioned respondent is said to be fully acquired when its chances of occurring after S_1 have become maximally certain. What is true for conditioned reflexes is true for many other behavioral and non-behavioral events. Sometimes a person will eat what is put before him, sometimes he will not. Sometimes a train will be late, sometimes it will be on time. Sometimes it rains on groundhog day, sometimes it doesn't. What we would like to have would be a ruler or measuring stick with which to represent and compare in a precise way the certainty of such events as *CR*'s, eating desserts, train arrivals, and rain showers. Fortunately, we find just such a measuring stick in the mathematical concept of *probability*. For present purposes we shall consider the probability of an event to be a number which we can associate with that event, a number which will characterize the event's relative certainty under well-defined conditions of observation.

In order to assign this number to an event we must first establish a standard set of conditions under which we are going to look for the event. One type of standard conditions involves a certain *operation* (procedure) that we perform, such as tossing a coin, presenting an S_1, or milking a cow. In a second type, the standard conditions are set by nature and we merely make our observations at standard times. Thus we may observe the sky on groundhog day, or we may observe whether or not the 7:34 local arrives on time, or we may observe the number of cars crossing the George Washington Bridge at a given hour. For convenience we shall henceforth refer to either type of standard conditions of observation as simply the *standard observation*.

The events of interest that turn up when we make standard observations we shall call outcomes. For example, in presenting a stimulus and looking for a respondent (a standard observation), we may observe the occurrence of a knee jerk (an outcome). In tossing a coin we may be interested in the occurrence of "heads" (an outcome). In general, whenever a given event or outcome is less than perfectly certain, this may be construed to mean that on making the standard observation *some other event* occurred, different from the one to which we were directing our primary attention. Thus if we were concerned with the "heads" event from flipping a coin, then the "tails" event is one that occurs whenever the "heads" event does not. To apply the notions of probability we find that we shall have to classify *all* the possible outcomes of a standard observation.

In the case of a two-sided coin, the possible outcomes are obvious. But how many possible outcomes could result from observing cars or milking a cow? In these latter cases we shall find it useful to classify the large number of possibilities into some small fixed number of categories. For instance, in measuring milk production we might find it expedient to concern ourself only with whether Elsie will give 0–½ gal, ½–1 gal, or more than 1 gal each morning when we milk her. The milking is the standard observation and we have arbitrarily broken the possible events into just three outcomes. It is apparent that this is an arbitrary procedure and that we could have chosen two (some milk or no milk), or more than three outcomes by inventing more categories. In conditioning experiments we often ask whether or not a conditioned response is observed following each presentation of a stimulus. Here the standard observation is the presentation of a stimulus and there are two outcomes—a response, or no response. But we could choose to examine a characteristic of the response (say its magnitude) and categorize that just as we did our morning milk output. The important point about all such classifications is that we are able to take each actual result from the standard observation and assign it to one or another outcome category.

Once we have fixed what the outcome categories of our standard observation shall be, our next step to measure the certainty of any particular outcome might well be to make the standard observation a few times to get some idea of how often the outcome in question will occur, *relative to the other possible outcomes*. This is a fundamental procedure in estimating probabilities. We might, for instance, flip a coin 100 times and note that we obtained 53 heads and 47 tails. Or we might note that in 50 presentations of an S_1, a CR was observed 45 times. If we now take the ratio of frequency of observed outcomes of the event in question to the frequency of total outcomes observed, we obtain a number between 0 and 1 that gives us some notion of the certainty of the event in question. Thus this *frequency ratio* of heads to total coin-tossing events is $53/100 = 0.53$. Analogously, the frequency ratio of CR's to S_1 presentations is $45/50 = 0.90$.

From these examples it should be clear that frequency ratios can be calculated whenever we have obtained frequencies of given outcomes, and frequencies of all outcomes. The idea of a frequency ratio brings us very close to our desired index of certainty. But one further characteristic of a frequency ratio must be noted. A frequency ratio is subject to the usual errors of measurement as discussed in section 2.6. That is, observed frequency ratios will vary somewhat in different blocks of standard observations. But as we take more and more standard observations, our calculated frequency ratio does a very interesting thing. It tends asymptotically to approach a limiting value. Figure 3–11 shows how this happens when we flip a coin and observe the values for the "heads" frequency ratio as more and more standard observations are made. Evidently we are getting closer and closer to an asymptote, in this case 0.50. *The asymptote of a frequency ratio is defined as the probability of the event.*

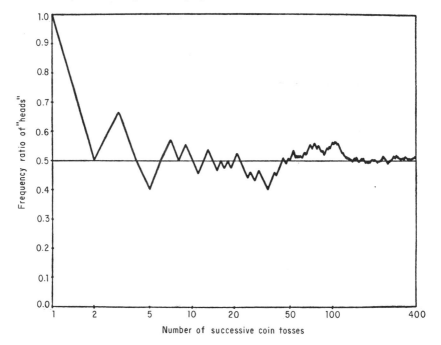

Figure 3–11. Frequency ratio for "heads" in a sequence of throws with a coin. Note the compressed (logarithmic) scale for the horizontal axis (Cramér, 1955).

The range of this number that we have called probability is from 0 to 1. A zero probability indicates that never in any previous standard observation has the event in question been observed. Generally, probabilities close to 0 are associated with the prediction that an outcome of the sort in question is unlikely to happen on any given trial of the standard observation and that in many trials in the future it will happen only a few times. Probabilities near 0.5 mean that the outcome in question occurs approximately half the time the standard observation is made, and hence this is our prediction for the future.

As the probability gets close to 1 we become correspondingly more certain that we shall observe the outcome in question and that finally at 1, we say that we are certain that the outcome will occur. Thus our confidence that the sun will rise tomorrow is given quantitative expression by a probability equal to 1.0, since every observation in the past has resulted in the outcome "sun comes up." The outcome "sun does not come up" however has, so far, a frequency of 0 and hence a probability of 0, and this value expresses our lack of confidence in predicting this outcome. A useful way to represent the probability scale is shown in Fig. 3–12.

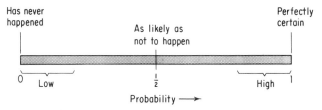

Figure 3–12. The scale of probability.

References for Chapter 3

Anrep, G. V. Pitch discrimination in the dog. *J. Physiol.,* 1920, **53,** 367–385.

Cramér, H. *The elements of probability theory.* Wiley: New York, 1955.

Dashiell, J. F. *Fundamentals of general psychology.* (3rd ed.) Boston: Houghton Mifflin, 1949.

Grant, D. A., and Norris, E. B. Eyelid conditioning as influenced by the presence of sensitized Beta-responses. *J. exp. Psychol.,* 1947, **37,** 423–433.

Hilgard, E. R., and Marquis, D. G. *Conditioning and learning.* New York: Appleton-Century-Crofts, 1940.

Keller, F. S., and Schoenfeld, W. N. *Principles of psychology.* New York: Appleton-Century-Crofts, 1950.

Long, Lillian D. An investigation of the original response to the conditioned stimulus. *Arch. Psychol.,* (New York) 1941, No. 259.

Mednick, S. A. *Learning.* Englewood Cliffs: Prentice-Hall, 1964.

Moore, A. U., and Marcuse, F. L. Salivary, cardiac, and motor indices of conditioning in two sows. *J. comp. Psychol.,* 1945, **38,** 1–16.

Mostofsky, D. (Ed.) *Stimulus generalization.* Stanford: Stanford Univer. Press, 1965.

Notterman, J., Schoenfeld, W. N., and Bersh, P. J. Conditioned heart rate response in human beings during experimental anxiety. *J. comp. physiol. Psychol.,* 1952, **45,** 1–8.

Osgood, C. E. *Method and theory in experimental psychology.* New York: Oxford Univer. Press, 1953.

Pavlov, I. P. *Conditioned reflexes.* London: Oxford Univer. Press, 1927.

Pavlov, I. P. *Lectures on conditioned reflexes.* New York: International Publishers, 1928.

Prokasy, W. F. (Ed.) *Classical conditioning: a symposium.* New York: Appleton-Century-Crofts, 1965.

Schlosberg, H. A study of the conditioned patellar reflex. *J. exp. Psychol.,* 1928, **11,** 468–494.

Wolfle, H. M. Conditioning as a function of the interval between the conditioned and the original stimulus. *J. gen. Psychol.,* 1932, **7,** 80–103.

Young, F. A. Studies of pupillary conditioning. *J. exp. Psychol.,* 1958, **55,** 97–110.

Zeaman, D., and Smith, R. W. Review of some recent findings in human cardiac conditioning. Chap. 19 in W. F. Prokasy (Ed.), *Classical conditioning.* New York: Appleton-Century-Crofts, 1965.

Chapter 4   **OPERANT STRENGTHENING**

Tнᴇ ʟᴀᴡꜰᴜʟɴᴇss ᴅᴇᴍᴏɴsᴛʀᴀᴛᴇᴅ ɪɴ ʀᴇꜰʟᴇx phenomena—both unconditioned and conditioned—illustrates the kind of order to be found between behavior and environment. Nevertheless, many of the activities of higher organisms do not appear to fit nicely into a reflex model of behavior. These include the actions of man, which were described long before Descartes as voluntary, spontaneous, willful, and purposeful, and which resisted experimental analysis until the turn of the twentieth century. An illuminating illustration of where reflexes end and these behaviors begin is found in the following passage:

> . . . when a cat hears a mouse, turns toward the source of the sound, sees the mouse, runs toward it, and pounces, its posture at every stage, even to the selection of the foot which is to take the first step, is determined by reflexes which can be demonstrated one by one under experimental conditions. *All the cat has to do is to decide* whether or not to pursue the mouse; everything else is prepared for it by its postural and locomotor reflexes (Skinner, 1957, p. 343, ital. added).

Hidden in the deceptively simple statement "all the cat has to do is to *decide*" lies the point of departure for a science of those behaviors whose occurrence is related neither reflexly to the immediate presence of an elicitor nor to a history of pairing of two elicitors.

4.1 INTRODUCTION TO PURPOSIVE BEHAVIOR

In the study of reflexes and conditioned responses, we found that scientific explanation and understanding came about by a progressive discovery and elaboration of the relations between certain aspects of behavior (the dependent response variables) and certain aspects of the environment (the independent stimulus and past-history variables). Each discovery of a new relationship or law of behavior was a prized event in the history of reflexes. As our laws began to pile up and intermingle we felt justified in speaking about a partial *understanding* of reflex behavior.

With behaviors which we shall for the moment call "purposive," experimental analysis has proceeded similarly. Dating from Thorndike's pioneer work on learning in cats and chicks, psychologists have progressively pursued a search for relationships between purposive behaviors and other events. In general, the search for these relations has not led us along the paths of the reflex. Nevertheless, a functional account has been initiated. Consider the problems in developing such an account: how do we go about finding variables or events to which purposive behavior might be significantly related? Initially, we must proceed by intuition and crude observation. If we are lucky we may find our task aided by forward-looking philosophical speculation. A quarter-century before Thorndike, the British philosopher Herbert Spencer wrote the following:

> Suppose, now, that in putting out its head to seize prey scarcely within reach, a creature has repeatedly failed. Suppose that along with the group of motor actions approximately adapted to seize prey at this distance . . . a slight forward movement of the body [occurs]. Success will occur instead of failure. . . . On recurrence of the circumstances, these muscular movements that were followed by success are likely to be repeated: what was at first an accidental combination of motions will now be a combination having considerable probability (Spencer, 1878).

In his statement that "those muscular movements that were followed by success are likely to be repeated," Spencer was emphasizing that what an organism *does* now is in some way related to the *consequences* of what the organism *did* in the past. Here then is the clue which Thorndike and later Skinner were to follow up extensively.

Purposive behavior is behavior that is almost *defined* by its consequences. Consider Table 4–1. In every act cited there, the purpose of the behavior is closely related to the consequences. We say that we tie

Table 4–1
SOME "PURPOSIVE" BEHAVIORS OF ANIMALS AND MEN,
THEIR SO-CALLED PURPOSES, AND THEIR ACTUAL PAST CONSEQUENCES

BEHAVIOR	PURPOSE	CONSEQUENCES
Tie a shoelace	*To* keep shoe on	Shoe stays on
Buy a raincoat	*To* keep rain off	Rain stays off
Enter a restaurant	*To* eat lunch	You get lunch
Turn on faucet	*To* get water	Water appears
Write a letter	*To* secure a reply	Reply obtained
Dig a hole	*To* escape the cold	Warmth obtained

a shoelace *to* keep our shoe on, but an equivalent statement is that we tie our shoe and yesterday when we *did* tie it, it *did* stay on. The statement that rats burrow into holes to escape the cold can equivalently be expressed by the statement that rats have often in the past burrowed into holes and found warmer temperatures.

EXERCISE 2.
Translate each of the behaviors and purposes in Table 4–1 into equivalent statements that merely state the present behavior and the past behavior with its consequences.

Apparently we have two ways in our language to represent the same behavior: (1), the purposive, in which we employ the term *to* (or, *in order to*) and imply the future tense; (2), the descriptive, in which we state the present behavior and conjoin it with what happened in the past. Redundancy in representation is wasteful and usually avoided by scientists. In the present account, we shall reject the purposive language and adopt the more descriptive language for a compelling logical reason. Behavior cannot be related to future events, that is, events that have not yet happened. A harsh reminder of this can be gleaned from the following illustration:

During the war the Russians used dogs to blow up tanks. A dog was trained to hide behind a tree or wall in low brush or other cover. As a tank approached and passed, the dog ran swiftly alongside it, and a small magnetic mine attached to the dog's back was sufficient to cripple the tank or set it afire. The dog, of course, had to be replaced (Skinner, 1956, p. 228).

Only one of the two possible descriptions is satisfactory here. The dog runs to the tank because of certain past consequences of running to tanks. (Presumably they were fed there, petted there, etc.) In this extreme example it is easy to reject the alternative statement, that the dogs ran to the tanks to be blown up. Yet the illustration is useful in establishing the general principle that the future does not determine behavior.

In brief, a very real and important class of behaviors, arising out of situations that seem to involve choice or decision, is called purposive behavior. Such behavior, it should be apparent at once, falls into Descartes' category of "voluntary" and constitutes action that the ancients called "willful." Our present analysis indicates that this behavior is in some way related to and thus governed by its consequences. For that reason we shall henceforth replace the older term purposive with Thorndike's term "instrumental," or Skinner's term "operant." To call behavior "instrumental" or "operant" suggests that, by operating on the environment, the behavior is instrumental in obtaining consequences. Neither of these terms implies the undesirable conceptual scheme that "purposive" does, yet both attempt to capture the fundamental notion that the past consequences of such behavior are one of its important determiners.

4.2 A PROTOTYPE EXPERIMENT

If a hungry laboratory rat is confined to the box shown in Fig. 4–1 and certain procedures are carried out, a number of interesting behavioral effects may be observed.

For the purposes of the present analysis, the significant features of the box are (1) a tray for delivery of a small pellet of food to the rat; and (2) a lever or bar, protruding from the front wall, which when depressed downward with a force of about 10 gm closes a microswitch, permitting the automatic recording of this behavior. The significant features of the rat are as follows: (1) It is healthy and has been accustomed to eating one meal each day at about the same hour as it currently finds itself in the box. (2) It has previously been acclimatized to this box during which time food was occasionally delivered into the tray; it now readily approaches the food tray and eats such food whenever it is available.

Consider the following experiment. The rat is carefully observed in

Figure 4-1. An experimental chamber based on the box originally used by B. F. Skinner for the study of instrumental behavior in the rat and other small mammals (Will Rapport).

this box for a period of 15 min. During that time no food is delivered to its tray. We shall not have to look hard to observe the occurrence of behaviors that we call exploratory. The rat noses the corners, noses the tray, occasionally depresses the lever, leans on the walls, and so forth. Furthermore, the animal frequently engages in "grooming" activities and in sniffing, and from time to time it remains almost completely immobile. All these activities are examples of what are usually labeled by psychologists as responses. We shall discuss the term response in greater detail in a later chapter; it is sufficient, at present, to observe the following caution: these behaviors are not respondents—no specific elicitor can be found for them. This is not to say that they do not depend to a great extent on the construction of the box for their occurrence. Still, they appear to be emitted in the absence of any specific stimulus. For that reason they are often referred to as *emitted responses*.

The observation of the emitted behaviors of an animal in a situation in which no special consequences are being provided for any response is known as *operant-level* observation. Operant-level recordings serve as an important baseline against which we shall later compare the effects of providing special consequences for one or a number of the emitted responses.

After 15 min of observation of these various emitted responses, we initiate the following procedure. Each time we observe the rat depressing the lever, we immediately deliver a pellet of food to its tray. Now, for the first time in this rat's history, lever-pressing behavior has the special consequence of producing food. We shall not have to wait long to see the effects of this new *contingency* on the rat's behavior. Soon the animal is busily engaged in lever-pressing and eating behaviors. Some very marked changes or modifications in its behavior have taken place in the space of a few short minutes.

In common parlance, the rat is said to have learned to press the lever *to* get food. Such a description adds little to the statement that the rat *is* pressing the lever frequently now and *is* getting food. What we wish to do is to describe in detail, and as quantitatively as possible, the changes in behavior that result from the simple *operation* of providing a special consequence for only *one* of an individual's normal ongoing activities in a situation. To do that, we shall consider four complementary ways of viewing the changes in the rat's behavior when, as here, one of its behaviors is selected out and given a favorable consequence.

4.3 ABSOLUTE RATE CHANGES

The experiment we have described is an instance of the prototype experiments on operant behavior performed by B. F. Skinner as early as 1930. One of the striking behavioral changes that occurs whenever a behavior like pressing a lever is followed by food is that the behavior increases very greatly in frequency. We might do well to regard the increase in frequency that occurs when already existing behavior incurs a special consequence as a *strengthening* of that behavior. Thus the process that we are now examining might well be called the strengthening of operant behavior, or more briefly, *operant strengthening*.

The changes in frequency of a given behavior are seen most clearly on Skinner's kymographic device that records in ink successive occurrences of the selected response and cumulates them vertically upward on a paper record, at the same time that the pen is moving continuously in time in the horizontal direction. To understand this device, which might justifiably be called the behaviorist's microscope, read the program in Table 4–2 step by step. Write your answers in the blanks provided. Proceed step by step until you come to the end.

Table 4–2

AN INSTRUCTIONAL SEQUENCE ON HOW TO READ A CUMULATIVE
RESPONSE RECORD (ADAPTED FROM SKINNER, 1959)

A broad strip of paper is unwinding from a roll. The end of the strip is moving slowly and steadily toward the left. A pen held against the paper in a fixed position has drawn a line beginning at _____ and ending at _____.

The slow movement of the paper under the fixed pen has drawn the horizontal line from _____ to _____. At b the pen suddenly moved a short distance upward to _____.

In the diagram to the left the paper has moved a short distance beyond the position shown in the diagram in the frame above. The fixed pen has drawn a second horizontal line from _____ to _____.

In the diagram of this frame the pen has been in the four positions a, b, c, d. It occupied position _____ first and _____ last.

In the diagram of this frame the time which elapsed between c and d was _____ than the time which elapsed between a and b.

Table 4–2 (continued)

In recording the responses made by an organism, the pen moves upward and draws a short vertical line each time a response is made. In the diagram to the left an experiment began when the pen was at a. The first response was made at ——.

In the diagram three responses were made fairly quickly, and at a steady rate at ——, ——, and ——.

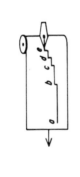

In the diagram to the left the three responses recorded at a were emitted —— rapidly than the three at b.

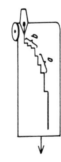

The more rapid the responding, the —— the pauses between responses.

The higher the rate of responding, the —— the horizontal line drawn by the pen between successive responses.

In the diagram of the last frame, the more rapid the responding, the —— the slope of the step-like line.

Rate of responding is shown by the —— of the step-like line.

Responding in the diagram at the left begins at a relatively high rate at a. The time between successive responses grows progressively ——.

In the diagram the slope of the first part of the curve drawn by the pen beginning at a is relatively ——.

Table 4-2 (continued)

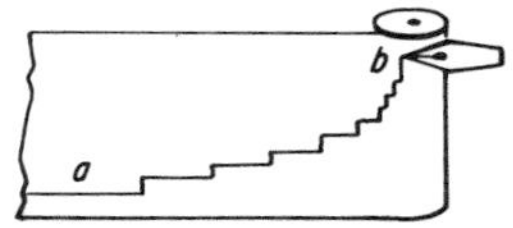

In this diagram the rate increases fairly steadily from a low value near ——— to a high value near ———.

An *increase* in rate is called *positive acceleration*. Positive acceleration is shown in this diagram/the diagram in the frame above (choose one).

Negative acceleration refers to a(n) ——— in rate.

Negative acceleration is shown in the diagram of this frame/the frame above (choose one).

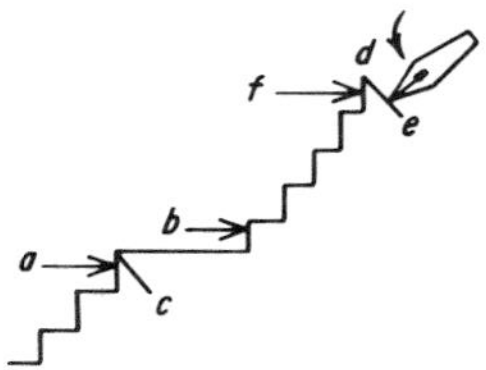

To record other events which occur while an animal is responding, the pen swings quickly "to the southeast" and back again. In the diagram to the left the pen has just drawn a line from ——— to ———. The point of the pen will immediately return to ———.

The short diagonal mark ("hatch" or "pip") at ——— was made by the same movement of the pen as shown at *d–e*.

The "southeast" mark or hatch is often used to indicate that a response has produced some special consequence. In the diagram of this frame these responses only were recorded by the *vertical* marks at ——— and ———.

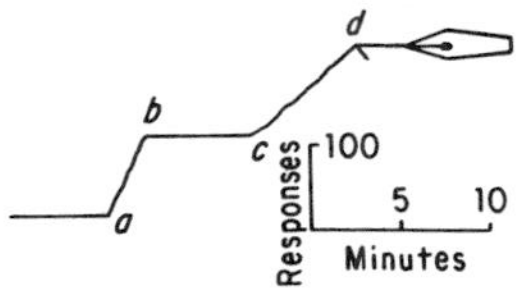

In the diagram of this frame a response received a special consequence at ———.

In practice, the vertical mark made by a single response is too small to be easily identified. However, we can still use the ——— of the curve at any point as a valid indicator of rate of responding.

In the diagram the rate was highest between ——— and ———, zero between ——— and ———, and of an intermediate value between ——— and ———.

69

Table 4-2 (continued)

When the steps are so small that we cannot count responses, we can still determine the number of responses between two points on the record by using a scale. In the diagram of this frame the vertical portion of the scale at the right tells us that approximately —— responses were made between a and b in the cumulative record at the left.

If the paper moves very slowly, we may not be able to measure accurately the time between two responses, but we can still determine the time elapsing between two chosen points. In the diagram of this frame the horizontal portion of the scale at the right tells us that responses at a and b in the cumulative record at the left occurred approximately —— minutes apart.

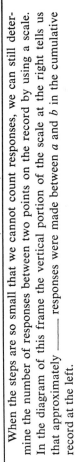

In the diagram to the left after completing about 100 responses, between a and b, the animal paused for a short period, —— to ——, and then emitted about —— responses between c and d.

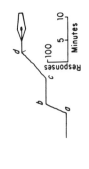

Sometimes a cumulative curve is used to record the progress of a moving automobile, and then the slope indicates the speed of motion. When a cumulative curve is used to record animal behavior the slope indicates ——.

"Rate of responding" means number of responses per unit time. In a cumulative record, number of responses can be determined from the distance traversed by the pen in a —— direction.

In a cumulative record, time is indicated by the distance traversed by the pen in a —— direction.

70

What do typical cumulative curves of the instrumental strengthening process look like? The curves shown in Fig. 4–2 are the records of four rats individually subjected to the procedure we have described above. The curves indicate that the strengthening process is abrupt. The effect

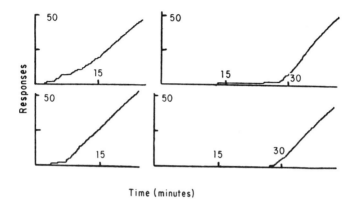

Time (minutes)

Figure 4–2. Some typical cumulative response curves obtained from hungry rats on the day of strengthening a bar-pressing response for the first time. Since every response produces a pellet of food, food pips are omitted (Skinner, 1938).

of the special food consequence does not always "take" right away but once it does, there is a precipitous change to a new and high response rate that is sustained for the remainder of the experiment.

4.4 RELATIVE RATE CHANGES

A second useful way of viewing the process of response strengthening is to consider the rate changes in the favored response against the background of rate changes that take place in the entire substrate of ongoing activities in the situation. For instance, in an undergraduate classroom demonstration of lever-press response strengthening at the Carnegie Institute of Technology, the following behaviors of a hungry rat were recorded over 15 min of operant level, and then over a subsequent 15 min of strengthening the lever pressing.

R_L = lever-press activities
R_S = sniffing
R_C = pulling of a small chain that dangled into the box from overhead

R_T = nosing the food tray

R_B = extending a paw to a lead block that rested in one of the far corners

R_I = remaining approximately immobile for 10 continuous seconds

The frequencies of these activities during operant level and during strengthening are represented in the histograms of Fig. 4–3. From

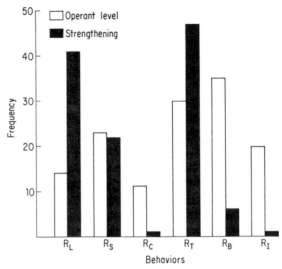

Figure 4–3. Relative frequencies of several behaviors occurring in an experimental box before and after strengthening of the lever-press behavior.

Fig. 4–3 it is apparent that not only is the rate of lever pressing increased, but the rates of other activities in the situation not associated with food are decreased.

4.5 SEQUENTIAL CHANGES IN THE ORDER OF RESPONDING

The behavioral modifications that accompany the strengthening of a given response extend beyond that response to many other activities. In particular, when food is given to the animal, all activities involved in food getting are also strengthened. But the strengthening is not confined merely to an increase in their frequency. A change in the order in which the animal emits certain behaviors occurs in instrumental strengthening. A particular order is quickly established and maintained. In the lever-pressing experiment the order is (1) press the lever, (2) approach the food tray, (3) pick up the food, (4) ingest it, (5) approach the lever, (1) press the lever. . . . In short, a continuous loop of behavior has been formed by the operation of making food contingent on bar pressing. This loop is markedly different from the pattern of response sequences seen in operant level. Two members of the established loop, 1 and 2, will serve to illustrate the point. Let us ignore for the moment all the other possible behaviors in the situation and confine our attention to (1) pressing the lever and (2) approaching the food tray. Prior to strengthening of the lever press, these two responses occur in such a way that when the animal performs one of them, he is likely to repeat that one again rather than perform the other (Frick and Miller, 1951). Thus a fairly typical operant level sequence of lever-press (R_L) and tray-approach responses (R_T) might be

$$R_L R_L R_T R_L R_L R_L R_L R_T R_T R_T \ldots$$

During strengthening, this sequence changes quickly to the alternation

$$R_L R_T R_L R_T R_L R_T \ldots$$

with hardly any other pattern to be seen (Millenson and Hurwitz, 1961). It is not known how quickly this process takes place, but under favorable conditions it seems likely that it is almost as instantaneous as the absolute rate change in lever pressing itself.

4.6 VARIABILITY CHANGES

An individual never emits an act in exactly the same way twice. Just as each time you write your name you do it slightly differently, so too the rat presses the bar each time slightly differently. Some presses are made with the left paw, some with the right, some with the nose, and some with the shoulder. Yet we group all these instances together and say that the class of responses we call lever presses is made up of all the possible ways of pressing a lever. During strengthening of such a response class we are actually strengthening these individual response instances, each one of which differs from its relatives slightly.

This strengthening of the members of the class of behaviors that make up lever pressing has a marked effect on the final form in which the behavior settles. Whereas initially, in operant level, the rat tends to press the bar in very many different ways, after strengthening the animal tends to press it in far fewer ways. In other words, the individual instances come to resemble each other more closely. We express this result by saying that the *topography* of the behavior narrows during instrumental strengthening. The topography of a response refers to the way that the animal makes the response. Strictly speaking, topography would seem to refer to the actual muscles used at the moment of occurrence of the response. Recording such events, however, presents difficulties. As an approximation, a camera may be employed to photograph the animal at the instant the response is completed. Guthrie and Horton (1946) made such photographs of cats and dogs when the behavior that produced a special consequence was that of tilting a pole that stood in the middle of the animal's box. Figure 4–4 illustrates some dramatic examples of the stereotypy of behavior after strengthening. Each animal adopts an idiosyncratic topography and departs from it on any given occasion only in details. A striking example of human stereotypy in learned instrumental behavior is shown in Fig. 4–5 on p. 75.

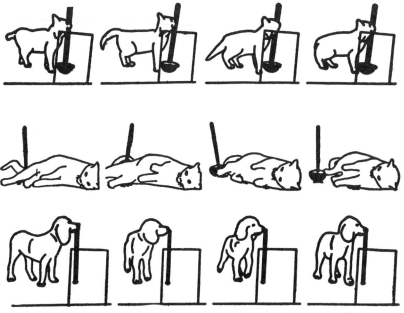

Figure 4–4. Tracings of the responses of two cats and one dog on successive emissions of a pole-tilting response. (From Kimble, 1956 after Guthrie and Horton, 1946.)

4.7 OPERANTS AND REINFORCING STIMULI

In summary, then, four effects of strengthening a response are:

1. to increase the rate of that response relative to its operant level,
2. to increase the rate of that response relative to the rate of other ongoing behavior in the situation,

3. to modify the pattern or sequence of responses involved to a loop that is repeated over and over, and
4. to increase the stereotypy of the actual response.

Figure 4–5. Ted Williams getting his 2,000th hit in the first inning and 2,001st hit in the fifth inning of a game played at Yankee Stadium on Aug. 11, 1955. (© The New York Times and Patrick A. Burns.)

Lever pressing, chain pulling, nose poking, pole tilting, and so forth are convenient acts chosen by experimentalists to study these effects. The suitability of these behaviors for studying operant strengthening depends critically upon their ability to be modified as described. Formally, these and other behaviors that are so strengthenable are defined as *operants*. The four strengthening effects themselves constitute what we shall henceforth call the laws of operant strengthening. Lever presses and other simple animal behaviors are chosen for studying these laws because they are easily observed and measured by the experimenter, and easily executed at various rates by the organism. Throughout the text we shall continue to extend the applicability of these laws and the term operant well beyond lever presses and rats.

In his law of effect, Thorndike stressed the importance of certain special consequences of behavior. Events which were "satisfying," he said, and which followed behavior, acted to stamp in that behavior. Although calling such events satisfying may at first glance seem to be a useful independent specification of the special consequences, it turns out that providing a satisfying definition of "satisfying" is difficult. In the case of the animal, we have no way of knowing whether an event is satisfying save by observing whether it works on behavior according to the laws of operant strengthening. In the case of a human, you might think that satisfaction could be more easily identified, but try to define the term. Satisfying things are those that we like, but what are the things we like? The things we like are, in the final analysis, the things that we will work for. But to say that we will work for them is just another way of saying that we will do for them what our rat will do "for" food. We are thus led to the conclusion that the definition of these special consequences is best framed in terms of their special effects on behavior.

In short, we have a set of special consequences that are special because when we use them in connection with operants, as we did in section 4.2, they result in characteristic changes of behavior.

A partial list of such consequences is instructive. For humans and higher animals

Food
Water
Sex
Warmth
Novelty

function in this way.

A consequence is always a change in an individual's environment. The delivery of food to our rat was a change in its previously foodless environment. The consequence of calling for a glass of water may be a new environment in which a glass of water appears in the hand of a friend. The consequence of picking up a telephone receiver is a new environment which now includes a dial tone. We could extend such examples indefinitely. Note, however, an interesting coincidence. Changes in a part of our environment were defined, in the context of reflexes and Pavlovian conditioning, as stimuli. It is thus apparent that in speaking of a certain special set of consequences we are doing nothing more than delimiting, by their special effects on operants, a certain subset of stimuli. We may conventionally define those stimuli, which when they follow operant behavior affect it by the laws of operant strengthening, as *reinforcing stimuli* (S^+) or simply, *reinforcers*. The operation of presenting a reinforcer we shall denote as *reinforcement*.

It is sometimes held that the terms operant and reinforcement are circular. It appears that each is defined in terms of the other. Reinforcers appear to be defined as those events that strengthen operants; but operants appear to be defined as those behaviors that are strengthenable by reinforcers. The little "thought experiment" which follows shows how the circularity can be broken.

Consider a naïve experimenter faced with a Martian. He observes an "organism" he has never seen before. The organism does something. The experimenter, from his bag of consequences, presents one at random. Does the organism perform that behavior again more frequently, or does the consequence have no effect? If not, perhaps he tries again with another consequence or perhaps he tries the same consequence but selects another behavior. By a process of trial and error, the experimenter may discover certain consequences and certain behaviors that function in the ways described in sections 4.3 to 4.6. Having discovered one special consequence, he can go on to use it to discover other operants; having found one operant, he can go on to use it to discover other consequences. Little by little, the persistent experimenter would build up his concepts of Martian "reinforcers" and Martian "operants" by just such operations.

4.8 THE OPERANT-STRENGTHENING PARADIGM

The matters that we have been discussing under operant strengthening are variously referred to in the literature of psychology as simple selective learning, trial-and-error learning, effect learning, instrumental learning, instrumental conditioning, acquisition, Type R (for response) conditioning, operant learning, and operant conditioning. We prefer to restrict the term operant strengthening to conditions in which the behavior that is reinforced exists in some strength, greater than zero, at the time that strengthening is begun. Nevertheless it is useful when examining other sources to recognize the equivalence of these various names for the strengthening process.

We are now in a position to give a comprehensive definition of the operant-strengthening paradigm. Like Pavlovian conditioning it has four aspects: a *Given,* a *Procedure,* a *Process,* and a *Result.*

GIVEN: 1. An operant response being emitted in greater-than-zero frequency.
2. A suitable reinforcer.

PROCEDURE: Follow each emission of the selected operant with the reinforcing stimulus.

It is helpful to notate the procedure of operant strengthening symbolically. The procedure may be represented simply as

$$R \rightarrow S^+$$

where R represents an operant response class (made up of $r_1, r_2, \ldots, r_n$), S^+ represents a reinforcing stimulus, and the arrow is read "produces" or "leads to."

PROCESS: An abrupt increase in the rate of the operant, its rapid incorporation into a loop of behavior, and a narrowing of the topography of the operant.

RESULT: Same as process.

4.9 VOCAL OPERANTS

The human activities that we call language constitute possibly the most complex of all human behavior patterns. At the present time, language behavior is still so unique to the human organism that it may well be taken as one of the principal defining properties of the species. The usual elements of all languages are sounds produced by the vibration of expelled air from the lungs moving through and across a set of muscles in the larynx called the vocal cords. The tension of these muscles as air moves over them is under the same kind of control that governs the movement of other parts of the body. Hence the sound production is operant behavior. The jaws, lips, and tongue act in combination with the larynx to mold the sounds and produce the more than forty different humanoid sounds known as *phonemes* that are used in various combinations in languages. Because the sounds of phonemes are directly dependent on the movements of the vocal apparatus, measurement of phoneme production constitutes an indirect measure of behavior in the same way that measurement of the depression of a lever constitutes an indirect measure of the movements used by the rat in depressing that lever.

Human language evolves from the crude sounds emitted by infants. Surprisingly, the human infant during the first 5 months of life emits every sound used in every human language—French nasals and trills, German gutturals, and so on (Osgood, 1953). These sounds are emitted independently of eliciting stimuli, and are to be distinguished from the actual crying of a baby. During the early months of life, a baby exhibits a very high operant level of sound production. He may lie for hours producing gargling sounds, sputterings, whistles, squeaks, and snorts. The technical term *babbling* is used to denote the spontaneous emission of these behaviors. An important advance in babbling occurs at about the sixth month when the sequential structure of babbling is altered so that the infant tends to repeat its own vocal production (uggle-uggle, oodle-oodle, luh-luh-luh, etc.).

The changes that occur from babbling to speaking are complex, and no single graph suffices to describe the progress in any completeness. However, one important change that takes place is the change in relative frequency of the different sounds uttered as the baby grows older. Thus, in France the phonemes involved in the French *r* and the nasal vowels are strengthened by the reinforcing community—the child's parents, its playmates, and eventually its teachers. In English-speaking countries, a different set of phonemes is shaped into words by a different reinforcing community. The result of this strengthening can be inferred from a set of histograms similar to that of Fig. 4–3, but more complicated. In Fig. 4–6, histograms of the relative frequencies of 12 vowel phonemes (see Appendix A to this chapter for their explication) are shown for infants at various ages, and the adult. We may infer that reinforcement of these sounds is adjusting their frequency to that of the adult community.

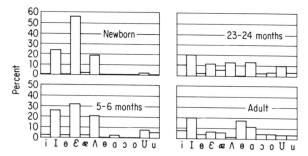

Figure 4–6. Vowel-phoneme frequency profiles showing gradual shift of relative frequency toward a pattern typical of adults in the infants' reinforcing community (Irwin, 1952).

A more direct proof of the effects of reinforcing infant sounds comes from laboratory experiments. In one experiment, the behavior of 3-month-old babies was observed while they lay in their cribs. During two observation sessions an adult experimenter leaned over the crib at a distance of a little more than a foot from the child and remained relatively motionless and expressionless. During this time a second observer recorded the frequency of sounds produced by the infant. In two subsequent sessions the procedure was the same, except that the first experimenter followed each non-crying sound with a "broad smile, three 'tsk' sounds, and a light touch applied to the infant's abdomen with thumb and fingers of the hand opposed" (Rheingold, Gewirtz, and Ross, 1959, p. 28). This is, of course, just:

$$R_{(babble)} \rightarrow S_{(smile,\ clucking,\ touch\ to\ abdomen)}$$

The effect of the procedure was to raise the frequency of babbling well above its operant-level rate during these strengthening sessions.

The experiment demonstrates the operant nature of human sounds. Many other animals make sounds, some of which are reinforceable and some of which are not. A chimpanzee was raised from birth with a family that tried to teach it to speak (Hayes, 1951). The task was difficult, because the ape made no operant sounds at first. The only sounds it made were reflex cries when food or other elicitors appeared, and *CR* sounds to stimuli which had previously been paired with some of these elicitors. Mrs. Hayes attempted to follow the procedure

$$S_1 \text{ (sight of food dish)} - CR \text{ (excited cry)} \rightarrow S^+ \text{(food)} \qquad [4.1]$$

in the hopes of strengthening *CR* (cry) by reinforcing it. The procedure was followed for many months but was ineffective, illustrating that conditioned-respondent behavior is not under the control of its consequences. Eventually an emitted "ahhhha" sound appeared spontaneously one day and it was found to be reinforceable. The ape learned eventually to say *Mama, Papa,* and *Cup* by procedures we discuss in a later chapter.

It is interesting to speculate on the importance of the history of [4.1] for the eventual production of the operant "ahhhha." Was [4.1] a necessary precursor for that operant, or, given the mere passage of time, would the ape have developed it anyway in the absence of [4.1]? One of the chief difficulties with developing speech (as we know it) in an ape is the absence of babbling. Whereas a human infant will babble to itself for hours on end, at a comparable developmental stage the baby chimpanzee lies quietly. Often for days the chimp will not utter a single sound. Clearly a non-zero operant level is a requirement for strengthening, for one must have something to reinforce.

Experiments with other animals have verified that the barking of dogs, the meowing of cats, and some of the sounds of birds are reinforceable. In these cases the frequency of sound production can be raised markedly by special consequences.

4.10 THE EXTENSION OF OPERANT STRENGTHENING

Operant strengthening is a phenomenon which is by no means limited to the simple animal and infant behaviors we have discussed so far. We study the animal because we can rigorously control its environment, past and present. But operant behavior—that is, behavior that can be strengthened by its consequences—constitutes a large proportion of the everyday activities of humans. When we kick a football, sew up a hem, discuss the latest in fashions, bemoan the weather, and wash the dishes we are constantly emitting operants in large numbers. In fact, we are emitting *some* operant at every moment of our waking life. True, our operants are often arranged in more complicated sequences than the simple repetitive loop of the rat in section 4.2; but as we shall see in later chapters, surprising complexity can also be generated at the level of the rat, cat, pigeon, and monkey.

It is not difficult to demonstrate operant strengthening in humans. Given the conditions of the operant-strengthening paradigm, we can perform demonstrations on our friends without great difficulty. The principal added consideration is that we will find the demonstration more dramatic and convincing if we prevent our human subject from "becoming aware" that we are performing such a strengthening experiment. For the subject to "become aware" is a way of saying that he is able to verbalize the procedure that is being followed. This verbal "awareness" is a sure index that the behavior which we are trying to strengthen will now be under the powerful control of years of past history, against which the application of a strengthening paradigm for 30 min or so with a weak reinforcer will have little possibility of competing.

In an interesting experimental design, based on earlier work by W. Verplanck (1955), an undergraduate research assistant was employed as an "actor" to try to strengthen certain conversational behavior in fellow undergraduate subjects (Centers, 1963). The assistant and subject were confined to a room, both ostensibly waiting to be called for a psychological experiment. Actually this was the experiment, and during this time the assistant engaged the unsuspecting subject in ordinary conversation, but at various periods reinforced several types of conversational content such as opinion statements, information statements, and questions, with agreement and special attention. Meanwhile, unknown to the subject, the conversation was being taped and observed through a one-way screen.

The experimental "conversation" lasted 30 min, broken up into three 10-min portions. During the first portion, or operant level, the assistant refrained from expressing agreement or providing informative answers to the subject's opinions and questions. During the second 10 min, the behavioral strengthening period, the assistant agreed with or paraphrased favorably all opinion statements that were voiced by the subject. He further expressed attention, sympathy, and understanding to all information statements, and reinforced all questions by either giving the information solicited or giving agreement or approval, if that was what the question indicated was desired. During the final 10 min the assistant either disagreed with the subject's opinions or remained silent after they were verbalized. He ignored information statements, and was as noncommittal as possible to questions.

The results of agreement reinforcement (strengthening) indicated clearly that the frequency of opinion and information statements relative to all statements increased. Furthermore, no subject noted this conditioning of his behaviors. For reasons not well understood by the experimenters, the question statements did not show any strengthening, and therefore according to our definition they do not constitute an operant class.

At a different level of development, Brackbill (1958) successfully strengthened a smiling response in 4-month-old babies, with physical contact as reinforcement.

The scientist himself is engaged in an enterprise that often demands the emission of many operants, only a few of which may be reinforced. Behaviors that bring about the statement of new relationships, or a new order among concepts, a discovery of a new phenomenon, and so on, are reinforced by the scientific community. Among the prominent reinforcers for the behaviorist, is the order observed when some behavior of an individual is seen to be lawfully related to its consequences, as was the lever pressing of the rat of Section 4.2. This reminder that the human investigator is just himself a behaving organism, subject to the laws of operant strengthening, characterizes the cartoon shown in Fig. 4–7.

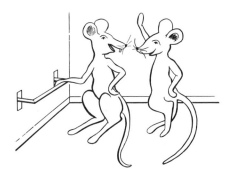

Figure 4–7. "Boy do we have this guy conditioned. Every time I press the bar down he drops a pellet in." (Adapted by permission from Jester, Columbia College.)

The verification of the laws of operant strengthening on human behavior is important, for it shows that despite very great apparent differences between man and animal, certain functional similarities exist. It is these similarities that in the end justify our study of psychology through the behavior of lower organisms. After all, the psychologist is usually interested principally in *human* behavior, or more accurately in behavior laws that are shared by both humans *and* higher animals. We very often utilize animal subjects in our experimental work for pragmatic reasons. We can more easily control an animal's immediate and past environment. We can deprive it of agents such as food and water in order to dole these agents out later as powerful reinforcers. Finally, we can continuously observe the animal for very long periods of confinement.

The use of animals in psychological research follows a long and respected tradition in science of controlling and isolating relevant conditions in order to reveal the basic lawfulness in nature. Perhaps our most important class of independent variables in psychology is concerned with the past history of the individual. A human subject comes to us with a long, complicated, and incompletely known past history. The fact that an hour or so of weak reinforcement of an only partially specified operant can result in detectable behavioral modification, as in the Centers (1963) experiment, must be taken as a tribute to the fundamental nature of the processes which we have isolated from animal study.

4.11 SUPERSTITION

To say that a reinforcement is contingent on a response may mean only that reinforcement follows the response and does not necessarily imply some direct physical linkage between the response and the reinforcer. The reinforcement may be mediated via the behavior of an experimenter, or via some other automatic device; the effect of reinforcement on behavior is indifferent as to the means by which the temporal correlation between R and S^+ is brought about. The automatic power of reinforcement to strengthen behavior reminds us that, like Pavlovian conditioning, whenever the temporal conditions for the operant strengthening procedure are met (in the jungle, in the home, in the laboratory), modifications in behavior are likely to result.

When we recall that the strengthening process is often virtually instantaneous, we may not be surprised to discover that strengthening of behavior can occur even in situations where there exists only a fortuitous coincidence between a given R and the occurrence of S^+. In an experiment by Skinner (1948) a hungry pigeon was confined to a box not unlike the one shown in Fig. 4–1. No lever was present in this box, however, and food consisted of a few bits of mixed grain that could be delivered via a food hopper. Every 15 sec food was automatically presented to the bird, regardless of what it happened to be doing at the time. Under these conditions 6 out of 8 birds soon developed characteristically different, but stereotyped, responses. One bird developed a counterclockwise circular movement, completing two or three turns between reinforcements. A second repeatedly thrust its head into an upper corner of the cage. Another exhibited a "head tossing" movement in the vertical plane. Three other birds developed a variety of other bizarre but characteristic movements of their heads and bodies.

The fortuitous strengthening process is usually apparent. The bird chances to be executing some response at the moment that grain is delivered. This coincidence strengthens that response and so makes it more likely to appear again and be reinforced a second time. Once begun, the process perpetuates itself. As Skinner points out, the experiment might be said to demonstrate a kind of superstition.

> The bird behaves as if there were a causal relation between its behavior and the presentation of food, although such a relation is lacking. There are many analogies in human behavior. Rituals for changing one's luck at cards are good examples. A few accidental connections between a ritual and favorable consequences suffice to set up and maintain the behavior in spite of many unreinforced instances. The bowler who has released a ball down the alley but continues to behave as if he were controlling it by twisting and turning his arm and shoulder is another case in point. These behaviors have, of course, no real effect upon one's luck or upon a ball halfway down an alley, just as in the present case the food would appear as often if the pigeon did nothing—or, more strictly speaking, did something else (Skinner, 1948, p. 171).

4.12 OPERANT CONDITIONING

Operant strengthening is a special case of what we shall later call more generally operant conditioning. The term conditioning is somewhat unfortunate in this context for it conjures up the elicited nature of respondent behavior. Nevertheless, operant strengthening and Pavlovian conditioning do have certain important similarities. In particular, the modifications of behavior seen in both paradigms *are conditional upon* some prior past history. In one case, the history is a pairing of an S_1 with an S_2. In the other, it is a history of a given R occurring just before an S^+. It is this conditional nature of the behavioral changes that justifies the use of the term conditioning for both. As long as the important differences between the two phenomena are kept always at hand, there is no danger in using the general term "conditioning," qualified by its appropriate adjective, Pavlovian or operant. However, to avoid the danger that lies in neglecting these differences, we shall generally confine the term conditioning to the Pavlovian paradigm, and provide other terms (for example, strengthening) to refer to the various operant modifications that we study in the succeeding chapters. Table 4–3 is useful for making some direct comparisons between the two types of behavioral modifications that are often called conditioning.

Table 4–3

COMPARISON BETWEEN PAVLOVIAN AND OPERANT CONDITIONING

	PAVLOVIAN CONDITIONING	OPERANT CONDITIONING
PARADIGM OR PROCEDURE	$S_1 \longrightarrow R_1$ $\searrow$ CR $S_2 \longrightarrow R_2$	$R \to S^+$
R CHARACTER	CR is under the control of S_1 (CR may have elements in common with R_2).	R is emitted.
PROCESS	CR gradually evoked by S_1.	R increases in frequency, its topography narrows, and it is incorporated into a loop of behavior
RESULT	Formation of some new behaviors (CR) to S_1.	Strengthening of an R already in behavioral repertoire.
HOW MEASURED	Probability of CR to S_1, magnitude of CR, latency of CR.	Rate of R, form of R, sequential order relative to other ongoing R's.
PHYSIOLOGICAL CORRELATES	Usually involves smooth muscles and glands.	Usually involves skeletal muscles.
IMPORTANCE TO PSYCHOLOGY	Involved in emotion. Possibly part of motivational substrate.	Basic building block for acquisition of complex problem-solving activities.

APPENDIX A

The following table is a key to the phonemes shown on the abscissa of Fig. 4–6.

Symbol	Example
j	the *y* in yet
ɪ	the *y* in hymn
e	the *a* in alone
ɛ	the *a* in dare
æ	the *a* in hat
ʌ	the *o* in son
θ	the *a* in rain
a	the *a* in father
ɔ	the *a* in tall
o	the *o* in toe
ʊ	the *o* in wolf
u	the *o* in move

References for Chapter 4

Brackbill, Yvonne. Extinction of the smiling responses in infants as a function of the reinforcement schedule. *Child Develpm.,* 1958, **29,** 115–124.

Centers, R. A laboratory adaptation of the conversational procedure for the conditioning of verbal operants. *J. abnorm. soc. Psychol.,* 1963, **67,** 334–339.

Ferster, C. B., and Skinner, B. F. *Schedules of reinforcement.* New York: Appleton-Century-Crofts, 1957.

Frick, F. C., and Miller, G. A. A statistical description of operant conditioning. *Amer. J. Psychol.,* 1951, **64,** 20–36.

Guthrie, E. R., and Horton, G. P. *Cats in a puzzle box.* New York: Rinehart, 1946.

Hayes, C. *The ape in our house.* New York: Harper and Row, 1951.

Irwin, O. C. Infant speech: development of vowel sounds. *J. speech hearing Disorders,* 1952, **17,** 269–279.

Mednick, S. A. *Learning.* Englewood Cliffs: Prentice-Hall, 1964.

Millenson, J. R., and Hurwitz, H. M. B. Some temporal and sequential properties of behavior during conditioning and extinction. *J. exp. Anal. Behav.,* 1961, **4,** 97–105.

Osgood, C. E. *Method and theory in experimental psychology.* New York: Oxford Univer. Press, 1953.

Rheingold, H. L., Gewirtz, J. L., and Ross, H. W. Social conditioning of vocalizations in the infant. *J. comp. physiol. Psychol.,* 1959, **52,** 68–73.

Skinner, B. F. *The behavior of organisms.* New York: Appleton-Century, 1938.

Skinner, B. F. Superstition in the pigeon. *J. exp. Psychol.,* 1948, **38,** 168–172.

Skinner, B. F. *Walden two.* New York: Appleton-Century-Crofts, 1948.

Skinner, B. F. A case history in scientific method. *Amer. Psychologist,* 1956, **11,** 221–233.

Skinner, B. F. The experimental analysis of behavior. *Amer. Sci.,* 1957, **45,** 343–371.

Skinner, B. F. *Cumulative Record.* New York: Appleton-Century-Crofts, 1959.

Spencer, H. *The principles of psychology.* New York: D. Appleton, 1878.

Verplanck, W. S. The control of the content of conversation. *J. abnorm. soc. Psychol.,* 1955, **51,** 668–676.

Chapter 5   **OPERANT EXTINCTION AND RECONDITIONING**

WHEN THE CONNECTION BETWEEN AN OPERANT response and its reinforcer is abruptly severed, a characteristic behavioral process results. The features of this process, which is called *extinction,* play an important part in the building and maintaining of complex behavior patterns, and they are therefore examined in some detail in this chapter.

Historically, the concept of extinction has had a slow and difficult evolution. The characteristic weakening of behavior (that is, decline in its frequency) seen under the extinction procedure was considered by early workers to be a mere artifact of the concurrent strengthening of some other "competing" behaviors. The realization that extinction could not be explained in terms of a concomitant strengthening operation elsewhere in the behavior stream has come only slowly with the discovery that extinction entails far more than the weakening (lowering in frequency) of a single response class.

When a previously reinforced operant is allowed to occur without the usual reinforcement consequence, numerous *unreinforced* responses follow. These responses are emitted at first with a frequency higher even than when they were being reinforced. This immediate increase in rate of response is correlated with changes in the topography and magnitude of the behavior that implicate them as emotional. A rat, previously trained to press a lever for food, will often vigorously attack and bite the lever when reinforcement is omitted. The rat, like the man unable to find his keys in the pocket where he has usually found them, exhibits effects that might be labeled "anger." In addition to these changes in response rate and topography, the formerly well-established loop of behavior degenerates toward the pattern of activities seen prior to strengthening. At the same time, as extinction continues, behaviors previously suppressed by the strengthening of the selected response begin to return to their old prominence in the animal's response repertoire. Many of these changes take place gradually, extending over a period of many hours. Indeed, the extinction process is so protracted following even a few reinforcements that it is safe to say that probably no study has ever traced the process in all its aspects to its endpoint.

5.1 CHANGES IN RESPONSE RATE DURING EXTINCTION

The decline in the rate of the once-reinforced response is the best-documented effect of extinction. The changes in rate are clearly seen in a cumulative curve where they appear as wavelike fluctuations superimposed on a general negative acceleration. In Fig. 5–1, such an extinction curve appears for the lever-press response of a rat previously accustomed to receiving a food pellet for each lever press. The response rate is highest at the start (just after reinforcement is withdrawn) and gradually diminishes over the period of an hour and a half. By the end of 90 min, the rat is responding at a rate only slightly higher than its operant-level rate. As Fig. 5–1 shows, the extinction curve is very irregular and contains many periods of high activity interspersed with periods of low activity (the flat portions of the curve). These latter

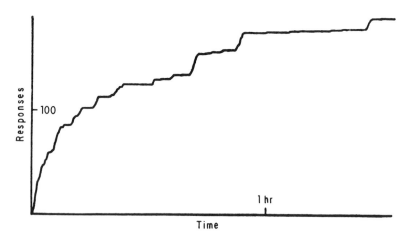

Figure 5–1. An extinction curve for a previously food-reinforced lever press. (From Skinner, 1938, data of F. S. Keller and A. Kerr.)

become more prominent towards the end of extinction. Some workers have supposed that the extinction process is due principally to a gradual increase in the number of these inactive periods over time, and that when the organism responds it does so at its usual high rate. Hurwitz (1957) has presented suggestive data in support of this notion. He analyzed a number of curves similar to Fig. 5–1, breaking them into successive 2-min time intervals. He then divided the intervals into two classes depending on how many responses were in them. Those containing zero or only a single response he called "silent" and those containing two or more responses he called "active." He found that the number of responses in the active periods failed to decline as extinction progressed but that more and more intervals became "silent." His results for a group of animals are summarized as Fig. 5–2.

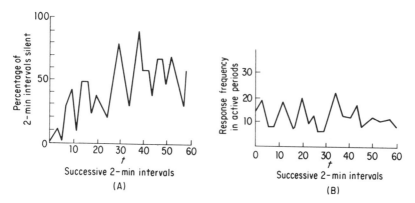

Figure 5–2. Analysis of responding during extinction. (*After Hurwitz, 1957.*)

5.2 TOPOGRAPHICAL AND STRUCTURAL CHANGES IN EXTINCTION

The effects of extinction are by no means confined to frequency changes in the selected response. In particular, marked changes occur in the *form* of the behavior during extinction. In a study by Antonitis (1951) in which a rat's poking its nose through a slot in the wall was the operant under study, the effects of several sessions of extinction interspersed by strengthening were measured. One wall of the chamber used by Antonitis contained a horizontal slot 50 cm long. Whenever the rat poked its nose into the slot a light beam was broken, causing a photograph of the rat to be made at the exact instant of the response. The position along the slot where the animal was at that moment and the angle that its body made with a perpendicular to the slot were measured. Figure 5–3 illustrates the apparatus.

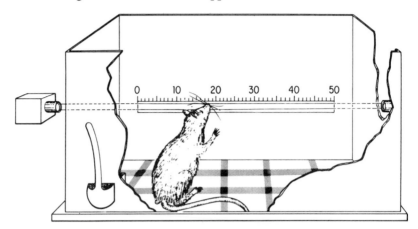

Figure 5–3. Pictorial representation of the response studied by Antonitis (1951).

By reinforcing nose poking with food, the frequency of this behavior was first increased above operant level. Subsequently, nose poking was extinguished, re-strengthened, re-extinguished, and re-strengthened again. Confirming Guthrie and Horton's (1946) results with pole tilting of cats and dogs, Antonitis found that response position and angle tended to become stereotyped during strengthening: the animal confined his responses to a rather restricted region of the slot. Extinction, however, produced variability in nose poking at least as great as that observed during operant level: the animal varied his responses over the entire length of the slot. Finally, re-strengthening resulted in ever more stereotypy (more restricted responses) than the original strengthening had produced.

Similar results were obtained by Notterman (1959), who studied the force with which rats pressed a lever during operant level, strengthening, and extinction. One additional finding emerged from Notterman's force data. Individual records revealed occasional forces, emitted during extinction, that exceeded *any* previously seen in either operant level or strengthening. We shall come back to this finding later in discussions of differentiation and skills.

The loop, or chain, of behavior established by reinforcement degenerates when reinforcement is withdrawn from the operants. Frick and Miller (1951) gave rats 300 reinforcements spaced over 5 sessions for pressing a bar in the apparatus shown in Fig. 5–4. (Note that the food tray in this apparatus was somewhat farther away from the bar than in the prototype chamber used by Skinner, described previously.) Immediately following the 300th reinforcement a 24-hr record of extinction was obtained for each rat. During extinction Miller and Frick observed the degeneration of the strengthened $R_LR_TR_LR_T$ . . . loop. As extinction progressed, lever presses began to follow lever presses (R_LR_L, etc.) and tray visits began to follow tray visits (R_TR_T, etc.). There was very little tendency for the pattern to become random during extinction. Rather, the strengthened pattern of $R_LR_TR_LR_T$ . . . gradually gave way to the operant-level pattern of repeated occurrences of the same response. Perhaps it should be stressed that this result was by no means logically forced. The loop of behavior could have simply declined in frequency during extinction, yet remained intact.

In summary then, the effect of the extinction procedure is to instigate a gradual behavior process whose changes include decline in frequency of response, increases in variability of form and intensity of the response, and breakdown in the sequential structure of the behavior. These are all-important properties of extinction and will be alluded to frequently hereafter as explanatory mechanisms.

5.3 RESISTANCE TO EXTINCTION

Were the extinction process allowed to go to completion, the operant-level states might eventually be reached. The time taken for this to occur is apparently an index of the individual's *persistence* in the face of extinction. In actual experiments, a return to operant level is rarely, if

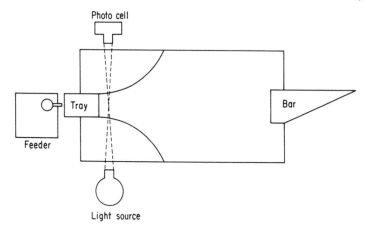

Figure 5–4. *Apparatus used to study the changes in behavior sequence during strengthening and extinction (Frick and Miller, 1951).*

ever, reached. Hence, more convenient and practical measures of persistence are based on how fast the response rate declines during extinction. For instance, the number of responses emitted, or the amount of time up until the point at which some low rate criterion is met, are called *resistance-to-extinction* measures.

The way in which actual values of these measures are arrived at is illustrated in Fig. 5–5, in which the extinction curve of Fig. 5–1 re-

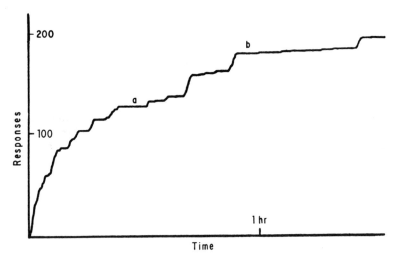

Figure 5–5. An extinction curve for lever pressing following strengthening. At the point a, no response had been emitted for five consecutive minutes (after Skinner, 1938, data from F. S. Keller and A. Kerr).

appears. Suppose we adopt the arbitrary criterion that if at any time during extinction more than 5 min elapse without an occurrence of the selected response, extinction shall be assumed for all practical purposes to be "complete," and we shall then terminate our experiment. Then, in examining Fig. 5–5, our experiment will end at *a*. At that point, no response has occurred for 5 min, 130 responses have been emitted, and 32 min have elapsed. Either of these latter two values, in conjunction with the specification of the low rate criterion (no responses for 5 min), serves as an index of the resistance to extinction.

A different criterion may affect the resistance-to-extinction result. In Fig. 5–5, for instance, a criterion of 5 min of no responding would have been rather lax, as many more responses, well above operant-level rate, were yet to be emitted. On the other hand, had we picked 10 min of no responding, the 90 min of Keller and Kerr's experiment would not have sufficed to meet our criterion, since no pause that long occurred. In order to avoid the arbitrary nature of an extinction criterion, many investigators carry out the extinction procedure until the *all-over slope* indicates that the function is close to its asymptote. Then the number of responses omitted at any arbitrarily convenient time thereafter may easily be read off the cumulative record as the resistance to extinction. This procedure is illustrated at point *b* in Fig. 5–5 where, at 1 hr, the resistance to extinction is defined as 190 responses.

Resistance to extinction provides a quantitative behavioral index whose relation to a number of experimental operations is of interest. On occasion we shall refer to studies in which resistance to extinction is the principal behavioral dependent variable. In everyday life we are often interested in how persistent a person will be in the face of no reward. A man whose resistance to extinction is low is said to "give up too easily" or to lack "perseverance" at a difficult task. On the other hand, too much resistance to extinction is sometimes undesirable. The man who spends too much time fruitlessly trying to patch up a broken love affair may miss a good chance for a new and better relationship.

One of the variables that was early suspected to affect resistance to extinction was the amount of previous strengthening. It seemed plausible that if many strengthening reinforcements were given, resistance to extinction might be greater than if only a few were given. This general hypothesis has been confirmed by several experiments (Williams, 1938; Perin, 1942; Hearst, 1961) which indicate that the resistance to extinction of an operant is low when only a few reinforcements have been given in strengthening, then gradually increases reaching a maximum after 50 to 80 reinforcements.

Another variable that would seem likely to affect the persistence of a response in extinction is the effortfulness of the response. Mowrer and Jones (1943) hypothesized that responses that required great effort to make would extinguish more quickly than would responses requiring less effort. This prediction has been confirmed in a study by Capehart, Viney, and Hulicka (1958) who trained rats to press a bar for food. They varied the force necessary to depress the bar during strengthening so that on some sessions a heavy bar was present and on others it was light or intermediate. The animals were then divided into three groups, one of which was extinguished on the heavy bar, another on the light bar, and the last on the intermediate bar. Using a criterion of no responses in 5 min as the index of resistance to extinction, they obtained the function shown in Fig. 5–6.

The design of this experiment is rather different from any we have considered up to the present. In the graphical representations of behavioral effects in this and previous chapters, we have presented data obtained from individual subjects. Sometimes the graphical representa-

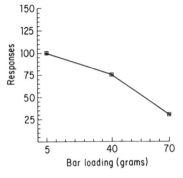

Figure 5–6. Resistance to extinction of a lever-press response as it is related to the weight of the bar (after Capehart, Viney, and Hulicka, 1958).

tions have been averages of several subjects but, in all cases, every subject underwent an identical and complete procedure. By complete is meant that the behavior of the subject was measured at every employed value of the independent variable. The use of several subjects and the averaging of the results was merely an attempt to cancel out random errors of measurement that perturb every experiment. In certain behavioral studies, however, it is impossible to subject the same individual to more than one value of the independent variable without introducing new confounding variables. Such is generally the case when resistance to extinction is the dependent variable. To measure the values of resistance to extinction for each of several values of our independent variable we would have to get several extinction curves from the organism. But after original strengthening at a given value of the independent variable there exists only *one* extinction curve. To get another one we should have either to restrengthen the behavior or to use another subject. The first course is justified only if successive extinction curves after repeated strengthening and restrengthenings are identical. It turns out, however (see section 5.6), that they are not; in fact they are systematically different. Thus we are usually left no recourse but to adopt the device of using a different subject or group of subjects for each experimental condition.

Hence, Capehart, Viney, and Hulicka extinguished one rat at a 5-gm loading, another at a 40-gm loading, and a third at a 70-gm loading. In this way they avoided the problem of how to get *initial* extinction curves from the same rat at all 3 bar weights. But in so doing, they introduced a new source of measurement error; that of individual differences among subjects due to such factors as genetic differences or uncontrolled differences in past history. To average out these individual differences among subjects, which might obscure whatever effect effort of response might have, the investigators essentially replicated their experiment 9 more times and averaged their results, thus using a total of 27 subjects altogether (9 rats per condition times 3 different conditions). Although the smoothness of their function relating resistance to extinction to bar loading attests to the success of their strategy, their results (and all such similar results) must be interpreted with caution. In their experiment, no single subject ever experienced all three values of the independent variable in extinction. Hence, the generalization of the result to any individual organism depends upon the assumption that if it were possible to obtain initial extinction curves for three different values of the independent variable in a single individual, the results of such a procedure would correspond to the results obtained by subjecting different individuals to the different experimental conditions. In general we tend to avoid this assumption whenever possible and hence resort to such group functions (of which Fig. 5–6 is an example) only when, as in this case, we seem to have no choice. Whenever we have a choice, it is usually preferable to perform a complete experiment on an individual subject, exposing him to all the conditions in which we are interested. Reliability of our results can then be assessed by complete replications of our experiment on additional subjects.

EXERCISE 3.

Without going to the psychological literature, see if you can design an experiment to test the effect of number of strengthening reinforcements on resistance to extinction. Did you have to use a group design (like Capehart, Viney, and Hulicka) or were you able to use an individual design (like Anrep's function in Fig. 3–10)?

5.4 SPONTANEOUS RECOVERY

Extinction may be extended until the rate of a formerly strengthened operant has reached a low level. If the subject (for example, a rat in a Skinner box) is then removed from the situation and returned a bit later, another (smaller) extinction curve will be obtained (see Fig. 5–7). Even

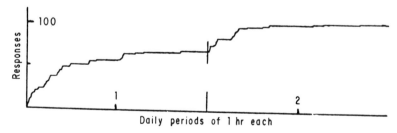

Figure 5–7. Spontaneous recovery from extinction of a rat's lever-press response. The portions of the curve to the right and left of the vertical line were separated by 47 hr during which the organism was out of the situation (Skinner, 1938).

though no restrengthening has taken place between the two extinction sessions, a certain amount of spontaneous increase in strength takes place.

The amount of spontaneous recovery (as measured by the resistance to extinction of the second extinction curve) depends, up to a limit, on the time lapse between the end of the first extinction and the beginning of the second one. Spontaneous-recovery effects can be seen with an interval as short as 15 min between the two extinction sessions in a lever-pressing situation. The effect increases up to about 2 hr, after which no further increase in spontaneous recovery is apparent. Spontaneous-recovery phenomena have been the subject of several speculative accounts, but their postulated mechanisms are beyond the scope of an introductory account.

5.5 SUCCESSIVE CONDITIONING AND EXTINCTION

In section 5.4 we mentioned that the first extinction after original strengthening is a unique phenomenon. Later extinctions (after re-strengthenings) differ from the first extinction in being more rapid and containing fewer total responses. The effect is documented by data from Bullock and Smith (1953). They exposed rats to 10 daily sessions of a procedure that reinforced the first 40 lever responses, followed directly by 1 hr of extinction. When the extinction curves were examined, it was found that they became progressively smaller over sessions 1 to 10. The effect is shown in Fig. 5–8. Whereas in session 1 the average resistance to extinction in 1 hr was 50 responses, by session 10 this had dropped to only 10 responses.

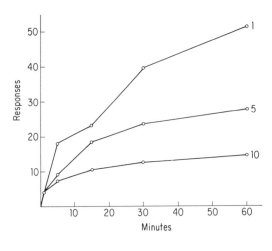

Figure 5–8. Averaged cumulative response curves for 1 hr of extinction. The numbers to the right of each curve identify the session (after Bullock and Smith, 1953).

These results can be extrapolated beyond ten sessions. It would seem that only a few more sessions would be needed before the animals would reach what is called *one-trial extinction*. In one-trial extinction, only a single response is emitted following the withdrawal of reinforcement. The change in behavior has become abrupt and it seems reasonable to conclude that the organism has come to discriminate the extinction procedure as such. Few responses in extinction are the rule at the human level. Many of our own responses show a rapid decrement when reinforcement ceases. We do not continue to insert coins into a faulty cigarette or candy machine when we fail to receive the payoff. When we open the mailbox and discover it empty we do not keep opening it. Like Bullock and Smith's rats, we have learned to wait for our reinforcement.

Results such as Bullock and Smith's leave no doubt that successive extinction processes are different. In fact, they form a progressive subprocess in their own right, as they tend to an asymptote of one response per extinction period. What happens, however, if each extinction period is prolonged all the way back to the point where operant-level rate is reached? Will each successive extinction still be a bit more rapid than the one preceding? Little information exists to answer the question with authority, but unpublished data collected by J. L. Kerr and J. R. Millenson (1957) showed that when a rat's lever pressing was extinguished back to the point where two consecutive sessions were equal to or less than operant-level rate, an effect similar to Bullock and Smith's was still obtained. Figure 5–9 shows the results of that procedure for one animal carried through four such conditioning-extinction cycles.

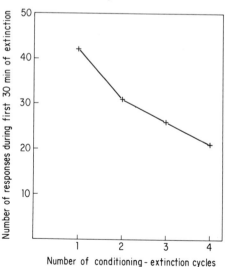

Figure 5–9. Resistance to extinction in one rat as a function of successive conditioning and extinctions back to operant level (from unpublished data of Kerr and Millenson, 1957).

5.6 FORGETTING AND EXTINCTION

Because extinction and forgetting are both associated with a weakening of behavior they are often confused. In extinction, the weakening is associated with the emission of unreinforced responses in the situation previously associated with reinforcement. In forgetting, the effect of reinforcement is weakened by a simple loss of time, during which the individual is not in the situation previously associated with conditioning. Forgetting can be studied by first strengthening an operant, then allowing a considerable period of time to elapse, and finally extinguishing that operant. When this is done under the controlled conditions of the Skinner box, the resulting extinction curve is very similar to ones obtained just after strengthening. Figure 5–10 shows a comparison between two averaged cumulative-response curves, one obtained from a group of rats extinguished 1 day after original strengthening, the other obtained from rats extinguished 45 days after original strengthening. The 44 days' difference in time lapse seems to have had only a very small effect compared with the effect of the actual extinction procedure itself.

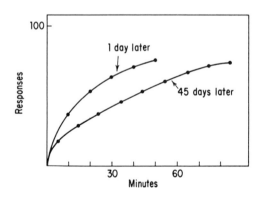

Figure 5–10. Extinction curves one day after original strengthening and 45 days after original strengthening (Skinner, 1938).

Even more impressive results are available in support of the notion that the mere passage of time between conditioning and extinction has surprisingly little effect. A group of pigeons was trained in the apparatus shown in Fig. 5–11 to peck a lighted key or disk for food. After strengthening of the key-peck response, the birds were transferred to the usual living quarters. Four years later they were returned to the apparatus and tested under the extinction procedure. Although the birds had not seen the disk for over 1400 days, they began to peck it immediately and gave hundreds of responses in extinction (Skinner, 1950).

A large literature exists on the forgetting of human verbal behavior. Before the turn of the twentieth century Ebbinghaus memorized lists of

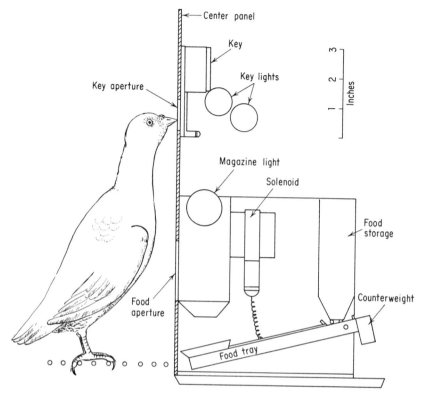

Figure 5–11. Apparatus used for the study of the pigeon's operant behavior.

what are called nonsense syllables (see Fig. 5–12) and noted what percentage of the syllables he could remember after various time lapses. The use of nonsense syllables rather than words was an attempt to eliminate factors of meaning and familiarity that might influence the results if ordinary words were used. Ebbinghaus found (see Fig. 5–13) that a marked drop in retention occurred during the first 8 hr after learning the lists; after that, the forgetting process very slowly approached an asymptote. Almost as much could be remembered 31 days after learning as 2 days after learning.

Figure 5–12. A list of nonsense syllables for the study of verbal learning and forgetting.

BIK	NAX
ZUR	KIB
JEK	VOD
ZOT	MEF
YIN	BEW

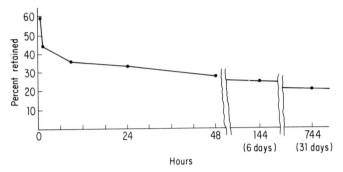

Figure 5–13. Ebbinghaus' curve of forgetting for non-sense syllables (after Ebbinghaus, 1885, from Keller and Schoenfeld, 1950).

Nonsense syllables are easily forgotten. Other verbal materials are not lost so quickly. Figure 5–14 shows forgetting curves for three types of materials: poetry, prose, and nonsense syllables.

Why is it that the animal extinction curves show such small effects after extended lapses, whereas a human may forget more than half of what he learns in a few hours? Is this an unsuspected superiority of the rat and pigeon over man? It may be, but a more convenient explanation lies in a consideration of the activity that intervenes during the time lapse in the two kinds of experiments. In the animal experiments, the animal is removed from the experimental situation and has little chance to make responses that resemble the strengthened operant. In its usual living

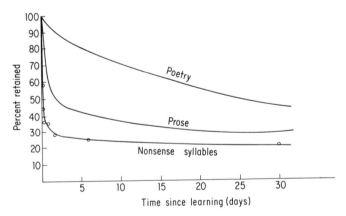

Figure 5–14. Forgetting curves showing retention for different kinds of materials (after Guilford, 1939, and Kendler, 1963).

quarters the animal does not experience any situations which closely resemble its training box. The human, on the other hand, after memorizing passages of words—be they nonsense words, prose, or poetry—is not then abruptly removed from his verbal environment. Rather, he continues to use words (learned) and to experience situations in some degree similar to the environment in which he did the original memorizing. Whenever situations do change radically after acquisition, forgetting is not so great. Typewriting skills are only a little affected after a year or so of disuse. Away from the typewriter, the chances of a person's being called upon to execute responses similar to typewriting are small. Swimming and riding a bicycle are two further illustrations of skills that are retained over long periods of disuse.

Whenever a special response is strengthened in a novel environment that is different from any found in the everyday situation, forgetting is reduced. This is true for both human and animal. It is difficult to transport a human abruptly from the learning situation to another completely different environment. An attempt to do this was made by Jenkins and Dallenbach (1924), whose subjects learned a list of nonsense syllables just before going off to sleep. The subjects were then awakened at various intervals after learning and asked to recall the list they had learned earlier. The results (Fig. 5–15) were compared with those obtained from a group of subjects who did not go to sleep after learning the list,

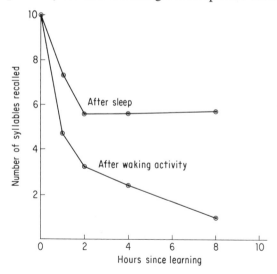

Figure 5–15. Curves showing the number of syllables recalled after sleep or waking activity (adapted from Jenkins and Dallenbach, 1924).

but continued with their usual daily activities. Apparently what one does during the time lapse is critical in determining how much forgetting takes place. We can usefully consider that in the most extreme case of "forgetting," normal and complete extinction takes place, that is, the response is emitted over and over, but without reinforcement until it ceases to occur. In other everyday cases, some weakening takes place due to the similarity of other behaviors with the learned behavior and due to the similarity of the environments during strengthening and forgetting.

5.7 A COMPREHENSIVE DEFINITION OF OPERANT EXTINCTION

The extinction procedure gives rise to the extinction process. As we have seen, the extinction process consists, in part, of a decline in response rate. A number of other behavioral processes such as fatigue, habituation, and satiation entail a similar decline, and we must be careful to distinguish them. If a decline in rate of response is all we happen to observe we are likely to find it difficult to say which decay process is involved. In later theorizing we may attribute a decline in rate of response to the extinction of certain other responses which are not being measured, but only hypothesized. This is an example of well-known concepts (for example, extinction) being used as building blocks to construct an explanatory edifice for a more complex and less well understood process. But we must be wary in attributing all rate declines to an assumed extinction. Where possible, resort to the comprehensive definition of extinction:

GIVEN: A previously strengthened operant response.
PROCEDURE: Withhold reinforcement from the operant. In symbolic notation:

$$R, \text{ or } R \nrightarrow$$

PROCESS: 1. A gradual, somewhat irregular, decline in rate marked by progressive increases in frequency of relatively long periods of non-responding.
2. An increase in the variability of the form (topography) and of the magnitude of the response.
3. A gradual disruption of the orderly loop of strengthened behavior.
RESULT: The behavior processes approach operant-level states as limiting values.

5.8 THE EXTENSION OF EXTINCTION CONCEPTS

The decline in response strength seen in experimental extinction is not confined to laboratory rats and pigeons. This is shown by the following original research report by C. D. Williams, here reproduced in its entirety from the *Journal of abnormal and social Psychology.*

THE ELIMINATION OF TANTRUM BEHAVIOR BY EXTINCTION PROCEDURES

CARL D. WILLIAMS, UNIVERSITY OF MIAMI

This paper reports the successful treatment of tyrant-like tantrum behavior in a male child by the removal of reinforcement. The subject (*S*) was approximately 21 months old. He had been seriously ill much of the first 18 months of his life. His health then improved considerably, and he gained weight and vigor.

S now demanded the special care and attention that had been given him over the many critical months. He enforced some of his wishes, especially at bedtime, by unleashing tantrum behavior to control the actions of his parents.

The parents and an aunt took turns in putting him to bed both at night and for *S*'s afternoon nap. If the parent left the bedroom after putting *S* in his bed, *S* would scream and fuss until the parent returned to the room. As a result, the parent was unable to leave the bedroom until *S* went to sleep. If the parent began to read while in the bedroom, *S* would cry until the reading material was put down. The parent felt that *S* enjoyed his control over them and that he fought off going to sleep as long as he could. In any event, a parent was spending from one-half to two hours each bedtime just waiting in the bedroom until *S* went to sleep.

Following medical reassurance regarding *S*'s physical condition, it was decided to remove the reinforcement of this tyrant-like tantrum behavior. Consistent with the learning principle that, in general, behavior that is not reinforced will be extinguished, a parent or the aunt put *S* to bed in a leisurely and relaxed fashion. After bedtime pleasantries, the parent left the bedroom and closed the door. *S* screamed and raged, but the parent did not re-enter the room. The duration of screaming and crying was obtained from the time the door was closed.

The results are shown in Fig. [5–16]. It can be seen that *S* continued screaming for 45 min the first time he was put to bed in the

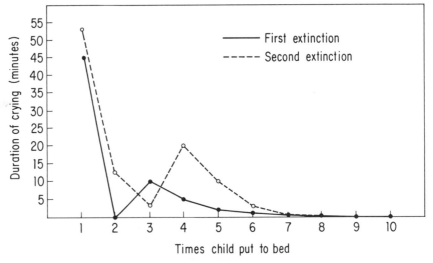

Figure 5–16. *Length of crying in two extinction series as a function of successive occasions of being put to bed (Williams, 1959).*

first extinction series. *S* did not cry at all the second time he was put to bed. This is perhaps attributable to his fatigue from the crying of Occasion 1. By the tenth occasion, *S* no longer whimpered, fussed, or cried when the parent left the room. Rather, he smiled as they left. The parents felt that he made happy sounds until he dropped off to sleep.

About a week later, *S* screamed and fussed after the aunt put him to bed, probably reflecting spontaneous recovery of the tantrum behavior. The aunt then reinforced the tantrum behavior by returning to *S*'s bedroom and remaining there until he went to sleep. It was then necessary to extinguish the behavior a second time.

Figure ⌊5–16⌋ shows that the second extinction curve is similar to the first. Both curves are generally similar to extinction curves obtained with subhuman subjects. The second extinction series reached zero by the ninth occasion. No further tantrums at bedtime were reported during the next two years.

It should be emphasized that the treatment in this case did not involve aversive punishment. All that was done was to remove the reinforcement. Extinction of the tyrant-like tantrum behavior then occurred.

No unfortunate side- or aftereffects of this treatment were observed. At three and three-quarters years of age, *S* appeared to be a friendly, expressive, outgoing child.

The use of the extinction procedure is general, then, for weakening the strength of any operant. In later chapters, we shall discover numerous other ways of manipulating the strength of behavior, but with just the simple application of two principal operations—reinforcement and extinction—we can cause the strength of behavior to vary widely. Strength of behavior is an important concept in psychology because of its close relation to probability of occurrence of behavior. When a response exists at high strength, its frequency is high and the probability that it will be emitted at any given time is also high. These are merely different ways of saying the same thing. This statement is true for the human or the animal. The analysis of operant behavior is very largely the study of the form and, more particularly, of the probability of occurrence of such behaviors. If we grant that reflex concepts can account for the sheer mechanics of executing such behaviors as posture, walking, and running, then the territory that remains for psychological exploration seems to be the *initiation* of the operants. Therefore, our interest centers on situations which provide for a choice in behaviors. Even in the simple Skinner box, where often only a single response is measured, choice is present in the animal's apparent "freedom" either to respond or not to respond. In general, our concern is with the causes of behavior or, to put it more technically, with the controls over the emission of responses. Though a sequence of behaviors may be reflexly integrated from start to finish, we may still be interested in *why it started at all.* Although this entire book is a series of proposed answers to that question, we can already perceive that the operations of conditioning and extinction provide two powerful explanatory principles. A response may fail to occur, for instance, because it has been extinguished.

> An aspiring writer who has sent manuscript after manuscript to the publishers only to have them all rejected may report that 'he can't write another word.' He may be partially paralyzed with what is called 'writer's cramp.' He may still insist that he 'wants to write,' and we may agree with him in paraphrase: his extremely low probability of response is mainly due to extinction. Other variables are still operative which, if extinction had not taken place, would yield a high probability (Skinner, 1953, pp. 71–72).

The notion of response frequency or strength is a very fundamental one for psychology, principally because so much behavior appears to be explainable in terms of the frequency with which bits of behavior occur.

> We say that someone is 'enthusiastic' about bridge when we observe that he plays bridge often and talks about it often. To be 'greatly interested' in music is to play, listen to, and talk about music a good deal. The 'inveterate' gambler is one who gambles

frequently. The camera 'fan' is to be found taking pictures, developing them, and looking at pictures made by himself and others. The 'highly sexed' person frequently engages in sexual behavior. The 'dipsomaniac' drinks frequently (Skinner, 1953, p. 62).

Although our account of extinction is very far from complete in this chapter, it illustrates some of the principal known effects of withdrawal of reinforcement on the strength of behavior.

Figure 5–17. The power of extinction. (Drawing by Opie, © 1961, The New Yorker Magazine, Inc.)

5.9 GRAPHICAL REPRESENTATIONS OF RESULTS OF EXPERIMENTS IN WHICH SEVERAL INDEPENDENT VARIABLES ARE STUDIED JOINTLY

In this text, the principal device for representing the results of experiments is the two-dimensional graph. In the simplest cases, such a graph is constructed from a table listing pairs of *x* and *y* values (see Tables 2–2 and 3–1). In the tables, each value of the independent variable is paired with a single value of the dependent variable (usually an average of several observed values). In a simple graph such as Fig. 5–6, three values of the independent variable (weight of bar) are paired with their respective observed averages of the dependent variable, resistance to extinction, and plotted as points. Then straight lines are drawn connecting (that is, interpolating between) the points. The resulting "curve" lets us see the results in a single picture, thereby interrelating the data in a way that the table cannot do. Cumulative records are more sophisticated. In Fig. 5–1, the independent variable (time) is continuous and interpolation is unnecessary since the cumulative recorder is actually sampling the occurrence or non-occurrence of a response (the dependent variable) at every instant in time, not just at a few selected points.

Occasionally an investigator desires to study the effects of more than one independent variable in the same experiment. The common method of representing the quantitative results of such experimental designs is still the graph, but the form is generalized somewhat. Consider the two functions of Fig. 5–18. One of these (A) is simply Fig. 5–6 reproduced here for convenience. The other is the Perin (1942)–Williams (1938) function relating

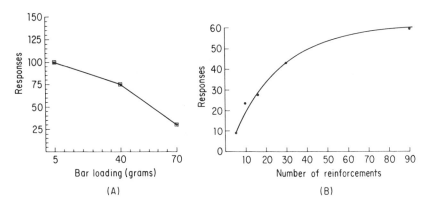

Figure 5–18. (*A*) *Resistance to extinction as a function of bar weight (Capehart, Viney, and Hulicka, 1958). (B) Resistance to extinction as a function of number of prior strengthening reinforcements (adapted from Perin, 1942, and Williams, 1938).*

lever-press resistance to extinction in the rat to the number of strengthening reinforcements. We shall suppose, for the purposes of the present discussion, that the experiments represented by (A) and (B) of Fig. 5–18 were carried out in the same laboratory, using the same apparatus, with the conditions controlled so that the only differences between (A) and (B) are in the independent variable manipulations indicated.

We may begin our analysis with the observation that both of these graphs correspond to our simple formula for an experiment: one independent variable coupled with one dependent variable. There is, however, an interesting relationship between the two examples of Fig. 5–18. Both (A) and (B) display the same dependent variable, resistance to extinction. Furthermore, close examination reveals that (A) and (B) have one point in common. To see this, consider the notion, implicit in (A), that many variables were held constant; only weight of bar was varied. Analogously, implicit in (B) is the notion that many variables were held constant; only number of strengthening reinforcements was varied. However, in (A) one of the variables held constant was the independent variable of (B); conversely, one of the variables held constant in (B) was the independent variable of (A). Specifically, all the subjects in (A) received 90 strengthening reinforcements, while all the subjects in (B) had a bar which weighed 15 gm. Therefore, each graph has one point in common with the other: the point representing 90 strengthening reinforcements with a 15-gm bar.

The link between (A) and (B) of Fig. 5–18 may be made more conspicuous by a graphical representation of both functions in the same coordinate system. Since there will be two independent variables and one dependent variable to portray, a three-dimensional coordinate system will prove useful. Examine the three-dimensional representation of (A) and (B) in Fig. 5–19. In that figure, Fig. 5–18A is shown as a shaded polygon in the

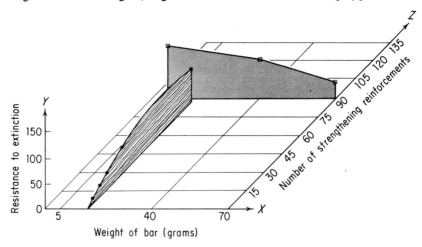

Figure 5–19. Representation of the two functions of Fig. 5–18 as two surfaces in a three-dimensional coordinate system.

xy plane, while Fig. 5–18B is shown as a hatched conic section in the *zy* plane. The two surfaces intersect at their common point, $x = 15$, $z = 90$. (The fact that the curves bounding the two surfaces do not precisely coincide may be explained by various differences in the two experiments beside the two variables under consideration.)

Figure 5–19 is a map showing the resistance-to-extinction territory staked out by these two independent variables. The map shows that the two functions of Fig. 5–18 provide behavioral information about the effects of bar weight and number of strengthening reinforcements in only a small region of the possible space.

The spatial representation of Fig. 5–19 suggests that the territory might be more efficiently studied by an experimental design in which both independent variables were manipulated jointly in such a way as to cover a larger portion of the experimental space. One such joint manipulation would be an extension of Capehart, Viney, and Hulicka's (1958) experiment in which number of strengthening reinforcements might be manipulated jointly with weight of bar. Assigning groups to the various combinations of independent variables might be accomplished by a scheme such as that described in Table 5–1.

Table 5–1

ASSIGNMENT OF GROUPS TO AN EXPERIMENT FOR STUDYING THE JOINT EFFECTS OF NUMBER OF PRIOR STRENGTHENING REINFORCEMENTS AND BAR WEIGHT ON RESISTANCE TO EXTINCTION

GROUP	NUMBER OF PRIOR STRENGTHENING REINFORCEMENTS GIVEN	BAR WEIGHT
A	50	5
B	50	15
C	50	30
D	100	5
E	100	15
F	100	30
G	300	5
H	300	15
I	300	30

The hypothetical curves of Fig. 5–20 are suggestive of the kind of result that might be obtained if groups receiving 30, 90, and 270 strengthening reinforcements had been studied using the three bar weights. In Fig. 5–20 the representation is two-dimensional, with the values of one of the independent variables (number of strengthening reinforcements) shown simply as a small numeral to the right of each curve. This representation is an

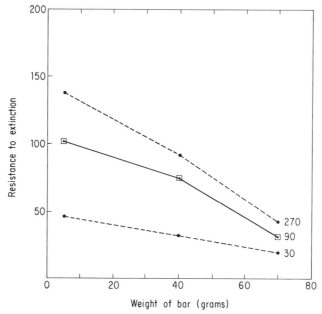

Figure 5–20. Two-dimensional representation of hypothetical results of manipulating bar weight jointly with number of strengthening reinforcements. The points at 90 are from Capehart, Viney, and Hulicka (1958). The other plotted points are hypothetical.

alternative form of that of Fig. 5–19. Two-dimensional representations such as Fig. 5–20 are frequently found in the literature and are known as families of curves, or the *parametric form* of functional representation. This latter terminology gives rise to the custom of speaking of the independent variables known to be, or believed to be, related to a given dependent variable as *parameters* of that dependent variable. "Parameter" is virtually a synonym for "independent variable" though it is used specifically with regard to the independent variables related to a common dependent variable. The parameters of resistance to extinction shown in Fig. 5–20 are therefore bar weight and number of strengthening reinforcements prior to extinction. Clearly the number of parameters of any given dependent variable may be very numerous. In any particular experiment, however, we rarely study more than one or two of them at a time.

EXERCISE 4.

Draw a parametric (*two-dimensional*) representation of possible results from an experiment similar to H. M. Wolfle's (*Fig. 3–6*), using four different values of intensity of the S_2. Let Wolfle's actual data be one of your four curves.

References for Chapter 5

Antonitis, J. J. Variability of response in the white rat during conditioning and succeeding extinction and reconditioning. Unpublished doctoral dissertation, Columbia Univer., 1950.

Antonitis, J. J. Response variability in the white rat during conditioning, extinction, and reconditioning. *J. exp. Psychol.,* 1951, **42,** 273–281.

Bullock, D. H., and Smith, W. C. An effect of repeated conditioning-extinction upon operant strength. *J. exp. Psychol.,* 1953, **46,** 349–352.

Capehart, J., Viney, W., and Hulicka, I. M. The effect of effort upon extinction. *J. comp. physiol. Psychol.,* 1958, **51,** 505–507.

Ebbinghaus, H. *Memory* (Translated by H. A. Ruger and C. E. Bussenius). New York: Teachers College, 1913.

Frick, F. S., and Miller, G. A. A statistical description of operant conditioning. *Amer. J. Psychol.,* 1951, **64,** 20–36.

Guilford, J. P. *General psychology.* Princeton: D. Van Nostrand, 1939.

Guthrie, E. R., and Horton, G. P. *Cats in a puzzle box.* New York: Rinehart, 1946.

Hearst, E. Resistance-to-extinction functions in the single organism. *J. exp. Anal. Behav.,* 1961, **4,** 133–144.

Hurwitz, H. M. B. Periodicity of response in operant extinction. *Quart. J. exp. Psychol.,* 1957, **9,** 177–184.

Jenkins, J. G., and Dallenbach, K. M. Oblivescence during sleep and waking. *Amer. J. Psychol.,* 1924, **35,** 605–612.

Keller, F. S., and Schoenfeld, W. N. *Principles of psychology.* New York: Appleton-Century-Crofts, 1950.

Kendler, H. H. *Basic psychology.* New York: Appleton-Century-Crofts, 1963.

Kimble, G. A. *Principles of general psychology.* New York: Ronald Press, 1956.

Mowrer, O. H., and Jones, H. M. Extinction and behavior variability as functions of effortfulness of task. *J. exp. Psychol.,* 1943, **33,** 369–386.

Notterman, J. M. Force emission during bar pressing. *J. exp. Psychol.,* 1959, **58,** 341–347.

Perin, C. T. Behavior potentiality as a joint function of the amount of training and the degree of hunger at the time of extinction. *J. exp. Psychol.,* 1942, **30,** 93–113.

Skinner, B. F. *The behavior of organisms.* New York: Appleton-Century, 1938.

Skinner, B. F. Are theories of learning necessary? *Psychol. Rev.,* 1950, **57,** 193–216.

Skinner, B. F. *Science and human behavior*. New York: Macmillan, 1953.

Williams, C. D. The elimination of tantrum behavior by extinction procedures. *J. abnorm. soc. Psychol.,* 1959, **59,** 269.

Williams, S. B. Resistance to extinction as a function of the number of reinforcements. *J. exp. Psychol.,* 1938, **23,** 506–522.

PART TWO

Fundamental Units of Analysis

6. RESPONSE AND STIMULUS CONTINGENCY NOTATION

7. INTERMITTENT REINFORCEMENT

8. RESPONSE SPECIFICATION

9. ENVIRONMENTAL CONTROL

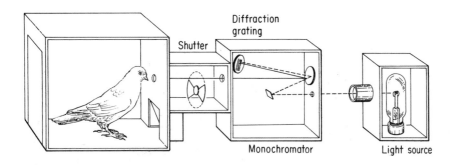

Shutter

Diffraction grating

Monochromator

Light source

Chapter 6

RESPONSE AND STIMULUS CONTINGENCY NOTATION

■LABORATE SYSTEMS OF SHORTHAND NOTATION, expressing relationships among procedures, concepts, and events, are not uncommonly developed in science. Such notational systems may serve as a convenience in describing operations. As an analytic device, notation may aid in recognizing similarities and differences between procedures and simplify their classification, paving the way for their eventual theoretical integration.

One such well-known and highly developed system exists in chemistry. By denoting a particular element by a particular symbol and defining relationships between elements (for example, + for *combine with;* → for *produces;* Δ for *apply heat*), a parsimonious description of a procedure and certain of its results may be quickly given and the relationship of this procedure to other similar procedures easily seen. It should be noted, however, that as in all notations used for summary purposes some information is lost. When sodium, for example, is added to water, hydrogen is released and sodium hydroxide is formed. This procedure and its result are conveniently and quantitatively expressed as

$$2Na + 2HOH \longrightarrow 2NaOH + H_2$$

This expression omits a great deal of detail for the sake of representing certain fundamental relations in a simple and concise way. It does not advise, for instance, that heat is generated by this reaction, it fails to give any information concerning the time course of the reaction, and it says nothing about the form (solid, liquid, gas) which the products will assume. Despite these limitations, the notation has proved useful enough to justify its continued inclusion in chemistry, for it conveniently describes a number of events with great generality. For example, the representation holds true for many different forms of sodium (powdered, solid, granular, crystalline), at any time of day, over a wide range of temperatures, over a large range of atmospheric pressures. Like most scientific generalizations, however, it is not universally valid. If the temperature is too low and the atmospheric pressure too high, the reaction will not occur. The representation also fails to inform that Na is not a unitary material but actually a number of related materials (isotopes); all of these behave similarly enough for most purposes to allow the label Na to be applied to them all as an approximation.

Psychologists are principally interested in the relationships between the activities of organisms and other events in the world. A system of notation employing environmental events and behavioral events as fundamental terms proves convenient in describing a number of psychological procedures and, as we shall show, makes possible an analytic comparison of operations. The notational scheme outlined in detail in this chapter is derived from a system first described by F. Mechner (1959) and elaborated by Vicki Mechner (1963). Unlike the chemical example, the behavioral notation we shall outline schematizes only *procedural* aspects of experimentation. In that way it resembles the notation of electronics. There, a circuit is represented by symbols, and the results of such a circuit, when a voltage is applied to it, must be described by functions relating independent and dependent variables operating in the circuit. In use, the present notation would similarly be supplemented typically with functions relating the independent variables (changes in the environmental events) to measures of behavior.

At the level of the present treatment we shall not attempt to give formal and rigorous definitions for the units that we shall employ to describe behavioral procedures: these may be found in other chapters. We shall be interested here only in making available in a concise format and with a minimum of comment the various notational tools, by providing examples and problems illustrating the principle powers, features, and limitations of the R and S notation that is used extensively throughout the text.

6.1 BEHAVIORAL EVENTS AND RESPONSES

The notation incorporates behavioral events in the form of instrumental (operant) responses, abbreviated R. These of course are behaviors which are governed by their consequences. For present purposes, we may define behavior as anything an individual organism does. Then we may further identify a response as a unit of behavior. The key word in the specification of behavior is the verb *do*. To behave, an organism must *do* something, it must act. Thus all the following are examples of behavior and also examples of what we shall call responses.

(1) John hit the ball.
(2) Mr. Mitty put the car into gear.
(3) I carried my tray to the table.
(4) The rat pressed the bar.
(5) The monkey scratched its back.
(6) George waited for the bus.

In all these examples some organism *did* something. In general we try to specify the response in terms of the movements that the organism makes rather than in terms of the consequences of these movements. Thus "John hit the ball" implies that John swung his arms in a certain prescribed way and in a certain correspondence with the path of an oncoming ball; as a consequence, the ball got hit. It is important at the outset to *separate behavioral events from their consequences*. Hence (1) is better written: "John swung the bat"; and (3) is better written "I moved my legs in such and such a direction, holding the tray in my hands, and eventually arrived at the table." Arriving at the table was a consequence of my leg-moving behavior.

Note that in each example an organism is identified. We shall follow the convention that each specification of an R will identify the organism for whom the event is an R. In this way we shall avoid confusing the R's of one organism with those of another.

A useful rule of thumb for identifying response events in ordinary language text is to pick out the action verbs. Since a response is a doing, action verbs will usually (though not invariably) be associated with response events.

The following counter-examples illustrate some events that are *not* response events.

(7)   The ball hit John.
(8)   The hurricane struck.
(9)   The government collapsed.
(10) Mrs. Brown died.
(11) The monkey fell asleep.
(12) George got tired of waiting.

In (7), John has not *done* anything. He has been acted upon. In (8), the hurricane is *not an organism,* hence cannot make responses in our sense. In (9), the government does not consist of an individual organism who has collapsed. The behavior of an individual is not being described by the government's collapse. We reject (10) because dying is a unique behavioral event for each organism and responses must be *repeatable* events. In (11), sleep, though an interesting behavioral phenomenon, is not to be construed as a response event. Finally, the statement that George "got tired" is a rough specification of some state within George, but *not* a description of anything he is doing and therefore not a response event.

We shall write response events in one of several ways. We may represent them as a capital R with a numerical or letter subscript and give elsewhere a key to their actual identity, as in the example

$$R_A$$
$$R_B$$

where R_A = John swung the bat
   R_B = John dusted off the plate

This simple example shows some important characteristics of the notation. In the first place each R in any particular example must be an R from the same organism. Thus R_A could not be an instance of something that John did and R_B an instance of something that George did. Another way of putting this is to note that we can only discuss the behavior of one organism at a time.

An alternate method of indicating the actual identity of R's is to subscript a word abbreviation of the behavior as in

$$R_{(swung)}$$

and

$$R_{(dusted)}$$

Both of these forms will be used.

6.2 ENVIRONMENTAL EVENTS AND SITUATIONS

Any behaving individual is surrounded and bombarded by a multiplicity of energies. Some of this energy is too far away to affect the organism. Thus a traffic light in Tokyo will have no effect on our behavior in New York. A man shouting to us from five miles away will similarly have no effect on us unless we happen to see him. Other energy will have no effect because the organism has no specialized receptors for receiving it. Radio waves and cosmic radiation surround us constantly but we do not detect these energies unless we are equipped with special instruments to translate them into sounds and pointer deflections, energies that we *can* detect. The organism is constructed to detect a sample of the energies around him and all these make up his environment. An environment at any given moment may be very complex, consisting of sounds, light patterns, odors, and all the configurations of these that we have come to call objects.

We shall often find that we need only specify the *changes* that occur in our environments. When John hit the ball, the ball traveled out in the general direction of the outfield. The rest of his environment remained relatively constant but the part involving the ball changed. The following ideas will prove useful. A description of an organism's environment at any given time and place and in reference to him will be designated a *situation,* abbreviated S. Furthermore, we shall call a change in a part or the whole of that organism's environment a stimulus. Since a stimulus is only a special case of a situation, we need no special symbol for it. We can use the S of situation. Here are some situations for several organisms:

(13) The ball came towards John . . .
(14) Walter Mitty in his 1962 grey Volkswagen, rain pouring down on it, his foot on the clutch, the motorist behind him hooting his horn . . .
(15) My tray laden with lunch . . .
(16) The rat in a Skinner box, a lever on the front wall, no food present . . .
(17) A flea biting the monkey . . .
(18) George at the bus stop . . .

Note that three dots follow each of these descriptions of situations. This is because any situation can always be described in indefinitely great detail. Fortunately, we need only describe the aspects of the situation in which we are interested. For the most part, these will be the *changes* in the environment that occur from one situation to another. Note also the absence of any action verbs in the description of the environmental situations. The next-to-last one, (17), appears to be an exception. Nevertheless, the bite is a situation (S) for the monkey (though it is a response for the flea). This illustration emphasizes the importance of always identifying for each R event or each S event just *which* organism's R's and S's we are talking about.

Situations (S's) are labeled much like R's. We may subscript a number or a letter as in

S_{16} = ball heading towards John
S_b = Walter Mitty in his car

or subscript as much of the actual situation as we deem necessary:

$S_{(rat\ in\ box,\ no\ food\ present)}$

It is important to note that situations may be *simple* as in the situation

$$S_{(dinner-gong\ ringing)}$$

or complex as in the situation

$$S_{24} = \text{bomb fell} + \text{street collapsed} + \text{people screaming} + \\ \text{air-raid sirens sounding} + \text{fire raging all around} \\ \text{me} + \cdots$$

However many changes occur in the environment at a given time, they all constitute one and only one situation: a situation with many changes. It should be apparent from this consideration that, logically, only one situation at a time can exist for any organism. We shall find it convenient to use a plus sign to combine separate changes in the same S event.

6.3 THE IDEA OF A BEHAVIORAL CONTINGENCY

Doing something often produces some important consequences. In the language of response and stimulus events, this statement means that R will often lead to an S of some consequence. The present notation is fundamentally a notation about the stimulus consequences of behavior. Whenever a behavioral event has been observed in the past to lead repeatedly to some specifiable environmental consequences, we are dealing with a *behavioral contingency*. Formally, a behavioral contingency is defined as a rule stating a conditional relationship between a response and its consequences. Examine a few examples of such rules.

(19) Pushing the starter button turns the motor over.
(20) If you say one more word, you'll be sent to bed without your dinner.
(21) Turn handle to left to open door.
(22) Drink your milk and you can have your dessert.
(23) Whenever the monkey presses the lever he receives a peanut.

Each of the five examples specifies a response event and a stimulus consequence for that R event. Consider (19): *If* you push, R, on the starter button, *then* the motor turns over, $S_{(turn\ over)}$. In (20): *If* you say a word, R, *then* you will find yourself in bed without your dinner, $S_{(in\ bed\ +\ no\ dinner)}$. Note that we change the form "you'll be sent" of (20) to the form "you will find yourself". The change stresses the critical idea that environmental events *happen* to the organism. In (20), sending you to bed might well entail response events on the part of another individual (for example, your mother) but since we are discussing *you*, this is an S event for you. It is very important to maintain a consistent frame of reference in notating contingencies. For the present, we shall assume that we can notate the R and S events of one and only one organism at a time. Thus, we cannot mix the behavioral events of two organisms in the same diagram and call them both Rs. In example (21), *if* the handle is turned to the left, $R_{(turn\ left)}$, *then* the door opens, $S_{(door\ opens)}$. Both examples (22) and (23) also fit the form *if R then S*.

In general, a contingency specifies the dependency of an environmental change on a prior behavior event. Although contingencies are very often stated in the future tense (see the previous examples) it should be evident that they are rules based on observations made in the past. We can usually read the dependency given by a contingency as *if R then S*. An equivalent way of describing this dependency of S on R is to observe that in a behavioral contingency R *leads to* S, or R *produces* S. These last forms are so generally useful that a special symbol, $\rightarrow$, exists which carries the meaning of *leads to* or *produces*. Hence we can write the contingency examples of (19) to (23) as follows.

(19a) $R_{(push)} \rightarrow S_{(motor\ turns\ over)}$
(20a) $R_A \rightarrow S_A$

where R_A = say a word and S_A = in bed.

(21a) $R_{16} \rightarrow S_1$

where R_{16} = turn handle to left and S_1 = open door.

(22a) $R_{(drink\ milk)} \rightarrow S_{(dessert)}$
(23a) $R_{(press\ lever)} \rightarrow S_{(peanut)}$

Each of these five cases is conveniently read R *leads to* S.

The notion of a behavioral contingency is not a difficult one, but it is important to note some of its characteristic features. First, the contingency describes the S consequences for making an R. It *does not* describe the occurrence of behavior. That is, it does not say that R *will* occur. It only says that S is conditional (dependent) upon R, that is, that R has occurred in the past and was then followed by S. Secondly, the behavioral contingency specifies only environmental consequences for behavior. There are a number of other kinds of contingencies which the notation is not designed to handle. Several of these are illustrated in the following counter-examples.

(24) The savages did a rain dance and the next day it rained.
(25) If the sun shines I'm going to the picnic.
(26) If he opens the book he will begin to read it.
(27) When I awoke I could hear Josella already moving around in the kitchen.
(28) If it rains any more, the crops will be ruined.

In (24), we are presented with a pseudo-contingency. $R_{(dance)}$ did indeed lead to ($\rightarrow$) $S_{(rain)}$. However, the statement does not imply that in the past such dancing also led to rain. Counter-example (24) is merely a statement of a unique sequence of R and S and the critical notion of a *rule* is absent. In (25) we have the idea that some behavioral event, $R_{(go\ to\ picnic)}$, is conditional upon some environmental event, $S_{(sun\ shines)}$. But this is the reverse of our idea of a behavioral contingency which states the dependency of an S upon a prior R. In (26) we have $R_{(read)}$ dependent on $R_{(open\ book)}$. But again, this is not a *stimulus* consequence of making an R. It is a behavioral consequence of making an R. Counter-example (27) is merely a descriptive statement of some events and neither states nor implies any *rule*. Finally, (28) describes two environmental events, the second, $S_{(crops\ ruined)}$, being dependent on the first, $S_{(rains\ more)}$. Such an S — S contingency fails to conform to the basic $R \rightarrow S$ model of a behavioral contingency.

The idea of S consequences being dependent on R's is fundamental in behavioral contingencies. The notation is uniquely equipped to represent such contingencies simply because, as the text elsewhere makes clear, controlling the past consequences of behavior is one of the most powerful ways of controlling behavior presently available to the psychologist. Hence it is not surprising that a notation should have been developed to represent the pattern of these consequences in relation to behavior, both in the laboratory and in the everyday world.

6.4 THE INITIAL SITUATION (S_A)

Clearly, every behavioral contingency is set in some environment. Another way of saying this is that contingencies are generally possible only in some given situation. Thus, in example (19), pushing the starter button is only possible when you are in your car, in reach of the button, and so forth. In (20), the contingency holds only when a second human being is present to hear your words and send you off to bed without your dinner. Similar considerations hold for the remaining contingency examples. In general, a given situation prevails at the time that a given contingency is in effect. Since this situation is changed by the occurrence of R (R leads to a new situation, the S consequence) it is often desirable for purposes of contrast to indicate this initial, pre-consequence situation. In the notation, this is done by writing the initial situation (often abbreviated S_A) vertically above the R. A bracket is then placed about the two terms S_A and R to indicate that the situation and contingency associated with R go into effect simultaneously. Consider

$$\left[\begin{array}{l} S_A \\ R \to S_B \end{array}\right. \qquad\qquad [6.1]$$

where S_A = milk in front of you
  R = you drink
  S_B = dessert

Diagram [6.1] is read: *When* the glass of milk is in front of you and *if* you drink it, *then* you will get dessert. Diagram [6.1] is the simplest possible type of contingency diagram to be written in the notation. It shows two situations, an initial one, and a second one—the consequences of R. It specifies one response event. Although succeeding diagrams will become more complicated, they all contain as elements the idea expressed in [6.1]. That is, in some S_A, *if* an R is made, *then* S_B will occur. Contingencies that conform to diagram [6.1] are best read

When or			
while or	S_A	$\left[\begin{array}{c}\end{array}\right.$ R	$\longrightarrow$ S_B
during or			
just after		*if*	*then*

If this phraseology is adopted, there will be little possibility of radically misrepresenting any particular problem.

6.5 MULTIPLE CONTINGENCIES IN THE SAME SITUATION

We seldom find ourselves in a situation in which there is only one thing we can do which will have consequences. There are usually very many behaviors we could perform in every situation, many of which might lead to significant environmental changes, or consequences. For instance, while seated at a typewriter, there might be forty or more keys that we could push, each leading to a different consequence. We might also be able to roll paper in and out, erase characters, change the ribbon, etc. Furthermore, if our telephone is near by, we could make calls. If a second person is at hand, we might call out requests which might be obeyed. One could continue indefinitely listing various activities possible in this situation, all with distinctive consequences. We deal with this problem in the notation by writing only as many of these contingencies as we desire to notate, and we do this merely by adding R's to our bracket. Thus if we were interested in notating the contingencies of pushing any key on our typewriter and obtaining a letter, or dialing a number on our nearby phone, or calling out for a glass of water to be brought to us, we could write

$$\left[\begin{array}{l} S_A \text{ (at typewriter, near phone, friend within earshot)} \\ R_1 \text{ (push key)} \rightarrow S_{\text{(letter)}} \\ R_2 \text{ (dial number)} \rightarrow S_{\text{(someone answers)}} \\ R_3 \text{ (call out for drink)} \rightarrow S_{\text{(glass of water brought)}} \end{array}\right. \qquad [6.2]$$

In general we may write as many R contingencies as we desire simply by appending R's and their consequences to a bracket.

$$\left[\begin{array}{l} S_A \\ R_1 \rightarrow S_B \\ R_2 \rightarrow S_C \\ R_3 \rightarrow S_D \\ R_4 \rightarrow S_E \\ \vdots \quad \vdots \end{array}\right. \qquad [6.3]$$

The triple vertical dots stand for "and so forth."

Note carefully that [6.2] and [6.3] are not representations of what behaviors we *will* engage in when seated at our typewriter. They are representations of what will happen *if* any of the R's are made. Diagrams [6.2] and [6.3] do not assert that any of these R's will in fact be made or that any behavior will take place at all. The best the notation purports to do is to show what consequences will happen *if* some behaviors do occur. This is a fundamental point and should be kept constantly in mind whenever R and S diagrams are examined.

A special case of a multiple contingency occurs when more than one R can lead to the same S consequences. In the expression "there is more than one way to skin a cat," we deal with a set of contingencies of the sort shown in diagram [6.4]:

$$\left[\begin{array}{l} S_A \\ R_1 \longrightarrow S_B \\ R_2 \\ R_3 \\ \vdots \end{array}\right. \qquad [6.4]$$

where S_A = intact cat
  S_B = skinned cat
  R_1 = one way of skinning cat
  R_2 = another way
  R_3 = yet another way
  $\vdots$

For a more specific example, consider the ways in which we might call a waiter to our table. We might call out "waiter," we might signal the nearest waiter with our hand, or we might merely glance in the waiter's direction fixing our eyes on his.

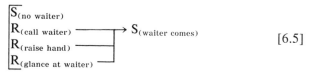

$$[6.5]$$

Diagram [6.5] illustrates a useful method of specifying S_A, the initial situation. In order to generate diagram [6.5], first write down all the behaviors entailed. Then write out the principle consequence, "waiter comes to us." Finally, to determine the best method of specifying S_A, merely ascertain what the opposite of the consequence would be. In this case, it is simply "no waiter at our table." When complex cases contain many S's, it is frequently useful to obtain the opposite of each S, for the opposite may provide a clue as to how to commence the diagram.

6.6 THE NULL CONTINGENCY

In diagrams [6.1] to [6.5], R's have led to S's. Whenever an R could lead to a new situation, that R was enclosed in a vertical bracket along with the current situation. But in these diagrams, the S consequences have been written alone, unbracketed. An S without a bracket around it usually indicates that no special contingencies (in which we are interested) hold in this situation. Thus the meaning of S_B alone in [6.1] is the same as

$$\boxed{S_B}$$

The inference here is that the R in question, $R_{(drink)}$, no longer has any special consequences once the organism reaches S_B. Thus, the *lack* of any given R in a bracket implies that *if* that R were made during that S, no special consequences would occur. The lack of any special consequences for an R defines a special case of a contingency and is called the *null contingency*. Thus the absence of any given R in any given bracket implies that the null contingency is in effect for that R during the S of that bracket. Furthermore, the appearance of an S without a bracket around it implies the null contingency in that situation for *all* the R's under consideration.

Occasionally, in some situation, say S_a, we wish to emphasize that an R which used to have consequences no longer does. One way to do this would be simply to omit the R from the bracket that includes S_a, but for emphasis it may be useful to write either

$$\boxed{\begin{array}{l} S_a \\ R \end{array}} \quad \text{or} \quad \boxed{\begin{array}{l} S_a \\ R \not\rightarrow \end{array}}$$

both of which are read: *During* S_a, R *no longer* leads to any special consequences. Both of the above are equivalent to

$$S_a \quad \text{or} \quad \boxed{S_a}$$

and all four forms illustrate different ways of writing the *null contingency*.

6.7 THE DURATION OF SITUATIONS AND CONTINGENCIES

Situations do not last indefinitely, whether or not we do anything to change them. We can climb on the bus only as long as the bus remains at our stop. We can beckon to the waiter while he is standing in our view, but eventually he will disappear and our signs will be to no avail. Children are often given a time limit in which to drink their milk. After that no dessert will be forthcoming whatever they do. The fact that many situations and contingencies have definite durations associated with them leads to the introduction of the symbol T, standing for time duration. The use of T is straightforward. A situation (S_1) that lasts T long is written

$$\boxed{\begin{array}{l} S_1 \\ T \rightarrow S_2 \end{array}} \qquad [6.6]$$

Several points must be made concerning the interpretation of [6.6]. First, T is the *duration* of S_1. Second, T always has an arrow leading from it. If one situation lasts T long, then a new situation *must* come into effect; that new situation will be found at the head of the arrow leading from T. Thirdly, T and its arrow are meant to represent "at the end of T units of time." Thus T is always a given duration of time. We find some examples of the uses of T in the following:

(29) The play lasts for 2 hr but there is a 10-min intermission between Act I and Act II. Act I lasts for 45 min.

$$\boxed{\begin{array}{l} S_{(Act\ I)} \\ T_{(45\ min)} \end{array}} \longrightarrow \boxed{\begin{array}{l} S_{(intermission)} \\ T_{(10\ min)} \end{array}} \longrightarrow \boxed{\begin{array}{l} S_{(Act\ II)} \\ T_{(65\ min)} \end{array}} \longrightarrow \boxed{\begin{array}{l} S_{(play\ over)} \\ \end{array}}$$

(30) The rat will be confined to this box for 1 hr.

$$\left[\begin{matrix} \overline{S_A} \\ T \end{matrix}\right. \to S_B$$

where S_A = rat in box
$\quad\quad$ T = 1 hour
$\quad\quad$ S_B = rat out of box

No contingencies have been written in these brackets since no consequences for any behaviors were specified. Had any been specified, then R's would have been added to the brackets.

Sometimes only an approximate value of T is known. Thus, if we are waiting for someone to get out of a phone booth so that we can make a phone call, we cannot be sure how long the situation of $S_{(phone\ box\ occupied)}$ will last. The best we might be able to do under these conditions would be to state an average waiting time, say 5 min on the average. An average T that is so specifiable is written $\tilde{T}$, where the $\sim$ indicates "on the average." $\tilde{T}$ is used in exactly the same manner as T. For example,

$$\left[\begin{matrix} \tilde{T}_{(5\ min)} \to S_{(box\ free)} \\ S_{(box\ occupied)} \end{matrix}\right. \quad\quad\quad [6.7]$$

Diagram [6.7] illustrates two further characteristics of the notation. First, arrows always come from T's (or R's), *never* S's. When one S succeeds another, the arrow must come from a T (or R). Second, the vertical position of T and S in a bracket is irrelevant. Either can be above or below the other. Events within a bracket all go into effect simultaneously.

6.8 MORE THAN A SINGLE RESPONSE REQUIRED FOR THE S CONSEQUENCE

When more than one instance of a given response is required to produce some S consequence, that fact may be indicated in one of two ways. First of all, the behavioral event associated with the contingency may be defined in terms of the number of elements required. Thus, the example "write a word on the blackboard 100 times and then you can go home," could be notated as

$$\left[\begin{matrix} R_a \to S_a \\ S_1 \end{matrix}\right.$$

where S_1 = confined to classroom
      R_a = write word 100 times
      S_a = permission to leave

Here the frequency requirement is built into the definition of R_a. Alternately this case could be notated as

$$\left|\overline{\begin{matrix} n R_a \to S_a \\ S_1 \end{matrix}}\right.$$

where S_1 = confined to classroom
      R_a = write word
      S_a = permission to leave
      $n = 100$

Like T, n may also be known only as an average value at times. When only the average number of responses required for an S change is known, we write $\tilde{n}$.

6.9 REPETITIVE CONTINGENCIES

In diagrams [6.1] to [6.5], responses produced environmental consequences. Yet all these contingencies could be described as one-shot. That is, once the specified R occurred, a new situation came about and the null contingency was then in effect for all the R's listed in the foregoing bracket. However, this is a condition that need not always be true. In [6.2] for instance, a gross oversimplification was made, since it is clear that almost immediately after hitting a key we can hit another key and get a letter. Evidently, we need some way of describing the repetitive nature of certain contingencies.

Perhaps the most common repetitive contingency is the one the typewriter illustrates. After we do something, we get a consequence, but we can do the same thing again if we wish and still get a consequence, and so on indefinitely. The simplest way to describe this case would be to diagram it in such a way as to indicate that the old contingency was again in effect soon after the consequence. This would be a faithful representation, for it is true that we cannot type a new letter at the moment the key strikes the platen. If we do, we get key jamming and other undesirable effects. The main idea is that we must wait a bit, if only for a fraction of a second. Thus the null contingency that is in effect at the moment of the consequence lasts only for a small fraction of a second, after which we are returned to our original contingency. In section 6.7 we discussed how time can lead to new situations. We need only extend this concept to permit time to lead *back* to old situations and old contingencies as well. This expansion of our ideas will permit a faithful representation of many repetitive contingencies. In the case of the typewriter, we may write

$$
\left[\,\rightarrow \boxed{\begin{array}{c} S_A \\ R_A \end{array}}_{1} \longrightarrow \boxed{\begin{array}{c} S_B \\ T \end{array}}_{2}\,\right] \qquad [6.8]
$$

where S_A = at typewriter, keys resting
$\quad\ R_A$ = strike a key
$\quad\ S_B$ = letter appears
$\quad\ T$ = small fraction of a sec

In diagram [6.8] we represent the fact that in one situation, S_A, we may strike a key and get a mark on our page; and in another, S_B, we cannot get this effect from striking a key. To refer to the two distinct contingencies (one of which, of course, is the null case) we subscript the small numerals 1 and 2 just below the brackets themselves. Other examples of simple repetitive contingencies are

(31) The bird gets a 3-sec presentation of grain for each disk peck.
(32) You can fill your fountain pen by dipping it into the ink and pushing the plunger. (Here the T of contingency 2 is fairly long, depending on how much you write.)
(33) Each pull on the trigger will cause a shot to be fired.

A second repetitive type of contingency occurs when a second response, rather than the sheer passage of time, returns the conditions to the first situation and its contingencies. When a rat is rewarded with a drop of milk for each lever press, a second lever press will not produce a second drop of milk until the first drop is consumed. Thus

$$
\left[\,\rightarrow \boxed{\begin{array}{c} S_A \\ R_A \end{array}}_{1} \longrightarrow \boxed{\begin{array}{c} S_B \\ R_B \end{array}}_{2}\,\right]
$$

where S_A = no milk
$\quad\ S_B$ = drop of milk
$\quad\ R_A$ = lever press
$\quad\ R_B$ = drink milk

represents those conditions. This kind of behavioral recycling is very common. Some small firearms are built to fire only when cocked between each firing.

$$
\left[\,\rightarrow \boxed{\begin{array}{c} S_{(gun\ cocked)} \\ R_{(pull\ trigger)} \end{array}}_{1} \longrightarrow \boxed{\begin{array}{c} S_{(fires)} \\ R_{(cock)} \end{array}}_{2}\,\right] \ .
$$

Similarly, you can get many bottles from a Coca-Cola machine by inserting dimes, but you must remove the one delivered each time for the next coin to be effective.

In summary, there are two principal ways of recycling a repetitive contingency, either through the passage of time (indicated by T⌐) or by means of a response event (indicated by R⌐).

6.10 FACILITATION

It occasionally happens that emission of a response, while leaving the environment unchanged, makes it possible for a second response to produce a stimulus. Thus when we come to the end of a line with our typewriter, the keys will no longer operate. If we push the Margin Release button the keys will then operate, but this response does not change our environment in any appreciable way. The typewriter looks exactly the same before and after Margin Release is pushed. The changes take place, of course, inside the typewriter, and they are revealed by the possibility of now obtaining letters by striking the keys. We notate this case as

$$\left[\begin{array}{c} S_{24} \\ R_a \\ \hline 1 \end{array}\right] \longrightarrow \left[\begin{array}{c} R_b \\ \hline 2 \end{array}\right] \longrightarrow \left[\begin{array}{c} S_{23} \\ T \\ \hline 3 \end{array}\right] \qquad [6.9]$$

where S_{24} = end of line
$\quad S_{23}$ = letter appears
$\quad R_a$ = depress Margin Release
$\quad R_b$ = strike key
$\quad\;\; T$ = small fraction of a second

Thus the appearance of R_b in bracket 2, without an S, implies that the S of the preceding bracket (S_{24}) is its S as well. And indeed that is correct. Cases such as [6.9] are indicated schematically as

$$R_1 \longrightarrow R_2 \longrightarrow$$

and are read *If R_1 then if R_2.* . . .

Human language behavior very often conforms to a representation similar to [6.9]. We often preface our remarks with "Listen to this," or "Have you heard this one?" These prefatory statements have the effect of gaining attention, though attention is not always revealed by any overt change in the faces of our audience, that is, in our environment. What does happen, however, is that our subsequent remarks are more likely to be heeded (that is, produce consequences) *if* they are prefaced by such statements.

In baking a cake we are advised to grease the bottom of the pan lightly. Then the cake will not stick later when we try to remove it from the pan. We cannot directly see the effects of greasing the pan once the cake is in it, but we can observe that the greasing response makes the removal response possible.

In more technical terms, facilitation is the production of a behavioral contingency via the occurrence of a response which by itself does not lead to any direct environmental consequence.

6.11 NEGATIVE CONTINGENCIES

Consequences for behavior are very often stated in the negative. *Unless* you drink your milk you will be sent to bed. If you *do not* pay your telephone bill, they will cut off your phone. Anyone who *does not* vote will be severely reprimanded. A common error is to take "not drinking," "not paying," "not voting," to be R's. Since behavior is something an organism *does,* such assignments are clearly in violation of our definitions. A solution to the specification of R lies in the observation that time invariably plays an important, though often camouflaged, role in these contingencies. Clearly, if a consequence is to occur for not doing something, the administrator of the consequence has to decide how long a time of not doing it constitutes "not doing it." Thus time is intimately bound up with negative contingencies, for it is always some duration of inactivity that leads to the consequences.

In dealing with negative contingencies, it proves useful to regard all the behaviors possible, *except the given R,* as a single class of behaviors. Though this class will in general be very diverse and not well specifiable, we can be sure that, at the very least, it will not include R as a member. To denote this complementary set of behaviors that does not include R as a member, we employ the symbol $\bar{R}$ (read "R bar") to refer to all behaviors *except* R. Since, as we noted, it is always a certain duration of $\bar{R}$ (not performing R) that leads to the consequences, we must always subscript a T to $\bar{R}$. Thus, "unless we pay our phone bill within two weeks of receiving the bill the phone will be cut off" is diagrammed as

$$\left. \begin{array}{l} \bar{R}_T \\ S_A \end{array} \right\rbrace \longrightarrow S_B \qquad\qquad [6.10]$$

where S_A = bill received
    R = pay the bill
    T = 14 days
    S_B = phone cut off

Note that $\bar{R}$ is not represented in the key as any specific behavior. However, its complement R *is* listed in the key, though it appears in the actual diagram only by implication (that is, if T amount of $\bar{R}$ fails to occur, then R must occur). Thus $\bar{R}$ is always defined relative to R so that one or the other *must* occur, but evidently both cannot occur. In [6.10], if T amount of $\bar{R}$ occurs, then the phone will be cut off; but if R occurs, then nothing special will happen. Since R is not represented in [6.10], it means that R is on a null contingency with respect to S_A and S_B, and indeed this is true. Paying the bill has no immediate consequence. Not paying it (two weeks of anything but paying it) results in the consequences.

As a general guide, it will often be found that S_B in these negative contingencies will be an aversive or undesirable event. Hence [6.10] can be thought of as a prescription for producing aversive events. Logically, of course, that means it is also a prescription for avoiding them, and that is precisely what we wished to notate when we introduced this kind of example.

6.12 PROBABILISTIC CONTINGENCIES

Sometimes the S consequences of a response vary. When we flip a coin we do not always get the same result. Half the time we get heads, half the time, tails. This case is notated by adding more than one arrow emanating from R and putting the probability values over each arrow. When more than one arrow from R is employed in this way, the designated probability values must add up to 1. In the unbiased coin we have

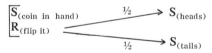

In general, when behavior may have one of a number of possible consequences, we must write

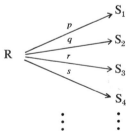

indicating the probability of each S consequence over its corresponding arrow. Naturally $p + q + r + s + \ldots$ must add up to 1.

Stimulus situations can also succeed each other probabilistically. When it rains on Monday, it is likely to rain again on Tuesday, but sometimes the weather changes over 24 hours and on Tuesday the sun shines:

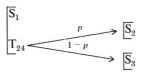

where S_1 = rain
T_{24} = 24 hr
S_2 = sunshine
S_3 = more rain

6.13 DISCRIMINATIONS

In all the diagrams we have presented, time was assumed to flow from left to right. That is, the temporal succession of S's and contingencies was from left to right. (Recycling contingencies are no exception, for the right-to-left recycle arrow is merely an abbreviation for writing out an infinite series of symbols yet further to the right.) The vertical dimension was used merely to indicate that events written within the same bracket went into effect simultaneously. Occasionally, it is useful to consider several contingencies which could be in effect simultaneously. Thus we might wish to discuss the contingencies that arise out of simple laboratory discriminations. If the light is red, the monkey must press a bar for food; but if the light is orange, the monkey must turn a wheel for food:

$$\begin{matrix} \overline{S}_{(red)} \\ R_{(press)} \\ 1 \end{matrix} \longrightarrow S_{(food)} \qquad [6.11]$$

$$\begin{matrix} \overline{S}_{(orange)} \\ R_{(turn\ wheel)} \\ 2 \end{matrix}$$

In [6.11] no rule is given for the order of red and orange; hence no recycling is shown. The appearance of the two brackets one above the other implies that, prior to reinforcement, either one or the other contingency will be in effect. Diagram [6.11] also illustrates the obvious fact that more than one R can lead to the same situation.

6.14 R AND S FUNCTIONALLY DEPENDENT

Complex cases of repetitive contingencies may involve more than a mere recycling to an original situation. Often the original situation is modified by each occurrence of the response event. When we pump up a bicycle tube, each pump inflates the tube a bit more. To notate this, we use the later letters of the alphabet (u, v, w, x, y, z, in lower case) as S subscripts, thus implying the variable and changing nature of the S. Thus in

$$\rightarrow \boxed{\begin{matrix} S_x \\ R \end{matrix}} \qquad\qquad [6.12]$$

where R = you pump
$\quad S_x$ = tire inflated x amount
$\quad x$ = a function of nR

we see that the amount of inflation is a function of the number of R's that have occurred. Diagram [6.12] is deceptively simple but a number of common cases use it as an element. When we chop down a tree, whip cream, and run a 100-yd dash, each response we make modifies the situation by a small amount. As soon as one R is made, modifying the situation, another R can be made immediately to modify it a little more, and so on. Eventually, toward the very end, a new set of contingencies will be in effect: we can put the felled tree on a truck, we can put the whipped cream on top of a piece of cake, we can receive a medal for our speedy run.

Sometimes the response that will produce consequences is a function of some aspect of the existing situation. In Chapter 10 we discuss a case in which the behavior of reaching out results in the encountering of an object. But the direction in which reaching out is effective is a function of where in space the object is located. This is a simple case in which both the R and the S within the same bracket require variable subscripts. The correct form of the R depends on the S, but unless the object is always found in the same place, S will be a variable. Diagram [6.13] represents this case as

$$\boxed{\begin{matrix} S_x \\ R_y \end{matrix}} \longrightarrow S_2 \qquad\qquad [6.13]$$

where $\ S_2$ = object in hand
$\quad R$ = reach out
$\quad y$ = direction in space
$\quad x$ = position of object
$\quad S$ = object at some distance from us
and $\quad y = f(x)$.

6.15 NESTED CONTINGENCIES

Time (T) has been used to refer to the duration of situations and contingencies. It is sometimes useful to represent, by a single T, the duration of an entire *set* of contingencies. To indicate this possibility, a new notational facility must be developed. Consider that blueberries are in season from

March to September, that is, for 7 months. If you go to your grocer during that time you will find blueberries advertised and on display. If you then ask for them you will get them. Of course, your grocer is not open all day. The shop opens at 9 A.M. and closes at 6 P.M. Here we have two independent time cycles. First, we have the blueberry season of 7 months on and 5 months off.

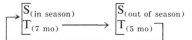

But we also have the grocer's 9-hr working-day schedule. This is

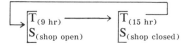

Somehow we must contrive to combine the situations and time cycles. Diagram [6.14] is such a representation. Here, brackets appear "nested" within

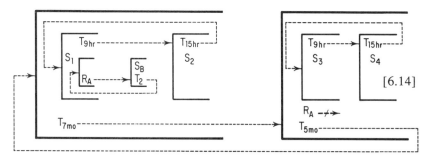

brackets. The 7-month T and the 5-month T apply to the duration of all the contingencies enclosed within them. T_2 is merely inserted to permit recycling of your request for blueberries. It probably lasts long enough for you to get the words out of your mouth and the first box in your hand. Then you can ask again and get another box. The example shows a triple nesting. Since one and only one situation can be present at any time, S_B includes many of the elements of S_1.

References for Chapter 6

Mechner, F. A notation system for the description of behavioral procedures. *J. exp. Anal. Behav.,* 1959, **2,** 133–150.

Mechner, Vicki. *A notation system for behavioral contingencies: an instructional program.* New York: Basic Systems, 1963.

Chapter 7 INTERMITTENT REINFORCEMENT

$\blacksquare$N THE OPERANT-STRENGTHENING PARADIGM, EACH emitted instance of a selected response class is typically followed by a reinforcing stimulus. This paradigm may be carried out by behavioral scientists, parents, teachers, friends, or nature itself. Whenever the procedure of operant strengthening is initiated, the typical result is an increase in response probability. The reinforcement of each instance of a selected response class within this paradigm is called continuous reinforcement (henceforth abbreviated *crf*). The term does not mean that reinforcement is continuously available. It simply means that a contingency of the form $R \rightarrow S^+$ prevails continuously between response and reinforcement.

In the civilized world and in the jungle, the relationships between emitted behaviors and subsequent changes in the environment are frequently far more complex than *crf*. On some days, often for obscure or unknown reasons, the same behavior that met with success on other days will meet with failure. This fortuitous character of the relation between operants and subsequent consequences can be avoided in the laboratory. There, by controlling the reinforcement of behaviors explicitly, we may decide for our human and animal subjects exactly which behaviors out of an emitted series will be successful. Typically, such control is described in the form of rules. These rules specify in detail the relationships that hold between certain operant responses and subsequent reinforcing stimuli. The rules are merely special cases of the behavioral contingencies of Chapter 6, but they incorporate as critical S events the special consequences we have elsewhere denoted as reinforcers.

Human behaviors in everyday situations reveal both continuous and intermittent reinforcement contingencies. Under normal circumstances much of our behavior is continuously reinforced. Light switches turn lights on and off with regularity. When we hear a voice and look in the direction from which it comes, we usually encounter the face of another person. When we ask a friend for the time, we regularly get an answer. Exceptions occur but they are infrequent enough to provide surprise and bewilderment when they do. In other situations, however, intermittent reinforcement is the rule. The patience of the fisherman casting his rod and reeling in his line for hours on end, without a bite, is developed through a history of intermittent reinforcement. In baseball, reinforcement in the form of a hit is considered adequate when seven out of ten or more trips to the plate result in outs. The inveterate moviegoer may rarely catch a good film, but his weekly film-going behavior remains strong. In the present chapter, we survey some of the principles of intermittent reinforcement that have been isolated in the laboratory with animal and human subjects, and sample a few of the many possible procedures.[1]

7.1 INTERVAL CONTINGENCIES

As a point of departure, recall the procedure of successive conditioning and extinction (see section 5.5). Typically, that procedure provided *n* continuous reinforcements for a response, followed by T hours of extinction. This characteristic cycle, consisting of a few reinforcements, and then a prolonged extinction, extended over one or more experimental sessions. When extinction had resulted in a marked reduction in responding, the cycle was repeated. Consider now a variation of this procedure, consisting of the reinforcement of a *single* response, followed by just a minute of extinction, followed by a second reinforcement, another minute of extinction, and so forth. In this variation, many cycles of conditioning and extinction are compressed into a single hour's session. Upon carrying out the procedure, a characteristic behavioral effect emerges, as shown in the stylized Fig. 7–1.

At first, abbreviated negatively accelerated extinction curves follow each reinforcement (Fig. 7–1, stage *a*). The response that produces reinforcement is often the last of a train of low-rate responses. This picture is transitory, however, and after a number of reinforcements have

---

[1] A word is in order concerning the design of the experiments on intermittent reinforcement discussed in this chapter. It is typical of these experiments that initially the subjects are *trained* on a *crf* schedule of reinforcement. Only when a steady rate of response has been established under *crf* conditions does the experimenter introduce the desired intermittencies.

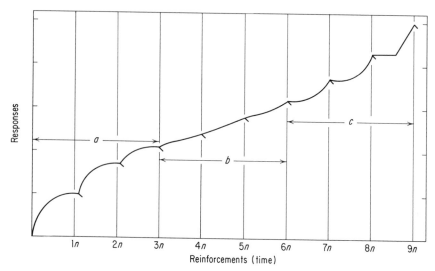

Figure 7–1. Stylized curve of the transition from crf to intermittent reinforcement at fixed periodic intervals. The use of n to label the abscissa suggests that the successive response segments might be associated not with successive reinforcements, but rather with successive multiples of reinforcements. For example, if n = 10, the segments would denote reinforcement nos. 10, 20, 30, etc.

occurred, a moderate and steady rate evolves (stage b). This too is an evanescent phase, giving way eventually to a third stage (c), characterized by a pause after each reinforcement which is followed by a gradual or abrupt shift to a moderately high rate of response sustained to the end of the 1-min interval. Transitional states b and c are illustrated with actual data in Fig. 7–2, which represents sessions 2, 3, and 4 of the disk (key)-pecking responding of a pigeon receiving grain on the conditioning-extinction procedure described above. The curves of Fig. 7–2 have been "stacked"; that is, they have been uprooted from their usual coordinate system and moved closer together horizontally to save space and facilitate comparison. The actual rates of response at any time, and also the cumulative number of responses made at any time, can be assessed by comparison with the small inset key at the lower right of the figure.

The procedure just described is one of the very many possible ways in which an experimenter can *schedule* reinforcement contingencies in relation to time. In the case at hand, the experimenter established a fixed interval of time between the last reinforcement and the reinstatement of the reinforcement contingency. Until this fixed interval had elapsed, no responses could be reinforced. Such a procedure, because it

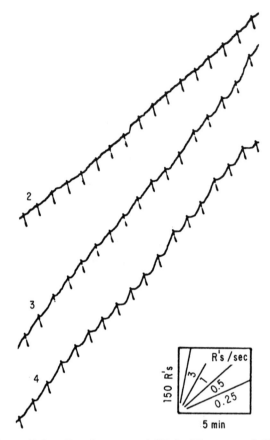

Figure 7–2. Development of FI–1 *(Ferster and Skinner, 1957).*

fixes the time between reinforcement and the next reinforcement contingency, is appropriately designated a *Fixed-Interval* (abbreviated *FI*) reinforcement schedule. Note, however, that the time between the receipt of any two actual reinforcements is *not* fixed. Although the *minimum* value of this interval is the fixed time between a reinforcement and the setting of a contingency, its actual value depends on just how soon a response occurs after the contingency goes into effect. The basic element appears in notation as

$$\begin{bmatrix} T_{(Fixed)} \to R \to S^+ \\ R \nrightarrow \end{bmatrix}$$

The principal effects of a fixed-interval (*FI*) schedule imposed after *crf* may be summarized as follows:

1. The behavior of the individual shows a gradual adjustment to the procedure, as shown by changes in the pattern of response rate. We have already discussed this effect.

2. The final pattern that emerges is wavelike (*scalloped*). On an *FI* schedule, the reinforcement is followed by a subsequent period of non-reinforcement. Extensive past history with this state of affairs results in the animal's pausing for an appreciable time following reinforcement. This cessation of responding is a natural consequence of the fact that, in the past, responding just after reinforcement was never reinforced. It is a form of *discriminated* extinction, which will be clearer later, when we discuss the behavioral process of discrimination.

3. Behavior can be maintained indefinitely under *FI*'s as short as a few seconds up to *FI*'s of several hours' duration.

In one experiment, hungry birds were exposed to *FI* 30-min grain reinforcement contingencies for 16 hr a day for 144 consecutive days, representing an experimental history of over 1300 hr. Key-pecking behavior was maintained throughout the experiment, and the transitional nature of certain *FI* effects was verified. In Fig. 7–3, changes in the

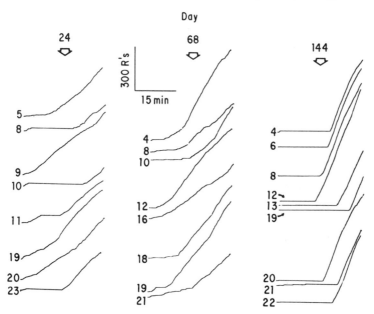

Figure 7–3. Stages in the development of behavior under a 30-min FI schedule. Selected inter-reinforcement data are presented for the indicated days. The number at the left of each segment gives the ordinal reinforcement number terminating that segment (after Cumming and Schoenfeld, 1958).

pattern of responding are illustrated by records of one bird's behavior during selected inter-reinforcement intervals taken from sessions 24, 68, and 144. The progressive change from a gradual to an abrupt scallop is evident.

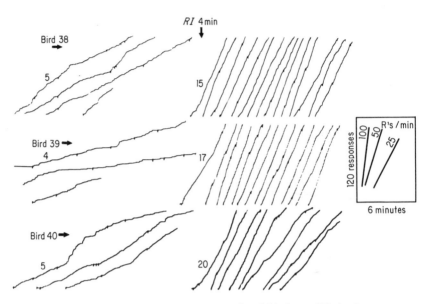

Figure 7–4. Cumulative records of birds on RI 4-min, taken at early sessions (4 or 5), and later sessions (15, 17, or 20) (Millenson, 1963).

Fixed-interval contingencies are not uncommon in everyday life. A pot boils at approximately a fixed time after heat is applied. Buses that run on schedule reinforce the waiting of passengers at stops on fixed intervals. The failure of *FI* to maintain a constant level of behavior over a period of time often is an important drawback to its use in the practical control of behavior. In college courses, in which the principal contingency set is a final examination, many students often do very little work throughout the term. A few days before the final exam, a frenzy of activity takes place.

Suppose the time intervals between reinforcement and the next rein-forcement contingency are made random in length and unpredictable. The result is a new type of procedure called a *Random-Interval* (*RI*) schedule. Such a schedule can only be specified by its *average* interval between reinforcement and reinstatement of the contingency. To give some indication of the variation in the intervals that may be encountered, in an *RI* 1-min schedule, for instance, about 95 per cent of the intervals between reinforcement and reinforcement contingencies will fall in the range 0 to 2 min. Initial exposure to an *RI* procedure after a history of *crf* yields only the first two transition stages described for *FI* in Fig. 7–1. The final result on *RI* is a stable and uniform overall response rate whose cumulative record shows no systematic deviations from a straight line (see Fig. 7–4).

Approximations to *RI* schedules are frequently encountered outside the laboratory. Radar operators who scan oscilloscopes for infrequent signals can be considered to be under an intermittency similar to an *RI* schedule. Their response is the behavior of scanning; their reinforcement is the discovery of a signal. A similar case occurs when an operator has to observe a meter for infrequent but critical deflections. In these examples, the overt behavior of scanning or observing may be assumed to follow the laws of operant behavior, but it is not always easily measured. In Holland's (1958) procedure, human subjects were instructed to examine a meter and report (by pressing a telegraph key) each observed deflection from a zero point. Both meter and subject, however, were in a dark room and the meter could only be seen by pressing a second telegraph key which provided illumination for a fraction of a second. In this way, Holland established a conveniently measured operant which correlated with the subject's "observing" behavior; to take a look at the meter, the subject had to press a key. To place the key-pressing behavior on an approximately random-interval schedule, the experimenter scheduled pointer deflections (reinforcements) various time intervals apart. The intervals were not quite random, but they were of variable lengths. The procedure is an example of what is called a *Variable-Interval* (*VI*) schedule. Under Holland's conditions, the schedule maintained key-pressing observing rates at higher than one per second. Holland investigated the effects of changing the average interval between scheduled pointer deflections. Beginning with a 15-sec mean interval, he progressively raised it to 30 sec, 1 min, and finally 2 min, over several consecutive sessions. Figure 7–5 shows the results given by one of his subjects, a U.S. Navy enlisted man. The picture of the rate patterns is in good agreement with animal studies of the behavioral effects of this schedule (Ferster and Skinner, 1957). Holland's results in Fig. 7–5 indicate, moreover, that *VI* yields overall response rates that tend to increase as the average interval between deflections (reinforcements) decreases. An interesting implication of this finding is that if the deflections happen to be transient (that is, if they last only a short time), then fewer deflections will be missed (that is, more will be observed) when the average interval between them is small. Thus, a man watching a radar screen on which signals *rarely* appear stands a good chance of missing a critical transient signal when it does come, because his observing rate is likely to be low. The results of Fig. 7–5 suggest the possibility of inserting supplementary artificial signals to keep observing rate up to a level that will insure detection of all critical signals.

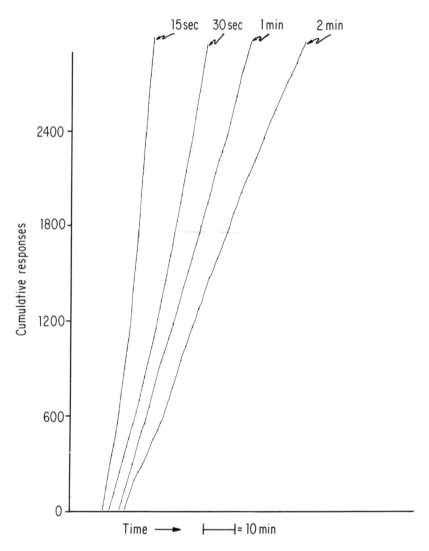

Figure 7–5. Cumulative response records for VI schedules of pointer deflections with average intervals of 15 sec, 30 sec, 1 min, and 2 min, respectively. All records are from the same subject. In each case, the record shown was made after previous sessions on the schedule (Holland, 1958).

7.2 PROBABILITY OF REINFORCEMENT

A reinforcement schedule may provisionally be defined as a procedure or plan that determines when and for how long a reinforcement contingency will be in effect. As such, it must be established and maintained by an experimenter. A schedule of reinforcement is therefore a laboratory phenomenon. Although there are schedules that approximate some of the intermittencies of reinforcement seen in nature, the concept of a schedule is independent of these matches and has implications that go far beyond them. A schedule of reinforcement may be considered an idealized case of a reinforcement intermittency.

A schedule of reinforcement is fundamentally a specification of the probability of reinforcement for a selected response at given times. In the previous section, we encountered contingencies that scheduled changes to and from the extreme values of that probability, 0 and 1. Evidently, extinction is another name for the extreme value, probability of reinforcement $= 0$; and continuous reinforcement is another name for the extreme value, probability of reinforcement $= 1$. In the interval schedules discussed above, contingencies specifying a reinforcement probability equal to 1 were established *after* fixed, random, and variable time intervals during which that probability had been 0. But the field of reinforcement schedules is by no means restricted to temporal admixtures, however complex, of the upper and lower extremes of reinforcement probability.

It is, for instance, possible to construct a schedule in which the probability of reinforcement for a given response is the same at all times. Certain real-life situations approximate these constant or uniform probability-of-reinforcement schedules. The outcomes of tossing an unbiased coin occur on such a probabilistic basis. In a wager, for instance, a series of tosses may be made and eventually one obtains the desired reinforcer, say a head. However, a head may not appear in a large number of tosses, although the probability of obtaining a head on any given toss is uniformly constant and equal to $\frac{1}{2}$. The unpredictability of a coin toss is characteristic of uniform probability of reinforcement contingencies. Betting and gambling in general are truly probabilistic in this way. If good weather is taken as a reinforcer and picnic behavior is under way, the reinforcement occurs probabilistically. We may consult the weather bureau to ascertain the number of fair days expected in June; but though the probability of finding good weather may be very high, our picnic behavior may still not meet a fair day.

We usually take it for granted that, in any given time period, it is to

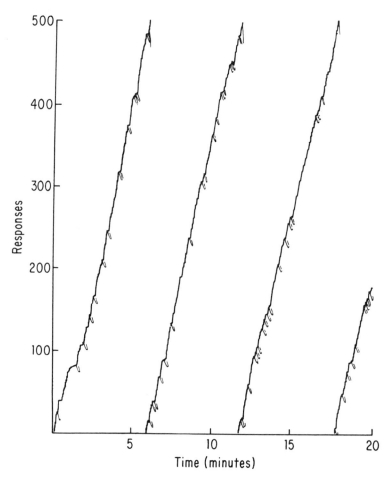

Figure 7–6. Cumulative response rates when key peck-ing is reinforced on a uniform probability schedule (data of J. Farmer).

the individual's advantage to gain as many reinforcements as possible. To the extent that this generalization holds, faced with a uniform probability schedule, the optimum strategy is to respond as frequently as possible. If we are paid to find pretty sea shells on a beach, then the more sea shells we examine, the more pretty ones we shall find. This is true *whatever* the probability of finding a pretty one may be. Some beaches may provide a higher probability of pretty shells than others, but on any beach it is to our advantage to examine as many specimens as we can. Another way of saying this is that it is advantageous for our examination behavior to be at its maximum rate.

A hungry pigeon, exposed to a uniform probability-of-food-reinforcement schedule of this sort, will quickly adjust to such an optimum strategy if the fixed probability is not too low. The schedule generates extremely high response rates (Brandauer, 1958). Figure 7–6 is a sample of some typical results obtained on this schedule when the probability of grain for pecking was ½₅. In some instances in Fig. 7–6, the pigeon was pecking at a rate of three or four responses a second for sustained periods. When Sidley and Schoenfeld (1964) exposed pigeons to various values of reinforcement probability, ranging from 1 down to ¼₆₀, they obtained the interesting function of Fig. 7–7. In their study, the overall response rate was highest when the probability of reinforcement was ¼₀. Both higher and lower probabilities of reinforcement led to reduced output which represents less than optimal strategy.

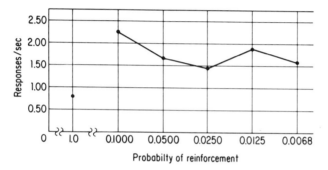

Figure 7–7. Overall response rates as a function of probability of reinforcement (after Sidley and Schoenfeld, 1964).

7.3 THEORETICAL NOTES ON REINFORCEMENT SCHEDULES

We may summarize much of the systematic import of sections 7.1 and 7.2 by observing that a schedule is a set of rules specifying: (1) *when* to establish a reinforcement contingency; (2) *how long* to keep it in force; and (3) *what* probability of reinforcement value to assign to it. When the variations on these three conditions are permuted with the diverse response parameters to be discussed in the next chapter, the possible procedural variations for maintaining operants become enormous. Under pressures to achieve economy of representation, theorists have evolved schemes such as Fig. 7–8 to describe and relate the various schedules. In Fig. 7–8, the probability of reinforcement for a response is shown as a function of post-reinforcement time for five of

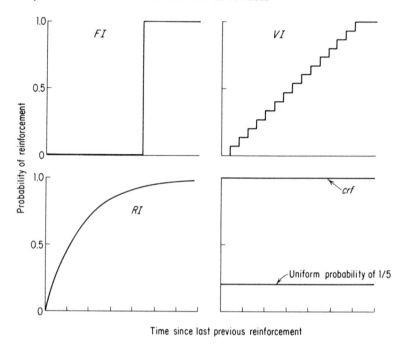

Figure 7–8. Probability of reinforcement for a response as a function of the time since the previous reinforcement.

the schedules we have been considering. (We may note, parenthetically, that universal agreement on the optimum representation of schedules has not yet been reached among research workers in this field. In consulting the literature, the advanced student must, therefore, be prepared to encounter other ways of conceptualizing the procedures of this chapter and Chapter 8.)

The task of describing or specifying the vast number of possible reinforcement procedures in terms of a few manipulable variables is but one of two related problems in the theoretical analysis of schedules. The other problem centers about the explanation of how schedules generate their characteristic effects on rate of response. Skinner (1953) has pointed out that schedules are only approximate ways of reinforcing rates of response. That is, schedules frequently arrange to provide reinforcements at a time when the individual is likely to have just been responding with a certain kind of rate—high or low, depending on the particular schedule. According to the familiar law of operant strengthening, whatever behavior occurs just before reinforcement is increased or maintained in probability. Our sea shell analogy led to the conclusion that, on a uniform probability schedule for instance, the higher the rate of response, the more likely a reinforcement becomes in any given small interval of time. On this kind of schedule, then, a high rate of response will frequently precede reinforcement.

Interval schedules, of course, present an altogether different picture. There, assuming the organism responds at least once per interval, higher rates do not increase the probability of reinforcement. This is because the establishment of a reinforcement contingency in an interval is independent of the animal's behavior. It is established by a clock in the case of an *FI* schedule, and by a geiger counter or some other random source in the case of an *RI* schedule. Nothing the animal does can speed up the delivery of reinforcement. In fact, the longer the organism *waits* before responding, the higher the probability of reinforcement when it finally does respond. In an *FI* schedule, for instance, the probability of reinforcement is unity if the organism waits out the entire *FI* period before responding (see *FI* panel, Fig. 7–8). These relations between waiting and then responding suggest that interval schedules act to retard rates of responding.

7.4 THE EFFECTS OF INTERMITTENT REINFORCEMENT ON RESISTANCE TO EXTINCTION

Intermittent reinforcement, when compared to *crf,* leads to a substantial increase in the resistance to extinction of the selected response. Thus, reinforcement schedules provide an important technique for increasing behavioral persistence. After continuous reinforcement of lever pressing or key pecking, the typical extinction curve reaches the commonly used extinction criteria in about an hour's time, during which at most only a few hundred responses are emitted. On the other hand, Fig. 7–9, recorded by a bird after a history of variable-interval (*VI*)

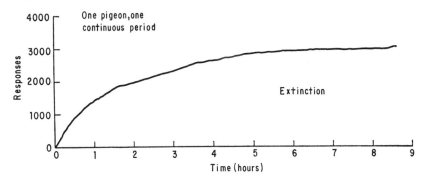

Figure 7–9. Extinction after VI *(Skinner, 1950).*

reinforcement, indicates that an asymptote of greater than 3000 responses is being only gradually approached after 8 hr.

Uniform probability-of-reinforcement schedules also produce higher resistance to extinction than *crf*. An experiment by Weinstock (1954) was concerned with the extinction of behavior after different values of reinforcement probability in training. A runway apparatus similar to that shown in Fig. 7–10 was employed. In such an apparatus, an animal is

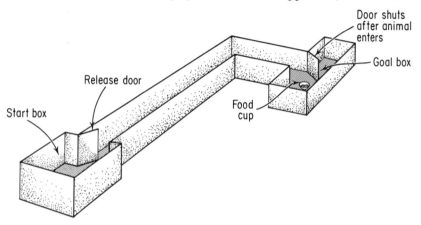

Figure 7–10. A runway apparatus used for studying the speed of instrumental behavior in small animals.

placed in the start box, the door is opened at an appropriate moment, and a timer started. When the animal enters the goal box, where food may be found, the timer is stopped and the animal removed when desired. This sequence of events is called a *trial*. Since each trial continues until the animal eventually finds its way to the goal box, frequency of response is not a useful measure of behavior in this instance. The time taken to get from start to goal, however, is relevant and easily measured. This measure is an instance of what we shall call a *reaction time*. It bears certain similarities to a latency in that it is the time between an environmental change (door being opened) and a response (entrance into goal box). But, whereas a latency is reserved for a description of respondents, a reaction time is reserved for the description of operants.

Weinstock (1954) trained four groups of rats to run down a runway similar to that in Fig. 7–10. Each group was assigned one of four different fixed probabilities for finding food in the goal box, $p = 1.0$, 0.8, 0.5, and 0.3. Thus the 1.0 group found food on each trial (*crf*), the 0.8 group found it on 80 per cent of the trials, and so on. After all the animals had been trained to run at what appeared to be their maximal speed, extinction was begun by removing the food from the goal box.

Only one trial was given per day. The results indicated that the 1.0 group was the fastest to extinguish; that is, after a very few trials (four or five), these animals took a very long time to traverse the runway, if they bothered at all. The order of extinction followed the reverse order of probability. The lower the probability, the longer conditioned running behavior persisted. The 0.3 group took the longest time for its running behavior to be weakened by extinction. Over the range of probabilities investigated, therefore, decreasing the probability of reinforcement *increased* the resistance to extinction, as measured by a return to the operant-level running speed. Note that this inverse proportionality cannot hold below some minimum value of probability, for if probability of reinforcement is made too small (approaches 0), original strengthening will be impossible.

Why do intermittent contingencies increase resistance to extinction? One explanation hinges on the observation that after an intermittent reinforcement history, extinction does not appear very different from the actual strengthening procedure. During intermittent reinforcement of any kind, there will occur periods of extinction, when no reinforcement is available for responding. In a sense, all of the animal's intermittent reinforcement history tells it that a period of extinction leads eventually to reinforcement. In effect the schedule has taught the animal perseverance.

7.5 OTHER BEHAVIORAL EFFECTS OF INTERMITTENT REINFORCEMENT

Schedules of reinforcement are very obviously procedures that manipulate rates of response. It is hardly surprising that most of our information about their behavioral effects is derived from analyses of response rates during and following exposure to them. Still, the question as to how such procedures affect the whole constellation of behaviors of an individual is a valid one. A partial answer would take the form of statements describing how schedules affect such behavioral properties as topography of response, magnitude of response, the sequential order of responding, and so forth.

Lane and Shinkman (1963) studied the effects of a *VI* schedule on amplitude and duration of chirping in the chick. The operant was first strengthened by reinforcing each chirp emitted by a hungry chick with a brief presentation of food. Following this training, chirping was intermittently reinforced on a *VI* 100-sec schedule. In a final phase of the experiment, chirping was extinguished. The results showed that the duration and amplitude of the chirping response were highly stereotyped during *crf*, becoming significantly more variable during the *VI* procedure.

But extinction produced a still higher level of variability in the response measures.

When the duration of a rat's lever pressing was examined under uniform probability schedules, it was found to be extremely stereotyped under *crf,* somewhat more variable during uniform probability contingencies, and maximally variable in extinction (Millenson, Hurwitz, and Nixon, 1963).

The data appear to support the generalization that variability of behavior appears to increase progressively under the conditions *crf,* intermittent schedule, and extinction, in that order.

7.6 BEHAVIORAL STEADY STATES

In much of our preceding analysis of behavior, we have emphasized the importance of certain behavioral procedures and the characteristic behavioral processes associated with them. In this fashion, we have examined the processes of Pavlovian and operant conditioning, and extinction. In the present chapter, we have found that the transitional states that are the initial products of exposure to a reinforcement schedule constitute another distinctive set of behavioral processes. Although such processes are important in the study of behavior, their endpoints are of at least equal importance. Thus a reinforcer is defined as much in terms of its ability to *maintain* behavior in the characteristic schedule patterns as it is in terms of its ability to *raise* rates of response during the operant strengthening process. The maintenance of behavior by intermittent contingencies brings us very close to our own daily behavior, much of which has been strengthened or acquired in the fairly distant past and sustained thereafter by intermittent reinforcements. In the laboratory, this sustained maintenance of behavior may best be described by so-called *steady states.* Behavioral measures settle into steady states at the end of their "process" or transitional aspect. For example, the curves of session 144 in Fig. 7–3 probably represent a stable state of behavior on *FI* contingencies. Similarly, the *VI* curves of Fig. 7–5 seem to be representative of the final performance on these kinds of schedules. A *VI* or *RI* schedule can generate steady moderate rates of responding for long sessions day after day, indefinitely.

The fact that schedules can lead to stable behavioral states which can be sustained indefinitely suggests that these states might serve as useful *baselines* from which to assess the effects of numerous variables on behavior. The notion of a baseline is familiar enough. Operant level was used as the baseline against which to determine whether strengthening of a response had occurred. We may use a performance that is currently being maintained by a schedule as a baseline. In later chapters, the effects of stimulus changes, interpolated contingencies, and other procedures on such baselines will help to define many important psychological concepts. As an illustration of the general technique, we shall content ourselves for the present with a demonstration of the effect of a tranquilizing drug on stable behavior. Dews (1955) studied the effect of pentobarbital on stabilized *FI* responding of pigeons. After having exposed pigeons to *FI* 15-min contingencies long enough for a stable pattern to emerge, Dews injected small amounts of the drug into the birds during certain sessions. He then observed the effects on the *FI* pattern. In this experiment, the independent variable was the amount of drug injected, and the dependent variable was the change in behavior from the normal *FI* state (see Figs. 7–2 and 7–3). To be certain that any effects observed could be attributed only to the drug and not to the disruption caused by an injection itself, a salt solution was injected into the birds on other sessions. Up to a certain level of concentration of the drug, Dews found no behavioral effects—performances continued to look like those under normal *FI*. With concentrations above 1 mg of pentobarbital, a significant change took place. The overall rate was reduced by about 75 per cent, and the characteristic scallop of *FI* was nearly lost, being replaced by a constant and very low rate of responding throughout the fixed interval.

This is a relatively simple example from a very large and expanding subfield of applied behavior science known as psychopharmacology, the study of the action of drugs on behavior. Many pharmaceutical firms now maintain behavioral laboratories exclusively for the study of the effects of new drugs on animal behavior. In the exploration of a new drug, many baselines may be used. A drug will not affect all behavior patterns in the same way. We have not dealt with many baseline states yet, but the following processes that we have studied terminate in statistical steady states that are amenable to use as baselines:

1. The interval schedules
2. Probabilistic schedules
3. Successive conditioning and extinction
4. Extinction itself
5. The behavioral sequence seen in simple loops of behavior
6. The topography and magnitude of behavior under *crf*

References for Chapter 7

Brandauer, C. M. The effects of uniform probabilities of reinforcement on the response rate of the pigeon. Unpublished doctoral dissertation, Columbia Univer., 1958.

Cumming, W. W., and Schoenfeld, W. N. Behavior under extended exposure to a high-value fixed interval reinforcement schedule. *J. exp. Anal. Behav.,* 1958, **1**, 245–263.

Dews, P. B. Studies on behavior. I. Differential sensitivity to pentobarbital of pecking performance in pigeons depending on the schedule of reward. *J. Pharmacol. exp. Ther.,* 1955, **113**, 393–401.

Ferster, C. B., and Skinner, B. F. *Schedules of reinforcement.* New York: Appleton-Century-Crofts, 1957.

Holland, J. G. Human vigilance. *Science,* 1958, **128**, 61–67.

Lane, H. L., and Shinkman, P. G. Methods and findings in an analysis of a vocal operant. *J. exp. Anal. Behav.,* 1963, **6,** 179–188.

Millenson, J. R. Random interval schedules of reinforcement. *J. exp. Anal. Behav.,* 1963, **6,** 437–443.

Millenson, J. R., Hurwitz, H. M. B., and Nixon, W. L. B. Influence of reinforcement schedules on response duration. *J. exp. Anal. Behav.,* 1961, **4,** 243–250.

Sidley, N. A., and Schoenfeld, W. N. Behavior stability and response rate as functions of reinforcement probability on "random ratio" schedules. *J. exp. Anal. Behav.,* 1964, **7,** 281–283.

Skinner, B. F. Are theories of learning necessary? *Psychol. Rev.,* 1950, **57,** 193–216.

Skinner, B. F. *Science and human behavior.* New York: Macmillan, 1953.

Weinstock, S. Resistance to extinction of a running response following partial reinforcement under widely spaced trials. *J. comp. physiol. Psychol.,* 1954, **47,** 51–56.

Chapter 8 **RESPONSE SPECIFICATION**

IN PREVIOUS SECTIONS, WE HAVE LIMITED OUR VIEW of behavioral modification to changes in behaviors that already existed at some strength greater than zero prior to conditioning. It is time now to remove that arbitrary simplifying restriction from the operant-conditioning paradigm by considering how new behavior, non-existent at one time in the individual's repertoire, comes to be acquired. Before proceeding to a study of this acquisition process, however, some further explication of the term operant response and its components is required.

8.1 THE DEFINITION OF RESPONSE CLASSES

One of the reasons that the science of behavior has been late in developing lies in the very nature of its subject matter. Unlike kidney tissue, salt crystals, batteries, and air foils, behavior cannot easily be held still for observation. Rather, the movements and actions of organisms appear to flow in a steady stream with no clear-cut beginning and end. When a rat moves from the front to the back of its cage, when you drive 500 miles non-stop in your car, when you sew on a button, it is difficult to identify points in the continuous behavioral stream where natural units of behavior could be said to fractionate. A further complication is that no two instances of an organism's actions are ever exactly the same, because no behavior is ever exactly repeated.

The problem of conceptualizing fundamental units out of a continuous, non-repetitive behavioral stream lies at the very foundation of the science. In order to subject behavior to a scientific analysis—that is, in order to be able to predict and control it—we must partition our subject

157

matter in such a way that something fixed and repeatable can be conceptualized. The methods of science are reserved for repeatable events. Both the term *event* and its qualifier *repeatable* are primitive scientific concepts. Thunderstorms, electric charges, fluids, molecules, planets, social institutions, etc., are the stuff of sciences. Although no two thunderstorms are exactly alike and no two democratic governments the same, it is necessary to group similar—though not identical—events into a single class and call them "thunderstorms" or "democratic governments." Through the use of such artifices, not only meteorology and political science, but all sciences, establish concepts in terms of which to frame their laws, generalizations, and predictions. Conceptualization of behavior in terms of such classes, analogous to the class concepts of other sciences is, therefore, a prerequisite for a science of behavior capable of making laws, predictions, and generalizations.

In behavior, we can sometimes begin by classifying into a single category a set of behaviors that are correlated with the same stimulus. Thus we can observe successive flexions of the leg in response to a well-defined tap on the knee and, although noting their differences, decide to call the knee-jerk response the class (set) of all movements (say) that occur with a duration between the limits ⅓ to 1 sec and that fall into the range of angles (α) 5–30 degrees (see Fig. 8–1). In adopting this class, our hope is to include all, or nearly all, the behaviors that are in fact correlated with that particular elicitor. We have obtained the successive movements by repeated elicitation, using the same eliciting stimulus with a fixed intensity, duration, locus, and so on. Although the class that is so formed appears to be a grouping of apparently similar movements, its formal definition is merely the class of movements that occurs to a given stimulus.

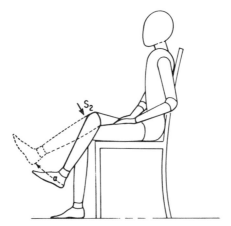

Figure 8–1. Schematic diagram of the movement range that includes all behaviors that are called "knee jerks."

Such a class is, of course, a respondent, and in this case it defines the knee-jerk respondent.

In defining such classes of behavior, it is necessary to conceptualize certain dimensions along which behaviors can be described and measured. Just as a table is exhaustively described by measuring its length, width, height, number of legs, color, weight, density of wood, number of drawers, and so forth, so a sample of behavior can be exhaustively described by measuring the position and orientation of the organism in reference to parts of its environment, the movements that are occurring, the time span they occupy, the intensity and frequency with which they occur, and so forth. Particular tables and particular samples of behavior can thus be described by their unique configuration of dimensional values. It appears therefore that the classes "tables" and "behavioral samples of type X" are established by setting *restrictions, limits,* and *requirements* along certain dimensions so that all "things" that we might conceivably wish to call tables and type-X behaviors, respectively, would fall naturally into our classes. Thus tables must have, say, one or more legs (a requirement), be made of solid rather than liquid or gaseous material (a restriction), have a flat top (a restriction), be greater than 1 ft but less than 40 yd long (a limit), and so on. Similarly, behaviors of type X might include, say, any downward movement (a restriction) of the left arm (a requirement) that is between 15 and 100 gm in force (a limit) and that does not exceed ½-sec duration (a restriction), and so on.

We have mentioned examples of behavioral dimensions such as position of response, duration of response, and force of response in earlier sections. These dimensions were used to describe the variability of behavior under operant level, strengthening, extinction, and schedules of reinforcement. Some of the dimensions such as position, angle, location, and orientation of behavior are said to be *topographical* dimensions, since a listing of their values at any given time will specify the precise form of the behavior. Specifying the value of these dimensions at any moment gives the kind of information provided by a photograph of the organism caught in action. Having captured the static form of the behavior by the topographical variables, we can use dynamic dimensions such as speed, force, duration, and repetition rate of the behavior to describe further a particular sample of behavior. In principle, a sample of behavior could be completely described by a statement of the values of all pertinent behavioral dimensions. It would, of course, stand in precisely the same relation to a more complete account that a snapshot stands to a film. In practice, an exhaustive description of behavior is rarely attempted. When topography or form is of primary interest, recourse may be made to photographing the behavior, but a quantitative account of one or two representative behavioral dimensions will often be preferred. In the case of the knee jerk, specification of the class of behavior in terms of just two dimensions seems to suffice for a useful approximation. One of these dimensions constitutes the angle of the leg from the resting position; the other dimension is the duration of the excursion movement. In general, the experimental specification of a piece of behavior is never more than partial, with the values of many dimensions left indeterminate.

To form the classes or units for expressing the laws, generalizations, and predictions of emitted behavior, a strategy different from that used to define respondents must be adopted. In non-elicited behavior, we may proceed at first to define a somewhat arbitrary set of behaviors that meet certain restrictions and requirements and that fall within certain limits along specified response dimensions. Our original criteria for grouping certain samples of behavior may be based on little more than superficial observation that the set of behaviors falling into what we described as type X might be a class of some interest. Having formed this arbitrary class, appeal must now be made—not to an elicitor, for there is none—but to a reinforcer, for confirmation that the class we arbitrarily selected will indeed function as a unit. That is, we proceed to apply the reinforcing operation to successive instances of the type-X behavior, as defined. Each instance of the class will of course be a little different from any other and for that reason is called a *variant*. We prepared ourselves for such differences by specifying *limits* (and not exact values) within which we would reinforce. If reinforcement now affects behavior in such a way as to selectively strengthen a class of behaviors, we are justified in speaking of this class as an *operant response* class, or more simply as an operant.

Consider some examples. We might define the limits of a certain class of movements and attempt to reinforce all movements within the limits. Reinforcement of a class of extensions of the limb occurs in reaching movements. Words are prominent examples of the formation of arbitrary response classes. All sounds that fall within certain acceptable limits (hence are made by musculature acting within certain acceptable limits) make up the spoken word *"please."* When a child enunciates and pronounces the word correctly (that is, emits a variant falling in the desired class), reinforcement is provided and the class of movements that produces *please* is strengthened.

In nature it seems unlikely that reinforcement is ever contingent on a restricted set of limits in the way described above. In the laboratory, reinforcement *could* be made contingent on a restricted subset of behaviors defined by dimensional limitations. But even there, units are more usually approximated by classing together all the movements that act, by the laws of simple mechanics, to produce a specified change in the environment. Thus all movements that depress a bar, or a disk, or a telegraph key, or that get the rat from the start to the end of a runway, turn a wheel, or get sugar into a cup of coffee, serve to limit effectively the topography of the organism in such a way that an approximation to a specified topographical class is achieved. This is true simply because there are limits on the possible ways of doing all these things. If we construct our apparatus carefully, the possible behaviors that could produce the specified environmental changes will be fairly circumscribed and therefore forced to be reasonably similar in form. (The behaviors in threading a needle are far more limited than those in shutting a door.) To the extent that we restrict our dimensions, the behaviors that make up the class will have topographical similarities in the way that respondents naturally do. *Nevertheless, the only formal requirement of an operant is that it be a class of behaviors that is susceptible, as a class, to reinforcement.* If we specify a class that fails to be strengthenable or maintainable by reinforcing its members, such a class does not constitute an operant response, its members are not response variants, and presumably it is not suitable for use in the study of operant behavior. This is true whether a specification of the boundaries of the behavior was in terms of dimensional limitations or some necessary environmental change that the behavior must produce. Operants, or operant responses (responses for short, *if* you remember that response does not mean "response-to") then, are the reinforceable classes of behavior that form the fundamental units of analysis of a large portion of human and animal actions.

In the definition of operants as classes of behaviors amenable to reinforcement, no logic bars the definition of subclasses or superclasses of operants contained in, or containing any particular previously defined operant class. This flexibility in the way the basic behavioral "packages" may be subdivided into smaller "packages" or combined to form larger "packages" will be of great importance when we examine the extreme limits to which operant concepts can be extended. In itself, the definition of an operant, therefore, places no restriction on how "big" or how "small" a response class may be in terms of the amount of behavior entering into it. As we shall see in section 8.5 below, classes consisting of muscle twitches too minute to be observable by the subject emitting them may come to function as operants. At the other extreme, lengthy sequences of actions appear to function as single operant classes. Under some conditions, it may be possible to speak of knitting a sweater, writing a book, or walking to work as operants. Extensions of the concept of the operant to such large-scale operants are only just being explored in the laboratory.

8.2 A SET THEORY DEFINITION OF OPERANT RESPONSE

An alternative definition of the operant, compatible with the preceding account, is provided here in set theory notation (see section 8.9).

Consider the set of all possible behavior samples,

In that set $\mathfrak{U}$, let us define the subset of behaviors, B, that fall within the preassigned limits L_a-L_b, M_c-M_d, . . . , and have restrictions or requirements such that the form of the behavior must be N, O, . . . , where the capital letters L, M, N, O, . . . , stand for behavioral dimensions, and the subscripts specify upper and lower limits of these dimensions. Then that subset may be represented by

As an alternative means of defining B, we may consider all the behaviors that accomplish a given environmental result, S, to constitute the subset B.

Consider an attempt to reinforce successive instances from the subset B. If strengthening of the members of a subset, R, of behaviors now occurs (as evidenced by a selective increase in their frequency, a change in their sequential order in relation to other behaviors, and so forth), then that subset R shall be known as an *operant* and the observed members of R shall be known as operant response *variants*. If no strengthening of a subset R occurs, then B is said merely to be a specified subset of behaviors, void of empirical import for the analysis of behavior.

Given an operant R, it is possible to define a subset, r, such that every member in r is also a member of R.

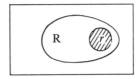

In practice, it may be found that many such subsets r_1, r_2, . . . , may be operants themselves by the previous definition. Since, however, the definition of an operant is dependent on observed strengthening by reinforcement and since strengthening is defined relatively to other behaviors (see section 4.4), the limit to which fractionation and/or subdivision of the class R can be extended is set by the point at which it is not possible to strengthen a given subset r_i without an equal strengthening of some other r_j. Evidently this determines the lower limit of definition of an operant class.

A converse operation is permissible. Given the operant R, it may be possible to discover (or create) a higher-order superset, R, which contains all the members of R in addition to other behaviors.

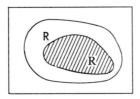

Thus, although the movements in pressing a bar may function as an operant, the movements in pressing a bar twenty-five times may function as a higher-order operant, R. Similarly, the movements of pressing a bar, followed by the movements of pulling a chain, may function as a higher-order operant. Again, the limits to which operants can be extended in this way are set only by the limits of reinforceability of behavior.

8.3 THE DIFFERENTIATION PARADIGM

The reinforcement of only those instances of behavior that fall within the limits and that meet the restrictions and requirements set on behavioral dimensions is known as the procedure of *response differentiation*. Thus, the strengthening of such behaviors as disk pecks by pigeons, lever presses by rats, and picking up of toys by children involves response differentiation. What we have been calling operant strengthening is a special case of response differentiation. In order to appreciate the various quantitative aspects of response differentiation, it is useful to examine a case in which the specification of the behavioral class to be reinforced is in terms of a single behavioral dimension.

In the definition of the lever press of a rat, the minimum force required to depress the lever may often be specified. This minimum force is an example of a lower limit of a behavioral dimension. If the minimum force is low enough, the operant level of lever pressing will be greater than zero and strengthening of the lever-press operant class will proceed exactly as described in Chapter 4. Hays and Woodbury (cited in Hull, 1943) conducted such a strengthening experiment, using a force minimum of 21 gm. After the strengthening process had stabilized, they obtained responses distributed along the force dimension as shown by the upper histogram of Fig. 8–2. Figure 8–2A shows no more than the

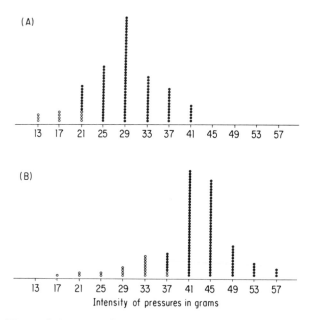

Figure 8–2. Distribution of response forces when all forces above 21 gm (A) and above 36 gm (B) were reinforced (after Hays and Woodbury, cited in Hull, 1943).

familiar variability that characterizes behavior, even when it is reinforced under *crf* conditions. In (A) the forces emitted are distributed approximately symmetrically about a point some 8 gm above the lower limit of the operant response class. Notice that a few presses (represented by the open circles of Fig. 8–2) do not adequately meet the criterion for a response and are therefore not reinforced. When the experimenters were satisfied that Fig. 8–2A represented the final stabilized state of the behavior under their conditions, they raised the minimum force requirement to 36 gm. The result of this change in the response class was the adjustment of the behavior of the rat to that shown by the histogram of Fig. 8–2B. The distribution of forces has moved upward and is now centered at approximately 41–45 gm. Conditioning of this new class of behavior has been successful; the necessary condition for conferring upon the class the status of an operant response has been met. There has been a further important consequence of this conditioning. Novel emitted forces, never before seen in the animal's repertoire (those over 45 gm), are now occurring with moderate frequency.

The differentiation procedure has resulted in the appearance and stabilization of a set of novel behaviors. How did this occur? Two complementary processes appear responsible. First, observe that, at the time it was put into effect, the new requirement of 36 gm encompassed some existing forces (see the right tail of Fig. 8–2A). The strengthening of these greater-than-36-gm force behaviors would be expected to maintain them. Had this condition not been met, normal extinction would almost certainly have occurred. Then, second, the 36-gm minimum excluded many forces previously reinforced. When lever presses of these previously reinforced forces were emitted under the 36-gm minimum procedure, they were extinguished. Recall that one of the results of the extinction procedure is an increase in the variability of behavior (section 5.2). Extinction of the previously reinforced 21–36-gm forces would, accordingly, tend to produce new forces both higher and lower than those usually emitted. The emission of very low forces would be of no consequence in the present experiment, but the emission of very high forces would be met with reinforcement and hence strengthened. Eventually, these two processes—(1) differential extinction and (2) differential strengthening—interacting along the force dimension, led to behavioral stabilization in the form of histogram (B) of Fig. 8–2.

Extinction has played a crucial dual role in this differentiation of more forceful lever depressions. (1) It has acted to bring about novel and exceptional response variants, some of which may be reinforced. (2) It has acted to weaken the behavior along the portion of the dimension where reinforcement is being withheld.

Like other important behavioral paradigms, *differentiation* finds a complete definition only in the specification of its given, procedure, process and result.

GIVEN: A class of behavior being emitted in some strength greater than zero.

PROCEDURE: Apply reinforcement to one subset of variants within that class and submit the rest to the extinction procedure.

PROCESS: The gradual strengthening of the variants being reinforced and the gradual weakening of the set of variants undergoing extinction.

RESULT: A stabilized distribution of reinforced variants whose strength exceeds that of the unreinforced variants.

The differentiation procedure need not necessarily be applied as it was in the Hays-Woodbury experiment. All that is required by our definition is that a subset of the variants be reinforced and a second subset extinguished and that, together, these two possibilities exhaust all the variants. In Fig. 8–3, several possibilities are shown schematically. Only (A) corresponds to the Hays-Woodbury case.

EXERCISE 5.

Predict the effects of the differentiation procedure applied as shown in each of the cases of Fig. 8–3 by drawing new response variant distributions.

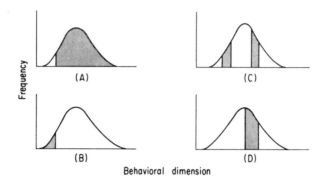

Figure 8–3. Some possible applications of reinforcement and extinction to R variants. Reinforced regions are shown shaded.

A case similar to that in Fig. 8–3D has been described by Keller and Schoenfeld (1950). A pinball machine was modified to permit precise measurement of how far back the plunger was pulled before its release. Variations in upper and lower limits on the response were explored when reinforcement for correct variants was a flash of light after release. The band of variants to which reinforcements are applied may be made so narrow that a selective strengthening of that particular band cannot be obtained. Instead, variants close to the reinforced band will be maintained at strengths equal to those in the reinforced band. In this situation, the experimenter has reached the minimal restrictions for the definition of a response class. Above these limits, however, the results conform to the law: *whatever is reinforced is also strengthened.*

Herrick (1963) designed the lever shown in Fig. 8–4 for studying the displacement of bar pressing. Presses made by a rat moved a T-bar through an arc while an electronic circuit sensed the maximum displacement achieved for each press. The maximum distance the lever moved

Figure 8–4. Lever used to study displacement of response.

with each press was categorized into one of eight zones. The lever was designed so that the higher the zone number, the greater the amount of work required from the rat. In one experiment Herrick (1964) first reinforced presses falling in any zone from 1 to 8. The results for one rat are shown in Fig. 8–5A. A wide range of displacements was obtained. The range of reinforced positions was then progressively narrowed. When

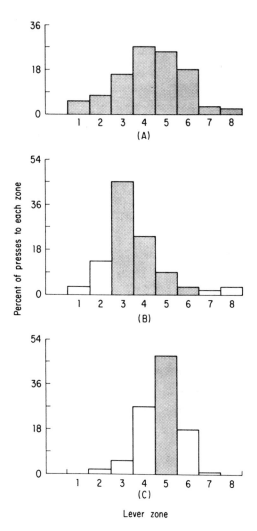

Figure 8–5.   Lever-displacement distributions as a function of the size of the reinforced region. Shaded sections of the histograms indicate the lever zones within the reinforcement region (after Herrick, 1964).

only positions 3–6 were reinforced the histogram of Fig. 8–5B resulted. The distribution of displacements had narrowed somewhat; still, the rat kept most of its presses within the reinforced limits. Later in the experimental series the only displacements reinforced were those in zone 5. The results are shown in Fig. 8–5C. The reinforced band of presses was at high strength, but numerous presses in unreinforced zones occurred. An interesting effect seen in the histogram of Fig. 8–5B is that the zones near the lower limits of reinforcement (zones 3 and 4) capture appreciably more behavior than the zones near the upper limits of reinforcement (zones 5 and 6). This phenomenon may be interpreted as a tendency for the rat to expend "least effort": given two reinforced zones, the one that has the lesser work requirement will show the most strengthening.

8.4 SUCCESSIVE APPROXIMATION

The great power of the differentiation procedure lies in its ability to generate and then sustain behaviors hitherto unobserved in the animal's repertoire. This power is extended very much further in cases in which progressive and gradual differentiations can be made to take place over time. In the Hays-Woodbury example and the examples from Fig. 8–3, a one-step differentiation was assumed. But a second differentiation procedure can follow on the results of the first, and so forth, so as to produce eventually behaviors which may be very different from the original forms. Unless the successive differentiation history were known, accounting for the appearance of these behaviors would be difficult. A baby begins life with a repertoire of all the basic sounds used in languages, but how unlike his babbling and gurgling is the smooth adult utterance of an English sentence. Yet the emergence of sentences was preceded by words, words by syllabic sounds, and these latter were differentiated out of the crude stream of noises emitted by the neonate. Progressive and gradual differentiations which build on the results of each previous differentiation and which gradually move the behavior to some final desired form are known as successive approximations to the final behavior, or more simply, the *shaping of behavior*. The process is represented schematically in Fig. 8–6. By the nth differentiation, a distribution of variants has emerged that to the casual observer might appear to bear no relation to the original response distribution. Nevertheless, the origins of the nth distribution lie in the successive strengthening and extinction of the ancestors of those variants. Without that causal history, the final distribution in Fig. 8–6 would never have emerged.

Successive differentiation must have an upper limit, determined by the capacity of the organism. But within the confines of these capacity

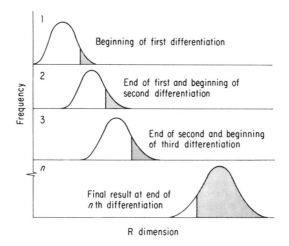

Figure 8–6. Schematic representation of progressive differentiations (successive approximation) along a quantitative response dimension. Shaded areas represent reinforced variants.

restrictions, successive approximation to a final form of behavior is an extremely powerful method for producing behavior. By such a process of successive approximation on the lever-force dimension, Skinner (1938) was able to train 200-gm rats to perform the Herculean feat of pressing a bar requiring a 100-gm minimal force.

Neither differentiation nor successive approximation is limited to changes along a quantitative response dimension. Even though topography, or form of behavior, is difficult to measure, the shaping of topography proceeds analogously to successive approximation along a quantitative dimension. Reference has been made earlier to the disk-pecking operant of pigeons. This response often has a zero operant-level frequency and hence must be shaped. In this case, the experimenter successively approximates the desired form of the behavior, beginning with a form that may not resemble key pecking at all. The experimenter may first reinforce all movements of the animal that occur in the vicinity of the wall containing the disk. The effect of this differentiation procedure is to strengthen the animal's movements in the vicinity of the disk. Then reinforcement is made contingent on movements of the head that are near the disk. When this contingency has had the effect of increasing these movements, reinforcement will be made conditional upon striking the disk with the beak. In this example, changing requirements of reinforcement are combined with progressively changing behaviors to shape out a novel act. The emergence of the disk-peck is due to a history of progressive differentiation from remote behavioral ancestors; to these the emergent disk-peck bears little superficial resemblance. This process is the one through which very many of our own skills are shaped. It is instructive to note that although nature arranges many selective reinforcement situations (the rabbit's running is reinforced only if it is fast enough to elude the fox; the fox's running will be reinforced only if he runs faster than the rabbit), it seems that successive approximation is a strictly human arrangement of contingencies. Teachers, parents, and friends follow such a procedure, though rarely as systematically as might be. It is in the laboratory, perhaps, that the greatest power of the procedure can be exploited, for it is there that we can best control and manipulate the many parameters, suggested by Figs. 8–3 and 8–6, whose effects on the process are still largely unknown.

8.5 EXTENSION OF THE CONCEPT OF THE OPERANT

A history of differentiation and successive approximation can make susceptible to reinforcement, classes of behavior that would have remained otherwise unavailable. In this sense, the procedures of differentiation and successive approximation are appropriately considered methods of creating operants. We are now in a position to understand why most of the operants we observe outside the laboratory, such as opening and closing doors, saying "please," operating machinery, baking cakes, sending morse code, and kicking footballs, appear to have a more unitary event-like structure than we intimated earlier was characteristic of the behavior stream. The very event-like status of these acts is conferred upon them by the fact that they are the products of differentiation. Differentially reinforced, at first in the form of arbitrary classes, these operants have become functional units through the action of selective reinforcement for their members and concurrent extinction for the members of all other behavior classes.

An important class of such created operants is the set whose members are made up of elements which themselves have previously been shaped up as operants. In the simplest case, reinforcement is made contingent on the emission of n successive repetitions of a previously reinforced operant. This procedure specifies a new higher-order operant made up of n successive instances of the previously reinforced class of behavior. When we describe such a higher-order operant, we refer to the instances of the previously reinforced class that make it up as its *elements* $(r_1, r_2, r_3, \ldots, r_n)$. Although the elements were themselves once unitary response classes, they are now being treated as components of a higher-order response class (Findley, 1962). The specification of an operant in terms of a fixed number of such repeated elements is known as a *Fixed-Ratio* (*FR*) operant. The term "ratio" refers to the fixed number of elements repeated per reinforcement. For instance, after having strengthened the telegraph key-pressing operant of a monkey, reinforcement may be made contingent upon 30 consecutive telegraph key presses. After shaping up the disk pecking of a pigeon, reinforcement can be made to occur only on every 50th disk peck. These cases are denoted *FR* 30 and *FR* 50, respectively. Such higher-order operants, being made up of easily observable and experimentally created components, are useful in permitting a comprehensive micro-analysis of operant behavior *structure*. Typically, the elements of *FR* operants are studied in much the same way that responses are studied in intermittent schedules of reinforcement. Thus, cumulative records of the elements of *FR* operants constitute a method for observing the temporal characteristics of highly magnified response classes.

The transition from reinforcement of a response class that has only one element to classes containing *n* elements represents a type of successive approximation along the dimension of number (*n*) of elements. Prior to changing the reinforcement requirement from a single element to *n* elements, there is, however, no information on the available variants along the *n* dimension. The only value of *n* previously examined (reinforced) in *crf* has always been 1. Thus, the differentiation is largely a matter of trial and error. Using the disk (key) pecking of pigeons, Ferster and Skinner (1957) were able to proceed from one element per reinforcement directly to reinforcement ratios of 40 and 50 elements without extinction occurring. When the differentiation of the new operant has stabilized (a few dozen hours), the rate pattern of the elements is such that high and uniform rates are frequent and a slight pause occurs after reinforcement. The differentiation of yet higher ratios requires a successive approximation by gradually increasing *n*. The ratio is increased by 5 or 10 and held at the new value for several sessions. A typical cumulative curve, showing a stable performance on *FR* 120 in a bird shaped in this way, is shown in Fig. 8–7. The curve shows the remarkable uniformity of behavior in time under *FR* specifications. Reinforcement is characteristically followed by pauses lasting as long as 5 or 6 min, after which the bird begins to peck at a uniform and high rate which is sustained until reinforcement. The pause after reinforcement is closely related to the size of the ratio. Large ratios are marked by long pauses. At short ratios, the pause may disappear altogether. The upper limit of the ratio differentiation is perhaps unknown. Skinner (1957) reports data by Morse and Herrnstein in which an *FR* operant containing 900 elements was stabilized through progressive differentiation.

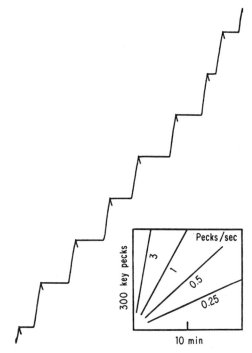

Figure 8–7. Cumulative curve of key pecking of a pigeon, reinforced after every 120th peck (Ferster and Skinner, 1957).

The notion that the ratio procedure defines a higher-order operant is supported by studies which have verified that this operant, like others, can be subjected to a schedule of reinforcement and maintained indefinitely in ways characteristic of the particular schedule. Ferster and Skinner (1957) reinforced *FR* 30 operants under uniform probability schedules. That is,

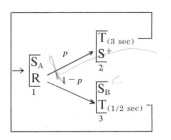

where   R = 30 key pecks
      S_A = normal illumination
      S_B = dimming of lights

The end of an unreinforced FR was signaled in Ferster and Skinner's experiment by a brief change in illumination (bracket 3 in the diagram). Probabilities of reinforcement (p) for FR 30 key-pecking behavior from 0.85 down to 0.50 maintained behavior. At 0.50, there was often a tendency for long pauses to occur between FR operants (not between elements) characteristic of a result found by Brandauer (1958), who used very low p values with a simpler operant, one key peck. Since Brandauer had to go down to probabilities of 1⁄600 to get the effect that was obtained here with 0.50, it seems that the amount of behavior involved in an operant modifies its responsiveness to a schedule.

The function relating resistance to extinction to FR size has received some experimental attention. Large FR's may require substantial work from the individual and for that reason might be expected to show less persistence in the face of extinction than small FR's. Boren (1961) and Weissman and Crossman (1966) have presented data which show that over the range FR 1 to FR 64, lever-pressing rats and key-pecking pigeons appear to give such an effect. Despite this decline in persistence of the operant as a function of its size, many more elements are actually emitted in the extinction of large FR's. In fact, within limits, the larger the FR in training, the greater will be the number of individual elements emitted during extinction.

An important conclusion follows. If we are interested in increasing the persistence of behavior in the face of extinction, the FR specification provides an alternative method to a schedule to produce perseverance. We may incorporate the behavior as an element of a higher-order FR operant.

In contrast to higher-order operants created by combining elements which themselves have been earlier demonstrated to be operants, Hefferline and Keenan (1963) have investigated a "miniature" operant, so small that electronic amplification must be employed to detect it. These workers have successfully extended the concept of the operant response class to behaviors so small in amplitude that the subject is generally not able to report observing his own responses. In one experiment, muscle-twitch potentials were recorded from the thumb of human subjects. Dummy electrodes were placed at other points on the subject's body to distract attention from the thumb response. Subjects were seated comfortably in a triply shielded, air-conditioned, sound-deadened cubicle and were under instructions only to relax. They were advised that reinforcements in the form of counts on a counter located near them might occur and that each count was worth 5 cents. But the subjects were never told how to produce counts. In one subject, thumb twitches, generating potentials in the range of 25–30 microvolts, were reinforced and then extinguished. Histograms, for 10 min of operant level, followed by 6 successive blocks of 10 min of strengthening, followed by a final 10 min of extinction, are shown in Fig. 8–8. The conditioning histograms show that the differentiation procedure was successful in selectively strengthening the reinforced class of behavior, and that even 10 min of extinction

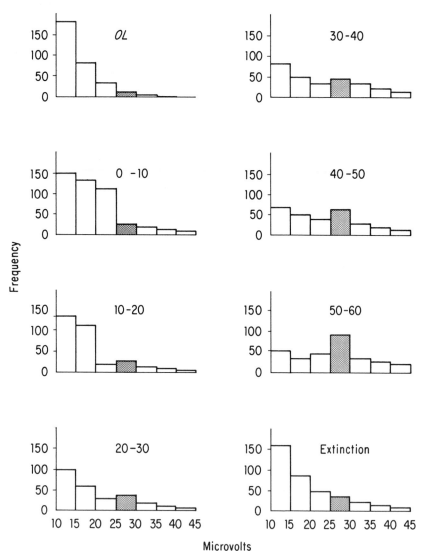

Figure 8–8. Frequency of response histograms for various categories of thumb contractions, measured in microvolts, during operant level (OL), conditioning, and extinction. The reinforced category is shown shaded (after Hefferline and Keenan, 1963).

caused a marked weakening in the class. Cumulative records taken of the reinforced muscle twitch show a typical rate of increase of the reinforced class but—as might be expected with an operant of such limited dimensions—the process is a gradual one, extending throughout the 60 min of conditioning. It differs, therefore, from the rather abrupt strengthening curves of the rat's lever press (Fig. 4–2).

Hefferline and Keenan's results are important in our analysis of behavior for a number of reasons. First, they show the lower limits to which our concept of operant may be pushed and yet still denote a functional unit of behavior. Second, they demonstrate that the subject's inability to verbalize the reinforcement contingencies in no way affects the lawful nature of conditioning and extinction. A third empirical phenomenon—typical of operant behavior in general—is demonstrated. In the muscle-twitch operant, the response class was defined as twitches between 25 and 30 microvolts. But close inspection of the histograms of Fig. 8–8 will show that neighboring classes of behavior, though actually unreinforced, were also somewhat strengthened. The incidental strengthening induced in behaviors not actually participating in the reinforcement contingency is called *response induction*. Response induction occurs during the strengthening of any operant but is not always so easy to verify. Although the experimenter may choose to limit reinforcement to a specified class of behavior, the strengthening may extend through induction well beyond the limits set. Rats that learn the movements necessary to traverse a complex runway are found to be able to swim the runway efficiently if it is flooded, although swimming requires a very different set of movements. Learning to write with the right hand trains the unused left hand, though to a lesser degree. Learning to speak Italian makes it easier to learn to speak Spanish. Response induction has been studied in the laboratory with the aid of the mirror-drawing apparatus shown in Fig. 8–9. The subject is given the task of drawing a figure from its image as seen in the mirror. Since the usual relationships between hand and eye are reversed, the first attempts are poor reproductions. Gradually the subject gets better and better at the task. Response induction may be measured at any time in the acquisition process by testing the amount of improvement shown by the left hand, with which no practice has been permitted.

8.6 RATE DIFFERENTIATION

In considering the effects of certain reinforcement schedules, appeal is often made to the fact that different rates of response happen to get differentially correlated with reinforcement. Thus, random-interval

Figure 8–9.   Schematic diagram of a mirror-tracing apparatus. The subject sits facing the star, which is visible to him only in the mirror (Mednick, 1964).

schedules *tend* to provide differential reinforcement after low rates, and uniform probability schedules *tend* to provide differential reinforcement after high rates. Since the effect of reinforcement is to strengthen whatever behavior comes before it, these schedules act indirctly to strengthen certain rates of behavior. If we wish, we can bring about a more direct and invariant differentiation by specifying rate limits, requirements, or restrictions of the operant that is to be reinforced.

In the *differential reinforcement of low rates (drl)*, an operant R is first specified and strengthened. When the R has been sufficiently strengthened, it is made an element in a new higher-order response specification: only response elements that are spaced apart from each other by at least a certain amount of time are now reinforced. Thus the *drl* procedure reinforces a certain behavior only when it is preceded by a pause. Wilson and Keller (1953) carried out such a *drl* procedure, requiring hungry rats to space out their lever presses for given minimum delays to obtain food. The minimum time specification of the operant was raised gradually in 5-sec steps from 10 to 30 sec over the course of 30 sessions. Fig. 8–10 shows that the different required pauses provided by the specifications produced different rates of lever pressing. As

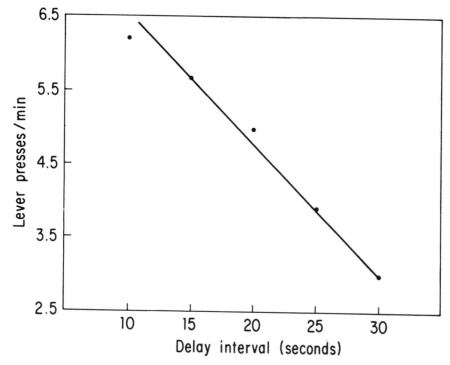

Figure 8–10. Average rate of bar pressing during the last session at each of five different values of the minimum delay interval necessary between reinforced presses (after Wilson and Keller, 1953).

the *drl* pause specification was increased, a systematic decline occurred in the rate of the lever-pressing elements. Another way of putting this is that as the delay requirement is lengthened, a systematic increase occurs in the average length of the pauses between presses.

The *drl* specification is a powerful operator for strengthening and maintaining low rates of some specified behavior. Cumulative curves of slow sustained key pecking of hungry pigeons, when only pecks preceded by a 3-min or longer pause are reinforced, are shown in Fig. 8–11. By appropriate adjustment of the *drl* specification, pigeons have been kept working slowly but steadily, 24 hr a day, for over two months.

The higher-order operant strengthened by the *drl* procedure consists of a rather well-specified topography (for example, a peck or a press) preceded by a poorly specified topography (for example, anything except a peck or a press). The class "anything except" is usually sufficiently broad that individual subjects come to form idiosyncratic, superstitiously reinforced behaviors during the enforced pause. Wilson and Keller report

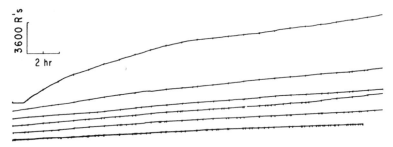

Figure 8–11. Key-pecking rates when only key pecks preceded by a 3-min or longer pause are reinforced (Skinner, 1957).

that each rat developed an easily recognizable and predictable form of collateral behavior made up of ritualistic grooming, nose poking, and trips between various parts of the experimental chamber, during the delay intervals.

The specification of the *drl* operant is conveniently expressed as a sample of behavior that includes for a certain duration any behavior other than some selected behavior, followed by the selected behavior. In set notation, we first define in $\mathfrak{U}$ the operant R. The portion of $\mathfrak{U}$ not included in R is called $\bar{R}$, and includes any behaviors except those falling into the class R. Evidently R and $\bar{R}$ exhaust the behavioral space, $\mathfrak{U}$. Under *drl* the new operant, *O,* is defined as consisting of: at least T min of $\bar{R}$, $+$ R.

The *drl* operant has been successfully maintained on interval schedules by Anger (1956) and Ferster and Skinner (1957).

In contrast to *drl,* very high rates of behavior can be generated by making reinforcement contingent upon the completion of the elements of a ratio operant within a specified time interval. If that interval is progressively shortened, or the ratio progressively raised, a shaping of extremely high rates of the component behaviors will occur. This procedure is known as the *differential reinforcement of high rates (drh).*

8.7 REINFORCEMENT OF CONTINUOUS RESPONDING

As we have seen, the creation of operants through the process of differentiation typically acts to impose arbitrary beginning and endpoints on behavior. The creation of discrete units of this sort is useful in measuring behavioral effects, for units lend themselves well to counting. Counting, of course, makes possible the calculation of a rate of response, and hence probability of response, with all the attendant advantages of these variables.

Nevertheless, this separation of operants into discrete events with clear beginning and endpoints is not a necessary condition for their definition. If it were, analysis of such interesting behaviors as standing still and its converse, moving continuously, would be outside the pale of operant behavior. That these behaviors are just as susceptible to reinforcement as are more obvious behavioral units is shown by the reinforcement of a continuous running response in the rat. The apparatus for studying running is a form of revolving cage similar to that shown in Fig. 8–12, but modified by the addition of a food magazine for automatic delivery of a pellet of food when required. For the purposes of establishing a class of behavior, a complete 360° revolution provides a convenient, though perfectly arbitrary, unit of behavior to be reinforced. If running (defined as one complete revolution) is reinforced on a fixed interval of 5 min (*FI* 5 min), only the first revolution after a lapse of 5 min is reinforced. The effects of reinforcement are to strengthen a pattern of running characteristic of responding under *FI* schedules (see Figs. 7–2 to 7–4). The rat pauses for several minutes just after a reinforcement,

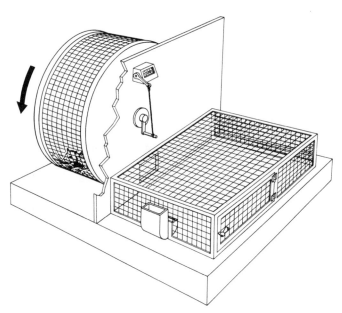

Figure 8–12. Revolving cage and automatic counter. The wheel turns in only one direction, counterclockwise.

then runs at a high rate until the next reinforcement, and so on (Skinner and Morse, 1958). Here the development of the *FI* pattern serves to verify the operant nature of running.

8.8 SUMMARY

The procedures of differentiation and successive approximation vastly increase our experimental control over behavior. These are procedures for selecting the aspects of behavior that we wish to reinforce and, indeed, for making the desired behaviors available for strengthening. The combination of schedules of reinforcement with various response specifications (including the higher-order specifications made up of previously conditioned operants) permits large samples of a laboratory organism's behavior to be maintained and studied over long periods of time. Ratio procedures permit the study of the ways in which the amount of work necessary for reinforcement can affect behavior. Between them, *drl* and *drh* procedures make available for study a wide range of rates of behaviors. In the pigeon, for example, these procedures yield a stabilizable range of key-pecking rates extending from less than 100 responses per hour up to 20,000 per hour. Frequently, ingenious response specifications may be used to establish behavioral baselines, analogous to schedule baselines, against which typical effects of drugs and other operations can be studied.

A number of characteristic human activities find counterparts in the laboratory investigation of various operant specifications. Piece work, in which a worker is paid for producing a fixed number of articles, is a clear *FR* specification. So too are activities like typing a large number of pages, preparing long assignments, or pounding a nail into a board. In many of these, if the amount of behavior involved is substantial, a pause before "getting down to work" is frequently seen. We may observe *drh* behavior in activities in which a premium is placed on rapid completion of work in a short time—it may be seen in waitresses at rush hour, or in the movements of a runner going down to first base. More "intellectual" kinds of behavior also fit differentiation paradigms. In a verbal argument, for example, there is usually a *drh* premium on "fast thinking" to guide rejoinders. On the other hand, in a quarrel, there is often a *drl* premium on *not* responding too hastily, and "saying things we will regret later."

A note is in order on the similarities between the effects of certain response specifications and the effects of certain schedules. Fixed ratio, for example, is not unlike *FI* in its effect upon behavior (compare Fig. 8–7 and Fig. 7–3). These similarities have occasionally led theorists to attempt to reduce schedules and differentiation to a common framework emphasizing probability of reinforcement parameters, and de-emphasizing response specification variables, or vice versa. The success of such enterprises is not yet assured, and for the present purposes we shall prefer to regard a schedule as a procedure for specifying probabilistic reinforcement contingencies in time, where the R class is given. On the other hand, we shall regard differentiation as the procedure for specifying what class of behavior shall be acted upon by a schedule of reinforcement. The observation that a certain definition of R under one schedule may give effects similar, or even identical, to another definition under a different schedule may indeed be interesting; nevertheless, such behavioral correspondences need not be taken to mean that in general either specification or schedule is reducible to the other.

8.9 THE LANGUAGE AND LOGIC OF SETS

A set is any well-defined collection of objects or conceptual entities. The term *"objects or conceptual entities"* is taken loosely to mean such things as trees, people, kitchen tables, outcomes of tossing a coin, color of hair, responses, or numbers. To say that a set is a *well-defined* collection refers to the fact that for any given object or conceptual entity we can give a definite yes or no answer as to whether it is in a particular collection. Some examples of sets are

(1) All the people in Kansas City with red hair.
(2) Those films in which Alec Guinness appears.
(3) The odd digits.
(4) The countries of the world with elected parliaments.
(5) All the behaviors that open a door.

For each of these sets, we can give a yes or no answer as to whether a given person, or film, or number, or country, or behavior, respectively, should be included in the collection. In the terminology of sets, the individual items that make up the collection are called the members, or *elements* of the set.

Sets are often symbolized by capital letters. Thus, the odd integers less than 10, taken as a set, might be symbolized by the letter I, and the set of common vowels in the English language by the letter V. Suppose we wish to indicate the members of a set. One method of writing out the collections we call sets is to enumerate each of the members of the set, separating each one by commas and enclosing the lot in braces. Thus the set of odd integers less than 10 is written

$$I = \{1, 3, 5, 7, 9\}$$

and the set of common vowels in the English language is written

$$V = \{a, e, i, o, u\}$$

Sometimes the set or collection is too large for us to conveniently write all its members, or elements. Then we may use triple dots after writing enough of its members to suggest the rule determining membership. For example we could write the set of governments, with elected legislatures, P, as

$$P = \{\text{U.S.A., Canada, U.K., France, Iceland, } \ldots\}$$

Two special sets are of interest. One is the *universal* set written as $\mathcal{U}$. The universal set $\mathcal{U}$ contains *all* the elements about which we shall have any reference in a given discussion. In terms of our previous examples, each of the following would be appropriate universal sets.

For (1) $\mathcal{U} = All$ the people in Kansas City.
(2) $\mathcal{U} = All$ films made.
(3) $\mathcal{U} = All$ numbers.
(4) $\mathcal{U} = All$ the countries of the world.
(5) $\mathcal{U} = All$ the behaviors of the individual.

$\mathcal{U}$ merely serves to delimit any particular discussion, to set its boundaries, and to define the topic or region from which various collections may then be made.

A second special set is one that lacks any members at all. Such an empty set is called the *null set*, ϕ. All the odd single-digit numbers greater than 10, all the countries of the world containing living dinosaurs, all the people in Kansas City with green hair, are presumably examples of the empty set, ϕ. Note that there is only one ϕ, whereas there are as many different universal sets as there are frames of reference for any given discussion.

Although a set may be made up of elements, some or all the elements may themselves be considered to be sets. Consider the universal set, $\mathcal{U}$, of all books, sentences, words, and letters. One element of that set is the present book. But this book itself contains a collection of sentences. These sentences make up a set: the set of sentences in this book. The analysis can be carried still further to words, then to letters. The sentences contain as elements words; yet words contain as elements letters. In this connection it is important to note that in enumerating the elements of a set we include only different elements. Thus the elements of the set L of letters making up the word "agreeable" is written

$$L = \{a, g, r, e, b, l\}$$

We do not duplicate the e or the a which occur more than once in the word, for they are identical elements. Of course if the word Agreeable were capitalized, then we might have to include a capital A as well as a small a as elements, depending on whether we had taken as our universal set the set of all letters, or just the set of lower-case letters.

The idea that sets can be partitioned into sets is embodied in the concept of a subset. A subset B of A is a set such that every member of B is also a member of A. The reverse is not necessarily true. Thus, if the set of all people living in the United States is the universal set, then the set of Kansas City people is a subset. Furthermore, the set of redheaded Kansas City people is a further sub-subset. Suppose all people to be the universal set, $\mathfrak{U}$. Then the set of males is a subset of that universal set. But the set of boys is a further subset. All boys are males, but not all males are boys.

To represent the fact that all the members of a given set B are also in the set A we write

$$B \subset A$$

meaning that every element of B is also an element of A.

To represent these kinds of ideas and to further our intuitions about the various simple manipulations and combinations of sets that we may wish to perform, diagrams known as Venn diagrams prove helpful. In a Venn diagram the universal set $\mathfrak{U}$ is represented as a rectangle and various sets and subsets within $\mathfrak{U}$ are depicted as circles, oblongs, or other irregular figures. Thus, in the earlier illustration concerning the set of people living in Kansas City, we draw

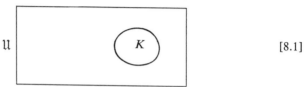

[8.1]

where K equals Kansas City people. If we wish to indicate redheaded Kansas City people we can draw two circles, letting them partially overlap, as in

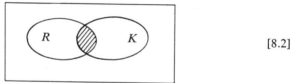

[8.2]

where the circles K and R stand respectively for Kansas City people and redheaded people. Not all redheaded people live in Kansas City, but the ones who do are those who are representd by the shaded overlapping region in [8.2], called the *intersection* of the two sets, R and K. The symbol Λ is used to denote the intersection of two sets. Hence [8.2] can be written as $R \Lambda K$.

Suppose we wish to refer to the two sets of animals, rats, R, and cats, C. Then if the universal set $\mathfrak{U}$ consists of all known animals, we have

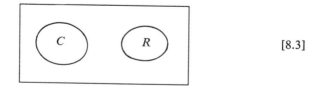

[8.3]

In [8.3], no element holds membership in both R *and* C. That is, there is no animal that is both a rat and a cat. Evidently then, $R \Lambda C = \phi$. Sets having no overlapping regions as in [8.3] are said to be *mutually exclusive* sets. Whether or not two sets overlap, we frequently have occasion to refer to the members of both sets taken together as a group. If we were interested in furry animals, then the rats and cats might be classed together. In Venn diagrams to refer to this collection we could write

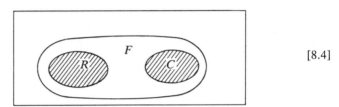

[8.4]

where F is the set of furry animals.

A set X such that any element x is either a cat *or* a rat is called the *union* of the two sets R and C and is written: $X = R \cup C$. It is the set X that is represented by the shaded areas in [8.4].

One final concept will find use. We often wish to discuss the *complement* of a set S, symbolized $\bar{S}$. The complement of a given set is that set which contains all the *non*members of the given set. Thus the complementary sets of each of our original examples are given

for (1) All non-redheaded people in Kansas City,
    (2) All films not containing Guinness,
    (3) All numbers except the odd digits,
    (4) All the countries of the world that do not have elected legislatures, and
    (5) All behaviors that do not open the door.

Note that the complement is formed by comparing the original set with the universal set and writing down as the complement what is left. Thus the complement of our set K in [8.1] is conveniently represented by the shaded area in [8.5].

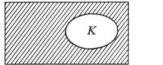

[8.5]

EXERCISE 6.
  Demonstrate that $S \cup \bar{S} = \mathfrak{U}$ *and that* $S \wedge \bar{S} = \phi$.

References for Chapter 8

Anger, D. The dependence of interresponse times upon the relative reinforcement of different interresponse times. *J. exp. Psychol.,* 1956, **52,** 145–161.

Boren, J. J. Resistance to extinction as a function of the fixed ratio. *J. exp. Psychol.,* 1961, **61,** 304–308.

Brandauer, C. M. The effects of uniform probabilities of reinforcement on the response rate of the pigeon. Unpublished doctoral dissertation, Columbia Univer., 1958.

Ferster, C. B., and Skinner, B. F. *Schedules of reinforcement.* New York: Appleton-Century-Crofts, 1957.

Findley, J. D. An experimental outline for building and exploring multi-operant behavior repertoires. *J. exp. Anal. Behav.,* 1962, **5,** 113–166.

Hefferline, R. F., and Keenan, B. Amplitude-induction gradient of a small-scale (covert) operant. *J. exp. Anal. Behav.,* 1963, **6,** 307–315.

Herrick, R. M. Lever displacement during continuous reinforcement and during a discrimination. *J. comp. Physiol. Psychol.,* 1963, **56,** 700–707.

Herrick, R. M. The successive differentiation of a lever displacement response. *J. exp. Anal. Behav.,* 1964, **7,** 211–215.

Hull, C. L. *Principles of behavior.* New York: Appleton-Century-Crofts, 1943.

Keller, F. S., and Schoenfeld, W. N. *Principles of psychology.* New York: Appleton-Century-Crofts, 1950.

Mednick, S. A. *Learning.* Englewood Cliffs: Prentice-Hall, 1964.

Skinner, B. F. *The behavior of organisms.* New York: Appleton-Century, 1938.

Skinner, B. F. The experimental analysis of behavior. *Amer. Sci.,* 1957, **45,** 343–371.

Skinner, B. F., and Morse, W. H. Fixed-interval reinforcement of running in a wheel. *J. exp. Anal. Behav.,* 1958, **1,** 371–379.

Weissman, N. W., and Crossman, E. K. A comparison of two types of extinction following fixed-ratio training. *J. exp. Anal. Behav.,* 1966, **9,** 41–46.

Wilson, M. P., and Keller, F. S. On the selective reinforcement of spaced responses. *J. comp. physiol. Psychol.,* 1953, **46,** 190–193.

Chapter 9 **ENVIRONMENTAL CONTROL**

I N DISCUSSING THE PROCEDURES OF OPERANT strengthening, schedules, and differentiation, we have paid little attention to the state of the prevailing environment. During the strengthening of a rat's lever press, a baby's crying, a pigeon's pecking, and a college student's voicing of opinions, our interest in the environment was confined to verifying that the operant was possible (that is, that levers, disks, and a past history with the English language were provided where necessary), and that reinforcement could be introduced when desired. Nevertheless it is apparent in considering the behavior of any organism at large that this neglect of prevailing environmental conditions must result in a very inadequate picture of behavior. In general, organisms emit responses selectively according to the state of their current or preceding environments. A child learns to cry only when a parent is home to reinforce crying. A dog will not beg for food in the absence of a human. We are unlikely to ask for a glass of water when nobody is in the room to hear (and hence to reinforce) us. All these cases illustrate a type of behavioral control on the part of the environment, but a type of control which differs in numerous ways from the manner in which eliciting stimuli control their respondents. In particular, we do not shout our restaurant orders louder and louder the larger the waiter. Conversely, a whispered warning may lead to violent activity if what is said is of such a nature as to warrant that kind of activity. In a word, the laws of the reflex are inapplicable to the environmental control of operants. A quite different set of laws, couched in terms of the past reinforcement history of the organism, governs the selective emission of operants. To formulate these

187

laws, however, we shall need to conceptualize a number of dimensions for specifying, analyzing, and in general, quantitatively describing the environment of organisms.

9.1 STIMULUS DIMENSIONS

The prevailing environment of an organism may be considered to be the pattern or configuration of all energies, present at any given time, that are capable of entering into lawful relationships with behavior. These energies are only a small subset of the energies studied by physicists. They are confined at most to those that can be detected by the specialized anatomical structures, *receptors,* that organisms have for receiving certain energies and for transforming them into electrical nerve impulses. The eye is specialized for the reception of a limited range of electromagnetic radiation, the ear for a limited range of air-pressure vibrations, the tongue and nose for certain chemical energies. There are receptors in the skin for detecting mechanical pressure, thermal changes, etc. There are receptors within the muscles and joints of the body that detect the movement of the muscles and joints in which they are embedded. A complete specification of the patterns of electromagnetic, mechanical, chemical, and thermal energies impinging on an organism's receptors at any time can rarely be undertaken. Fortunately it is not usually necessary. Since behavior can come under the selective control of limited parts or features of the energy configurations that make up what we call the environment, only a small and selected part or single feature of the environmental energy is varied in experimental work. The remainder of the environment is held as constant as possible. These experimentally manipulable features or parts of the environment are what we more usually call stimuli. Of all the behavioral laws that stimuli participate in, we have so far encountered only the laws of elicitation and the laws of reinforcement; others will make up the content of this and the subsequent chapters.

The stimulus is the arbitrary environmental unit. When we manipulate or change limited aspects of the environment and bring them into correlation with behavior, we are manipulating these units. In manipulating the visual environment, for instance, we frequently confine our experimental changes to one of the fundamental dimensions by which physicists describe light. For our purposes, light may be considered to be a limited range of electromagnetic disturbance radiated at 186,000 miles/sec in wave form. Light waves may be represented as in Fig. 9–1. Wavelength (λ, read "lambda") is one important stimulus dimension to which dif-

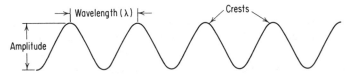

Figure 9–1. The regular wavelike character of pure light. Wavelength (λ), that is, the difference between successive wavecrests, is inversely proportional to the frequency in time of the waves, and is correlated with what we call the color, or hue, of light. Amplitude is related to light intensity.

ferent responses called color names have been correlated. The wavelengths that make up light form only a very small portion of the entire electromagnetic spectrum. In Fig. 9–2 a more complete electromagnetic dimension of λ is shown.

Nearly all organisms respond to differences in amplitude or intensity of light waves, but only a limited number of species have receptors specialized for detecting changes in λ. Pigeons, men, snakes, and monkeys are examples of organisms that do. Others, such as the rat and dog are said to be color blind because differences in λ alone cannot control differential responding. The receptor we call the eye is conveniently compared to a camera, for both have certain functional similarities (see Fig. 9–3). Both admit light through an adjustable diaphragm; in the eye, this diaphragm is called the iris. Both the eye and the camera have lenses through which light passes and which serve to focus the light onto a sensitive surface. In the camera, that surface constitutes the emulsion of the film. In the eye, the surface consists of nerve cells making up the retina. These retinal cells transform light into nerve impulses.

When the light waves of Fig. 9–2 strike the eye, they are sometimes referred to as pure spectral lights. These are the lights that occur in a rainbow and can be produced in the laboratory by a device called a monochromator. They are said to be pure because they contain only one wavelength. Most lights, including reflected light that reaches the eye from surfaces such as tables, chairs, blackboards, and lawns, are far from pure in this sense. Generally, even the light from a homogeneously colored surface or a lamp is made up of a large mixture of different wavelengths. Those wavelengths that are predominant usually determine the color-naming response we make. Some mixtures of light, however, are not named by their predominating wavelengths. The word "purple" is never used to name a pure spectral light of one wavelength. "Purple" is the color name for a mixture of red and blue. The lights we call white and the surfaces we call gray radiate heterogeneous mixtures of nearly all visible wavelengths. No single wavelength predominates in such lights, but the label "colorless" often given them would seem a misnomer.

Visual stimulus dimensions are not confined to different wavelength distributions and intensities of isolated patches of light. Relevant dimensions that can control behavior may be defined to include spatial combinations of the fundamental dimensions of wavelength and intensity. For instance, the relative intensities of two adjacent light regions can be a powerful controlling stimulus dimension determining the brightness response that an observer will make to a portion of the pattern. A look at Fig. 9–4 will show that when the amount of light reflected from the background surround varies, different brightness responses occur to the unchanging center triangle; that is, the observer will report different brightnesses of the triangle. (This phenomenon is called brightness contrast.) In fact, to produce an unchanging brightness response to the triangle, one would have to vary it in such a way that as the surround intensity is raised (surround made lighter) the triangle would also have to be raised proportionately in intensity (triangle made lighter also). In the situation illustrated by Fig. 9–4, an identical brightness response to the different triangles is obtained only when the *ratio* of intensities of triangle to surround is the same (Wallach, 1948). The functional control of the brightness response to the triangles in Fig. 9–4 is clearly located in a compound environmental variable. As this lawfulness between environment and behavior is the basis on which we assign the status of stimulus to environmental events, we need not be embarrassed to call this compound variable a stimulus. This designation, of course, does not preclude that with other contingencies prevailing, the triangle alone, or the surround alone, may also function as individual stimuli.

Another instance of complex stimulus control is shown by the lines of Fig. 9–5, commonly referred to as the Müller-Lyer "illusion." The two horizontal line segments are judged to be of unequal lengths because the stimulus variable controlling the judgment is not just the simple variable of horizontal line length. Instead, the relevant stimulus dimension is compound, composed of length of horizontal line and angle of attached wings.

Sound stimuli, like light stimuli, may also be analyzed into a set of constituent dimensions. Sound bears a superficial resemblance to light in displaying certain wave properties. But the waves of sound are slowly propagated (700 ft/sec) disturbances in air pressure, rather akin to the waves in the sea that are the products of disturbances in surface water pressure. Changes in the amplitude of sound waves constitute changes in

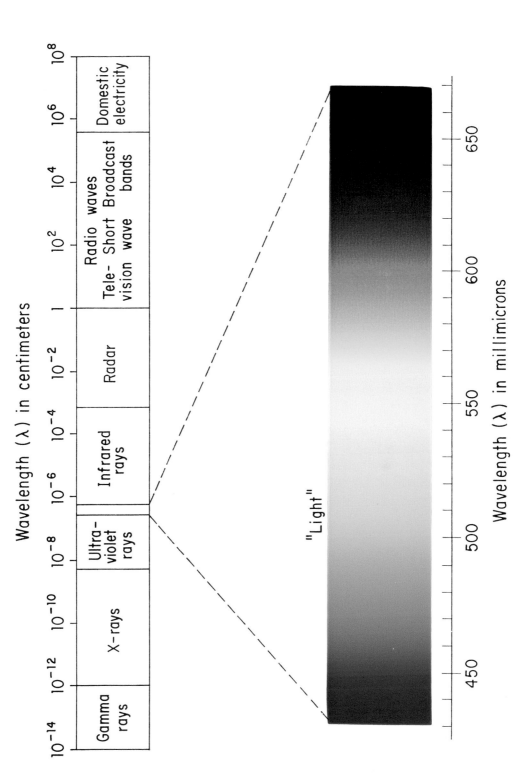

Figure 9-2. The electromagnetic spectrum. Note that the region that can enter into relationships with behavior ("light") is relatively small.

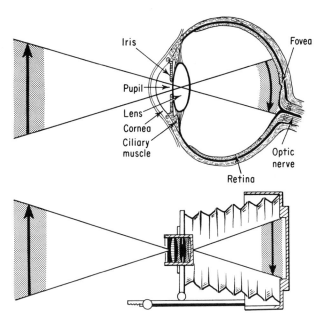

Figure 9–3. The eye compared functionally and schematically with a camera (after Wald, 1950).

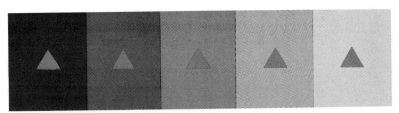

Figure 9–4. An example of how relations between two
parts of the visual field influence responses (after Boring,
Langfeld, and Weld, 1948).

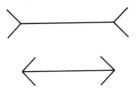

Figure 9–5. The Müller-Lyer illusion.

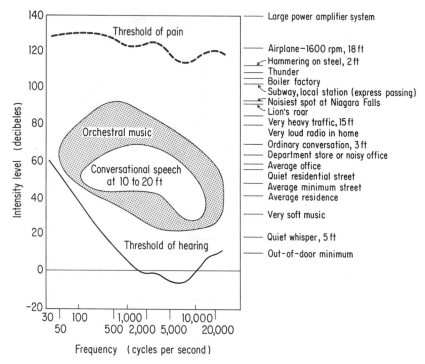

Figure 9–6. The intensity of some familiar sounds (after Lewis, 1963).

the intensity of the energy, and are associated with different loudness responses. Figure 9–6 indicates various sound intensities in terms of a logarithmic scale called decibels; the figure provides some common examples of the sources of these intensities.

The wavelength dimension proves useful in further describing sound stimuli. Sound, however, is conventionally described by the number of crests or *cycles* per second (cps) rather than by the λ. The number of cycles per second, or the *frequency* of the sound, is the dimension on which responses of pitch naming are based. Man is capable of making differential pitch responses over the range of about 20–20,000 cps. Other animals, such as dogs and bats, have been shown to detect frequencies two or three times our maximum upper frequency limit. The way in which pitch responses vary with frequency is illustrated by Fig. 9–7, which gives the principal frequency of various notes of the piano.

Just as a pure light containing only one λ is rare, so too is a pure tone containing only one frequency. Tuning forks and laboratory oscillators are sources of pure tones. The tones of musical instruments contain a mixture of frequencies, and the pitch is generally determined by the

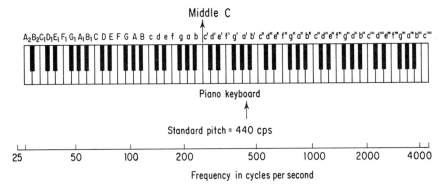

Figure 9–7. Sound frequencies of various piano tones (after Boring, Langfeld, and Weld, 1948).

predominant frequencies. Everyday sounds such as barks, traffic roar, speech, and music represent very complex admixtures of many different frequencies. Sound containing a fairly generous distribution of all audible frequencies in approximately equal intensities (such as applause and radio static) is termed *white noise,* on analogy with white light.

Dimensions have been conceptualized for describing the energies that make up the chemical, mechanical, and thermal portions of our environments. Smell and taste responses are based on differential changes in concentration and molecular structure of gases in the nose and solutions on the tongue, respectively. Changes in surface temperature are detected by certain receptors that are situated in the skin.

Describing the stimuli arising from muscle and tendon movements, called *proprioceptors,* poses experimental problems. Measurement of internal environmental changes is difficult without surgically invading the organism. The location of proprioceptors and their associated receptors makes such internal environmental changes relatively inaccessible for either measurement or manipulation. In practice, internal stimuli are, therefore, more often inferred than actually observed.

Note that in this discussion we use one set of terms to describe stimulus dimensions, and another set to describe corresponding behavioral responses. Although there are lawful correlations between these stimulus and response dimensions (described at length in the branch of psychology called psychophysics), labels for stimuli and responses should not be confused. Frequency and intensity of light energy are stimulus dimensions; color and brightness are response dimensions. Frequency and intensity of sound energy are stimulus dimensions; pitch and loudness (or volume) are response dimensions. Smell, taste, temperature, and weight are response terms associated with the stimulus dimensions of chemical structure, thermal energy, quantitative force, and so on. Recognition of the difference between the terms appropriate for describing stimuli and those for describing responses will prevent a great deal of confusion and unnecessary argument.

9.2 STIMULUS GENERALIZATION

The importance of having quantitative dimensions available with which to describe and manipulate the environments of organisms is shown clearly in quantifying the behavioral phenomenon known as stimulus generalization. This phenomenon is seen in crude form when a child learning to speak refers to all furry objects as "cats," and refers to all male adults as "Daddy." It is exemplified in our own behavior when we hail a stranger mistakenly because he appears to resemble a friend. In such examples similarity of stimuli seem clearly involved, but until we can specify the quantitative dimensions on which to relate such objects as cats, rabbits, and fur coats, a precise evaluation of the degree of similarity of any two stimulus situations is difficult. The availability of stimulus dimensions of the sort described in section 9.1 permits a more systematic study of this kind of similarity, which may be experimentally reinterpreted as follows. After a response has been strengthened in the presence of a particular environmental configuration, it will also occur, but to a lesser extent, when the environment is changed slightly in some way. The response may cease to occur at all when the change in the environment is very large. The import of these statements is to affirm the remarks made in the introduction to this chapter: The particular state of the environment at the time of operant strengthening is an important factor in governing the emission of the response.

The method of assessing the importance of the environment prevailing during conditioning is simple in principle. A given operant of some organism must be strengthened with the environment in a particular state or configuration. After the acquisition process is complete, variations can be made in some well-controlled single aspect of the environment, and the strength of the response tested in the new environmental configuration. In practice, the experiment offers enough complications to warrant a somewhat more detailed description.

A hungry pigeon may be confined to a box of the sort described elsewhere (Fig. 5–11). The apparatus is modified as shown in the illustration to Part (2) on p. 115 (from Guttman, 1956) so that pure light from a monochromator transilluminates the pecking disk. The monochromator permits the precise selection and presentation of any one of a very large number of visible wavelengths. The apparatus also includes provision for rapidly changing from one wavelength to another. In an experiment performed by Guttman and Kalish (1956), birds were shaped to peck the disk which was transilluminated by a yellow-green light (see Fig. 9–2) of 550 mμ (mμ = millimicron = 10^{-6} cm: a measure of λ, wavelength). Following some *crf* training, the birds were shifted to a variable-interval schedule (*VI* 1 min). When behavior had stabilized under *VI*, tests were made to determine to what extent the specific 550-mμ light on the disk was controlling behavior. This test consisted of an extinction procedure in which the birds were exposed to a randomized series of successive 30-sec presentations of 11 different wavelengths, only one of which was the 550 mμ actually used in training. No other changes were made in the bird's environment. (The procedure is shown in notation in the diagrams below.)

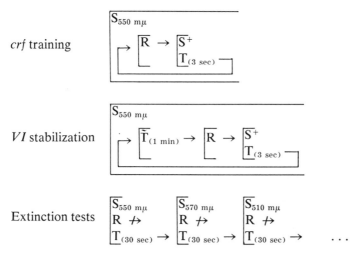

When the numbers of extinction responses emitted under each of the different stimuli were examined, they were found to take the form of Fig. 9–8. This figure indicates that the birds gave the maximum number of extinction responses only at their training stimulus, and gave progressively fewer responses at the test stimuli located progressively farther away from the training stimulus along the λ dimension. This gradation of responding, seen when response strength is assessed in environments somewhat different from the environment in which original strengthening took place, is known as the *generalization gradient*. In technical terms, "the generalization gradient is operationally defined by a succession of decrements from the established value of response strength" (Guttman, 1956).

The Guttman-Kalish technique illustrates nicely how procedures such as schedules of reinforcement and extinction can be combined to assess

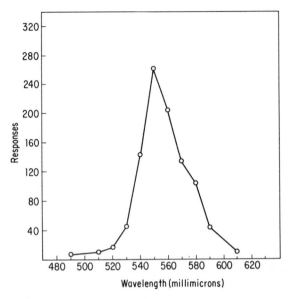

Figure 9–8. Extinction responses emitted in the presence of 11 different wavelengths projected one at a time on the bird's key. Training took place only at 550 mμ (Guttman, 1956).

certain fundamental behavioral phenomena. For example, consider the purpose of the *VI* schedule in training. A glance back to Fig. 7–9 (p. 151) will confirm that *VI* produces a very great persistence in the face of extinction. Several thousand responses may occur before the extinction rate begins to decline appreciably. In generalization, we are concerned with the spread of response strength to stimulus conditions other than those under which reinforcement actually took place. To make the necessary tests to assess this spread, we must never reinforce in the presence of the new, somewhat different stimulus conditions; otherwise, any responding that we might observe could be attributable to direct reinforcement in the presence of the new stimuli. But the use of the extinction procedure weakens behavior. How can we test as many as 11 different stimulus values in the face of this weakening? The solution to this problem lies in (1) making the presentation of each different test stimulus short (about 30 sec), (2) randomizing the order of presentation of the different test stimuli, and in (3) using a *VI* schedule in training to develop a persistence of several thousand potential extinction responses before marked signs of weakening begin to occur.

The results of Fig. 9–8 confirm the value of representing stimuli quantitatively. Suppose the experiment of Guttman and Kalish had been performed before it was known that light could be represented by waves and measured by wavelength. If the pigeon had been trained to peck at a disk covered with green paper, and then tested during extinction with green and then other colored papers on the disk, say blue, violet, red, orange, and yellow, differences in responding to these various colors would certainly have occurred. But consider how a graph such as Fig. 9–8 could have been drawn. The fact that no quantitative (numerical) dimension existed for relating the different colors, one to another, would have precluded such a functional representation. In our hypothetical example we have no basis for interpolating values of response strength between any two colors actually used. In the function of Fig. 9–8 we did this easily, just by connecting response strengths for two quantitatively adjacent stimulus values with a straight line. This interpolation by straight lines enables us to predict the amount of generalization to lights not even used in the actual experiment. The best that we might have been able to do with an experiment conducted prior to the discovery of the numerical specifications of light by its wavelength would have been to draw a bar graph of the sort shown in Fig. 9–9. In the absence of a better rationale, the colors of Fig. 9–9 are arranged alphabetically along the abscissa. The fact that no independent variable can be assigned to the X axis of Fig. 9–9 shows how deficient such a representation would have been. Here we are provided with some notion of the importance of quantitative dimensions in specifying and relating the independent variables of any science. Moreover, the example is useful in showing how one science (psychology in this instance) often borrows the methods and findings of another (physics in this instance) and exploits them for its own uses in contexts entirely different from those in which the methods were originally developed.

The actual shape of the generalization gradient will vary according to the particular stimulus dimensions used, the schedule and type of reinforcement in training the organism under study, and even the value of

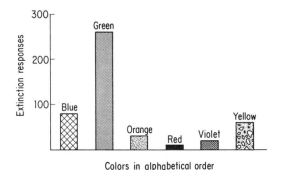

Figure 9–9. Hypothetical extinction responses emitted at various colors after training in the presence of green.

the particular training stimulus on a given dimension. Hence, any search for *the* generalization gradient must be abandoned. Sometimes a "gradient" may even fail to appear, and a flat generalization curve is obtained. When frequency of sound is used in an experimental design similar to that of Guttman and Kalish, the generalization gradient of the pigeon for sound frequencies assumes the form of Fig. 9–10. The curves of Fig. 9–10 are essentially flat. Although disk pecking was originally

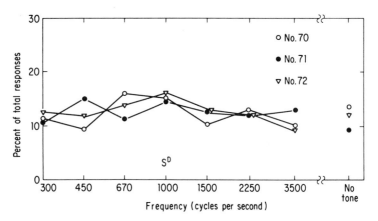

Figure 9–10. Generalization gradients along the frequency-of-sound dimension for three birds. A 1000-cps tone was present during strengthening of the disk-peck response (Jenkins and Harrison, 1960).

strengthened exclusively at 1000 cps, all tones between 300 and 3500 (and also no tone) have acquired equal power to control the emission of the response. Were it not for the fact, known from other experiments, that the pigeon *can* differentially detect these various sounds, we might be inclined to call the frequency dimension a behaviorally irrelevant one. As such it would be analogous to the portion of the λ dimension around the gamma-ray radiation region, or the dimension describing the level of traffic on a Tokyo street in relation to this bird pecking in New Jersey. We are forced to postpone, however, a detailed discussion of the variables responsible for the differences between Fig. 9–8 and 9–10 until the principles of the next chapter are introduced.

Even along the light-wavelength dimension itself, the use of training stimuli differing from 550 mμ produces gradients different in shape. Blough (1961) obtained the data represented in Fig. 9–11 when he trained three groups of birds at 530 mμ, 550 mμ, and 570 mμ, respectively. As the figure indicates, the actual shape of the obtained gradient varies depending on where the training stimulus lies on the λ dimension.

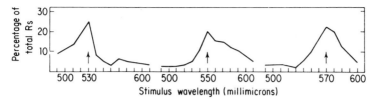

Figure 9–11. Generalization gradients around each of three different training wavelengths. Eight birds contributed to the curves—two at 530 mμ, four at 550 mμ, and two at 570 mμ (Blough, 1961).

At 530 mμ, the bulk of the gradient lies to the left of the training stimulus; at 550 mμ, on the other hand, it lies to the right. Only 570 mμ shows a symmetrical gradient. Note that the gradient around 550 mμ in Fig. 9–11 differs somewhat from the one originally obtained by Guttman and Kalish in 1956 (and shown in Fig. 9–8). The reason for the difference appears to be that Blough introduced an added precaution in taking his data. Because it is known that the pigeon's eye is more sensitive to some wavelengths than others, he used slightly different intensities of each test stimulus. The shape of Blough's gradients suggests that there are circumscribed *regions* along the λ spectrum in which generalization occurs more readily. "Trained near the middle of such a region the bird would generalize within the region, producing a symmetrical, flat-topped gradient. Trained at the edge of such a region the bird would generalize into the region; in the other direction its curve would fall more rapidly, to yield an asymmetrical gradient" (Blough, 1961, p. 38). The three curves of Fig. 9–11 suggest that two such regions are centered at approximately 515 mμ and 570 mμ, respectively. It is tempting to equate the presence of these regions with the "bands of colors" that the human being discriminates in the spectrum. These and other results indicate that the study of behavioral generalization holds promise for elucidating fundamental properties of the eye of infra-human organisms.

The simple generalization paradigm may be extended by examining the effects produced when more than one training stimulus is used. In one experiment Kalish and Guttman (1957) alternated lights of 530 mμ and 560 mμ during initial strengthening and subsequent *VI* stabilization. Testing for generalization was accomplished in the usual way. The curve obtained is shown in Fig. 9–12. It appears that this gradient is a composite of the individual gradients. Later work (Kalish and Guttman, 1959) has indicated that it probably represents a simple overlapping of two generalization gradients. An important feature of this procedure of training at more than one stimulus value is its ability to widen the generalization gradient. By using even more than two training stimuli, that

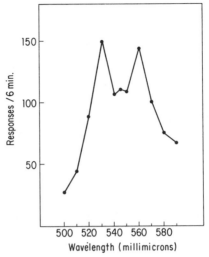

Figure 9–12. Generalization gradients along the wavelength dimension, after training in the presence of two stimuli, 530 mμ and 560 mμ (after Kalish and Guttman, 1957).

gradient may be broadened to any extent we please, a consideration that, as we shall see later, has significance in teaching general concepts to children.

Outside the laboratory, of course, generalization is never confined to a single environmental dimension. When naïve occidentals observe that all orientals look alike, and naïve orientals observe that all occidentals look alike, generalization is occurring from one complex stimulus (the first oriental or first occidental ever seen) to other "test" stimuli (new orientals, or new occidentals). A stimulus might be said to be complex when even its partial description involves more dimensions than would be practical to enumerate. Complex generalizations, as seen outside the laboratory, may be inferred as being based upon spreads of the Fig. 9–8 type along each dimension that the training and the test stimuli share. We may attempt to verify this hypothesis, partially at least, by extending our experimental test stimuli to include changes made simultaneously along two dimensions of a test stimulus. Illuminating a pigeon's disk with pure lights of various wavelengths establishes one well-controlled stimulus dimension, λ, as we have seen. In Fig. 9–13, light on a pecking disk is formed into a bar pattern. If this bar pattern is made to rotate about the center of the disk to any of several positions, we add a second independent dimension to the stimulus—angular orientation of the light pattern. Suppose a bird is trained and subsequently stabilized on a *VI* schedule

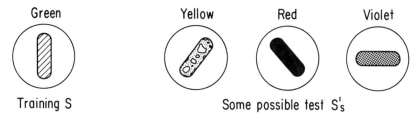

Figure 9–13. *Stimuli created by independently ma-nipulating two physically defined environmental dimen-sions.*

in the presence of a stimulus which may be described by a given value of wavelength (say 550 mμ, "green") and by a given angular orientation (say 0°, "vertical"). Then by using test stimuli that differ in *both* angle and wavelength during extinction, a generalization gradient extending over two dimensions may be determined. Detailed treatment of the quantitative results of such an experiment is beyond the scope of the present account; suffice it to note that an orderly generalization decrement occurs to test stimuli that differ in two dimensions from the original training stimulus. The decrement is a complex function of the remoteness of *both* dimensional values of the test stimulus from the initial values of the original training stimulus (Butter, 1963).

9.3 GENERALIZATION OF EXTINCTION

Just as the strengthening effects of reinforcing a given response in a given stimulus configuration spread to embrace other stimulus con-figurations, so too the weakening effects of extinction spread to stimulus conditions other than the particular one under which extinction was carried out. This phenomenon is called the generalization of extinc-tion. To observe it we must start with an operant existing at high strength in the presence of a range of stimuli. Extinction is then carried out in the presence of only one of the stimuli. When the extinction process is complete for that one stimulus, other stimuli from all along the range are tested to see the extent to which they still have the power to control the emission of the response. This procedure can be summarized in four phases:

Phase I. Initial strengthening of some operant in some stimulus situation.

Phase II. Maintenance of that operant (usually by a *VI* schedule) in the same and other stimulus situations.

Phase III. Protracted extinction of the operant in only one of the previously used stimulus situations.

Phase IV. Extinction tests conducted with all the stimuli used in Phase II.

Honig (1961) performed such an experiment and obtained the results plotted in Fig. 9–14. The portion labeled *baseline* was obtained in

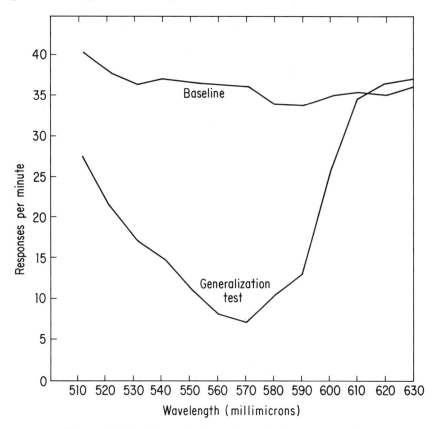

Figure 9–14. Generalization of extinction across the wavelength continuum. VI training was given at 13 values from 510 to 630 mμ. Extinction took place at 570 mμ (after Honig, 1961).

Phase II. In that phase hungry pigeons pecked the disk under a *VI* reinforcement schedule which was in force at 13 different wavelengths over the course of training. This procedure is an extension of Kalish and Guttman's (1957) training with two different wavelengths (see Fig. 9–12) and produces a generalization curve that is nearly flat across the entire spectral continuum. In Phase III, Honig carried out extinction exclusively at 570 mμ. Finally, the U-shaped gradient shown in Fig. 9–14 was obtained by testing the response rates in extinction at the other 12 stimuli. Under the conditions of this experiment, an inverted and somewhat flatter generalization gradient is produced than those of section 9.2. It is difficult to say whether the difference in flatness indicates a fundamental difference between generalization of extinction and generalization of reinforcement. In Honig's study, extinction at 570 mμ was not carried to completion in Phase III; the trough of the U function of Fig. 9–14 shows that at 570 mμ, response rate in testing is well above the nominally zero operant level normally associated with the key-pecking operant.

Stimulus generalization of extinction and stimulus generalization of reinforcement are inverse procedures. One involves a spread of weakening and the other involves a spread of strengthening. Table 9–1 contrasts their defining procedures.

Table 9–1

A PROCEDURAL COMPARISON OF STIMULUS GENERALIZATION OF REINFORCEMENT AND STIMULUS GENERALIZATION OF EXTINCTION

| | *GENERALIZATION* | |
	REINFORCEMENT	EXTINCTION
AT START	R strength *low* over a range of S's	R strength *high* over a range of S's
FUNDAMENTAL OPERATION	Strengthen R at *one* S value	Weaken R at *one* S value
TESTING	Numerous S's along the range presented and the extinction procedure constantly in effect	

9.4 SOME IMPLICATIONS OF GENERALIZATION

Early in section 9.2 we briefly noted a few non-laboratory examples of stimulus generalization. These examples of children confusing one situation with another through indiscriminate responding are cases in which generalization appears to hinder the adaptation of an organism to its world. But generalization is equally often a very useful property of behavior. For instance, skills learned in one environmental situation can be used in new environmental situations. Having learned to catch a ball thrown from a distance of 5 ft, we will catch it pretty well at 10, 20, and maybe even 40 ft. Parents who teach their children to say "thank you" at home are implicitly relying on generalization to see to it that "thank you" will be emitted outside the home. Our educational system is predicated on the assumption that the skills acquired in school will spread to environments outside the school. Still, the generalization *gradient* is there to remind and caution educators that the more closely a training situation resembles the situation in which the behavior will later be needed, the more effective will be the training. Schools and other agencies use this principle when they make the teaching situation as near to "real life" as possible.

The results shown in sections 9.2 and 9.3 support the inevitable conclusion that both reinforcement and extinction are somewhat specific to the state of the environment prevailing when they occur. The term "somewhat" is given precise meaning in the shape of the generalization gradients that can be observed when controlled changes in one or two physically specified stimulus dimensions are made. Generalization of this sort is a static concept. Unlike many of our previously familiar behavioral phenomena (conditioning, extinction, differentiation) generalization itself is not a process. That is, it is *not* a change in behavior over time with a fixed procedure held constant. Rather, it is a phenomenon that can be observed after strengthening or weakening by the use of a certain sequence of operations (for example, the phases of section 9.3). In a true behavioral process, *time* appears as the independent variable. But in the generalization gradients, the difference between training and test stimuli is the independent variable. Though static in this sense, we shall see in the next chapter how the generalization of weakening and strengthening combine in the discrimination paradigm to yield one of the most fundamental behavioral processes known.

Laboratory findings in generalization carry certain implications for an old philosophical problem, that of the meaning of *similarity*. C. E. Osgood's lucid comments are instructive of the manner in which the experimental method in psychology can occasionally provide a fresh reinterpretation of traditional philosophical problems.

> Suppose we ask (as has been asked in many an introductory class in philosophy), Which is more nearly similar to a red square—a green square or a red circle? The empirically oriented psychologist quickly tires of discussing matters like 'the relatedness of unique qualities' and dashes off to the laboratory to 'find out'! After setting up a reaction, any reaction, to the red square, he tests his human

subject for generalization to the green square and the red circle. Does the red circle show more generalization? If so, the red circle is more nearly similar to the red square than the green circle! Does this mean that we now have an objective scale for measuring 'similarity'? *Only when we are interested in similarity as defined by the behavior of an organism.* And it must be a specific type of organism at that, since similarity for the rat, thus defined (or for the Australian Bushman, for that matter), would not necessarily parallel those for Western *Homo sapiens.*

This brings up a minor matter of psychological jargon that most of us take periodic cognizance of but never observe in totality. We follow the impetus of our language and say that 'there is more generalization between these two stimuli *because* they are more nearly similar,' and then (like the brash young psychologist cited above) claim that 'these two stimuli are more nearly similar *because* there is more generalization between them.' Both statements are quite valid, depending on one's definition of similarity. Using a wave-frequency analyzer, we may measure the *physical* similarity (nearness on the frequency continuum) of two tones and then measure generalization as a function of this similarity. Conversely, we may use a group of organisms as measuring instruments for the similarity of tones, as in psychophysics, which is really measuring physical continua in terms of generalization and discrimination. Observe carefully, however, that there is no guarantee that the two measures of similarity will be parallel; in fact, they seldom are. The clearest illustration of this lies in the phenomenon of *octave generalization.* For both the rat and the human, at least, generalization of response to tones one octave apart is greater than to tones nearer on the physical frequency continuum, and they sound more nearly 'similar.' But, of course, there are those who would say that the concept of similarity is meaningful only in terms of the behavior of organisms. In this case, we must be content with as many modes of similarity as there are species, and cultures within species (Osgood, 1953, p. 361).

9.5 NOTES ON DESIGN FOR EXPERIMENTS IN PSYCHOLOGY USING ANIMAL SUBJECTS

The use of animals as subjects of psychological experiments can be conveniently dated from Thorndike's early experiments on trial-and-error learning. Thorndike's own comments on the rationale of animal subjects for psychological experiments make good reading even today. Where it is desirable to obtain better control of an organism's past and present history than is feasible with a human being; where it is desirable to investigate wide ranges of variables such as intense electric shocks, bright light, and so forth; and where we demand a more rigorous investment of time from our subject than a college student's schedule may permit, we can often turn to one or another of the widely available animal species without great loss of generality of our results. The purpose of the present notes is not so much to consider the problem of generalizing results from animal experiments to human beings, but rather to provide a general format for the design of animal experiments in psychology.

Note A. We must begin with a suitable animal. (In general, we want our results to be applicable to a wide range of species, including man.) That is, first, if the psychological problem under investigation is one that entails choice behavior or instrumental behavior (and practically all do), then we must choose an organism that emits such behavior. We must, in other words, choose an organism that exhibits operants. According to this criterion we may therefore choose annelid worms, camels, or dolphins; we must not choose protozoa, sponges, or clams, since these latter organisms have never been shown to exhibit behaviors that follow the laws of operant strengthening. We need not necessarily pick an animal very close to us on the phylogenetic scale, unless our experiment intends to study behavioral characteristics exhibited only by these phylogenetically advanced organisms. For many problems in learning, discrimination, differentiation, or chaining, animals as humble as the rat or common pigeon will do.

Note B. Having selected our species, we must deal with the problem of the kind of past experience that the particular animals should (or should not) have had if they are to be suitable subjects. Evidently, if we are designing an experiment to examine the acquisition process and our animal has already acquired the selected response—or a very similar one—he will not be a useful subject. Similarly, if we are interested in extinction results, an animal with a previous history of extinction with the given response will behave very differently from one lacking that history. Often, rather than keep a record of particular histories, psychologists choose animals that lack any experimental history, and that have been bred under controlled conditions. These animals, when used for the first time, are said to be experimentally "naïve." It is not always necessary to use such naïve animals; but we must satisfy ourselves that the particular past history that our animals have will not unduly disturb our results. The uniformity of our results will be our final justification.

Note C. Finally, we must motivate our animal. Here the problem of control and measurement is very much easier than with a human. We may deprive our pigeon of food for 22 hr, say, whereupon we may then use small bits of food as a convenient reinforcer; or we may chill our rats' compartment down to near freezing level, whereupon we may then use a brief blast of warm air as a reinforcer.

Notes *A, B,* and *C* supply hints for procuring a representative animal to serve as an experimental preparation for behavioral study.

References for Chapter 9

Blough, D. The shape of some wavelength generalization gradients. *J. exp. Anal. Behav.,* 1961, **4,** 31–40.

Boring, E. G., Langfeld, H. W., and Weld, H. P. *Foundations of psychology.* New York: Wiley, 1948.

Butter, C. M. Stimulus generalization along one and two dimensions in pigeons. *J. exp. Psychol.,* 1963, **65,** 339–345.

Guttman, N. The pigeon and the spectrum and other complexities. *Psychol. Rep.,* 1956, **2,** 449–460.

Guttman, N., and Kalish, H. I. Discriminability and stimulus generalization. *J. exp. Psychol.,* 1956, **51,** 79–88.

Guttman, N., and Kalish, H. I. Experiments in discrimination. *Sci. Amer.,* Jan. 1958, **198,** 78–79.

Honig, W. Generalization of extinction on the spectral continuum. *Psychol. Rec.,* 1961, **11,** 269–278.

Jenkins, H. M., and Harrison, R. H. Effect of discrimination training on auditory generalization. *J. exp. Psychol.,* 1960, **59,** 246–253.

Kalish, H. I., and Guttman, N. Stimulus generalization after equal training on two stimuli. *J. exp. Psychol.,* 1957, **53,** 139–144.

Kalish, H. I., and Guttman, N. Stimulus generalization after training on three stimuli: a test of the summation hypothesis. *J. exp. Psychol.,* 1959, **57,** 268–272.

Lewis, D. J. *Scientific principles of psychology.* Englewood Cliffs: Prentice-Hall, 1963.

Osgood, C. E. *Method and theory in experimental psychology.* New York: Oxford Univer. Press, 1953.

Wald, G. Eye and camera. *Sci. Amer.,* Aug. 1950, **182,** 32–41.

Wallach, H. Brightness constancy and the nature of achromatic colors. *J. exp. Psychol.,* 1948, **38,** 310–324.

PART THREE

Compounding Behavioral Units

10. DISCRIMINATION
11. ACQUIRED REINFORCERS
12. CHAINING

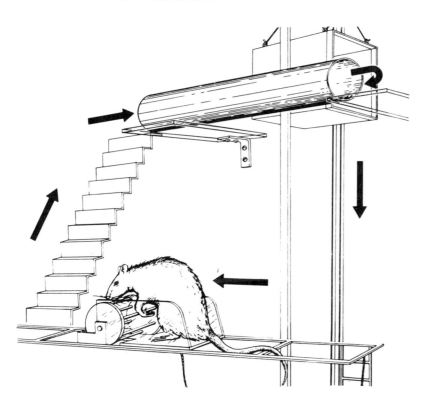

Chapter 10 **DISCRIMINATION**

A STRIKING CHARACTERISTIC OF ORGANISMS IS
their ability to form discriminations. Defined as differential responding
in the presence of different situations, discrimination is to be contrasted
with generalization, defined as similar responding in different situations.

Discriminations are demonstrated at the human level by the ability to
"tell two or more things apart." Some of us, for instance, discriminate
the paintings of Monet from those of Manet, butter from margarine, two
sets of similar fingerprints, two similar morse code characters. In "telling
these things apart," we are doing nothing more nor less than showing
differential responding in their respective presences.

In distinguishing objects in this way, a certain specific past history
appears to be a prerequisite. We make these and other discriminations
so casually and so naturally, however, that we are often apt to overlook
the necessity for this past history. Recall from the previous chapter that,
having strengthened a response in the presence of one stimulus, the
response will show strength, though less so, in the presence of other
related stimuli. If a given stimulus is very similar to the training stimulus,
it may control the response nearly as well as the actual training stimulus.
The discrimination procedure is a method for breaking down the
generalized control over responding held by a broad class of situations,
so that very similar situations come to be associated with very different
behaviors.

In terms of quantitative generalization along a single stimulus dimension, this breakdown amounts to narrowing a particular response strength
gradient sharply about one stimulus value; a bird is trained to peck only
at a green disk and no others, a child is trained to restrict the name

"cat" to a single subset of furry animals. The procedure by which such effects are obtained is straightforward: reinforcement for given behavior is restricted to a given situation. Although this procedure of making reinforcement of a particular operant conditional on the existence of a particular stimulus situation is sufficiently general to embrace all discriminations, there are enough variations to merit a classification of discriminations according to complexity, as indicated by the number of stimulus situations and associated response correlations entailed. In each of the four examples that follow, differential behavior is associated with different environments.

1. The discriminating movie-goer does not go to every film that arrives at his neighborhood cinema. He goes (R) to some (S_A), and does not go (absence of R) to others (S_B).

2. We say that some groups of people are discriminated against when they are treated differently from the way that other people are treated. That is, the discriminated group (S_A) is treated one way (R_A), and other people (S_B) are treated another way (R_B).

3. The professional winetaster can discriminate a variety of wines that all taste the same to the novice. The professional's discrimination is evidenced by his ability to give a unique name $(R_1, R_2, R_3, \ldots, R_{1000})$ to each one of a thousand different wines $(S_1, S_2, S_3, \ldots, S_{1000})$.

4. In the fine discriminations that a watchmaker must make as he places (R_y) each one of a dozen tiny screws into its proper place (S_x), the difference between correct and incorrect positioning is measured in fractions of millimeters.

Each of these four examples illustrates a progressively more complex level of discrimination. In the technical discussions that follow, refer back, when necessary, to the corresponding example for intuitive support.

10.1 TWO STIMULUS CONDITIONS, ONE RESPONSE CLASS

In analyzing the simplest of all possible discriminations we find that an organism emits a certain behavior with high strength in one situation, and does not emit that behavior in another situation. The basic operation for establishing such a discrimination between two situations is to reinforce a given operant in the presence of, or after, one stimulus (S^D); but to withhold reinforcement for that same operant in the presence of, or after, another stimulus (S^Δ, pronounced "ess-delta"). Two stimuli used in this fashion are called a pair of discriminative stimuli, one positive (S^D), the other negative (S^Δ).

In experimental practice, the procedure is usually complicated by the addition of several control techniques. Some of these insure that the discrimination is formed between the two desired stimuli and not some other spurious environmental changes. Others provide ways and means for quantitative and continuous measurement of response strength during the discrimination process. The need for these refinements can be seen in the simple example of providing a peanut for each chain pull that a monkey makes during a 3-min period in which a green light is on, then turning off the light and withholding peanuts for chain pulling during the next 3 min . . . , and so on repeatedly. Three faults can be detected in this experiment:

1. If the S^Δ interval is held constant, then a time discrimination can be made, allowing responding to come under the control of the fixed time period of S^Δ, and not the environmental properties of S^D. Recall that *FI* reinforcement schedules demonstrate that time correlated in this way with reinforcement contingencies comes to control behavior quite effectively.

2. In this procedure, the reinforcement contingencies in S^D are *crf*. In *crf* each of a series of responses is reinforced and *rate* of response becomes a meaningless measure. For all practical purposes, the rate in *crf* is determined entirely by how long it takes the animal to eat each peanut. Thus, any changes that might occur in response strength during S^D go undetected.

3. The monkey could close its eyes, never look at the lights, and still make a good discrimination by just responding sporadically. The first occurrence of a reinforcement for a sporadic response would signal that all further responses would then be reinforced for a while. Similarly the first failure of a response to be reinforced would signal that all further responses would be extinguished for a while. Thus the animal could base a discrimination on the presence or absence of reinforcement rather than on the presence or absence of the green light.

Herrick, Myers, and Korotkin (1959) employed an instructive procedure with rat subjects in studying discrimination between randomly alternating light (S^D) and dark (S^Δ) periods. To avoid fault 1 they used variable-length S^Δ periods (30, 60, or 90 sec). To avoid fault 2, and obtain a meaningful response-rate measure during the formation of the discrimination, they used *VI* 30-sec reinforcement in S^D. The *VI* schedule in S^D also precluded a discrimination based on reinforcement or non-reinforcement (fault 3) since (i) failure to be reinforced did not necessarily signal S^Δ, and (ii) the obtaining of a reinforcement did not signal that subsequent responses would necessarily be reinforced.

To help simplify inspection of the behavioral process that results from a discrimination procedure of this sort, responses in S^D and responses in

S^Δ may be recorded on separate cumulative recorders. The S^D recorder runs only while S^D is in effect, and the S^Δ recorder runs only in S^Δ. Figure 10–1 shows one rat's records of lever pressing from sessions 1, 6, 11, 21, and 40 on Herrick, Myers, and Korotkin's procedure. The

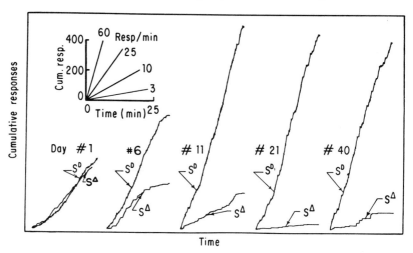

Figure 10–1. Sample daily records of one rat during samples of forty days of discrimination training (Herrick, Myers, and Korotkin, 1959).

reinforced response was lever pressing. Day 1 is essentially a generalization test: the rat had been trained originally in S^D and then on day 1, S^Δ was introduced for the first time in alternation with S^D. Figure 10–1 indicates that S^D and S^Δ rates were nearly identical on day 1; complete generalization of response rate from S^D to S^Δ occurred (see Fig. 9–10 for a comparable case). As discrimination training was continued, however, the S^D and S^Δ rates drew apart. S^D slope appears to increase, and S^Δ slope continues to decrease throughout the 40 days of the discrimination procedure.

Several remarks are in order concerning the two behavioral processes associated with S^D and S^Δ, respectively. The increase in S^D rate is probably an example of the fact that exposure to an interval schedule after *crf* always initiates, among other things, a gradual increase in rate (for example, see the *RI* curves of Fig. 7–4, p. 144) that eventually reaches an asymptote. Russell (1960) has shown that if 19 sessions of *VI* training are given in S^D *prior* to commencing discrimination training, then no increase in S^D rate is seen during the discrimination proper. The S^D rate change seen in Fig. 10–1 is evidently not peculiar to the discrimination procedure.

The second behavioral change, the decline in S^Δ rate, is merely the familiar process of extinction. In S^Δ, lever pressing is never reinforced and so is being continuously extinguished. The extinction process in S^Δ is undoubtedly prolonged because of generalization effects resulting from the concurrent maintenance of lever-pressing strength in S^D. The response strength incurred in S^D spreads to S^Δ by the usual principles of generalization. Therefore the discrimination process, a procedure in which a response is reinforced under one stimulus (S^D) and not under another (S^Δ), is represented by the gradual drawing apart of the strengths of response in the two stimulus situations.

To measure the state of the discrimination process at any given time, a useful compound variable can be formed, made up of both S^D and S^Δ rates. We may define the *discrimination index* (I_D) as

$$I_D = \frac{S^D \text{ rate}}{S^D \text{ rate } + S^\Delta \text{ rate}}$$

Evidently when S^D rate $= S^\Delta$ rate $= k$ (that is, when response strength generalizes completely from S^D to S^Δ), the index becomes

$$I_D = \frac{k}{2k} = \frac{1}{2}$$

As discrimination progresses, S^Δ rate approaches operant level ($\rightarrow 0$) and S^D rate remains constant (k), or approximately so, and the index approaches

$$I_D = \frac{k}{k} = 1$$

Thus the useful range of the discrimination index is from 0.5 (perfect generalization, no discrimination) to 1.0 (perfect discrimination, no generalization). Intermediate values indicate intermediate degrees of discrimination. Values less than 0.5, if reliable, would indicate a rate preference for the S^Δ condition.

Compound variables like the discrimination index play an important role in scientific theory construction. The physicist defines the *density* of a substance to be equal to its mass per unit volume ($D = m/v$). The average velocity of a moving body is the ratio of the distance that the body travels to the period of time ($V = d/t$). Rate of response, the number of response instances/time, is itself a compound variable, since it involves the ratio of two simpler variables. The rationale for forming a compound variable is purely practical. If the laws that relate the compound variable to certain other variables in the science are simpler and more informative than those for the component variables taken singly, then the compound variable is said to be "useful." In the case of the discrimination index it seems clear that neither the S^D rate nor the S^Δ rate alone would give a good approximation to our concept of discrimination. On the other hand, some ratio of these two rates would seem to be closely related to discrimination concepts, and we may well expect that the ratio will turn out to be "useful" in the formal sense described. For example, Fig. 10–2 shows that in Herrick, Myers, and Korotkin's study, the index is in fact lawfully related to the number of sessions of discrimination training. We are led to infer from Fig. 10–2 that the discrimination process is virtually complete by session 15, at which time the index seems to have reached its asymptote ($I_D \approx 0.93$).

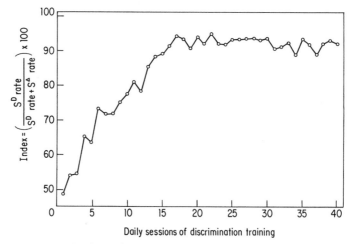

Figure 10–2. *Changes in the discrimination index over forty sessions of discrimination training of a light-dark discrimination (after Herrick, Myers, and Korotkin, 1959).*

The discrimination we have illustrated is termed "simple" because it involves the minimum number of responses (one) and the minimum number of different stimulus conditions (two) necessary to demonstrate a discrimination. Despite its simplicity, such a procedure has proven useful in assessing discriminative abilities and limitations in animals. Pfaffman, Goff, and Bare (1958) have used the technique to measure the rat's ability to detect odors. In S^Δ a controlled concentration of odorant gas was released into the rat's Skinner box. In S^D, no odorant was present. Moreover, in S^D lever presses were intermittently reinforced with food, whereas in S^Δ reinforcement was withheld. High values of the discrimination index would indicate that the rat was discriminating the experimentally introduced gas. Values of the index near 0.5 would indicate that little or no discrimination was being made. With the index at 0.5 the rat may be said to fail to detect any odor since the animal is then responding in the S^Δ situation as though gas were absent. That is, its S^Δ rate is the same as its S^D rate. The *threshold* for odorant detection may be defined as that concentration of odorant which produces a value of the discrimination index reliably greater than 0.5. By gradually decreasing the concentration of a gas until I_D has fallen to where it is no longer significantly different from 0.5, the threshold (minimum detectable value) of any experimentally introduced odorant may be determined (Goff, 1961).

EXERCISE 7.

Design an experiment to determine the weakest sound that a chimpanzee can hear. Use only a single response class and be sure not to incur any of the three listed faults.

10.2 THE DISCRIMINATION PARADIGM

The prototype of all discriminations is the paradigm defined by the simplest case. We have the

GIVEN: 1. One response class
           2. Two stimulus conditions
PROCEDURE: Reinforce the response in one of the stimulus conditions (S^D) and extinguish the response in the other stimulus condition (S^Δ)
PROCESS: The response strengths in S^D and S^Δ gradually draw apart, with a prolonged extinction process taking place in S^Δ
RESULT: The organism comes to respond in S^D and not in S^Δ

In notating the discrimination procedure, we desire to express the notion that a different contingency exists under S^D than under S^Δ.

$$\left[\begin{array}{l} S^D \\ R \overset{p}{\to} S^+ \\ \scriptstyle 1 \end{array} \right.$$

and   [10.1]

$$\left[\begin{array}{l} S^\Delta \\ R \not\to \\ \scriptstyle 2a \end{array} \right. \quad \text{or} \quad \left[\begin{array}{l} S^\Delta \\ \\ \scriptstyle 2b \end{array} \right.$$

In Diagram [10.1] contingency 1 is read: "in the presence of S^D, *if* R, *then* sometimes S^+ is produced." Contingencies 2a and 2b (both are ways of representing the same thing) are read: "in the presence of S^Δ, *if* R, *then* no environmental change." Contingency 2*b* is perhaps read more conveniently as "in S^Δ no responses are reinforced." Evidently in terms of the notation the simple discrimination procedure may be defined as the alternation of the two kinds of contingencies and their associated stimuli, as represented by brackets 1 and 2 of [10.1].

10.3 TWO STIMULUS CONDITIONS, TWO RESPONSE CLASSES

Over the years, psychologists have devised a variety of apparatus to test the discriminative capacities of animals. Many of these involve at least two responses, and at least two stimulus conditions. A popular apparatus at one time was Lashley's jumping stand (Fig. 10–3). In

Figure 10–3. One form of Lashley's jumping stand for testing discriminative reactions of rats (after Lashley, 1938, from Munn, 1950).

this apparatus, a hungry rat standing on an elevated platform faces windows on his right and left which are covered by cardboard cards on which designs have been drawn. In preliminary training, the elevated platform is close to the windows, both of which are open, the cards having been removed. The rat has only to step from the platform through either window to reach food located at the rear of the apparatus. When the rat has eaten, it may be picked up and returned to the elevated platform for another trial. Gradually the jumping stand is moved further away from the windows until a true jump response has been successively approximated (shaped). Then the cards that will be used as discriminative stimuli are gradually inserted to cover the windows, at first partially, and then completely. One card (sometimes called the + card) will be supported lightly by a spring that releases it if the rat jumps against it; after the jump, the rat finds itself facing a delicious bowl of bran mash. The other card (sometimes called the − card) is locked in place, however, so that if the rat jumps against it, the animal is repelled into the net below. This consequence serves as punishment for that jump, in addition to providing an extinction trial.

Consider an experiment in which two cards are used:

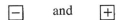

These cards will be randomly alternated from side to side on successive trials, and whichever window contains 🞧 will always be unlocked, while whichever window contains the ⊟ window will always be locked. The rat will adjust to a procedure of this sort in a few dozen trials, as shown by a gradual increase from 0.5 to 1.0 in the probability of responses to the correct card.

Describing the contingencies entailed in such discriminations is not difficult; the key is first to evaluate all possible stimulus situations. The individual cards are *not* stimuli in and of themselves. Their particular pattern and relative positions only help define the stimulus situation at any time. In the present example, prior to jumping, there are two possible stimulus situations:

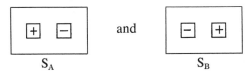

Since the experimenter will endeavor to hold every other feature in the rat's environment constant from trial to trial, we do not bother to include these constant features in the description of the two stimulus situations. Let us call the two situations S_A and S_B. If we ignore the net, the contingencies are

$$\begin{array}{c}\overline{\left|\begin{array}{l}S_A\\R_L \rightarrow S^+\\R_R \nrightarrow\end{array}\right.} \quad \text{and} \quad \overline{\left|\begin{array}{l}S_B\\R_L \nrightarrow\\R_R \rightarrow S^+\end{array}\right.}\end{array} \qquad [10.2]$$

where R_L = left jump

R_R = right jump

S^+ = food

Comparison of the notations for the simple discrimination of [10.1] and the present case shown in [10.2] leads to the conclusion that [10.2] is a double discrimination. If we consider the relation of only one response at a time to food reinforcement, we see that [10.2] resembles [10.1] closely, but instead of a null contingency prevailing in one of the two situations, we have a second contingency acting in conjunction with a second response class. Diagram [10.2] confirms that the terms S^D and S^Δ are always *relative* to a given response, and must therefore be carefully qualified when they are used outside of the simple paradigm of [10.1]. Here, in [10.2] for example, we might reasonably say that S_A is the S^D for jumping left as well as the S^Δ for jumping right. Equally, S_B is the S^D for R_R and the S^Δ for R_L. In general, when referring to any particular situation as an S^D or S^Δ, the response class for which it so serves should be stated or at least implied by the context.

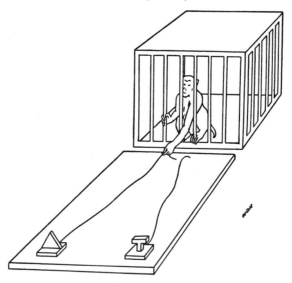

Figure 10–4. Pull-in apparatus for monkeys. One of the blocks attached to a string will have food hidden behind it (Harlow, 1948).

Although the specific design of the discrimination apparatus of the two response, two stimulus type will vary for different species of animals, depending on their response capabilities, the discrimination contingencies invariably take the general form of [10.2]. Monkeys, chimpanzees, baboons, and children lend themselves conveniently to apparatus that requires manipulative responses (see Fig. 10–4). The fact that the organism's response may be directed towards the physical aspect of the environment along which the discriminative stimulus may happen to be defined should not be permitted to distract attention from the common contingencies in all discriminations. In section 10.1, we examined an experiment in which rats pressed a bar when a light was present, but at some cost in experimental convenience they might just as well have been required to run towards the light. In Fig. 10–4, the animal's behavior is directed "towards" one of the blocks, and furthermore certain stimulus properties associated with the blocks themselves control this responding. But in both cases the correlation of different behaviors with different environments marks them as discriminations.

10.4 _m_ STIMULUS CONDITIONS, _n_ RESPONSE CLASSES

Increasing the number of discriminative stimuli used increases the complexity of the discrimination. Consider a case in which a single positive card ⊞, and two negative cards, ⊟ and ⊡, may appear. The possible situations prior to responding (assuming that in each situation one and only one response can be reinforced) are

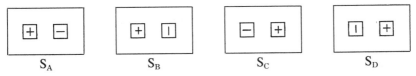

S_A S_B S_C S_D

In S_A and S_B jumping left will be reinforced, while in S_C and S_D jumping right will be reinforced. Using additional negative and/or positive cards creates still more situations, and the degree of complexity of the discrimination might be said to increase correspondingly.

Discriminations may be complicated further by specifying contingencies for more than just one or two response classes. In the Wisconsin General Text Apparatus (shown in Fig. 10–5), right, left, and center reaching movements are frequently specified. Food may be placed in shallow wells located under any of three objects. The arrangement of these objects serves to define discriminative stimuli. If the monkey is

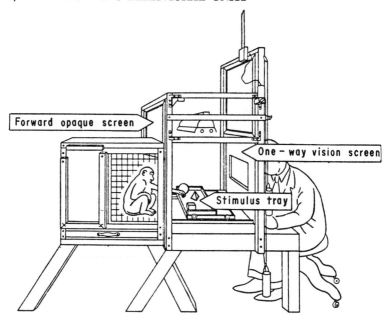

Figure 10–5. The Wisconsin General Test Apparatus. The experimenter's responses are confined to presenting and retracting the stimulus tray, shuffling the objects on the tray, and placing food in wells under some blocks. The subject's responses are confined to pushing aside any one block and picking up the food (if any) in the food well under the displaced block (after Harlow, 1949).

presented with the task of choosing a cube rather than a pyramid or a sphere, and assuming that each object must be present on each trial, then the possible stimulus situations are

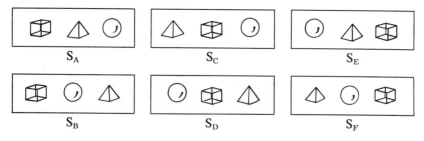

arranged in three groups, depending on the spatial location of the cube.

It should be apparent that as the number of specified responses and stimuli increases, discriminations of any degree of complexity desired may be studied in the laboratory.

10.5 CONTINUOUS CHANGES IN BEHAVIOR AS A FUNCTION OF CONTINUOUS CHANGES IN A STIMULUS DIMENSION

In correctly picking up an object from any location on a table, we engage in a discrimination that cannot easily be described by a fixed number of responses, in relation to a fixed number of discriminative stimuli. For every position on the table, one and only one response set is optimally reinforced. But there are many possible positions. As an approximation, we might represent a table as divided into a checkerboard of i rows and j columns, and in that way artificially designate a limited number of response classes and possible discriminative stimuli (see Fig. 10–6). Suppose we locate each of the possible discriminative stimulus classes uniquely by its row number (i) and its column number (j).

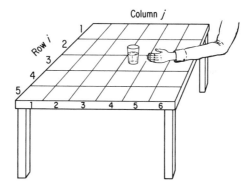

Figure 10–6

Then the object currently rests at row 3 and column 4. The discriminative stimulus class representing that condition is $S_{3,4}$, and the class of reaching movements that will be reinforced by contact with the object is correspondingly denoted as $R_{3,4}$. This analysis may be generalized as the contingency

$$\left.\begin{array}{c} S_{i,j} \\ R_{i,j} \end{array}\right| \to S^+ \tag{10.3}$$

where S = object at position i,j
R = reaching movement
S^+ = contact with object
i = the row number
j = the column number

Since i and j are variable, Diagram [10.3] represents an example of the functional representation of section 6.14. The spatial coordinates of the reinforced response class are a continuous function of the spatial coordinates of the stimulus object. In the present example, the angle and extent of the reaching-out response depends upon the spatial position of the object. The function is complicated, but there is no reason to suspect that the basic discrimination procedure used in every other section of this chapter is not the method for forming such a discrimination, or rather, set of discriminations. Reaches of given values of angle and extent falling with certain small limits are reinforced only when the object is in a certain position relative to the organism. Reaches whose values of angle and extent deviate from these limits are not reinforced. (One "misses" the object.) Such a past history and the subsequent control over behavior that it imparts to spatial position is immediately apparent when we "grope" for a flashlight in the dark, or when we search for a pencil dropped under a table out of sight.

The behavior involved in an operator's "tracking" a moving target is a more sophisticated example of such discriminations. In steering a car or aiming a gun at a rapidly moving object, a set of responses is required which must vary continuously with constantly changing stimulus conditions. However complex such discriminations may be, they are acquired through a history of appropriate reinforcement contingencies. Project ORCON (ORganic CONtrol), the outgrowth of a World War II research project, is illustrative of the discriminative subtleties that may be imparted to an organism as undistinguished as the pigeon. The goal of ORCON was to train pigeons to guide missiles to selected targets (Skinner, 1960). The birds were mounted in the nose cone of a missile, facing a screen on which was projected the simulated image of a possible enemy target. Harnessed in special jackets, the birds were immobilized except for their neck and head. A gold electrode covered the tip of each bird's beak. As the screen on which the bird had been trained to peck was made of a semi-conducting material, the exact location of pecks could be sensed by an electronic circuit in the missile. The information thus obtained was to be used to steer the missile.

During training, reinforcement was made contingent upon pecking only at the center of a selected target. Since a missile moving at speeds in excess of 600 mph would rapidly move the target off the screen should the bird pause for more than a few seconds, an intermittent schedule was used, maintaining a high rate of pecking. Some frames from a simulated approach are shown in Fig. 10–7. The target comes into view at the top and the bird begins pecking. The animal continues to hold the missile on course for several minutes, as shown in the next three frames. The birds were successfully trained to ignore spurious signals appearing

Figure 10–7. Frames from a simulated missile approach to strategic target. A pigeon's pecking is providing the control signal (from Swartz, 1963, after Skinner, 1960).

on their screens, such as anti-aircraft flak and clouds, and to close course on only one of several particular strategic targets which might come into view.

10.6 DISCRIMINATION WITHOUT S$^\Delta$ RESPONDING

In early work with the simple discrimination procedure, Skinner (1938) reported that the process of discrimination was made much more rapid if the discrimination procedure was instituted simultaneously with original strengthening of the operant. In certain dramatic cases Skinner was able to show that rats could form a light-dark discrimination immediately.

The following explanation is offered to account for this effect. A discrimination *process* such as that described in section 10.1 is prolonged, mainly due to the extinction process that must take place in S$^\Delta$. But one of the principal variables affecting the extent of any extinction process is the number of reinforcements obtained in acquisition (see section 5.9). If few reinforcements are given prior to extinction, the extinction process will be rapid. In discrimination training, responding in S$^\Delta$ is due to the generalization of strengthening from S^D. The *gradient* of generalization implies that the potential S$^\Delta$ responding generated by acquisition will be less than or equal to that established at S^D. In this analysis, a hypothetical family of generalization gradients such as those in Fig. 10–8 is assumed. The parameter of Fig. 10–8 is the number of strengthening reinforcements during acquisition. Notice that the fewer strengthening reinforcements administered, the closer S$^\Delta$ can be to S^D without incurring any strength by generalization.

In Skinner's procedure, discrimination training commenced with a light (S^D) present. The first operant-level bar press that was emitted was reinforced, and S^D was immediately replaced with a 5-min dark period (S$^\Delta$). After the 5-min S$^\Delta$ period, S^D was reinstated and again the first emitted response reinforced, followed by the onset of S$^\Delta$ and its extinction contingencies. This cycle was repeated throughout discrimination training. Under these conditions, generalization to S$^\Delta$ is negligible, so there is little or nothing to extinguish in its presence. Because S$^\Delta$ responding is absent in the acquisition of such discriminations they are appropriately called "errorless."

H. S. Terrace (1963a, b) has extended this technique to demonstrate errorless discriminations between discriminative stimulus pairs very close together on the generalization gradient. In Terrace's work the principle of minimal initial strengthening is combined with a technique of using initially disparate stimuli as S^D and S$^\Delta$, and then progressively

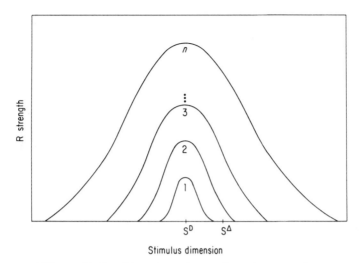

R strength

S^D   S^Δ

Stimulus dimension

Figure 10–8. Hypothetical family of generalization gradients with the parameter of number of original strengthening reinforcements. Each curve represents a different number of training S^D reinforcements from 1, 2, 3, . . . to n.

reducing the physical differences between them. Discrimination training is first begun with an S^Δ remote enough from the S^D to preclude generalization (see Fig. 10–8). As discrimination training progresses, the differences between S^D and S^Δ are gradually reduced by making S^Δ more and more similar to S^D. This amounts to bringing S^Δ closer and closer to S^D on their common stimulus dimensions.

In one of Terrace's procedures, key pecking at a red disk was shaped and given a few reinforcements. A discrimination between red (S^D) and green (S^Δ) was established with virtually no pecking in S^Δ by the following method:

> The key-peck is conditioned to a red key-light (S^D). Following each of the first five reinforcements the key-light was always red. After the fifth reinforcement the key was darkened for 2 sec. after which the red light came on again. Following the next 20 reinforcements the (dark) interval was progressively lengthened until a maximum interval of 30 sec. with a mean of 15 sec. was achieved. At this point, S^Δ was introduced. Initially, S^Δ was a faint green light of 1 sec. duration. During successive S^Δ trials the duration and intensity of S^Δ was progressively increased until the duration of S^Δ was 5 sec. and the brightnesses of S^D and S^Δ were equal (Terrace, 1963b, p. 224).

The *minimal S^D strengthening, progressive reduction of $S^D - S^\Delta$ differences* method of discrimination training seems to have a number of merits. In the first place, it appears that such discriminations are formed far more quickly than those using the procedures of sections 10.1–10.5. Second, the asymptotic value of I_D is probably closer to 1.0 with this technique. Third, since few or no responses ever occur in S^Δ, the emotional effects characteristic of extinction are lacking in these errorless discriminations. The disturbances that characterize these emotional effects (discussed more fully in Chapter 18) are generally undesirable in the everyday learning of skills and discriminations. Hence the errorless method of discrimination training may find important uses in educational technology.

10.7 DISCRIMINATIVE REACTION TIMES

The $S^D - S^\Delta$ history characteristic of discrimination training establishes stimulus control over operants. As S^D comes progressively to control its operant, the time between S^D onset and the occurrence of the operant declines. This time, analogous to reflex $S_2 \rightarrow R_2$ latency, is called the discriminative *reaction time* (*RT*). Under certain conditions the discriminative *RT* may be an index of the strength of a response, or of the state of a discrimination process. During $S^D - S^\Delta$ training of the sort described in sections 10.1 and 10.2, *RT* declines progressively, approaching—with the rat—an asymptote of about 1 sec.

There exists a large literature on asymptotic human discrimination *RT*'s as they are related to complexity of the stimulus situation, number of possible contingencies, difficulty in discriminating S^D from S^Δ, intensity of S^D, drug administrations, etc. The discriminative *RT* in applying brakes when the situation of an impending accident occurs has been of some interest to road safety investigators. As is well known, this *RT* can vary from a small fraction of a second to several seconds, depending on such factors as the concentration of alcohol in the blood, number of hours of previous driving, and presence or absence of caffeine in the blood. In the laboratory, reaction times are often measured by instructing a human subject to press a telegraph key as quickly as he can, after receiving a signal. Reaction times of the order of small fractions of a second (200–500 msec) are obtained by such a procedure, particularly if a "get ready" signal precedes the actual "respond" signal.

In everyday behavior, most of our responses are not emitted under such favorable conditions as those of the laboratory; and the demand for high-speed reactions is made only occasionally, as in athletics, military combat, and the control of such machines as the airplane and the automobile. For several reasons, the values reached in human reaction time experiments are seldom approximated, even in these pursuits. Warning signals are often lacking; one may not know from what direction the stimulus is coming; one is usually engaged in doing something else when the response is suddenly demanded; the response may involve the action of large, rather than small muscle groups; the stimulus may be very weak, or so strong as to cause 'freezing'; and so on. Thus, a group of football players in uniform may average as much as 400 millisec. in getting off a scrimmage line at an auditory signal; and the reaction time of automobile drivers may rise to several seconds when an impending accident requires a shift of the foot from gas pedal to brake (Keller and Schoenfeld, 1950, p. 146).

10.8 THE IMPLICATIONS OF OPERANT STIMULUS CONTROL

Proceeding from the simple to the complex, we have attempted to show the methods by which the state of the immediate environment comes to control operant responding. Operants under such control are said to be *discriminative operants*. When the rat jumps to the correct card, when the monkey pulls in the correct string, when the child picks up an object, and when we apply the brakes at a red stop-light, the particular response emitted is under powerful stimulus control. It is, therefore, a discriminative operant and its stimulus control will depend, in each case, on a prior history with the kinds of reinforcement contingencies described in sections 10.1 to 10.5.

The nature of operant stimulus control is such that not only the gross occurrence of a response, but certain properties of a response as well, can come to be controlled by the stimulus, given a particular reinforcement history. In the control of respondents by elicitors, response properties such as magnitude, duration, and latency are a fixed function of the elicitor, being determined by the laws of the reflex. In operant stimulus control, there is no single relation between S^D intensity and response properties such as duration and RT. For example, the reinforced response magnitude can be, within wide limits, whatever the contingencies specify it to be. Thus, we *could* build a discriminative operant that would mimic the laws of the reflex. By appropriately reinforcing any given response, lever pressing or the word "please," for example, in the presence of a light or a tone, for example, the force of that reinforced response could be differentiated to be proportional to the intensity of the prevailing stimulus. We may represent this, in notation, as

$$\begin{bmatrix} R_y \\ S_x \end{bmatrix} \to S^+ \qquad [10.4]$$

where y is the force of the response and x the intensity of the stimulus, and y is defined to be proportional to x. An observer, watching an organism so trained, but who did not know its history with the contingencies of [10.4], might be inclined to call the observed response, R_y, a respondent. Note that his mistake stems from neglecting to uncover the relevant past history of this organism. To avoid such misinterpretations, caution must always be observed when considering non-laboratory examples of everyday behavior. Often the relevant past history cannot be discovered. Our own discriminative behavior, for example, is so familiar, so automatic, that we are likely to forget how it was acquired.

As an instructive exercise, consider a contingency rule in which the *inverse* of the law of reflex magnitude would be obtained, by making the y of [10.4] $= 1/x$. The result now would be to create an R whose magnitude would be an inverse function of the intensity of the discriminative stimulus in which it occurred. Perhaps it is clear from this example why magnitude of response is not an appropriate measure of operant strengthening. Response magnitude can be shaped arbitrarily, depending on the reinforcement contingencies.

Once an operant discrimination of any sort has been formed, controlling the occurrence of S^D is a way of controlling the occurrence of the response. After 40 sessions of discrimination training, in order to get rats like those of Herrick, Myers, and Korotkin to press a lever, we need only present the light. Similarly, to get rats like those of Pfaffman, Gore, and Bare to press the lever we need only flush the odorant from their chamber and present fresh air. To get a man to move we ask him to move. In all these cases, responding is under the control of a prior stimulus (the light, the fresh air, or the request), but the relationship of the response to the stimulus differs markedly from that of the respondent to its elicitor. In the first place, the laws of the reflex fail to hold between the S^D and its R. Increases in the intensity of S^D would, if anything, decrease the probability of R according to the principle of generalization. (Try shouting your requests at people.) In the second place, the relation between S^D and R *depends* upon the discrimination history. This history can hardly be ignored, for without it, an S^D could not obtain its status as a controlling variable of behavior. To distinguish between the kind of control that elicitors have over their respondents, and the kind of control that S^Ds have over their operants, we say that an S^D *sets the occasion for* a response; that is, the occasion is set for the emission of R to produce reinforcement.

10.9 SIGNIFICANCE OF DIFFERENCES BETWEEN TWO MEANS

There are times when behavior in S^D and S^Δ is so similar that ascertaining the presence or absence of differential responding, the *sine qua non* of a discrimination, may be difficult. Very similar S^D and S^Δ responding may occur when the organism has not acquired appropriate observing behavior, when S^D and S^Δ are very similar, when distracting influences are present, and so forth. If the differences between S^D and S^Δ response rates are slight, the experimenter may be unsure whether any discrimination at all is being made.

The problem of evaluating small numerical differences transcends discriminations. Whenever two sets of measurements of any sort are very similar, or there is a great deal of variability within them, so that they overlap appreciably, a need arises for an objective evaluation of the numerical differences that are observed. Are the observed differences, however slight, attributable to the subtle, but possibly theoretically important effects of different experimental conditions, or are they just the product of chance errors of measurement?

Consider the data in Table 10–1, plotted as histograms in Fig. 10–9. These data are 60 fictional response rates that might have been obtained in 60 1-min presentations of haphazardly alternating S^D and S^Δ conditions. If it aids to make the discussion concrete, regard S^D as 1-min periods of fresh air, S^Δ as 1-min periods of a very low concentration of odorant gas, and the fictional subject to be one of Pffafman, Gore, and Bare's rats discussed in section 10.1. The data from S^D and S^Δ conditions are conspicuously similar. There is a substantial overlap between the two histograms of Fig. 10–9. Many re-

Table 10–1

NUMBERS OF RESPONSES RECORDED IN 60 ONE-MIN PERIODS OF S^D AND S^Δ, HAPHAZARDLY ALTERNATING. S^Δ VALUES ARE IN BOLDFACE (DATA HYPOTHETICAL)

25	**21**	13	24	29	24	27	16	**24**	27
30	**25**	25	23	22	29	**23**	**26**	**26**	**25**
27	26	25	**0**	**15**	28	19	27	23	**19**
11	27	**11**	30	28	**19**	6	**26**	**6**	16
37	22	**25**	25	20	**32**	**23**	23	26	**24**
26	**25**	**8**	27	**20**	31	**21**	29	**22**	25

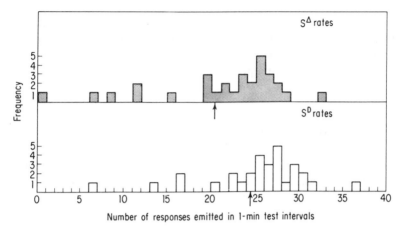

Figure 10–9.   Histograms of number of responses emit-ted in 30 one-min S^Δ periods (upper) and 30 one-min S^D periods (lower). Data fictional.

sponses are emitted in S^Δ; the discrimination between odorant and fresh air, if any, is marginal. Nevertheless, there are hints of a difference between S^D and S^Δ responding. The S^Δ distribution lies somewhat to the left of the S^D distribution; the S^Δ distribution contains the lowest rate (0 responses), whereas S^D contains the highest rate (36 responses); the modes of the two distributions are not identical; the mean of the S^Δ distribution is 20.7 responses/min, and that of the S^D distribution is 24.7 responses/min.

Are these differences in the two distributions the result of chance errors of measurement, or are they, in fact, significant indications of a slight discrimination? At this point, we shall find it helpful to recall a few pertinent features of the so-called normal curve, discussed in section 2.6, and reproduced in Fig. 10–10. In particular, we wish to recall that within plus or minus a certain number of standard deviation units, σ, from the center, lies a certain percentage of the measurements falling in the area under such a

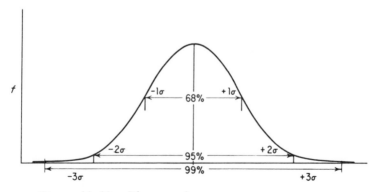

Figure 10–10.   The normal curve.

curve. To review, 68 per cent of the measurements lie in the area under the curve within $\pm 1\sigma$ from the central mean. An alternate way of expressing this property is to say that if we were sampling measurements at random from this normal distribution, the probability of getting a measurement that lies within this region would be 0.68, and the probability of getting a measurement that lies outside this region would be 0.32. Similarly, 95 per cent of the measurements lie within $\pm 2\sigma$ from the mean. Thus, the probability of a sample measurement lying outside this $\pm 2\sigma$ region is only 0.05.

Now suppose that our measurements of response rate in S^D and S^Δ in Fig. 10–9 represent sample measurements drawn from a population of tens of thousands and more potential measurements, and whose distribution would look rather like the normal curve in Fig. 10–10. That normal distribution would have a certain σ associated with it which would describe its variability due to errors of measurement. If we had that distribution available, and we were then given yet another single response-rate measurement about which we were told nothing except its value, and if we were subsequently asked whether it might have come from that distribution, we could give a meaningful answer in terms of probabilities. We need merely see by how many σ units this new measurement deviates from the mean of the normal distribution and then state the probability that it did come from it. Suppose the single measurement happened to lie in the region under the curve just outside the boundary line of exactly 2σ above the mean; then the probability is only 0.05 that it might have come from this distribution, because 0.95 (95 per cent) of the values from this distribution will lie in the region between $\pm 2\sigma$, and only 0.05 (5 per cent) will lie outside it. This statement does not say that the maverick measurement did not come from this distribution; it might have. It just says that it was somewhat unlikely to have come from it.

Our present problem has some elements in common with evaluating a single new measurement in reference to a known distribution. In evaluating our discrimination data we have not just a comparison of one measurement with a distribution of measurements but a comparison of two separate distributions (S^D and S^Δ) of measurements. What we should like to know is whether this S^Δ distribution differs systematically, however slightly, from this S^D distribution.

A profitable way to approach this problem is to inquire whether the *means* of the two distributions differ reliably from one another. In other words, does the difference of 4.0 between 20.7 and 24.7 represent merely chance fluctuations in moment-to-moment rate of responding that happened to get "caught" in our arbitrary partitioning of the session into "S^D" and "S^Δ" periods and, so far as the rat is concerned, S^D and S^Δ constitute identical treatments? Or, is this difference of 4.0 the result of S^D conditions actually having a different effect from S^Δ on tendency to respond?

A laborious way of determining the more plausible interpretation would be to run many more additional and identical sessions of our experiment, but using a value for S^Δ that we know to be too close to S^D to be discriminably different from it (for example, $S^D = S^\Delta$), so that any differences in S^D and S^Δ rates would *have* to be due to chance alone. These additional sessions would give us a host of new S^D and S^Δ response rate means. We could subtract the S^D mean from the S^Δ mean for session 1 and get a difference; we could subtract the S^D mean from the S^Δ mean for session 2 and get yet another difference; and so on, for all the sessions we had the patience to run.

We would end up with a set of numbers, differences between S^D and S^Δ means. We could plot a distribution of these differences between means (statisticians assure us it will turn out to be normal) and calculate its standard deviation, the sigma of the differences between sample means, σ_{M_d}. Note that this distribution of differences between sample means ought to center about zero if, in holding our experimental conditions constant from session to session, no discrimination was possible between S^D and S^Δ. The observed differences between means obtained from session to session would in that case be just those resulting from fluctuations in responding due to uncontrolled, but presumably non-systematic influences which are as likely to be positive as negative at any given moment. Over the long run they would cancel each other out, leaving us an average difference between means of zero.

Once in possession of this distribution of differences between mean response rates during periods of undiscriminable S^D and S^Δ, we would be in a position to compare our present observed value of 4.0 with that distribution of chance differences between means to see whether 4.0 lies further than $2\sigma_{M_d}$ units from the center at zero. The method would be the same as the method by which we compared a single measurement with a known distribution.

In fact, it is impractical and uneconomical to repeat such control experiments enough times to obtain a fair estimate of what the distribution of differences between sample means would look like in the case where we had arranged in advance that the samples could not conceivably differ except by chance. In practice, we may avail ourselves of a derivation from mathematical statistics showing that an estimate of that critical standard deviation, σ_{M_d}, can be obtained with a bit of arithmetic applied to our original 30 S^D and 30 S^Δ measures.

What we have to do is first calculate the standard deviation of the set of 30 observed S^D rates and the standard deviation of the set of 30 observed S^Δ rates from the data of Table 10–1. We then combine these two standard deviations and obtain a pooled standard deviation (call it σ_D to distinguish it from other standard deviations) which for the data of Table 10–1 turns out to be $= 9.15$. It is at this point that we apply a statistical formula, the origin of which need not concern us, to obtain an estimate of σ_{M_d}, the standard deviation of the differences between means of S^D responding that we would expect to obtain if we repeated the experiment over many sessions. The formula states that σ_{M_d} is estimated by $\sigma_D/\sqrt{N}$, where N is the number of pairs of measurements we happen to have; in this case, 30. The result, $9.15/\sqrt{30} = 1.67$, can be put to use to determine the probability that our particular observed mean difference, 4.0, arose only by chance errors involved in measuring S^D response rates.

Evidently, 4.0 is greater than two units of size 1.67. That is, our obtained difference, $+4.00$, lies in the region $(+4.00/1.67)$ σ_{M_d} units above the mean of the theoretical distribution of differences to be expected by chance alone. (Remember that the mean of this theoretical distribution, for the case when there are only chance errors in S^D to perturb measurements of the S^D response rate, is zero.) Indeed, a difference as great as 4.0 between two S^D means would be expected to arise by chance less than 5 per cent of the time. An observed difference so unlikely to arise by chance errors of measurement is conventionally said to be statistically *significant*. It is in this technical sense that, when referring to numerical results in this text, the word significance is used.

We began with a certain small difference between two response rate distributions. By utilizing certain properties of normal curves, and certain derivations of mathematical statistics, we were able to find the probability that a difference between the means of two observed distributions of data would be as large as it was through chance errors alone. In so doing we assessed the statistical significance of our difference. The technique used was to find, first, a pooled standard deviation representing the variability in both S^D and S^Δ, and second, from that statistic to derive the σ_{M_d}. The method assumed that equal numbers of measurements were made in the two conditions. This restriction can be circumvented by the use of other, somewhat less intuitive, formulae found in any elementary statistics book. In general, the methods for estimating the probability that observed differences between two means are due to chance errors of measurement find use where (1) the differences observed are small, (2) the variability of measurements is high as a result of uncontrolled or uncontrollable perturbations, (3) time does not permit replication of the experiment over and over enough times to provide an empirical basis for estimating the reliability of the differences found between experimental conditions.

References for Chapter 10

Goff, W. R. Measurement of absolute olfactory sensitivity in rats. *Amer. J. Psychol.,* 1961, **74,** 384–393.

Harlow, H. F. Studying animal behavior. Chap. 12 in T. G. Andrews (Ed.), *Methods of psychology.* New York: Wiley, 1948.

Harlow, H. F. The formation of learning sets. *Psychol. Rev.,* 1949, **56,** 51–65.

Herrick, R. M., Myers, J. L., and Korotkin, A. L. Changes in S^D and S^Δ rates during the development of an operant discrimination. *J. comp. physiol. Psychol,* 1959, **52,** 359–363.

Keller, F. S., and Schoenfeld, W. N. *Principles of psychology.* New York: Appleton-Century-Crofts, 1950.

Lashley, K. S. The mechanism of vision XV. Preliminary studies of the rat's capacity for detail vision. *J. gen. Psychol.* 1938, **18,** 123–193.

Millenson, J. R. Random interval schedules of reinforcement. *J. exp. Anal. Behav.,* 1963 **6,** 437–443.

Munn, N. L. *Handbook of psychological research on the rat.* Boston: Houghton Mifflin, 1950.

Pfaffman, C., Goff, W. R., and Bare, J. K. An olfactometer for the rat. *Science,* 1958, **128,** 1007–1008.

Russell, I. S. Analysis of the responding during operant discrimination. Unpublished doctoral dissertation, Indiana Univer., 1960.

Skinner, B. F. *The behavior of organisms.* Chapter 5. New York: Appleton-Century, 1938.

Skinner, B. F. Pigeons in a pelican. *Amer. Psychol.,* 1960, **15,** 28–37.

Swartz, P. *Psychology the study of behavior.* Princeton: Van Nostrand, 1963.

Terrace, H. S. Discrimination learning with and without "errors." *J. exp. Anal. Behav.,* 1963a, **6,** 1–27.

Terrace, H. S. Errorless transfer of a discrimination across two continua. *J. exp. Anal. Behav.,* 1963b, **6,** 224–232.

Chapter 11 **ACQUIRED REINFORCERS**

▌T IS APPARENT FROM EVEN A CURSORY EXAMINATION of the world about us that some of the special consequences we have been calling reinforcers have a more natural or biological primacy than others. Few would dispute that food, water, and sex fall into a different—more "basic"—category than books, money, and automobiles. Yet organisms at one time or another work for all of these. We can distinguish between these two categories by the manner in which the organism comes to possess a reinforcement susceptibility. For each individual there exists a class of reinforcers whose powers are a biological consequence merely of the individual's membership in a certain species. These reinforcers are as much a property of the species as are the leopard's spots, the cat's fur, the dog's tail. Reinforcement susceptibilities which come built into the organism this way define the *primary* or unconditioned reinforcers; they are discussed in subsequent chapters under Motivation. For the present, we address ourselves to a second group of "secondary" reinforcers which appears more variable and less predictable from individual to individual than the primary set.

Money, cars, pencils, newspapers, prestige, honor, and the countless other arbitrary things that human beings work for constitute a vast source of reliable and potent reinforcers. But these things have no value for us at birth. Clearly, they must have *acquired* their capacity to reinforce at some time during each individual's past history. An individual past history is a prerequisite; witness the occasional adult for whom some of the conventional reinforcers seem to hold no value. Moreover, gold has little importance for a Trappist monk, primitive man would hardly have fought for a copy of the *New York Times,* not everybody likes Brahms.

Money, newsprint, and the works of particular composers lack the universal value of food, water, and sex, yet for any given individual their appeal may seem equally strong. As we show below, the acquired reinforcers get their power to strengthen and maintain behavior by virtue of a past history of association with primary reinforcers. It is their dependence upon this *conditional* history for their power to reinforce that gives them the name of *conditioned reinforcers*.

Conditioned reinforcers appear to be especially pervasive in the maintenance of human behavior; indeed, they are tied up with the very notion of human culture. Nevertheless, they are easily cultivated with animal subjects in the laboratory, where the exact conditions of their establishment and the precise measurement of their relative strengths can be quantitatively studied.

11.1 THE REINFORCING PROPERTIES OF POSITIVE DISCRIMINATIVE STIMULI

Prior to strengthening the lever-press response of a hungry rat or the disk peck of a hungry pigeon, care is generally taken to precede each instance of food delivery with a brief click and a light flash emanating from the place where food is delivered. Since food is only available following the click-light combination, this procedure suffices to make the click-light a positive discriminative stimulus (S^D) for the food-tray approach response. But in addition to making the click-light situation an S^D, an inevitable by-product of this discrimination procedure is to give the click and light the power to reinforce. This power is exploited by permitting lever pressing or disk pecking to produce the S^D. In this way, more immediate special consequences can be provided for the response than is possible with food itself. It takes some time for the rat to move from the bar to the food tray and eat; but the click-light stimulus may reach it before it has even lifted its paws from the bar. This kind of immediate reinforcement, provided by the click-light secondary reinforcer, is essential to produce rapid operant-strengthening (see Fig. 4–2).

The procedure for demonstrating the reinforcing power of the click-light combination may be represented as a two-phase notation: (1) Establish the click-light as an S^D by the usual discrimination method:

$$\left[\begin{matrix} S^\Delta \\ R_1 \end{matrix}\right. \nrightarrow \quad \text{and} \quad \left[\begin{matrix} S^D \\ R_1 \end{matrix}\right. \rightarrow S^+$$

where S^D = click-light
  S^Δ = absence of click-light
  S^+ = food
  R_1 = approach tray

(2) Then, in S^Δ, permit a previously unstrengthened response, for instance, lever pressing, to produce the positive discriminative stimulus, S^D, at the same time withhold the final primary reinforcer.

$$
\begin{array}{ll}
\overline{S^\Delta} & \overline{S^D} \\
R_1 \nrightarrow & R_1 \nrightarrow \\
\underline{R_2} \longrightarrow & \\
\quad 2 & 1
\end{array}
\qquad\qquad [11.1]
$$

where R_2 = press lever

To test the effectiveness of the click-light S^D as an independent reinforcing agent, the primary reinforcer must be absent. As long as food occurs at the end of the sequence, strengthening of a new operant (in [11.1], lever pressing) may be due entirely to the action of the primary reinforcer; the click-light itself may be irrelevant.

It is apparent that, during the test of [11.1], extinction of the food-tray approach response will proceed concurrently with any strengthening effects the procedure might be exerting on the lever press. Yet the experimental result of [11.1] is unequivocal. The lever-press response, previously existing at a low operant-level rate, is quickly strengthened by the click-light S^D alone. The lever response is conditioned *despite the fact that no food is being presented,* and despite the fact that the tray response is simultaneously undergoing extinction. In Fig. 11–1, cumulative curves are shown for four rats on this procedure. For the first time in the rats' conditioning history, each lever press produced a special consequence—the S^D for food approach. During the time that Fig. 11–1 was recorded, food itself was never forthcoming. Compared with curves of strengthening by primary (for example, food) reinforcement, the curves are more variable and more negatively accelerated (see Fig. 4–2). From observation of the overall increase in rate of lever pressing seen in Fig. 11–1, however, there is no doubt that making the S^D contingent upon the lever press serves temporarily to condition the operant. The curves of strengthening by the click-light alone take the general shape of extinction curves. This is hardly surprising for, simultaneously with the conditioning of R_2 (lever press) by S^D, R_1 (tray approach) is being extinguished. Therefore S^D is concurrently losing its power to act as an S^D for R_1 and, by inference, its acquired reinforcing value as well. That loss is an inevitable consequence of testing for secondary reinforcement.

11.2 AMPLIFYING THE DURABILITY OF CONDITIONED REINFORCERS

The principle of acquired reinforcement was received enthusiastically by the early behaviorists who saw in it the key to the explanation of

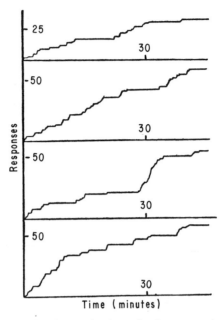

Figure 11–1. Strengthening of a lever-pressing operant in four hungry rats when the only reinforcement is the S^D that previously set the occasion for approaching the food tray (Skinner, 1938).

those complex social activities which, in man, seem to thrive in the absence of primary reinforcement. Conditioned reinforcement seemed a ready explanation for social behaviors such as gregariousness or co-operation, and social values such as the achievement of prestige, power, or wealth. But in the rush to extrapolate the laboratory concepts of conditioned reinforcement to the social field, it was rarely made clear that powerful experimental demonstrations of secondary reinforcement remained conspicuously absent. Skinner's (1938) curves (Fig. 11–1) were a genuine enough demonstration that S^D's do become secondary reinforcers. But the output of behavior sustained by the S^D as a conditioned reinforcer was on the order of some 50 responses over 45 min—a paltry yield indeed, certainly not a very convincing demonstration that the conditioned reinforcers of the laboratory might even remotely underlie the social incentives of human life. For some time, attempts by investigators, using runways, mazes, and levers, to produce more powerful secondary reinforcers, which would shape and sustain behavior over long periods without primary reinforcers, met with little success. It is only relatively recently that techniques have been discovered for amplifying the durability of conditioned reinforcers to a level where the experimental concept could reasonably be assigned a major role in a theory of human activity.

The ability to demonstrate acquired reinforcement in a convincing way awaited the development of intermittent reinforcement procedures, that is, schedules of reinforcement, and higher-order operant specifications. Intermittency plays two critical roles in amplifying the effects of conditioned reinforcers. (1) Used to schedule primary reinforcement (for example, food) for a discriminative operant in S^D — S^Δ training, it can build up a high resistance to extinction of the discriminative operant (R_1 in the chain of [11.1]). The method is simply to alternate the set of contingencies

$$\boxed{\begin{array}{l} S^D \\ R_1 \end{array}} \overset{p}{\to} S^+ \quad \text{and} \quad \boxed{\begin{array}{l} S^\Delta \\ R_1 \end{array}} \nrightarrow$$

The result is to confine the emission of R_1 to S^D and moreover, since contingency 2 is probabilistic, to develop a very strong potential resistance to extinction of R_1 in S^D. (2) Used in testing the reinforcing value of the S^D, an intermittency imposed between the new R to be conditioned and the contingent S^D conserves the power of the secondary reinforcer. The method is simply to let the new R produce S^D probabilistically, $R_2 \overset{p}{\to} S^D$; or alternately, incorporate R into a higher-order operant, $nR \to S^D$. A well-chosen intermittency here will not only conserve the power of S^D but will maintain a high rate of R_2 as well. The conservation of power of S^D in this procedure derives from its infrequency of occurrence. S^D will not lose its control over R_1 until a certain number of instances of R_1 have occurred (without reinforcement) in the presence of S^D. If S^D appears infrequently, R_1 has only infrequent opportunities to weaken.

In a variant of this method, used by D. W. Zimmerman (1957, 1959), hungry rats were first trained to run down a runway, obtaining food in a goal box at the end. A runway trial began when the rat was placed in the start box. A buzzer was briefly sounded, the door to the runway alley raised, and the rat allowed to run to the goal box. The reaction time (RT) between the buzzer's sounding and the response of entering the goal box was measured. So far this procedure is just

$$\boxed{\begin{array}{l} S^D \\ R_1 \end{array}} \longrightarrow S^+$$

where S^D = buzz in start box and door opened
   R_1 = run to goal box
   S^+ = food

When the RT had become asymptotically short (after about 30 trials), food was omitted on some trials; that is, the discriminative running operant was placed on a probabilistic reinforcement schedule:

$$\left[\begin{array}{l}\overline{S^D}\\R_1\end{array}\right. \xrightarrow{p} S^+$$

Over the next 60 trials, this probability was gradually lowered from 0.5 to about 0.2. That is, by the end of the 90 trials of runway training, only about one run in five ended with food. On the other four runs, the rat found an empty goal box. Yet the running *RT* to the buzzer remained short; the buzzer–door opening continued to act as an S^D for vigorous and speedy runway responding. The situation at this point is reminiscent of our own behavior in answering a ringing telephone. Though only a few of the calls may actually be directed to us, answering behavior remains (like the running behavior of Zimmerman's rats) at high strength.

Following these 90 trials of runway training, food was permanently removed and a lever installed in the start box. A trial began with the rat being placed in the start box as usual, but now the buzzer and door opening were made contingent solely upon lever pressing. Using the buzzer–door opening S^D as the only reinforcement, Zimmerman progressively shaped an *FR* operant of 15 lever presses over three 90-min sessions. During the following 11 sessions, *FR*-15 responding was maintained completely by the contingent S^D; meanwhile, on each trial, the subsequent runway behavior was slowly weakening due to its extinction. This stage is represented as

$$\left[\begin{array}{l}\overline{R_2}\\S^\Delta\end{array}\right._2 \longrightarrow \left[\begin{array}{l}\overline{S^D}\\R_1\end{array}\right._1 \not\longrightarrow \qquad\qquad [11.2]$$

where S^D = buzz in start box and door opened
$\quad$ S^Δ = no buzz in start box, door closed
$\quad$ R_1 = run to goal box
$\quad$ R_2 = 15 lever presses

Except for the differences in specific elements, the procedures of [11.2] and [11.1] are identical. Yet before the power of the conditioned reinforcer was depleted, Zimmerman's rats had emitted thousands of lever presses and continued working for 20 hr spaced over several sessions. Cumulative curves of lever pressing in the start box on sessions 1, 5, 11, and 14 are shown in Fig. 11–2. The shape of these curves indicates clearly that the use of the S^D in Zimmerman's procedure acted in a manner similar to primary reinforcement, in *generating and main-*

taining the characteristic effects of an *FR* response specification. Pauses followed by high rates of pressing are seen. As extinction continues, the pauses increase; yet when the organism responds, the entire *FR* operant is typically run off quickly and smoothly.

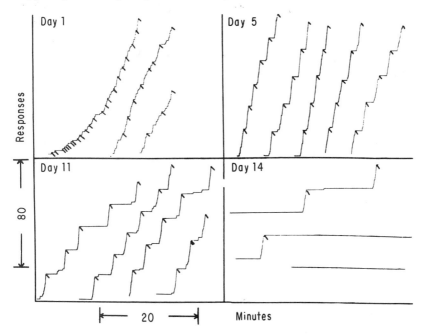

Figure 11–2. FR–15 bar-pressing based on conditioned reinforcement only. The pips represent buzzer and door opening. The recorder ran only while the animal was in the start box prior to producing the S^D (Zimmerman, 1959).

The performances sustained by Zimmerman's rats are to be contrasted with the behavior of Skinner's rats (Fig. 11–1), who emitted only about 50 presses for the S^D, and by the end of 45 min had ceased to respond. The difference in potency between the conditioned reinforcers in the two cases may be attributed to the double intermittency used by Zimmerman in training and testing. (1) The probabilistic connection between the discriminative operant (R_1) and its primary reinforcement (food) in Zimmerman's runway training greatly increased the resistance to extinction of the runway response to the S^D (buzzer–door opening). Thus the S^D itself remained in control of behavior for a much longer period of time than in [11.1] and therefore retained its conditioned reinforcing power far longer. Zimmerman's results imply that Skinner would have obtained more lever presses had he probabilistically reinforced tray approach to click-light. (2) By incorporating individual lever presses into a higher-order operant made up of 15 elements, the overall behavioral output, as measured by the number of lever-press elements emitted, was greatly increased (Weissman and Crossman, 1966). At the same time, the infrequency of occurrence of S^D conserved its discriminative function in controlling running.

Zimmerman's results suggest that, so long as the conditioned reinforcer remains potent, the effects of making it contingent on a response appear indistinguishable from the effects of making a primary reinforcer contingent on the response. The results of other experiments concur. Kelleher (1961) made the operating click of a food magazine an S^D for magazine-approach behavior in pigeons. When the click alone was used as a reinforcer for key pecking on *FI* schedules, and *FR* and *drl* specifications, the birds generated patterns of responding typical of these procedures under primary reinforcement.

11.3 TOKEN REWARDS

The operation of a typically human kind of conditioned reinforcement is demonstrated in studies in which poker chips ("tokens") were used to reward primates (Wolfe, 1936; Cowles, 1937). The chips were made S^D's for various manipulative responses, including the act of inserting them into the slot of a vending machine to produce grapes, oranges, peanuts, and other primary reinforcers. It was this history of association with primary reinforcement that transformed the chips into "tokens" (money) possessing the power to reinforce.

In some of Wolfe's (1936) experiments, chimpanzees were trained to insert a white chip into a vender and thereby produce a grape. The insertion response was shaped through successive approximation. A token was inserted partway in the vender slot by the experimenter, and any operant-level push by the chimp caused the token to drop and produce a grape. The shaping procedure continued until the animals would retrieve white chips from the floor and insert them into the grape vender.

$$\boxed{\begin{array}{c}S_F\\R_2\end{array}} \longrightarrow \boxed{\begin{array}{c}S_W\\R_1\end{array}} \longrightarrow S^+$$

where S_W = white chip in hand
  S_F = white chip on floor
  S^+ = grape
  R_1 = insert chip in vender
  R_2 = pick up chip

The animals were later taught to pull a weighted lever to produce chips, a task they learned to do easily.

$$\boxed{\begin{matrix} S_0 \\ R_3 \end{matrix}} \longrightarrow \boxed{\begin{matrix} S_F \\ R_2 \end{matrix}} \longrightarrow \boxed{\begin{matrix} S_W \\ R_1 \end{matrix}} \longrightarrow S^+$$

where S_0 = no chips present
   R_3 = pull lever

Later a further discrimination was established between brass chips which were worthless—that is, they did not operate the vender if inserted—and the white chips. A brief history with this set of contingencies sufficed to make the animals indifferent to the brass chips.

In other experiments (Cowles, 1937), with an apparatus analogous to the Lashley jumping stand of Fig. 10–3, animals learned pattern and spatial discriminations where the only reinforcement consisted of tokens. In Cowles' experiments the response was merely to push aside the card depicting the correct pattern. Vending machines were located in another room where, *after* the discrimination had been learned ($I_D \rightarrow 1.0$), the accumulated chips could be exchanged.

In these various experiments the chimps acquired new behaviors when the only immediate reinforcement was the chips. The chips are distinguishable from any other secondary reinforcer only by their physical properties, which make them manipulable, storable, etc. Of course, not only is a "token" the S^D for an inserting response; it also provides the actual physical means by which such a manipulative response can be emitted. A chip both implies reinforcement for inserting and makes inserting possible. Nevertheless, "tokens," like buzzers and clicks, come to be S^D's simply because a certain response is reinforced in their presence.

11.4   GENERALIZED   REINFORCERS

Many positive discriminative stimuli set the occasion for more than a single kind of response to be emitted and reinforced. Some S^D's in fact control numerous responses, each of which may lead to a different primary reinforcer. Outside the laboratory, such situations are encountered frequently. Money is a prime example. Having money, many responses can be made, each leading to its own distinct reinforcer.

$$\begin{matrix} S_{(money)} \\ R_{(buy\ theater\ ticket)} \longrightarrow S_1^+ \\ R_{(purchase\ new\ coat)} \longrightarrow S_2^+ \\ R_{(order\ a\ meal)} \longrightarrow S_3^+ \\ \vdots \qquad\qquad \vdots \end{matrix} \qquad\qquad [11.3]$$

"Attention" is sometimes used as a name for a similar kind of S^D; in order to obtain reinforcement for various verbal responses, it is often necessary for a person to obtain another's "attention." When the attention S^D has been procured, many responses (requests, demands, etc.) may then be emitted which stand a chance of being reinforced. In the absence of "attention," we would say that such requests go unheard, or unnoticed, which is the equivalent of saying that they are being subjected to extinction.

Discriminative stimuli that can set the occasion for more than one response-reinforcement sequence are based upon a history of association with more than one primary reinforcer. In diagram [11.3] for instance, money has previously been associated, through $S^D — S^\Delta$ training, with entertainment, warmth, food, etc. Discriminative stimuli associated in this manner with more than a single primary reinforcer and whose availability is then made contingent upon new behavior are termed *generalized reinforcers*. Although they appear to play an important role in mediating complex human behavior, such generalized reinforcers have not been extensively studied in the laboratory.

EXERCISE 8.

Describe a method to create a generalized reinforcer for chimpanzees. Use, as primary reinforcers, food, water, and removal from the experimental situation. Employ a different discriminative operant for each primary reinforcer. Use "tokens" as the generalized S^D. Once the animal possesses the token, what will determine the discriminative operant that he will make?

11.5 OBSERVING RESPONSES

Discriminative stimuli are sometimes said to have the property of carrying information regarding the state of the environmental contingencies effective at a given time. Thus, when a rat's lever presses are reinforced only in the presence of a light, the light may be said to provide the information that a certain reinforcement contingency is in effect. Similarly, the presence of an all-clear siren conveys the information that enemy bombers have retired, and it is safe to come out. Token reinforcers carry information as well, but here the informative function is overshadowed by the physical properties of the tokens which make possible the actual responses. When the automatic lock of an apartment door buzzes after you ring the bell, you are informed both that you may open the door and that when you do you will find somebody at home.

A different kind of information is provided by signs indicating "out of order" and "gone to lunch," red traffic lights and busy signals. These are notices that certain behaviors will go unreinforced; as such they constitute S^Δ's for these behaviors. Can the information about reinforcement provided by the S^D's and S^Δ's in these examples be thought of as reinforcing itself? The answer may best be given by reference to experiments.

In Herrick, Myers, and Korotkin's (1959) discrimination procedure of section 10.1, rats learned to discriminate between randomly alternating light and dark periods. The contingencies were *VI* reinforcement during S^D (light) and extinction during S^Δ (darkness). Imagine that instead of being provided automatically with a bright light as S^D and darkness as S^Δ, another group of animals was trained in a midway condition of dim illumination, *which did not change when each period of VI began and ended, nor when each period of extinction began and ended.* In the vernacular, these animals might be said to have no way of telling whether they were in *VI* or in extinction. If the extinction period is not too prolonged, rats trained under these conditions will adjust by producing a fairly constant rate of response in both *VI* and extinction.

Suppose that after such stabilization a new contingency is introduced for the first time. If now the rat should happen to pull a cord located in his compartment, the dim light would immediately be replaced either by darkness (S^Δ) or by the bright light (S^D), depending on the contingency which happens to be in effect at that moment. What we have done is to give the organism the *option* of producing discriminative stimuli. The behavioral result of the option is clear. The contingency acts quickly to condition the cord-pull response (Wyckoff, 1952).

When a response enables an organism to observe a situation correlated with the state of its reinforcement contingencies, we speak of it as an *observing response.* In merely observing an aspect of its environment correlated with certain reinforcement contingencies, the animal does not modify any of them, but it now has the opportunity to refrain from unreinforced responding.

Observing responses are among the most common of our own daily activities. In discriminating a genuine bill from one that is counterfeit, certain very detailed observing responses are required. A large part of the training of counterfeit and fingerprint experts involves the strengthening of observing responses which usually remain unconditioned in the layman. The expert must learn which aspects of a situation to study in order to distinguish between different stimuli which may be present. In the same way that the rat can check significant aspects of its environment by pulling a cord which produces S^D or S^Δ, so the counterfeit expert can check the significant print on a banknote which will identify it as genuine or fake. In both cases, the observing response, pulling the cord or examining the print, enables the organism to make a discrimination which increases the probability of its being reinforced.

The ability of experts to make discriminations, be it between wines, fingerprints, or paintings, is often viewed with some astonishment by the novice. For the latter, two cases reliably discriminated by the expert look, sound, or taste "alike." Observing behavior in the novice has not been strengthened, enabling him to "know where to look for the differences." In strengthening observing behavior in the human, we may often successfully "point out" the differences in situations. In pointing to the aspects of the situation on which the differences between S^D and S^Δ depend, we capitalize on a past history in which reinforcement has previously been contingent on looking in the direction the finger points.

Analogous contingencies shape up listening responses, as well as observing behavior in other sense modalities. In general, a principal characteristic of an observing response is that it enhances the probability of reinforcement for behavior. This is certainly true of the rat given the option of producing its S^D's and S^Δ's. If the animal's discrimination is good, S^D and S^Δ presentations will at least enable responding to be confined to S^D. This has the effect of increasing the overall probability of reinforcement for responding well above what it would be if no distinctive S^D and S^Δ were available. The batter who observes a minute but characteristic movement of a pitcher about to throw a curve ball stands a better chance of a hit than he would without such an S^D. Often the S^D's and S^Δ's produced by observing behavior are crucial for the occurrence of any reinforcement at all. Try to thread a needle blindfolded, or answer an examination question without first reading it. In both examples probability of reinforcement is so small as to be effectively zero in the absence of appropriate observing behavior.

Observing behavior is often covert, as when a man sits silently in the presence of a radio. Is he listening or not? That is, is he observing or not? In general, the answer can only be obtained by setting reinforcement contingencies in which the probability that the individual might emit certain words would be negligibly small in the absence of prior observing behavior. If we ask what was said on the radio, the response of repeating what was in fact said is taken as *prima facie* evidence that observing behavior must have occurred.

EXERCISE 9.

Notate the contingencies that prevail when an organism is given the option of producing S^D and S^Δ, as described at the beginning of this section. To make the exercise simpler, assume that a uniform-probability schedule alternates with extinction.

11.6 THE NECESSARY AND SUFFICIENT CONDITIONS FOR CREATING CONDITIONED REINFORCERS

The content of sections 11.1–11.5 has implied that a *sufficient* condition for making a stimulus a conditioned reinforcer is to make it an S^D

via the discrimination procedure. There is somewhat less evidence that making a stimulus an S^D is both a *necessary* and sufficient condition for making it a conditioned reinforcer. (Myers, 1958; Kelleher and Gollub, 1962). On several occasions we have observed that as a stimulus loses its S^D function it also loses its potency as a conditioned reinforcer. Dinsmoor (1950) established that the resistance to extinction of a discriminative operant was the same whether the operant was extinguished in the presence of its S^D, or extinguished with its S^D made contingent upon it. Another experiment (Notterman, 1951) showed that the less discrimination training the subject received, the less reinforcing value an S^D took on. These observations suggest that the discriminative and reinforcing functions of an S^D are closely allied, if not directly parallel.

Schoenfeld, Antonitis, and Bersh (1950) showed that merely associating an environmental event with a primary reinforcer is in itself insufficient to make the event a conditioned reinforcer. Rats were trained to approach their food tray for a pellet of food. After the rat had picked up the pellet and was already eating it, a brief (1-sec) light was presented. One hundred such light-food associations failed to impart any potential reinforcing value to the light, for in subsequent testing, the animal would not press a lever to produce this light alone.

Clues to the necessary and sufficient associations for producing acquired reinforcers have been provided by Egger and Miller (1962, 1963). The schematic representation in Fig. 11–3 of three environmental events, S_1, S_2, and S^+, will prove an aid to comprehending their results. Assume that S^+ possesses the power to reinforce behavior,

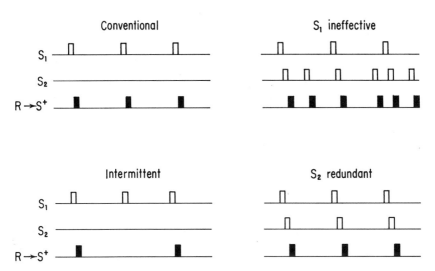

Figure 11–3. Some possible pairing arrangements of neutral stimuli with reinforcement.

whereas S_1 and S_2 originally lack this power. Assume also that the emission of a given R is necessary to produce S^+. Some of the associations in Fig. 11–3 bear close correspondences to some of the time relations in Pavlovian conditioning, as described in Fig. 3–5. They would, therefore, be expected to result in classical conditioning of some respondents along with any acquired reinforcing value that they lend to S_1 or S_2.

The top left case in Fig. 11–3 represents the conventional paradigm for creating conditioned reinforcers. Each presentation of S_1, if succeeded closely by R, is followed by S^+. When S_1 is not present, responses are not reinforced. This is the case of the click-light example of section 11.1 and token rewards, and, in general, describes a large class of $S^D — S^+$ pairings. Clearly, in this case, S_1 undergoes a discrimination history with respect to R.

In the bottom left case, S^+ comes after *some* S_1's, but not all. If responses are reinforced at all, however, they must occur after S_1. This is Zimmerman's intermittent case, and it too establishes S_1 as both an S^D and a conditioned reinforcer.

In the top right case, a reinforcement contingency *may* occur after S_1, but also at certain other times. If S^+ occurs as often as 50 per cent or more of the time without S_1, this case fails to impart reinforcing power to S_1 (Melching, 1954). S_1 fails to become an S^D presumably because responses are reinforced in its absence—a violation of the discrimination paradigm. Note, however, that S_2 becomes a conditioned reinforcer, because it bears the same relation to $R \rightarrow S^+$ as S_1 does in the conventional case of the top left.

In the bottom right case, the two neutral events are paired closely in time (within a few seconds), after which a response can produce primary reinforcement. This case will impart conditioned reinforcing value to S_1, but not to S_2 (Egger and Miller, 1962, 1963). It appears that S_2 is redundant here, providing no new information about the occurrence of the reinforcement contingency. This result would explain Schoenfeld, Antonitis, and Bersh's failure to make their light a conditioned reinforcer. In their experiment, the light was S_2, having already been preceded by S_1, the sight of the pellet, or the pellet in the mouth, etc.

A general analysis of the four cases of Fig. 11–3 indicates two salient facts. (1) Various paradigms exist for the establishment of S^D's, and all S^D's so established also acquire conditioned reinforcing power. (2) Only when a stimulus is informative (that is, correlated nonredundantly with a reinforcement contingency) does it become either an S^D or a conditioned reinforcer. The arguments advanced in this section should be taken provisionally; for their generality depends upon confirmation with additional temporal paradigms, responses, and primary reinforcers.

11.7 SECONDARY REINFORCEMENT IN SOCIAL BEHAVIOR

A stimulus controlling behavior as an S^D, or [conditioned reinforcer] need not stem from the inanimate environment alone. Other organisms (or, the stimuli emanating from them) can act in these ways too, and therein lies a fact of utmost significance to human as well as other biological life. Social behavior may be described as *behavior for which the reinforcing or discriminative stimuli are, or have been, mediated by the behavior of another organism.* By 'mediated' we mean 'arising from, or in connection with,' and there is no intention of straining the word's connotation. We would neither (1) include as social the delivery of a pellet by the experimenter to a bar-pressing rat—it may be a social situation for the experimenter, but it is not for the rat; nor (2) exclude as non-social the behavior of the marooned sailor who speaks to himself or makes clothes out of skins, since both activities have been socially acquired.

From birth on, social stimuli play a large part in the life of human beings. Many scientists, indeed, have thought that society itself has its origins in the protracted and utter dependence of the human infant. However that may be, parents, and especially the mother, are among the first secondary reinforcers of a social sort to enter the infant's ken. Their discriminative and reinforcing potency are quickly established by their continual association with food, warmth, relief from pain, and the like. If, however, the child is reared by a nurse, then she becomes the ever-present secondary reinforcement, and it is commonly seen that attachment to the nurse replaces that to the mother. Psychiatrists have pointed out that, in adolescence and before, the first sexually interesting objects may be the parents, brothers, or sisters. Within the relatively restricted social environment of the child, the few organisms who serve as the accompanying stimuli when reinforcement is given or withheld can acquire an over-spreading and life-long grip on his behavior. With increasing age, the child's widening excursions beyond the home provide an increasing range of secondary reinforcers to control his reactions. School, friends, clubs, and related activities of all sorts —these push upon him the stimuli which are the ever-present signals and accompaniments of ultimate reinforcement, the S^D's and the [conditioned reinforcers] which are the warp and woof of his life in society (Keller and Schoenfeld, 1950, pp. 257–258).

A rat taught to imitate another rat is demonstrating a rudimentary social skill and exhibiting the action of a social reinforcer. Miller and Dollard (1941) trained hungry rats to traverse the elevated T-shaped runway shown in Fig. 11–4. Some rats were trained to run to either a

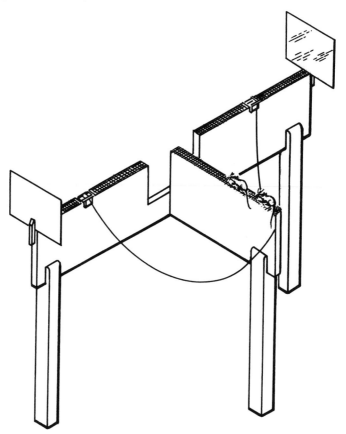

Figure 11–4. An elevated T runway for studying imitation in the rat (after Miller and Dollard, 1941).

white or a black card. The position of the cards was randomized on successive trials. Other rats were trained merely to run consistently to the right or to the left. When the rat made a correct run, it found food in a well just at the base of the card. These rats were designated "leaders" and were given training until they ran 20 consecutive trials correctly.

A second group of rats was trained to follow the leaders. On any trial where they followed the leader rat, the "followers" found food uncovered in a small well midway up the arm. On any trial where they failed to follow the leaders they were removed from the runway for a short wait and later given another trial.

The contingencies were effective in producing followers. The rats were found to imitate the turns of the leaders in the presence or absence of the white or black cards, to imitate leaders who had been trained to go right or left, and to imitate indiscriminately white rats or grey rats.

The social relationship between a teacher and a pupil is probably several orders of magnitude more complex than any single social skill such as imitation, but the rudiments of this relationship lend themselves to experimental analysis. From the standpoint of social reinforcement we may consider that the behavior of the teacher is reinforced by changes in the behavior of the pupil. The pupil must often be more directly reinforced, either by the promise of attainment of certain useful skills, or by the threat of punishment.

The contingencies involved in the usual educational setting are complex and often only loosely formalized. But the fundamental idea—one organism strengthening or imparting behavior to another organism—can be demonstrated in the pigeon in a way that exposes the critical processes involved.

In Fig. 11–5 two birds are separated from each other by a clear plastic partition. Before the demonstration, both birds have been trained to eat from their respective feeders. In addition, the "teacher" has been trained to peck the disk on the partition for intermittent food reinforcement. The demonstration begins with the birds placed together for the first time. Each time the teacher now strikes the disk, food is delivered to the "pupil." The teacher is itself reinforced for pecking only when the pupil is standing in the front left corner. Consonant with its history, the teacher begins by pecking rapidly, and indiscriminately with respect to the position of the pupil. At first, therefore, few of the teacher's pecks are reinforced. Gradually, however, as the demonstration progresses, more and more times as the teacher strikes the disk, both birds are fed. The behaviors of both birds are undergoing modification by the social interaction. Soon, an almost comical performance has evolved. The teacher will be watching the pupil as if waiting for it to move to the left-hand corner. Meanwhile, the pupil has confined its activities to a repetitive shuttle from feeder to corner. As soon as the pupil is stationed appropriately the teacher pecks, both birds eat, and the pattern is repeated.

The teacher might be said to be manifesting a kind of primitive social discrimination. Its behavior is reinforced only when the pupil is performing a certain act—standing in the left corner. It is this act on the part of the pupil that provides the S^D for the teacher to strike the disk.

As such, this precise situation functions as a conditioned reinforcer for

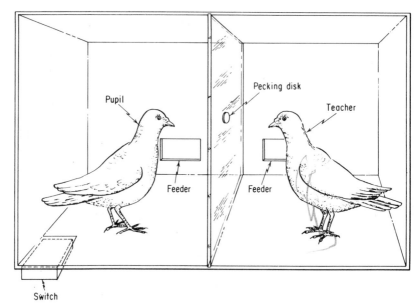

Figure 11–5. By striking the disk with its beak, the "teacher" feeds the "pupil." The teacher is also fed if the pupil happens to be standing on the switch when the disk is struck (Herrnstein, 1964).

the teacher as well. If the teacher is to obtain food, it must find a way to produce this situation reliably, for initially the pupil will rarely be standing in the favorable spot. A subtle social interaction is present: any pecking that the teacher does when the pupil is elsewhere results in food only for the pupil. Indiscriminate pecking is thus likely to strengthen behaviors on the part of the pupil other than going to the left corner. "Waiting" for the pupil to go to the left corner remains the only behavior the teacher has available to direct the responses of its pupil. The pigeon teacher is quick to discover the value of patience.

The simple demonstrations of this section illustrate the continuity that is to be found between social and non-social behavior. No new principles are needed to account for the results of the imitation contingencies, or the results of the pigeon teacher-pupil interaction. Imitative running behavior of follower rats is indistinguishable by topography, precision, or complexity from any other running operant under discriminative control. Likewise, the behaviors acquired by the pigeon teacher and pupil are only the familiar operants we have treated in detail throughout the text. The subtleties of social behavior lie in large part in the controlling contingencies arising from the complex source of stimulation provided by another organism.

References for Chapter 11

Cowles, J. T. Food-tokens as incentives for learning by chimpanzees. *Comp. psychol. Monogr.*, 1937, **14**, 1–96.

Dinsmoor, J. A. A quantitative comparison of the discriminative and reinforcing functions of a stimulus. *J. exp. Psychol.*, 1950, **40**, 458–472.

Egger, M. D., and Miller, N. E. Secondary reinforcement in rats as a function of information value and reliability of the stimulus. *J. exp. Psychol.*, 1962, **64**, 97–104.

Egger, M. D., and Miller, N. E. When is a reward reinforcing? An experimental study of the information hypothesis. *J. comp. physiol. Psychol.*, 1963, **56**, 132–137.

Herrick, R. M., Myers, J. L., and Korotkin, A. L. Changes in S^D and S^Δ rates during the development of an operant discrimination. *J. comp. physiol. Psychol.*, 1959, **52**, 359–363.

Herrnstein, R. J. "Will." *Proc. Amer. Phil. Soc.*, 1964, **108**, 455–458.

Kelleher, R. Schedules of conditioned reinforcement during experimental extinction. *J. exp. Anal. Behav.*, 1961, **4**, 1–5.

Kelleher, R., and Gollub, L. A review of positive conditioned reinforcement. *J. exp. Anal. Behav.*, 1962, **5**, 543–597.

Keller, F. S., and Schoenfeld, W. N. *Principles of psychology*, New York: Appleton-Century-Crofts, 1950.

Melching, W. H. The acquired reward value of an intermittently presented neutral stimulus. *J. comp. physiol. Psychol.*, 1954, **47**, 370–374.

Miller, N. E., and Dollard, J. *Social learning and imitation*. New Haven: Yale Univer. Press, 1941.

Myers, J. L. Secondary reinforcement: a review of recent experimentation. *Psychol. Bull.*, 1958, **55**, 284–301.

Notterman, J. M. A study of some relations among aperiodic reinforcement, discrimination training, and secondary reinforcement. *J. exp. Psychol.*, 1951, **41**, 161–169.

Schoenfeld, W. N., Antonitis, J. J., and Bersh, P. J. A preliminary study of training conditions necessary for secondary reinforcement. *J. exp. Psychol.*, 1950, **40**, 40–45.

Skinner, B. F. *The behavior of organisms*. New York: Appleton-Century, 1938.

Skinner, B. F. A case history in scientific method. *Amer. Psychologist*, 1956, **11**, 221–233.

Weissman, N. W., and Crossman, E. K. A comparison of two types of extinction following fixed-ratio training. *J. exp. Anal. Behav.*, 1966, **9**, 41–46.

Wolfe, J. B. Effectiveness of token-rewards for chimpanzees. *Comp. psychol. Monogr.,* 1936, **12,** 1–72.

Wyckoff, L. B., Jr. The role of observing responses in discrimination learning: Part I. *Psychol. Rev.,* 1952, **59,** 431–442.

Zimmerman, D. W. Durable secondary reinforcement: method and theory. *Psychol. Rev.,* 1957, **64,** 373–383.

Zimmerman, D. W. Sustained performance in rats based on secondary reinforcement. *J. comp. physiol. Psychol.,* 1959, **52,** 353–358.

Chapter 12 CHAINING

IN SECTION 11.1 WE SAW HOW, THROUGH THE USE
of token rewards acting as acquired reinforcers, simple sequences or
chains of behavior could be created. The simplest of these chains were
constructed from (1) a new, previously unstrengthened, response; (2) a
previously established S^D; and (3) the operant controlled by that S^D. In
general, chains of any desired length may be formed by indefinitely
compounding more and more such elements.

12.1 THE ELEMENTS OF BEHAVIORAL CHAINS

A chain of operant behavior is succinctly described as a sequence of
operant responses and discriminative stimuli such that each R produces
the S^D for the next R. The successive R's in a chain are its *members;* the
successive S^D's are its *links.* In the simplest chains, the number of members and the number of links are identical. The loop of behavior involving lever pressing and approaching a food tray, our prototype of operant
strengthening, constitutes such a simple repetitive chain. The behavior
of the rat is established by the procedure

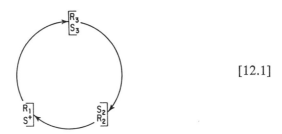

[12.1]

257

where S_3 = no food $\quad$ R_3 = press lever
$\quad\quad$ S_2 = click-light $\quad$ R_2 = approach tray
$\quad\quad$ S^+ = food $\quad\quad$ R_1 = eat

The loop of [12.1] is a special case of a behavioral chain, one in which the chain is repeated indefinitely. A loop may be regarded as a chain that is "closed" by permitting the "last" response to produce the S^D for the "first." For example, in the loop of 12.1, eating is the last response and produces the S^D, no food, for the first response, pressing the lever.

The loop of [12.1] is represented as being composed of three response members. Thus it is conventionally described as a three-membered chain. But the actual number of members used to represent a behavioral sequence is arbitrary, being dictated principally by descriptive convenience. In discussing the behavior observed and reinforced, three members serve adequately to illustrate the chained nature of the act. At the same time, three members are not too many to overwhelm us with a mass of details. Still, for other purposes, we may wish to represent the act as being made up of more members. For example, in further resolving the topography of the act, we could double the number of members considered and expand [12.1] to

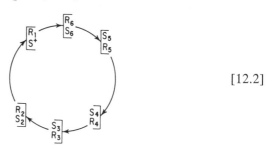

[12.2]

where S_6 = no food $\quad\quad\quad\quad\quad$ R_6 = rise up on lever
$\quad\quad$ S_5 = on lever $\quad\quad\quad\quad\quad\quad$ R_5 = depress lever
$\quad\quad$ S_4 = click-light, lever down $\quad$ R_4 = release lever
$\quad\quad$ S_3 = click-light, lever up $\quad\quad$ R_3 = enter tray
$\quad\quad$ S_2 = in tray $\quad\quad\quad\quad\quad\quad\quad$ R_2 = seize food
$\quad\quad$ S^+ = food in paw $\quad\quad\quad\quad\quad$ R_1 = put in mouth

Diagram [12.2] represents the same behavior and the same set of contingencies as [12.1], but the magnification power has been doubled in [12.2]. With attention to still more subtle topographical details and to still more minute stimulus changes, the resolution could easily be extended further. In general, the composition of a behavior chain may be represented as an indefinite number of operants. The number is not infinite, because a point will inevitably be reached in successive conceptual subdivision where the specification of two adjacent topographical classes will be so nearly similar that the two classes cannot be observed to function independently of each other. That is, their members will show complete overlap; the animal cannot be brought under any conditions to differentiate them. At that point we will have reached a logical limit to response resolution. In the main, behavior is subdivided to a level which serves illustrative and procedural purposes best. Without any special instrumentation, lever presses and tray approaches are easily observed, measured, and reinforced. In the last analysis, these are the considerations that justify their status as conceptually discrete units.

A chain may be compressed as well as expanded. In principle, we might well write [12.1] as

$$\left[\begin{array}{l} R_{(\text{press lever,}\atop \text{go to food tray})} \longrightarrow S^+ \\ S_{(\text{no food})} \end{array} \right. \qquad [12.3]$$

The criteria for defining a response class are that the class be specifiable (as it is in [12.3]) and that it be strengthenable or maintainable *as a class* by reinforcement. The question of whether the R specified in [12.3] is reinforceable is an experimental question. The answer will depend on many factors, such as the weight and height of the lever, its spatial distance from the food tray, the distinctiveness of any intermediary cues that are used to signal the delivery of food, individual differences among rats, and so on. Of course if this R has already been successively approximated and strengthened, [12.3] is a perfectly defensible way of abbreviating the contingencies that will subsequently *maintain* this behavior. Unfortunately, however, diagram [12.3] represents the contingencies of reinforcement often used when the experimenter has little time to devote to the actual shaping of the response. The procedure of [12.3] amounts to "throwing the rat in the box and waiting for conditioning to take place on its own accord." The school child expected to learn by merely being told or shown, or the college student given a book and told to learn Chapter 12, are the all too frequent victims of contingencies like [12.3]. The result is the same for both rat and human— some individuals acquire the desired behavior, and some do not. We might almost say in reference to [12.3], as compared with a more deliberate arrangement of the contingencies, that the organism learns *in spite of* the loose connection between the behaviors required and the reinforcement provided.

12.2 THE DEVELOPMENT OF A COMPLEX CHAIN

The significant behavioral principles used in establishing chains are (1) the successive approximation of each member, (2) bringing each member under discriminative control, and (3) the use of stimuli with the dual role of discriminative cue and conditioned reinforcer to link each member to the next. Various proliferations of these principles can produce chains of striking complexity and length, even in the rat. The behavior that can be acquired often surprises the untutored, yet the principles are merely those operating in the acquisition of lever presses or disk pecks. In general, great complexity in behavior does not result from any complexity in the topography of responding, nor even from the discriminations required, but rather from the complex ways in which various contingencies may be permuted.

Consider how a hungry rat might be trained to pick up a marble from the experimenter's hand, deposit it into a hole located some distance away, then pull a miniature trapeze dangling into its box, and finally press a lever (see Fig. 12–1). It is useful to delineate five response classes,

$$R_5 = \text{pick up marble}$$
$$R_4 = \text{carry and position marble over the hole}$$
$$R_3 = \text{drop marble}$$
$$R_2 = \text{pull trapeze}$$
$$R_1 = \text{press lever}$$

and note that we shall wish them chained in the order R_5, R_4, R_3, R_2, R_1. The necessary stimulus situations are more conveniently introduced in the text. The following hints will prove helpful.

1. Strengthen the members that occur nearest to primary reinforcement first; that is, build the chain from back to front.
2. Bring each operant under stimulus control; that is, make each operant a discriminative operant before going on to add another member to the chain.
3. Let the S^D for the operant just strengthened act as the reinforcer for the next response to be added. In this way, add members to the chain one at a time.

In accord with hint 1, R_1 may be conditioned by the usual methods of operant strengthening (see section 4.2). Then, applying principle 2, R_1 may be converted into a discriminative operant by reinforcing it in the presence of one situation (S^D), and not in the presence of a second situation (S^Δ). It will prove useful, as we shall see in a moment, to choose a situation for S^D that has at least two conveniently manipulated stimulus dimensions. A small light in combination with a soft buzzer will do. Let the buzzer be on continuously, and let the light-off serve as S^Δ for R_1. When discrimination has progressed to the point where the light controls the lever press discriminatively, hints 3 and 1 may be used to let trapeze pulling (R_2) produce the light. The result of this procedure will be, of course, the strengthening of R_2. Until now the buzzer has sounded continuously, regardless of the state of illumination. But after R_2 is strengthened, the buzzer can be turned on and off, and R_2 permitted to be effective in producing the light *only* when the buzzer is present. In this way trapeze pulls, R_2, will soon come under the discriminative control of the buzzer, while remaining under the reinforcing control of the light.

Adding the remainder of the response members (R_3, R_4, and R_5)

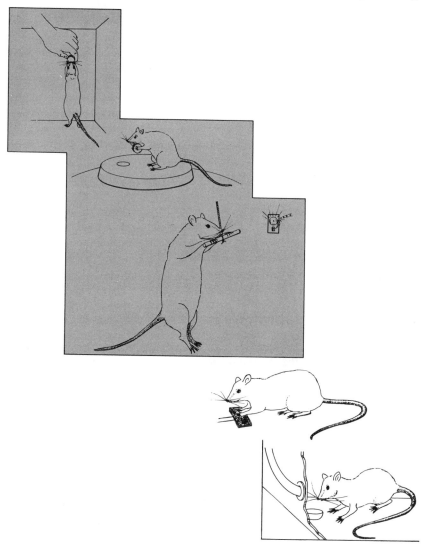

Figure 12–1. A rat executing a chain of behavior (after Michael, 1963).

proceeds similarly, although a certain amount of successive approximation is necessary. Begin with the marble placed near the hole, with the
stimulus conditions being buzzer-off/light-off. Responses progressively
nearer the marble are reinforced immediately by the production of the
buzzer, and the subsequent running off of the chain. By successive
approximation, the responses of touching the marble, then raising the
marble, then raising and dropping it, are established, all reinforced by
the buzzer onset. The final step is the addition of R_5. This is done by
gradually moving the marble further and further from the hole and
requiring longer and longer carrying responses. Eventually the chain is
complete. The marble is in the experimenter's hand; the rat, when placed
in the cage, advances to the experimenter, takes the marble, carries it
to the hole, and drops it in. The buzzer sounds and the rat then pulls the
trapeze. The small light goes on, the rat presses the lever, and food is
delivered. The contingencies are

$$\begin{array}{ccccc} \boxed{\begin{array}{c} S_5 \\ R_5 \end{array}} & \boxed{\begin{array}{c} S_4 \\ R_4 \end{array}} & \boxed{\begin{array}{c} S_3 \\ R_3 \end{array}} & \boxed{\begin{array}{c} S_2 \\ R_2 \end{array}} & \boxed{\begin{array}{c} S_1 \\ R_1 \end{array}} \\ 5 \quad\longrightarrow & 4 \quad\longrightarrow & 3 \quad\longrightarrow & 2 \quad\longrightarrow & 1 \quad\longrightarrow S^+ \end{array}$$

where S_5 = marble in experimenter's hand, buzzer off, light off
          S_4 = marble in paws, buzzer off, light off
          S_3 = marble over hole, buzzer off, light off
          S_2 = no marble, buzzer on, light off
          S_1 = no marble, buzzer on, light on
          S^+ = food

After training, the complete chain will be smoothly executed, with
little jerkiness remaining to suggest the individual units that were used in
its development. Yet without the original partitioning of behavior into
these smaller units, the complex sequence could never have been
developed.

In analyzing the human vocal chains that constitute spoken language,
there is a tendency to forget the extended past history that makes it possible to reel off long sentences made up of what were, long ago, units in
themselves: phonemes, syllables, words, and phrases. The apparent continuity (fluency) of a speech episode should not distract us from the fact
that speech is the product of a past history of chaining not in principle
different from that of the educated rat just described.

In tying his shoe, the child engages in a chain different only in details
from the rat's chain. Each individual operant in the tying chain serves
to advance the lace to a position where a slightly different response can
be made and reinforced. The final reinforcement is a secure knot. In
training a child to tie a shoe, the same principles operate as in training a

rat to execute a chain. Optimally, the chain should be begun from the end, with the shoe all tied save the final tug on the bow. When that response is strengthened, the lace is untied slightly and any response that produces the S^D for the final tug will be reinforced. Inappropriately executed responses will merely loosen the tie and thus be extinguished. In practice, children are rarely taught optimally, but more in the manner of [12.3]. Parents are often dismayed at the lack of what they call intelligence when a child fails to master such "simple" tasks quickly. The deficit is not in the child's problem-solving ability, but rather in the parents' appreciation of the principles of chaining. A child *can* learn from scratch to tie a shoe in a matter of minutes, if these principles are carefully followed. Ideally, the process might be automated with the use of perhaps several dozen shoes, each one in a progressively more untied state.

The student may wonder, where are the lights and buzzers in the shoelace chain? Why were they needed for the rat and not the child? The discrepancy is only apparent. In tying a shoelace, each response in the chain naturally produces a different stimulus situation, a lace that is closer to being a knot. In the Skinner box, lever pressing or cord pulling does not naturally affect the environment this way, so that the experimenter is obliged to add stimulus changes somewhat artificially. But in both chains, S^D's and S^Δ's are the binding forces. When the lace is in a particular state, only certain responses can advance it to the next state. Thus, any given lace state is the S^D for a particular response class, and an S^Δ for all the rest. (Note that the child has to learn to observe the current state of the lace to pick out the relevant S^D's.) Both for the shoelace behavior and the rat's movements, the status of chaining remains a sequence of operant responses interspersed with their S^D's.

Pierrel and Sherman (1963) have described the training of an exotic sequence of rat behavior. The rat climbed a spiral staircase, crossed a narrow bridge, and mounted a ladder. It then pulled in a chain attached to an open toy car, clambered aboard the car, and pedaled it to a second staircase (see p. 209). After ascending these, it squirmed through a tube, and entered an elevator. The weight of the rat lowered the elevator slowly to the starting platform, where, in something of an anticlimax, the animal pressed a lever and received a food pellet for its efforts. After eating, the rat was in a position to begin the sequence again. The casual observer is likely to marvel at the rapid and confident performance of this chain by an organism as undistinguished as the rat. An examination of the history behind such a performance, however, reveals that only the well-established principles of Chapters 4–11 were employed. The rat's behavior was acquired by the principles of discrimination and shaping, and chained by a judicious use of conditioned reinforcers.

12.3 MAZE LEARNING AS CHAINING

The maze apparatus has long been associated with psychology. In early experiments dating from the turn of the century, hungry animals were placed in devices such as those shown in Fig. 12–2 and allowed to find their way to food. The maze was adapted for blindfolded human subjects by letting the individual trace his way with a stylus through tortuous paths, with many choice points, cut in wood or etched in metal.

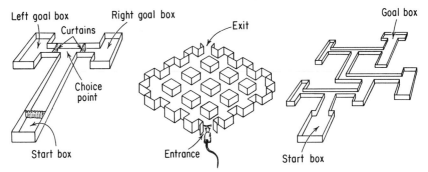

Figure 12–2. *Representative mazes. Each maze has a start box, and one or more goal boxes or exits where food may be found. A point in the maze where two possible paths may be followed is called a* choice point.

Response strength was inferred from changes in (1) the number of errors, or entrances into blind alleys, and (2) the reaction time (*RT*) from start box to goal box. After a varying number of training trials, individuals placed at the start point came to run these mazes quickly and without errors. The curves obtained when errors or *RT*'s were plotted against number of trials were of various sorts, depending on the particular maze structure used. Generally, as more and more trials were given, errors progressively decreased to zero, and *RT*'s progressively shortened, approaching an asymptote.

Great hopes were originally held that the study of animals in mazes would unlock the secrets of instrumental action and provide fundamental information concerning the acquisition process. Unfortunately, history has confirmed few of these hopes. Compared with the topography of a lever press or a key peck, the maze sequence constitutes a long complex chain, whose acquisition involves an unanalyzed mixture of discrimination, differentiation, and conditioned reinforcement. Because all these aspects of behavior are inextricably intermingled during training, it is not surprising that acquisition in the maze is gradual rather than abrupt.

Mazes still find a use in psychological research for specialized problems where the degree of analysis required is minimal; but the confounding of a host of acquisition factors invites difficulties in interpretation of behavioral results. The student is advised to regard maze behavior as a chain of *heterogeneous* (that is, different) response elements which only gradually become cemented into unitary response sequences.

12.4 THE EFFECTS OF SELECTIVE EXTINCTION AT DIFFERENT POINTS IN THE CHAIN

Although we may agree that complex sequences of operant behavior are acquired as gradually lengthening chains, it is still relevant to ask whether, once it is well formed, an act retains any chained aspects. For example, do the original response members preserve their unitary status as responses? Experiments in which the extinction procedure is applied selectively to the original members of a well-conditioned act are instructive.

Skinner (1938) chained lever-pressing and tray-approach responses in the usual loop (phase *a*).

Phase *a*:
$$\hookrightarrow \begin{bmatrix} R_{(lever\ press)} \\ S_{(no\ food)} \end{bmatrix}_3 \longrightarrow \begin{bmatrix} S_{(feeder\ sound)} \\ R_{(tray\ approach)} \end{bmatrix}_2 \longrightarrow \begin{bmatrix} S^+ \\ R_{(eat)} \end{bmatrix}_1$$

When this sequence had been well conditioned, extinction was introduced by no longer permitting lever pressing to produce the sound of the feeder (phase *b*). This extinction operation breaks the chain between links 3 and 2.

Phase *b*:
$$\begin{bmatrix} R_{(lever\ press)} \\ S_{(no\ food)} \end{bmatrix}_3 \nrightarrow$$

Under these conditions, the S^D's for the final two members (tray approach and eating) could not be produced, and of course lever pressing in link 3 weakened. When lever responding had reached a low level, the chain was reinstated to include link 2, by permitting lever pressing to produce the sound of the feeder. But no further contingencies of the chain were restored (phase *c*).

Phase *c*:
$$\begin{bmatrix} R_{(lever\ press)} \\ S_{(no\ food)} \end{bmatrix}_3 \longrightarrow \begin{bmatrix} S_{(feeder\ sound)} \\ R_{(tray\ approach)} \end{bmatrix}_2 \nrightarrow$$

The results of these selective extinction operations appear in the double extinction curves of Fig. 12–3.

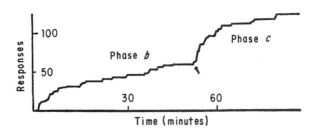

Figure 12–3. The separate extinction of members of a chain. Extinction of $R_{(lever\ press)}$ was conducted until the arrow. After the arrow, both $R_{(lever\ press)}$ and $R_{(tray\ approach)}$ were extinguished (after Skinner, 1938).

From the figure, it appears that upon re-introduction of the magazine sound (phase c), the lever-press response regained strength promptly, and a second extinction curve was generated. The interpretation of this result is as follows. During extinction phase b, the lever-press response (in link 3) declined in strength; but the tray-approach response (in link 2) did not, because the latter was principally under the control of the magazine-sound stimulus which was prevented from occurring in this phase. Since it was absent in phase b, the magazine stimulus did not lose its S^D properties then, *nor apparently its conditioned reinforcing properties either.* The reinstatement of contingency 3 in phase c therefore restored to lever pressing its customary source of conditioned reinforcement, the feeder sound. During phase c, the discriminative tray-approach response gradually weakened through extinction, and the magazine sound correspondingly lost its S^D properties, since it was no longer being paired with food (S^+).

Skinner's demonstration suggests that, in extinction, only the members of a chain up to the point of the fracture decline in strength. The strength of members and S^D's beyond that point is preserved.

Extinction may be applied in a rather different manner to demonstrate further the chained nature of established behavior. Rats are first trained to run a T-shaped maze (Fig. 12–2) for food placed in one of the goal boxes (say the right). When the rats go to the right side consistently and quickly they are ready for the next phase of the experiment. All food is removed from the goal box, the rats are then placed directly in the now empty goal box (where they had formerly found food after running the maze) and allowed to remain there for a while. In a final testing phase, the rats are placed in the start box with food still unavailable in the goal boxes; the time taken to run from start to goal is measured. The maze running of those rats having had this history of being placed in the empty goal box shows abnormally rapid extinction. In testing, these rats run the maze more slowly and make more errors than they would have, had they not had the opportunity to "discover" that their goal box was now empty.

This reduction in response strength defines a phenomenon known as "latent extinction." The choice of this phrase to describe the behavior is based on a debatable interpretation of the intermediate phase of the experiment, in which the animals are placed directly in the empty goal box. "Latent extinction" implies that this intermediate phase is a period during which extinction of the running behavior is taking place implicitly, or latently. There is a temptation to say that the rats quickly stop running the maze in extinction because, having already had ample time to "investigate" the empty goal box, they "know" in advance of running that they will find it empty. Unfortunately, that explanation relies on the future as the controlling factor in the behavior, and harbors all the pitfalls of such "explanations" mentioned earlier (section 4.1). A simpler, albeit more austere, interpretation is based on "manifest" extinction and losses in conditioned reinforcement. In training, the rats were taught to run the maze.

Training: $\overline{S}_{(start\ box)}$ $\overline{S}_{(choice\ point)}$ $\overline{S}_{(goal\ box)}$
$\underset{3}{\underline{R}_{(run)}} \longrightarrow \underset{2}{\underline{R}_{(turn\ right)}} \longrightarrow \underset{1}{\underline{R}_{(go\ to\ food\ cup)}} \longrightarrow S^+$

In the intermediate phase, the rats were in the *now empty* goal box, resulting in some very real extinction of R_1.

$\overline{S}_{(goal\ box)}$
$\underset{1}{\underline{R}_{(go\ to\ food\ cup)}} \longrightarrow\!\!\!/\!\!\!\rightarrow$

In testing, the entire chain was subjected to a standard extinction procedure.

Testing: $\overline{S}_{(start\ box)}$ $\overline{S}_{(choice\ point)}$ $\overline{S}_{(goal\ box)}$
$\underset{3}{\underline{R}_{(run)}} \longrightarrow \underset{2}{\underline{R}_{(turn\ right)}} \longrightarrow \underset{1}{\underline{R}_{(go\ to\ food\ cup)}} \longrightarrow\!\!\!/\!\!\!\rightarrow$

The response members associated with contingencies 3 and 2 were seen to be significantly weakened by the intermediate phase. The explanation of this decrement in strength is found in the drastic reduction in reinforcing power of the goal box which took place in this phase. In "latent extinction," this reduction appears to extend back throughout the entire portion of the chain, lowering the reinforcing power of all prior S^D's.

The results of "latent extinction" and Skinner's selective extinction experiment suggest the following two-part generalization. All the members in a chain *up to* the point in that chain where a member has been subjected to extinction undergo a weakening, whether or not these members have actually been emitted; on the other hand, none of the members *beyond* the point of extinction is weakened. The generalization offers some appeal as a practical method for reducing unwanted behavior by merely extinguishing the conditioned reinforcers upon which it depends. If the unwanted behavior consists of long and time-consuming sequences, such a principle, should it hold for chains of any length, might be welcomed by educators who find it desirable to extinguish old points of view before teaching new ones.

12.5 CHAINED SCHEDULES

Assessing the strengths of the various responses and conditioned reinforcers in an established chain of the sort we have described is not always easy.

(1) *The problem of measurement.* Responses in these chains are heterogeneous—that is, successive responses in the chain differ from one another in form. When a rat rolls a marble to a hole, pulls a wire, and presses a lever, these heterogeneous behaviors will be unlikely to occur at identical rates. The responses vary in topography, duration, and work effort required, so that it would be surprising if their rates of occurrence were comparable. But a chain whose members occur at varying rates because of varying topographies is poorly suited as a means for studying the quantitative effects that various experimental operations such as drugs, physiological insult, and reinforcement schedules might be expected to exert on chained behavior.

(2) *The problem of sensitivity.* When these chains are well established, they come to function as units. That is what we meant when we referred to their members' being "welded" into what amounts to a higher-order operant. The unitary structure of these chains is a consequence of maintaining the members under functional control of reinforcement, as we do for a simpler operant. Although we have seen that selective extinction is a way of revealing the essentially chained structure of such acts, many experimental operations seem to affect the sequence as a unit. The chain *as a whole* may vary in strength as a function of these different experimental variables, but the relative strengths of the individual members of the chain remain insensitive to these variables.

In contrast to a simple chain, the *chained schedule* (Ferster and Skinner, 1957) provides a baseline for assessing properties of chains that is both quantitative and sensitive. Like the chains described already, chained schedules consist of a succession of linked contingencies. But unlike these chains, chained schedules specify that each response member produces the succeeding contingency probabilistically. Thus, in any single link, a number of responses may have to be emitted to advance the chain to the next link. The advantage is that, in any such probabilistic link, the rate, frequency, or pattern of responding provides a sensitive dependent variable that can be studied independently of the rate, frequency, or pattern of the response members in a link elsewhere in the chain. Moreover, since the individual members in the chained schedule may conveniently be specified as identical (homogeneous) response classes, the measurement problem associated with heterogeneous topographies in simpler chains is bypassed.

Consider a homogeneous two-link chained schedule. Recall that the term *link* refers to the successive S^D's of the schedule. In notation, the successive brackets of a diagram denote the links. In a simple chain, every link is associated with one and only one response, but in the chained schedule this one to one correspondence between response and link is absent.

A representative chained schedule is abbreviated in [12.4]. Key pecking by a pigeon in the presence of a red light produces, on an *RI* schedule, a green light; key pecking in the presence of the green light produces, on an *FI* schedule, food reinforcement.

$$\begin{bmatrix} S_{(red)} \\ R_{(peck)} \end{bmatrix}_2 \xrightarrow{RI} \begin{bmatrix} S_{(green)} \\ R_{(peck)} \end{bmatrix}_1 \xrightarrow{FI} S^+ \qquad [12.4]$$

Diagram [12.4] depicts a two-link chain, but one that typically generates many key-peck responses per reinforcement. Furthermore, different response patterns develop in the different links, each pattern appropriate to the specific contingency of the link in which it occurs. Thus the curves in Fig. 12–4A show that typical *RI* effects result in the second link, the red-light situation; the curves in Fig. 12–4B show that typical *FI* effects are generated in the first link, the green-light situation. Two recorders were used to obtain Fig. 12–4. Pecks in the presence of the red light (link 2) registered on one recorder; pecks in the presence of the green light (link 1) registered on the other. When the bird was in the situation associated with a given link, only the recorder appropriate to that link was activated.

The chained-schedule procedure finds application in assessing in quantitative detail the reinforcing power of a conditioned reinforcer. In section 11.2 we were concerned with the durability of a conditioned reinforcer: that is, how long an acquired reinforcer retains its power to

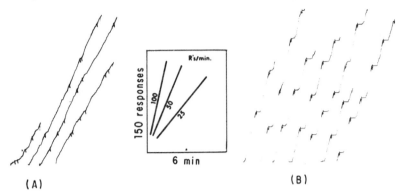

Figure 12–4. Responses produced on a chained RI-45 sec—FI-45 sec schedule. The responses are key pecks of hungry pigeons. The appearance of a green light associated with the FI contingency is the reinforcement in (A). Food is the reinforcement in (B) (unpublished data of J. R. Millenson).

maintain behaviors. But the *strength* of a conditioned reinforcer at any given time is often of equal interest. In colloquial language, the strength of a reinforcer is proportional to how hard an animal will work to get the reinforcer. A complete discussion of the strength of reinforcers is left to Chapter 15. For the present, it suffices to note that the rate at which an organism works in a situation (where his working there has led in the past to the reinforcer) is one measure of such strength. In general, a man who wants something "badly" will work very hard for it. So will a pigeon. When the *FI* of the first link in [12.4] is lengthened, or shortened, the bird's overall pecking rate in *that FI* link is hardly affected at all. But its pecking rate in the preceding *RI* link alters systematically. The function is a smooth one and is shown in Fig. 12–5. The function was obtained with a procedure like that in [12.4]. Over several months of daily experimentation four values of *FI* in link 1 were studied. According to Fig. 12–5, the larger the *FI*, the less the bird is inclined to work to produce the link associated with it, and therefore, by inference, the less the reinforcing value associated with it.

Chained schedules may be combined with higher-order response specifications to get chains such as *VI-FR, VI-drl,* and *FR-FI.* The number of permissible links may go well above two; *VI-VI-VI-VI-VI* chains have been shown to maintain behavior (Kelleher and Gollub, 1962). Many interesting behavioral phenomena occur by chaining together a variety of procedures; the interested student is referred to Ferster and Skinner (1957) and Kelleher and Gollub (1962) for additional details.

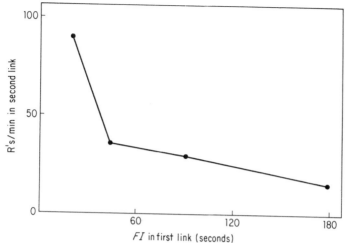

Figure 12–5. Responses per minute in the second link of a two-link chained schedule as a function of the FI *schedule in the first link (unpublished data of J. R. Millenson).*

12.6 EVERYDAY HUMAN BEHAVIOR AS CHAINING

In human behavior, nearly every action or skill, from walking across a room to whistling a tune, takes the form of an operant chain. Are such chains pieced together in the way that the series of movements were combined by the rats described in section 12.1? Do S^D's separate each simple movement in human performance and serve to bind the sequence together as a whole? Analysis suggests affirmative answers to both questions.

In the behavior known as walking, one leg is lifted, extended, and allowed to touch the ground. The other leg then repeats a similar pattern. The chain is clearly something like

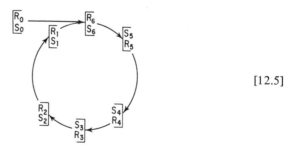

[12.5]

where S_0 = both legs on ground R_0 = lift left leg
    and feet together

S_6 = left leg off ground R_6 = extend left leg

S_5 = left leg extended R_5 = lower left leg

S_4 = left leg on ground R_4 = lift right leg
    and left foot forward

S_3 = right leg off ground R_3 = extend right leg

S_2 = right leg extended R_2 = lower right leg

S_1 = right leg on ground R_1 = lift left leg
    and right foot forward

In this chain the descriptions of the stimuli may be questioned on practical grounds. When we walk, we do not usually continuously observe the position of our legs in reference to each other. In any case, we walk quite adequately in the dark. Evidently there exist events inside the organism that are part of the S's in each of the brackets of [12.5]. These internal elements of each situation of [12.5] arise from the very movements of the body itself. We mentioned briefly in section 9.1 the receptors known as proprioceptors which lie embedded in muscles and tendons. These receptors have the property of responding differentially to various muscle and tendon movements. Thus, each S in [12.5] may be more completely described by noting not only the state of the limb in reference to the external environment as we have done, but also the exact state of tension of the particular sets of muscles being used. In ordinary walking, these states are used as the principal cues to maintaining a smoothly coordinated sequence of movements.

All the same, the muscle sense is not always sufficient, especially in the acquisition of more complex sequences, for optimum management of behavior. In learning a new dance step, an instructor may have to caution us not to look at our feet. Our observing behavior is an obvious way to insure that we place our feet "where they are supposed to be" during the dance. But visual observing behavior is discouraged by dancing masters, for it violates certain aesthetic standards, delays the acquisition of appropriate control by proprioception, and makes it nearly impossible for two persons to dance together. In certain diseases or injuries to the spinal cord, the proprioceptive receptors are rendered inoperative. In such cases, persons continue to walk, but only by observing visually the position of their legs.

The duplication of cues and informational overlap commonly found in situations is exploited in the technique known as "fading." Chains are often built using rather gross elements of situations as preliminary S^D's. Then, as acquisition progresses, the controls are gradually shifted to more and more subtle portions of the situations. This may be done by refusing reinforcement when gross observing behavior is detected, as in the dancing example, or it may be done by gradually removing certain aspects of the situation. For instance, in being taught to drive a car, the novice may first depend upon verbal commands issued by his driving instructor to maintain a smooth chain of behavior. These commands are shown in quotation marks in [12.6] labeling the S^D's.

$$\boxed{\begin{matrix} S_A \\ R_A \end{matrix}} \longrightarrow \boxed{\begin{matrix} S_B \\ R_B \end{matrix}} \longrightarrow \boxed{\begin{matrix} S_C \\ R_C \end{matrix}} \longrightarrow S_D \qquad [12.6]$$

where S_A = "Put it in low gear" + *car not moving*
R_A = push gear lever to low
S_B = "Press accelerator" + *gear in low*
R_B = press accelerator
S_C = "Let out clutch" + *motor revving moderately*
R_C = release clutch
S_D = "Good!" + *car moves forward*

The instructor can gradually begin to omit the verbal elements of the situations, so that the cues arising from the clutch pedal and gear lever take hold directly. Teachers may be inclined occasionally to forget that in the world outside the classroom, spoken and written *prompts*—as the "instructions" of [12.6] are often called—are rarely present. Thus in formal teaching it is important that prompts used at the start be dropped out before the student is regarded as trained. It is this gradual elimination of portions of an S^D situation, leaving only minimal aspects of the stimulus in control, that is known as *fading*.

Other cases of fading arise when a musician learns a piece of music by rote. Initially, the individual notes written on the score provide the S^D's. In the passage

a chain, $R_{(play\ F)}$, $R_{(play\ A)}$, $R_{(play\ B)}$, $R_{(play\ E)}$, is prescribed. At first the individual members of the chain are controlled by the score. Eventually, however, the score is faded, observing responses directed at the score are discouraged by the instructor, and finally the note sounds themselves provide all the necessary S^D's. In general, the S^D for playing a note will not necessarily be the sound of just the immediately preceding note, but rather a combination of the sounds of several earlier notes—a passage. Thus, for instance, the playing of note E above will not in general be cued by the previous B alone, but will be under the control of a long series of preceding notes, with B being only the last of these. As would be expected, therefore, the hardest passages to play are those that are similar, that is, those that contain runs of identical notes ending in a different terminal note. To obtain the correct note, the only available S^D is located some distance away (in very similar passages perhaps a half-dozen or more notes earlier) and the immediately preceding notes must, for the moment, be ignored.

A breakdown in chaining explains the hesitation a performer sometimes exhibits in commencing a passage. There is no unique S^D at the very beginning of a piece. A similar problem may arise in memorizing poetry. Once begun, each spoken word is the occasion for the next word, but one must often be prompted to begin. In reciting poetry, children are frequently observed to get "stuck" between lines. This is the result of memorizing line by line, so that the last word of the previous line fails to acquire sufficient S^D power for the first word of the next line.

12.7 VOCAL CHAINS

Not only poetry, but all human verbal (communicative) behavior is chained. The sentence is a chain of words, each spoken word being a response which produces an S^D (the sound of that word) setting the occasion for the next word. We have never distinguished the noises emitted by humans as being fundamentally different from other human and animal operants. In an earlier chapter (sections 4.10 and 4.11) we described experiments indicating that the vocal behavior of human infants and college students waxed and waned according to appropriate reinforcement contingencies. We wish to expand that account in this section, indicating at the same time how language behavior achieves a typically chained status.

The extent to which language is so intimately a part of human art, science, and culture generally has led scholars and scientists from various disciplines to apply their different points of view and techniques to the analysis of language. The resulting body of knowledge constitutes linguistics. In the present text we confine our interest to three "psychological" problems of language: (1) What constitutes a useful behavioral description of language? (2) How is that behavior acquired? (3) What is the "meaning" of language? In this section, we restrict attention to the first two of these problems, postponing "meaning" analysis (which is better described as enumerating the specific conditions that control particular language sequences) until a later chapter on concept acquisition.

In section 4.10 we noted that very early in a child's life the relative-frequency distribution of various phonemes comes to resemble the phoneme histograms for the community in which that child is being raised. The correspondence is presumably the effect of selective reinforcement contingencies peculiar to that community. While such distributions may tell us which basic sounds we are most likely to hear enunciated by a given individual, they provide little information on the structure of language behavior. That structure is conveniently described as chains of words. Furthermore, spoken words themselves are conveniently represented as chains of syllables or phonemes. Of course, like the response members in the rat's loop of behavior about the lever press, the units of verbal chains also merge into smoothly flowing (fluent) sequences. Under certain circumstances the chained nature of words is readily demonstrable. In the acquisition of a new and difficult word, for instance, we rely on hearing the separate parts spoken slowly in order to repeat the word correctly. The Delaware Indian word <Monongahela> is difficult for foreigners to pronounce. When the word is represented as a chain, the sound S^D's and speech R's are conveniently described as syllables (Diagram [12.7]). Initially, the sounds may be

$$R_{<mo>} \to \begin{bmatrix} S\,_{\text{``mo''}} \\ R_{<non>} \end{bmatrix} \to \begin{bmatrix} S\,_{\text{``non''}} \\ R_{<ga>} \end{bmatrix} \to \begin{bmatrix} S\,_{\text{``ga''}} \\ R_{<he>} \end{bmatrix} \to \begin{bmatrix} S\,_{\text{``he''}} \\ R_{<la>} \end{bmatrix} \to S_{\text{``la''}} \qquad [12.7]$$
$$\phantom{R_{<mo>} \to }\quad\; 4 \qquad\qquad 3 \qquad\qquad 2 \qquad\qquad 1$$

produced by the vocal apparatus of a coach or, in principle, by a machine. The responses of [12.7] are those of the organism learning to pronounce the word. In the notation, the spoken (R) elements of words are placed between oblique brackets < >; while the sounds (S) of the words are placed between quotation marks " ".

Early in acquisition, the S^D's of any given link in [12.7] are not sufficiently in control of the R's of that link to produce reliable behavior. The coach may have to prompt the desired syllable. For instance, after the common error <mogonga>, the coach may advise a return to the beginning and, after the learner's response of <mo>, may himself prompt "non." Under appropriate instructions to imitate, $S_{\text{``non''}}$ is likely to control $R_{<non>}$. Of course, the coach will eventually fade out these prompts so that the correct pronunciation becomes independent of his presence.

A note on imitation is here inserted parenthetically. Imitation is unquestionably a valuable method of guiding behavior. But as a short cut for a full acquisition process it may often be overrated. Student teachers are frequently surprised to find that telling a pupil a piece of information frequently fails to teach the student anything. The complicated performance of a dancer, a skilled acrobat, or a musician cannot be brought into the novice's repertoire of behavior through sheer imitation. Watching someone drive a car or fly an airplane does not in itself impart these skills to the observer. Imitation is often useful for bringing up the strength of previously acquired responses, but less useful for chaining the members into a sequence of any length or complexity.

The chained nature of words is neatly exposed by experiments which tamper with the normal succession of S^D's. If syllabic responses of the sort shown in [12.7] fail to produce their characteristic S^D's immediately, the speech pattern becomes broken and chaotic. The subject may begin to stutter and, in extreme cases, is unable to speak at all. In delayed auditory feedback, the normal $R \rightarrow S^D$ relations in speech are disrupted by delaying the subject's sound reception form each of his own speech R's by about ⅕ sec (Lee, 1950). The term feedback is borrowed from the language of electronics where part of an output signal (for example, in your record player, some of the amplified energy that would ordinarily go to your loudspeaker) is *fed back* to the input (the place where you plug in your phonograph cartridge) of the same circuit. By analogy, a response can be considered to be the output of a behaving system; the environment can be considered the input to that system. When an organism operates on its environment by emitting operants, the changes in the environment produced by the organism's own responses can be considered to be fed back to the organism. The word "feedback," stripped of its electronic disguise, is analogous to those special consequences that we have called primary and secondary reinforcers.

Consider a subject confined to a soundproofed room. Snugly fitting headphones and sound-absorbing walls and ceiling prevent him from hearing his own voice through normal air conduction routes. (A very diminished reception is possible through bone conduction.) The sounds produced by speech responses go to a tape recorder via a microphone. They are delayed by the simple procedure of first recording them and then a fraction of a second later playing them back amplified to the subject. Amplification serves to override most of the weak bone-conduction S^D's. The effect obtained is an exaggeration of that observed by a speaker talking into a public address system when the loudspeaker is located at some distance from his microphone.

In a typical case of the speech distortion produced by this kind of sound delay, the pronunciation of Monongahela becomes <Monongahelala>. Consider this effect in reference to the chain of diagram [12.7]. At contingency link 1, the subject has just uttered $R_{<la>}$ and under normal circumstances would immediately hear $S_{\text{"la"}}$, the final S^D in the chain. But due to the delay he hears $S_{\text{"he"}}$, which controls yet another $R_{<la>}$. The effect is most pronounced at the end of the chain because, in normal speech, the behavior in the middle of the word chain is held together by the immediately antecedent movements of the speech apparatus in addition to the sound effects produced by these movements. The final R, a deliberate pause, is most dependent on the sound of the terminal syllable. (The surest way to know that you have finished speaking a word is to hear its last syllable.)

The delayed auditory feedback method with a fixed delay may not be optimal for breaking the speech chain. With practice, it seems likely that the subject could come to use the delayed S^D's since they still bear a fixed relation to previous behavior (always ⅕ sec later). If the delay were an average *randomized* one of ⅕ sec, however, varying from instant to instant, more complete disruption of the chain of spoken language would be expected.

Sentences may be analyzed analogously to words. During childhood, sentence acquisition is built up by linking longer and longer combinations of words. Aside from the problem of meaning, sentence chains differ from the rat behavior chains so far considered in that their response members (words) are combined in many different permissible sequences. (This is true also of the syllable chains that make up words.) The chain "Dog bites Man" is controlled by a very different situation from the chain "Man bites Dog." Hence the basic units of sentences (words) cannot be learned in any single fixed sequence in the way the rat of section 12.2 learned the members of its chain. The sentence is built piecemeal, using individual words as units. As children grow older, the average length of their spoken sentences increases as shown by Table 12–1.

Table 12–1
THE AVERAGE LENGTH OF SPOKEN SENTENCES AT VARIOUS AGES
(FROM McCARTHY, 1954)

Age (years)	1.5	2.0	2.5	3.0	3.5	4.0	4.5
Number of words	1.2	1.8	3.1	3.4	4.3	4.4	4.6

How are the word units organized into sentences? The mechanism seems to be a chaining of discrete discriminative operants. For instance, a child's verbal behavior may be shaped (according to the principles of Chapters 7 and 8) in such a way that the word "ball" comes to be pronounced on demand in the presence of spherical, bouncy objects. Similarly, reinforcement may be made contingent on the child's emitting certain noises (<blue>, <red>, <green>, etc.), in the presence of appropriately colored objects. Finally, the child may be trained to vocalize <I have . . .> under conditions in which he is in possession of a certain object for which he has earlier learned a name, as he learned "ball." The key to this analysis is that each word or set of words comes under the control of a specific environmental situation, or more accurately, a set of situations:

$$\begin{array}{lll} \overline{S}_{(ball)} & \overline{S}_{(red\ object)} & \overline{S}_{(in\ possession\ of\ ...)} \\ R_{<ball>} \longrightarrow S^+, & R_{<red>} \longrightarrow S^+, & R_{<I\ have\ ...>} \longrightarrow S^+ \end{array}$$

Although the child may never have previously integrated this list, the question "What do you have there?" may produce the novel chain, $R_{<I\ have>}$ [a] $R_{<red>}$ $R_{<ball>}$ if the elements of the list—in conjunction with certain grammatical rules concerned with indefinite articles and their positions with respect to other words, and rules governing the order of adjectives and nouns—are already in the behavioral repertoire. There is, of course, no need for the child to be able to verbalize those rules; he need merely use them appropriately. Typically, the behavior of verbalizing grammatical rules is saved for Professors of English Composition to strengthen.

12.8 BRANCHING CHAINS AND FLOW-DIAGRAM REPRESENTATION

In the study of "token rewards" with chimpanzees, a discrimination was established between "valuable" white chips and "worthless" brass chips (section 11.3). In one procedural variation, the chimps had to pull a lever to obtain chips. Sometimes they got a white chip for their efforts, but at other times they got a brass one. When they received a white chip, they inserted it into a vender which then delivered a grape or an orange slice. But on those occasions when they received a brass chip, the animals discarded it and went back to their lever for another try. They had learned that inserting brass chips in the venders never led to reinforcement.

The chimpanzees' lever-pulling contingencies resemble in some ways those of a motorist approaching an intersection. The behavior the driver emits at the intersection will depend on whether he finds a green light, a red light, a yield sign, or a traffic policeman. The stimulus consequences of the approach behavior of the motorist and the lever-pulling behavior of the chimpanzee are subject to a degree of uncertainty. In both cases, a given response—lever pulling or intersection approach—can lead to one of several possible situations. And the appropriate response that follows in the chain (insert chip or pull lever again; stop or go) will depend on which particular situation did in fact occur.

When a response within a chain of behavior may lead in this way to one of several possible situations, the contingencies at that point are said to branch. We notated simple branching contingencies in previous sections by drawing several arrows from an R, and indicating the probabilities of each stimulus consequence. Many everyday problems are more complex than those faced by the chimpanzee and the motorist. In such cases, solutions are reached only by traversing a complex chain of such branching contingencies. In the typical problem, contingencies are compounded to form a complex network of branches, subloops, interconnections, dead ends, and alternate routes.

It will prove instructive to analyze the arrangement of reinforcement contingencies in a case of more complex problem solving. In finding the difference between two numbers, a child is solving a "problem." To the sophisticated adult, of course, such a subtraction exercise seems an almost trivial execution of a straightforward behavioral sequence. That the flavor of a "problem" has long been lost, however, is all the more reason why analysis should prove enlightening. In fact, a breakdown of the simple exercise reveals a fairly complex chain of contingencies, in which at least three behavioral subskills participate.

Consider the sample problem

$$\begin{array}{r} 60,048 \\ -152 \\ \hline \end{array}$$

For the purposes of analysis, we shall refer to the integers 6, 0, 0, 4, and 8, which appear in the upper number, as the upper integers, or simply the "uppers"; and those integers, 1, 5, and 2, which appear in the lower number, as the lower integers, or simply the "lowers." We assume that any spaces present under an "upper" (for example, those under the 6 and leftmost zero of the sample problem) are to be understood as zeros.

We may identify three operants that must be available in the individual's behavioral repertoire in order to execute the various chains that will lead to a "solution" to the problem.

1. A repertoire of simple subtraction responses must be available. A child is trained to respond "three" to the command "subtract four from seven"; to respond "eight" to the command "take nine from seventeen"; and so on. In general, a list of discriminative operants is acquired such that the child can correctly give the answer to any subtraction where the "upper" is not larger than 18 and the "lower" is not larger than 9. (Above these limits, a subtraction will be "solved" by the process to be described.) This list of responses constitutes a set of discriminative operants usually acquired by rote learning and said to be "memorized." The responses could of course be prompted from a table, but they are used so often in arithmetic problems that a table look-up would drastically delay the execution of the solution chain.

2. Borrowing behavior must previously have been acquired. Given a "lower" greater than its "upper,"

$$\begin{array}{r} 60,048 \\ 152 \end{array}$$

one must be able to examine the next non-zero "upper" lying to the left (6̲0048), and take 1 from it. One must then transform any zeros intervening between the two "uppers" in question to nines (599**4**8), and finally add 10 to the "upper" whose "lower" originally exceeded it (599[**14**]8).

3. The individual must be able to discriminate the larger of two integers. This discrimination consists of first directing an observing response at a "lower" and then at the "upper" just above it. If the "lower" is greater than the "upper," then one response (borrowing) must be at strength; otherwise, another response (subtraction) must be at strength.

When we try to represent, by R's, S's, and brackets, the contingencies that will combine these three component skills in such a way as to produce a solution, we encounter a difficulty. This arithmetic problem is relatively simple compared with many other numerical and non-numerical problems. Nevertheless, its contingencies comprise so many branches, subloops, interconnections, and alternate routes, that our notation is taxed to provide a manageable representation. A less cumbersome representation of the behavioral structure of such tasks is needed.

The responses and discriminations that an individual makes in solving a problem like subtraction bear certain resemblances to the operations that a digital computer performs in solving similar problems. The machine and the human may not employ identical methods, but both reach a solution by application of component skills at appropriate times and places. Computer scientists have developed a notation for describing the sequential flow of their machine operations. The elements of this notation are the test box (Fig. 12–6) with one entry and two exits, corresponding behaviorally to a discrimination; and the operation box (Fig. 12–7) with one entry and one exit, corresponding behaviorally to a fixed sequence of responses.

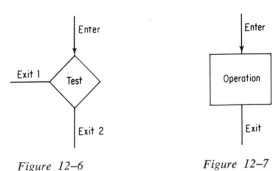

Figure 12–6   *Figure 12–7*

Figure 12–8 is a flow diagram of tests and operations describing the steps leading to the solution of our problem of finding the difference between two numbers. A subloop (shown dotted) describes the observing behavior that precedes the actual problem-solving process. Be-

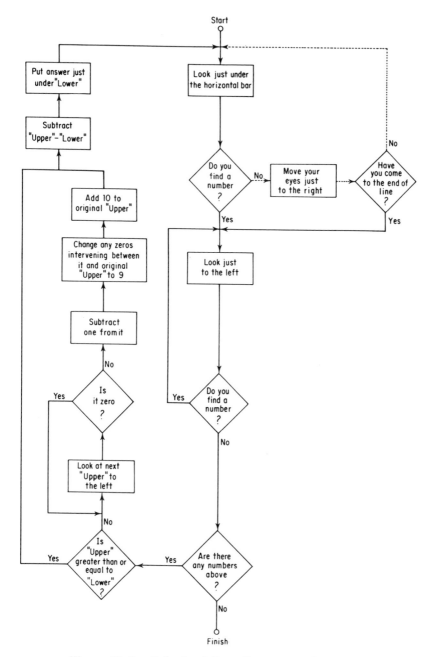

Figure 12–8. Behavioral flow diagram for finding the difference between two numbers.

havior may go round and round in this loop before reaching the S^D conditions that permit the chain to advance. Borrowing is shown as a path that may have to be traversed, depending on the results of the lower leftmost test of the diagram.

The arrangement of the component skills into the structure shown in Fig. 12–8 guarantees a "solution" to the problem as defined. Behaviorally, a "solution" constitutes the production of a situation (S^D) with certain properties. In the present case, that S^D is a number that, when added to 152, gives 60,048. When a set of contingencies, tests, and operations can be arranged to guide behavior to the inevitable production of a solution S^D, we speak of the resulting chain as an *algorithm*. Many everyday practical problems, from dressmaking and cookery to calculus and draftsmanship, are dealt with by such algorithmic chains of behavior.

12.9 COVERT BEHAVIOR CHAINS

One of the principal characteristics of language chains is their ability to become covert, so that it is difficult to tell by direct observation what a person is doing, if anything, when he is solving a problem "to himself." Since we have repeatedly referred to behavior as anything an individual can be *observed* to do, there exists a real problem of definition here. Are we dealing with behavior when a child solves a subtraction problem "to himself"? By inference, there is every reason to believe that a branching chain of the type of Fig. 12–8 is indeed going on, even though close observation of the child reveals no movements of the lips, tongue, eyes, or mouth. The value of such an inference, of course, lies in its ability to predict and explain other behaviors.

One of John B. Watson's (1914, 1920) most intriguing theories was the equation of the phenomenon known as thinking with covert behavior chains. Watson was able to cite in support of this theory the fact that children, if not punished for it, often think out loud. In fact, a history of successively approximating ever more silent responses is necessary to get children to "talk to themselves." Furthermore, when adults solve difficult problems their lips often move, and if the problem is very hard the individual may resort to open talking. Watson reasoned that evidence of covert speech would probably be found by sensitive instruments attached to the very muscles that are used in everyday speech. He suggested that in thinking about such activities as riding a bicycle and driving a car, small-scale responses ought to be found in the muscles of the body normally used in these activities.

Watson's theory was not without historical precedents. Plato had observed that thought and language were closely allied, and several nineteenth-century commentators came close to anticipating Watson. But nobody before Watson had dared advance the thesis that *all thought* was covert responding. Viewed from the modern vantage point, Watson's position may appear more or less extreme, depending on one's philosophical preconceptions. But scientifically speaking, the proposed equation between thought and muscle twitches is unnecessary, and perhaps even untestable. However, the notion that chains of behavior can become reduced in magnitude until they are unobservable with the naked eye stands as a scientific proposition capable of generating experiments, whether or not all, some, or no "thought" is to be identified with these chains. It is in this sense that Watson's hypothesis stands as an important creative development in the history of behavioral science.

Unfortunately, little conclusive experimentation has resulted from Watson's hypothesis. In his own time, sensitive recording devices had not yet been perfected to the extent necessary to make the required measurements. Two experiments, however, done in the 1930's, provide some preliminary evidence that covert responding goes on in appropriate muscles when instructions to "think" are given to subjects.

In one experiment, electrodes were attached to various parts of the subject's body (right and left biceps) and the subject instructed to imagine movement of a limb (Jacobson, 1932). Electrical responses of muscles were recorded on fast-moving kymographs (of the non-cumulative type). In Fig. 12–9, records taken from the right biceps are jux-

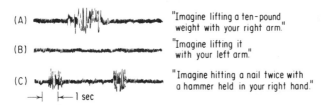

(A)   "Imagine lifting a ten-pound weight with your right arm."

(B)   "Imagine lifting it with your left arm."

(C)   "Imagine hitting a nail twice with a hammer held in your right hand."

→| |←— 1 sec

Figure 12–9. Muscle potentials recorded from the right biceps after several kinds of instructions (after Jacobson, 1932).

taposed with the various instructions preceding them. The instructions clearly had a selective effect on muscle activity and, as record (B) shows, the effect was located in the right arm only when the right arm was to be "imagined." During the recording of (A), (B), and (C), the experimenter was unable to detect any actual movement of the arm with the naked eye.

In another experiment, electrodes were attached to the muscles of the tongue and under lip. Under instructions to "imagine" counting, or recalling poems or songs, or multiplying numbers, muscle potentials occurred in the speech musculature. The form of the electrical activity, though reduced in amplitude, was much like that of the electrical activity that took place when the instruction "imagine" was replaced by the instruction "whisper."

In other independent experiments, electrodes were attached to the arms of deaf-mute subjects whose language takes the form of gestures with the hands and fingers. When the mutes were instructed to "think" words or solve multiplication problems covertly, muscle potentials generally appeared in the forearm region. Muscle potentials from subjects who could hear and speak were used as a basis of comparison. Under similar instructions to the normals, potentials were absent in their forearm regions (Max, 1937).

In conclusion, Watson's theory provides a certain intellectual comfort for the behavioral scientist: thought is given a place in the scheme of things behavioral, and may then be dismissed like other "mental" ghosts of the past. But experiments do not immediately flow from Watson's position, perhaps only partly because of the difficulties of recording from muscles. Theories, even the best, may often lend a complacency that, rather than furthering research, can act to discourage it. It would seem that there are numerous inherently interesting problems concerned with covert chains of responding, how they are acquired, their advantage in efficiency over corresponding overt chains, questions of their maintenance, and so forth. But so long as covert responding is considered merely an "explanation" for "thinking," these problems remain buried. In this connection, the work of Hefferline and Keenan (1963) referred to in section 8.5 is encouraging, for it provides the kind of theoretical neutrality that promises to bring these problems to light, and re-open the issues of covert responding so boldly introduced by Watson over a half-century ago.

References for Chapter 12

Ferster, C. B., and Skinner, B. F. *Schedules of reinforcement.* New York: Appleton-Century-Crofts, 1957. Chapter 12.

Hefferline, R. F., and Keenan, B. Amplitude-induction gradient of a small-scale (covert) operant. *J. exp. Anal. Behav.,* 1963, **6,** 307–315.

Jacobson, E. The electrophysiology of mental activities. *Amer. J. Psychol.,* 1932, **44,** 677–694.

Kelleher, R., and Gollub, L. A review of positive conditioned reinforcement. *J. exp. Anal. Behav.,* 1962, **5,** 543–597.

Lee, B. J. Effects of delayed speech feedback. *J. acoust. Soc. Amer.,* 1950, **22,** 824–826.

McCarthy, Dorothea. Language development. In L. Carmichael (Ed.), *Manual of child psychology.* New York: Wiley, 1954.

Max, L. W. Experimental study of the motor theory of consciousness. IV. Action-current responses in the deaf during awakening, kinaesthetic imagery and abstract thinking. *J. comp. Psychol.,* 1936, **24,** 301–344.

Michael, J. *Laboratory studies in operant behavior.* New York: McGraw-Hill, 1963.

Pierrel, Rosemary, and Sherman, J. G. Train your pet the Barnabus way. *Brown Alumni Monthly,* Feb. 1963, pp. 8–14.

Skinner, B. F. *The behavior of organisms.* New York: Appleton-Century, 1938.

Watson, J. B. *Behavior, an introduction to comparative psychology.* New York: Holt, 1914.

Watson, J. B. Is thinking merely the action of language mechanisms? *Brit. J. Psychol.,* 1920, **11,** 87–104.

PART FOUR

Complex Contingencies

13. CONCEPT ACQUISITION

14. PROBLEM SOLVING AND
    INTELLIGENCE

Chapter 13 CONCEPT ACQUISITION

$\blacksquare$HE PRINCIPLES ELABORATED IN THE PRECEDING
chapters permit us to describe and classify a large fraction of the learned
behavior of animal and human organisms. But were we to terminate our
account of behavior with the operations of simple acquisition, discrimination, differentiation, chaining, secondary reinforcement, and generalization, we should still be forced to admit that the bulk of complex human
behavior had been left untouched. The activities that might be classified
as complex human behaviors are, of course, extremely diverse; the one
characteristic they all seem to share, however, is a close affiliation with
language. Indeed, an implication of the preceding chapters is that possession and use of language is perhaps the sole behavioral attribute remaining to man which sets him apart from his lower relatives. Although
we might agree that early language behavior is acquired through the
process of successive approximation, and that words come to serve as
S^D's, still, the "meaning" of language appears to go beyond the concepts derived from animals in the laboratory. The very term "meaning"
presents numerous problems in definition; nevertheless, the aspects of
human behavior to which it refers constitute very real phenomena. Furthermore, it is clear that any science of behavior which pretends to be
at all comprehensive must eventually address itself to the description of
these phenomena. We cannot ignore complex human behaviors simply
because they are poorly specified. Indeed, a principal reason that they
are so poorly specified is that they await description in terms of a
general, comprehensive, and yet rigorous language. Thus, the description of such complex behaviors in terms of the conceptual structure of

simple behavioral phenomena would result in their being simultaneously understood and clarified.

In the present chapter, therefore, we extend behavioral analysis into this field of complex human behavior. We choose as our point of departure the area known as *concept formation*. So many characteristically human activities have been related to concepts—thinking, understanding, word meaning, reasoning, problem solving—that we can be sure that if experimental contact can be established here, we shall be in a favorable position to move toward an analysis of many forms of complex human behavior.

We begin with a consideration of a type of behavior, developed in the animal laboratory, which shares certain important properties with our own human conceptual behavior. Yet this laboratory behavior arises from a configuration of the familiar operations of acquisition, extinction, discrimination, and generalization. Because of its relations to both simple and complex behaviors, it seems to represent an important bridge between the two classes. The relative simplicity of the laboratory phenomena will help us to identify the term *concept* with certain precise characteristics of behavior. Once having anchored this key word, a number of simple human experiments, in which the special features of language are not utilized, will further elaborate the general logic of concept behavior. Eventually, guided by our experimental paradigms, we can turn briefly to explore the complex human behaviors associated with terms such as understanding, meaning, instruction, perception, and (in the next chapter) problem solving.

13.1 SIMPLE LEARNING SETS

In Chapter 10 (Discrimination) we noted that one class of discriminations entailed two situations and two responses, and we described experimental apparatus useful for setting such contingencies. One such apparatus, the *Wisconsin General Test Apparatus*, was shown in Fig. 10–5. In the WGTA, a monkey or other primate subject may be presented with several objects on a movable tray, one object concealing a peanut in a well beneath it. Suppose two objects to be in use, a solid wooden cross and a solid wooden U-shaped object. The peanut is always to be found under the cross figure, whether the latter appears on the left or on the right. The two possible contingencies may be diagrammed as[1]

---

[1] Throughout this chapter R_L, R_C, and R_R refer to reaching left, center, and right.

$$
\left[\begin{matrix} \overline{S} \\ \boxed{+ \, \mathsf{U}} \\ R_L \to S^+ \end{matrix}\right]_1 \quad \text{and} \quad \left[\begin{matrix} \overline{S} \\ \boxed{\mathsf{U} \, +} \\ R_R \to S^+ \end{matrix}\right]_2 \qquad [13.1]
$$

where contingency 1 represents the cross on the left and contingency 2 represents the cross on the right. An "incorrect" response (that is, R_R in 1, or R_L in 2) leads to removal of the tray. After a short delay, one of the two contingencies is again put into effect. A "correct" response (that is, R_L in 1 or R_R in 2) produces a peanut (S^+). Following a short delay, one of the two contingencies is again set. Let us agree to call a *trial* the single presentation by the experimenter of one or the other of the situations and contingencies of [13.1]. From what we know about discrimination, we may be sure, given a number of such trials, that a behavioral process will take place. During the early trials, the animal's behavior will not be under the control of the cross object, and hence incorrect R's will occur: R_R in 1 and/or R_L in 2. Eventually, however, as more trials are given, the animal's behavior will gradually come under the control of the location of the cross. Since this process is a gradual one, tens to hundreds of trials, depending on species and individual differences, may be necessary to reach an asymptotic value of near or at 100 per cent "correct" responses.

So far, we have merely described a set of 2S — 2R discrimination contingencies. Let us call a single such set of contingencies (as in [13.1]) a discrimination *problem*. Suppose, once the discrimination process has reached its asymptote, we present a new set of contingencies. That is, suppose we present a new discrimination problem. We choose the new problem so that it differs from the old contingencies only in the objects used to make up its 2 S's; for example, a solid wooden sphere and an inverted wooden cone. The problem is otherwise identical. What will be the nature of this *new* discrimination process? In fact, it is very similar to the first process. The animal begins by performing little better than chance would predict; but it eventually comes to choose the correct object (now the sphere) on each and every trial. Closer inspection of these two processes might reveal, however, a slightly more rapid shift toward the asymptote in the second case.

This comparison of two successive discrimination processes suggests an interesting general experimental design. Evidently we are not limited to one, or two, or even a few, such discrimination problems. We can continue to present new problems, one after the other, as long as we can find different objects and as long as our patience holds out. Fortunately for the latter, we discover that as we do present more and more problems, the discrimination processes become appreciably more rapid. Although tens to hundreds of trials may have been necessary to reach asymptotic performance on the early problems, perhaps less than a half-dozen trials are necessary for errorless performance by the time 100 discriminations have been learned. Eventually, after several hundred problems, we discover a remarkable outcome. The monkey is now able to solve any new problem of this sort immediately. If, by chance, it chooses the correct object on trial 1, it thereafter continues to choose the correct object. If, by chance, it chooses the wrong object on trial 1, it reverses response pattern immediately and chooses the correct object from trial 2 on. In both cases, the monkey's performance is nearly always perfect by trial 2. In effect, presentation of a long series of similar problems has eradicated the gradual discrimination process. We are left with an animal that solves new discriminations immediately.

The preceding example illustrates the development of a *learning set* (L-set), a general paradigm studied extensively and named by H. F. Harlow. Figure 13–1 displays more precisely the results of the L-set procedure obtained from typical rhesus monkey subjects. Each curve in Fig. 13–1 is the average of a number of discrimination processes. The

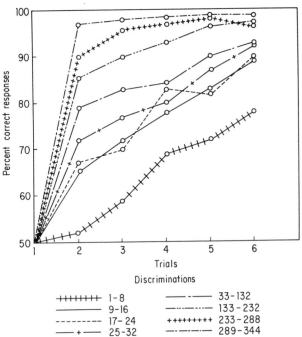

Figure 13–1. Changes in successive blocks of 2S—2R discrimination processes. The curves are the average scores of eight monkeys, but we may assume that they are representative of a single subject (after Harlow, 1949).

processes are shown through trials 1–6 only. The key just below the graph tells exactly which discriminations are averaged in each curve. Figure 13–1 thus shows in detail the changes in the form of successive averaged discrimination processes. Discrimination process 1–8 is gradual and $\int$ shaped, and it is clear that its asymptote would lie well beyond the six acquisition trials shown. The average process for problems 9–16 is less gradual; the curve is steeper and will reach its asymptote more quickly. Subsequent processes are still steeper, until, after 232 problems, there is no "process" as such. There is only the result: on trial 2 the monkey is nearly always correct.

It is this behavioral result of presenting successive similar discrimination contingencies—an acquired ability to solve any one of a class of similar discrimination problems with maximum efficiency—that is usually described as a learning set (L-set). The acquired nature of such an ability suggests that it may have a characteristic process of its own. And indeed, the curve that describes the development of an L-set can be derived from Fig. 13–1 if we use the performance on trial 2 as an index of its progress. Maximum efficiency for solving this sort of discrimination would be indicated by errorless performance on trial 2. It should be clear that performance on trial 1 cannot possibly be above 50 per cent correct. In advance, the monkey has no basis for discriminating which of two new objects is correct, and so it will pick the correct object on a chance, 50–50 basis only. Figure 13–2 shows the performance level on trial 2 as a function of the number of problems previously presented. The figure is, then, a convenient description of the L-set acquisition process. An important feature of the process shown in Fig. 13–2 is its gradual and continuous character. *Thus the ability to solve a discrimination problem in one trial is itself acquired by a gradual process.*

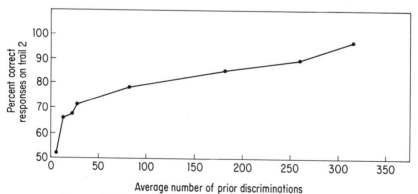

Figure 13–2. *An L-set process derived from the data of Fig. 13–1 based on performance on trial 2.*

In contrasting the discrimination processes of Fig. 13–1 and the L-set process of Fig. 13–2, note that in discrimination, the independent time variable over which the behavior changes with continued exposure to a constant procedure is called trials. In the L-set process, on the other hand, the independent time variable over which the behavior changes is called problems. Note also that the *result* of each individual process of Fig. 13–1 is called a discrimination; but the *result* of the process of Fig. 13–2 is an L-set—the ability to solve a type of discrimination immediately.

We must not suppose that L-sets are restricted to the particular type of discrimination described in our example. In the discriminations of Figs. 13–1 and 13–2, behavior is gradually brought under the control of one of two objects—the object that covers the peanut reinforcer on trial 1. But the general notion of an L-set consists of an acquired ability to solve discriminations of a given class on first contact. Thus, bringing behavior under the control of the larger of two objects, the green or the triangular one of two objects, constitutes other simple 2S — 2R L-sets which may conveniently be established by a procedure similar to that described. In general, we may assume that the L-set procedure is applicable whenever it is possible to devise a set of *related* discrimination problems. After the animal has been exposed to a subset of these problems, it may eventually acquire the ability to solve them all.

If we attempt to formulate the L-set paradigm, we discover that it has a

PROCEDURE: A series of related discriminations is presented to the organism;

PROCESS: The individual discrimination processes gradually change their form from slow and gradual to sudden and abrupt; and

RESULT: New, but related, discriminations are solved with maximum efficiency.

This actual term L-set is usually taken to refer to the result of this paradigm.

13.2 SOME VARIABLES AFFECTING L-SET ACQUISITION

Harlow (1959) has summarized investigations of L-set formation using various species of organisms, including children. Children tested in L-set procedures typically surpass chimpanzee and monkey subjects in overall performance, but they too exhibit a continuous L-set acquisition process. Primates lower on the phylogenetic scale than rhesus monkeys—squirrel monkeys and marmosets, for example—show a more gradual L-set acquisition process than Fig. 13–2 depicts. Even after 1000 or more problems, the asymptote of their L-set process is significantly lower than perfect L-set performance. Other animals, like rats and cats, show some steepening in successive discrimination processes, but they never reach sophisticated L-set results within the limits of the experiments that have been performed. However, we recommend caution in concluding that true L-sets are a privileged ability of primates, in view of the methodological difficulties in establishing comparable arrays of discrimination "problems" for lower animals.

The number of trials alloted to each problem markedly affects L-set acquisition. Since the early discrimination processes are the most gradual, a large number of trials is required on early problems to bring behavior to any given criterion, say 70 per cent correct performance. As more and more problems are given, the discrimination process steepens, and fewer trials are necessary to reach that same criterion. This difference was considered in obtaining the curves of Fig. 13–1. The early problems were run for 50 trials, later ones for only 6 or 9 trials. It is worthy of note, however, that even when as few as 6 trials are given for *all* problems, the L-set still emerges; correspondingly, more problems are, of course, required to offset the fewer trials per problem. The ideal trial-problem combination has yet to be worked out.

The rate of L-set acquisition is a function of the difficulty of successive discrimination problems. Harlow kept all problems within the same series uniformly difficult. A gradual progression from easy to difficult discrimination might yield the L-set more efficiently.

13.3 MORE COMPLEX L-SETS

We have avoided using the term "concept" in the preceding L-set discussions, but it seems natural to wonder whether an organism possessing an L-set for the larger of two objects, or for the green one of two objects, might reasonably be said to exhibit the concept "larger of two", or "green one of two." Such speculations would find themselves in good company, for Professor Harlow himself has hypothesized that "all concepts such as triangularity, middle-sizedness, redness, number, and smoothness evolve only from L-set formation" (Harlow, 1959, p. 510). We postpone for the moment a rigorous definition of the term concept, and merely suggest that the "concept" acquired in Figs. 13–1 and 13–2 is "the object of two which had the peanut under it on the previous trial." Its verbal description is longer than those concepts mentioned by

Harlow; a single-word identifier is lacking perhaps because the contingencies that comprise this concept are rare in the world outside monkey behavior laboratories. An example of a more complex L-set will prove useful in illuminating the close relation between L-sets and concepts.

An important class of L-sets consists of "oddity" discriminations. In these discriminations, a group of objects is presented. Reinforcement is contingent upon picking out a single object which differs in some way from the other objects of the group. Such a discrimination might consist of the contingencies shown in Table 13–1. These entail two kinds of

Table 13–1
A SET OF ODDITY CONTINGENCIES

	SITUATIONS	REINFORCED RESPONSE
S_1	○ △ △	R_L
S_2	△ ○ ○	
S_3	△ ○ △	R_C
S_4	○ △ ○	
S_5	△ △ ○	R_R
S_6	○ ○ △	

objects, six situations, and three responses. Once the primate subject has acquired the discrimination at a certain criterion level, a new problem is presented. Two new object types are used in the new problem but the contingencies remain such that the position of the odd-shaped one of three is again correlated with reinforcement. After a series of many such problems, the monkey acquires an L-set which we could call "choosing the odd-shaped one of three." The well-trained subject in the illustration to Part Four, p. 287, is demonstrating the behavior typifying this L-set. The sophisticated performance of the rhesus monkey is achieved only after the presentation of many similar problems. These results indicate the degree to which L-set procedures can succeed in bringing the operant behavior of animals under the control of rather subtle relationships existing within situations.

Such behavioral control in humans is often the basis upon which we assign the word "concept." For instance, we agree that a child has the concept of ownership when he can discriminate his own possessions from those of anyone else. We say that a child has the concept of a noun phrase when he can pick out the noun phrases from unfamiliar sentences. Similarly, we credit him with the concept of equality of number when he can identify equal quantities in unfamiliar settings, as when he can match the number of beads in one jar to the number of apples on a table. However, these illustrations are, at best, merely suggestive. Clearly we require a more rigorous definition of a "concept" if we wish to examine in detail the relation between L-sets and concepts. It will prove fruitful therefore to turn to some of the very earliest concept-formation experiments with human subjects. It is here that we find an explicit attempt to translate human concept formation into behavioral terms, with the systematic question "What does a person *do* when he is said to exhibit a concept?" When that question can be given a satisfactory answer, we shall be in a position to determine the procedures by which such conceptual behaviors are acquired.

13.4 SIMPLE HUMAN CONCEPT-FORMATION EXPERIMENTS

C. L. Hull (1920) took as his point of departure for the study of concept formation the history by which a child comes to acquire the concept of "dog."

> A young child finds himself in a certain situation, reacts to it by approach say, and hears it called 'dog.' After an indeterminate intervening period he finds himself in a somewhat different situation and hears that called 'dog.' Later he finds himself in a somewhat different situation still, and hears that called 'dog' also. Thus the process continues. The 'dog' experiences appear at irregular intervals (Hull, 1920, p. 5).

As a result of these "experiences," a time arrives when the child is said to have the concept of dog. Hull's interpretation of this concept was a "characteristic more or less common to all dogs and not common to cats, dolls, and 'teddy bears' " (Hull, 1920, p. 6).

If a concept consists of a characteristic common to a diverse group of situations, it should be possible to set up laboratory conditions to study how behavior comes under the control of the common characteristics of a group of situations. As the elements for his experimental concepts, Hull chose the 144 Chinese characters shown in Fig. 13–3. The unfamiliarity of these characters to his American university student subjects assured that none of the experimental concepts could have been previously acquired. In order to produce groups of situations containing a common characteristic, groups of characters were selected containing certain common elements. Note, for instance, that in Fig. 13–3 all the characters

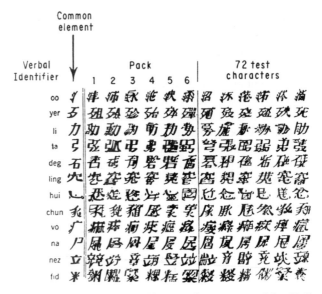

Figure 13–3. The 144 Chinese characters used by Hull to study concept acquisition. The verbal identifying response and the common element are shown for each series (Hull, 1920).

in row 1 have embedded in their different overall structures the common brush strokes 彳. In general, each character in a given horizontal row is related to every other character in that same row via the possession of some common element. In the experiment, the characters were combined into packs (vertical columns of Fig. 13–3) such that each pack contained one and only one of the characters having a particular common element. Subjects were then shown the characters of pack 1, one at a time, and were asked to give the appropriate verbal identifying response as shown under the left column in Fig. 13–3. The correct name was spoken by the experimenter a few seconds after presentation of each character. The subject's task was to name the character before the experimenter did so. The first trial was, of course, unique, for it acquainted the subject with the set of verbal identifiers. When the criterion of two perfect trials had been reached, that is, when the subject had correctly named all the characters of pack 1 twice in a row, the characters of pack 2 were presented until they were all identified, then those of pack 3, and so forth, through pack 6.

Once the subject had learned to identify these 72 Chinese characters (6 packs × 12 characters per pack), the experimenter made a generalization test. He presented the remaining 72 characters, but no longer spoke the identifier. Is the subject capable of identifying them, even though he has never seen them before? Hull found that the subjects correctly identified over 70 per cent of these new characters. In fact, correct identifications were often made even though the subject was unable to verbalize the rule for inclusion in the particular class.

In Hull's experiment, each member of a given S class had a certain brush stroke in common. Smoke (1932) pointed out that concepts in the real world rarely if ever consist of a class of situations with such explicit common elements. Concept formation more generally would seem to involve a response under the control of *relationships* common to a group of stimulus patterns. Consider, for example, the figures of Fig. 13–4 generated by a rather artificial relation suggested by Smoke. All the figures in the left-hand box of Fig. 13–4 are members of the S^D class named "dax," while none of the figures in the right box of Fig. 13–4

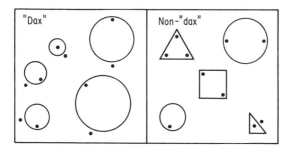

Figure 13–4.   Samples of "dax" S^D's and "dax" S^Δ's (from Kimble and Garmezy, 1963, after Smoke, 1932).

is a "dax" figure. The rule for "dax" is a circle and two dots, one dot being inside the circle, the other outside it. Smoke found that human subjects readily acquired the generalized behavior of categorizing "dax's" from other patterns even though their only prior "discrimination training" was a presentation of some appropriately labeled "dax's" and non-"dax's" with instructions to note the differences. Though they were frequently unable to verbalize the rule for class inclusion, subjects could still correctly identify new instances of "dax" which they had never seen before.

In both the Hull and Smoke experiments, subjects are said to acquire certain concepts. We may now ask in what way these experiments demonstrate concept learning:

1. In both the Hull and Smoke experiments, subjects acquire the ability to pin a common verbal label on any member of a class of situations.

2. The acquired behavior generalizes to new situations to which the subjects have never before been exposed.

3. The class of situations is bound together by some common relationship—a brush stroke, or a complicated geometric rule.

From these findings, we are led to two conclusions about concept behavior. First, an organism is said to exhibit a concept when he can identify any member of a set of related situations. Second, the organism acquires that ability via an explicit reinforcement history (or instructions relying on a previous reinforcement history) in the presence of a subset of the situations.

We are now in a position to see the relation of the L-set paradigm to concept formation. The L-set procedure is merely a systematic way of ordering the reinforcement history that leads to concept behavior. Though the monkeys do not speak, the behavior they acquire from L-set procedures seems precisely analogous to what human subjects in concept-formation experiments do, using verbal responses. The monkey picks the odd object from a set of objects he may never have seen previously. The human picks the "dax" from a set of patterns which he may never have seen previously. In real life, it would seem that we rarely acquire our concepts by the orderly advance from one related problem to another, the sequence characteristic of L-sets. The child in school, at home, and at play acquires his concepts concurrently, and in a far more haphazard fashion than any laboratory procedure arranges. Nevertheless, when he can identify a new dog as a dog, or a new social situation as one that requires "company manners," he is engaging in behaviors of the sort produced by the various procedures we have described.

Note that the term concept, as described, does not refer to a thing. Like discrimination, conditioning, and extinction, the term refers to certain behavioral facts and certain relationships between behavior and environment. The word "concept" denotes the behavioral fact that a given response is under the control of a class of related S^D's. An interesting corollary of this definition is that it does not separate a concept from a discrimination. We may recall that a discrimination (Result) is a name for the behavioral fact that an S^D has come to control an operant response. But we know that generalization renders it impossible to discover a perfect case of discrimination in which only a single S^D controls a response. Prolonged discrimination training may narrow down the class of environmental events that sets the occasion for the response, but the class remains a class. If we have been trained to say "yellow" in the presence of a certain wavelength of light, the probability of the "yellow" response remains high when slight changes in wavelength are made. Such results, indicating the persistence of generalization even after long discrimination training, are expressions of the limitations on the capacity of the organism to make infinitely fine discriminations.

If a concept also refers to a class of S^D's controlling the emission of a response, how does it differ from a discrimination? Evidently the difference is one only of degree; at its borders the distinction is fuzzy and arbitrary. It is therefore plausible to speak either of the *concept* of yellow, or of the *discrimination* of yellow. Our word usage in a particular case will be determined merely by the broadness of the class of controlling S^D's. If the class of S^D's seems relatively narrow, we call the behavior a discrimination; if it seems relatively wide or broad, we are more likely to call the behavior a concept.

While the notion of broadness *per se* is too imprecise to permit a rigorous distinction between concepts and discriminations on the basis of the behaviors exhibited, it does suggest that the distinction between the two can be made procedurally. Suppose we were interested in training an organism to make finer and finer discriminations between a given triangle (S^D) and all other triangles. Our procedure would be to present triangles gradually more and more similar to the S^D triangle, while withholding reinforcement in their presence. In effect, we sharpen the discrimination by broadening the class of experienced S^Δ's. In forming the *concept* of triangularity, on the other hand, we would present and reinforce responses to triangles similar to the original triangle, thus broadening the S^D class. This is just what Hull did for "oo," Smoke did for "dax," and Harlow did for oddity. All these procedural variants serve gradually to build up the aggregation of S^D's that control a given response, be the behavior saying "oo," saying "dax," or selecting the odd-shaped object. The procedures for forming concepts and discriminations begin similarly with reinforcement in the presence of a single S^D, but they diverge thereafter to achieve their different effects. Discrimination training narrows the class of controlling S^D's, while concept formation broadens the class of controlling S^D's. Keller and Schoenfeld's (1950) "discrimination between classes, generalization within classes" is a handy phrase for summarizing the behavior characteristic of a concept, and reminds us of the processes that went into its evolution.

13.5 ANIMAL STUDIES IN CONCEPT-FORMATION

According to the analysis presented up to this point, a concept represents the control acquired over a given response by a set of related situations (S's). In the preceding section, we suggested that the general method for establishing this control was the prior use of a subset of the S's as S^D's in a discrimination paradigm. Such a description fits the specific training procedures of Harlow and Hull, who presented a series of related discrimination contingencies. The description fits Smoke's procedure too, as long as we are willing to assume that his instructions resulted in his subjects giving themselves discrimination training with S^D

and S^Δ instances of the geometric figures they were given to look at. These three experiments represent only a small sample of the training procedures that satisfy the definition of a concept-acquisition procedure. There are many ways to arrange a history of discrimination with a subset of the members of a broad class of related S^D's. In the present section we consider a few such additional procedures, at the same time calling attention to the variety of concepts that have been established at the infrahuman level.

Kelleher (1958) reinforced telegraph key presses of hungry chimpanzees (on a $p = 0.01$ probabilistic schedule of food reinforcement) only when certain visual patterns were present on a 3×3 array of small plexiglass windows above the key. Other patterns were associated with extinction contingencies for key pressing. In concept training, 13 S^D patterns and 13 S^Δ patterns were shown in a haphazard sequence. Figure 13–5a shows a sample of three of the S^D patterns and three of the S^Δ patterns. The accompanying cumulative-response records below these patterns show a typical performance achieved after extensive training under this procedure. The three sample S^D patterns illustrate that the S^D class was bound by the rule "bottom three windows illuminated." The

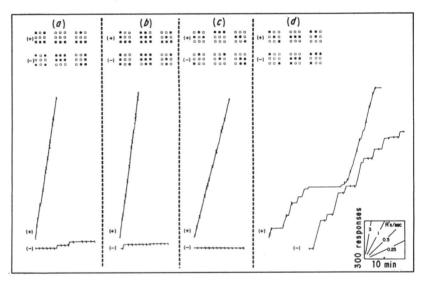

Figure 13–5. Representative stimulus patterns and cumulative-response curves for two concept problems. The dark squares correspond to illuminated windows. The pips represent changes from one stimulus to another. S^D patterns and responses are labeled $(+)$; S^Δ patterns and responses are labeled $(-)$ (Kelleher, 1958).

behavior of Fig. 13–5a represents a stable advanced discrimination, with responding principally confined to the occasions when S^D patterns were present. In (b), a test was made for concept behavior by substituting 6 unfamiliar S^D patterns and 6 new S^Δ patterns into the stimulus sequence without altering the reinforcement contingencies. Three of each of the new patterns are shown in Fig. 13–5b. As the cumulative records in Fig. 13–5b show, the behavior was unperturbed, indicating that concept formation was obtained. The behavior established by a prior discrimination history with a subset of instances had generalized to new members of the S^D class.

Like Hull's concept of common brush strokes, these S^D patterns of Fig. 13–5a and b share common elements—illumination of the three bottom windows. A somewhat different result was obtained when the experimenter attempted to develop a concept based on the *number* of windows illuminated. The stimulus patterns in the upper section of Fig. 13–5c illustrate the training contingencies of the second concept. Here the S^D class is bound together by the rule "illumination of three windows." On the other hand, S^Δ patterns contained two or four illuminated windows. The cumulative records of Fig. 13–5c indicate the excellent discrimination achieved in training, using a sequence of 13 S^D patterns and 13 S^Δ patterns. However, when 6 new S^D and S^Δ patterns were introduced (Fig. 13–5d), performance markedly deteriorated. Substantial responding occurred in the presence of the new S^Δ patterns, while decreased responding occurred in the presence of the new S^D patterns. The critical test for concept behavior failed, for the animal's responding could not be shown to be under the general control of the S^D class "three windows lit."

This negative result serves to emphasize the criterion for the existence of concept behavior. After establishing discriminative control of an R with a subset of the members of an S class, we look to see whether the discriminative control has generalized to incorporate the remaining members of the S class. The examples described in the previous sections met the required test; hence their designation as concept behavior. This was not true of Kelleher's second concept problem (Fig. 13–5d); hence we conclude that the second problem resulted only in a discrimination, not a concept. However, there are $9!/3!6! = 84$ possible S^D patterns conforming to the three-windows-lit rule, and it is possible that training with a subset of more than 13 S^D patterns would be successful in establishing the concept (Ferster, 1964).

It is instructive to compare the procedure of Kelleher's experiment with the L-set paradigm, for both purport to be concept paradigms. In the L-set procedure, the subset of S^D and S^Δ instances is arranged in terms of "problems," each of which contains a few repeated contingencies. A new problem generally is not presented until the previous one has been acquired to criterion. In Kelleher's procedure, the entire subset of S^D and S^Δ instances is presented in a single "problem." But it would be easy to redesign Kelleher's experiment casting it in an L-set format, by using a series of 2S — 1R discrimination problems. For concept 1, we might first present

Problem 1: S_1^D 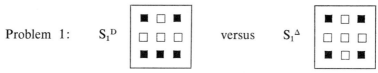   versus S_1^Δ

until the discrimination index had reached some arbitrarily high value. Then we would present

Problem 2: S_2^D 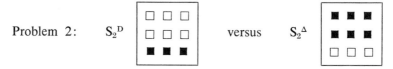   versus S_2^Δ

and so on. Our test for concept acquisition automatically proceeds with the initiation of each problem, for it is then that the organism is presented with S^D's and S^Δ's never previously seen.

Too few systematic experiments have been performed to test which combination of all possible procedures most efficiently trains concept behavior. The L-set paradigm has the virtue of yielding a concept-acquisition curve (see Fig. 13–2) which is an estimate of the degree of concept attainment at any time during the experiment. But it should be apparent that in the everyday world we learn our concepts more in the manner of Kelleher's chimpanzees, for whom numerous instances of both S^D's and S^Δ's appeared in haphazard order.

The chimpanzees' failure to acquire the three-windows-lit concept suggests that the size of the subset of S^D members used in training is an important variable in concept learning. This seems to be well documented. Andrew and Harlow (1948) trained monkeys to discriminate a single triangle from a circle. The monkeys were subsequently tested in a number of different situations which included changes in orientation of the original triangle as well as new triangles of different sizes and angles. The monkeys gave little indication of having formed the concept "triangle" from their history with a single member of the class of triangles. In Hull's Chinese-character study, one group of subjects learned to identify only three packs of characters instead of the usual six. To offset their exposure to fewer numbers of packs, the subjects were given twice as many trials on these three packs. Nevertheless, the three-pack subjects did far worse in identifying characters they had never seen. Within limits, it would seem that concept formation depends directly on the number or variety of training S^D's employed.

The experimental technique known as *matching to sample* provides a set of discrimination contingencies well suited for the study of concept behavior in animals. Matching-to-sample behavior is conveniently studied in the pigeon, using an apparatus that provides three pecking disks, each of which may be transilluminated by colors or patterns. In the study of hue matching, the sequence of events is described schematically by Fig. 13–6. During preliminary training the two side keys are occasionally illuminated with lights of different colors. Pecking at either key is then reinforced. When pecking is reliably brought under the control of the lighted side keys, the chain of behavior can be extended. The side keys are darkened and only the center key lit with colored light (Fig. 13–6, top). When the lighted center key is pecked, both the side keys are illuminated and the center key goes dark. One of the side keys—sometimes the left, sometimes the right—will display the same hue that the center key displayed just the moment before (Fig. 13–6, middle). A peck to the side key exhibiting this matching hue is reinforced. An incorrect choice, however, is followed by darkening of all lights and

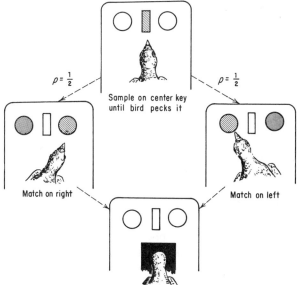

Figure 13–6. The sequence of events in matching to sample. Illumination is indicated by cross-hatched or stippled keys.

time-out from all contingencies for a few seconds. After either reinforcement or time-out, the center key light comes on again and a new matching trial begins. Experiments with two or three hues indicate that the
pigeon can be trained to match hues with better than 90 per cent
accuracy (Cumming and Berryman, 1961). No experiments have yet
attempted to build a general concept of "matching" using many hues and
many patterns. To establish such a general concept of matching, side-key
behavior would have to be brought under the control of *any* pattern just
previously presented on the center key. When such matches are made
with patterns never seen in training, we may describe the behavior as
exhibiting a general matching concept.

Matching is only one of a number of subtle relational concepts that
can be studied experimentally by this three-key technique. In the contingencies indicated by Fig. 13–7, a somewhat more complicated concept
is called for. The bird must peck the figure that is rotated 90° counterclockwise from the sample figure. The establishment of such laboratory
concepts in animals is still in the preliminary stage; there is reason to
expect that their production awaits appropriate combinations of the
familiar procedures of acquisition, discrimination, and successive approximation, rather than any new principles of behavior.

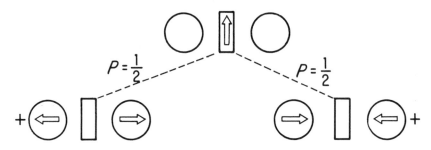

Figure 13–7. Stimuli for establishing the relational
concept of "90° counterclockwise rotation." The + indicates the key to where a peck will be reinforced (Goldiamond, 1966).

That such concepts are probably not beyond the reach of the pigeon
is suggested by an interesting demonstration by Herrnstein and Loveland
(1964). These investigators trained birds to peck a plastic key for food
only when a translucent plate near the key was illuminated. The pigeons
quickly acquired the discrimination of pecking when the plate was lit,
and not pecking when it was dark. In the terminal procedure, the plate
was illuminated with projections of 35 mm color slides containing photographs of natural settings, including countryside, towns, bodies of water,
trees, and meadows. Each slide was presented for about a minute. In

half of the slides people in various postures and positions were present, and these projections were made the occasion for intermittent reinforcement of key pecking. The other slides contained no people and these slides were S△'s for key pecking. Hundreds of different slides were shown over several months of training with these contingencies. Eventually the birds came to confine their pecking to the occasions when slides with people were projected. When a batch of new slides was presented, the birds continued to peck predominantly when people were present, though they had never seen these slides before. Since the slides containing people varied greatly in the number of people shown, their dress, whether they were near or distant, children or adults, it might be said that the pigeons were demonstrating a sophisticated concept of "person." Even the occasions when the pigeons erred were instructive. They occasionally pecked when the slide depicted objects frequently associated with people such as houses, boats, and automobiles.

13.6 ARBITRARY S^D CLASSES: DISJUNCTIVE CONCEPTS

In the previous sections we have alleged that when the behavior of organisms comes under the discriminative control of the members of a broad class of S^D's, these organisms are demonstrating conceptual behavior. We have indicated several different kinds of discrimination histories that serve to bring about such complex control. In the concepts discussed, the controlling S^D classes may be described as a set of stimuli bound together by a common relation of spatial arrangement or topological structure. Thus, however unique each animal that constitutes the S^D class "cat" may be, each member of this class shares certain physical relations in common with every other member. The same holds true for the Chinese characters grouped in the "oo" concept, the "dax" figures, etc. In general, such common relations characterize our object concepts such as "house," "book," "table," and the printed letter "E." In other concepts, such as "bigger than," "comes from," "to the right of," "is a member of," "leads to," and "threeness," the common relations binding all the S^D's are not spatial structure but other types of relations that are named by the very verbal responses they occasion. Thus, "bigger than" is a verbal response that names the relation shared by the members of the controlling S^D class.

It should be apparent that relational concepts are very pervasive. Nevertheless, behavior frequently may be observed to come under the control of broad classes of stimuli whose members seem to lack common stimulus relations. An obvious physical stimulus relation, for instance, is absent in the S^D's for "food." A carrot, a pea, a leaf of spinach, and a glass of milk appear as extremely diverse objects. From its visual characteristics alone, a pea is more like a marble than it is like a leaf; a carrot is more like a stick than it is like a glass of milk. A similar heterogeneity is present in the white crystals of iodine, the red liquid bromine, and the colorless gas known as chlorine, which partially constitute the class "halogen." The set of situations collected in Fig. 13–8 all control stopping behavior yet they bear little resemblance to one another.

Figure 13–8. Physically different stimulus situations that all control the same response: stopping (Goldiamond, 1966).

Evidently, dissimilarity in the members of a broad S^D class is no deterrent to their ability to control a similar response. We may demonstrate experimentally the control illustrated by broad, but heterogeneous, S^D classes with an L-set procedure. If we train a monkey to choose *either* the triangular *or* the spherical of two objects and agree never to present a triangle and a sphere together, the monkey's behavior will come under the control of "triangles *or* spheres." Moreover, the control will generalize to both new triangles and new spheres. Here, the controlling S^D class consists of two very different subclasses. The triangular members are all bound together by their common geometrical relation, and the spherical members by theirs. Yet a common relation is lacking *between* spheres and triangles. By extending the procedure to additional diverse S^D's, we may broaden the monkey's S^D class to an indefinite list of heterogeneous objects. If we are careful to keep the new S^D elements unrelated to the old ones, there will be no reason to expect the monkey to generalize to any novel S we decide to add to the class.

The examples of everyday heterogeneous S^D classes, and the behavior of the monkey cited in the last paragraph, illustrate what are known as disjunctive concepts. The members of the S^D class are *either* triangles *or* spheres; *either* carrots, *or* peas, *or* spinach, *or* milk, . . . ; *either* a policeman at an intersection, *or* a red light; and so forth. In each case, a response is under the control of a broad class of S^D's, and therefore meets one of the important criteria of concept behavior; nevertheless, the lack of a single common relation, a thread linking all the members of the class, prevents the generalization to new members that is typical of other concepts.

The difficulty in bringing in new members of a disjunctive S^D class on the basis of generalization may be one of the reasons why mankind is sometimes said to abhor disjunctive concepts (Bruner, Goodnow, and Austin, 1956). Fortunately, it is frequently possible to find an *underlying* relation among the members of a disjunctive S^D class which can provide the basis for generalization. For example, different though foods may be in appearance, all have the common property of being substances which are ingested by living organisms and changed into vital bodily constituents. Similarly, bromine, chlorine, and iodine have the common property of combining with metals to form white crystalline salts which in fact are closely related to each other.

In these and many other disjunctive concepts, an underlying relation is revealed by a behavioral operation that transforms the originally heterogeneous and diverse members of an S^D class into a new set of homogeneous and similar members. These new situations share a common relation, and that relation provides the basis for normal generalization. Sometimes the operation that is required is simple. To discover whether a certain substance is a food, we need merely ingest it and wait for the resulting transformed situation. To discover whether some new substance is a halogen, we let it interact with sodium and see whether a white crystalline "halogenic" salt is produced.

More frequently, resolving disjunctive classes into underlying relational concepts may be arduous. A significant part of scientific activity consists in trying out operations on superficially unlike events in the hope of transforming them into situations that are in fact similar. Much of this book is devoted to illustrating underlying relations discovered in behavioral events that, on the surface, look very different. A bird pecking a disk and a student voicing an opinion are shown to have an underlying relation.

Searches for underlying relations are by no means confined to science. Consider the long attempt to discover the absolute standard for great art or great music. Such a standard, if it could be found, would be a rule for relating the extremely diverse instances of what we identify as good art or music. The failure to find such rules may force us in exasperation to conclude that good music is what the critics say is good; or, to cite an illustration from psychology, intelligence is sometimes said to be "what the intelligence tests measure." No one has yet found an operation to perform on paintings or musical compositions that generates a set of situations in which the great and the mediocre are unequivocally distinguished. The concept of greatness remains disjunct. "When to stop" also retains a certain arbitrariness. No operation can be found to transform the diverse elements of Fig. 13–8 into those exhibiting a common stimulus relation. The class is man-made and the choice of stimulus elements arbitrary. For this reason, there is no basis for generalization when a new S is introduced; all one can do is test each new instance as it comes along, determining class inclusion by the reinforcement contingencies alone. Such a class is built in much the way that we built the monkey's concept of "triangle-or-sphere."

In the final analysis, the only relation common to all kinds of disjunctive concepts is that their dissimilar members govern the same response. Some disjunctive concepts, for example, food and halogens, have the further property that their diverse members can be so transformed as to show a common underlying relation. Other disjunctive concepts such as great music and intelligence *may* have an underlying relation; others still, such as the experimental "sphere-or-triangle" concept, remain entirely arbitrary and dissimilar.

13.7 MEANING AND UNDERSTANDING CONSIDERED AS INTERRELATIONS BETWEEN CONCEPTS

The meaning of a word (verbal response) has long been held to be related to concept formation, but the lack of a systematic framework for describing concepts has hampered an analysis of the exact relationship. In his discussion of how a child evolves the concept of a dog, Hull equated the formation of the concept with the idea of meaning. A child has the meaning of a dog when he can appropriately identify new objects as dogs. We may agree that appropriate use of a verbal response to identify the members of a concept's S^D class is part of what is meant by having the meaning for the verbal response. But we are likely to feel that something is missing in equating meaning with discriminative behavior. Consider the concept of milk. Would we be willing to agree that a child has the meaning of milk when he can correctly identify bottles of milk, glasses of milk, and spilt milk? The child might be said to have a limited meaning of milk if all he can do is identify instances of the S^D class, but we shall be inclined to say that his understanding of the concept does not go very deep. Analogously, a chimpanzee may be trained to pick out triangles from any group of objects, but few psychologists would be willing to use terms like meaning or understanding in describing the observed behavior. Meaning and understanding are, however, things we try to teach in schools. Even science and art are sometimes said to be quests for them. Hence it may be appropriate to ask what further behaviors may be involved when an organism is said to have the meaning of, or to understand, a concept.

We must first examine the notion that an organism may acquire a concept which is itself made up of two or more concepts. In the present terminology, a response (verbal or otherwise), may be controlled by a broad S^D class which can itself be partitioned into two or more S^D classes, each controlling its own unique response. Consider, for instance the concept "ice," which we shall take as equivalent to "frozen water." The S^D class for ice is evidently the intersection of the set of frozen objects (F) and the set of water objects (W). Ice is therefore represented by the shaded region in the Venn diagram of [13.2]. Few of our everyday con-

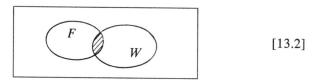

[13.2]

cepts are as simple as this diagram indicates, but the majority of the concepts acquired by human organisms do lend themselves to analysis in terms of other concepts. Thus, an operant is the <set of responses> under <the control of> their <consequences>. A harbor is a <sheltered> <body of water> with <piers>. Father is a <male> <parent>. We may even invent such concepts, as in the example tiglon = the <offspring> of a <male> <tiger> and a <female> <lion>. Many of these concepts are generalized forms of [13.2].

Whenever the S^D classes of a concept are made up of the intersection, or what is more often called the conjunction, of two or more S^D classes, we speak of the concept as a *conjunctive* concept. The compound nature of a conjunctive concept suggests an experimental question, namely, whether a prior history with its component concepts affects the acquisition of such a conjunctive concept. An experiment by Kendler and Vineberg (1954) indicates that when its components are previously conceptualized, a concept based on their conjunction is more quickly acquired. In that experiment, each of the 32 figures in Fig. 13–9 was drawn on a card and the subjects' task was to sort a haphazard arrangement of the 32 cards into two classes. Sorting responses were reinforced with "right" or "wrong" according to a rule which differed for different

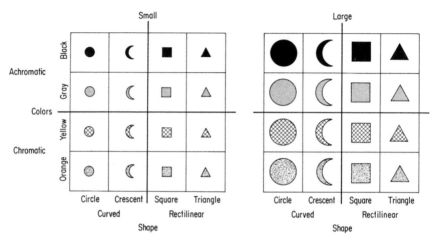

Figure 13–9. The 32 figures used by Kendler and Vineberg (1954) to study the acquisition of conjunctive concepts.

groups of subjects. Two groups of subjects were reinforced for sorting all curved figures in one pile and all rectilinear figures into another pile. A third group of subjects was reinforced for sorting all achromatic (lacking color) figures into one pile and all chromatic (colored) figures into another pile. Thus the three groups of subjects first learned shape, or color classifications. When these had been well learned, the rules for reinforcement were changed. Subjects of the first group were now reinforced for sorting all large figures into one pile, and all small figures into another pile, that is, a size sort. The second group was now reinforced for color sorts, and the third group for sorting all triangles and crescents into one pile, and all circles and squares into another. At the end of this training, all groups had learned two concepts, as shown by the first and second concept columns of Table 13–2. In the terminal procedure, all subjects were reinforced for sorting the cards into *four* piles: small-curved, large-curved, small-rectilinear, large-rectilinear. Such a sort is made on the basis of conjunctive concepts consisting of size and shape concepts. Group 1 learned this final sort the most rapidly, Group 2 next, and Group 3 last. The authors conclude that the rate of acquisition of the conjunctive concept is directly related to the number of component concepts previously learned.

Table 13–2
THE TRAINING CONDITIONS USED BY KENDLER AND VINEBERG
(1954) TO STUDY CONJUNCTIVE CONCEPT ACQUISITION

	FIRST CONCEPT	SECOND CONCEPT	THIRD CONCEPT
Group 1	Shape	Size	Size and shape
Group 2	Shape	Color	Size and shape
Group 3	Color	△ ℂ vs ○ □	Size and shape

In Kendler and Vineberg's final concept task, two component concepts (size and shape) were related by conjunction to form a new concept (size-shape). Conjunction is, however, only one of the many ways that concepts may be related, and it is an analysis of such inter-concept relations that is most pertinent for the meaning or understanding of a concept. We argued earlier in this section that a child who could identify instances of the concept milk, or a monkey who could press a lever whenever he was presented with a triangle, cannot fully be said to exhibit all the behavior necessary for us to class it as exhibiting understanding. The kind of additional behavior that seems required is represented schematically in Fig. 13–10 for the concept of milk.

Figure 13–10 is explicated as follows. Each of the circles of the diagram refers to a class of S^D's of the sort we have previously described. Thus the child, for whom Fig. 13–10 might be said to be a meaningful structure, can identify bottles of milk, cups of milk, spilt milk, and so on. But he can also identify (with different verbal responses) cows of various sorts, cereals of one kind or another, cheeses, ice creams, and milkmen. If he is a high school student studying nutrition, then he is likely to be able to identify fluids, butterfat, and calcium too. But, equally important, the sophisticated human organism can give a *relational* identifier for a compound situation consisting of one S^D from milk and one from any of the other S^D classes indicated. This further conceptual skill is indicated by the lines between circles with the statements describing the relation. Each relational statement is, however, also a concept; indeed, it is the sort of concept we have met frequently in previous sections. The training required for such relational concepts as "comes from" and "is a component of" is precisely analogous to the training given the monkey when such concepts as the "odd one," "the taller," "the one rotated 90 degrees," were acquired. A child is said to have a more complete meaning of milk, or a more complete understanding of the concept of milk, therefore, when he can identify the relations between members of the S^D class making up milk and the members of various other S^D classes.

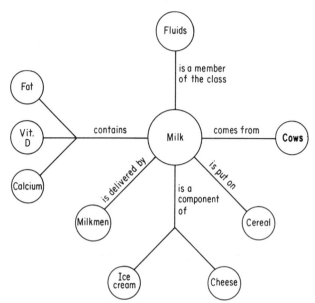

Figure 13–10. A schematic representation of the concept of milk and its relation to several other concepts.

It should be clear that the structural representation of meaning of Fig. 13–10 is artificially isolated. We have in fact shown only the relations between a single concept and a group of others, neglecting the interrelationships of each peripheral concept to the others, and to all other concepts the organism exhibits. A complete representation of the conceptual repertoire of any given individual would seem an insurmountable task, though a limited sample of concepts and their interrelations might feasibly be described (Reitman, 1965; R. Quillian, unpublished manuscript).

Figure 13–10 does give us a way of crudely representing varying degrees of understanding. The more dense the interconnections, and the more S^D classes that can be tied together, the more likely we are to say that an individual understands a concept. The understanding a child has of milk differs principally from that of the dairy manager, or the nutrition expert, in the smaller number of concepts to which the child can relate milk. My understanding of my car is very incomplete compared with that of my garage mechanic, who can relate the word car to thousands of other S^D classes including, in particular, what we call the parts of the vehicle. Yet his understanding may end with the mechanics of engines. An interesting case is provided by the physicist who may be able to analyze such concepts as friction, acceleration, work, and energy at a far more basic level than could the mechanic. But when his car refuses to start, the physicist will be helpless in repairing it unless he also possesses such concepts as rocker arm, spark plug, cylinder, distributor, and their various interrelations. The interrelationships between concepts for any given individual depend on that individual's past history: the automobile driver's contingencies are affiliated with a certain set of situations, the mechanic's with another, and the physicist's with still another. The differences between their conceptual repertoires suggest a distinction in level, though it is often very difficult in practice to establish the relative levels of concepts.

Numerous authors have studied one or another of the relations between concepts in an attempt to clarify in general the relational structure between concepts. Many of our own concepts show an interesting hierarchical structure (Welch, 1947; Brown, 1958a, b). That is, the concept dog, for instance, may contain as members poodles, dalmatians, hounds,

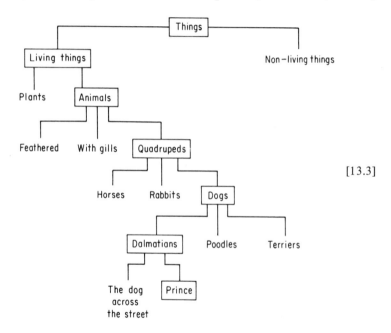

[13.3]

terriers, and so forth. But <my dalmatian, Prince> is a complete concept too. Consider all the situations in which we might use the word "Prince" to identify them: Prince in the house, Prince outside chasing a cat, Prince asleep, etc. Hierarchical structure extends in both ways. Prince is not only a dog—he is a quadruped, an animal, and a living thing (Brown, 1958a). Evidently the S^D classes that make up our concepts may be both sets containing other concepts as well as subsets of other concepts. (For instance, see Diagram [13.3].) Acquiring the verbal repertoire that will put a concept in its proper place in a hierarchy is an important part of what we mean by understanding a concept.

It is in responding to the interrelations between concepts, or S^D classes, that language responses have a special advantage over other forms of behavior. In teaching a child that milk comes from cows, it is not necessary for us to bring a sample of milk and a cow to the child and reinforce picking out the milk under a set of contingencies analogous to the "matching" contingencies we used in the pigeon. If the child has already acquired the concepts $<$cow$>$, $<$milkmen$>$, and $<$comes from$>$ that is, uses the words "cow," "milkmen," and "comes from," in appropriate situations, we may deal directly with the verbal behavior. We may first prompt, and then reinforce, the compound sentence: "Milk comes from cows." The unique advantage of language is that, unlike levers, keys, and buttons, it provides a portable response repertoire which the organism can carry away from the original situations in which the behavior was shaped. Moreover, when the language responses of an organism can be brought under the discriminative control of the arbitrary situations that make up printed words, or the spoken words of a second organism, this advantage is further enhanced. But this great flexibility in both control and emission of the system of behaviors we call language can be a disadvantage too, for it presents the possibility of acquisition of verbal chains without the accompanying broad environmental S^D control characteristic of concepts. A child may acquire what we call empty verbalisms. John Dewey, a well-known educational theorist of Thorndike's generation, once asked a group of school children what they would find if they dug deep into the earth. He was greeted with blank stares. The teacher quickly explained to Dewey that he had asked the wrong question. "What is the state of the center of the earth?" she asked. The answer came in a chorus: "Igneous fusion." Here, a verbal sequence has been brought under the discriminative control of a second organism's (the teacher's) spoken words, but it appears that no child would have been able to identify any of the members of the S^D classes $<$igneous$>$ or $<$fusion$>$, or relate the concept of the $<$center of the earth$>$ to $<$digging at the surface$>$. Such are the chief differences between what many educators call rote memorization and meaningful learning. Many a child has learned the Pledge of Allegiance without understanding a word of it; that is, without being able to identify examples of the concepts represented by the various words of the Pledge.

The present analysis helps to clarify the role of *definition* within a language. Consider the familiar definition that an operant = a response that is under the control of its consequences. Such a definition is a statement of a compound concept made up of $<$response$>$, $<$under the control of$>$, and $<$consequences$>$. Students are sometimes tempted to acquire the verbal chain on the right-hand side of the equals sign in preparation for being presented with the left-hand term alone on a quiz. But most instructors will hope for more. A definition is said to be understood when it can be parsed, that is, broken down into its component concepts. If this analysis is carried on successively, concept by concept, a point is eventually reached where the components of the original concept have all been reduced to simple rather than compound concepts. Each of these simple concepts can only be specified by listing some of the actual situations from the environment that make up its S^D class. At this level, a concept is sometimes said to be primitive. We illustrate this kind of conceptual parsing in Fig. 13–11. This figure, like Fig. 13–10, is merely another way of representing a partial meaning structure. It would appear that the great power of a definition lies in its ability to encode a vast number of concepts and their interrelations into a single unit of verbal behavior. The typical definition would appear to be a very complex example of the kind of concept studied by Kendler and Vineberg.

The notes in this section provide a clue as to what is lacking from the experimental analyses of concept behavior presented in earlier sections. There, in training their animals by means of the L-set or other concept-

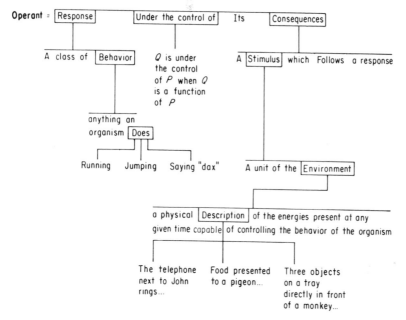

Figure 13–11. A partial parse of the definition of the word Operant into some of its component concepts. The important behavioral concepts are boxed and further parsed.

training procedures, investigators have in general endeavored to establish only a single concept. In order to simulate the simplest form of understanding, at least three concepts seem required: two independent S^D classes, and a further S^D class which would contain among its elements compound situations consisting of one element from each of the first two S^D classes. This would be equivalent to two concepts and a relational concept linking their members. The behavioral technology remains to be developed for bringing a number of behaviors under the kind of control illustrated by Figs. 13–10 and 13–11, but a promising start in this direction is illustrated in the behavior of the monkey in the two panels of Fig. 13–12. In the lower panel, the monkey is shown choosing the odd-*shaped* object of three, and his behavior is partly under the control of the color of the tray. When this color is changed, as in the upper panel of Fig. 13–12, the monkey chooses the odd-*colored* of the same three objects. Here, two relational concepts have been developed by L-set procedures: "odd-shaped" and "odd-colored," and they have both been brought under the discriminative control of the tray color. But even these demonstrations fall well short of simulating the complex interrelationships characteristic of "understanding." In these and the other experiments with animals described in this chapter, only a limited response repertoire is developed. It would appear that the experimental analysis of concept relationships will require the development of more extensive response repertoires, which could play a role analogous to the verbal behaviors of the human organism.

13.8 THE ACQUISITION OF CONCEPTS THROUGH PROGRAMMED INSTRUCTION

Much of the previous section was of necessity speculative, since behavioral technology has not yet developed to the stage where a detailed assessment of complex concept acquisition and concept interaction can be made in lower organisms. We might hope to supplement our experimental information about concept acquisition by examining human learning. But when we turn to the place where the most systematic human concept learning is supposed to take place, the school, we find many broad generalizations but few principles. Everyone is for meaningful learning and against rote memorization. Concepts, it is universally agreed, are what we want taught rather than "empty facts." Yet few would deny that while many school children do acquire the basic concepts that are the objectives of their school courses, many others do not. This is hardly for any lack of conceptual material, for the school curriculum

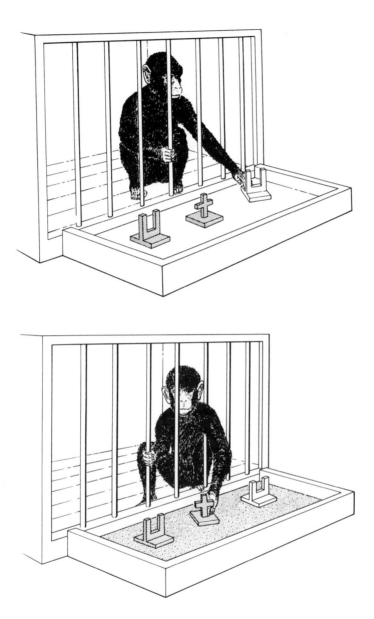

Figure 13–12. Complex conceptual control by one ele-ment of the total situation (adapted from Harlow and Kuenne, 1949).

is filled with an unmatched variety of concepts. Consider a few adapted from Brownell and Hendrickson (1950): nation, government, constitution, citizen (social studies); law, element, magnet, reagent, cell, osmosis, mass, acid, ion (science); erosion, latitude, region, map (geography); voice, tense, number, sentence, paragraph (language); division, fraction, exponent, equation, number base (arithmetic); scale, pitch, key, interval, harmony (music). Amid this diversity of conceptual material it would seem surprising if we failed to glean something from a critical examination of how such concepts are taught. Unfortunately a twin difficulty presents itself: (1) No traditional method of teaching guarantees concept acquisition, yet (2) some children seem to acquire concepts no matter what the method. It thus proves impossible to extract from the traditional methods of teaching the necessary and sufficient conditions for producing concept acquisition. Methods appropriate to the heterogeneous classroom group fail to provide adequate control over individual reinforcement contingencies to insure the desired performance in each organism.

The implications of this fact led B. F. Skinner (1954, 1958, 1961) to consider the possibilities of a method that would permit somewhat better control over each individual student's conditions of learning. Skinner proposed to program the contingencies entailed in teaching school subjects in small systematic steps, and to provide immediate reinforcement for correct behaviors. Skinner noted that traditional methods do not guarantee responding from the student. In lecturing to a student, in assigning him a book to read, or even with the more exotic audio-visual aids such as televised classrooms, the teacher cannot be sure the student is listening or reading carefully. In the language of behavior, the teacher cannot be sure that the student is actively responding.

Skinner's programmed contingencies tacitly assumed that the kinds of intellectual skills acquired in schools, and traditionally viewed as ideas, understanding, interests, associations, knowledge, and so on, were complex operant behaviors. If so, then their acquisition and maintenance ought to follow all the laws of behavior we have described. But a program of teaching based on the principles of successive approximation, discrimination, etc., requires a more systematic attention to individual contingencies than the traditional schoolroom provides. Skinner advanced a solution to this problem in the form of a machine for serially presenting teaching material and for setting contingencies of reinforcement for behavior. The machine incorporated three essential aspects. (1) Material is presented to the student in small discrete portions, called *frames*. (2) This material sets the occasion for some discriminative operant on the part of the student, such as writing a word or sentence, completing a blank, or choosing an answer. (3) Provision is made for immediately reinforcing the behavior emitted by making available the correct "answer" as soon as the student has responded, thus permitting him to advance to the next frame. One such machine used by Skinner is shown in Fig. 13–13. In this version, frames are written on a rotary disk, and one frame at a time appears in the center window. After reading the frame, the student writes his response on a paper strip exposed through the opening on the right. He then lifts a lever at the front of the machine, thus moving what he has written under a transparent cover and revealing the correct response in the center window. The individual frames are organized in small sequential steps. The student can move at his own pace through such a succession of frames, called a *program,* making very few errors.

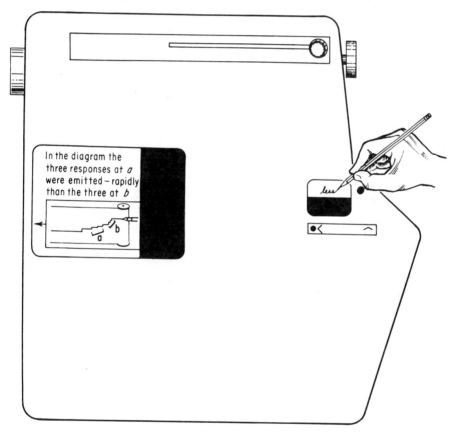

Figure 13–13. A teaching machine. The student reads the frame and makes a written response, then moves a lever to uncover the correct answer for comparison with his response (after Skinner, 1958).

Programs of this sort are not restricted to machine presentation. The critical aspects—small sequential steps, active responding, and immediate reinforcement—can be organized in book form. A sample of such *programmed text* is found in this book in Chapter 4.

Much has been written regarding the merits and possibilities of programmed instruction. The writing of a program is a delicate art, and when a program is perfected the teacher-programmer is in a position to contact an indefinite number of individual students via intimate reinforcement contingencies. Despite its automated nature, the method bears certain resemblances to that of an individual tutor who proceeds slowly and methodically, making sure each point is understood before progressing to the next. The repeated testing and revising of a program on individual learners, until it succeeds in teaching what it is meant to, is a characteristic of programming which is all too frequently lacking in traditional methods of teaching. These benefits of programmed instruction could well be the basis for upgrading more conventional modes of teaching. When a suitable program is available to teach fundamentals, the teacher is free to discuss the subtle points, to lead the students in creative problem solving, and to rehearse the skills acquired by machine in a somewhat more lifelike context. Programming is in too nascent a stage at present to permit us to estimate exactly how radically it will change our educational practices. In any case, our present interest lies elsewhere. We are concerned with the program as an experimental vehicle for the acquisition of concepts.

It is useful to classify the verbal subject matter constituting a frame into two types of statements: rules and examples (Evans, Homme, and Glaser, 1962). A rule may be considered to be a general specification or definition of an S^D class, whereas an example may be considered to be an instance of one of the members of the S^D class. An instructional program may be viewed as an arrangement of various rules and examples, with portions of each rule or example missing, thus requiring behavior on the part of the learner for completion. It should be apparent that a presentation of a subset of examples associated with a given rule is analogous to the presentation of a subset of individual S's from a broad S^D class and the reinforcement of a given identifying response, say the word milk, or a reaching response in the direction of the odd object.

Consider the four frames of a student program for teaching certain concepts of imagery in poetry shown in Fig. 13–14. Prior to these frames, the concepts of image, object, and likeness had been taught by examples. Frames 48, 49, and 50 are three examples from the S^D class which is to be identified as *simile*. Note that each frame is so arranged that the contextual cues enhance the probability of the required response. The three frames used as S^D's for simile have certain similarities but also certain differences. Since the programmer desires the concept

Figure 13–14. Four frames of a program designed to teach concepts concerned with imagery in poetry (courtesy of Susan Stitt).

---

48. An image that expresses a likeness between objects of different classes, but does not mean exactly what it says, is called a *simile*. The image "the girl is like a flower" is a _____.

Answer. simile

---

49. Because it expresses a likeness between objects of different classes, but does not mean exactly what it says, the image "the man's face lit up like the sun" is a _____.

Answer. simile

---

50. A simile is not only introduced by the word like, but by the words as, as if, or as when. Thus the image "the man is as red *as* a beet" is a _____.

Answer. simile

---

51. On the other hand, a phrase which expresses identity between two objects, but does not mean exactly what it says, is not a simile. Thus the image "her eyes are stars" (is/is not) a simile.

Answer. is not

---

of simile to be as broad as possible, the reinforcement contingencies are set in the presence of a wide variety of examples from the S^D class. Frame 51, however, is an S^Δ instance. In human as well as animal concept acquisition, it is important to present situations which are not members of the S^D class and withhold reinforcement for the response or, as in this case, reinforce an incompatible response. Frame 51 helps establish what a simile is not.

Another example of concept formation is shown in the frame of Fig. 13–15. Later on in this program, the student will encounter pictures of other organisms with and without six legs, and with many other features that vary. But the word insect will be cued and reinforced only in the presence of pictures of six-legged organisms. Eventually, the concept of insect will generalize to the broad class of organisms with six legs via this history with a subset of the members.

Still another example in the field of behavior analysis itself is provided in the frames of Fig. 13–16. The concept to be acquired is that of a response event. Note that the four frames provide S^D and S^Δ instances for the concept. Eventually, a frame will appear in which the programmer will ask the learner to induce the general definition from his past history with numerous examples.

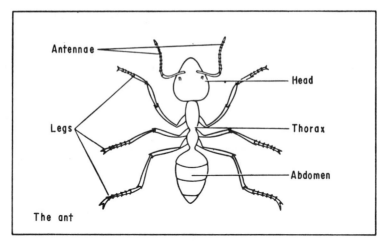

Figure 13–15. A frame illustrating a member of the S^D class "insect" (Lysaught and Williams, 1963).

The examples of concept formation via programmed instruction indicate that the fundamental notions of concept acquisition discussed in earlier sections are applicable to human learning as well. The examples shown represent fairly simple illustrations of how control of a verbal response (simile, insect, response-event) by a broad class of S^D's can be brought about by systematic presentation of examples, with reinforcement[1] for the desired verbal response. It is clear that the concepts evolved are compound concepts made up of others. Simile is composed of certain relations between the concepts of object, image, and likeness; insect is the conjunction of organism and six legs; response event is a compound of action and actor. In a complete program, each concept to be acquired is established via a suitable set of contingencies with a subset of its members, and many of the acquired concepts are then related to each other via suitable compound examples. It is this web of concepts which appears to be the hallmark of true understanding of a subject matter.

Programming concept acquisition raises a number of systematic questions concerning the role of certain variables that the programmer has under his control. The programmer may control the number of S^D examples and S^Δ counter-examples; he may control their diversity and their sequences. In developing a number of different concepts, he may choose one concrete multi-dimensional example, presenting it from various points of view, or he may use numerous simpler examples, presenting each from a single point of view. Little systematic information

---

[1] Note that for normal humans "getting the answer right" is often a sufficient reinforcer. See, for instance, the program in section 4.3.

Figure 13–16. A series of frames designed to establish the concept of response-event. The correct R's are indicated by the small letters to the right of the frame (Mechner, 1963).

1. Your being born *was not* a "response-event" for you. Your throwing your rattle out of your crib *was* a "response-event" for you. Check those sentences below that describe a response event for the person or animal *named* in it. (Note: You can check any number of sentences.) a. ☐ Clara dyed her hair red. b. ☐ Herman died. c. ☐ John had a cavity. d. ☐ Harold went to the dentist. e. ☐ The cat meowed.	a d e
2. When you hit someone, it is *your* response-event. When the other person hits you back, it *is not* your response-event. For each sentence below, check the box if it describes a response-event for the organism named in it. a. ☐ Philip ran fast. b. ☐ Gregory was run over. c. ☐ Alice cheated on the exam. d. ☐ Mary was caught cheating. e. ☐ The canary lost all its feathers. f. ☐ The dog caught the fudge on the first bounce.	a c f
3. Check the statements that describe response-events for *you*. a. ☐ You solved a hard math example. b. ☐ Your teacher gave you a good report card. c. ☐ You are a dentist. d. ☐ You are studying to be a dentist.	a d
4. The sentence "A cat runs" refers to a response-event. The sentence "A person runs" refers to a response-event. The sentence "A color runs" does not refer to a response-event. Check the response-events below: a. ☐ The hurricane struck here yesterday. (for the hurricane) b. ☐ Tom struck Harry. (for Tom) c. ☐ Tom struck Harry. (for Harry) d. ☐ The clock struck ten. (for the clock) e. ☐ You eat a carrot. (for you) f. ☐ A mosquito bites you. (for you) g. ☐ A mosquito bites you. (for the mosquito)	b e g

is available concerning any of these variables, but it is as an experimental medium that programming possesses important potentialities for elucidating fundamental relations in concept acquisition.

13.9 THE PERCEPTUAL CONSTANCIES

The notion of a "thing" as an unchanging entity is so strongly ingrained that it may come as a surprise that things as primitive as objects may be described as concepts. Consider that the face of a friend is not a single visual stimulus. At times it appears in shade, at other times in sunlight. At times it is smiling, at times frowning. Sometimes you see the profile, at other times you see the front view. Yet profile and front view are themselves a collection of profiles and front views, no single one of which is ever exactly repeated. In spite of the fact that you never see the same face twice you have no difficulty identifying your friend. In technical language, your friend is a broad class of S^D's and you respond similarly to all the members.

Consider the object shown in Fig. 13–17. All four sketches represent "the same door," yet the various patterns that reach the eye, and that constitute the four situations we call "door," are vastly different. It is clear that for doors, or any other object we wish to imagine, our concept of the given object consists not of a single situation, but a broad class of situations. The examples we have just given are instances of what might be called *object constancy*. In spite of rather marked changes in the situation, we retain a constant response in the presence of all its variants.

What kind of a concept is represented by object constancy? Taken individually, the four sketches of Fig. 13–17 suggest that the object concept is disjunctive, since these four situations look so different. But Fig. 13–17 is only a sample of the infinite set of situations ranging from open to shut, all of which control the response "door." And all

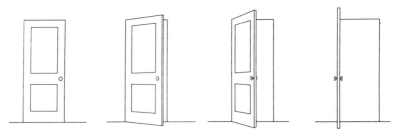

Figure 13–17. Four members of the S^D class "door"
(Gibson, 1950).

these situations are related one to the other by the fact that one "door" situation may be continuously transformed into another. Such a series of transformations relates the situations of any given object.

Object constancy is merely one of a class of what are generally called perceptual constancies. Another example is shown by the two pieces of coal resting on white paper illustrated in Fig. 13–18. We call the coal "black" and the paper "white" regardless of the absolute intensity of light that either the coal or the paper alone reflects. In shadow, the piece of coal in the left panel of Fig. 13–18 reflects only 1 millilambert of light,

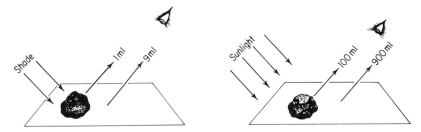

Figure 13–18. A case of neutral color constancy. A piece of coal rests on a sheet of white paper (Hochberg, 1964).

while the same piece of coal in the sun (right panel of Fig. 13–18) reflects 100 times as much light. Still we call the coal black, even though now it reflects more than ten times as much light as did the white paper in the shade. The neutral color response (shade of gray) depends on the relative illumination of the object to its background or immediately surrounding region. Thus "black" appears as a concept since it is the response in the presence of a broad class of related S^D's: object 1 unit of light, background 9 units of light; object 10 units, background 90 units; object 100, background 900; and so forth.

A final example is provided by the phenomenon known as *size constancy*. As a person walks towards you, you are unlikely to report that his visual image is increasing in size. Yet, as he approaches, his image is growing in size on your retina in a way that is approximately inversely proportional to his distance from you. Within limits, you report him as the same size regardless of the size his image makes on your retina. It turns out that one's concept of size is dependent on an S^D class where the rule for class inclusion is a complex function of the retinal size of the object plus the values of numerous other visual variables that vary with the distance of an object. Figure 13–19 shows that the concept of constant size is not controlled by constant retinal size. The three cylinders of Fig. 13–19 are all the same size (measure them) but we tend to class

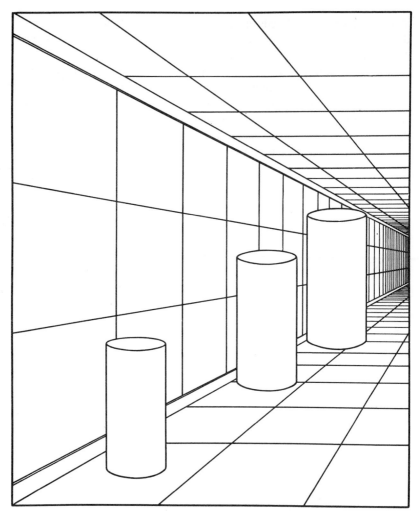

Figure 13–19. Size response as determined by distance variables (Gibson, 1950).

them as progressively larger from left to right because of the changes in linear perspective, one of the variables that ordinarily changes progressively with distance.

It is, of course, no accident that the object, neutral-color, and size constancies have developed. Reinforcing contingencies are very often correlated with "objects" (a bird had best keep clear of all the situations we call "cat" if it is to live to a ripe old age), as well as the compound stimulus variables controlling achromatic color constancy and size constancy. It is rarely of use to regard an object as changing its color or size when its illumination or distance changes. On the other hand, it is very useful to classify that animal moving rapidly towards you as "big" even though its image size is still very small. Our concepts mirror the reinforcing contingencies of nature, though it remains an interesting speculation whether these perceptual concepts are generally re-acquired in each individual's past history or whether, having been so well acquired by his ancestors, they are now a permanent part of his visual response equipment.

References for Chapter 13

Andrew, G., and Harlow, H. F. Performance of macaque monkeys on a test of the concept of generalized triangularity. *Comp. psychol. Monogr.,* 1948, **19,** 1–20.

Brown, R. How shall a thing be called? *Psychol. Rev.,* 1958a, **65,** 14–21.

Brown, R. *Words and things.* Glencoe, Ill.: Free Press, 1958b.

Brownell, W. A., and Hendrickson, G. How children learn information, concepts and generalizations. In *Learning and instruction,* 49th Yearb., Nat. Soc. Study Ed., 1950, Part I.

Bruner, J., Goodnow, Jacqueline J., and Austin, G. A. *A Study of thinking.* New York: Wiley, 1956.

Cumming, W. W., and Berryman, R. Some data on matching behavior in the pigeon. *J. exp. Anal. Behav.,* 1961, **4,** 281–284.

Evans, J. L., Homme, L. E., and Glaser, R. The ruleg system for the construction of programmed verbal learning sequences. *J. educ. Res.,* 1962, **55,** 513–518.

Ferster, C. B. Arithmetic behavior in chimpanzees. *Sci. Amer.,* May 1964, **210,** 98–106.

Gibson, J. J. *The perception of the visual world.* Cambridge: The Riverside Press, 1950.

Goldiamond, I. Perception, language, and conceptualization rules. In B. Kleinmuntz (Ed.), *Carnegie Institute of Technology annual symposium on cognition,* New York: Wiley, 1966.

Harlow, H. F. The formation of learning sets. *Psychol. Rev.,* 1949, **56,** 51–65.

Harlow, H. F. Learning set and error factor theory. In S. Koch (Ed.), *Psychology: a study of a science,* Vol. 2. New York: McGraw-Hill, 1959.

Harlow, H. F., and Kuenne, M. Learning to think. *Sci. Amer.,* 1949, **181,** 36–39.

Herrnstein, R. J., and Loveland, D. H. Complex visual concept in the pigeon. *Science,* 1964, **146,** 549–551.

Hochberg, J. E. *Perception.* Englewood Cliffs: Prentice-Hall, 1964.

Hull, C. L. Quantitative aspects of the evolution of concepts. *Psychol. Monogr.,* 1920, **28,** Whole No. 123.

Kelleher, R. Concept formation in chimpanzees. *Science,* 1958, **128,** 777–778.

Keller, F. S., and Schoenfeld, W. N. *Principles of psychology.* New York: Appleton-Century-Crofts, 1950.

Kendler, H. H. *Basic psychology.* New York: Appleton-Century-Crofts, 1963.

Kendler, H. H., and Vineberg, R. The acquisition of compound concepts as a function of previous training. *J. exp. Psychol.,* 1954, **48,** 252–258.

Kimble, G. A., and Garmezy, N. *Principles of general psychology.* (2nd ed.) New York: Ronald Press, 1963.

Lysaught, J. P., and Williams, C. M. *A guide to programmed instruction.* New York: Wiley, 1963.

Mechner, F. *Science education and behavioral technology.* New York: Basic Systems, 1963.

Reitman, W. R. *Cognition and thought: an information processing approach.* New York: Wiley, 1965.

Skinner, B. F. The science of learning and the art of teaching. *Harvard educ. Rev.,* 1954, **24,** 86–97.

Skinner, B. F. Teaching machines. *Science,* 1958, **128,** 969–977.

Skinner, B. F. Why we need teaching machines. *Harvard educ. Rev.,* 1961, **31,** 377–398.

Smoke, K. L. An objective study of concept formation. *Psychol. Monogr.,* 1932, **42,** Whole No. 191.

Welch, L. A behaviorist explanation of concept formation. *J. genet. Psychol.,* 1947, **71,** 201–222.

Chapter 14 PROBLEM SOLVING AND INTELLIGENCE

The term "problem" has arisen occasionally in previous discussions. Thorndike placed cats in a puzzle box containing a latch that could be opened by various movements (Fig. 1–1). Cats lacking a previous history with the contingencies of this apparatus were said to be faced with a problem—escaping from the box. The acquisition of any instrumental behavior can thus be said to contain elements of problem solving. In the learning sets of the last chapter, we described the successive sets of discrimination contingencies presented during training as a series of discrimination problems. Monkeys solve these problems, and as a result achieve the ability to solve new and similar problems with increasing efficiency.

14.1 THE STRUCTURE OF A PROBLEM AND THE NATURE OF A SOLUTION

The problems faced by Thorndike's cats and Harlow's monkeys differed in several respects, but particularly in the contingencies extant. The contingencies set for the cats were predominantly differentiations; those for the monkeys, discriminations. It appears, therefore, that the notation of a "problem" does not denote any particular class of reinforcement contingencies. Both discriminations and differentiations can be problems. Whether a set of contingencies is or is not to be construed as a problem for an organism depends upon the behaviors that are at strength when the organism first faces the problem situation. Thorndike's cats evidently found the puzzle box a problem on their early trials.

Eventually, as the behavior that led to opening the latch was repeatedly reinforced, the situation lost its problematic character. No sooner were the cats placed in the box than they were out again. A similar development occurs in L-set formation. A monkey with a well-formed oddity L-set solves any new oddity discrimination immediately. The oddity situation can no longer be described as a "problem" for this organism.

These simple ideas are not limited to the artificial problems set animals in psychological laboratories. For a second grader

$$\begin{array}{r} 25 \\ -18 \\ \hline \end{array}$$

constitutes a problem, but a year or so later that will no longer be the case. Similarly, you may not find $\int e^{-3x}\, dx$ a problem, depending on whether you possess certain behaviors usually taught in first-year calculus texts. At the extreme end of the continuum, we may all be said to find "how to end wars" a problem since a universal solution remains to be demonstrated. In summary, no class of contingency, nor any particular contingency, can be described as a problem until we know what behavior the organism has available in the presence of that contingency. Let us now attempt to describe this view more rigorously. To do so, we shall find the concepts of chaining introduced in Chapter 12 indispensable.

In a chain of behavior, an organism emits operants in a sequential order. The particular order is governed by the consequences set for each individual operant. In solving a division problem, a well-trained child performs multiplication, subtraction, borrowing, carrying, etc., in a certain sequence that is dependent on the result of various discriminations. A child without the component skills cannot perform the required chain. This second child illustrates the possibility that in any given situation there may not exist any chain at strength that will produce the situation associated with reinforcement. This may arise in one of two related ways. (1) The organism has not in the past acquired a part or all of the chain necessary to lead it from the present situation, S_A, to the reinforcing situation, S_B, though such a chain may be known to other organisms. (2) No known chain exists whose execution guarantees the transformation of S_A to S_B. Let us now examine several representative problems.

The puzzle-box problem reveals a number of interesting features in problem solving. The cats were placed in an initial situation, the locked box, S_A. A number of behaviors was immediately generated. The cats thrashed about, meowed, put their paws through the bars, scratched at large openings, looked in various directions, and so forth. Many of these behaviors represent operants generalized from a past reinforcing history within similar situations. When confined to a small space in the past, the cat usually escaped by looking around the environment, advancing towards any opening, scratching at loose parts of the environment, and so forth. Some other behaviors, such as meowing, are undoubtedly built into the structure of the cat. Regardless of how they became strengthened, a number of behaviors, R_1, R_2, R_3, R_4, . . . , arise in the initial problem situation. Furthermore, though these behaviors are not random, they are not yet patterned into the well-ordered sequence that is emitted when the cat eventually solves the problem. The cat's initial repertoire consists of a selective set of behaviors which it brings to the situation and with which it operates on it. Eventually, one of these R's may succeed in opening the latch; when that happens, the cat has transformed the situation from door closed to door open.

$$\left| \begin{array}{l} \overline{S}_A \text{ (door closed)} \\ R_1 \\ R_2 \\ R_3 \\ R_4 \\ \cdot \\ \cdot \\ \cdot \end{array} \right. \rightarrow \left| \begin{array}{l} \overline{S} \text{ (door open)} \\ R \text{ (go through door)} \end{array} \right. \rightarrow S_{B\,\text{(out of box)}}$$

In the new situation, $S_{\text{(door open)}}$, the cat has a well-established response sequence at strength, advancing through the open door. This simple problem illustrates several important aspects of problem solving in general. (1) An organism brings a set of responses $\{R_1, R_2, R_3, \ldots\}$ to the situation, either by virtue of its past history with similar situations, or by virtue of its genetically determined structure. (2) These R's are not all equally likely to occur; some (scratching at openings, meowing) exist at higher strength than others (exploring the roof of the box, standing still). (3) Once a given response succeeds in transforming the situation into a familiar one, a well-established sequence can carry the animal to the reinforcing situation, S_B.

Thorndike, as others before him, referred to the first two aspects described as *trial-and-error* responding. The animal emitted ("tried") many responses in the problem situation, most of them being "errors"; eventually it chanced upon the "correct" R, and thereby achieved "success." Köhler (1925) very early criticized this characterization of problem solving. He argued that Thorndike's situation was not representative of problems in general. The cats, maintained Köhler, could not initially observe the relation between the latch and the open box. But many actual problems, he argued, permit the organism to observe more aspects and relations in the situation than was the case for these cats. Köhler, therefore, set animals the following problem (Fig. 14–1). A banana was located outside an ape's cage. There were two hollow bamboo sticks

Figure 14–1. Köhler's two-stick problem.

inside the cage, but neither stick was long enough to reach the banana. One stick, however, was smaller in diameter and could easily be inserted into either end of the other stick, thereby making a single stick long enough to reach the banana. Köhler's apes, when placed in this situation, initially exhibited behaviors which had been reinforced in the past. They extended one or the other stick, moving it back and forth just short of the banana. After a certain amount of extinction, this responding weakened. At this point, some animals were observed to sit quietly for a time, after which they suddenly put the two sticks together and drew in the banana.

> Sultan first of all squats indifferently on [a] box, which has been
> left standing a little back from the railings; then he gets up, picks

up the two sticks, sits down again on the box and plays carelessly with them. While doing this, it happens that he finds himself holding one rod in either hand in such a way that they lie in a straight line; he pushes the thinner one a little way into the opening of the thicker, jumps up and is already on the run towards the railings . . . and begins to draw a banana towards him with the double stick (Köhler, 1925, p. 27).

Köhler called this sudden solution an *insight* and suggested that it was a typical property of problem solving. He maintained that Sultan and other subjects solved the problem because the structure of the problem became readily apparent, and not because the behavior of putting the two sticks together was an operant of high strength in the situation. Birch (1945), however, was able to show that a certain past history is critical in solving this kind of problem. Köhler had not specified his apes' past histories in detail.

Birch undertook to see whether prior stick manipulation was essential. He took a group of apes who had never had experience with sticks and set them identical problem contingencies. Contrary to Köhler's finding, none of these subjects was able to solve the problem in a 30-min session. Birch then allowed the apes several sessions of play with short straight sticks. He observed the animals gradually come to use the sticks as extensions of their arms for poking, prying, digging, raking, and other similar operations. On a second test, all the animals solved the two-stick problem in less than half a minute. The conclusion is inescapable. Previous manipulation of sticks is essential in the solution of a problem requiring this as a component skill; the logical structure of the situation will not aid an organism that possesses no skills in utilizing that structure.

The chained nature of the component behaviors constituting the solution to a problem helps us explain the sudden character of solutions observed by Köhler and others. Once the organism has produced a situation that is the cue for a well-established sequence of behavior, the problem has ended. Once Sultan turned those two short sticks into one long one, the problem had come to an end; for we may reasonably suppose that Sultan had had a previous history of raking in objects with sticks of varying lengths.

14.2 PUZZLES

In studying human problem solving, psychologists have set their subjects a variety of tasks. Some of these have been in the form of puzzles. A well-known puzzle is shown in Fig. 14–2. The subject is instructed to draw through each of the nine dots with four straight lines without taking his pencil off the paper and without retracing a line. Lines can cross

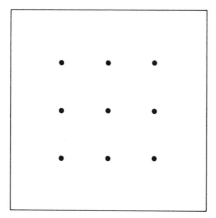

Figure 14–2. The nine-dot puzzle.

each other if necessary. Most subject meet the problem with a set of operants for connecting up points by drawing around the periphery. This sequence fails, however, and another response at high strength usually emerges—the drawing of a diagonal. This new behavior is of little aid since the diagonal plus three peripheral lines still leave one dot unaccounted for. Very quickly, then, the subject exhausts his usual repertoire for dealing with such "problems"; it is at this point that he will agree that it is indeed a puzzle. A solution to the nine-dot problem consists of the extension of the lines beyond the confines of the dot matrix (see appendix to this chapter).

That such a simple solution requires such a great deal of time, and frequently is not achieved at all, points to an important feature of puzzles. Many problems or puzzles are difficult to solve because they tend to control very strong but inappropriate responses. Puzzles frequently resemble past situations in which certain responses were appropriate and reinforced. The nine-dot problem, for instance, is very similar to a situation containing only eights dots (imagine the center dot of Fig. 14–2 to be missing), which could easily be "solved" by drawing four lines along the periphery. The repeated emission of inappropriate behavior in a problem situation is usually called *set,* used in the sense that we say someone is "set in his ways." Confining line-drawing responses to the boundaries of the nine-dot matrix is an example of such a set. Many problems can only be solved by unusual responses, so it is frequently useful to instruct problem solvers in such a way that their variability of behavior increases. It is easy to demonstrate that set is under the control of the organism's reinforcement history. Luchins (1942) asked subjects to solve a number of numerical problems calling for the measurement of quantities of water by means of several measuring jars. Table 14–1 shows 11 of these problems. Problem *1* was an introductory example.

Table 14–1
LUCHINS (1942) WATER-JAR PROBLEMS

	CAPACITIES OF JARS			
PROBLEM NUMBER	*A*	*B*	*C*	REQUIRED AMOUNT
1	29	3	—	20
2	21	127	3	100
3	14	163	25	99
4	18	43	10	5
5	9	42	6	21
6	20	59	4	31
7	23	49	3	20
8	15	39	3	18
9	28	76	3	25
10	18	48	4	22
11	14	36	8	6

The subject was shown that in order to obtain 20 units of water (the value in the rightmost column), he would have to fill the 29-unit jar and pour 3 units from it, 3 times. The subject then worked at the other ten problems. Note that (excluding the introductory example) all problems except number *9* conform to the rule *B* minus *A* minus 2*C*: first fill the large jar, *B*, then pour off 1 *A*-jarful and 2 *C*-jarfuls. Problems *7–11,* however, have an alternative solution using only two jars, which might be interpreted as a simpler chain of behavior. Nevertheless, subjects from grade-school to university graduate level rarely used the two-jar solutions. Their reinforcement history on problems *2–6* brought the three-jar sequence to such high strength that it dominated all other chains.

The idea of set appears in the celebrated two-string problem of Fig. 14–3. The initial situation, S_A, consists of two strings hanging from the ceiling of an otherwise practically bare room. The terminal reinforcing situation, S_B, consists of the two ends of the strings tied together. However, the distance between the strings is too great for the subject to reach over and grasp one string while holding on to the end of the other. In one version of the problem, the only loose object present in the experimental room was an electromagnetic relay. A solution to the problem is shown in Fig. 14–4. The subject has attached the relay to the string and has set the weighted string in motion as a pendulum. Once caught, the end of the swinging string can be joined to the other string, and the two strings can easily be tied. Subjects given a prior

Figure 14–3. The two-string problem. The two strings are to be tied to each other, although they are too far apart for one to be held while the other is grasped.

Figure 14–4. A solution to the two-string problem. The subject has tied the relay to one string and has set it swinging.

session in which they were instructed in using the relay as an electrical-circuit component were markedly deficient at solving this problem (Birch and Rabinowitz, 1951). Here again, a certain past history (using the electrical component as an electrical component) overrode the behaviors needed for solving the problem (using the electrical component as a weight).

As a final example, consider the matchstick problems of Fig. 14–5. The matchstick problems illustrate a feature common to many problems, namely, that the solution to be arrived at is specified only in general form. The legend of Fig. 14–5 tells what general properties the solution must have; it does not specify in detail the terminal situation, S_B. Except for

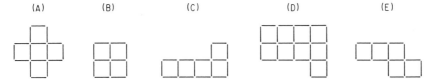

(A)   (B)   (C)   (D)   (E)

Figure 14–5. Katona's (1940) matchstick problems. In A–C move three matches to produce a new figure that has one less square than the original figure. In D, produce a new figure with only five squares by moving three matches. In E, move two matches to produce a figure with four squares. (See solutions in appendix to this chapter.)

the nine-dot problem, our previous problems and puzzles specified the exact reinforcing situation, S_B, rather than its general structure. The monkey solved the problem when the banana was in the cage; the two-string problem was solved when the strings were tied together. But the matchstick problems are solved only when the box count is the required number. For these problems, there are several acceptable solutions, with many ways to arrive at them. (See appendix to this chapter.)

14.3 HEURISTIC SEARCH STRATEGIES

Our general characterization of problems emphasized their chained, or component, nature. But analysis of most of the sample problems from the previous sections does not require detailed chaining. Let us therefore broaden the concept of a "problem." Consider the combination lock of Fig. 14–6. Most combination locks of this type have 50 or 100 discrete positions, but 5 will suffice for our illustration. A man for whom such a lock bars the entrance to some reinforcing situation may be said to be faced with a problem if he does not have the sequence of behaviors available to open the lock. On the other hand, a systematic algorithm (see

Figure 14–6. A five-position combination lock.

section 12.8) can be given for opening the lock: try every combination until you succeed. This is probably the notion of trial-and-error behavior that Köhler and other psychologists attributed to Thorndike when they criticized his analysis of problem solving as lacking the elements for a structured solution. Yet Thorndike never reported that the cats engaged in every possible behavior in every possible sequence. In fact, the cats confined their attention to the slots and moving parts of the puzzle box, exhibiting a highly *selective* set of behaviors. But a combination-lock problem illustrates much more pure trial-and-error responding. Thus, a lock with 50 numbers, which opens when the correct sequence of 3 numbers is dialed, will require $50^3/2$ ($= 62,500$) sequences to be tried on the average before it will open. If each sequence takes 6 sec to dial, the average time to open such a lock would be about 4 days' continuous work. It is obvious why such a lock serves as a protection, even though nearly everyone has at strength a suitable algorithmic chain that could eventually open it.

An upside-down tree structure is a useful way of representing the behavior sequences in this kind of problem (Fig. 14–7). The circles or

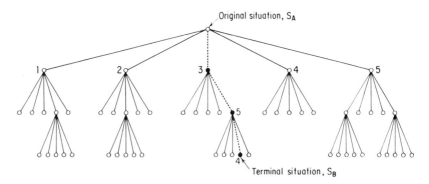

Figure 14–7. A tree structure representing some of the behaviors and resulting situations arising from dialing the numbers of the lock of Fig. 14–6. The "combination" (3, 5, 4) is shown as dotted lines joining the filled circles. For reasons of space, only a few of the third (lowest) level branches are shown.

nodes in a tree structure represent the situations that may be produced by various responses available to the organism. Thus the top node is the original situation, with no number dialed as yet. The first 5 possible numbers are shown as nodes one level lower. Analogously, the 25 nodes at the next level represent the set of situations that result from dialing yet another number. The possibilities at the lowest level, reached by dialing a third number, are so numerous (125) that we can conveniently represent only a sample of these in the diagram. In the tree of Fig. 14–7, the lines represent the operant dialing responses of the organism. The structure gives us a way of representing the possible situations that may arise when all the available responses in a problem are specified, and all their resulting consequences known. It is apparent from inspection of Fig. 14–7 that a man who wishes to open this lock is going to have to make his way through very many branches before he chances upon the correct one.

Many other problems can be represented in the form of a tree of operant sequences and their resulting situations. If a simple 5 numeral turn lock can lead to so many possible branches (125), we may well wonder how an individual ever solves really difficult problems, such as finding a good move in chess, integrating a function, proving a theorem in logic. The possible situations resulting from only a dozen distinct types of responses carried to a sequence level of 12 is 12^{12}. Evidently, pure trial and error could never suffice to solve a problem of any difficulty.

Suppose that there were some way for the problem solver to limit his alternative operations. That is, suppose that in Fig. 14–7 the individual was told that the first number in this kind of lock is usually 3. His search then might be profitably limited to the small portion of the tree stemming from the node 3. In general, problems that are soluble do have associated with them various rules or *heuristics* that permit the organism to narrow down his response topography to a certain likely set of operations. These heuristics are generally characterized as rules of thumb that help limit the behavior sequence. Unlike an algorithm, their use does not guarantee a solution, but it does frequently aid in finding a solution. We may think of Thorndike's cats as exhibiting such heuristics when they confined their attention to the slots and moving parts of the puzzle box. In the past, such responses paid off more frequently than other behaviors. A possible heuristic for the combination-lock problem might be to note that people sometimes fasten a lock and leave the last number of the combination still standing. This is not invariably true, but it might serve as a useful heuristic. In complex problems, it is helpful to be able to diagnose whether progression towards or recession away from the solution is occurring; that is, whether one is "getting warmer." As one moves away from S_A, it is often possible to interpret the intermediate situations (nodes) as bringing one either closer to or further away from the terminal situation, S_B. Suppose we blindfold a man, confine him to a large room, and tell him that his task is to throw a dart into a bull's-eye. The location of the box of darts and of the target is unknown to him. We permit our subject two responses, walking, and throwing darts. We agree to advise him, however, after every step he takes, whether or not he is getting closer to the dart box. Furthermore, once he gets there and starts throwing darts, we shall advise him whether his successive throws are closer or farther from the target. This is just a version of the "you're getting warmer" game, and if our target is not too small, our subject will solve this problem very quickly. But it is obvious that a man who is not supplied with the progressive S^D's ("advice") along the way may never solve the problem.

In general, an analysis of problem solving takes the form of (1) noting the suitable heuristics that narrow the response topography to be used and the situations that are worth exploiting; (2) noting the important intra-problem discriminations that must be made in order to detect whether a response has moved the organism closer to or further away from the terminal situation.

If these are indeed the critical components of problem-solving behavior, it ought to be possible to incorporate them into the structure of a machine which could then solve similar problems. The behavior of such a machine might be of interest for several reasons. First, it could act as a check on the sufficiency of the set of heuristics and discriminations we might hypothesize to be necessary for any given set of problems. Second, by varying features of the machine, we might discover ways to develop a more efficient problem solver, and then apply these discoveries to educational practice. Because of its rapidity of operation (25,000 or more operations per sec), the digital computer is ideally suited for the exploration of such models of problem solving. Representations of situations can be programmed, various operations corresponding to organismic responses can be simulated, and a strategy for successively transforming one situation into another can be built into the machine. Newell and Simon (1963) have described a computer program called the General Problem Solver (GPS) for treating certain puzzles and problems. The program uses a variety of heuristic search strategies and discrimination tests for evaluating whether newly created situations represent progress toward the terminal situation, S_B.

One of their problem environments is the domain of symbolic logic. The machine may be asked to prove that $(R \supset \sim P) \cdot (\sim R \supset Q)$ is equivalent to $\sim (\sim Q \cdot P)$. The machine is given the same information that a college-student subject is faced with, namely, a dozen rules for transforming symbols by adding terms, deleting terms, changing connectives, changing signs, changing groupings, and so forth. The program that turns the computer into a problem solver provides it with the ability to apply these rules (respond) and to discriminate differences among the situations it produces. Perhaps most important, the program provides it with a number of heuristics to guide its search through a problem tree. One useful heuristic restrains GPS from trying to transform a situation (node) if that situation is more difficult to transform than a previous situation (node) was. GPS has its own built-in criteria of difficulty of transformation. GPS expects differences between its successively generated situations, S_1, S_2, S_3 . . . , and the terminal situation, S_B, to decrease as GPS proceeds to work its way through a series of transformations. If that does not prove to be the case, GPS returns to a higher level (back towards S_A) and sets off along a new branch. Another heuristic forces GPS to abandon a branch when it gets below a given depth (the vertical dimension in Fig. 14–7) and situation S_B has not yet turned up. GPS seems to solve its problems about as well as the college-student subjects, and, more important, perhaps, often makes the same kinds of errors. Other programs for solving geometric proofs, playing chess and checkers, performing integration, and balancing assembly lines have been devised, all making use of the ideas of heuristic search strategies.

14.4 CONCEPT IDENTIFICATION

When an individual has acquired a set of concepts by the methods of Chapter 13, his skill in inducing or *identifying* any particular concept from inspection of only a few of the S^D members of the concept may be of interest. Despite certain procedural similarities between concept acquisition and concept identification, the latter is properly treated in the context of problem solving. In concept identification, we deal with a subject who has already acquired all the concepts employed in the experiment. The process of concept acquisition is well behind him. Suppose we show a subject a picture of a bird, an airplane, and a balloon and ask him to "identify" (name) the "concept" (the S^D class) that these exemplify. The subject has long ago acquired the concept of a "flying object" through a discrimination history with such objects; now his task is merely to display the acquired verbal behavior by giving the name "flying object." In general, the subject's task in concept identification usually consists of examining a number of situations, and inducing the concept from them (that is, stating the general rule for the S^D class). He is told for each situation whether or not it is an instance of the unknown S^D class. In such a task the subject typically employs strategies, or systematic sequences of responses, that lead to the correct identification.

Bruner, Goodnow, and Austin (1956) presented subjects with the 81 cards shown in Fig. 14–8. These cards varied in four ways: (1) the number of figures (1, 2, or 3), (2) the color of the figures (red, green, or black), (3) the shape of the figures (cross, circle, or square), and (4) the number of borders (1, 2, or 3). The subject was first shown a given card (say the one with three red circles and two borders, $3R\bigcirc2b$) and told that this was a positive instance of a concept that he was to identify. The subject was then advised that he could choose additional cards from the 80 remaining to obtain more information. After each

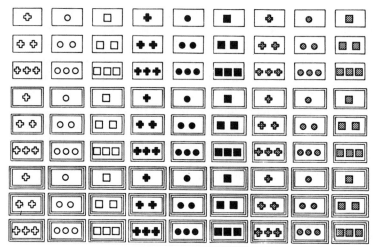

*Figure 14–8. A set of cards used to study concept iden-
tification. The forms varied in (1) number, (2) shape,
(3) color, and (4) number of borders (Bruner, Goodnow,
and Austin, 1956).*

choice, he was advised whether the particular card he chose was or was
not an instance of the concept. When the task consisted of identifying
conjunctive concepts (red circles, two green figures, etc.), the majority
of subjects adopted a strategy which consisted of choosing cards which
varied in one and only one dimension from the known initial positive
card. In this way, each selection eliminated one or more concepts. An
example of the kinds of choice sequences made using this strategy might
be as follows:

3R○2b   (+)   the initial given positive example.
2R○2b   (+)   first choice: eliminate "three" figures as a relevant
              element.
3G○2b   (−)   second choice: retain "red" as a relevant element.
3R+2b   (−)   third choice: retain "circle" as a relevant element.
3R○1b   (+)   fourth choice: eliminate "two borders" as a relevant
              element.

Ergo: concept is "red circles."

Bruner, Goodnow, and Austin were able to show that a number of
variables, such as the kind of concept to be identified, the manner in
which the 81 cards were displayed, and the number of examples the
subjects were permitted to choose, affected the type of systematic strategy
employed.

14.5 THE MEASUREMENT OF PROBLEM-SOLVING ABILITIES: INTELLIGENCE TESTS

Perhaps no word carries more mystique in all of psychology than "intelligence." It is a word everyone uses but hardly anyone defines. Since 1905, psychologists have been in the curious "position of devising and advocating tests for measuring intelligence and then disclaiming responsibility for them by asserting that 'nobody knows what the word really means'" (Wechsler, 1958). We shall find that problem solving provides a useful vehicle for treating the topic of intelligence. In every case of a test that purports to measure intelligence, we shall find only a series of problems set a subject, and various measures of his performance recorded.

The idea of an intelligence test, or as we shall be inclined to view it, a problem-solving test, arose originally from purely practical considerations. In 1904, the French psychologist Alfred Binet was commissioned to devise a test which would pick out those children whose deficiencies in problem solving made it unlikely that they would profit from regular school instruction. Binet's resulting test was a series of problems using pictures, wooden blocks, peg boards, etc., designed to be administered to one child at a time. It proved to be the first successful intelligence test. During the First World War, there arose a pressing need in the United States to evaluate the problem-solving skills of several million draftees as quickly as possible. Pencil-and-paper tests that could be simultaneously administered to a group of inductees were developed to meet this need, and found their application in selecting men for various tasks. With time, such group tests have achieved more universal use. Many schools now use their results to stream students; colleges and graduate schools rely heavily upon their scores for admission decisions. Our concern, however, is not with the practical applications of such tests; we wish, rather, to inquire into certain contributions the intelligence tests have made to our analysis of human problem-solving behaviors.

What is the nature of the problems used in the tests of "intelligence"? There is no better way to describe them than by example. In the typical test, there appear a number of subtests designed to assess various problem-solving skills. A sample set of items is shown in Fig. 14–9. The items in Fig. 14–9 test a variety of skills. Some problems rely heavily on language skills, others on discrimination and perceptual skills. For the most part there is an attempt to use items that test general problem-solving

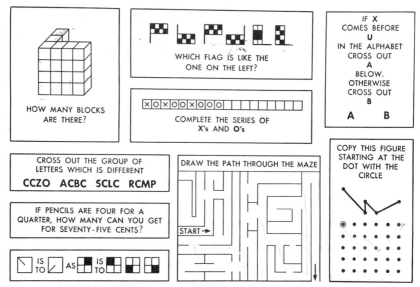

Figure 14–9. Sample items of the sort used in group paper-and-pencil tests of problem-solving ability (Kimble and Garmezy, 1963).

skills and the ability to apply broad concepts and L-sets. This ideal, however, is never completely realized.

The scores obtained from problem-solving tests of this sort tell us something about the relative problem-solving skills of individuals within a given cultural setting. In the remainder of this section (1) we examine some of the variables to which the scores have been related, and (2) we undertake a more detailed analysis of the scores themselves.

One of the best-documented results is the function relating problem-solving scores to age of the subject. Typical curves illustrating the basic relation for five subjects who were tested and retested at various ages are shown in Fig. 14–10. The five very different individuals of Fig. 14–10 continued to advance in their problem-solving ability over a 25-year period. By age 25 the rate of increase in problem-solving ability has begun to taper off for some of the subjects, but not all. The population at large shows a sharp tapering off in the late teens, and only a very slight advance in problem-solving ability between ages 20 and 50.

Suppose we wish to relate an individual's problem-solving score to that of his peers. To do that, we might administer a given test to many individuals of the same age. Once we had the scores of the group, we could compare the scores of any given individual with those of the others in the group. An interesting feature of such test scores is that they turn

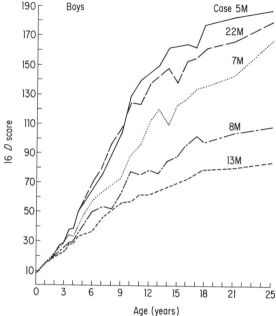

Figure 14–10. Problem-solving ability as a function of age (Bayley, 1955).

out to be approximately normally distributed. That is, if we test enough individuals, the relative frequencies with which various possible scores occur may be described by the bell-shaped curve in the top portion of Fig. 14–11. In sections 2.6 and 10.9, we noted that there is a very intimate relationship between the standard deviation and the percentage of measurements falling in various regions of the normal curve. This relationship permits us to establish the percentile scale shown just below the curve. If, for example, we inspect Fig. 14–11 closely, we find that the point $+2\sigma$ from the mean corresponds to 98th percentile. A score at the 98th percentile point indicates that only 2 per cent of the scores are greater than its value. Similarly, the $+1\sigma$ point is at the 84th percentile, the mean at the 50th percentile point, and so on.

A still more common method of expressing relative problem solving ability is to find an "Intelligence Quotient," defined as

$$IQ = 100 \left(\frac{\text{obtained problem-solving score}}{\text{average problem-solving score}} \right)$$

The individual's own score is the numerator of this quotient. The denominator of the quotient is the average problem-solving score for the individual's appropriate age group. (Children's scores are generally compared with those of other children of the same age; adults' scores are usually compared with those of other adults irrespective of age, on the assumption that average problem-solving ability changes very little after the teens.) If the individual's score is the same as the group average, then numerator = denominator and the calculated IQ is 100. The relation between IQ index and percentile rank is shown in Fig. 14–11. It appears that the standard deviation of the IQ index is about 16 IQ points. Thus an individual whose IQ is calculated to be 116 is about $+1\sigma$ above the mean of his age group, and therefore stands at the 84th percentile point; only 16 per cent of his peers will score higher.

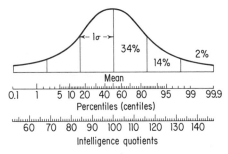

Figure 14–11. Relations among problem-solving scores, percentiles, and the IQ index (after Cronbach, 1963).

Many workers have criticized the derivation and subsequent use of a single number, such as the IQ, from performance on problems like those in Fig. 14–9. Two individuals might well obtain identical IQ scores of 116 (say) though their problem-solving abilities might be radically different. To illustrate by reference to Fig. 14–9, one subject might solve the hidden-block problems with a high degree of proficiency, but do very poorly on the problems requiring the completion of letter series. The other individual might exhibit a reverse repertoire—superior letter-series skills combined with little ability to solve the spatial-relations problems. But adding up the scores for both tests we get the same total for the two individuals. A large part of the resistance to more refined analysis of performance on different types of problems has probably been due to the historical idea that "intelligence" represents a fixed capacity within the organism for solving problems of all kinds. The evidence is not all in, but recent studies indicate that an individual's problem-solving ability is better represented as a group of problem-solving abilities. Thurstone (1945) has suggested what he calls a profile analysis (see Fig. 14–12). An individual's problem-solving abilities are characterized as being made up of the eight basic skills shown at the top of Fig. 14–12. This profile

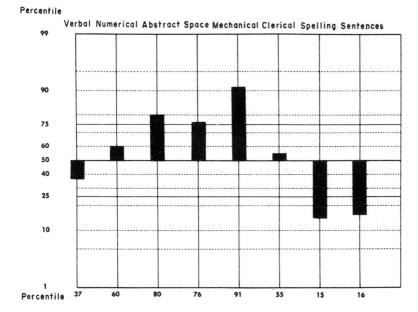

*Figure 14–12. A typical problem-solving abilities pro-
file of a hypothetical individual (Bennett, Seashore, and
Wesman, 1951).*

provides much more information about the problem-solving skills of an
individual than any single IQ score could, but the analysis may still be
insufficient. Some workers now suggest that 120, rather than 8, basic
problem-solving skills may be necessary to describe an individual's
performance satisfactorily. With a number as large as 120, we may well
wonder in what sense the word "basic" can be applied.

The context in which intelligence testing has developed has seldom led
workers to seek ways in which to modify the problem-solving behaviors
they have isolated. Nevertheless, it is well known that "coaching," or
training in the special skills entailed in IQ problems, can raise the scores
significantly. If Fig. 14–10 is inspected carefully it will be seen that the
age when the increase in problem-solving ability begins to taper off coincides with the precise time that many individuals cease their formal
school training. But though formal education contributes greatly to the
increase in general problem-solving ability with age, no full-scale attempt
has been made to "shape" problem-solving skills of the sort evaluated in
IQ tests. It would seem that if such skills are in any sense basic, a systematic program, begun at an early age, for shaping them by the techniques of the previous chapters would be desirable.

14.6 CORRELATION, TEST RELIABILITY, AND VALIDITY

In various places throughout the text, the term "correlation" has been used in the sense of "relationship." Reflexes were said to consist of correlations between elicitors and respondents; reinforcement was said to be correlated with the occurrence of a specified operant. The usage has been one signifying relation or dependency. Pupillary contraction is closely related to (dependent upon) light flashes; delivery of grain is closely related to (dependent upon) key pecking. In general, when one variable is dependent upon another, it can be said to be correlated with it; the converse, as we shall show, need not be true. In describing particular correlations or relations between two variables more fully, we are typically led to graphical representation. The correlations that constitute the laws of the reflex are described by functions relating elicitor properties to respondent properties. The correlations that constitute the laws of operant strengthening take the form of plots of response rate against time.

When we speak of two variables being correlated, it is important to separate the ideas of *how* they are correlated from *how well* they are correlated. To ask *how* two variables are correlated is to inquire about the *form* of the relationship between them. As one variable increases, does the other increase, decrease, or remain unchanged? Is the relationship best represented by a straight line, a simple curve, or a complex curve with valleys and peaks? The previous pages may be consulted for samples of a wide variety of forms.

To ask *how well* two variables are correlated is to inquire about the *accuracy* with which we are able to predict the value of one of them knowing the value of the other. The answer to "how well" is independent of the answer to "how." The form of the relationship could be linear, curvilinear, or what have you, yet the variability in measurement might be so great that little more than gross prediction could be achieved. The contrast between a highly defined *form* and a low *degree* of correlation is illustrated in the hypothetical data of Fig. 14–13. Nine measurements of Y appear at each X value in Fig. 14–13. The median values of the Y's are connected by a straight line. X is clearly directly related to Y, and the form of the relationship is indisputably linear. The degree of correlation is, however, low. Where the value of X is 2, for instance, the measured values of Y range from less than 1 to more than 3. In general, prediction of Y from X in Fig. 14–13 is poor. To improve the degree of correlation in Fig. 14–13 the values of Y at any X value would have to fall much more closely together; that is, the Y values would have to be much less variable.

In the various graphical relationships, or correlations, to be found on the previous pages, the variable on the horizontal axis is typically an independent variable (measured and manipulated), whereas the variable on the vertical axis is typically a dependent variable (measured, but not directly manipulated). In treating such functional relationships, we directed our attention

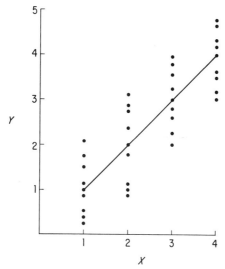

Figure 14–13. Hypothetical linear relationship between two variables.

principally to the *form* of the correlations, that is, "how" the variables were related. The *degree* of correlation, that is, predictive ability or "how well" the variables are related, was assumed to be high by virtue of careful experimental control, accurate measurement devices, and so on.

It is sometimes the case that there are no experimental manipulations available to determine how one variable is influenced by systematic changes in another. In these cases we may be forced to rely upon relationships between two dependent variables. The degree of correlation between the variables in such dependent-dependent variable relationships cannot be taken for granted. Neither variable is under direct experimental control and, since we are often unable to control influences that may affect one or the other in complex ways, far more variability in measurement must be expected. We have rarely had occasion to discuss dependent-dependent variable relationships in this text, but their evaluation is a common enterprise, frequently having practical import. The scores an individual earns on a standardized pencil-and-paper test of problem solving and his rate of progress as a job trainee are both dependent performance variables. Yet if the two variables are highly correlated, predictions about one can be made knowing the value of the other.

The degree of correlation between two dependent variables may range from very low, where knowing the value of one is of little help in predicting the other, to very high, where knowing the value of one makes it possible to predict closely what the value of the other will be. Within these extremes lie all degrees of intermediate correlations. For instance, there is some degree of correlation between height and weight (both dependent variables); tall people *tend* to weigh more than short people. But the degree of correlation is far from perfect, since one can only approximately predict a man's weight from his height. Statisticians have developed a numerical index, or *coefficient,* for denoting degree of correlation. The coefficient ranges from −1 through 0 to +1. Plus 1 represents the case where two variables are directly related and perfectly predictable each from the other. High values of one accompany high values of the other, intermediate values accompany intermediate values, and so on. Minus 1 represents the case where two variables are inversely related and perfectly predictable. High values of one accompany low values of the other and vice versa. A correlation of 0 represents a random relation between two variables; knowing the value of one is of no help whatsoever in predicting the value of the other. Intermediate coefficients represent intermediate degrees of predictability. Figure 14–14 indicates graphically the kinds of relationships that are associated with various values of the coefficient of correlation. Our X and Y could be any two related dependent variables: for example, paper-and-pencil test score (X) *versus* job achievement (Y), or height (X) *versus* weight (Y).

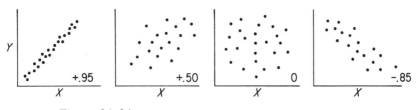

Figure 14–14

Correlations between two dependent variables often present problems of interpretation that are absent when the X variable of a relationship is an independent variable. Problem-solving ability in the growing child is known, for example, to be correlated with length of the big toe. As a child grows, his capacity for solving problems increases at the same time that his bones are growing in length, and the two therefore show a significant correlation. This may help the student to see that, though a correlation shows a causal relation *somewhere,* it does not necessarily mean that one of the two things correlated causes the other (Hebb, 1958, p. 237). Here there is a third and independent variable lurking in the wings, the individual's age, which is functionally related to both dependent variables, thus bringing about a correlation between them.

Two correlations underlie the concept and measurement of intelligence. (1) An individual's relative ability to solve a particular type of problem at one time correlates to some degree with his relative ability to solve that type of problem at some later time. Were it not for this within-class consistency in problem-solving ability, there would be no *concept* of intelligence. (2) From how well an individual solves problems a, b, c, . . . , n, we can predict how well he will solve problems a′, b′, c′, . . . , n′. Without this between-class consistency in problem solving there would be no *measurement* of intelligence. Since Binet, the prevailing treatment of intelligence has been a continuing attempt to improve the degree of between-class correlation through better and better selections of the $a, b, c, \ldots, n$ problems. That is, psychologists have been concerned with establishing standard sets of problems ($a, b, c, \ldots, n$, called the *test problems*, or the IQ tests) whose correlation with other sets of problems ($a', b', c', \ldots, n'$, usually school, or university, or job achievement, or even other IQ tests) is high.

The measurement of intelligence, like all measurement, hinges on two further requirements which, upon analysis, are seen to involve correlations. The first requirement stipulates that the measuring instrument be *reliable*, namely, that repeated uses of it give similar results. A ruler is reliable when its repeated measures of a table yield results which are in close agreement with each other. Similarly, if a problem-solving test is a reliable measuring instrument, its repeated use ought to yield the same value for problem-solving ability for a given individual. The reliability requirement is, in effect, a demand for a high degree of correlation between test results on different occasions. Given a single measure, we should be able to predict the next: it should be almost the same. Reliability depends partially on constant measurement conditions, and partially on the act of measurement itself negligibly affecting the thing being measured. The reliability of a problem-solving test is generally lower than that of a ruler because many operations can easily occur between measurements that change an individual's problem-solving performance. For instance, extensive practice on various problems will affect the agreement of repeated IQ measures. Furthermore, the measuring instrument somewhat affects the thing being measured: giving IQ tests repeatedly is likely to affect the scores—the subject becomes "test-wise."

A second requirement imposed on measurements is that they be useful for whatever purpose they are made. Usefulness in the context of measurement is called *validity*. If we have a piano on the street and we want to make sure before carrying it up three flights of stairs that it will pass through a certain door, we had better measure its widest side. By comparing that measure with the dimensions of the door, we shall be able to predict whether we can get the piano inside. We could make many other measurements on the piano—we could determine its market value, or weigh it—but none of them would be valid for our present purposes; they would not be useful for what we wish to do at the moment with the piano. It follows, therefore, that they would not be valid measures of "get-through-the-doorability."

Validity is a disguised form of correlation for, in the example just described, the width of the piano is the variable most highly correlated with ability to pass through the door. Weight is far less correlated, and unless market value and size happen to be related in pianos, market value will probably bear a random (0) relation to this ability.

Sometimes validity can take the form of estimating the degree of correlation between a measurement dimension (D_1) whose usefulness is already well established, and a different, less well-established measurement dimension (D_2). Such a problem often arises when the established measurement method entails practical difficulties, and a second, simpler, or abbreviated method is proposed. If we wish to measure a large plot of land, we find it impractical (but not impossible in principle) to measure its perimeter with a ruler. Instead, we adopt an altogether different and more rapid measuring procedure, using optical surveying equipment. The justification for the surveying method is its high correlation with the results obtained when rulers are actually used to check the surveyed values.

The validity demanded of an intelligence-test score is of this type. Certain established measurement dimensions exist in the form of school performance, job skills, and so forth. But it is often impractical to assess all of a child's problem-solving abilities, or to measure an individual's entire problem-solving repertoire on the job. We might even like to predict a man's performance before he takes the job. The IQ test is proposed as an abbreviated measuring device that attempts to measure features of a complex problem-solving dimension in a simpler way, through pencil-and-paper operations. The degree to which the IQ test does so is given by the degree of correlation between its scores, and on-the-job or in-the-classroom problem-solving performance. The higher that degree of correlation, the greater the validity (usefulness) of the pencil-and-paper score.

APPENDIX TO CHAPTER 14

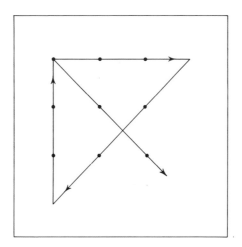

Figure 14–15.   Solution to the nine-dot puzzle.

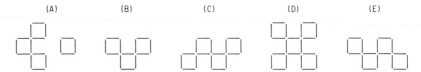

Figure 14–16.   Solutions to matchstick problems.

References for Chapter 14

Bayley, Nancy. On the growth of intelligence. *Amer. Psychologist,* 1955, **10,** 805–818.

Bennett, G. K., Seashore, H. G., and Wesman, A. G. *Counseling from profile. A case book for the Differential Aptitude Tests.* New York: Psychological Corp., 1951.

Birch, H. G. The relation of previous experience to insightful problem solving. *J. comp. Psychol.,* 1945, **38,** 367–383.

Birch, H. G., and Rabinowitz, H. S. The negative effect of previous experience on productive thinking. *J. exp. Psychol.,* 1951, **41,** 121–125.

Bruner, J. S., Goodnow, Jacqueline J., and Austin, G. A. *A study of thinking.* New York: Wiley, 1956.

Cronbach, L. J. *Educational psychology.* New York: Harcourt, Brace and World, 1963.

Hebb, D. O. *A textbook of psychology.* Philadelphia: Saunders, 1958.

Katona, G. *Organizing and memorizing: studies in the psychology of learning and teaching.* New York: Columbia Univer. Press, 1940.

Kendler, H. H. *Basic psychology.* New York: Appleton-Century-Crofts, 1963.

Kimble, G. A., and Garmezy, N. *Principles of general psychology.* (2nd ed.) New York: Ronald, 1963.

Köhler, W. *The mentality of apes.* New York: Harcourt, Brace, 1925.

Luchins, A. S. Mechanization in problem solving: The effect of *Einstellung. Psychol. Monogr.,* 1942, **54,** No. 248.

Newell, A., and Simon, H. GPS, a program that simulates human thought. In E. A. Feigenbaum and J. Feldman (Eds.), *Computers and thought,* New York: McGraw-Hill, 1963, pp. 279–293.

Thurstone, L. L. Testing intelligence and aptitudes. *Hygeia,* 1945, **53,** 32–36.

Wechsler, D. *The measurement and appraisal of adult intelligence,* Baltimore: Williams and Wilkins, 1958.

PART FIVE

Reinforcement Dynamics

15. MOTIVATION I

16. MOTIVATION II

17. AVERSIVE CONTINGENCIES

18. EMOTIONAL BEHAVIOR

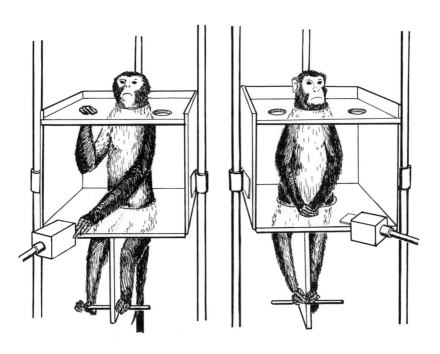

Chapter 15 **MOTIVATION I**

$\blacktriangle$PPEALS TO THE MOTIVATION OF BEHAVIOR ARE generally construed to refer to the determinants or the *causes* of behavior. But it should be obvious from previous chapters that elaboration of the causes of behavior is the province of all psychology. From reflexes to complex problem solving, a unifying aim of the science has been an experimental elaboration of the causes or "laws" of behavior. The topic "motivation," if it is to be distinguished from the procedures and processes in previous chapters, must comprise causes of behavior so far neglected, or must offer fresh phenomena for analysis. Before turning to an experimental treatment of motivation, it is appropriate to insert a few notes on cause and effect in science in general, and in psychology in particular.

15.1 CAUSE AND EFFECT AND THE IDEA OF SCIENTIFIC LAW

The terms "cause" and "effect" have a long history of usage in all systematic attempts to explain nature, philosophical as well as scientific. The terms are part of our everyday language for describing aspects of hurricanes, revolutions, epidemics, assassinations, and airplane crashes, as well as the more pedestrian events of day-to-day commerce. We may, therefore, be surprised to discover in turning to the contemporary scientific literature that these terms are conspicuously missing. In their place, we can find reference only to relationships between variables, correlations of events, and "laws" relating phenomena. It is not that the scientist has lost interest in the causes of his phenomena. It is simply that all he finds upon performing experiments are relations between events or variables. For him, finding the causes of a phenomenon y has become equivalent to finding which other variables, $u, v, w, x,$ and so forth are systematically (*functionally*) related to y.

Every science is filled with examples of functional relationships that purport to replace more ordinary notions of cause and effect. Consider Hooke's law: so long as the elastic limit is not exceeded, the extension of a body is directly proportional to the force applied to it. The law may be summarized as the relation between two variables, *Force → Extension*. The relation would be more extensively described by a graph in which units of force (the independent variable) are plotted against units of extension (the dependent variable). We may, if we wish, consider the cause of any particular extension to be the particular force acting on the body. But in calling the force the cause of extension, we add no additional information to the functional relation itself. In fact, while the law describes the exact form of the relationship for a host of forces and extensions, the assignment of cause is confined to the logical statement— *if* a force, *then* extension.

In the relationship

Heat water to 212°F → Water boils

the application of heat may be considered to be the cause of the boiling. But if we persist in asking "why" water boils when heated sufficiently, we shall be referred to further functional relationships between the vapor pressure of water and temperature. At exactly 212°, we are told, the vapor pressure of water equals that of the atmosphere. This may or may not satisfy our curiosity about boiling water, but in any case the form of the answers we shall obtain to all further "why" questions will always be the same—more functional relationships.

Relationships are equally central to the explanatory process in biological science. The mating of male and female white-eyed fruit flies invariably yields white-eyed offspring.

Mate white-eyed parents → White-eyed offspring

A functional relationship exists between the color of the parent's eyes and the color of the offspring's eyes.

All these functional relationships exhibit a common logic. If we regard the antecedent variable in these relationships as x, and the consequent that is produced as y, their logic seems to be

                        If x, then y

and its corollary

                        If not y, then not x

Thus, *if* a force (*x*) is applied, *then* we shall observe extension (*y*). But *if* no extension was observed (*not y*), *then* force must not have been applied (*not x*). Similarly, *if* the temperature of the water rises to 212° (*x*), *then* water will boil (*y*). Furthermore, *if* the water is not boiling (*not y*), *then* the temperature must be below 212° (*not x*). Finally, *if* both parents have white eyes (*x*), *then* all offspring will have white eyes (*y*). But *if* the offspring's eyes were not white (*not y*), *then* the parents could not both have had white eyes (*not x*).

We must not be disappointed to learn that scientific laws give an accurate representation of nature only when certain conditions are met. Scientific laws hold in context, sometimes broad, sometimes narrow, depending on the generality of the particular relation; but no scientific law is true under *all* conditions. Beyond the elastic limit, Hooke's law fails, and extension is no longer proportional to the applied force. Unless certain variables such as atmospheric pressure and purity of the water are held constant, water does not boil at 212°. Irradiation of the parent fruit flies complicates hereditary relationships.

In the laws described, the *x* and *y* terms of the functional relationships are concepts based on *observable* quantities. The intimacy by which such concepts are tied to observables is the reason that such laws are said to be *empirical*. We may observe and measure events which we conceptualize as forces and extensions of bodies, temperatures and states of water, sexual reproduction and eye-color of fruit flies. The kinds of explanation afforded by empirical laws are to be contrasted with pre-scientific and non-scientific explanations. Prior to the discovery of laws relating micro-organism activity to disease, illness was often attributed to the presence of demons lodged within the body. Animal and human behavior was long believed to be due to animal spirits and souls. In these pre-scientific explanations illness and behavior were related to hypothetical events (demons, souls) which were free to take on almost any property the theorist wished to give them. The lack of restrictions placed on the hypothetical nature of these concepts made it possible for them in principle to explain everything; yet, their immunity to disconfirmation by any procedure put them in the paradoxical position of in fact explaining nothing.

In contrast to the emptiness of such fictional explanations, the functional relationship of science possesses powerful abilities for the prediction, interpretation, and control of nature. When a functional law exists between *x* and *y*, knowing the value of *x* we may *predict* the value of *y*.

Having the law in hand, whenever we suspect that we see x and y acting in the everyday world, we are in a position to *interpret* actual non-laboratory events. Finally, if we can manipulate x at will, then we have the means of *controlling* y at will. In the model of the functional relationship we have the power and versatility of the scientific enterprise revealed in a striking way.

15.2 FICTIONAL CAUSES OF BEHAVIOR

When we come to examine traditional accounts of behavior, we find that three principal classes of fictional causes have occupied the field.

In one, behavior is explained by reference to observable events that are fortuitously correlated with it, such as the position of the planets at birth, the direction of lines in the palm, the relative prominence of various bumps on the skull. Although both behavior and the "causal agent" are observable, any relation between them is non-systematic and therefore qualifies as "chance" rather than "lawful."

In the second, behavior is frequently attributed to events supposedly located in the central nervous system (the brain and spinal cord). When we say a man is clever because he has brains, that he cannot work because his nerves are exhausted, or that he needs his head examined when he acts strangely, we are invoking causal events apparently located inside the nervous structure. In practice, however, actual observation of these events is rarely made. In these examples, the nervous system exists only as a repository for fictional explanations of behavior. The properties of the hypothetical causes are specified in only the grossest manner, and no specific relations are either observed or theorized between them and the observed behavior.

In the third, behavior is commonly "explained" by hypothetical inner mental processes. We are said to close a door because we "want" it closed, to whistle a tune because we have an "urge" to whistle, to read a book because we "feel" like reading. Because such statements seem so natural and harmless, we are unlikely to notice that they imply a form of cause and effect which differs markedly from the laws of section 15.1. Yet in each an unobservable inner "want," "urge," or "feeling" is being subtly assigned the status of a cause of some behavior. Here again these "causes" are given no independent properties which might be related either by theory or by observation to the actual behavior to be explained. The "want" and the "urge" are fictional because they are inferred entirely from the behavior which they are proposed to explain.

The emergence of a scientific psychology is, to a large extent, a shift from fictional to functional causes of behavior. We need only to examine the various procedures and processes of previous chapters to find a number of such functional relationships. As a prelude to the analysis of motivational phenomena, it will prove useful to review some of these familiar behavioral paradigms in such a way as to emphasize how their procedures constitute a major class of behavioral causes.

15.3 PAST HISTORIES WITH CONDITIONING AND EXTINCTION CONTINGENCIES AS CAUSES OF BEHAVIOR

To the extent that a past history with the various operant-conditioning paradigms is a reliable way of modifying an organism's behavior, a particular history must be considered a genuine cause of behavior. Thus prior reinforcement may cause the appearance of a behavioral chain, and it may cause the decline of other behavior in the situation. Conversely, the non-reinforcement (extinction) of behavior may lead to the absence or low probability of some behavior. Combining the procedures of extinction and conditioning, we pass to more complex causes. The control over behavior exerted by S^D's can be understood only by reference to a past history of operant-discrimination training. The emergence of a novel form of behavior can often be explained only by the special reinforcement conditions set up in successive approximation. Certain characteristic temporal patterns of responding require a specific past history with a schedule of intermittent reinforcement.

The causes of, or controls over, behavior in these examples are found in the way that behavior *has been* related to reinforcement in the past. Like the causes of extension in a spring, boiling of water, and the color of a fruit fly's eye, these causes are best described in the form of functional relationships. Here, the relations are between a given set of contingencies, previously applied, and the appearance of behavioral changes. The changes in behavior that are associated with these past histories characteristically take place over time; hence the curves we called behavioral processes are the primary descriptions of these laws.

A prevailing idea in all these causes is the notion that certain behavioral effects are conditional upon a certain history of conditioning and extinction. A few general cases are summarized in Table 15–1 in such a way as to include the operant paradigms of previous chapters. Note that each case may be reduced to a combination of only two ingredients: conditioning and extinction. The variety of behaviors that can be acquired and maintained through their use, and the complexity of the environmental controls over behavior that their correlation with stimuli can induce, testify to the remarkable potency of these two opposing operations.

Table 15-1

SOME CAUSES OF BEHAVIOR THAT LIE IN THE PAST
REINFORCEMENT HISTORY OF THE ORGANISM

CAUSE	SYMBOLICALLY	EFFECT
1. A response has a history of being followed with reinforcement	$R \rightarrow S^+$	R strength high
2. A response has had a history of extinction	$R \nrightarrow$	R strength low
3. A past history with the discrimination procedure	$\begin{bmatrix} S^D \\ R \rightarrow S^+ \end{bmatrix}$ $\begin{bmatrix} S^\Delta \\ R \nrightarrow \end{bmatrix}$	S^D controls the occurrence of R, and has become a reinforcer
4. The behavior (R_n) owes its existence to a previous history of reinforcing its related ancestors	$\begin{bmatrix} R_1 \rightarrow S^+ \\ R_2 \rightarrow S^+ \\ \cdot \\ \cdot \\ R_n \rightarrow S^+, \end{bmatrix}$ $\begin{bmatrix} R_1 \nrightarrow \\ R_2 \rightarrow S^+ \\ \cdot \\ \cdot \\ R_n \rightarrow S^+, \dots \end{bmatrix}$ $\begin{bmatrix} R_1 \nrightarrow \\ R_2 \nrightarrow \\ \cdot \\ \cdot \\ R_n \rightarrow S^+ \end{bmatrix}$ (successive stages in time $\rightarrow$)	A new unit of behavior is added to the repertoire
5. A past history with a particular probabilistic contingency	$T \rightarrow R \xrightarrow{p} S^+$	A characteristic pattern of responding in time

15.4 MOTIVES AND REINFORCERS

For all their power, the procedures of Table 15–1 are worthless unless the environmental consequences that they provide for behavior are of the special sort that we have called reinforcing. In previous discussions, we have taken for granted the reinforcing power of such events as food and water, postponing until now an analysis of the variables that modulate their reinforcing properties. It is the elaboration of these variables that constitutes the field of motivation.

We may question at the outset what this definition of motivation has in common with more classical conceptions of motivation as the study of needs, wants, aspirations, interests, urges, drives, and other energizers or *motives* of behavior. For the present, we note only that needs and wants and other motives seem to be closely related to the concept of reinforcers. When an organism is said to "need" food or water the inference of need is usually made from the observation that an organism which has been without food or water for a period is especially likely to eat and drink. A person is said to "want" a drink if he asks for it, or otherwise engages in behavior that has previously produced water. The needs and wants refer to the fact that, by a period of their absence, food and water have been made reinforcers.

We set a restriction on our experimental analysis of motivation by identifying as its domain the analysis of *primary* reinforcers alone. The restriction serves to exclude those reinforcers whose reinforcing power depends upon a past history of conditioning, in particular, upon the discrimination paradigm. In everyday discourse, of course, motives are not sharply distinguished on the basis of whether they refer to primary or secondary reinforcers. In fact, a motive can refer to almost any of the "whys" of behavior. A need to excel over others, a desire for attention, and a hankering after an expensive car or social status may all qualify as legitimate motives. Common usage notwithstanding, the laws governing such motives are just the laws governing acquired reinforcers. Consequently, such acquired motives are treated more appropriately as conditioning phenomena. Money, a good example of such a motive, is satisfactorily described as a generalized acquired positive reinforcer. Its reinforcing significance depends on its history in discrimination paradigms where its presence has set the occasion for R's that lead eventually to primary reinforcers. Attention; need for power, affiliation, achievement; competitiveness; and many other social motives seem to fit the secondary reinforcement paradigm described in Chapter 11. We shall, therefore, have little new to add to their analysis in this chapter.

The problem of how to study acquired motives was solved in Chapter 11 by formulating a set of principles for converting any arbitrary stimulus situation into a conditioned reinforcer. In studying primary reinforcers we shall be concerned to elaborate a number of variables that have been found to be intimately related to the waxing and waning in value of such reinforcers. As an aid in broadening the student's concept of primary reinforcement, we shall, in the discussions that follow, introduce a variety of different primary reinforcers.

15.5 DRIVE OPERATIONS

A cardinal operation that affects the reinforcing power or *value* of all known primary positive reinforcers is the procedure of depriving the organism of the reinforcer for a time. To a first approximation, the reinforcing value of a reinforcer increases directly as the length of its deprivation increases.

Previous discussions of conditioning effects (Pavlovian and operant) took for granted that deprivation variables had been regulated to impart moderate reinforcing value to the stimuli used as reinforcers. Although working behind the scenes until now, deprivation variables in fact play a central role in making possible the behavioral processes we have studied. The existence of this new set of variables, upon which behavior so critically depends, has two implications for behavioral analysis which we can no longer ignore. (1) Behavior is multi-determined. A horse may not drink water to which it has been led because it has not been deprived of water. Or the horse may not drink because it has never acquired the behavior of drinking from a trough. But if it does drink, then it must be that it possesses the necessary behavior *and* has been deprived of water. Neither deprivation nor past conditioning alone will be sufficient to cause behavior patterns.

(2) A deprivation operation raises the reinforcement value of a class of stimuli on which many chains of behavior may depend. When we deprive a man of food we increase the probability that he will eat. But we also increase the probability that he will ask for food, that he will walk down a certain street where a restaurant is located, that he will enter a grocery shop, and so on. In traditional accounts of motivation this concomitant rise in strength of many behaviors has been the basis for regarding deprivation as a way to "drive" the organism to the reinforcer. Nevertheless, used in this way, the "drive" concept has little more than metaphorical value. If the organism has not acquired behavior that will get it *to* the reinforcer, deprivation in itself will not result in reinforcement.

It is convenient to strip the term *drive* of its workaday connotations and give it a technical redefinition which emphasizes the ability of certain operations to establish reinforcers. The word drive is used to denote that, as a result of some operation performed on an organism (for instance, deprivation), some S becomes a reinforcer, S^+. So defined, drive is a word like reflex, standing for a certain relationship between variables. If we agree to use the word only in this technical sense we shall be careful to avoid saying that the organism responded *because of* a drive. Being already a relationship between some operation and behavior, a drive cannot cause any behavior.

Appropriate deprivation operations may be found for each primary reinforcer. Casual observation suggests, and experiment confirms, that many other operations have deprivation-like effects on reinforcers. Enforcing exercise, lowering room temperature, injecting insulin, making surgical lesions in a localized region of the brain, stimulating another region of the brain, administering certain drugs, offering appetizers, introducing another eating animal can all make food a reinforcer, and hence are drive operations.

Just as there are diverse operations that establish and raise the value of reinforcers, so there are drive operations that reduce or eliminate reinforcing value. We might call these reinforcer-reducing operations. The most universal of these is *satiation*—repeatedly presenting the reinforcer until it loses its power to reinforce. Certain drugs, the injection of blood from satiated animals, emotion-producing events, lesions in a localized part of the brain, and stimulation in another region of the brain reduce the reinforcing value of food.

Each of the primary reinforcers has its own particular reinforcer establishing and reducing operations. Diagram [15.1] schematizes some of the operations that make water a reinforcer.

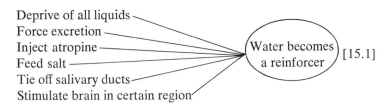

Deprive of all liquids
Force excretion
Inject atropine
Feed salt
Tie off salivary ducts
Stimulate brain in certain region
→ Water becomes a reinforcer [15.1]

The tendency is strong to say that these drive operations make the organism "thirsty," and *therefore* it drinks. But "thirsty" is a dubious causal agent. All we see is that a number of operations have a similar effect—they make water a reinforcer. As explanatory concepts, the term "thirst," and its counterpart "hunger," are probably never defensible, simply because they fail to point to any empirical or theoretical relationships between behavior and other observed or specified events. Even as descriptive terms they may trap the unwary. When we say a man is "thirsty" when we see him drink, or "hungry" when we see him eat, we are inferring that water and food have been made reinforcing by some deprivation-like operation. But in fact people eat and drink for many reasons. They may find various social pressures to do so, they may do it to reduce anxiety, or they may do it much as a child drinks its milk or eats its spinach to progress to reinforcers like dessert.

15.6 PERIODICITIES IN REINFORCEMENT VALUE

Consider the following alphabetized list of some of the best-known primary reinforcers for humans and certain other higher animals:

Activity	Novelty
Air	Sex
Food	Sleep
Love and affection	Warmth
Maternal activities	Water

The experimental study of primary reinforcers begins with the observation that all the items of this list sometimes are, and sometimes are not, reinforcers. This variability is easily seen for a reinforcer like food whose reinforcing value undergoes cycles measured in hours; it is less easily seen for air, whose periodicities are the short breathing cycles of animals, measured in seconds or less. Nevertheless the general fact is clear—sometimes food, water, air, sex, and so forth are reinforcers; sometimes they are not. The experimental analysis of motivation is a systematic attempt to relate this variability to observable variables in the organism's past or present environment. In short, we search for the behavioral laws of motivation.

The determination of the cyclical nature of primary reinforcers is a first step in such an analysis. Neither animals nor men eat continuously. When provided with an inexhaustible supply of food, the normal mouse eats periodically. The cyclic nature of the eating is shown in Fig. 15–1. Each lever-press response made by the mouse produces a small pellet of food and a continuous reinforcement contingency is held permanently in effect. It will be observed from Fig. 15–1 that a "meal" begins as a

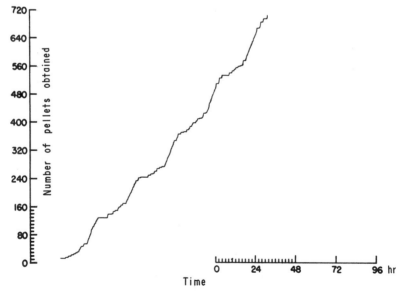

Figure 15–1. Cyclical feeding behavior exhibited by the mouse (Anliker and Mayer, 1956).

3–5-hr sustained constant rate of pressing (therefore eating). Thereafter the pressing-eating rate declines, terminating usually in a complete cessation of pressing-eating for up to 6 hr.

Left to drink water whenever it chooses, the rat produces characteristic cycles of drinking and no drinking, as the cumulative drinking curves of Fig. 15–2 indicate. There is relatively little drinking between 6 A.M. and 6 P.M., the daylight hours. Drinking then gradually increases and is usually at its peak around midnight.

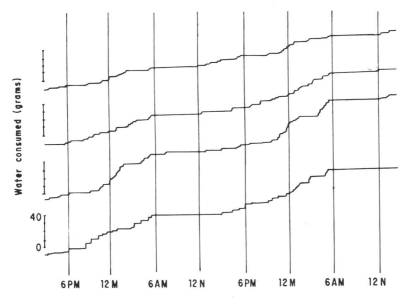

Figure 15–2. Cumulative drinking curves for four rats. The graph shows periods of drinking and non-drinking of distilled water which was constantly available (Young and Richey, 1952).

Human sleep is characterized by periodicities that change at various ages. Figure 15–3 depicts graphically the way the cycles change as the human grows older. The cycle changes both its period (the number of "naps" per day) as well as its phase (when the first "nap" commences) with age.

15.7 DEPRIVATION AND SATIATION PARADIGMS

The discovery of a lawful periodicity in reinforcement value represents only the beginning of an experimental analysis of motivation. More progress is made when direct control is obtained over the cycles. The

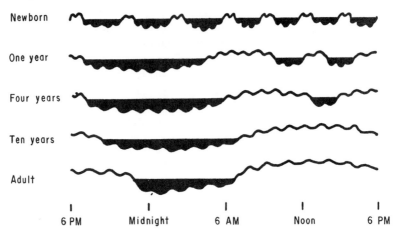

Newborn

One year

Four years

Ten years

Adult

6 PM   Midnight   6 AM   Noon   6 PM

Figure 15–3. Cycles of sleep at different ages (Kleit-man, 1963).

operation of deprivation is strongly identified with motivation because the withholding of primary reinforcers is a universal method for varying the reinforcing value of all known primary reinforcers. When we deprive an organism of a class of primary reinforcers for a fixed period of time, and then permit access to the reinforcer, we may observe the effect that our deprivation operation has had upon behavior. In the case of food and water, the actual behavior of consuming the reinforcer is often of interest. After a period of deprivation, an animal eats and drinks a certain quantity of food or water, and then ceases. We say that the animal is then satiated. The behavioral description of this satiation process conveniently takes the form of the change in rate of a response that produces food or water on *crf* contingencies. Since each response is reinforced, the rate of eating is indexed by the rate of emission of this response.

Food-satiation curves do not all take the same form, but the most common form seems to be that of a constant rate of eating followed by a fairly abrupt cessation (Smith and Smith, 1939; Reese and Hogenson, 1962). In Fig. 15–4, several satiation curves from a pigeon pecking a key for grain are shown. The curves were taken after various lengths of food deprivation, as indicated.

In their decline in rate, satiation curves may bear a superficial resemblance to extinction curves. The form of a satiation curve is, however, characterized by a much more abrupt cessation of rate (see Fig. 15–4). Furthermore, if the chain of acquired behavior is examined in detail, it will be found to remain intact as the process progresses. The extinction process, on the other hand, is associated with a marked disintegration of the chain of behavior.

The satiation paradigm may be schematized as follows:

GIVEN: 1. Deprivation of a primary reinforcer (or some other suitable reinforcer-establishing operation).
2. A suitable behavior previously strengthened by that reinforcer.
PROCEDURE: $R \rightarrow S^+$.
PROCESS: A fairly constant R rate, followed by an abrupt termination.
RESULT: Cessation of R rate.

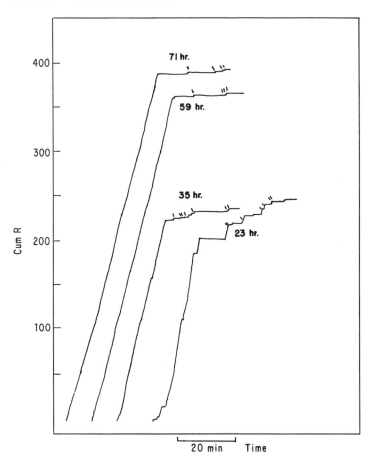

Figure 15–4. Individual food-satiation curves. Curves are labeled with number of hours of prior food deprivation. A pip above the curve indicates that the bird did not eat following that pecking response (Reese and Hogenson, 1962).

Note that in general the *result* also differs from the extinction result. Whereas extinction returns the behavior to operant level, satiation returns the behavior to a near-zero level—which may be lower than the operant level. Satiated for all other reinforcers, organisms frequently go to sleep.

15.8 THE MEASUREMENT OF DRIVES

We frequently refer to the fact that an individual is more strongly motivated at some times than at other times, and indeed we infer a continuum of motivational strength. We may translate this statement to an equivalent one about a continuum of drive strength. The notion that a drive may vary in strength from a very low to a very high value seems, upon analysis, to refer principally to the observation that primary reinforcers can vary in their strengths from very low to very high values. Thus, we speak of a person as being strongly motivated for food when food is a strong reinforcer for that person's instrumental behavior. Similarly, a person who is highly sexed frequently engages in behavior that leads to sexual reinforcers. Note that even though in these examples we talk in terms of a high strength of motivation, all we actually observe is the ability of a particular set of primary reinforcers to strengthen and maintain behavior. To the extent that this ability can be demonstrated to be graded from low to high, depending on circumstances, we may denote its value by a variable we name the primary *reinforcing value* of stimuli.

How can we measure the reinforcing value of stimuli? There appears no way to measure it save by measuring the behavioral effects of stimuli when they are made contingent upon operant responses. In measuring drive we find that we come finally to measuring behavior. Thus, many of the familiar behavioral measures of previous chapters, such as response rate and resistance to extinction, will be useful in assessing the strength of motivation. A curious implication of this versatility follows. The behavior that the experimenter chooses to measure cannot alone and in itself determine what phenomenon is under study. Bar pressing, key pecking, and vocalizing "I'm hungry" take on meaning only when they are associated with other events. More generally, this is the reason why the very discipline of psychology cannot be defined solely as the study of behavior, but is more appropriately considered the study of behavior as it is related to the environment. In earlier chapters, the response rates of representative operants were used frequently to study conditioning, extinction, discrimination, chaining, and other phenomena, depending on the particular procedure that was being imposed on the organism when the behavior was being measured. Now we discover yet another use for operant measures. When conditioning parameters are held constant, and the behavior is related to drive operations, the properties of the behavior being emitted may serve as a measure of the relative reinforcing value (or strength) of primary reinforcers. Note carefully how this experimental strategy is the converse of one used in previous chapters, where drive operations were always held constant, and reinforcement contingencies were manipulated. Using that methodology, the rate of behavior was generally taken to represent the strength of behavior. In motivational methodology, the rate of behavior will often be taken to represent the strength of the reinforcer. Evidently the "meaning" of behavior is derived only by considering the variable or variables to which the behavior is being related. We discuss below a number of behavioral techniques that have been used to measure the primary reinforcing value of stimuli, and therefore, by inference, motivation. At the same time, we illustrate a variety of different responses and primary reinforcers.

1. *Resistance to Satiation.* Our intuitions tell us that the "thirstier" we are, the more water we can consume, and the "hungrier" we are, the more food we can eat. How can we quantify these impressions? One way is to examine the properties of the satiation process in relation to the duration of time that an individual has been previously denied access to all the reinforcers in a certain class. In effect, we look at satiation curves obtained at various degrees of deprivation. Suppose, after a period of deprivation, we set a contingency so that some arbitrary chain of behavior can lead to reinforcement. Then, either the time it takes the organism to reach some arbitrary low-rate criterion, or the number of reinforced responses emitted before reaching the low-rate criterion, would provide a measure of the *resistance to satiation.* It is evident that if *crf* contingencies are in effect, and if each reinforcement is held constant in amount, this last measure is equivalent to the amount of reinforcement substance consumed. Resistance to satiation is calculated analogously to resistance to extinction (section 5.5). Using the resistance-to-satiation method, Siegel (1947) measured the amount of water drunk by rats in a 5-min period as a function of how long the animals had been deprived of water. The relationship obtained is shown in Fig. 15–5. From 0- up to 48-hr deprivation, the resistance to satiation, as measured by the amount of water consumed, increased. The *rate of increase,* however, appears to fall off after 12 hr. Similar results may be obtained for food deprivation. At very long periods of deprivation, however, the amount of food eaten will decline, presumably as a result of shrinkage of the stomach and inanition. Within limits, however, resistance to satiation increases as deprivation time increases.

Resistance to satiation, although a useful technique, is not always entirely satisfactory for measuring reinforcing value. One difficulty lies

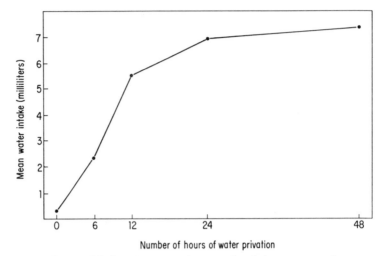

Figure 15–5. Amount of water drunk by rats in a five min test period as a function of the number of hours that they were denied access to all liquids (after Siegel, 1947).

in the physiological complications that occur at long deprivation times, sometimes causing reduced intake. Another difficulty arises if we wish to know how strong the reinforcer is at various points in the satiation process. At any level of deprivation, an organism may eat or drink at a constant high rate until the process comes to an abrupt halt (Fig. 15–4). Hence, the momentary strength of the reinforcer is difficult to assess by inspection of the satiation process. Satiation curves tend to differ principally in their point of termination, rather than in their slopes (Fig. 15–4). Hence we are forced to wait until satiation has been reached to know how hungry or thirsty the animal was at the beginning.

2. *Rate of Intermittently Reinforced Responses.* A more generally useful technique for measuring reinforcement value is to observe the rate of response generated by the organism when behavior is being intermittently reinforced. An interval schedule, for instance, can be arranged to provide a low enough reinforcement rate so that behavior can be maintained without the occurrence of satiation for a very long period. Skinner (1938) used this technique to assess the behavioral effects of feeding specified amounts of food to rats prior to testing. Rats were at first deprived of food for 23 hr, and then, on various days, fed different amounts of food just prior to testing on interval contingencies. The results for one of these rats appear in Fig. 15–6. The numbers associated with each curve refer to the amount of food in grams fed the rat previously. It is clear that the more the rat was fed immediately prior to working, the lower the response rate on the schedule.

F. C. Clark (1958) studied the effects of various degrees of food

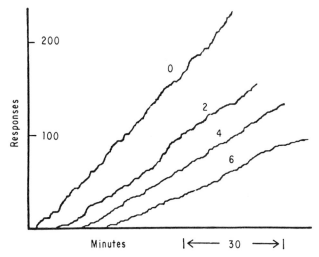

Figure 15–6. Four daily records for one rat under interval contingencies, 23-hr deprived then fed different amounts of food immediately prior to testing (Skinner, 1938).

deprivation on "stabilized" *VI* response rates of rats. Several different *VI*'s were used. Clark obtained the curves of Fig. 15–7 when he plotted the rats' response rate against hours of deprivation. The effect of increasing deprivation was to increase the response rate under all *VI* schedules. The way in which deprivation and reinforcement schedule interacted to determine the response rates of Fig. 15–7 is of some interest. The similarity in shape of the curves of Fig. 15–7 means that deprivation interacted with the *VI* schedule so that at all deprivation levels the ratio of the rate at one *VI* to that of the rate at another *VI* was a constant. For example, at 5-hr deprivation, the rate of *VI*-3 was about 4 R/min, and at *VI*-1, it was 2.5 times that, about 10 R/min. When deprivation was increased to 20 hr, the two rates were approximately 6 and 15, respectively, so that the *VI*-1 rate was still 2.5 times greater than the *VI*-3 rate.

In Clark's experiment the maximum deprivation interval was 23 hr. Heron and Skinner (1937) investigated protracted starvation in rats which extended until the death of the animal. They found that *FI* food reinforced response rate increased progressively throughout the starvation period until it reached a maximum, after which it declined rapidly, and death soon followed as a result of inanition. The maximum rate did not occur at the same point for all rats. In Heron and Skinner's experiment, it ranged from 4 to 12 days. The result bears on theories that equate motivation with bodily deficit ("need"). Although the rat's food deficit continues to increase throughout deprivation, it would appear that

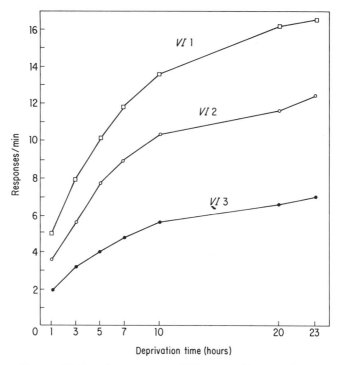

Figure 15–7. Average rate of VI *responding as a function of deprivation time. The parameter is the mean* VI *(Clark, 1958).*

the reinforcing value of food does not. We shall see later that other behavioral measures substantiate this conclusion.

3. *Resistance to Extinction.* The rate of response during extinction, and other measures of resistance to extinction (section 5.5) have frequently been used to measure the behavioral effects of deprivation and other deprivation-like operations. Crocetti (1962) trained 7-hr food-deprived rats to press a lever for food. The subjects were then distributed into five groups, and each group was extinguished after a different duration of deprivation. In Fig. 15–8, the total number of responses emitted by each group after 3 hr of extinction is shown. The curve shows the usual increase in response rate as deprivation time increases; but observe that the shape of this curve differs from those of Fig. 15–7. Differences such as these raise the systematic problem of which behavioral index best represents reinforcement value. At present, there is no clear-cut solution to this problem, and theorists are often forced to take the position that the measures that correlate the best with each other represent reinforcement strength best.

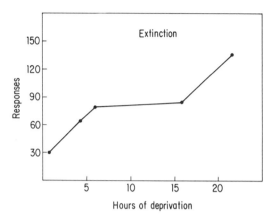

Figure 15–8. The relation of hours of food deprivation to the number of bar-pressing responses during extinction (after Crocetti, 1962).

4. *Acquisition.* We might expect that with an increase in the power of the reinforcer, there would be a concomitant increase in the speed of the acquisition process. When the acquisition entails a long chain of responses (for instance, behavior in a runway) or a discrimination, this prediction is verified. Broadhurst (1957) ran rats in the underwater equivalent of a **Y** maze. Rats were submerged in a start box and confined there for a few seconds, then permitted to swim underwater to the choice point. There they were presented with a light-dark discrimination, with contingencies of the sort discussed in relation to the Lashley jumping stand (section 10.3). If, at the choice point, the rat then swam to the bright side, it found an unlocked door which led out to dry land. If, however, it swam to the incorrect side, it encountered a locked door and had to swim back to the choice point, and then down the other branch of the **Y** to get out. The entire procedure was run underwater. The procedure schematically is

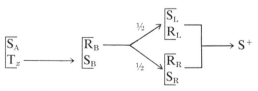

where S_A = in start box, door closed
S_B = in start box, door open R_B = swim to choice point
S_R = ■□ R_R = right turn
S_L = □■ R_L = left turn
S^+ = dry land

where T_x is the independent variable, the deprivation of air for T_x seconds. Broadhurst also varied the intensity difference between the two parts of the visual choice-point stimulus. The greater this difference, the easier the discrimination task (Frick, 1948). Hence, a large difference in the illumination corresponds to an "easy" discrimination, a small difference in the illumination corresponds to a "difficult" discrimination.

The results of the acquisition are shown in Fig. 15–9. The number of correct choices in 100 acquisition trials is shown for the two discriminations. When the illumination difference was large ("easy" discrimina-

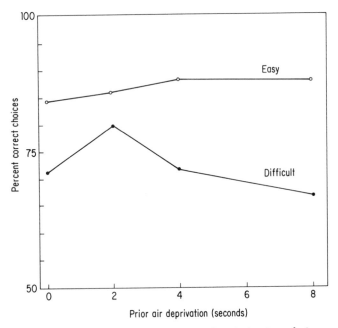

Figure 15–9. Number of correct discrimination choices in 100 acquisition trials as a function of prior air deprivation. The data are for three discriminations varying in difficulty (after Broadhurst, 1957).

tion), we may summarize the results by saying that the longer the deprivation time for air, the more efficient was the acquisition performance. But when a small illumination difference was used ("difficult" discrimination), acquisition was most efficient at a middle value (2 sec) of air deprivation, and less efficient at both shorter and longer deprivations. If this result can be generalized, it appears that with difficult tasks it is possible to have too much motivation for optimum performance. Certainly, the differences in shape between the two curves of Fig. 15–9 indicate that the acquisition method must be used cautiously as a measure of reinforcing strength. For instance, a rather different result was obtained in a situation requiring a straight underwater swim without discrimination contingencies. Then, over the range of prior air deprivations from 0 to 10 sec, rats swam faster the greater the previous air deprivation.

5. *Overcoming Obstructions.* The more reinforcing a stimulus, the more obstructions, barriers, and hindrances an organism would be expected to overcome to produce the reinforcer. That is the rationale for the Columbia Obstruction Box shown in Fig. 15–10. A rat is placed in the start box and an electrically charged grid is interposed between it and food, water, or a mate located in the goal box. (The rat has previously been trained to run to the goal box without receiving any electric shocks.) If the rat crosses the grid, it is given brief access to the reinforcer and then returned to the start box for another trial. The number of crossings of the electrified grid in 30 min provides a measure of the strength of the behavior. Warden (1931) investigated several primary reinforcers and deprivation procedures with this apparatus. He believed it was a way of comparing objectively the maximum strengths of the various primary reinforcers. One interesting set of Warden's functions

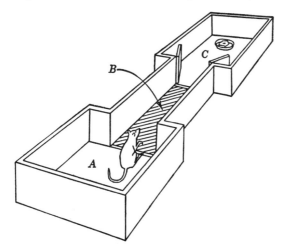

Figure 15–10. The Columbia Obstruction Box. A charged grid (B) stands between the rat's compartment (A) and a reinforcer placed in the goal box (C) (after Warden, 1931, from Harlow, 1948).

appears in Fig. 15–11. From these we see that if deprivation operations are carried out long enough, the behavior that leads to the reinforcer rises to a maximum strength, then eventually declines. Warden thought that the relative heights of the maxima could be interpreted to mean that the water and food drives were stronger than the sex drive. But is such a conclusion justified? We must remember that behaviorial functions

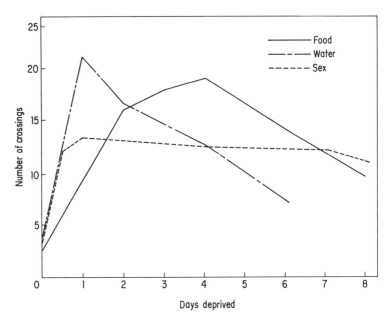

Figure 15–11. The number of crossings of a charged grid as a function of days of deprivation of the appropriate primary reinforcer (after Warden, 1931).

depend on many variables other than the particular one the experimenter happens to be investigating. Reinforcement value, in particular, depends on such factors as the quality and quantity of the reinforcement. Warden's conclusion assumed that somehow these factors had been equated for sex, food, and water, so that deprivation was the only *variable* in the situation. But in what sense, except the most trivial, can (say) a 10-sec exposure to a female rat, a dish of water, and a piece of cheese be said to be equal? And even if some way were found to equate two reinforcers, the satiation processes associated with each class of reinforcer are almost certainly so different that the average crossings in a 30-min session would reflect a different composite of reinforcement values for each reinforcer. These considerations indicate that Warden's ranking of water, food, and sex drives probably should not be taken too seriously. The question of which drive is the strongest may not even have experimental meaning.

6. *Maximum-Work Technique.* The maximum-work technique is similar in outlook to the obstruction box, but avoids one of the latter's undesirable side effects—contamination of the results by emotional effects of electric shocks. The maximum-work technique is based on the idea that the stronger the reinforcer, the more work an individual will do to obtain it. Hodos (1961) devised an ingenious procedure in which an organism works on a ratio schedule of reinforcement in which the actual

value of the ratio is progressively increased with each successive reinforcement. In one experiment, the session began with a ratio of 2, and
each successive reinforcement increased the ratio by an additional 2, so
that animals were required to emit 2 responses for the first reinforcement,
4 for the second, 6 for the third, and so on. A ratio is eventually reached
which is so high that the animal refuses to go on working. The point
at which this occurs is named the "breaking point," defined in Hodos'
work as 15 min of no responding. Using rat subjects, and sweetened
condensed milk as reinforcement, Hodos manipulated the deprivation
schedule of his subjects by feeding them each day only enough food to
keep their body weights at a fixed percentage of their free-feeding weights.
Thus, a rat kept at 80 per cent of its normal body weight is strongly
deprived; a rat kept at 95 per cent of its normal body weight is only
mildly deprived. This procedure is commonly used to control deprivation
in experimental subjects, and is thought by some to give slightly better
control of motivation than maintaining subjects at a fixed duration of
deprivation, say 23 hr. The measure of behavior used by Hodos was the
number of responses in the last completed ratio prior to the breaking
point. This final ratio is the maximum ratio that the rat would complete
under the conditions of the experiment. Figure 15–12 shows that as the
rats were more deprived they completed a larger maximum ratio. We
interpret this to mean that with greater deprivation the rat will put out
more total work.

7. *Adulteration of Reinforcer.* When we are only slightly hungry, we
are very selective about what we will eat. Eventually, as we grow increasingly hungry, our standards of what we will accept go down. If
we are starving, we will eat almost anything. These impressions suggest

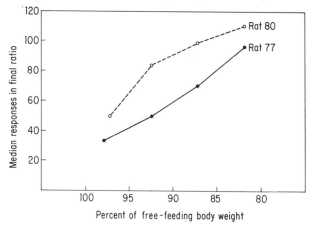

*Figure 15–12. Maximum ratio run leading to milk that
rats will emit as a function of degree of food deprivation
(Hodos, 1961).*

that drive might be measured by the quantity of an unpalatable substance that must be mixed with food in order to stop the organism from working for or consuming the adulterated food.

Investigators with interests in brain-behavior relationships have commonly resorted to experimental destruction (lesions) of small localized regions of the nervous system in order to pinpoint specific brain regions associated with specific behaviors. In one vicinity deep in the brain (the ventromedial nuclei of the hypothalamus) such experimental damage produces an animal that upon recovery from surgery eats voraciously. In 2 months' time it will double its weight if given continuous access to food (Teitelbaum, 1955). Though such "operated" rats will eat enormous quantities of food and grow obese, Miller, Bailey, and Stevenson (1950) had earlier shown that these rats would not work as hard to obtain food on ratio schedules as would normal rats. This is one of several findings that amount of food consumed (resistance to satiation) and work done for food are not perfectly correlated. Miller, Bailey, and Stevenson took the ratio findings to mean that the obese rats were not as "hungry" as normal rats, though if food were freely available they would eat relatively much more of it.

Teitelbaum used the method of adulterating the rat's food with a fixed small amount of quinine (a substance that humans find bitter) to examine further Miller, Bailey, and Stevenson's interpretation. He found that during the 2 months after the operation, as the rats were growing obese, the quinine did not deter their abnormally large consumption of food. In other words, during this period in which the rats grew very fat food was a strong reinforcer. But once the rats had become obese, an amount of quinine too small even to affect the normal rat's food consumption completely deterred the obese animals from eating. It appears that food is less reinforcing for the fully obese rat than it is for the normal rat. Even so, if given continuous access to non-adulterated food, the obese animal will eat a great deal more—its resistance to satiation is higher than normal.

8. *Preference.* Suppose it is possible for either but not both of two chains of behavior to be emitted. To the extent that an organism emits behavior leading to one reinforcer rather than emitting behavior leading to another, we speak of a *preference* being shown for the first reinforcer. If the amount of effort in completing both chains is approximately the same, such a preference could be regarded as an expression of a higher reinforcing value of the first reinforcer. Hence, preference behavior becomes a method of assessing the relative reinforcing value of two or more reinforcers.

When the adrenal glands of rats are surgically removed, a drastic change occurs in sodium and potassium ion balance. Unless a large quantity of sodium is ingested daily, the animal will soon die. When the operation is performed, rats change their normal preference for water over salt (sodium chloride) solutions, and ingest large quantities of salt solution, thereby managing to stay alive and healthy. This changed behavior is evidence that the operation acts to increase the reinforcing value of salt.

Summary. We have briefly described several methods showing that behavior of several sorts varies in an orderly fashion with changes in deprivation, satiation, and allied operations. There appears to exist a set of behavioral measures which, within limits, covary with deprivation of the reinforcer. For instance, increased deprivation of food results in an individual working faster on an interval schedule of food reinforcement, doing more total work (progressive ratio), overcoming more obstacles and adulterations of the reinforcer, or acquiring a new skill faster. We summarize these in Diagram [15.2].

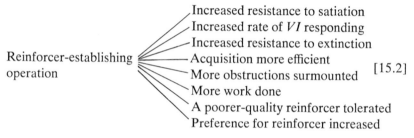

Reinforcer-establishing operation

Increased resistance to satiation
Increased rate of VI responding
Increased resistance to extinction
Acquisition more efficient
More obstructions surmounted
More work done
A poorer-quality reinforcer tolerated
Preference for reinforcer increased

[15.2]

The systematic covariation in a number of independent behavioral measures in relation to a single operation (for example, deprivation) provides grounds for the introduction of a concept which will summarize and stand for this covariance. The term reinforcement value, for which we intentionally postponed a formal definition until now, is just such a concept. Reinforcement value may be said to denote the covariance of the behaviors on the right side of [15.2]. We are now in a position to merge Diagrams [15.1] and [15.2], for the meaning of the right-hand side of [15.1] is more accurately expressed by [15.2]. Similarly, the left-hand side of [15.2] is more adequately spelled out in [15.1].

The actual concept of a drive itself may now be formally defined as the conjunction (relationship) of the terms of Diagrams [15.1] and [15.2]. That is, a drive remains a relation between a reinforcement-establishing operation and the reinforcing value of a class of stimuli. But we may now appreciate the great diversity of information that the term "drive" contains. The concept carries with it a degree of complexity that must not be forgotten when using the single word drive. In fully understanding its status as an abstract summarizing concept, we shall be unlikely to use it metaphorically as a "goad," or a force that "drives the organism," or as a cause of behavior. Similarly, we avoid references to its "location" (for an abstraction has no "location") or its "satisfaction" (for how can an abstraction be satisfied?). None of the metaphors in common use is appropriately applied to the concept of drive that we have here explicated. The term stands for a complex relationship and means no more and no less than Diagrams like [15.1] and [15.2].

References for Chapter 15

Anliker, J., and Mayer, J. Operant conditioning technique for studying feeding patterns in normal and obese mice. *J. appl. Physiol.,* 1956, **8,** 667–670.

Broadhurst, P. L. Emotionality and the Yerkes-Dodson law. *J. exp. Psychol.,* 1957, **54,** 345–352.

Clark, F. C. The effect of deprivation and frequency of reinforcement on variable interval responding. *J. exp. Anal. Behav.,* 1958, **1,** 221–228.

Crocetti, C. P. Drive level and response strength in the bar-pressing apparatus. *Psychol. Rep.,* 1962, **10,** 563–575.

Frick, F. C. An analysis of an operant discrimination. *J. Psychol.,* 1948, **26,** 93–123.

Harlow, H. F. Studying animal behavior. Chap. 12 in T. G. Andrews (Ed.), *Methods of psychology,* New York: Wiley, 1948.

Heron, W. T., and Skinner, B. F. Changes in hunger during starvation. *Psychol. Rec.,* 1937, **1,** 51–60.

Hodos, W. Progressive ratio as a measure of reward strength. *Science,* 1961, **134,** 943–944.

Kleitman, N. *Sleep and wakefulness.* (rev. and enlarged ed.) Chicago: Univer. of Chicago Press, 1963.

Miller, N. E., Bailey, C. J., and Stevenson, J. A. F. Decreased "hunger" but increased food intake resulting from hypothalamic lesions. *Science,* 1950, **112,** 256–259.

Reese, T. W., and Hogenson, Marilyn J. Food satiation in the pigeon. *J. exp. Anal. Behav.,* 1962, **5,** 239–245.

Siegel, P. S. The relationship between voluntary water intake, body weight loss, and number of hours of water privation in the rat. *J. comp. physiol. Psychol.,* 1947, **40,** 231–238.

Skinner, B. F. *The behavior of organisms.* New York: Appleton-Century, 1938.

Smith, Margaret F., and Smith, K. U. Thirst-motivated activity and its extinction in the cat. *J. gen. Psychol.,* 1939, **21,** 89–98.

Teitelbaum, P. Sensory control of hypothalamic hyperphagia. *J. comp. physiol. Psychol.,* 1955, **48,** 156–163.

Warden, C. J. *Animal motivation studies.* New York: Columbia Univer. Press, 1931.

Young, P. T., and Richey, H. W. Diurnal drinking patterns in the rat. *J. comp. physiol. Psychol.,* 1952, **45,** 80–89.

Chapter 16 **MOTIVATION II**

DRIVES ARE OFTEN SAID TO (1) ENERGIZE OR activate the organism, and (2) direct it to a goal. In view of our definition in the previous chapter of a drive as a summary relationship between two sets of observables (see Diagrams [15.1] and [15.2]), we are forced to reject as metaphorical the notion that a drive itself can either activate or direct an organism. Nevertheless, we must not be too hasty in rejecting all of the ideas behind activation and direction. Upon analysis, some may refer to fundamental properties of behavior which we have hitherto neglected in our account of motivation.

16.1 ACTIVATION AND DIRECTIONAL ASPECTS OF MOTIVATION

In the present terminology, activation can be construed as an increase in the so-called diffuse general activity of the organism. Such activity in the rat comprises grooming, locomotion, sniffing, changes in position, "exploration," and the like. Indeed, unconditioned operant-level responding, studied in previous chapters, is a form of this kind of activity. Since neither the past nor the present reinforcement for these activities is readily apparent, the behaviors are often spoken of as spontaneous activities. "Spontaneous" is probably a misnomer since, as we shall show, these activities can be experimentally controlled to some extent. We refer to them hereafter as general activities.

An apparatus known as the running wheel (or activity wheel) has been in use since the beginning of the century for the study of general activity in small mammals (rats, hamsters, mice). The wheel (Fig. 16–1) is

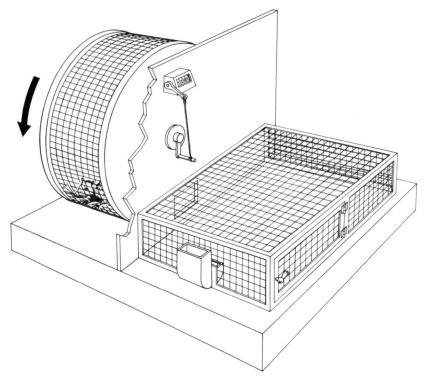

Figure 16–1. A running wheel.

frequently attached to the organism's living cage and the animal is free to enter the wheel at any time and run. The question of whether motivation is related to activation is approached in a straightforward way by studying the relation of various drive operations to running activity in the wheel. A representative result is Richter's (1922) finding that activity steadily increases with food deprivation up until the third day of deprivation (72 hr), after which time continued starvation results in a decrease in running activity.

Very little work has been done to explore the effects of water deprivation on running-wheel activity. The existing evidence suggests a progressively increasing activity as a function of increased deprivation (Hall, 1961).

In section 15.6 we saw that the reinforcing value of primary reinforcers is periodic. The periodicities that a female rat shows in sexual receptivity are correlated with periodicities in sexual hormone secretion and ovulation (called the estrus cycle) and are mirrored very clearly in running activity. A typical activity cycle of a mature female rat appears in Fig. 16–2. It can be seen that approximately every 4 days the female rat

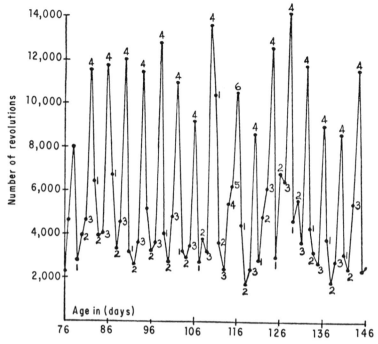

Figure 16–2. Typical activity of a female rat (Richter, 1927).

is extremely active. Corresponding physiological measurements show that it is precisely during this active period that ovulation occurs, rendering the female maximally susceptible to insemination. During this period, the female is said to be "in heat" and is then most receptive to sexual advances from the male. During the low-activity portions of the cycle, however, the female is likely to resist copulation and fight off advances by the male. Thus, for the female rat, there exists an intimate correlation between general activity and the reinforcing value of sex.

Another apparatus that records a somewhat different set of general activities than the wheel is the stabilimeter (Fig. 16–3). The stabilimeter consists of a cage (often triangular) whose floor is mounted above a pneumatic suspension system. Slight movements about the cage, and shifts in balance by the animal, tilt the floor slightly, changing the air-pressure balance. These changes are transmitted to recording pens that permit a permanent record of activity to be kept. The movements recorded are not necessarily the same type as the movements in wheel running, so we must not necessarily take it as a paradox that some investigators have reported that food and water deprivations affect only slightly, or not at all, the activities recorded from stabilimeters. In gen-

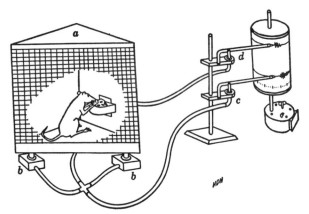

Figure 16–3. A stabilimeter for recording movements of small animals (Harlow, 1948).

eral, the kinds of activities measured by the wheel appear to be enhanced by deprivation, whereas those in the stabilimeter are much less affected. Bolles (1963) suspected that this difference meant that different specific activities were differentially affected by deprivation. With the aid of several assistants, he periodically observed the activities of two groups of rats for a number of days in their home cages. Once each hour, the experimenters glanced briefly at each rat, and classified what it was doing as one of six activities: sleeping, resting quietly, standing in one location, grooming, eating, drinking. One group (hungry) was fed 10 gm of food once a day. As a result, this group experienced a 15 to 20 per cent loss in free-feeding body weights. The other group had unrestricted access to food and was therefore called the *ad lib* group. The food-deprivation regimen resulted in deviations from the *ad lib* pattern of activity. The hungry rats both made more movements (standing and locomotion) *and* rested quietly more than *ad lib* rats. In turn, they slept less and groomed less than *ad lib* rats. Food deprivation appears therefore to change the pattern of activity, increasing some activities and decreasing others.

Operant-level responding, that is, pre-strengthened operant activity, is sensitive to deprivation operations. Crocetti (1962) obtained the curve shown in Fig. 16–4, when he recorded the operant level of rats pressing a lever under five different values of food deprivation. Comparison of the curve of Fig. 16–4 with that of Fig. 15–8 (both containing data from the same rats) shows that food deprivation affected the operant level of bar pressing much in the same way that it affected the resistance to extinction of the response following its experimental strengthening.

The evidence presented from several sources suggests that some drive operations do increase certain activities, even though these activities may never have been directly related to the primary reinforcer associated with the drive operation in use. While this statement can be generalized to include many primary reinforcers, it is not true for all. For example, certain vitamin deficiencies are associated with a decrease rather than an increase in activity (Hall, 1961). In trying to understand how deprivation operations are related to activity, some workers appeal to the evolution of the species. In the evolutionary history of the species, it would seem that a species that became increasingly active as it was increasingly deprived of vital substances might have a certain survival advantage over a species that lacked this tendency. Becoming more active might lead the organism to happen upon food or water which a more quiescent individual might never discover.

When we turn to an analysis of the so-called directive property of drive operations, we find that the idea expressed is less one of experimental fact than one of interpretation. A drive operation is directional to the extent that it acts selectively on behavior associated with a given class of reinforcers, rather than on all behaviors equally. Thus food deprivation affects food-reinforced behaviors maximally, water deprivation affects water-reinforced behaviors maximally, and so on. By selectively affecting reinforcers, certain behaviors are made more likely to occur than others. For instance, when a chimpanzee that has been highly deprived of food and only slightly deprived of a mate is placed in a situation where it can perform either a chain of behavior leading to food (say pressing a lever) or one leading to a mate (say entering a compartment where its mate is confined) it is likely to do the former. This is the essence of direction, and indeed the direction does lie partly in the drive operation. But another critical condition for direction lies in the past condi-

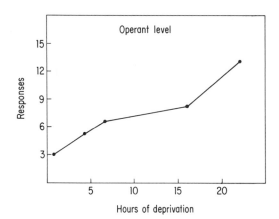

Figure 16–4. Operant-level bar-pressing rate related to hours of food deprivation (after Crocetti, 1962).

tioning history. Unless behavior exists for getting to the reinforcer, the drive operation will not direct the organism there. The best it will do is to change the pattern of general activity, or make acquisition take place more quickly; but by itself, the drive operation is powerless to direct.

The chimpanzee example raises the interesting problem of what happens if two drive operations are performed simultaneously, and the chains of behavior made topographically incompatible. That is, consider a chimpanzee strongly deprived of both food and sex, and placed in a situation where performing a behavior that leads to one reinforcer precludes obtaining the other. If the animal runs to its mate, it turns off its food S^D. If it begins to press a lever for food, a door falls blocking the path to its mate. This is one of the situations frequently described as a conflict of motives. How many times have we found ourselves forced to choose between one reinforcer or another? In the present terminology, the situation reveals itself to be similar to the preference method used to assess relative reinforcing values. The conflict is thus perhaps best described as a conflict between reinforcing values.

16.2 INCENTIVE

The *quality* and *quantity* of a reinforcer, a pair of related variables, are closely associated with reinforcing value. We have already seen how a food can be adulterated with quinine to lower its reinforcing value. The quality of a food reinforcer can also be adversely affected by mixing it with non-metabolized bulk cellulose. This constitutes, in effect, a dilution of the reinforcer, and as such is a way of varying reinforcer value while holding the volume of substance ingested constant. Dilution, of course, is particularly convenient for manipulating the reinforcing value of liquids. Guttman (1953) reinforced the lever pressing of hungry rats with a drop of sucrose solution on a *VI* schedule. As the concentration of sucrose in the solution increased, the lever-pressing rate rose, reaching a maximum when sucrose concentration was 32 per cent. Concentrations above this value produced a decline in response rate.

The behavioral effects of quantity of reinforcer may be studied in several ways. If the reinforcer is food, and the quality is kept uniform, the volume may be varied. In general, rats acquire maze chains faster and stabilize at a lower asymptote of errors per run when they receive more food for their performance. Quantity may also be studied by varying the access time to the reinforcer. Rat subjects run faster to a mate if allowed to spend more time with it; pigeons peck faster if allowed more access time to the contingent grain reinforcer.

The behavioral effects of varying quality and quantity of primary reinforcement may be categorized under the label of *incentive* functions. As a noun, incentive is a synonym for reinforcer; but as an adjective, we may use it to denote the class of variables that change reinforcing value through changes in the stimulus properties of the reinforcer. For a summary and interpretation of the diverse behavioral effects that incentive variables may have, the interested student may consult Cofer and Appley's (1964) readable account.

16.3 PHYSIOLOGICAL FACTORS IN MOTIVATION

We have had little occasion to mention the properties of the nervous system in the present treatment of behavioral principles. This neglect should not be taken as a denial that nervous structures and functions underlie the various behaviors we have described. Rather, it stems from the recognition that the tremendous volume of information which constitutes behavioral science must of necessity be partitioned into somewhat arbitrary divisions. Psychology, sociology, and anthropology constitute such divisions; so do the hybrid disciplines of behavior genetics and physiological psychology. Although we have elsewhere noted that the laws of behavior cannot be subsumed or replaced by laws of physiology (or chemistry, or mechanics, or particle physics) the nervous system is intimately involved in all behavioral phenomena. An intact, functioning brain and spinal cord are a prerequisite for all the laws of operant strengthening and many of the laws of the reflex.

Evidently, natural phenomena transcend the arbitrary boundaries of disciplines. Thus behavior involves a complex of physical, biochemical, physiological, psychological, and sociological events. The position we have adopted is dictated by convenience: psychology concerns itself with lawful relations between environment and behavior. Laws relating behavior to nervous function carry us outside the strictly psychological province into physiology. But whenever behavior is the dependent variable of physiological studies, they contribute to our knowledge of behavior *and* physiology; hence the designation physiological psychology. In an introductory treatment of psychology, however, physiological psychology must be regarded as an advanced specialty, and cannot be treated in any degree of depth. We elect to introduce certain of its findings in the context of motivation, because the picture that is emerging of the physiological mechanisms underlying reinforcement helps in understanding the behavioral concept of drive. Physiological studies promise to give the concept of reinforcing value a physical referent in various anatomical structures, and to tie together a number of environmentally diverse drive operations by discovering their common effects within the organism.

Eating and Drinking Mechanisms. In the gradual elaboration of the bodily mechanisms associated with eating, we find a representative example of the search for physiological events underlying behavioral phenomena. More precisely, that search concerns itself with certain internal events and processes that accompany changes in the reinforcing power of food. The state of the stomach was thought from antiquity to recent times to play a major role in the control of the reinforcing value of food. The fact that "hunger pangs" often accompanied reports of great hunger[1] in humans led to investigations of the relationship between hunger pangs, stomach contractions, and hunger. Cannon and Washburn (1912) studied stomach contractions using an ingenious technique in which a human subject swallowed a small rubber balloon. Once in the stomach, the balloon was inflated, and any stomach contractions that occurred squeezed the balloon. The resulting air-pressure variations within the balloon were in turn transmitted to a pen-recording device. The subject depressed a telegraph key whenever he felt hunger pangs. Cannon and Washburn showed that the contractions were closely correlated with reports of hunger pangs, and concluded that these contractions were the *cause* of hunger. The hypothesis won immediate attention because it seemed to offer such a simple and straightforward mechanism for hunger and eating. But it was soon shown that patients lacking stomachs altogether ate in normal ways, and reported "hunger" even though they never had stomach contractions. The implications behind these observations were extended in experiments which showed that rats ate normally even though the nerves from the stomach were surgically isolated from the brain. Other observations showed that hunger contractions were abolished by the first few morsels of food, yet food continued to have a high reinforcing value long after the contractions had ceased. In the end the stomach-contraction theory of hunger had to be abandoned, for it failed to explain enough of the facts of eating behavior.

A more complicated mechanism was indicated by the early experiments of Tschukilshew (cited in Templeton and Quigley, 1930) in which blood transfusion from food-deprived animals to well-fed animals augmented the stomach motility of the recipient. More recent experiments have shown that transfusing the blood between hungry and satiated rats (Fig. 16–5) affects the food intake of these animals. Feeding and fasting appear to

[1] The terms "hunger" and "thirst" in the following account are used in their descriptive sense as shorthand words meaning that food and water, respectively, have high reinforcing value.

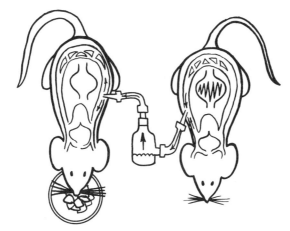

*Figure 16–5. When blood is transfused between hungry
and satiated rats, food intake is altered (Sanford, 1961).*

change some aspect of the blood, which change could in turn affect brain
mechanisms leading to a change in the reinforcing value of food. One
theory (Mayer, 1953) holds that a possible mediating variable is the
relative arterial to venous glucose concentration, and that the cells in the
brain where this concentration may be "metered" lie in a restricted region
of the hypothalamus (Fig. 16–6).

Independent experimental work has confirmed that certain structures
in the hypothalamus are intimately related to the reinforcing power of
food. In a previous subsection, we described behavioral effects caused
by experimental damage in the ventromedial region of the hypothalamus.
Rats with damage in this ventromedial region overeat and grow obese.
Electrical stimulation of this brain region also has effects on food-
motivated behavior. Tiny electrodes can be implanted in the brain with
fairly precise localization, yet without damaging surrounding structures.
The electrodes are guided into brain tissue through a hole drilled in the
skull, then secured in a plastic block which is cemented to the skull
covering the hole. Finally the scalp is resewn. Following a few days of
recovery from the operation, such an implanted animal regains complete
health. The animal appears in no way inconvenienced by the addition
of the electrodes, and lives normally. Through the implanted electrodes,
minute electrical currents can be applied to the brain structure where
the tips of the electrodes lie. The behavioral effects of such electrical
current are then measured. When the ventromedial region of the hypothalamus is so stimulated, food intake decreases. Other areas in the brain
have been found where stimulation causes a "satiated" animal to begin
eating. The picture of physiological mechanisms behind deprivation and

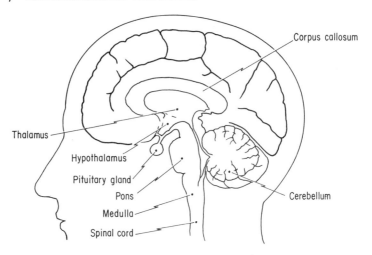

Figure 16–6. Schematic diagram of the human brain (Rosenzweig, 1962).

eating is complex and still fragmentary. No single bodily structure mediates the reinforcing value of food. The stomach, the blood, the brain, and probably other bodily systems interact to determine when food shall be reinforcing.

An analogous experimental history can be narrated for drinking mechanisms, but we can only indicate it briefly. The earliest explanations centered on the role of the relative dryness of throat and mouth membranes and the importance of salivary secretions. Dry mouth and pharynx were equated with thirst. Later work showed that salivation could not be crucial since animals both drank and ceased to drink normally even when their salivary ducts were tied off. Conversely, in experiments in which the water that dogs drank never reached their stomachs but ran out from a fistula in the throat (Fig. 16–7), water-deprived dogs continued to drink indefinitely, although their throats and mouths were thus being kept constantly wet. Experimental attention gradually shifted to the role of the water content of body cells. A very slight deficit from the normal water concentration in the body's cells and blood appears to be a critical factor in drinking (Gilman, 1937). Recent work has focused on localizing brain centers in the hypothalamus that regulate drinking and cessation of drinking behavior.

We turn now to describe briefly some methods by which physiological psychologists undertake to discover the logic of internal bodily mechanisms. Their principal techniques are (1) stimulation of nerve tissue by electrical current or by chemicals or drugs, (2) surgical or pharmacological destruction or isolation of areas believed to be crucial, (3) recording of local electrical activity of the brain, (4) modifying *some* of the

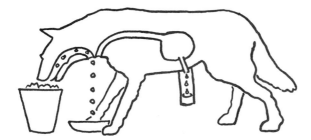

Figure 16–7. (From Rosenzweig, 1962.)

stimulation encountered in normal functioning while leaving other aspects intact (such as the sham drinking experiment of Fig. 16–7), (5) measurement of numerous physiological variables in relation to behavior (such as blood glucose level and water content of cells), (6) comparison of behavioral processes with physiological processes (for example, comparison of the satiation process with stomach contractions showed that the two were not parallel, indicating that one probably did not underlie the other).

The methods of physiological psychologists may lead to important behavioral discoveries. Olds and Milner (1954) implanted electrodes deep in the rat's brain with the aim of seeing whether stimulation in a region associated with sleep would facilitate or hinder simple operant acquisition. The investigators were surprised to find that the stimulation itself had a marked effect on the rat's behavior.

> In the test experiment we were using, the animal was placed in a large box with corners labeled *A, B, C* and *D*. Whenever the animal went to corner *A*, its brain was given a mild electric shock by the experimenter. When the test was performed on the animal . . . it kept returning to corner *A*. After several such returns on the first day, it finally went to a different place and fell asleep. The next day, however, it seemed even more interested in corner *A*.
>
> At this point we assumed that the stimulus must provoke curiosity; we did not yet think of it as a reward. Further experimentation on the same animal soon indicated, to our surprise, that its response to the stimulus was more than curiosity. On the second day, after the animal had acquired the habit of returning to corner *A* to be stimulated, we began trying to draw it away to corner *B*, giving it an electric shock whenever it took a step in that direction. Within a matter of five minutes the animal was in corner *B*. After this, the animal could be directed to almost any spot in the box at the will of the experimenter. Every step in the right direction was paid with a small shock; on arrival at the appointed place the animal received a longer series of shocks (Olds, 1956).

Evidently the brain stimulation was acting like a reinforcer with which operant behavior could be quickly shaped. Eventually the animal was placed in a Skinner box (Fig. 16–8) and allowed to stimulate its own brain at whatever rate it chose. High rates of response were emitted under *crf* contingencies. The similarities between brain-stimulation re-

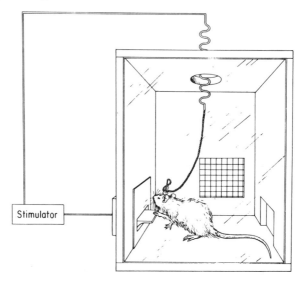

Figure 16–8. Rat self-stimulating in a Skinner box (after Olds, 1956).

ward and more conventional positive reinforcers such as food and water are pronounced. Like other positive reinforcers, brain-stimulation reward maintains *FR* operants, generates high resistance to extinction after intermittent contingencies, and permits powerful schedule control (Pliskoff, Wright, and Hawkins, 1965). On the other hand, the deprivation-satiation cycles of brain stimulation reward appear to be measurable in seconds rather than hours or days.

Additional work by Olds and others indicates that there is not one but a number of places in the brain where electrical stimulation exerts reinforcing effects (Olds, 1962). Many of these are the very places that seem, from other experiments, to be linked to the effectiveness of food, sex, activity, and other primary reinforcers.

16.4 ADDITIONAL PRIMARY REINFORCERS

Most of the principles of behavior elaborated in previous chapters have come from studies in which the primary reinforcer consisted of food for food-deprived organisms, or occasionally water for water-

deprived individuals. Food and water are powerful and dependable reinforcers and their deprivation provides a straightforward and reliable
operation for activating their strength. Nevertheless there are a host of
other primary reinforcers which, unlike food and water, are not essential
to the life of the organism. In the present section we shall briefly consider
primary reinforcers such as activity, novelty, exploration, manipulation,
affection, and bodily contact. The importance of some of these primary
reinforcers has been recognized only in recent years. In many cases, we
still have much to discover about the operations that determine their
reinforcing strengths. In other cases, such as exploration, novelty, and
affection, the actual specification of the class of reinforcing stimuli is far
from established. Though these problems present real difficulties for the
development of drive concepts in terms of these reinforcers, they do not
detract from the empirical importance of such reinforcers in modifying
and controlling behavior. Much of the behavior of human beings, living
in a society where starvation and extreme deprivation of liquids are rare,
seems far removed from the drives associated with food or water deprivation. Analysis of additional primary reinforcers is likely to prove essential
in interpreting complex human motivation.

1. *Activity.* In a previous section we considered several techniques
used to measure the so-called activation properties of food, sex, and water
deprivation. Apart from these controls over general activity, it appears
that deprivation of activity itself serves as a drive operation for activity.
For instance, a rat confined to a small chamber where its movements are
restricted will, upon being given access to a running wheel, run an
amount very nearly proportional to the time previously confined.
Activity is therefore an increasing function of hours of confinement
(Hall, 1961). The increased reinforcing value of activity after confinement can be demonstrated by a stabilimeter (tilt-cage) apparatus as
well. When placed in a tilt cagé after long periods of enforced inactivity
rats move about far more than usual. Kagan and Berkun (1954) have
shown that rats will press a lever to obtain access to a wheel in which
they can run. Apparently activity can serve as a primary reinforcer for
operant responses.

2. *Exploration.* Other things being equal, organisms will often prefer
to put themselves in novel situations. This is particularly true where the
novel situation presents an opportunity for "exploration." It is well
known that a hungry rat, when introduced into a novel situation that
contains food, will invariably "explore" the situation before eating. This
suggests that the reinforcing value of exploration exceeds that of food,
at least initially. As an experimental demonstration of this reinforcer,
imagine a T maze in which one arm contains an elaborate checkerboard
maze (Fig. 12–2), and the other arm contains a smaller ordinary end
box. Rats that are neither food nor water deprived will come to run

consistently to the side containing the checkerboard maze if they are permitted a brief time to "explore" the checkerboard maze when they get to it.

Novel stimuli need not be as complicated as a checkerboard maze. Rats and mice will press a lever if each press produces a brief flash of light or even a soft click. Prior deprivation of light or darkness is an important variable in whether a rat prefers to press a lever that turns *on* a light, or to press another lever that turns *off* a light (Lockard, 1963).

Reinforcers capable of strengthening behavior somewhat loosely called "curiosity" were demonstrated by Butler (1953). Young monkeys were placed in a dimly lit opaque box with two covered windows, one blue and the other yellow. Pushing against the yellow window had no effect, but pushing against the blue window opened it for 30 sec, revealing various scenes (Fig. 16–9). Some scenes, such as a large growling dog, were not reinforcing and led to little pushing. Other scenes, such as views of the laboratory and the experimenter, other monkeys, and moving toy objects, had appreciable reinforcing value. The confined monkey quickly discriminated panel color and produced the reinforcing scenes frequently. This behavior appears to bear some relation to deprivation, since the longer the animal was confined to the box without the opportunity to produce a scene, the higher his response rate when

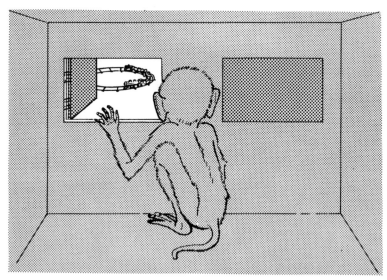

Figure 16–9. Young rhesus monkey in visual exploration apparatus. The reinforcer, a 30-sec view of a toy train, was obtained by the discriminated operant of pushing a blue panel (from Murray, 1964, based on description in Butler, 1953).

given the opportunity. Butler (1957) found the function shown in Fig. 16–10 when panel pressing was reinforced on a *VI* schedule with a 12-sec view of the monkey colony.

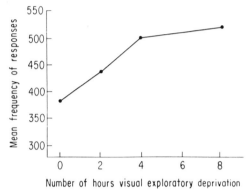

Figure 16–10. Rate of VI *responding reinforced by a brief exposure to a visual scene as a function of hours of visual deprivation (Butler, 1957).*

Young children spend a lot of time in "play" and manipulation of objects. This manipulation seems to have intrinsic reinforcing properties and need not be dependent on association with other primary reinforcers. Harlow (1950) has shown that monkeys will disassemble mechanical puzzles of the sort shown in Fig. 16–11, with no additional reinforcement. It appears that monkeys will solve problems merely for the sake

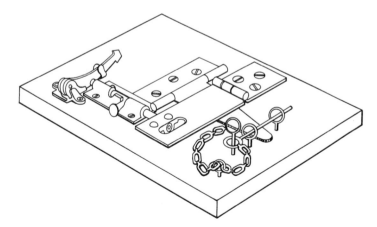

Figure 16–11. Mechanical puzzle that monkeys will solve without any additional reinforcement (Harlow, 1950).

of solving them. This is why such reinforcers are called intrinsic. Over a 10-hr observation period Harlow found that the number of puzzles opened decreased progressively, suggesting a satiation process.

3. *Physical Contact for Young Organisms: "Affection" Reinforcers.* One might suspect that physical contact with the mother might well be a strong reinforcer for a young organism. Such a reinforcer would have the obvious biological utility of keeping the young organism close to its mother where food, shelter, and protection would be found. Research by Harlow has shown that the body-contact reinforcer is a very powerful one, and furthermore does not depend on the additional primary reinforcers of food, shelter, and protection with which it is normally associated. Contact is itself a powerful and specific primary reinforcer. Harlow (1960) reared young monkeys in total isolation from their mothers. From observations of the clasp reflex in baby monkeys (Fig. 16–12),

Figure 16–12. Clasp reflex in newly born rhesus monkey elicited by cylindrical object (Harlow, 1960).

Harlow suspected that a "surrogate" (substitute) mother could be constructed which could provide certain aspects of the physical contact that a real mother supplies. The clasp reflex of clinging and contacting is elicited by a cylindrical object; hence objects of the sort shown in Fig. 16–13 were provided in the baby monkeys' cages from birth onwards. These cylindrical objects (surrogate mothers) were identical in construction, save for their heads (a feature later found to be irrelevant) and their surfaces. Both objects were constructed from a wire frame, but the frame of one was covered with a thick layer of terry cloth, whereas the wire frame of the other was exposed. Harlow referred to the object covered with soft terry cloth as the "cloth mother"; the other object he called the "wire mother." Monkeys reared in cages containing both these surrogate mothers spent much of their young life in contact with the "cloth mother," clinging to "her" much in the fashion of the clasp reflex of Fig. 16–12. On the other hand, they virtually ignored the "wire mothers."

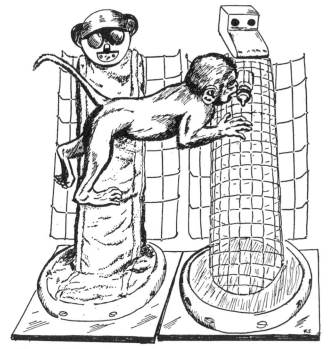

Figure 16–13. Young rhesus monkey nursing from a wire cylindrical object while clinging to a similar object covered with terry-cloth (Harlow, 1960).

To determine whether the constant-contact reinforcer provided by the "cloth mother" depended on a history of association with food reinforcement, some monkeys were nursed by a bottle inserted in the "chest" of the wire monkey and the rest were nursed by bottle from the cloth monkey. But associating the wire mother with food did not modify the infant monkey's preference for clinging to the cloth mother. The number of hours spent on the two mothers for two groups of monkeys is shown in Fig. 16–14. The monkeys fed on the wire monkey spent no more time on her than did the monkeys fed on the cloth mother. In Fig. 16–13 we see how some monkeys solved the problem of feeding from one mother while contacting the other. In other experiments, Harlow showed that the reinforcing value of the cloth mother extended for as long as 2 years. This finding attests to the great durability of this reinforcer. The critical reinforcing properties of the surrogate appear to be (1) its cylindrical shape and (2) its softness. When a flat board covered with terry cloth was used, it failed to generate the effects shown by the cloth cylinder of Fig. 16–13. "Clinging" was not possible with the board.

Harlow has indicated that depriving baby monkeys of their mothers, or of suitable mother surrogates, can interfere markedly with later

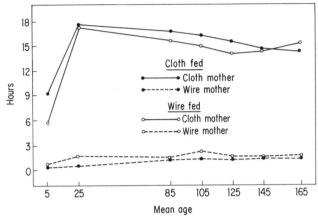

Figure 16–14. Hours per day spent on cloth and wire surrogate mothers at various ages in days (Harlow, 1960).

emotional responsiveness and mating patterns. Evidently, availability of the contact reinforcer at an early age is critical for the normal occurrence of certain behavior patterns in adulthood. Harlow's work provides an impressive start on this very difficult problem of the effects of early experiences on later mature behaviors. Since Freud, psychoanalysts have stressed that certain critical early experiences are of great importance in the emotional adjustment patterns of adult humans; but controlled experimentation exploiting these ideas has been difficult to carry out. Harlow's paradigm may provide a useful framework for testing some of these ideas.

16.5 ACQUIRED DRIVES

In the present treatment of motivation we have completely excluded a discussion of acquired reinforcers. We have justified (p. 365) this exclusion on the grounds that the properties of conditioned reinforcers are well explained by a certain past history with the behavioral contingencies of discrimination. In this chapter and Chapter 15 we have confined our attention to operations, other than those in an organism's past conditioning history, that affect reinforcers. If, however, it were possible to create a reinforcer that (1) gave every evidence of being the terminal reinforcer of a behavioral chain and (2) once created, was sensitive to various establishing and reducing operations much in the way that primary reinforcers are, we should have to concede that such a reinforcer meets the necessary conditions for an acquired drive. Unlike the secondary reinforcers of Chapter 11, *these* acquired reinforcers would not be dependent on subsequent primary reinforcement for their continuing strength. Two behavioral phenomena, drawn from somewhat different contexts, seem to warrant tentative consideration as acquired drives of this sort.

1. *Imprinting.* Certain moving objects, if presented at an early age, may acquire reinforcing properties for species whose young are capable of locomotion soon after birth. The earliest reports described the behavior exhibited by goslings, ducklings, chicks, and other fowl of "following" certain moving objects. Hess (1958) describes the early observations of the Austrian zoologist Konrad Lorenz:

> On an estate near Vienna Lorenz divided a clutch of eggs laid by a graylag goose into two groups. One group was hatched by the goose; the other group was hatched in an incubator. The goslings hatched by the goose immediately followed their mother around the estate. The goslings hatched in the incubator, however, did not see their mother; the first living thing they saw was Lorenz. They then followed Lorenz about the estate (Hess, 1958, p. 81).

This phenomenon, in which an early experience of the goslings influenced their later behavior, Lorenz called *imprinting.* It was soon established that the experience had to occur during a critical period in the organism's early life for it to be effective. Subsequent work devoted to imprinting has shown that the kinds of objects that might call forth such following behavior are as arbitrary as moving cardboard boxes or spheres. This later work has attempted to quantify the conditions under which imprinting will occur. It has indicated also that "following" is simply one manifestation of the fact that a certain object has become a powerful reinforcer. *Any* instrumental behavior that brings the young bird in closer proximity with the object is strengthened.

The apparatus used by Hess (1959) (shown in Fig. 16–15) consists of a circular Plexiglass-enclosed runway around which a decoy duck can be moved by a motor at various speeds. A duckling, hatched a few hours

Figure 16–15. An apparatus used in the study of imprinting. It consists of a circular runway about which a decoy duck can be moved. In the drawing a duckling is shown following the decoy (Hess, 1959).

previously, is placed in the runway and the model begins to move around the runway. In some experiments, a sound emanates from a loudspeaker inside the model. The imprinting operation consists of 1-hr, or less, exposure to the moving object. Later, the goslings are tested by determining preference responses for the imprinting model as opposed to other objects. A striking finding is that the imprinting operation must occur during a very limited age span to be effective in determining preference. Figure 16–16 shows this graphically. For the case of wild mallard ducklings, an age of 13–16 hr after hatching gives maximum imprinting. It appears that beyond 30 hr after hatching imprinting is not possible in this species.

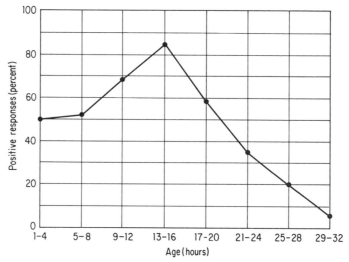

Figure 16–16. Positive test preference responses to the test object (Hess, 1959).

In order to establish that the imprinted object acts like other reinforcers, Hoffman, Searle, Toffey, and Kozma (1966) shaped a key-peck response which produced a brief (5-sec) illumination of the moving imprinted object. In their study, the arbitrariness of the imprinting object was emphasized. The object was a white milk bottle being shunted back and forth on model-train track. Ducklings given a prior imprinting exposure to the milk bottle later acquired key-peck R's when each peck produced the brief appearance of the moving milk bottle as reinforcer. Subsequently, 5–1 ratio behavior was sustained. Subjects given no previous imprinting exposure to the bottle did not peck the key, showing that the imprinting operation was essential for the creation of this kind of reinforcer.

Although the imprinted object appears to acquire reinforcing properties, these may not last indefinitely. Hoffman, Toffey, Searle and Kozma measured the amount of time that imprinted ducklings, living constantly in the apparatus, kept the milk bottle in view by key pecking. The experimenters discovered that as the animals aged they tended less and less to work for the object. Some typical results are shown in Fig. 16–17. By 60 days, the value of the moving object as a reinforcer had almost completely dissipated. Interestingly, the reinforcer could be temporarily reinstated by shocking the ducklings, or presenting other emotion-arousing stimuli.

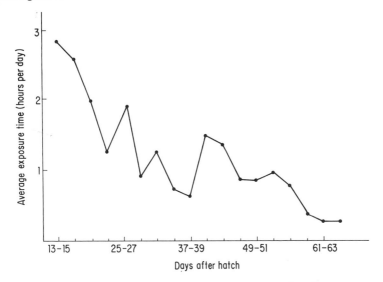

Figure 16–17. Average amount of time per day that a moving object was kept in view as a function of ducklings' age. The imprinting operation with this object had been performed earlier. Each point represents a 3-day average across three subjects (H. S. Hoffman, unpublished data).

The results of the imprinting studies indicate that the imprinting procedure is an operation for creating a class of reinforcers which resemble the imprinted object. Because this new reinforcer is the terminal reinforcer in a chain of behavior, its properties resemble those of primary reinforcers rather than secondary reinforcers. Unlike a conditioned reinforcer, it is not subject to an extinction procedure, nor does it serve as an S^D for a response that produces a subsequent, more primary reinforcer.

2. *Addiction.* It is well known that repeated administration of certain drugs creates a dependence on their continual administration. Further, these drugs (such as opium and its derivatives morphine, heroin, and demorol) come to acquire powerful reinforcing properties. Humans who develop such dependencies, called addictions, will go to great lengths to obtain injections of the drug. Despite its prevalence in modern society,

the conditions controlling addiction (its causes and cures) are not well understood. Recent studies with animal subjects have utilized the techniques of free-operant responding to study the reinforcing power of these drugs after addiction. A principal aim of these studies is to clarify the conditions that are related to addiction.

The operation that creates the addiction reinforcer consists of repeated presentation (usually by injection) of morphine or other compounds in gradually larger doses. As a consequence of this series of administrations, the drug acquires powerful reinforcing properties. Experimental addiction has been produced in rats and monkeys by this method of gradually increasing drug dose. The properties of the acquired drug reinforcer were studied by permitting an addicted rat the means to administer the narcotic to himself (Weeks, 1964). The addicted rat worked in a Skinner box where each lever press initially produced controlled injections of a selected narcotic. The injection system consisted of a tube arrangement and a cannula by which the drug was led in

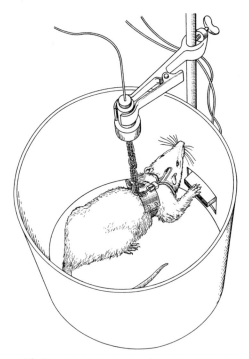

Figure 16–18.   Addicted rat takes drug injection at will by pressing the lever. The drug solution comes down the tube and then through a chronically implanted cannula into the rat's jugular vein. A sprocket chain and clamp prevent the tube from twisting as the animal moves about its cage (after Weeks, 1964).

solution directly into the jugular vein of the rat (Fig. 16–18). The results showed that addicted rats would acquire the lever-press R when this led to various amounts of morphine. Typical *FR* curves associated with ratios ranging from 10 to 400 lever presses for a single injection demonstrated the extremely powerful nature of the morphine reinforcer. Although short-term periodicities in reinforcing value occurred (satiation effects), the long-term duration of the acquired reinforcer was indefinite. A monkey working under conditions similar to those described above for the rat remained addicted for 21 months (Weeks, 1964). The technique shows promise of yielding results that may suggest the procedures to be used in controlling the reinforcing properties of the drugs once addiction has taken place. The control of the addiction reinforcers has obvious implications for the control of human addictions.

References for Chapter 16

Bolles, R. C. Effect of food deprivation upon the rat's behavior in its home cage. *J. comp. physiol. Psychol.,* 1963, **56,** 456–460.

Butler, R. A. Discrimination learning by rhesus monkeys to visual-exploratory motivation. *J. comp. physiol. Psychol.,* 1953, **46,** 95–98.

Butler, R. A. The effect of deprivation of visual incentives on visual exploration motivation in monkeys. *J. comp. physiol. Psychol.,* 1957, **50,** 177–179.

Cannon, W. B., and Washburn, A. L. An explanation of hunger. *Amer. J. Psychol.,* 1912, **29,** 441–452.

Cofer, C. N., and Appley, M. H. *Motivation: theory and research.* New York: Wiley, 1964.

Crocetti, C. P. Drive level and response strength in the bar-pressing apparatus. *Psychol. Rep.,* 1962, **10,** 563–575.

Gilman, A. The relation between blood osmotic pressure, fluid distribution, and voluntary water intake. *Amer. J. Physiol.,* 1937, **120,** 323–328.

Guttman, N. Operant conditioning, extinction, and aperiodic reinforcement in relation to concentration of sucrose used as reinforcing agent. *J. exp. Psychol.,* 1953, **46,** 213–224.

Hall, J. F. *Psychology of motivation.* New York: Lippincott, 1961.

Harlow, H. F. Studying animal behavior. Chap. 12 in T. G. Andrews (Ed.), *Methods of psychology,* New York: Wiley, 1948.

Harlow, H. F. Learning and satiation of response in intrinsically motivated complex puzzle performance by monkeys. *J. comp. physiol. Psychol.,* 1950, **43,** 289–294.

Harlow, H. F. Primary affectional patterns in primates. *Amer. J. Orthopsychiat.,* 1960, **30,** 676–684.

Hess, E. H. Imprinting in animals. *Sci. Amer.,* 1958, **195,** 81–90.

Hess, E. H. Imprinting. *Science,* 1959, **130,** 133–141.

Hoffman, H. S., Searle, J. L., Toffey, Sharon, and Kozma, F. Behavioral control by an imprinted stimulus. *J. exp. Anal. Behav.,* 1966, **9,** 177–189.

Kagan, J., and Berkun, M. The reward value of running activity. *J. comp. physiol. Psychol.,* 1954, **47,** 108.

Lockard, R. B. Some effects of light upon the behavior of rodents. *Psychol. Bull.,* 1963, **60,** 509–529.

Mayer, J. Glucostatic mechanism of regulation of food intake. *New England J. Med.,* 1953, **249,** 13–16.

Murray, E. J. *Motivation and emotion.* Englewood Cliffs: Prentice-Hall, 1964.

Olds, J. Pleasure centers in the brain. *Sci. Amer.,* Oct. 1956, **195,** 105–116.

Olds, J. Hypothalamic substrates of reward. *Physiol. Rev.,* 1962, **42,** 554–604.

Olds, J., and Milner, P. Positive reinforcement produced by electrical stimulation of septal area and other regions of rat brain. *J. comp. physiol. Psychol.,* 1954, **47,** 419–427.

Pliskoff, S. S., Wright, J. E., and Hawkins, T. D. Brain stimulation as a reinforcer: intermittent schedules. *J. exp. Anal. Behav.,* 1965, **8,** 75–88.

Richter, C. P. A behavioristic study of the activity of the rat. *Comp. Psychol. Monogr.,* 1922, **1,** No. 2.

Richter, C. P. Animal behavior and internal drives. *Quart. Rev. Biol.,* 1927, **2,** 307–343.

Rosenzweig, M. The mechanisms of hunger and thirst. Chap. 3 in L. Postman (Ed.), *Psychology in the making.* New York: Knopf, 1962.

Sanford, F. *Psychology, a scientific study of man.* Belmont, Calif.: Wadsworth, 1961.

Templeton, R. D., and Quigley, J. P. The action of insulin on the mobility of the gastro-intestinal tract. *Amer. J. Physiol.,* 1930, **91,** 467–474.

Weeks, J. R. Experimental narcotics addiction. *Sci. Amer.,* Mar. 1964, **210,** 46–52.

Chapter 17 AVERSIVE CONTINGENCIES

⬤UR DISCUSSIONS OF OPERANT BEHAVIOR HAVE SO far dealt exclusively with cases in which, by manipulating the correlation between a specified response class and events such as food and water, certain lawful changes in behavior occur. Acquisition, discrimination, schedules of reinforcement, differentiation, successive approximation, and chaining are labels for specific procedures that dictate the precise form of the response-reinforcement correlation. The term "drive" subsumes variations in operant behavior that are under the control of operations which change the reinforcing value of these reinforcers. In all of the diverse procedures treated, behavior has been maintained by reinforcers that are defined as stimuli having the ability to increase the probability of responses they follow. We turn in this chapter to a new class of reinforcing stimuli that do not meet this definition of positive reinforcers, yet do modify and maintain behavior in characteristic ways.

17.1 NEGATIVE REINFORCERS

Little more than casual observation is needed to detect that, under appropriate circumstances, the *removal* of certain environmental events exerts powerful behavioral effects. We see that birds find shelter during rainstorms, dogs move to shady spots when the summer sun beats down upon them, and people close windows when the roar of traffic is loud. In these instances, behavior is emitted that removes or terminates some environmental event such as rain, heat and light, and noise. Such observations suggest the existence of a distinctive class of reinforcing events. Because the operation that defines these events as reinforcing (their removal) is opposite in character to that of positive reinforcers (defined by their presentation), they are known as *negative reinforcers* (S⁻). In general, negative reinforcers constitute those events whose *termination* (or reduction in intensity) will strengthen and maintain operants.

Negative reinforcers include the events that, in common parlance, we call "annoying," "uncomfortable," "painful," "unpleasant," "noxious," and so forth. Most of these terms connote a non-behavioral domain of reference which we are unlikely to find useful in a functional analysis. As a synonym for negative reinforcement, the term "aversive" is more neutral than any of these adjectives, and is valuable in suggesting the appropriate notion of "averting," "moving away from," or "escaping from" a situation. In the laboratory, aversive stimuli typically take the form of electric shocks, prolonged immersion in water, and certain intensities of light, sound, and temperature.

17.2 ESCAPE CONDITIONING

We may verify the aversive quality of any stimulus by making its removal contingent upon a hitherto unconditioned operant. If the

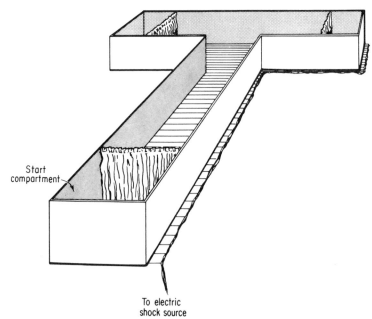

Start
compartment

To electric
shock source

Figure 17–1. **T**-*maze for the study of escape behavior (after Muenzinger and Fletcher, 1936).*

strength of that operant subsequently increases, the stimulus is said to be aversive.

An experiment by Muenzinger and Fletcher (1936) is representative of this *escape* procedure. A rat was placed in a T-shaped maze which contained an electrically charged grill floor. The floor was wired so that as long as the animal remained on the grill a continuous shock was administered to its paws (Fig. 17–1). A cover over the maze (not shown) prevented the rat from escaping the shock by jumping out of the apparatus. One escape route remained—the animal could find safety by running consistently to a designated arm of the T.

Behavior in the T maze is usually measured on each trial by timing the rat from start to safe, or by tallying the "incorrect" turns ("errors") into the non-safe arm of the T. On early trials, the rat is equally likely to run right or left, but as acquisition of the response of turning to the safe side proceeds, responses to the "incorrect" side decrease. We see the average trend for 25 rats in Fig. 17–2. We may infer from the declining error curve in Fig. 17–2 that, after 100 trials of escape training, acquisition of the turning response leading to safety has occurred.

The behavioral process represented in Fig. 17–2 requires that we expand our concept of operant strengthening. Responses may be strengthened either by producing positive reinforcers (S^+), or by terminating negative reinforcers (S^-). The latter variant is

$$\boxed{\begin{array}{l} S^- \\ R \end{array}} \longrightarrow S_o$$

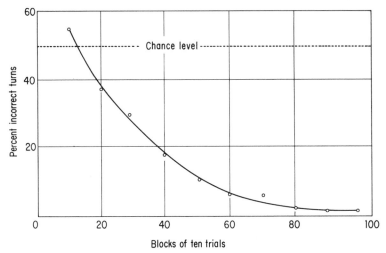

Figure 17–2. Percent incorrect turns in 100 trials of escape training (after Muenzinger and Fletcher, 1936).

A response (R) takes the organism out of an aversive situation, S⁻, into a different, less aversive one, S_o.

17.3 PARAMETERS OF S⁻

Figure 17–3 schematizes the events, variables, and relationships inherent in negative-reinforcement escape contingencies. The independent variables of principal interest in Fig. 17–3 are (1) the intensity of the

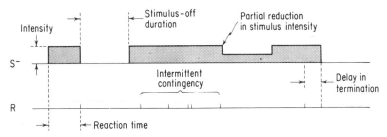

Figure 17–3. Variables in escape contingencies.

prevailing aversive stimulus, (2) the duration of the stimulus-off time, (3) the amount by which the intensity is reduced after responding, (4) the nature of the intermittency, if any, existing between R and the termination or reduction in S⁻, and (5) the delay, if any, that intervenes between an R and subsequent stimulus termination or reduction.

If a source of aversive stimulation is added to the Skinner-box apparatus, lever pressing becomes a convenient response for the study of negative reinforcement. The Skinner box has the merit of freeing the animal to respond at any time; hence rate of response becomes available as a sensitive, wide-ranging dependent measure of the behavioral effects in individual subjects. For special purposes, reaction time, *RT,* (see Fig. 17–3) may supplement such rate measures.

A procedure used by Dinsmoor and Winograd (1958) will serve as a prototype demonstration, as well as an illustration of the action of some of the parameters of S⁻. Rats learned to press a bar when this was the only behavior that turned off electric shocks delivered through the grid floor of their experimental compartment. Shock was terminated for 2 min following a lever press (stimulus-off duration), after which the aversive stimulation was reinstated. Presses in the absence of shock had no special consequences. The procedure is simply

When the RT between S^- and R had declined to a low asymptotic value, a VI 30-sec contingency was added to the procedure:

$$\hookrightarrow \boxed{\begin{array}{c}\widetilde{T}_{30\ sec} \\ S^-\end{array}} \longrightarrow \boxed{\begin{array}{c}(S^-) \\ R\end{array}} \longrightarrow \boxed{\begin{array}{c}T_{2\ min} \\ S_o\end{array}} \longrightarrow$$

Responses were effective in escaping shock only after shock had been on for an average duration of 30 sec. The procedure generated a moderate and sustained rate of bar pressing in the presence of shock. The pattern of the behavior resembled VI food-reinforced responding.

Dinsmoor and Winograd explored the effects of varying intensities of S^- on this baseline of VI escape responding. Their technique was to begin a session with a given intensity of S^- present, say 100 μamps, observe the frequency of responding for a long enough period to obtain a reliable rate measure, then change to a different value of S^-, say 400 μamps, and repeat the process. In a 2-hr session they were thus able to obtain escape-rate measurements from as many as six different values of S^- intensity.

One rat's behavior during a portion of such a session appears in Fig. 17–4. The cumulative record shows that each shock intensity value controls a unique rate of escape responding. The behavioral effect of changing from one intensity value to another (at the hatch marks) is almost instantaneous: regardless of its prior rate, the animal abruptly shifts to a new rate appropriate to the new shock intensity.

When the overall function of response rate against shock intensity is

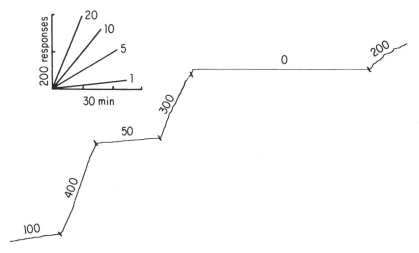

Figure 17–4.   Cumulative VI *escape responding at different shock intensities (Dinsmoor and Winograd, 1958).*

plotted, Fig. 17–5A results. This function was obtained from the same rat whose cumulative curves appear in Fig. 17–4. Figure 17–5A indicates that, over the range studied, as shock intensity increased, escape response rate continuously increased as well.

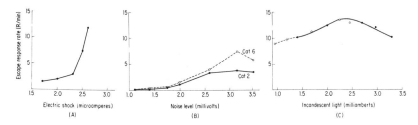

Figure 17–5. Escape response rate as a function of the intensity of the aversive stimulus. The abscissa is in logarithmic units. [(A) Dinsmoor and Winograd, 1958; (B) Barry and Harrison, 1957; (C) Kaplan, 1952].

Figures 17–5B and 17–5C document the results of similar experiments with other aversive agents. Figure 17–5B illustrates the effects of increasing the intensity of a sound on *VI* lever-pressing escape rate of cats. The results of Fig. 17–5C were obtained from a group of rats whose pushing of a panel on *FI* contingencies terminated lights of various intensities. Both the (B) and (C) panels of Fig. 17–5 demonstrate that maxima in escape behavior occur if the aversive-stimulus intensity is made very great. The decline in responding associated with very intense aversive events is not well understood; it is thought to be due to a general suppressive (emotional) effect of strong aversive stimuli.

It will prove instructive to draw an occasional parallel between negative and positive reinforcement. To what variable in the field of positive reinforcement, we may ask, does aversive-stimulus intensity correspond? Superficially, the intensity of a negative reinforcer seems analogous to the magnitude of a positive reinforcer. Intensity of S^- and magnitude of S^+ are both stimulus properties of the reinforcer, and increases in both variables generate increases in responding (see section 16.2). But closer analysis of the functional role these two variables play in negative and positive reinforcement, respectively, suggests that the analogy is only superficial. The principal effect of raising the intensity of a light, or a sound, or a shock from a low to a high value is that the reinforcement of behavior is made possible through termination of the new intensity. Increasing the intensity of an S^- has, therefore, the logic of a reinforcement-establishing operation; it makes possible the strengthening of behavior. Thus, in the presence of a weak intensity of light, a rat will not show conditioning of a response that terminates the light; so too, with a small value of food deprivation, a response that produces food will not be strengthened. Conversely, high values of both shock intensity and food deprivation make it possible to use shock termination and food presentation as reinforcers for conditioning operants. If the functions of Figs. 17–5 and those in section 15.8 are examined, a close parallel will be found in the way that hours of deprivation and S^- intensity control behavior. Such considerations imply an interesting conceptual status for aversive stimuli. Their presentation is simultaneously drive arousing *and* negatively reinforcing.

There is, of course, a variable in the negative-reinforcement field that corresponds to S^+ magnitude. Consider the duration of time that elapses between the termination of an aversive stimulus and its subsequent reinstatement, labeled the stimulus-off duration in Fig. 17–3. Here is an independent variable that corresponds closely to magnitude, or duration, of S^+. The longer the duration of the aversive stimulus-off time, the greater the strength of escape responding. Using a *crf* escape contingency, and measuring bar-press *RT* to S^-, Dinsmoor and Hughes (1956) found the gradient of escape reinforcement reproduced in Fig. 17–6. When lever presses produced long shock-off times, the rat responded promptly to the onset of shock. But when short shock-off times were a consequence of pressing, *RT*'s to shock-onset were long, indicating that such short values of shock-off time provide little or no reinforcement.

An operant need not completely terminate an aversive stimulus to exhibit strengthening. Merely reducing the level of stimulus intensity is

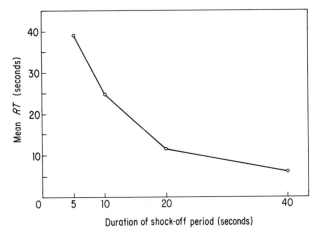

Figure 17–6. Escape reaction time (RT) *as a function of several values of shock-off duration* (*after Dinsmoor and Hughes, 1956*).

often sufficient to condition and maintain operant behavior. Small reductions in intensity, when contingent upon lever pressing, form the basis of a procedure for measuring the level of aversive stimulation an organism will tolerate (Weiss and Laties, 1959, 1963). In this procedure, each lever press produces a small decrement in the intensity of a prevailing aversive stimulus. A fixed period of time without a single lever press produces a small increment in the intensity of the stimulus. The relations between R and S⁻ are illustrated schematically in Fig. 17–7. The first R

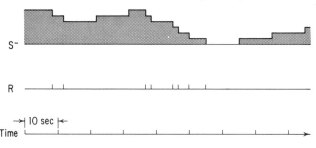

Figure 17–7

emitted in Fig. 17–7 reduces the intensity of S⁻ by one step. A second R follows closely on the heels of the first R, and the intensity falls another step. The criterion time then elapses without a response occurring, as a result of which S⁻ is incremented one step. A further such period elapses without an R, and yet another increment in S⁻ occurs. The next 6 R's occur frequently enough to drive the aversive intensity down to zero. Subsequently the intensity rises three steps anew in the absence of further emitted responses.

This procedure acts to bring about a state of equilibrium. The organism maintains a rate of responding that holds the S⁻ intensity within a small range of (usually low) intensities. When S⁻ is electric shock, this equilibrium is spoken of as the *shock-tolerance level*. The actual level maintained varies with a number of procedural parameters, and is sensitive to the administration of certain pharmacological agents such as analgesics and anaesthetics. Figure 17–8 illustrates the typical behavioral stability that this procedure generates. In addition, the figure shows the behavioral result of intravenous administration of a small quantity of morphine to a rhesus monkey working on such a procedure. (Figure 17–8 amounts to a much reduced and extended record of the S⁻ contour of Fig. 17–7.) Injection of morphine is rapidly followed by a rise in shock tolerance to a new intensity level which is held throughout the remaining 40 min shown. The effect confirms the well-known clinical properties of morphine, and suggests that the procedure provides a useful experimental tool for measuring the analgesic properties of various drugs.

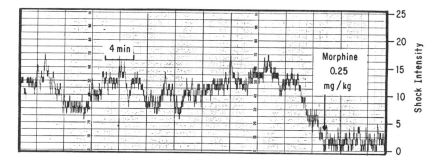

Figure 17–8. Effect of intravenously administered morphine sulfate, 0.25 mg/kg, on shock-tolerance level. Record reads from right to left (Weitzman, Ross, Hodos, and Galambos, 1961).

17.4 CONDITIONED AVERSIVE STIMULI

When we dodge an oncoming car, duck from an intended blow, and leave the golf course at the appearance of thunder clouds, our behavior takes the form of escaping stimuli that are not in themselves aversive. Oncoming vehicles, a cocked arm, and a dark cloud are events whose significance must be acquired in some way. There appears to be a class of acquired aversive stimuli, which might appropriately be called *secondary* negative reinforcers. In examining the manner in which stimuli take on secondary negative reinforcing properties, we shall be obliged to call upon the concepts of classical conditioning. It develops that an originally neutral environmental event acquires aversive properties if it is paired in Pavlovian fashion with such events as shocks, intense sounds, and light. The latter aversive agents exhibit a dual behavioral function. They hold status both as primary negative reinforcers (S^-), as well as unconditioned elicitors (S_2) for increased heart rate, rapid breathing, and other respondents. When an S_1 is paired with one of these S_2^- events, the S_1 comes (1) to evoke a *CR* similar to R_2 by the laws of respondent conditioning; and (2) to acquire aversive power.

The manner in which negative-reinforcing properties are conferred upon previously neutral situations may be experimentally demonstrated in the rat with the apparatus shown in Fig. 17–9. Two compartments are separated by a door which may be raised, leaving a low hurdle between the two compartments. Each compartment is fitted with a grid floor through which shock may be delivered. Lamps and loudspeakers deliver signals when desired. Since special consequences may be made contingent on jumping over the hurdle from one compartment to the other, that is,

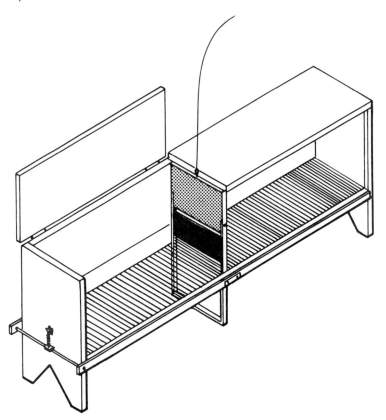

Figure 17–9. A shuttle box for the study of aversive stimulus control (after Miller, 1951).

shuttling back and forth between the compartments, the apparatus is commonly known as a shuttle box.

Brown and Jacobs (1949) confined rats to one compartment of a shuttle box and paired a pulsating tone+light (S_1) with an inescapable 6-sec shock (S_2^-). Twenty-two pairings of S_1, S_2^- were administered over a 2-day period. Shock was then permanently disconnected and S_1 was tested for aversive properties. The door between the compartments was raised, S_1 presented, and a contingency set such that any jumps into the other compartment terminated the tone-light S_1. The effect of the test trials was to condition hurdle jumping. Since shock was never present in testing, this conditioning must have been the consequence of escape from the tone-light S_1. And since rats do not normally trouble to escape from the kinds of tones and lights used in this experiment, the operation of pairing the tones and lights with shock must have been critical.

In testing for conditioned positive reinforcement (section 11.1), we may recall, a new operant was allowed to produce an S^D, but the primary reinforcement was withheld. The new operant was initially strengthened by virtue of the contingent S^D, but as time went on the S^D gradually lost its power as a conditioned reinforcer since it no longer set the occasion for obtaining a primary reinforcement. This loss showed up as an eventual decline in strength of the new operant. A similar rise and fall in the probability of a new operant takes place in testing the power of a conditioned aversive stimulus. In the shuttle-box test, each time the tone+light is presented without shock, a Pavlovian extinction trial occurs; that is, the tone+light loses some of the eliciting properties conferred by previous pairings with shock. Along with extinction of the eliciting power of S_1 comes a gradual reduction in the power of S_1 to negatively reinforce a response. The result, of course, is that eventually the rats cease to jump over the hurdle when S_1 is presented. In Brown and Jacobs' experiment, the *RT* of hurdle jumping to S_1 onset shortened over the first 20 testing trials; then, over a subsequent 20 trials, the *RT* began to lengthen, indicating that the tone-light's power to control behavior was fading. We shall need to bear these delicate relationships in mind in dealing with the phenomena of subsequent sections.

17.5 AVOIDANCE CONDITIONING

The phenomenon of avoidance behavior raises a general problem concerning the place of purpose in scientific methodology. We say that we turn the wheel of a skidding car opposite to the direction of the skid *to* avoid a crash, that one builds a bridge in a certain way *to* avoid its collapsing, that a deer flees *in order to* avoid a pursuing wolf. The term "to," or "in order to," imputes a certain purposive quality to the behavior. The purpose of a given act, and hence its apparent explanation, is given in a statement of the aversive or undesirable consequences that might have occurred, had the act not averted them. Purposive or teleological explanations are generally rejected by scientists on the grounds that such explanations purport to let a future (and therefore nonexistent) event be the cause of a present (existing) event; and because purposive explanations add nothing to the bare facts. To say, for instance, that a stone falls to the ground *in order to* return to its natural resting place, the earth, tells no more than the purely descriptive statement: stones fall to the earth. And yet, by seeming to be a sufficient explanation, the teleological statement tends to discourage further examination of the phenomena, thus postponing a functional analysis.

Explanation in science is a complex and many-sided matter, but some commentators feel that it can be reduced to (1) extensive descriptions of the events in question, including their relationships to other events; and (2) familiarity with these descriptions and relationships.

Scientific explanation, according to this view, is largely a matter of providing interlacing relationships between the phenomena of sense experience. Eventually these relationships become so familiar that they seem a matter of course, or self-evident. Thus one generation's "radical reformulations" are the next generation's "common sense." Compare this kind of explanation with the purposive account. Peculiar as it may seem to us, 300 years after Galileo, to think of rocks possessing a will to return to the earth, we are often still content to regard behavior as being directed by purpose or will. Nevertheless, just as purpose is irrelevant in "explaining" falling stones, so is it irrelevant in the analysis of behavior. To say that organisms make responses to (in order to) produce reinforcers conveys no more information than to say that they *do* make responses when these responses have been frequently followed by reinforcers.

Teleological explanations are frequently proposed for avoidance behavior. When we say that we take shelter when we see a thundercloud *to* prevent getting wet, we are implicitly invoking a purposive explanation for our behavior. Nevertheless, our statement (or belief) does not constitute an explanation in the technical sense described (namely, a statement of some functional relationship between the behavior being described and some other variable), but is merely a restatement of the facts—when the sky darkens and thunder sounds, we move in a certain way. The avoidance of an environmental event that has not yet happened (the rain shower) can hardly govern present behavior. To assume that it could is to create the logical problem of how to account for an event in terms of another event that has not yet happened. Instead, we seek an explanation (description) of the behavior in terms of variables that (1) act at the time of the behavior, and (2) have acted in the past under similar conditions. In doing this, we shall build our account on concepts introduced in the previous three sections.

We begin our analysis of avoidance behavior with an experimental demonstration of the phenomenon. Perhaps through careful scrutiny of the behavioral events that occur in the avoidance situation, we shall find some invariant relationships on which to base a more acceptable explanation of the phenomenon.

Brogden, Lipman, and Culler (1938) placed guinea pigs in individual activity wheels. A 1000-cps tone was presented to the animal, and 2 sec later a shock was administered through the floor of the cage. If the animal ran in the wheel, causing it to turn an inch or more when the sound began, it could avoid the shock. Turning the wheel by running also terminated the tone. Note the basic structure for avoidance paradigms. First, there occurs some "warning" environmental event (the tone); then, after a lapse of time, there follows a second and aversive environmental event. Meantime, there is a contingency established—

either by an experimenter or by nature—such that if a specified response occurs between the onset of the first stimulus and the onset of the aversive stimulus, the aversive stimulus is omitted and the first stimulus terminated.

In Brogden, Lipman, and Culler's experiment, the guinea pigs learned to turn the wheel and thereby avoid shock on nearly every trial. Figure 17–10 relates the observed increasing percentages of wheel-turning responses to the average day that each particular percentage was attained.

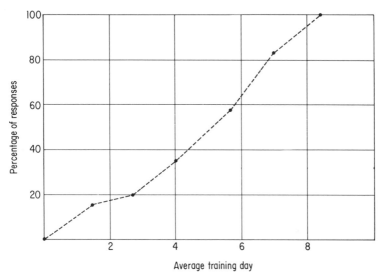

Figure 17–10. Acquisition of avoidance behavior. Data from four guinea pigs (after Brogden, Lipman, and Culler, 1938).

The facts of avoidance are clear, but their representation is another matter. It is evident that the observed strengthening of behavior is not operant conditioning by positive reinforcement, since no positive reinforcer was made contingent on the response. It seems unlikely that wheel turning was classically conditioned since the response has an emitted character. But it will prove instructive to entertain the possibility. The paradigm

$$S_1 \nearrow R_1$$
$$\searrow CR \qquad\qquad [17.1]$$
$$S_2^- \longrightarrow R_2$$

where S_1 = 1000-cps tone
   S_2 = electric shock
   R_1 = not measured
   R_2 = running, jumping, squealing, etc.
   CR = similar to R_2

apparently fits. Note, however, that Diagram [17.1] fails to describe the effect that running in the wheel (CR) has on shock (S_2^-). In true Pavlovian conditioning, the CR does not prevent the occurrence of S_2. When a dog comes to salivate to a tone, salivation does not prevent the occurrence of food.

That the conditioned response in avoidance prevented the occurrence of S_2 may or may not have been significant. Brogden, Lipman, and Culler reasoned that if the running they observed was actually a true CR, then omitting shock ought to have made no difference to the running behavior. The Pavlovian procedure is merely a prescription to pair two elicitors. A second experiment was therefore performed in which the 1000-cps tone came on, and 2 sec later the shock was given as in the first experiment. In the second experiment, however, running responses occurring before shock *had no effect on the subsequent delivery of shock*. The experiment thus provides a strict pairing of an S_1 and S_2^-. If the response of running is conditioned by Pavlovian principles, we should expect the new reflex, $S_1 — CR$, (*Tone — Running*) to increase in strength.

The results of the experiment, shown in Fig. 17–11, are strikingly different from those of the first experiment shown in Fig. 17–10. Over the course of the second experiment, the strength of the running response fluctuated, rising slowly to a maximum (about 50 per cent of the daily trials by day 13), then declining to a low level, near zero, by the twentieth day (500th trial) when the experiment ended. Contrast this result with

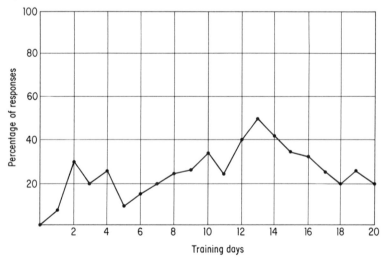

Figure 17–11. *Percent running responses when running does not avoid* S_2^- (*after Brogden, Lipman, and Culler, 1938*).

the 100 per cent performance of the animals in the first experiment (Fig. 17–10) after only just over 8 days (120 trials). The failure to condition running by means of a Pavlovian procedure eliminates the possibility that avoidance conditioning is a type of respondent conditioning.

Avoidance conditioning is neither positively reinforced operant strengthening nor an instance of Pavlovian conditioning; might it be a kind of escape training? If we examine closely the two experiments of Brogden, Lipman, and Culler, we discover that both provide the necessary conditions for establishing a secondary negative reinforcer. In the first experiment, the avoidance experiment, running before the presentation of shock terminated the tone. In section 17.4 we showed that this contingency

$$\boxed{\begin{array}{l} S_1{}^- \\ R \longrightarrow S_o \end{array}}$$

where $S_1{}^- =$ a conditioned aversive stimulus
$\quad\quad R =$ an operant
$\quad\quad S_o =$ a situation in which S_1 is not present

served to strengthen the operant, R.

These conditions, it is now claimed, are exactly those that are to be found during avoidance conditioning. In Brogden, Lipman, and Culler's first experiment, shock was avoidable; but (critical to this analysis) the 1000-cps warning tone was also terminated by the operant response. Through being paired with shock on the trials prior to the development of avoidance behavior, the tone had acquired conditioned aversive character. Thus, it was the termination of the conditioned aversive stimulus, the tone, and not the non-occurrence of shock that reinforced the running response. *Avoidance of S_2 was a by-product of the escape from the secondary negative reinforcer.*

We may now set down the procedure for avoidance conditioning. It reduces to an escape contingency in which an operant is reinforced by the termination of a secondary negative reinforcer:

$$\boxed{\begin{array}{l} S_1 \\ T \longrightarrow S_2{}^- \\ R \longrightarrow S_o \end{array}}$$

We can now see that remaining outside in the presence of clouds and thunder provides stimuli that have in the past been correlated with drenching rain. Taking shelter permits us to escape these warning stimuli, the avoidance of the rain being a by-product. Similarly, the deer that fails to run from the wolf (S_1) is bitten ($S_2{}^-$); if the deer is still alive the next time a wolf appears, any response the deer makes which removes the wolf from its immediate environment is reinforced through the termination of a secondary negative reinforcer.

A significant implication of avoidance behavior must be examined. When the response that removes S_1 occurs, S_2^- is thereby omitted. By breaking the S_1, S_2^- correlation in this way, we expect that S_1 will gradually lose its conditioned aversive properties, as a result of which the avoidance response will eventually fail to be emitted, thus permitting S_2^- to reappear. Through being paired again, S_2^- now renews S_1's aversive character. Experimental data support the theoretical prediction that avoidance behavior is, in fact, cyclical (Wertheim, 1965). The occasional restoration of aversive properties to S_1 means that the S_1, S_2^- pairing is actually intermittent. This intermittency probably preserves the aversive strength of S_1 far better than if S_1 were correlated each time with S_2^-, for the same reasons that a stimulus intermittently paired with food is a more durable secondary positive reinforcer. As avoidance training progresses, the pairings of S_1 and S_2^- become less and less frequent, while the aversive durability of S_1 continues to increase. Eventually a point might be reached where an individual's remaining lifetime is not long enough for the S_1, S_2^- correlation ever to occur again.

This discussion of avoidance has been restricted to the cases where the terminated S_1 has been an external warning stimulus. More subtle cases of avoidance conditioning occur when the organism's own behavior comes to take on aversive character, as in the set of contingencies known as the Sidman procedure (Sidman, 1953). We can only provide a sketch here of what is perhaps the simplest variant of this procedure. If a brief aversive stimulus is delivered to an organism after T units of time without the appearance of a given response, we have the following contingency in effect.

$$\rightarrow \begin{array}{c} \boxed{\begin{array}{c} T_x \longrightarrow \\ R \end{array}} \quad \boxed{\begin{array}{c} S^- \\ T_{1/2 \text{ sec}} \end{array}} \end{array} \qquad [17.2]$$

In [17.2] S^- could be electric shock, R could be lever pressing, T_x could be any fixed value from a few seconds up to several minutes. Electric shocks are delivered *unless* a response is emitted. The procedure defines an avoidance contingency that lacks an explicit warning stimulus (S_1) prior to the occurrence of S_2^-. Animals adapt to this procedure by responding at a sustained moderate rate, taking only a few of the possible shocks that could be delivered (Verhave, 1959). Figure 17–12 shows cumulative records of the behavior generated by this procedure. Evidently, the lack of an explicit warning S_1 does not prevent the acquisition and maintenance of efficient avoidance responding.

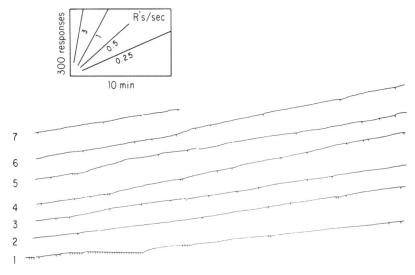

Figure 17–12. Cumulative records of lever press avoidance during the first session of training. The vertical marks indicate shocks. The value of T_x *was 30 sec (Verhave, 1959).*

Our earlier account of avoidance behavior turned so critically on the idea of an S_1 being paired with an S_2^- that we may at first wonder how Sidman avoidance fits into this picture. Even in the Sidman procedure, however, there exists the possibility of a pairing of certain events with S_2^-. Consider the behavior of the rat early in training, prior to the development of efficient avoidance behavior. Shocks are being delivered frequently; occasionally, an operant-level lever press is emitted, thus postponing the shock. Let us turn our attention to what the rat is doing at the moment it is shocked. It may be poking its nose in the corners of the cage, investigating the walls of the box, resting motionless, and so forth. Although we cannot say with any certainty exactly what the animal will have just done when it receives a shock, we can say with great certainty what it will *not* have just done. It will not have just pressed the lever. If it had, it would not be getting the shock. Clearly, *all* behavior except lever pressing can be paired with shocks much in the way that every occurrence of the warning S_1 in conventional avoidance situations is first paired with shock. The effect of this pairing of behaviors with shock in the Sidman avoidance situation is to make a large portion of the animal's own behavior take on conditioned aversive properties. After a time, much of the rat's own behavior, except for its lever pressing, acquires the status of a self-administered warning S_1. If the rat is to "escape" its own aversive behavior, there remains nothing it can do but press the lever. In pressing the lever it obtains the usual by-product of escape from conditioned aversive events—namely, avoidance of an unconditioned negative reinforcer.

17.6 PUNISHMENT

When a negative reinforcer is made contingent on an operant we speak of the *punishment* of that operant. A child reaching towards a flame is burned, a man crossing a street against traffic is hit; both organisms are punished for acting in a given manner in a given situation. In the laboratory, the punishment contingency may be established by providing a controlled aversive stimulus following the occurrence of a response. For example, lever presses or key pecks previously raised above operant level by positive reinforcement may be punished by now following their occurrence with electric shocks to the skin. Society has used and still uses the punishment procedure in a variety of ways to discourage certain behaviors of its members. The birch rod has not entirely disappeared from our schools; we spank our offspring when they "mis"behave; and punishment is still the principal instrument of justice. The punishment procedure appears to be frequently used, not because it works so well, but rather because (1) it has an immediate effect, and (2) its delivery and/or side effects are often positively reinforcing to the person administering the punishment. Clinical psychologists and psychiatrists speak of individuals who find positive reinforcement in punishing others as sadistic. We postpone discussion of the conditions that may give rise to sadistic behavior until the next chapter.

The immediate effects of punishment are easily observed. A child giggling in church can be silenced immediately by being pinched; a dog that jumps on visitors can ordinarily be restrained by a swat with a rolled-up newspaper. Both the child and the dog are not likely to be permanently cured of their undesirable behaviors through punishment. For the moment, however, the undesirable behavior is temporarily suppressed, and this suppression serves to give immediate positive reinforcement to the behavior of the punisher, thus making it more likely that he will punish in the future.

The temporary suppression of behavior produced by punishment can be readily demonstrated in the laboratory, where its quantitative characteristics may be ascertained. In an early experiment by Skinner (1938), hungry rats were trained to press a lever leading to food on a fixed-interval schedule of reinforcement. Lever pressing was then extinguished through the withholding of food. Some of the rats were punished during the first 10 min of extinction. The punishment was in the form of a sharp slap delivered by the bar itself to the forepaws after each press. The slap was a rapid and forceful reverse movement of the bar transmitted to it by a hammer that struck it sharply after each press. The effects of this 10-min slapping can be seen from comparison of the extinction processes of two groups of rats in Fig. 17–13. It is clear from

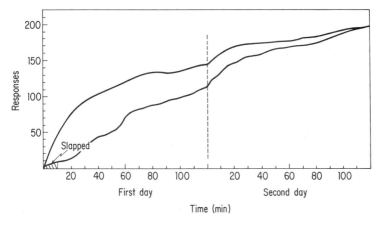

Figure 17–13. The effects of mild punishment (slapping) on the operant extinction process (Skinner, 1938).

Fig. 17–13 that the slapping immediately depressed responding well below its normal extinction rate. Following the slapping, the rate of the response remained, for the first day, well below that of non-punished rats. This response suppression is a typical result of punishment, and is a partial specification of the emotional effects of punishment. So far, the result confirms our intuitions about punishment—it suppresses behavior and it takes effect immediately. On the second day of extinction, however, the punished group responded *more* rapidly than the non-punished group, so that by the end of two days, the total output of extinction lever-press responses for the two groups was the same.

We have to conclude that mild punishment, such as slapping the paws for a few minutes, does not permanently suppress the operant-extinction process; it merely postpones it. Were it our desire to eliminate lever pressing entirely, we could not use this procedure since its effect is transient.

We must be careful not to over-generalize from this single demonstration. Punishment has no one simple effect on behavior. Its effects depend on many parameters of the aversive stimulus itself—its strength and duration, for example. Had a powerful electric shock been used instead of a mild slap, and/or had the punishment contingency prevailed for several hours instead of a few minutes, behavior would have been suppressed far longer than it was. Moreover, the total number of responses in the extinction process would have been significantly attenuated, although the time to reach operant level might not have been affected. Unless the punishment has been extremely intense, however, once it is terminated behavior eventually re-emerges. Only with extremely strong aversive stimulation can punishment permanently reduce behavior to zero level (Holz and Azrin, 1963). The different effects that punishment can have on responding, depending on the strength of the aversive stimulus, signal caution in making any sweeping generalizations about *the* effects of punishment.

In the procedure used by Skinner, only a single response, lever pressing, could lead to positive reinforcement. When several responses can produce positive reinforcement in the same situation, punishment of one response may facilitate a shift in behavior and, if arranged judiciously, thereby aid acquisition of new behavior patterns. In an experiment by Whiting and Mowrer (1943), hungry rats learned to run the maze shown in Fig. 17–14. Rats released in the start box quickly acquired the chain of running to the goal box via the short path to food. The behavior conforms to the Law of Least Effort: given two or more alternate chains to the same reinforcer, the organism chooses the one requiring the least work. Following acquisition, three procedures were compared for their ability to force the rats to use the long path. For one group of rats, *A*, a glass barrier was placed midway up the short path so that these animals could only reach the goal box by way of the long path. For a second group, *B*, reinforcement was withheld for short-path runs and given only if the rats used the long path. For a

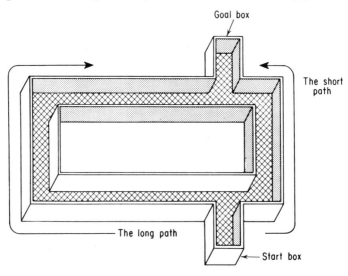

Figure 17–14. Representation of the maze used by Whiting and Mowrer (1943).

third group, C, an electrically charged plate midway up the short path delivered a shock to the rats attempting to use it; nevertheless, if the rats did run through the shock, they found food. Whiting and Mowrer found marked differences in the rates of adjustment to these procedures. The punished rats of Group C came to use the long path after an average of only 6 encountered shocks. The barrier group went 82 times to the barrier before they consistently shifted to the long path. Group B, under simple extinction, ran 230 times to the empty goal box via the short path before coming to prefer the long path. Evidently, punishing one response can greatly aid the acquisition of another *available* response.

This result has been corroborated by other experiments. If incorrect turns are punished and correct turns are positively reinforced in a T maze, acquisition is more rapid than if only positive reinforcement for correct turns is used (Warden and Aylesworth, 1927). One caution must be noted in interpreting such results. Although acquisition of behavior may be speeded up by punishing undesirable response forms, there exists little evidence to indicate what happens to the newly acquired behavior when punishment of the undesired behavior is terminated. In the Warden and Aylesworth study, for example, we may well wonder whether there would have been a temporary increase in "errors" if shock for incorrect responses had been terminated after acquisition.

These studies do suggest a practical conclusion. If punishment is employed in an attempt to eliminate certain behavior, then whatever reinforcement the undesirable behavior had led to must be made available via a more desirable behavior. Merely punishing school children for "misbehavior" in class may have little permanent effect, save to engender a long-lasting hatred for learning. The reinforcers for "misbehavior" must be analyzed and the attainment of these reinforcers perhaps permitted by means of different responses, or in other situations. If schoolchildren are denied sufficient opportunity for physical activity, for instance, they are likely to be over-active in the classroom, with disruptive effects on teaching. Frequent recesses, contingent on productive work, in conjunction with consistent punishment of undesired activity would appear to be a practical application of Whiting and Mowrer's results. Eventually, the need for administering aversive stimulation would disappear as the punished behavior disappeared and was replaced by more desirable forms of behavior. But for this to happen, it appears important to provide a rewarded alternative to the punished response.

One class of behavior for which punishment may have very complicated effects is behavior that has itself been acquired and maintained by aversive contingencies. What, for instance, is the effect of punishing established avoidance behavior of the sort described in Fig. 17–12? The evidence we have at present indicates that if the behavior is punished with the same stimulus that the animal was previously trained to avoid, this punishment does not aid in reducing the strength of the behavior; rather, it may raise its strength! If the punishment is a different aversive stimulus, however, it will have its usual suppressing effect (Church, 1963; Solomon, 1964).

A critical point to be gleaned from the present discussion of punishment is the complexity of its results. The effects of punishment depend on too many factors for us to write a simple paradigm of Procedure, Process, and Results. The Processes and Results of the punishment Procedures are variable and conditional upon the type of behavior being punished as well as upon the states of many variables operating both in the past and present environment of the punished individual. Until the general laws of punishment are worked out, the emotional by-products accompanying aversive stimulation would suggest that its use in the practical control of human behavior be undertaken with extreme caution.

Much of what we call punishment in human affairs takes a form somewhat different from the presentation of a primary (unconditioned) aversive stimulus. When we punish a child for lying by depriving him of his dinner, or when we send a man to jail for stealing, our punishing consequences are in the form of the withdrawal of positive reinforcers (conditioned and unconditioned). Ferster (1958) studied some behavioral effects of making the withdrawal of a positive discriminative stimulus contingent upon certain responses. In preliminary training, the lever pressing of hungry chimpanzees was food-reinforced on a variable-interval schedule in one situation (S^D), but was never reinforced in a second situation (S^Δ). The situations were alternated periodically. This is a standard discrimination procedure, with intermittent reinforcement in S^D. Once a stable discrimination had been established, the procedure was modified so that S^Δ only appeared (S^D only terminated) following high response rates. The withdrawal of the S^D was contingent on a certain kind of lever-press responding, namely, high rates. By inhibiting rapid responding the chimpanzees were able to avoid S^Δ periods. The effect of Ferster's contingency was to produce abnormally low lever-press rates (inhibition of high rates) which only returned to normal when the "punishment" contingency was withdrawn. "Punishment" of this sort may possibly avoid some of the undesirable emotional side effects of unconditioned aversive stimuli, and deserves more study as a useful behavioral control technique.

17.7 MASOCHISM

Certain individuals are said to seek out punishment. Clinical psychologists and psychiatrists refer to such individuals as masochistic. What kind of conditioning history could have endowed the primary aversive stimuli used in punishment with positively reinforcing properties? That such a reversal of reinforcement value can occur even at the infra-human level has been shown by Muenzinger (1934). He trained hungry rats to run in T mazes and both shocked and then fed them for turning into a designated arm. These rats acquired the maze chain faster than did control rats that were fed but not shocked for turning the designated way. In this experiment and other similar ones, shock is being used as an S^D for responses that are subsequently positively reinforced. A correct turn in the maze is followed by shock which sets the occasion for continuing on to food. This procedure is thus to be contrasted with that of shocking S^Δ or "incorrect" responses. The abbreviated contingencies are

$$R_{(correctly\ turn)} \rightarrow \begin{array}{l} S^- \\ R_{(approach)} \rightarrow S^+ \end{array}$$

Under these conditions, even moderately strong shocks can acquire the status of S^D's for approaching food, and thus the status of conditioned positive reinforcers. In a conventional S^D — S^Δ discrimination paradigm, Holz and Azrin (1961) shocked the food-reinforced key-pecking of birds in S^D but not in S^Δ. They found that the punishment element in S^D came to control appreciable rates of responding. In tests, when punishment was administered during S^Δ, the animals began to work rapidly, as though they were in S^D, even though no food was ever given for such S^Δ responding. These animals of Muenzinger and Holtz and Azrin might indeed have appeared to be masochistic. They appeared to work to get punished. When we appreciate the history that makes electric shocks into S^D's for responses that may be positively reinforced, we are perhaps on the way to understanding the causes of human masochism.

References for Chapter 17

Barry, J. J., and Harrison, J. M. Relations between stimulus intensity and strength of escape responding. *Psychol. Rep.,* 1957, **3,** 3–8.

Brogden, W. J., Lipman, E. A., and Culler, E. The role of incentive in conditioning and extinction. *Amer. J. Psychol.,* 1938, **51,** 109–117.

Brown, J. S., and Jacobs, A. The role of fear in the motivation and acquisition of responses. *J. exp. Psychol.,* 1949, **39,** 747–759.

Church, R. M. The varied effects of punishment on behavior. *Psychol. Rev.,* 1963, **70,** 369–402.

Dinsmoor, J. A., and Hughes, L. H. Training rats to press a bar to turn off shock. *J. comp. physiol. Psychol.,* 1956, **49,** 235–238.

Dinsmoor, J. A., and Winograd, E. Shock intensity in variable interval escape schedules. *J. exp. Anal. Behav.,* 1958, **1,** 145–148.

Ferster, C. B. Control of behavior in chimpanzees and pigeons by time out from positive reinforcement. *Psychol. Monogr.,* 1958, **72,** Whole No. 461.

Holz, W. C., and Azrin, N. H. Discriminative properties of punishment. *J. exp. Anal. Behav.,* 1961, **4,** 225–232.

Holz, W. C., and Azrin, N. H. A comparison of several procedures for eliminating behavior. *J. exp. Anal. Behav.,* 1963, **6,** 399–406.

Kaplan, M. The effects of noxious stimulus intensity and duration during intermittent reinforcement of escape behavior. *J. comp. physiol. Psychol.,* 1952, **45,** 538–549.

Miller, N. E. Learnable drives and rewards. Chap. 13 in S. S. Stevens (Ed.), *Handbook of experimental psychology.* New York: Wiley, 1951.

Muenzinger, K. F. Motivation in learning: I. Electric shock for correct responses in the visual discrimination habit. *J. comp. Psychol.,* 1934, **17,** 439–448.

Muenzinger, K. F., and Fletcher, F. M. Motivation in learning, VI. Escape from electric shock compared with hunger-food tension in the visual discrimination habit. *J. comp. Psychol.,* 1936, **22,** 79–91.

Sidman, M. Two temporal parameters of the maintenance of avoidance behavior by the white rat. *J. comp. physiol. Psychol.,* 1953, **46,** 253–261.

Skinner, B. F. *The behavior of organisms.* New York: Appleton-Century, 1938.

Solomon, R. L. Punishment. *Amer. Psychologist,* 1964, **19,** 239–253.

Verhave, T. Avoidance responding as a function of simultaneous and equal changes in two temporal parameters. *J. exp. Anal. Behav.,* 1959, **2,** 185–190.

Warden, C. J., and Aylesworth, M. The relative value of reward and punishment in the formation of a visual discrimination habit in the white rat. *J. comp. Psychol.,* 1927, **7,** 117–127.

Weiss, B., and Laties, V. G. Titration behavior on various fractional escape programs. *J. exp. Anal. Behav.,* 1959, **2,** 227–248.

Weiss, B., and Laties, V. G. Characteristics of aversive thresholds measured by a titration schedule. *J. exp. Anal. Behav.,* 1963, **6,** 563–572.

Weitzman, E. D., Ross, G. S., Hodos, W., and Galambos, R. Behavioral method for study of pain in the monkey. *Science,* 1961, **133,** 37–38.

Wertheim, G. A. Some sequential aspects of IRTs emitted during Sidman-avoidance behavior in the white rat. *J. exp. Anal. Behav.,* 1965, **8,** 9–15.

Whiting, J. W. M., and Mowrer, O. H. Habit progression and regression —a laboratory investigation of some factors relevant to human socialization. *J. comp. Psychol.,* 1943, **36,** 229–253.

Chapter 18 **EMOTIONAL BEHAVIOR**

◯NE OF THE OLDEST OF DISTINCTIONS IS THE broad classification of human behavior into emotions and passions on the one hand and rational and voluntary acts on the other. Yet this venerable and compelling dichotomy has done little to further the experimental analysis of the behaviors regarded as emotional. Too often these have remained merely behaviors that could not be explained by known causes. Emotion has, in effect, been a wastebasket category of behavior and the various phenomena discarded there have shown a strong resistance to systematic integration. Indeed, many present-day psychologists, discouraged by the persistent failures to formulate a positive concept of emotional behavior, would like to drop the term "emotion" altogether from the conceptual vocabulary of the science. They would prefer to construe emotional phenomena as special states of motivation or general activity. None of these attempts proves completely satisfactory because, as we shall see, a careful conceptual dissection of emotional behavior reveals certain unique features not incorporated by other unifying behavioral rubrics. In the present account, therefore, we retain the concept of emotion, using it to refer to certain widespread changes in ongoing operant behavior that result from the application of well-defined environmental operations. But before elaborating these relationships, we discuss a number of traditional solutions to the problems that have been assigned to the field of emotion.

18.1 IS EMOTION A CAUSE OF BEHAVIOR OR A BEHAVIORAL EFFECT?

Prior to the end of the nineteenth century, emotion was thought of as an internal state of the organism that, when induced, caused appropriate

433

behavior on the part of the organism. Thus, in the traditional or classical view, emotion was a cause of behavior. When, for example, a deer saw a bear (S), fear (a bodily state) was aroused, and was followed by an appropriate R, running. Similarly, a man when thwarted (S) became angry (bodily state) and his anger made him aggressive, R.

The overt behaviors supposedly induced by emotional states were classified very early, and Charles Darwin wrote a classic treatise describing their biological usefulness. Fear, for instance, in inducing caution, must have saved the life of many an animal in evolutionary history. So too anger might have been useful in destroying certain physical barriers preventing the completion of a chain of behavior leading to a reinforcer of biological significance. Other emotions, such as joy, Darwin though useful for the purpose of communicating to other nearby organisms that no aggressive action would be forthcoming, and therefore cooperative, sexual, and other behaviors would now be safe and reinforced. Darwin described the elaborate postures and respondents by which the emotions of rage, fear, and joy are "expressed" in animals (Fig. 18–1). Well-defined response patterns could be identified which were in some respects peculiar to the species, and yet showed common elements between species. The curl of a man's lip in rage, revealing his canine teeth, was construed as a vestige of the retraction of the animal's gum preparing its sharp teeth to attack an aggressor. We rarely bite in anger today, but this vestigal pattern is with us still.

Darwin's account emphasized what we might call the topographical

Figure 18–1. *Hostility and friendliness in animals. (1) Hostility in the dog. (2) Friendliness in the dog. (3) Hostility in the cat. (4) Friendliness in the cat (from Darwin, 1872, after Young, 1961).*

features of emotional behavior. William James, writing at the end of the nineteenth century, was more interested in the *sequence* of cause and effect in emotion. In particular he was concerned with refuting the idea that internal states cause emotional behavior. James proposed that the bodily changes in emotion (the physiological respondents) were not the cause of overt behavior at all, but were the result of the patterns of behavior which were directly elicited by the situation. "Common sense says, we lose our fortune, are sorry and weep; we meet a bear, are frightened and run; we are insulted by a rival, are angry and strike" (James, 1890). James argued, however, "that the more rational statement is that we feel sorry because we cry, angry because we strike, afraid because we tremble and not that we cry, strike, or tremble, because we are sorry, angry, or fearful, as the case may be" (James, 1890). Thus James reversed the classic sequence of events in emotion.

In James's account, as well as in all traditional ones, the "feeling" of emotion, be it a cause or an effect, played a critical role.

> What kind of an emotion of fear would be left if the feeling neither of quickened heart-beats nor of shallow breathing, neither of trembling lips nor of weakened limbs, neither of goose-flesh, nor of visceral stirrings, were present it is quite impossible for me to think. Can one fancy the state of rage and picture no ebullition in the chest, no flushing of the face, no dilation of the nostrils, no clenching of the teeth, no impulse to vigorous action . . . ? In like manner of grief, what would it be without its tears, its sobs, its suffocation of the heart, its pang in the breastbone? (James, 1890).

James' description implied that the bodily states accompanying emotional behaviors offered a basis on which to define the emotions.

In the 1920's and 1930's Walter Cannon, a physiologist, disputed James' suggestion that emotions were distinguished by special bodily states. Cannon argued that (1) the physiological states for many different emotions were very similar, and could not be distinguished; rage and anxiety, for instance, gave identical changes in many respondents. (2) The respondents of emotion occurred in non-emotional states such as exposure to an icy wind, heavy exercise, and fever. (3) The drug adrenalin when injected into humans produces the respondents typical of fear (dilation of the bronchioles, constriction of blood vessels, liberation of sugar from the liver, increase in heart rate, cessation of gastrointestinal function, etc.) yet the individuals so injected gave no reports of emotion (Cannon, 1927).

Cannon adduced other evidence to prove that the "feeling" of emotion could not be the result solely of the respondent changes that occur in emotional situations, and then offered a theory of his own. The internal events we report as "feelings" are mediated by a special region of the brain, the thalamus. His hypothesis was based on the effects of lesions and electrical stimulation of this brain region on emotional behavior.

18.2 THREE CONCEPTS OF EMOTION

Private Events. Despite the differences among the theories of Darwin, James, and Cannon, in each one unobservable private events ("feelings"), accessible only to the experiencing individual, occupy a prominent position. The diagrams of Fig. 18–2 summarize these historical views. (Read → as "leads to.")

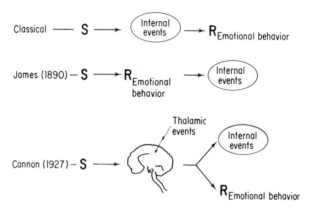

Figure 18–2. Schematic representation of three historical theories of emotional causation.

A methodological problem emerges in determining how to treat the so-called "feelings" of emotion, those events so vividly described by James on p. 435. We may all agree that such feelings do indeed characterize emotion, but how are we to measure and control them? And in the absence of direct observation, how can we even be sure that the feeling of fear that Smith says he has is the same as the feeling of fear that Jones says he has? An individual acquires such verbal responses as "I am afraid," "I am sorry," "I am happy," through reinforcement by parents and other adults when, as a child, he vocalizes these statements in the presence of certain environmental situations. For example, seeing a child tremble and cry in the presence of an unfamiliar object, a parent might be inclined to say "you are afraid," and the child could thereby acquire the response, "I am afraid." An analogous history would prevail for other "emotions." But the community shaping our verbal repertoire of "emotion" words never looks inside us to make reinforcement contingent on discriminative responding in the presence of a particular and well-specified physiological state. Whatever the internal S^D elements may be that were present at the time of early reinforcement, they are *presumably* the same internal events that are present when the adult later reports his emotional state; but those discriminative events are private and remain forever private for each of us.

The inaccessibility of our feelings to others' scrutiny does not render them altogether irrelevant. As hints to the individual scientist for where and when to look for the significant variables, relationships, and concepts of emotional behavior they remain invaluable. It is as scientific data that they fail to meet the observability criterion of science, for this criterion stipulates that the data on which science builds its laws shall be accessible to all who wish to observe them. When emotion—like learning, memory, motivation, and other psychological phenomena treated in previous chapters—finds a translation in behavioral terms which everyone can validate, the stage is set for its experimental analysis.

The problem of private events is particularly emphasized in emotion simply because overt emotional behavior is frequently accompanied by intense and widespread visceral (stomach, heart, lungs, etc.) and glandular changes. Whether or not these events are strongest when behavior is said to be "emotional," the methodology of emotion study remains fundamentally the same as that of the other behavioral processes. The feelings that may accompany visceral events always present the problem of privacy and hence of scientific exclusion, however vivid they may be to the person experiencing them. A reasonable assumption is that the inaccessible private events we call feelings are correlated with particular physiological states which are accessible to observation, given the necessary instrumentation. To turn to the inside of the organism and investigate the properties of physiological processes concomitant with overt behavior is indeed commendable and plays an important part in developing a comprehensive picture of any behavioral phenomenon. But such physiological investigation does not replace the need for firm information about behavior and its environmental determinants.

Reflex Patterns. If we turn our attention away from private events, we discover that the problem of the sequence of situation, feeling, and behavior no longer concerns us in the way it did James and Cannon. Since the actual feelings are not measurable or directly manipulable, whether they come before, after, or at the same time as behavior is not of critical interest to us. J. B. Watson, the man who prepared psychology in so many ways for modern behavior analysis, seems to have been among the first to see this, and in his writings viewed emotions as special patterns of responses elicited initially by unconditioned stimuli. These patterns, he noted, could be attached to previously neutral stimuli via

Pavlovian conditioning procedures. From studies on new-born babies, Watson concluded that there were only three such patterns that legitimately qualified as emotions, patterns X, Y, and Z. Table 18–1 summarizes Watson's scheme. Evidently the three primary emotional patterns in Table 18–1, X, Y, and Z, are the prototypes of what we more usually call rage, fear, and joy. According to Watson, all other emotions were based on these three, as mixtures or combinations brought about by complex Pavlovian conditioning procedures.

Table 18–1

THE WATSONIAN DEFINITION OF THE INFANTS' EMOTIONS
AS REFLEX PATTERNS (COMPILED BY TOLMAN, 1923)

ELICITORS	RESPONDENTS
Rage (X)	
Hampering the infant's movements by holding its face or head; or holding its arms tightly to its sides	Crying, screaming, body stiffening Coordinated slashing or striking movements of hands and arms Feet and legs drawn up and down Holding breath
Fear (Y)	
Suddenly removing all means of support (dropped from the hands to be caught by an assistant) Loud sound Sudden push or slight shake (when just falling asleep or just waking up) Sudden pulling of supporting blanket (when just going to sleep)	Sudden catching of breath Clutching (grasping reflex) Blinking of eyelids Puckering of lips Crying
Joy (Z)	
Stroking or manipulation of an erogenous zone Tickling, shaking, gentle rocking Patting Turning on stomach across attendant's knee	If the infant is crying, it stops crying A smile appears Gurgling and cooing

Watson arranged a simple demonstration to show how conditioning extends the controls of emotion. To an infant, Albert, aged 11 months, Watson showed a rat (S_1), never previously feared, and paired the presence of the rat with a few presentations of a sudden loud sound (S_2^-), produced by striking a steel bar with a hammer. The sound frightened the infant (Watson's syndrome Y), and served as the unconditioned elicitor in a Pavlovian paradigm. Eventually the rat (S_1) came to elicit a CR in Albert that was very similar to Y behavior: crying, whimpering, withdrawal, etc. The conditioned form of fear may or may not be exactly identical to unconditioned fear. To emphasize this point, the CR based on unconditioned fear reflexes is generally referred to as *anxiety*. In later experiments, Watson showed that this conditioned anxiety could be slowly extinguished by the usual method—presentation of the S_1 (the rat) without the S_2^- (the loud sound).

One of the important advances of Watson's treatment of the emotions over that of his predecessors was that he asked the question, what are the external causes of emotional behavior? As Watson himself remarked, "It never occurred to James, or any of his followers for that matter, to speculate, much less experiment, upon the genesis of the emotional forms of response" (Watson, 1930, p. 142). Watson's demonstration that emotions were allied to Pavlovian conditioning principles was a key first step to their experimental analysis. Indeed, the present chapter might well be called *Some complex effects of Pavlovian conditioning,* but we follow tradition in discussing these effects as "emotions."

Disrupted Operants. Another conceptual step must be taken to simplify the experimental analysis of emotional phenomena. Watson subscribed to the view (as had Darwin) that the primary emotions were complex unconditioned response patterns, and he picked out three such patterns as "fundamental." But what justification did he have for confining himself to just these particular three? A loud sound, for example, a pistol shot at close range, will produce the startle pattern (Fig. 18–3) and a host of other respondents. The pattern is completed in about ½ sec, and contains many of the features of a brief bout of emotion. But why is it not called an emotion? So too, the cough, the hiccough, the sneeze, the tearing of the eye to a dust particle, the allergic symptoms called hay fever, the panting and flushing of heavy exercise, and indigestion from over-eating all involve complex patterns of respondents. Yet few would be disposed to call them emotions. What is special about the X, Y, Z reactions that they, rather than these other patterns, should be raised to special status and called "emotions"? No satisfactory answer has ever been given to this question. Useful criteria that might distinguish emotional reflexes from non-emotional reflexes have never been found. In their absence we may suppose that the definition of emotion lies elsewhere than in the special characteristics of certain reflex patterns.

A prime feature of all emotions is the disruption, disturbance, enhancement, or general change that takes place in any of a host of arbitrary behaviors in which an individual might be engaged at the

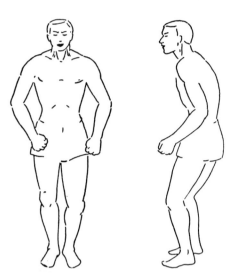

Figure 18–3. The startle response to a pistol shot (Landis and Hunt, 1939).

moment when what we call an emotional situation occurs. Indeed, a man made afraid is more easily identified by the marked depression of all his usual activities than by special cardiac, respiratory, or digestive changes. An angry man is the epitome of a man disrupted. The very angry individual is unlikely to go on with what he was doing before he was made angry. Now he turns to new behaviors; he is especially likely to damage things near him, to make verbal retorts, and to emit operants with unusual force. Give a child a promise of an especially attractive activity and he may literally jump with joy. Many of the child's present behaviors are temporarily disrupted, others may be enhanced. It is the special character of these widespread changes, not of the reflex patterns, nor of the bodily states, that will prove the most convenient framework for the study of the emotions.

The operations that bring about these widespread changes consist of two main types: (1) the presentation or termination of powerful primary reinforcers, and (2) the presentation of stimuli which have previously been associated with such powerful reinforcers through Pavlovian conditioning. The widespread changes in many operant behaviors associated with these operations could well be interpreted as simultaneous changes in the reinforcing value of practically all the organism's primary reinforcers. Destruction and damage take on such strong reinforcing value for the angry individual that momentarily nothing else is important. The man who is afraid or grief-stricken loses his appetite and his sexual desire. People in love are often so wrapped up in their new-found reinforcers that they "live on love" exclusively for a time, neglecting to eat and engage in other routine activities. It would appear that emotion, like motivation, classifies a set of operations that modulate the reinforcing value of primary reinforcers, and change the general activity of the organism. So we must not be surprised to learn that many authorities currently treat the two topics as a unified area. Nevertheless, there are differences in the kinds of operations historically assigned to the two fields. The universal antecedent operations associated with motivation are deprivation and satiation. In emotion, the antecedent operations are abrupt stimulus changes. Moreover, fear, anger, and joy imply diffuse, non-specific changes in the value of all reinforcers; hunger and thirst imply somewhat more specific changes in a more restricted set of reinforcers.

18.3 THE ANXIETY PARADIGM

A significant portion of the analysis of emotion as a disruption of an individual's routine operant activities comes from studies of a laboratory phenomenon known as experimental anxiety. The anxiety is produced by a variant of Watson's variation of Pavlovian conditioning: an originally non-aversive stimulus (S_1) is paired with an aversive stimulus (S_2^-). The anxiety is measured by observing what effects the pairing has on any operant activities in which the organism might be engaged. Since we are limited in the range of aversive stimuli we would want to present to a human organism, we shall generally find monkeys, rats, and pigeons to be the subjects of choice. To engage these animals in operant activities for sustained periods, we may deprive them of food or water, and then train them to press a lever or peck a key for intermittent positive reinforcement. Once this training is complete, we have an organism that will maintain a moderate rate of operant behavior for long periods, a preparation to which we may administer Pavlovian conditioning procedures.

A classic experiment on conditioned anxiety is that of W. K. Estes and B. F. Skinner (1941) using a Pavlovian procedure superimposed over an intermittently reinforced operant, as we have outlined. Certain procedural refinements were introduced by Hunt and Brady (1951, 1955) and it is their experimental technique that we describe. They trained liquid-deprived rats to press a lever for water and then placed the behavior on a *VI* schedule of water reinforcement. When the *VI* behavior had become stable, Pavlovian pairings were given periodically, with a clicker (S_1) sounding for 5 min, followed by a brief electric shock (S_2^-) to the rat's feet.

Some of the typical behavioral changes that ensued can be seen by examining the cumulative lever-pressing curves of Fig. 18–4. These curves describe disturbances in the ongoing water-reinforced operant that were brought about by the Pavlovian pairing of S_1 with S_2^-. In Fig. 18–4A, the rat was working steadily on the lever. Water reinforcements are not shown but several were delivered during the period shown

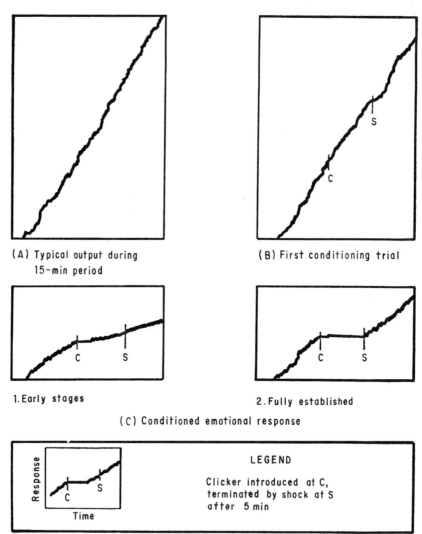

(A) Typical output during 15-min period

(B) First conditioning trial

1. Early stages

2. Fully established

(C) Conditioned emotional response

Response

Time

LEGEND

Clicker introduced at C, terminated by shock at S after 5 min

Figure 18–4. The conditioned anxiety response (CAR) in the rat, as it typically appears in the ongoing intermittently and positively reinforced operant lever-pressing behavior (Hunt and Brady, 1951).

in (A). The first Pavlovian conditioning trial (S_1, S_2^-) is shown in (B). Note that at this stage the clicker, S_1, had no noticeable effect on ongoing lever pressing. The shock, however, when it came resulted in a brief lowering of rate, but soon the rat was again working steadily. The pairing procedure was repeated at intervals. After a few pairings, a change took place which can be seen in the middle left portion of Fig. 18–4. The rat began to respond erratically and at a reduced rate during the clicker. Meanwhile, the original response to shock began to *adapt* (section 18.9) so that the shock itself affected the ongoing lever pressing less and less. After a number of pairings (lower right of Fig. 18–4), nearly complete cessation of lever pressing occurs in the clicker period. Ongoing operant behavior was almost completely disrupted by the pairings; conditioned anxiety had developed, taking the form of a *conditioned suppression* of the positively reinforced lever pressing. Observation of the rat during the clicker period revealed the reflexes characteristic of fear: crouching, trembling, panting, immobility, defecation, and urination.

Conditioned anxiety has been verified in a number of species and with a number of baseline positive reinforcement schedules. The general result is a suppression of ongoing responding developed during the warning stimulus. The suppression is long lasting: pigeon subjects retained it over a 2-year rest period (Hoffman, Fleshler, and Jensen, 1963). Clearly, then, the effects of the anxiety procedure are consistent and durable; but is there any reason to believe that what we are studying in laboratory animals has anything to do with anxiety as we know it in man?

It remains to be seen whether what is termed anxiety by the laboratory worker has relevance to speculations about anxiety in man. Certainly we do not understand from the clinical standpoint precisely what anxiety is in man, whereas the laboratory worker can specify a meaning. To borrow the word anxiety for our experiments, reflects the judgment that the experiments contain the basic features of what is believed, though without adequate proof as yet, to be involved in human anxiety (Schoenfeld, 1950, p. 75).

Let us turn to a few additional features of conditioned anxiety. It is easy to verify that conditioned suppression occurs maximally to the particular warning stimulus (S_1) that was used in the Pavlovian pairing. But some suppression also occurs to stimuli similar to S_1, even though these were never previously paired with shock. A gradient of generalization can be demonstrated for conditioned suppression by testing for the extent of suppression to stimuli related to, but different from, the actual S_1 used in training. Hoffman and Fleshler (1961) studied this generalization of conditioned suppression in pigeons maintained on *VI* 2-min food

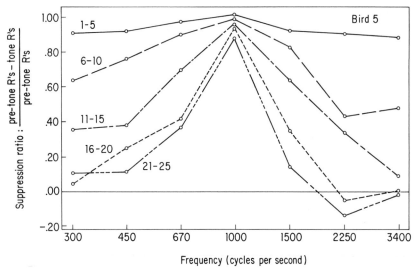

Figure 18–5. Generalization of suppression gradients. The numbers to the left of each gradient indicate the sessions included. The index of suppression used has the following properties. When the index is at 1.0, suppression in S_1 is total; when at 0, there is no disturbance during S_1; and when less than 0, there is enhancement of VI rate during S_1 (Hoffman and Fleshler, 1961).

reinforcement for key pecking. A 1000-cycle tone was used as S_1, and an electric shock to the bird's body as S_2^-. Following repeated pairings of S_1 and S_2^-, key pecking became suppressed in S_1. Then shock was permanently discontinued, tones of various frequencies were presented throughout 25 testing sessions, and any suppression to them was measured. Figure 18–5, from one typical bird, shows that throughout sessions 1–5 (the topmost curve), nearly complete suppression occurred to a wide range of tones; the gradient was flat. In the subsequent sessions, the gradient became gradually sharper, as the bird resumed its key pecking in the presence of those tones most remote from the training S_1. But even after 25 sessions without shocks, nearly perfect suppression was still occurring to the original training S_1. These generalization gradients indicate first that anxiety may spread to conditions very different from those that originally produced it, and second that conditioned anxiety, once produced, may be extremely resistant to extinction.

We may summarize the information presented on experimental anxiety in its paradigm.

GIVEN: An operant, previously strengthened with positive reinforcement, an unconditioned aversive elicitor, a "neutral" stimulus.

PROCEDURE: (1) An operant is maintained on an intermittent schedule of positive reinforcement, for example, $R \xrightarrow{P} S^+$.

(2) While the positive reinforcement contingencies remain in force, S_1 is occasionally paired with S_2^-.

PROCESS: A gradual suppression of the rate of R takes place whenever S_1 is presented.

RESULT: R is suppressed to some measurable extent during S_1 and other related S's.

Our survey of the experimental anxiety paradigm reveals that pairing a previously neutral stimulus with an aversive stimulus while the organism is engaged in other activities produces certain drastic and durable effects on those ongoing activities. For the most part, the "other activities" have been restricted to behavior maintained by intermittent schedules of positive reinforcement. A more complete profile of emotional effects would include information from discrimination, differentiation, chaining, problem solving, avoidance, and other behavioral baselines. There are reasons to expect characteristic effects in each of these cases. Mild anxiety is often said to facilitate problem solving, whereas strong anxiety is thought to hinder it. Conditioned-anxiety procedures provide objective tests of these and other intuitions. The effects of the conditioned-anxiety procedure are sure to be more complex than any simple statement of "suppression." Already it is known that the S_1, S_2^- pairing procedure, when superimposed on an avoidance baseline, may generate facilitation rather than suppression of ongoing responding (Sidman, 1960).

Experimental anxiety, in the form of suppression of intermittently reinforced responding, has proved a useful practical tool for studying various experimental variables. Brady and Hunt (1955) found they could temporarily eliminate experimental anxiety by sending sufficient current through the rat's brain to produce convulsions (a procedure called *ECS* or "electroconvulsive shock," and common in psychiatric practice). Conditioned suppression is predictably affected by tranquilizers that control human anxiety symptoms. Other workers have studied the effects of various brain lesions on conditioned suppression, in the search for the central nervous structures that are critical for emotional behavior (Brady, 1961, 1962).

18.4 ANGER

Anxiety is concerned with the presentation of negative reinforcers. Quite a different form of behavioral disturbance occurs when positive reinforcers are withdrawn. We had occasion to refer earlier (section

5.1) to the brief increase in response rate that occurs when a chain of operant behavior is abruptly broken by extinction. In the rat, this increase in rate of the strengthened response is accompanied by a variety of other behaviors whose characteristics—biting the response manipulandum, extreme agitation, violent excitement—implicate them as emotional.

These observations have their counterpart in the aggressive behaviors exhibited by angry humans. Gates (1926) interviewed women college students, and asked them to list the circumstances that typically led them to become angry. The girls cited refusals of requests, tardiness of friends keeping dates, getting a wrong number on the telephone, failure in operation of watches, pens, and typewriters, delays in buses or elevators, and loss of money as the most common precipitators. Each of these situations produced strong tendencies to make verbal retorts, do physical injury to someone else, damage objects, vigorously withdraw from the situation, scream and swear. Each of the cited causes implies a sudden extinction of previously reinforced behavior, the abrupt breaking of a behavior chain.

Azrin, Hutchinson, and Hake (1966) devised a technique for experimentally measuring the duration and frequency of aggressive behaviors that result from breaking a chain of behavior. In their technique, a hungry bird was first trained to peck a disk for food. When the experimental bird had acquired key-pecking behavior, a second "target" bird, immobilized in a specially designed box, was introduced into the experimental compartment (Fig. 18–6). The box holding the target bird was mounted on an assembly that caused a switch underneath to close whenever the box was jiggled vigorously. The assembly was carefully balanced so that normal spontaneous movements of the target bird were insufficient to close the microswitch, whereas any forceful attacks that the experimental bird might direct against the exposed body of the target bird would be recorded. Attacks occurred predictably. Whenever its reinforcement contingencies were abruptly changed from *crf* to extinction, the experimental bird invariably attacked the target bird. The attacks were vicious and aggressive, lasting up to 10 min.

The parallel results of breaking a chain of reinforced behavior in both the animal and the human confirm the generality of the *frustration* paradigm. Its procedure is merely abrupt operant extinction following continuous reinforcement. Its results are widespread changes in the topography of behavior, accompanied by changes in the reinforcing value of destruction, damage, and other aggressive acts.

Are these angry behaviors conditionable in the manner that fear was shown to be conditioned in the previous section? In one relevant study, Leitenberg (1966) trained rats to press a lever for positive reinforce-

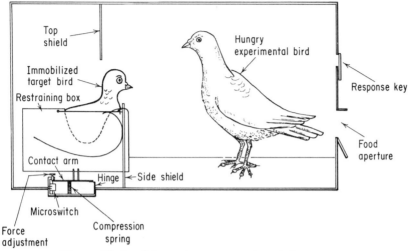

Figure 18–6. Schematic representation of the apparatus for measuring attack (Azrin, Hutchinson, and Hake, 1966).

ment on a *VI* schedule. During the session a "warning" stimulus (S_1) was presented, followed a few minutes later by a second stimulus (S_2^Δ) which indicated that a period of extinction for lever pressing had just come into effect. The procedure is analogous to the conditioned-anxiety procedure, but a stimulus correlated with extinction (S^Δ) is here substituted for shock (S^-). After a few pairings, Leitenberg's rats increased their responding in the "warning" stimulus, though such rate increases did not bring about more reinforcement.

We may speculate that this facilitation of response rate represents a "conditioned rage response," but Leitenberg's procedure is only suggestive. Not enough aspects of behavior were measured for us to be certain whether, during the warning stimulus, the likelihood of aggressive behaviors such as attack or abnormally forceful responding might also have been increased.

18.5 ELATION

Fear and anger are appropriately described as negative emotions since they depend on presentation of negative reinforcers or withdrawal of positive reinforcers. But emotional behavior is not purely confined to negative instances. Watson identified "syndrome Z" as an unconditioned reflex pattern resulting from stimulation of erogenous zones or associated with feeding (suckling). In casual discourse we identify behaviors as joyful, excited, pleasant, and so forth. Our aim here will be to show that these terms imply the existence of yet another set of operant disturbances which, like anxiety, are closely associated with certain Pavlovian conditioning procedures.

Everyone has seen a child delighted by a promise of good things to come. Even the adult can be "thrilled" by good news. The dog has a built-in mechanism, the tail wag, to indicate its enthusiasm when greeting its master or when about to be fed or petted. Such observations suggest that the effects of positive reinforcement are not confined to strengthening and maintaining operant behavior. An S^+, or a stimulus that precedes S^+, seems to generate some behavior disturbance, which we may call "joy" or "elation." We may easily conceive of a conditioned elation procedure in which an S_1 is paired with an $S_2{}^+$ while the organism is working at an operant activity. It is less easy to predict the effects of this operation. The businessman hard at work on his daily agenda when he learns that he has just made a killing on the stockmarket and the housewife in the midst of baking a cake when she learns that she has won a free all-expenses-paid round trip to Hawaii are likely to be disrupted in their ongoing activities. Nevertheless, it is an experimental question how *this* disruption differs from those disruptions called anxiety and anger. The question implies a systematic program of research involving numerous baselines and perhaps many different $S_1, S_2{}^+$ pairing procedures. At present, we have only the scantest experimental information to offer for the reality of conditioned elation.

Herrnstein and Morse (1957) trained pigeons to peck a key for food, and then stabilized key pecking by a procedure that generated a very low rate of pecking. They reinforced only those pecks spaced at least 5-min apart (*drl* 5-min, see section 8.6). When the rate of response appeared to be stable, a Pavlovian paradigm was superimposed on the operant contingencies. S_1 was a change in key color followed after a time by $S_2{}^+$, a "free" food delivery, identical to the reinforcement used to maintain the ongoing baseline, except that the "free" food delivery was not contingent on a key peck. Herrnstein and Morse's procedure produced a dramatic change in the ongoing rate of key pecking during S_1. Prior to the Pavlovian procedure, a very low and nearly constant rate of pecking had been maintained. After the Pavlovian procedure had been in effect for a few sessions, however, high rates of pecking developed during S_1. Figure 18–7 shows the cumulative records on session 11 for six subjects. At *a* the S_1 was presented. (*f* indicates the presentation of $S_2{}^+$, food.) In this experiment, S_1 was continued for 1 min beyond $S_2{}^+$, and terminated at *b*, though we are here concerned only with the rate effects from *a* to *f*. Figure 18–7 indicates that most birds show a

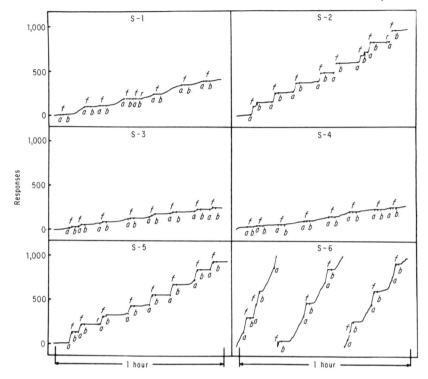

Figure 18–7. One-hour segments of conditioned "elation" (Herrnstein and Morse, 1957).

rate increase at a (S_1) lasting at least until f ($S_2{}^+$). The rapid appearance of the effect seems to rule out the possibility that the rate increase is due to any superstitious correlations of pecking with the free reinforcement.

Similar experiments using a food-reinforced *VI* baseline and positively reinforcing brain stimulation (see section 16.3) as the $S_2{}^+$ also demonstrate conditioned enhancement (Fig. 18–8) during a stimulus that consistently precedes the brain stimulation (Brady, 1961).

A still more subtle effect of this general type was observed by Pliskoff (1963). Behavior may be sustained on several different alternating *VI* schedules, each *VI* in effect for a limited time, and each *VI* correlated with a special stimulus. If a warning stimulus (S_1) is given prior to the change (S_2) from a *VI* with a higher mean interval between reinforcement opportunities to one with a shorter mean interval (say *VI* 2 min to *VI* ½ min), certain changes may occur in responding during the warning stimulus. When the change is from long mean interval to short, as just described, the organism is in effect moving from a less favorable schedule to a more favorable one. Pliskoff's procedure led to a mild suppression

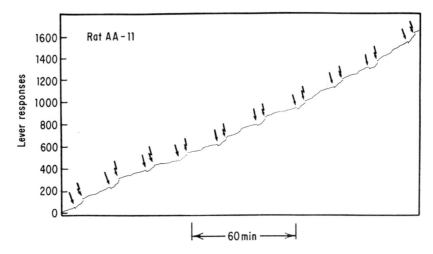

Figure 18–8. Conditioned enhancement on a food-rein-forced VI *baseline resulting from pairing an* S_1 *with a positively reinforcing brain shock (Brady, 1961).*

in response rate during the warning stimulus, suggesting that an "elation" operation may not always enhance ongoing operant activities.

Establishment of the general conditions that produce suppression and the ones that produce enhancement awaits further experimental work on the general emotional effects of S^+'s, and of pairing S_1's with S^+'s, on other behavioral baselines. The few studies described indicate how the positive emotions can be viewed as conditionable changes in ongoing operant behavior.

This section and the two preceding ones complete our survey of the behavioral effects of three categories of emotion-producing operations. The operations have been reflex, the behaviors operant. Yet unlike ordinary operant phenomena, these we have called "emotional" refer to changes in ongoing operants not brought about directly by altering their reinforcement consequences. None of the anxiety, anger, or elation effects makes positive reinforcement more likely, or negative reinforcement less likely. The "anxious" rat in Fig. 18–4 gets shocked whether he suppresses or not. The "angry" pigeon that pecks its companion viciously does not thereby reinstate reinforcement. Brady's "elated" rat (Fig. 18–8) cannot hasten the occurrence of brain stimulation by rapid responding. Thus, although the changes in behavior being measured are changes in the rates of operants, the changes are not governed directly by the reinforcement contingencies of any of the affected operants.

That an emotional effect is not useful here and now in the animal's laboratory environment or the man's civilized environment in influencing the probability of reinforcement does not mean that it may not have *once* been useful in influencing reinforcement probability or that it might not be useful in other environments. In particular, emotional behavior may well have been extremely useful for the ancestors of the individual whose emotional behavior we are now witnessing. Darwin's suggestions concerning the biological usefulness of emotional behaviors in the natural environment have already been noted (p. 434). Such speculations fit with the known facts that emotional respondents are mediated by parts of the nervous system that are, to a large extent, phylogenetically older than the parts of the nervous system governing the capacities to acquire complex operant behavior. Emotional behaviors seem to be among those primitive behaviors whose potentialities are built in; and, like other reflexes, they are under the control of Pavlovian rather than operant principles.

18.6   A MODEL FOR REPRESENTING AND INTERRELATING EMOTIONAL PHENOMENA

We have described three patterns of disturbances in ongoing operant behaviors which are closely allied to withdrawal or presentation of reinforcers, yet which, in many cases, are intimately related to Pavlovian conditioning procedures. Since the behavioral effects produced seemed to resemble, in certain ways, behaviors that in ourselves we call anxiety, anger, and elation, we retained those names as labels for these three paradigms. Our intuitions tell us, however, that even if these three paradigms do correspond to human phenomena, they do not begin to exhaust the field of emotion. Words like sorrow, humiliation, chagrin, guilt, shame, misery, embarrassment, pity, love, tenderness, contentment, and euphoria suggest that there are many subtle emotional variants not accounted for by our gross experimental classification of fear, anger, and elation.

A variety of different accounts has been provided by philosophers and psychologists to schematize and represent various emotional phenomena (Plutchik, 1962). The theoretical scheme to be elaborated here borrows from two historical ideas: (1) that certain emotions differ from each other only in intensity, and (2) that certain emotions can be considered as compounds of other, more fundamental ones. The first idea is straightforward. Rage, anger, and annoyance, for instance, are words that seem to denote different intensities of a similar kind of disturbance. The second notion, mixing "pure" emotions to form others, is more subtle. Three centuries ago Descartes argued that all emotions were derived from six basic "passions": love, hate, desire, joy, sadness, and admiration, though he gave no justification for choosing these six in particular as basic. Other writers have given other lists of varying lengths from three to several dozen basic emotions. No satisfactory criteria for selecting the fundamental or primary emotions have ever been agreed upon, nor have the methods for mixing been closely analyzed.

Our account begins with the claim that the three patterns cited by Watson (Table 18–1) and described as operant changes in the preceding three sections constitute the three fundamental emotional patterns. Their fundamental status derives from the facts that (1) in their unconditioned form, their procedures exhaust the possibilities for presentation and withdrawal of primary positive and negative reinforcers, and (2) in their conditioned form their procedures exhaust the possibilities for simple Pavlovian paradigms. Table 18–2 summarizes the Pavlovian operations and some of their known behavioral effects. In Table 18–2,

Table 18–2

THE PRIMARY EMOTIONAL OPERATIONS
AND SOME OF THEIR BEHAVIORAL EFFECTS

PAVLOVIAN PAIRING OPERATION	COMMON NAME OF "EMOTION"	EFFECTS ON ONGOING OPERANT ACTIVITY
S_1, S^-	Anxiety	Suppression of positively reinforced operants. Facilitation of negatively reinforced operants
$\begin{cases} S_1, S^+ \\ S_1, \cancel{S}^- \end{cases}$	Elation	Enhancement of some operants. Little information available
$S_1, \cancel{S}^+$	Anger	Increases in magnitude of some operants. Reinforcing value of attack and destruction raised

a diagonal slash through S is a notational abbreviation indicating termination of the reinforcing stimulus event. It will be observed that the left column of the table exhausts the possible combinations of an S_1 with the presentation or termination of an S^+ or S^-. There are four logical possibilities, but we group two of them together on the premise that the behavioral effects of terminating a negative reinforcer or presenting a positive reinforcer are similar enough to permit similar conceptual treatment. A second simplifying assumption is made in neglecting differences between particular positive or negative reinforcers. Thus the "elation" produced by pairing an S_1 with a sexual reinforcer is not distinguished in the scheme of Table 18–2 from the "elation" produced by pairing an S_1 with a food reinforcer. These assumptions constitute working hypotheses whose usefulness only future experimentation can determine.

Having established three "primary" emotions, we can turn to the problem of representing other emotions. In Fig. 18–9, the three primary

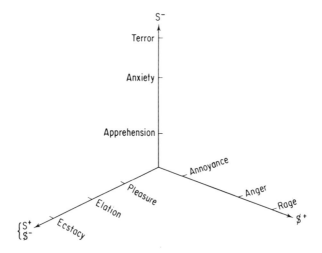

Figure 18–9. The emotional coordinate system. A model for representing intensity differences in the fundamental emotional operations.

emotions appear as vectors of a geometrical model. This framework permits us to represent the idea that some apparently different emotions can be considered to correspond to differences in the intensity of the positive or negative reinforcer on which they are based. The emotions portrayed at the extremes of each vector are based on the strongest values of the relevant unconditioned reinforcers and the terms used to describe the behaviors are chosen appropriately. As we move in the direction of the origin, the intensity declines. We follow Plutchik (1962) in assuming that as the intensity declines, the behavioral effects tend to merge and be less clearly distinguishable. This is indicated by choosing a system that converges towards a point (the origin) where the three emotions meet. It should be clear that a great number of terms from the ordinary language of emotion could be fitted in at some point in this structure, only three levels of which (high, medium, low) are shown.

Many behavioral phenomena to which we apply the term emotion do not find a place in Fig. 18–9, whatever intensity level we might choose. These, we suggest, can be considered as cases of mixed primaries. How do primaries come to be mixed? In two principal ways: (1) A given S_1 is paired successively with two or three primaries, schematically (for example),

$$S_1,S^+; S_1,S^-; S_1,S^-; S_1,S^+; \ldots$$

(2) A given S_1 is paired with an S_2 that comprises two or more different primary reinforcers, schematically (for example)

$$S_1,S^\pm; S_1,S^\pm; S_1,S^\pm; S_1, S^\pm; \ldots$$

As an example of the first mixture, consider the effect that occurs when a child steals a cookie. The cookie in hand is an S_1 for the S^+ of cookie in mouth; but it is also an S_1 for punishment (S^-) that has a high probability of occurring. This particular combination (an S_1 paired first with an S^+ and later with an S^-) occurs frequently enough in nature for its effects to be given a unique name, *guilt*. Plutchik's analysis suggests that in an analogous way pride may be a mixture of anger and joy. Clearly, more complicated cases can occur with other mixtures of the three primaries. In some cases, the effects do not fuse and we speak of having mixed emotions. By independently varying the probabilities of occurrence of each of the S_2's, further subtleties in emotional behavior patterns can be acquired. Just as the chemist now prepares compounds that do not exist naturally, experimental emotions that do not ordinarily arise in the natural world might be generated by various compound conditioning operations.

The case in which S_2 is made up of both positive and negative elements ($S_2^\pm$) illustrates a type of psychological *conflict* situation. If a given situation includes both positive and negative elements, then both approach and avoidance behaviors may exist at high strength, and there is said to be a conflict between the two incompatible chains of behavior: approach versus retreat. A child who ordinarily avoids or escapes spinach may be placed in a conflict situation if told that dessert depends on eating spinach. Making spinach-in-the-stomach the S^D for dessert-producing responses gives spinach a certain positive reinforcing strength which may or may not overcome the original aversion. An example of a still stronger conflict appears in an experiment by a psychiatrist, Jules Masserman (1946). Hungry cats were placed in a box with food at the far end. The cats soon came to approach and eat the food whenever they were placed in the box. In later trials a tube for conducting compressed air was positioned near the food in such a way that just as the cat was about to pick up and eat the food, a strong air blast was directed at the animal's head. Masserman describes the behavioral effect of this pairing of positively reinforced approach behavior with an aversive stimulus as "panic." The next day, and subsequently, these cats refused to approach the food. The air blast was then removed permanently (Pavlovian extinction), but many cats never again went near the food, preferring to starve. Masserman characterized such cats as "neurotic," and suggested that a conflict procedure of this sort might be the underlying factor in many human neuroses. An interesting side observation was made. Prior to beginning the experiment, the alcoholic preferences of the cats were tested by offering them plain milk in one saucer and milk laced with alcohol in another. Before experiencing the conflict procedure, the cats invariably preferred plain milk, but after experiencing the conflict procedure Masserman's cats showed a marked preference for the "spiked" milk.

Emotional mixtures or compounds may be produced by yet more complicated Pavlovian procedures. Certain emotional patterns, it would appear, depend on rather complex conditioning operations, many of which might not be possible without other, still earlier complicated conditioning histories. Consider the case of removing not just a single S^+ but a generalized reinforcer (section 11.4). By removing such a reinforcer we effectively remove a host of positive reinforcers; but without the history that first makes an S a generalized reinforcer, the particular emotional effects of its removal are not possible. The case in point, we claim, bears a close relationship to the phenomenon we call "sorrow." The death of a friend, the loss of a good job, and similar events provoke sorrow because at one fell swoop a host of reinforcers is lost. It seems reasonable that this pattern is rarely seen in animals because generalized reinforcers are most commonly created in human societies. But everyone is familiar with the dog who, at the death of its master, shows behaviors remarkably like our own sorrowful behavior. To the extent that the operations are feasible, it may be possible to generate these or similar behaviors in other species. The emotions we usually think of as human-like may be peculiar to us, not because animals are incapable of them, but because their generating conditions rarely if ever arise outside human societies.

18.7 PSYCHOSOMATIC MEDICINE

We have defined emotion as the association between certain widespread changes in ongoing operant behaviors and the presentation or removal of reinforcers. As an abstract relation between events, "emotion," like drive, cannot therefore *cause* anything—feelings, behaviors, or physiological changes. Nevertheless, the operations that give rise to certain emotional behaviors can, if implemented frequently, provoke acute pathological bodily changes. Thus strong and prolonged emotion may be correlated with hypertension, bronchial asthma, gastrointestinal ulcers, headaches, and other ills. It has been recognized for some time that certain bodily illnesses have their origins in "stressful" situations; that is, situations that feature strong and/or prolonged aversive stimuli which give rise to strong and prolonged emotional behavior. Executives are prone to ulcers and certain cardiovascular diseases. The onset of asthma is sometimes associated with a frightening event in childhood and can subsequently be instigated by mildly frightening circumstances. In general, chronic anxiety is often correlated with a number of pathological bodily symptoms, ranging from acne to severe gastrointestinal upset.

Psychosomatic medicine specializes in the diagnosis and treatment of illnesses which appear to result from the very same procedures that produce certain conditioned emotional behaviors. The reality of psychosomatic illness can be demonstrated dramatically in the animal laboratory, where aversive emotional situations can be produced whose effects are lethal to the subject. In Brady, Porter, Conrad, and Mason's (1958) experiments, monkeys were trained to avoid electric shocks by pressing a lever using a procedure similar to the Sidman avoidance procedure shown in Diagram [17.2]. Shocks were programmed every 20 sec, and the monkeys were exposed to the procedure for 6 consecutive hours, then given a 6-hr rest, then 6-hr avoidance, and so on, indefinitely, day after day. A red light was correlated with the 6-hr avoidance periods.

Typical avoidance behavior generated by this procedure is shown in Fig. 18–10. Note how few shocks were actually administered in the 6-hr avoidance period. After a few weeks, the unexpected death of many of the subjects brought the experiment to an abrupt halt. Autopsy revealed that the animals had succumbed to perforated duodenal ulcers. When these results were first obtained, they suggested that the avoidance procedure might have been the causal agent in the ulcer production and eventual death of the monkeys. But another possibility was that the ulcer was a result of the effects of electric shocks being delivered day after day, and that the avoidance contingency was superfluous.

> To test this possibility we set up a controlled experiment, using two monkeys in 'yoked chairs' in which both monkeys received shocks but only one monkey could prevent them. The experimental or 'executive' monkey could prevent shocks to himself and his partner by pressing the lever; the control monkey's lever was a dummy. Thus both animals were subjected to the same physical stress (i.e., both received the same number of shocks at the same time), but only the 'executive' monkey was under the psychological stress of having to press the lever (Brady, 1958).

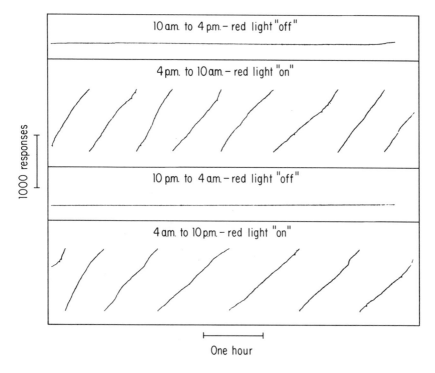

Figure 18–10. A sample cumulative lever-pressing curve showing avoidance behavior on the 18th consecutive experimental session of the 6-hr on, 6-hr off repetitive avoidance procedure. Shocks are indicated by small vertical pips on the records (Brady, Porter, Conrad, and Mason, 1958).

A picture of the apparatus in which the two animals were restrained for several weeks during avoidance testing is shown in the illustration to Part Five, p. 357. The executive animal typically emitted a high rate of avoidance responding during the 6-hr avoidance periods and responded little during the 6-hr "rest" times. The control monkey, on the other hand, rarely pressed its lever throughout the avoidance or "off" period since its lever was associated with the null contingency. In the yoked-control experiment, however, only the executive animal succumbed from ulcers. The control monkeys, sacrificed on the day of the death of their "executive" partners, showed no ulcer production whatsoever, thus suggesting that the lethal factor was indeed the prolonged avoidance contingencies, and not shock itself. Subsequent studies indicated that a critical factor for the production of ulcers by this method is the choice of a 6-hr on-off cycle. Other cycles failed to produce ulceration (Brady, 1958).

From the point of view of the present analysis of emotional behavior, we note that the executive animal is the only one of the two receiving a consistent Pavlovian pairing procedure. For it alone, failing to press the lever for 20 sec ($\bar{R}_{20''}$) suffices to provide a situation (S_1) which is consistently paired with shocks. Its yoked control partner, however, receives occasional shocks, but these are never consistently paired with any given situation (S_1) in its environment; hence the conditioned anxiety paradigm is fulfilled only for the executive monkey.

18.8 THE AUTONOMIC NERVOUS SYSTEM

Sir Charles Sherrington remarked that of the places where physiology and psychology meet, one is emotion. Certainly no analysis of emotion would be complete without some description of the very great physiological changes that take place under the Pavlovian paradigms of emotion. Some psychologists subscribe to the view that the psychological territory of emotional phenomena is exhausted by the analysis of the reflex patterns and perturbations of ongoing operants that are produced by the procedures we have discussed in previous sections. Such a view may technically be correct, depending on one's definition of psychology, but it imposes arbitrary disciplinary boundaries that have no counterparts in the natural phenomena themselves. We have noted elsewhere in this text that the borders between scientific disciplines are often very arbitrarily drawn, and it is obvious that a scientist interested in emotional phenomena can draw from behavioral analysis, from reflex physiology, from endocrinology, and from neurophysiology as well as from other related disciplines. In an introductory account of psychology, our obligation is to describe the principal behavioral effects of various environmental changes; but we do not go very far afield in noting briefly some of the neurophysiological data which help paint a more complete picture of the phenomenon under discussion.

The idea that each emotion is associated with a unique pattern of autonomic respondents appears in the passage by William James cited earlier (p. 435). Nevertheless, these various patterns may often be very similar, and a rather detailed measurement of many respondents may be needed to discern their differences (Ax, 1953). In our introductory discussion of reflexes and simple Pavlovian conditioning, we pointed out that Pavlovian procedures seem most applicable to those internal respondents that are mediated by a part of the nervous system called the *autonomic* ("self-regulating") nervous system (*ANS*), depicted diagrammatically in Fig. 18–11. The *ANS* carries electrical impulses *from* the brain and spinal cord *to* the visceral organs, never the reverse. The

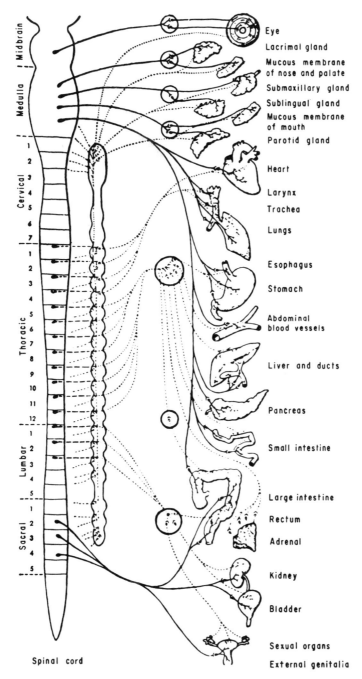

Figure 18–11. The right side of the human autonomic nervous system (Kimble and Garmezy, 1963).

ANS breaks down functionally into two divisions. One of these is called the *sympathetic* system and is shown as dotted lines in Fig. 18–11. The other, the *parasympathetic* (para meaning alongside of), lies anatomically above and below the sympathetic and is shown as solid lines in Fig. 18–11.

The following facts are of importance. First, the organs served by the *ANS* are precisely those which, we have elsewhere indicated, yield respondents, conditioned and unconditioned. The respiratory respondent, the salivary respondent, and heart rate are old friends from Pavlovian conditioning. Over the past half-century, Russian investigators have painstakingly shown that the functioning of nearly every organ in this diagram is susceptible to classical conditioning procedures. The *ANS* is so intimately linked with Pavlovian conditioning that it might be thought of as the anatomical apparatus for conditioning of this kind.

A second point of interest is the difference of function subserved by the two divisions of the *ANS*. Note that the solid-line fibers (parasympathetic) typically come from *unique* origins and go straight to their organs without interconnecting or interacting. This anatomical fact is reflected in the physiological fact that different parts of the parasympathic system operate individually. The sympathetic (dotted) fibers, however, go first to a common junction chain (the long vertical structure shown along the right side of the spinal cord in Fig. 18–11), where they interact before they reach their organs. This anatomic fact is reflected by a unity of the sympathetic system such that its fibers affect all the organs at once.

Finally we can observe that each individual organ in Fig. 18–11 has both dotted and solid fibers leading to it and is therefore subject to influences from both the sympathetic and the parasympathetic divisions. But the effects on each organ of these two divisions are not the same. In fact, they are typically opposite. This is partly because the two divisions liberate different chemicals at their terminal points on the organ. The sympathetic system liberates a substance very like adrenalin, while the parasympathetic nerves liberate a different substance called acetylcholine. Table 18–3 summarizes some of the main effects of the two divisions of the autonomic system.

At one time it was thought that anxiety and fear were principally sympathetic effects, whereas anger was principally a parasympathetic effect. It is now believed that the picture is much more complex, and that the result of all emotional operations is to produce sympathetic *and* parasympathetic effects. What physiological differences there are between emotions must be due to different patterns of respondents; that is, to subtle differences in sympathetic and parasympathetic action. These patterns of autonomic respondents associated with emotional behavior make up what is sometimes called the *autonomic substrate* of the emotions.

Table 18–3

AUTONOMIC RESPONDENT ACTION (AFTER P. T. YOUNG, 1961)

SYMPATHETIC NERVES	BODILY STRUCTURES	PARASYMPATHETIC NERVES
Dilates the pupil	Iris	Constricts the pupil
Inhibits secretion	Salivary glands	Facilitates secretion
Erects (pilomotor reflex)	Hair	
Augments secretion	Sweat glands	
Constricts	Surface arteries	
Accelerates	Heart	Inhibits
Dilates bronchioles	Lung	Contracts bronchioles
Secretes glucose	Liver	
Inhibits gastric secretion and peristalsis	Stomach	Facilitates gastric secretion and peristalsis
Constricts, giving off erythrocytes	Spleen	
Secretes adrenalin	Adrenal medulla	
Inhibits smooth-muscle activity	Small intestine	Facilitates smooth-muscle activity
Constricts	Visceral arteries	
Relaxes smooth muscle	Bladder	Contracts smooth muscle to empty
Relaxes smooth muscle	Colon and rectum	Contracts smooth muscle to empty
Constricts, counteracting erection	Arteries of external genitals	Dilates, causing erection
Contracts at orgasm	Vasa deferentia	
Contracts at orgasm	Seminal vesicles	
Contracts at orgasm	Uterus	

It must be mentioned that a number of demonstrations show that artificially inducing the respondent substrate of emotion does not typically produce the other behavioral properties of emotion. For example, injecting the drug adrenalin (which acts to mimic sympathetic activation) into animals does not give rise to the operant disruptions characteristic of anxiety, anger, or joy. Humans injected with adrenalin report sham emotion: they feel "as if" they were angry, "as if" they were joyful, "as if" they were afraid, and so forth. A demonstration by Schacter and Singer (1962) indicates that such artificial induction of the respondent substrate of emotional behavior will bias an individual's sensitivity to emotional situations. Thus college students injected with adrenalin showed *angrier* behavior in an anger-producing situation, but they also showed more euphoric behavior in a joyful situation than non-injected college students. It appears that inducing the respondents of emotion can sensitize the organism to the operations of emotion.

18.9 EMOTIONAL CONTROL, EMOTIONAL MATURITY, AND PATHOLOGICAL EMOTIONAL BEHAVIOR

If emotions entail elicited behaviors, then what kind of self-control can be exercised over them? Because our operants are under the control of their consequences, and because we are able to observe that fact, we are inclined to translate this as a control that "we" have over them. But respondents are not under the control of their consequences. We have already noted how the suppressing and enhancing effects of emotional procedures are often so unrelated to reinforcing consequences as to appear non-adaptive and useless. But one's emotional reflexes are often aversive to other individuals and to oneself, and civilized society demands some control over emotional behavior. The usual change in emotional patterns from childhood to adulthood is characterized by greater increase in control over emotional behavior, often called emotional maturity. How is it achieved? Apparently there are at least three major ways of achieving such control.

When a situation that produces emotional behavior is repeatedly presented, the magnitude of the response declines over time. This is the phenomenon known as *adaptation* or habituation, referred to in our earliest discussions of operant conditioning. Introducing an organism to a novel situation often produces fear behavior: crouching, freezing, defecation, urination, etc. But repeatedly introducing the organism to that same situation results in a gradual lessening of the effects. The individual is said to have adapted, or habituated to the situation.

In society, an important method of modifying emotional behavior is to adapt it. An organism subjected to the extinction procedure after an intermittent schedule of reinforcement does not show the increased rate of response or other changes we called anger. After such an organism has had a history of extinction in intermittent reinforcement, his angry behavior is absent because it has adapted out long ago, and we now say he has a "high frustration tolerance." We see analogous effects in human conduct. Children cry and scream when their toys are removed. Adults (usually) exhibit more moderate reactions. The typical adult has had a longer history of losing things; he has had some years of adaptation to the hardships of extinction, and reacts correspondingly less. We often speak of outgrowing our fears, indicating that habituation of them occurs in due time. Adaptation is not confined to aversive events, however. Even the good things in life can lose their appeal if we get "used" to them.

A second form of control occurs when we mask our respondents by overlaying them with opposed operants. Thus a child is told not to whimper and whine, however he may "feel." In Western society, men must restrain tears, but women may cry. Overt fear behaviors are often chided and we are induced to bring operants to bear that hide our fears. Whenever we are advised to keep a stiff upper lip, we are encouraged to counteract, with an opposed operant, the reflexive respondent of dropping the lip that occurs in grief. The "dead pan" face is a necessary skill for all good poker players, but it is unlikely that enough habituation ever occurs to abolish completely the unseen respondent substrate generated by a royal flush. This survival of autonomic respondents in the absence of other behaviors (such as facial expression) characteristic of emotion is the basis of the lie detector, which is actually an autonomic respondent detector. This device consists of apparatus for measuring heart rate, respiration, skin resistance, muscle tension, and other respondents. When questions are put to a suspect, his answers may consist of operants that mask any overt emotional reaction. But measurement of his autonomic respondents may give him away if he is "lying," since a man who has recently committed a crime is especially likely to show selective anxiety effects to words descriptive of the scene and the events of the crime.

A third form of control over emotion consists of avoidance, on the one hand, or production, on the other, of the situations that call out the emotional behavior. When we avoid an enemy who is likely to make us angry, or stop playing golf because we continually play poorly, or when we go to a restaurant where we have often had a good meal, we avoid or produce certain reinforcers; but as a by-product we may also escape or produce certain of our own emotional behaviors. In that sense, we may be said to be exerting control over our emotions.

It is evident from the brief consideration of these three methods of emotional control that our regulation over our emotional respondents falls somewhat short of the degree of control we have over our arms, legs, or vocal cords. It is perhaps useful to appreciate this difference in our upbringing of children and our dealings with each other.

Society is fraught with numerous anger- and anxiety-producing situations. From childhood onward we meet prohibitions and conflicts, threats and frustrations. Some are capricious; others seem necessary to the orderly running of human affairs. Most individuals manage to emerge from this history with a repertoire of skills for avoiding aversive events and producing positive reinforcers that is sufficient to keep anxiety and anger at tolerable levels. But some individuals, perhaps because their history contains an unusual amount of aversive control, or perhaps because genetically they are more sensitive to anger- or anxiety-producing operations, fail to acquire sufficient skills to make a satisfactory adjustment to society's contingencies. We have already discussed the cases that fall within the province of psychosomatic medicine. Many other human individuals show drastic effects of prolonged anxiety and anger operations that cannot quite be called illnesses in the way that ulcers, hypertension, and asthma can. A prolonged lack of elation-producing situations may have adverse effects also, especially if the impoverishment occurs early in life. Infants that are raised from birth in institutions often receive sufficient food and care for their general health, but may not receive the fondling and affectionate stimulation that other children get from parents. If this affectionate stimulation is lacking during the first 6 months of life, these infants frequently grow up to become extremely apathetic children and adults (Spitz, 1957). The infants become dejected, detached, show stupor, lack of appetite, and retarded physical development. Such infants appear to lack the usual intensity of joy behavior as well as fear and anger behavior. In short, all their emotional behaviors appear to be highly attenuated. Some of them never develop normal levels of positive reinforcers, so that they have to be kept institutionalized for their entire lives.

There are numerous other pathological behavior states to which humans are prone for which the causes are still more subtle and poorly understood. Persons who show the behavioral effects of anxiety over long periods of time in the complex situations that arise in their daily lives are often called "neurotics." Prolonged emotional behavior of the sort called anxiety constitutes a marked interference with other ongoing operants, and a neurotic might be said to be "maladjusted" simply because, instead of engaging in operants that might gain him positive reinforcers, he displays the suppressions characteristic of anxiety. If the suppressions persist for long periods, his efficiency in normal ongoing activities may be greatly reduced. Other individuals develop patterns of behavior that are so pathological or dangerous to the society at large that these persons have to be institutionalized for their own safety or that of society. In a broad class of behavior pathology known as *psychosis,* normal positive reinforcers may be disrupted in value, or absent altogether. Some psychotics have to be spoon fed, others have no "interest" in anything, others report the appearance of situations that are not in fact present (hallucinations), others show a generalization of anxiety to nearly all situations, yet others exhibit at high strength behaviors such as murder and rape which are lacking in the typical civilized repertoire. The rehabilitation and cure of individuals who display behavior pathologies of these magnitudes are pressing social problems, yet the precise causes of most of these behavior pathologies remain obscure.

During the middle ages, bizarre behaviors were put down to the influence of the devil, and persons exhibiting such behaviors were burned as witches, incarcerated in prisons, and subjected to other hardships designed to exorcise the devil. Man's cruelty to his own kind is nowhere clearer than in the early story of his treatment of disordered individuals. During the nineteenth century, a more enlightened attitude emerged; individuals displaying behavior pathologies began to be viewed as "sick" rather than possessed. Instead of prisons, such individuals were sent to hospitals.

Hospitals are a vast improvement over jails; but a significant implication can be drawn from modern psychology: the causes and cures of behavior pathologies differ markedly from those of organic diseases. Only very recently have behavior pathologies come to be seen as the products of unusual conditioning histories. As such, their cures demand, not medical, but behavioral treatment. It was the Viennese psychiatrist Sigmund Freud who recognized that the causes of certain behavior pathologies lie in the distant past history of the individual. Furthermore, Freud stressed that often the individual was unable to describe the critical past events that led to the pathology. A principal feature of Freud's psychoanalytic method therefore involved supplying verbal S^D's to increase the probability of the patient's reporting incidents from his past that might bear upon the present disorder. It seemed obvious to Freud that treatment partly consisted in making known to the patient himself what his relevant history was. Such a point of view is very much in keeping with what we know about the extinction and adaptation of emotional effects.

We cannot pretend that we have arrived at a clear understanding of exactly what kinds of histories lead to the different pathologies, and what kinds of action should be taken to re-educate individuals into more reinforcing life patterns. Nevertheless, basic behavioral principles of the sort described in this book will surely help to lay a solid experimental foundation for clinical psychology and psychiatry. For, just as the practice of organic medicine derives from the discoveries of fundamental chemical, biochemical, and physiological processes, so must the practice of psychotherapy derive from the discoveries of fundamental behavioral processes.

18.10 AN INDEX OF EMOTIONAL CHANGE

We give a simple method of measuring ongoing operant response-rate suppression or enhancement due to pairing an S_1 with an S^+ or S^-. The method relies on observing the rate of ongoing responding in the period just before S_1 is presented, and then comparing that rate with the rate of responding during S_1. For instance, if S_1 lasts 5 min, we could conveniently measure the rate during the 5 min immediately preceding S_1 and compare that with the rate during S_1 itself. In Fig. 18–12 that would be a comparison in rate from a to b with the rate from b to c. A useful index of behavioral disruption during S_1 is

$$I_e = \frac{c - b}{(c - b) + (b - a)}$$

where I_e is defined as the index of emotional change. It should be clear that $c - b$ is the number of responses during S_1, and $b - a$ the number of responses in a control period immediately before S_1 and of equal duration to S_1. When S_1 and the control period responding are equal (no effect of S_1) then $I_e = 0.5$. When $c - b < b - a$, suppression has occurred and I_e lies between 0 and 0.5, depending on how complete the suppression is. In the case where responding in S_1 happened to be enhanced, $c - b > b - a$, then $1.0 \geq I_e > 0.5$. Evidently I_e ranges from 0 (complete suppression) to 1.0 (complete enhancement: no responding in control period, all in S_1).

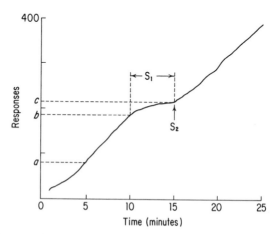

Figure 18–12. The calculation of a suppression index.

EXERCISE 10.

Why is it difficult to define an emotion as a particular behavior pattern?

EXERCISE 11.

Discuss the similarities and differences between emotion and motivation.

EXERCISE 12.

Notate the procedure attributed to Pliskoff in section 18.5.

References for Chapter 18

Ax, A. F. The physiological differentiation between fear and anger in humans. *Psychosom. Med.,* 1953, **15,** 433–442.

Azrin, N. H., Hutchinson, R. R., and Hake, D. F. Extinction-induced aggression. *J. exp. Anal. Behav.,* 1966, **9,** 191–204.

Brady, J. V. Ulcers in executive monkeys. *Sci. Amer.,* 1958, **199,** 95–100.

Brady, J. V. Motivation-emotional factors and intracranial self-stimulation. Chap. 30 in D. E. Sheer (Ed.), *Electrical stimulation of the brain.* Austin: Univer. of Texas Press, 1961.

Brady, J. V. Psychophysiology of emotional behavior. Chap. 10 in A. J. Bachrach (Ed.), *Experimental foundations of clinical psychology.* New York: Basic Books, 1962.

Brady, J. V., and Hunt, H. F. An experimental approach to the analysis of emotional behavior. *J. Psychol.,* 1955, **40,** 313–324.

Brady, J. V., Porter, R. W., Conrad, D. G., and Mason, J. W. Avoidance behavior and the development of gastroduodenal ulcers. *J. exp. Anal. Behav.,* 1958, **1,** 69–72.

Cannon, W. B. The James-Lange theory of emotions: a critical examination and an alternative theory. *Amer. J. Psychol.,* 1927, **39,** 106–124.

Darwin, C. *The expression of the emotions in man and animals.* London: Murray, 1872.

Estes, W. K., and Skinner, B. F. Some quantitative properties of anxiety. *J. exp. Psychol.,* 1941, **29,** 390–400.

Gates, G. S. An observational study of anger. *J. exp. Psychol.,* 1926, **9,** 325–336.

Herrnstein, R. J., and Morse, W. H. Some effects of response-independent positive reinforcement on maintained operant behavior. *J. comp. physiol. Psychol.,* 1957, **50,** 461–467.

Hoffman, H. S., and Fleshler, M. Stimulus factors in aversive controls: the generalization of conditioned suppression. *J. exp. Anal. Behav.,* 1961, **4,** 371–378.

Hoffman, H. S., Fleshler, M., and Jensen, P. K. Stimulus aspects of aversive controls: the retention of conditioned suppression. *J. exp. Anal. Behav.*, 1963, **6**, 575–583.

Hunt, H. F., and Brady, J. V. Some effects of electro-convulsive shock on a conditioned emotional response ("anxiety"). *J. comp. physiol. Psychol.*, 1951, **44**, 88–98.

James, W. *Principles of psychology.* Vol. II. New York: Holt, 1890.

Kimble, G. A., and Garmezy, N. *Principles of general psychology.* (2nd ed.) New York: Ronald, 1963.

Landis, C., and Hunt, W. A. *The startle pattern.* New York: Farrar and Rinehart, 1939.

Leitenberg, H. Conditioned acceleration and conditioned suppression in pigeons. *J. exp. Anal. Behav.*, 1966, **9**, 205–212.

Masserman, J. *Principles of dynamic psychiatry.* Philadelphia: Saunders, 1946.

Pliskoff, S. S. Rate change effects with equal potential reinforcements during the "warning" stimulus. *J. exp. Anal. Behav.*, 1963, **6**, 557–562.

Plutchik, R. *The emotions: facts, theories, and a new model.* New York: Random House, 1962.

Schacter, S., and Singer, J. E. Cognitive, social, and physiological determinants of emotional state. *Psychol. Rev.*, 1962, **69**, 379–399.

Schoenfeld, W. N. An experimental approach to anxiety, escape, and avoidance behavior. Chap. 5 in P. Hoch and J. Zubin (Eds.), *Anxiety.* New York: Grune and Stratton, 1950.

Sidman, M. Normal sources of pathological behavior. *Science,* 1960, **132**, 61–68.

Spitz, R. A. *No and yes.* New York: International Univer. Press, 1957.

Tolman, E. C. A behavioristic account of the emotions. *Psychol. Rev.,* 1923, **30**, 217–227.

Watson, J. B. *Behaviorism.* (rev. ed.) Chicago: Univer. of Chicago Press, 1930.

Young, P. T. *Motivation and emotion.* New York: Wiley, 1961.

INDEX TO REFERENCES

Italicized bracketed numerals after each entry indicate the pages on which the reference is cited.

Andrew, G., and Harlow, H. F. Performance of macaque monkeys on a test of the concept of generalized triangularity. *Comp. psychol. Monogr.*, 1948, **19**, 1–20. [*304*]

Anger, D. The dependence of interresponse times upon the relative reinforcement of different interresponse times. *J. exp. Psychol.*, 1956, **52**, 145–161. [*178*]

Anliker, J., and Mayer, J. Operant conditioning technique for studying feeding patterns in normal and obese mice. *J. appl. Physiol.*, 1956, **8**, 667–670. [*368*]

Anrep, G. V. Pitch discrimination in the dog. *J. Physiol.*, 1920, **53**, 367–385. [*38, 39*]

Antonitis, J. J. Variability of response in the white rat during conditioning and succeeding extinction and reconditioning. Unpublished doctoral dissertation, Columbia Univer., 1950. [*91*]

Antonitis, J. J. Response variability in the white rat during conditioning, extinction, and reconditioning. *J exp. Psychol.*, 1951. **42**, 273–281. [*91, 92*]

Ax, A. F. The physiological differentiation between fear and anger in humans. *Psychosom. Med.*, 1953, **15**, 433–442. [*458*]

Azrin, N. H., Hutchinson, R. R., and Hake, D. F. Extinction-induced aggression. *J. exp. Anal. Behav.*, 1966, **9**, 191–204. [*446, 447*]

Barry, J. J., and Harrison, J. M. Relations between stimulus intensity and strength of escape responding. *Psychol. Rep.*, 1957, **3**, 3–8. [*414*]

Bayley, Nancy. On the growth of intelligence. *Amer. Psychologist*, 1955, **10**, 805–818. [*347*]

Bennett, G. K., Seashore, H. G., and Wesman, A. G. *Counseling from profile. A case book for the Differential Aptitude Tests.* New York: Psychological Corp., 1951. [*349*]

Birch, H. G. The relation of previous experience to insightful problem solving. *J. comp. Psychol.*, 1945, **38**, 367–383. [*335*]

Birch, H. G., and Rabinowitz, H. S. The negative effect of previous experience on productive thinking. *J. exp. Psychol.*, 1951, **41**, 121–125. [*338*]

Blough, D. The shape of some wavelength generalization gradients. *J. exp. Anal. Behav.*, 1961, **4**, 31–40. [*198–199*]

Bolles, R. C. Effect of food deprivation upon the rat's behavior in its home cage. *J. comp. physiol. Psychol.*, 1963, **56**, 456–460. [*388*]

Boren, J. J. Resistance to extinction as a function of the fixed ratio. *J. exp. Psychol.*, 1961, **61**, 304–308. [*173*]

Boring, E. G. *A history of experimental psychology.* New York: The Century Company, 1929. [*8, 12*]

Boring, E. G., Langfeld, H. W., and Weld, H. P. *Foundations of psychology.* New York: Wiley, 1948. [*191, 193*]

Brackbill, Yvonne. Extinction of the smiling responses in infants as a function of the reinforcement schedule. *Child Develpm.*, 1958, **29**, 115–124. [*82*]

Brady, J. V. Ulcers in executive monkeys. *Sci. Amer.*, 1958, **199**, 95–100. [*456, 457*]

Brady, J. V. Motivation-emotional factors and intracranial self-stimulation. Chap. 30 in D. E. Sheer (Ed.), *Electrical stimulation of the brain.* Austin: Univer. of Texas Press, 1961. [*445, 449–450*]

Brady, J. V. Psychophysiology of emotional behavior. Chap. 10 in A. J. Bachrach (Ed.), *Experimental foundations of clinical psychology.* New York: Basic Books, 1962. [*445*]

Brady, J. V., and Hunt, H. F. An experimental approach to the analysis of emotional behavior. *J. Psychol.*, 1955, **40**, 313–324. [*441, 445*]

Brady, J. V., Porter, R. W., Conrad, D. G., and Mason, J. W. Avoidance behavior and the development of gastroduodenal ulcers. *J. exp. Anal. Behav.*, 1958, **1**, 69–72. [*456–457*]

Brandauer, C. M. The effects of uniform probabilities of reinforcement on the response rate of the pigeon. Unpublished doctoral dissertation, Columbia Univer., 1958. [*149, 173*]

Broadhurst, P. L. Emotionality and the Yerkes-Dodson law. *J. exp. Psychol.*, 1957, **54**, 345–352. [*377–378*]

Brogden, W. J., Lipman, E. A., and Culler, E. The role of incentive in conditioning and extinction. *Amer. J. Psychol.*, 1938, **51**, 109–117. [*420–423*]

Brown, J. S., and Jacobs, A. The role of fear in the motivation and acquisition of responses. *J. exp. Psychol.*, 1949, **39**, 747–759. [*418–419*]

Brown, R. How shall a thing be called? *Psychol. Rev.*, 1958a, **65**, 14–21. [*315*]

Brown, R. *Words and things.* Glencoe, Ill.: Free Press, 1958b. [*315*]

Brownell, W. A., and Hendrickson, G. How children learn information, concepts and generalizations. In *Learning and instruction,* 49th Yearb., Nat. Soc. Study Ed., 1950, Part I. [*320*]

Bruner, J. S., Goodnow, Jacqueline J., and Austin, G. A. *A study of thinking.* New York: Wiley, 1956. [*309, 343–344*]

Bullock, D. H., and Smith, W. C. An effect of repeated conditioning-extinction upon operant strength. *J. exp. Psychol.*, 1953, **46**, 349–352. [*98–99*]

Butler, R. A. Discrimination learning by rhesus monkeys to visual-exploratory motivation. *J. comp. physiol. Psychol.*, 1953, **46**, 95–98. [*398*]

Butler, R. A. The effect of deprivation of visual incentives on visual exploration motivation in monkeys. *J. comp. physiol. Psychol.*, 1957, **50**, 177–179. [*399*]

Butter, C. M. Stimulus generalization along one and two dimensions in pigeons. *J. exp. Psychol.*, 1963, **65**, 339–345. [*201*]

Cannon, W. B. The James-Lange theory of emotions: a critical examination and an alternative theory. *Amer. J. Psychol.*, 1927, **39**, 106–124. [*435–436*]

Cannon, W. B., and Washburn, A. L. An explanation of hunger. *Amer. J. Psychol.*, 1912, **29**, 441–452. [*392*]

Capehart, J., Viney, W., and Hulicka, I. M. The effect of effort upon extinction. *J. comp. physiol. Psychol.*, 1958, **51**, 505–507. [*95–97, 109, 111, 112*]

Centers, R. A laboratory adaptation of the conversational procedure for the conditioning of verbal operants. *J. abnorm. soc. Psychol.*, 1963, **67**, 334–339. [*81, 83*]

Church, R. M. The varied effects of punishment on behavior. *Psychol. Rev.*, 1963, **70**, 369–402. [*430*]

Clark, F. C. The effect of deprivation and frequency of reinforcement on variable interval responding. *J. exp. Anal. Behav.*, 1958, **1**, 221–228. [*374–376*]

Cofer, C. N., and Appley, M. H. *Motivation: theory and research.* New York: Wiley, 1964. [*391*]

Cowles, J. T. Food-tokens as incentives for learning by chimpanzees. *Comp. psychol. Monogr.*, 1937, **14**, 1–96. [*244–245*]

Cramér, H. *The elements of probability theory.* Wiley: New York, 1955. [*58*]

Crocetti, C. P. Drive level and response strength in the bar-pressing apparatus. *Psychol. Rep.*, 1962, **10**, 563–575. [*376, 388–389*]

Cronbach, L. J. *Educational psychology.* New York: Harcourt, Brace and World, 1963. [*348*]

Cumming, W. W., and Berryman, R. Some data on matching behavior in the pigeon. *J. exp. Anal. Behav.*, 1961, **4**, 281–284. [*306*]

Cumming, W. W., and Schoenfeld, W. N. Behavior under extended exposure to a high-value fixed interval reinforcement schedule. *J. exp. Anal. Behav.*, 1958, **1**, 245–263. [*143*]

Darwin, C. *The expression of the emotions in man and animals.* London: Murray, 1872. [*8, 434*]

Dennis, W. *Readings in the history of psychology.* New York: Appleton-Century, 1948. [*18*]

Dews, P. B. Studies on behavior. I. Differential sensitivity to pentobarbital of pecking performance in pigeons depending on the schedule of reward. *J. Pharmacol. exp. Ther.*, 1955, **113**, 393–401. [*155*]

Dinsmoor, J. A. A quantitative comparison of the discriminative and reinforcing functions of a stimulus. *J. exp. Psychol.*, 1950, **40**, 458–472. [*249*]

Dinsmoor, J. A., and Hughes, L. H. Training rats to press a bar to turn off shock. *J. comp. physiol. Psychol.*, 1956, **49**, 235–238. [*415*]

Dinsmoor, J. A., and Winograd, E. Shock intensity in variable interval escape schedules. *J. exp. Anal. Behav.*, 1958, **1**, 145–148. [*412, 413, 414*]

Ebbinghaus, H. *Memory* (Translated by H. A. Ruger and C. E. Bussenius). New York: Teachers College, 1913. [*100–102*]

Egger, M. D., and Miller, N. E. Secondary reinforcement in rats as a function of information value and reliability of the stimulus. *J. exp. Psychol.*, 1962, **64**, 97–104. [*249–250*]

Egger, M. D., and Miller, N. E. When is a reward reinforcing? An experimental study of the information hypothesis. *J. comp. physiol. Psychol.*, 1963, **56**, 132–137. [*249–250*]

Estes, W. K., and Skinner, B. F. Some quantitative properties of anxiety. *J. exp. Psychol.*, 1941, **29**, 390–400. [*441*]

Evans, J. L., Homme, L. E., and Glaser, R. The ruleg system for the construction of programmed verbal learning sequences. *J. educ. Res.*, 1962, **55**, 513–518. [*322*]

Fearing, F. *Reflex action: a study in the history of physiological psychology.* Baltimore: Williams and Wilkins, 1930. [*5*]

Ferster, C. B. Control of behavior in chimpanzees and pigeons by time out from positive reinforcement. *Psychol. Monogr.*, 1958, **72**, Whole No. 461. [*430*]

Ferster, C. B. Arithmetic behavior in chimpanzees. *Sci. Amer.*, May 1964, **210**, 98–106. [*303*]

Ferster, C. B., and Skinner, B. F. *Schedules of reinforcement.* New York: Appleton-Century-Crofts, 1957. [*142, 145, 171, 172, 178, 268, 270*]

Findley, J. D. An experimental outline for building and exploring multioperant behavior repertoires. *J. exp. Anal. Behav.*, 1962, **5**, 113–166. [*171*]

Frick, F. C. An analysis of an operant discrimination. *J. Psychol.*, 1948, **26**, 93–123. [*378*]

Frick, F. C., and Miller, G. A. A statistical description of operant conditioning. *Amer. J. Psychol.*, 1951, **64**, 20–36. [*73, 92, 93*]

Garrett, H. *Great experiments in psychology.* New York: Appleton-Century-Crofts, 1951. [*9*]

Gates, G. S. An observational study of anger. *J. exp. Psychol.*, 1926, **9**, 325–336. [*446*]

Gibson, J. J. *The perception of the visual world.* Cambridge: The Riverside Press, 1950. [*326, 328*]

Gilman, A. The relation between blood osmotic pressure, fluid distribution, and voluntary water intake. *Amer. J. Physiol.*, 1937, **120**, 323–328. [*394*]

Goff, W. R. Measurement of absolute olfactory sensitivity in rats. *Amer. J. Psychol.*, 1961, **74**, 384–393. [*217*]

Goldiamond, I. Perception, language, and conceptualization rules. In B. Kleinmuntz (Ed.), *Carnegie Institute of Technology annual symposium on cognition,* New York: Wiley, 1966. [*306, 308*]

Grant, D. A., and Norris, E. B. Eyelid conditioning as influenced by the presence of sensitized beta-responses. *J. exp. Psychol.*, 1947, **37**, 423–433. [*46*]

Guilford, J. P. *General psychology.* Princeton: D. Van Nostrand, 1939. [*102*]

Guthrie, E. R., and Horton, G. P. *Cats in a puzzle box.* New York: Rinehart, 1946. [*74, 92*]

Guttman, N. Operant conditioning, extinction, and aperiodic reinforcement in relation to concentration of sucrose used as reinforcing agent. *J. exp. Psychol.*, 1953, **46**, 213–224. [*390*]

Guttman, N. The pigeon and the spectrum and other complexities. *Psychol. Rep.*, 1956, **2**, 449–460. [*194, 195, 196*]

Guttman, N., and Kalish, H. I. Discriminability and stimulus generalization. *J. exp. Psychol.*, 1956, **51**, 79–88. [*195*]

Guttman, N., and Kalish, H. I. Experiments in discrimination. *Sci. Amer.*, Jan. 1958, **198**, 78–79. [*207*]

Hall, J. F. *Psychology of motivation.* New York: Lippincott, 1961. [*386, 389, 397*]

Hall, G. S., and Hodge, C. F. A sketch of the history of reflex action. *Amer. J. Psychol.*, 1890, **3**, 71–86; 149–173; 343–363. [*7*]

Harlow, H. F. Studying animal behavior. Chap. 12 in T. G. Andrews (Ed.), *Methods of psychology.* New York: Wiley, 1948. [*220, 379, 388*]

Harlow, H. F. The formation of learning sets. *Psychol. Rev.*, 1949, **56**, 51–65. [*222, 292*]

Harlow, H. F. Learning and satiation of response in intrinsically motivated complex puzzle performance by monkeys. *J. comp. physiol. Psychol.*, 1950, **43**, 289–294. [*399*]

Harlow, H. F. Learning set and error factor theory. In S. Koch (Ed.), *Psychology: a study of a science,* Vol. 2. New York: McGraw-Hill, 1959. [*294–295*]

Harlow, H. F. Primary affectional patterns in primates. *Amer. J. Orthopsychiat.*, 1960, **30**, 676–684. [*400–402*]

Harlow, H. F., and Kuenne, M. Learning to think, *Sci. Amer.*, 1949, **181**, 36–39. [*319*]

Hayes, C. *The ape in our house.* New York: Harper and Row, 1951. [*80*]

Hearst, E. Resistance-to-extinction functions in the single organism. *J exp. Anal. Behav.*, 1961, **4**, 133–144. [*95*]

Hebb, D. O. *A textbook of psychology.* Philadelphia: Saunders, 1958. [*352*]

Hefferline, R. F., and Keenan, B. Amplitude-induction gradient of a small-scale (covert) operant. *J. exp. Anal. Behav.*, 1963, **6**, 307–315. [*173–175, 284*]

Heron, W. T., and Skinner, B. F. Changes in hunger during starvation. *Psychol. Rec.*, 1937, **1**, 51–60. [*375*]

Herrick, R. M. Lever displacement during continuous reinforcement and during a discrimination. *J. comp. Physiol. Psychol.*, 1963, **56**, 700–707. [*166*]

Herrick, R. M. The successive differentiation of a lever displacement response. *J. exp. Anal. Behav.*, 1964, **7**, 211–215. [*167*]

Herrick, R. M., Myers, J. L., and Korotkin, A. L. Changes in S^D and S^{Δ} rates during the development of an operant discrimination. *J. comp. physiol. Psychol.*, 1959, **52**, 359–363. [*213–216, 247*]

Herrnstein, R. J. "Will." *Proc. Amer. Phil. Soc.*, 1964, **108**, 455–458. [*254*]

Herrnstein, R. J., and Morse, W H. Some effects of response-independent positive reinforcement on maintained operant behavior *J. comp. physiol. Psychol.*, 1957, **50**, 461–467. [*448–449*]

Herrnstein, R. J., and Loveland, D. H. Complex visual concept in the pigeon. *Science*, 1964, **146**, 549–551. [306].

Hess, E. H. Imprinting in animals. *Sci. Amer.*, 1958, **195**, 81–90. [403]

Hess, E. H. Imprinting. *Science*, 1959, **130**, 133–141. [*403–404*]

Hilgard, E. R., and Marquis, D. G. *Conditioning and learning.* New York: Appleton-Century-Crofts, 1940. [*50*]

Hochberg, J. E. *Perception*, Englewood Cliffs: Prentice-Hall, 1964. [*327*]

Hodos, W. Progressive ratio as a measure of reward strength. *Science*, 1961, **134**, 943–944. [*380–381*]

Hoffman, H. S., and Fleshler, M. Stimulus factors in aversive controls: the generalization of conditioned suppression. *J. exp. Anal. Behav.*, 1961, **4**, 371–378. [*443–444*]

Hoffman, H. S., Fleshler, M., and Jensen, P. K. Stimulus aspects of aversive controls: the retention of conditioned suppression. *J. exp. Anal. Behav.*, 1963, **6**, 575–583. [*443*]

Hoffman, H. S., Searle, J. L., Toffey, Sharon, and Kozma, F. Behavioral control by an imprinted stimulus. *J. exp. Anal. Behav.*, 1966, **9**, 177–189, [*404*]

Holland, J. G. Human vigilance. *Science*, 1958, **128**, 61–67. [*145–146*]

Holz, W. C., and Azrin, N. H. Discriminative properties of punishment. *J. exp. Anal. Behav.*, 1961, **4**, 225–232. [*431*]

Holz, W. C., and Azrin, N. H. A comparison of several procedures for eliminating behavior. *J. exp. Anal. Behav.*, 1963, **6**, 399–406. [*428*]

Honig, W. Generalization of extinction on the spectral continuum. *Psychol. Rec.*, 1961, **11**, 269–278. [*202*]

Hull, C. L. Quantitative aspects of the evolution of concepts. *Psychol. Monogr.*, 1920, **28**, Whole No. 123. [*297–298*]

Hull, C. L. *Principles of behavior.* New York: Appleton-Century-Crofts, 1943. [*163, 164*]

Hunt, H. F., and Brady, J. V. Some effects of electro-convulsive shock on a conditioned emotional response ("anxiety"). *J. comp. physiol. Psychol.*, 1951, **44**, 88–98. [*441–442*]

Hurwitz, H. M. B. Periodicity of response in operant extinction. *Quart. J. exp. Psychol.*, 1957, **9**, 177–184. [*91*]

Irwin, O. C. Infant speech: development of vowel sounds. *J. speech hearing Disorders*, 1952, **17**, 269–279. [*79*]

Jacobson, E. The electrophysiology of mental activities. *Amer. J. Psychol.*, 1932, **44**, 677–694. [283]

James, W. *Principles of psychology.* Vol II. New York: Holt, 1890. [*435–436*]

Jenkins, H. M., and Harrison, R. H. Effect of discrimination training on auditory generalization. *J. exp. Psychol.*, 1960, **59**, 246–253. [*198*]

Jenkins, J. G., and Dallenbach, K. M. Oblivescence during sleep and waking. *Amer. J. Psychol.*, 1924, **35**, 605–612. [*103*]

Kagan, J., and Berkun, M. The reward value of running activity. *J. comp. physiol. Psychol.,* 1954, **47,** 108. [*397*]

Kaplan, M. The effects of noxious stimulus intensity and duration during intermittent reinforcement of escape behavior. *J. comp. physiol. Psychol.,* 1952, **45,** 538–549. [*414*]

Kalish, H. I., and Guttman, N. Stimulus generalization after equal training on two stimuli. *J. exp. Psychol.,* 1957, **53,** 139–144. [*199–200, 202*]

Kalish, H. I., and Guttman, N. Stimulus generalization after training on three stimuli: a test of the summation hypothesis. *J. exp. Psychol.,* 1959, **57,** 268–272. [*199*]

Kantor, J. R. *The scientific evolution of psychology.* Vol. 1. Chicago: Principia Press, 1963. [*3*]

Katona, G. *Organizing and memorizing: studies in the psychology of learning and teaching.* New York: Columbia Univer. Press, 1940. [*339*]

Kelleher, R. Concept formation in chimpanzees. *Science,* 1958, **128,** 777–778. [*302–304*]

Kelleher, R. Schedules of conditioned reinforcement during experimental extinction. *J. exp. Anal. Behav.,* 1961, **4,** 1–5. [*244*]

Kelleher, R., and Gollub, L. A review of positive conditioned reinforcement. *J. exp. Anal. Behav.,* 1962, **5,** 543–597. [*249, 270*]

Keller, F. S., and Schoenfeld, W. N. *Principles of psychology.* New York: Appleton-Century-Crofts, 1950. [*39, 47, 50, 51, 102, 166, 228–229, 251, 301*]

Kendler, H. H. *Basic psychology.* New York: Appleton-Century-Crofts, 1963. [*102*]

Kendler, H. H., and Vineberg, R. The acquisition of compound concepts as a function of previous training. *J. exp. Psychol.,* 1954, **48,** 252–258. [*311–313, 317*]

Kimble, G. A. *Principles of general psychology.* New York: Ronald, 1956. [*74*]

Kimble, G. A., and Garmezy, N. *Principles of general psychology.* (2nd ed.) New York: Ronald Press, 1963. [*299, 346, 459*]

Kleitman, N. *Sleep and wakefulness.* (rev. and enlarged ed.) Chicago: Univer. of Chicago Press, 1963. [*370*]

Köhler, W. *The mentality of apes.* New York: Harcourt, Brace, 1925. [*333–335*]

Landis, C., and Hunt, W. A. *The startle pattern.* New York: Farrar and Rinehart, 1939. [*440*]

Lane, H. L., and Shinkman, P. G. Methods and findings in an analysis of a vocal operant. *J. exp. Anal. Behav.,* 1963, **6,** 179–188. [*153*]

Lashley, K. S. The mechanism of vision XV. Preliminary studies of the rat's capacity for detail vision. *J. gen. Psychol.* 1938, **18,** 123–193. [*218*]

Lee, B. J. Effects of delayed speech feedback. *J. acoust. Soc. Amer.,* 1950, **22,** 824–826. [*276*]

Leitenberg, H. Conditioned acceleration and conditioned suppression in pigeons. *J. exp. Anal. Behav.,* **9,** 205–212. [*446–447*]

Lewis, D. J. *Scientific principles of psychology.* Englewood Cliffs: Prentice-Hall, 1963. [*192*]

Lockard, R. B. Some effects of light upon the behavior of rodents. *Psychol. Bull.,* 1963, **60,** 509–529. [*398*]

Long, Lillian D. An investigation of the original response to the conditioned stimulus. *Arch. Psychol.,* (New York) 1941, No. 259. [*44*]

Luchins, A. S. Mechanization in problem solving: the effect of *Einstellung. Psychol. Monogr.,* 1942, **54,** No. 248. [*336–337*]

Lysaught, J. P., and Williams, C. M. *A guide to programmed instruction.* New York: Wiley, 1963. [*324*]

McCarthy, Dorothea. Language development. In L. Carmichael (Ed.), *Manual of child psychology.* New York: Wiley, 1954. [*277*]

Masserman, J. *Principles of dynamic psychiatry*. Philadelphia: Saunders, 1946. [*454–455*]

Max, L. W. Experimental study of the motor theory of consciousness. IV. Action-current responses in the deaf during awakening, kinaesthetic imagery and abstract thinking. *J. comp. Psychol.*, 1936, **24**, 301–344. [*284*]

Mayer, J. Glucostatic mechanism of regulation of food intake. *New England J. Med.*, 1953, **249**, 13–16. [*393*]

Mechner, F. A notation system for the description of behavioral procedures. *J. exp Anal. Behav.*, 1959, **2**, 133–150. [*118*]

Mechner, F. *Science education and behavioral technology*. New York: Basic Systems, 1963. [*325*]

Mechner, Vicki. *A notation system for behavior contingencies: an instructional program*. New York: Basic Systems, 1963. [*118*]

Mednick, S. A. *Learning*. Englewood Cliffs: Prentice-Hall, 1964. [176]

Melching, W. H. The acquired reward value of an intermittently presented neutral stimulus. *J. comp. physiol. Psychol.*, 1954, **47**, 370–374. [*250*]

Michael, J. *Laboratory studies in operant behavior*. New York: McGraw-Hill, 1963. [*261*]

Millenson, J. R. Random interval schedules of reinforcement. *J. exp. Anal. Behav.*, 1963, **6**, 437–443. [*144, 214*]

Millenson, J. R., and Hurwitz, H. M. B. Some temporal and sequential properties of behavior during conditioning and extinction. *J. exp. Anal. Behav.*, 1961, **4**, 97–105. [73]

Millenson, J. R., Hurwitz, H. M. B., and Nixon, W. L. B. Influence of reinforcement schedules on response duration. *J. exp. Anal. Behav.*, 1961, **4**, 243–250. [*154*]

Miller, N. E. Learnable drives and rewards. Chap. 13 in S. S. Stevens (Ed.), *Handbook of experimental psychology*. New York: Wiley, 1951. [*418*]

Miller, N. E., and Dollard, J. *Social learning and imitation*. New Haven: Yale Univer. Press, 1941. [*252*]

Miller, N. E., Bailey, C. J., and Stevenson, J. A. F. Decreased "hunger" but increased food intake resulting from hypothalamic lesions. *Science,* 1950, **112**, 256–259. [*382*]

Moore, A. U., and Marcuse, F. L. Salivary, cardiac, and motor indices of conditioning in two sows. *J. comp. Psychol.*, 1945, **38**, 1–16. [*51*]

Mostofsky, D. (Ed.) *Stimulus generalization*. Stanford: Stanford Univer. Press, 1965. [*46*]

Mowrer, O. H. and Jones, H. M. Extinction and behavior variability as functions of effortfulness of task. *J. exp. Psychol.*, 1943, **33**, 369–386. [*95*]

Muenzinger, K. F. Motivation in learning: I. Electric shock for correct responses in the visual discrimination habit. *J. comp. Psychol.*, 1934, **17**, 439–448. [*431*]

Muenzinger, K. F., and Fletcher, F. M. Motivation in learning, VI. Escape from electric shock compared with hunger-food tension in the visual discrimination habit. *J. comp. Psychol.*, 1936, **22**, 79–91. [*410–411*]

Munn, N. L. *Handbook of psychological research on the rat*. Boston: Houghton Mifflin, 1950. [*218*]

Murray, E. J. *Motivation and emotion*. Englewood Cliffs: Prentice-Hall, 1964. [*398*]

Myers, J. L. Secondary reinforcement: a review of recent experimentation. *Psychol. Bull.*, 1958, **55**, 284–301. [*249*]

Newell, A., and Simon, H. GPS, a program that simulates human thought. In E. A. Feigenbaum and J. Feldman (Eds.), *Computers and thought,* New York: McGraw-Hill, 1963, pp. 279–293. [*342*]

Notterman, J. M. A study of some relations among aperiodic reinforcement, discrimination training, and secondary reinforcement. *J. exp. Psychol.,* 1951, **41,** 161–169. *[249]*

Notterman, J. M. Force emission during bar pressing. *J. exp. Psychol.,* 1959, **58,** 341–347. *[92]*

Notterman, J., Schoenfeld, W. N., and Bersh, P. J. Conditioned heart rate response in human beings during experimental anxiety. *J. comp. physiol. Psychol.,* 1952, **45,** 1–8. *[43]*

Olds, J. Pleasure centers in the brain. *Sci. Amer.,* Oct. 1956, **195,** 105–116. *[395–396]*

Olds, J. Hypothalamic substrates of reward. *Physiol. Rev.,* 1962, **42,** 554–604. *[396]*

Olds, J., and Milner, P. Positive reinforcement produced by electrical stimulation of septal area and other regions of rat brain. *J. comp. physiol. Psychol.,* 1954, **47,** 419–427. *[395]*

Osgood, C. E. *Method and theory in experimental psychology.* New York: Oxford Univer. Press, 1953. *[47, 78, 204–205]*

Pavlov, I. P. *Conditioned reflexes.* London: Oxford Univer. Press, 1927. *[37, 40, 46, 53–54]*

Pavlov, I. P. *Lectures on conditioned reflexes.* New York: International Publishers, 1928. *[7, 38]*

Perin, C. T. Behavior potentiality as a joint function of the amount of training and the degree of hunger at the time of extinction. *J. exp. Psychol.,* 1942, **30,** 93–113. *[95, 109]*

Pfaffman, C., Goff, W. R., and Bare, J. K. An olfactometer for the rat. *Science,* 1958, **128,** 1007–1008. *[216]*

Pierrel, Rosemary, and Sherman, J. G. Train your pet the Barnabus way. *Brown Alumni Monthly,* Feb. 1963, pp. 8–14. *[263]*

Pliskoff, S. S. Rate change effects with equal potential reinforcements during the "warning" stimulus. *J. exp. Anal. Behav.,* 1963, **6,** 557–562. *[449]*

Pliskoff, S. S., Wright, J. E., and Hawkins, T. D. Brain stimulation as a reinforcer: intermittent schedules. *J. exp. Anal. Behav,* 1965, **8,** 75–88. *[396]*

Plutchik, R. *The emotions: facts, theories, and a new model.* New York: Random House, 1962. *[451, 453]*

Prokasy, W. F. (Ed.) *Classical conditioning: a symposium.* New York: Appleton-Century-Crofts, 1965. *[51]*

Reese, T. W., and Hogenson, Marilyn J. Food satiation in the pigeon. *J. exp. Anal. Behav.,* 1962, **5,** 239–245. *[370–371]*

Reitman, W. R. *Cognition and thought: an information processing approach.* New York: Wiley, 1965. *[314]*

Rheingold, H. L., Gerwitz, J. L., and Ross, H. W. Social conditioning of vocalizations in the infant. *J. comp. physiol. Psychol.,* 1959, **52,** 68–73. *[79]*

Richter, C. P. A behavioristic study of the activity of the rat. *Comp. Psychol. Monogr.,* 1922, **1,** No. 2. *[386–387]*

Richter, C. P. Animal behavior and internal drives. *Quart. Rev. Biol.,* 1927, **2,** 307–343. *[387]*

Romanes, G. J. *Animal intelligence.* (4th ed.) London: Kegan Paul, 1886. *[8]*

Rosenzweig, M. The mechanisms of hunger and thirst. Chap. 3 in L. Postman (Ed.), *Psychology in the making.* New York: Knopf, 1962. *[394]*

Russell, I. S. Analysis of the responding during operant discrimination. Unpublished doctoral dissertation, Indiana Univer., 1960. *[214]*

Sanford, F. *Psychology, a scientific study of man.* Belmont, Calif.: Wadsworth, 1961. *[393]*

Schacter, S., and Singer, J. E. Cognitive, social, and physiological determinants of emotional state. *Psychol. Rev.*, 1962, **69**, 379–399. [*462*]

Schoenfeld, W. N. An experimental approach to anxiety, escape, and avoidance behavior. Chap. 5 in P. Hoch and J. Zubin (Eds.), *Anxiety*. New York: Grune and Stratton, 1950. [*443*]

Schoenfeld, W. N., Antonitis, J. J., and Bersh, P. J. A preliminary study of training conditions necessary for secondary reinforcement. *J. exp. Psychol.*, 1950, **40**, 40–45. [*249*]

Schlosberg, H. A study of the conditioned patellar reflex. *J. exp. Psychol.*, 1928, **11**, 468–494. [*50*]

Siegel, P. S. The relationship between voluntary water intake, body weight loss, and number of hours of water privation in the rat. *J. comp. physiol. Psychol.*, 1947, **40**, 231–238. [*373–374*]

Sidley, N. A., and Schoenfeld, W. N. Behavior stability and response rate as functions of reinforcement probability on "random ratio" schedules. *J. exp. Anal. Behav.*, 1964, **7**, 281–283. [*149*]

Sidman, M. Two temporal parameters of the maintenance of avoidance behavior by the white rat. *J. comp. physiol. Psychol.*, 1953, **46**, 253–261. [*424*]

Sidman, M. Normal sources of pathological behavior. *Science*, 1960, **132**, 61–68. [*445*]

Skinner, B. F. *The behavior of organisms*. New York: Appleton-Century, 1938. [*15, 71, 90, 94, 97, 100, 169, 240, 265–266, 374–375, 426–427*]

Skinner, B. F. A review of C. L. Hull's Principles of behavior. *Amer. J. Psychol.*, 1944, **57**, 276–281. [*14*]

Skinner, B. F. Superstition in the pigeon. *J. exp. Psychol.*, 1948, **38**, 168–172. [*83–84*]

Skinner, B. F. Are theories of learning necessary? *Psychol. Rev.*, 1950, **57**, 193–216. [*100, 151*]

Skinner, B. F. *Science and human behavior*. New York: Macmillan, 1953. [*107–108, 150*]

Skinner, B. F. The science of learning and the art of teaching. *Harvard educ. Rev.*, 1954, **24**, 86–97. [*320*]

Skinner, B. F. A case history in scientific method. *Amer. Psychologist*, 1956, **11**, 221–233. [*64*]

Skinner, B. F. The experimental analysis of behavior. *Amer. Sci.*, 1957, **45**, 343–371. [*61, 178*]

Skinner, B. F. Teaching machines. *Science*, 1958, **128**, 969–977. [*320–321*]

Skinner, B. F. *Cumulative Record*. New York: Appleton-Century-Crofts, 1959. [*67–70*]

Skinner, B. F. Pigeons in a pelican. *Amer. Psychol.*, 1960, **15**, 28–37. [*224–225*]

Skinner, B. F. Why we need teaching machines. *Harvard educ. Rev.*, 1961, **31**, 377–398. [*320*]

Skinner, B. F., and Morse, W. H. Fixed-interval reinforcement of running in a wheel. *J. exp. Anal. Behav.*, 1958, **1**, 371–379 [*180*]

Smith, Margaret F., and Smith, K. U. Thirst-motivated activity and its extinction in the cat. *J. gen. Psychol.*, 1939, **21**, 89–98. [*370*]

Smoke, K. L. An objective study of concept formation. *Psychol. Monogr.*, 1932, **42**, Whole No. 191. [*299*]

Solomon, R. L. Punishment. *Amer. Psychologist*, 1964, **19**, 239–253. [*430*]

Spencer, H. *The principles of psychology*. New York: D. Appleton, 1878. [*62*]

Spitz, R. A. *No and yes*. New York: International Univer. Press, 1957. [*464*]

Swartz, P. *Psychology the study of behavior*. Princeton: Van Nostrand, 1963. [*225*]

Teitelbaum, P. Sensory control of hypothalamic hyperphagia. *J. comp. physiol. Psychol.*, 1955, **48**, 156–163. [*382*]

Templeton, R. D., and Quigley, J. P. The action of insulin on the mobility of the gastro-intestinal tract. *Amer. J. Physiol.*, 1930, **91**, 467–474. *[392]*

Terrace, H. S. Discrimination learning with and without "errors." *J. exp. Anal. Behav.*, 1963a, **6**, 1–27. *[226]*

Terrace, H. S. Errorless transfer of a discrimination across two continua. *J. exp. Anal. Behav.*, 1963b, **6**, 224–232. *[226–227]*

Thorndike, E. L. Animal intelligence. *Psychol. Rev. Monogr. Suppl.* 1898, No. 8. *[9, 331, 339–340]*

Thurstone, L. L. Testing intelligence and aptitudes. *Hygeia*, 1945, **53**, 32–36. *[348]*

Tolman, E. C. A behavioristic account of the emotions. *Psychol. Rev.*, 1923, **30**, 217–227. *[438]*

Toulmin, S., and Goodfield, June. *The architecture of matter.* New York: Harper and Row, 1962. *[4]*

Verhave, T. Avoidance responding as a function of simultaneous and equal changes in two temporal parameters. *J. exp. Anal. Behav.*, 1959, **2**, 185–190. *[425]*

Verplanck, W. S. The control of the content of conversation. *J. abnorm. soc. Psychol.*, 1955, **51**, 668–676. *[81]*

Wald, G. Eye and camera. *Sci. Amer.*, Aug. 1950, **182**, 32–41. *[191]*

Wallach, H. Brightness constancy and the nature of achromatic colors. *J. exp. Psychol.*, 1958, **38**, 310–324. *[190]*

Warden, C. J. *Animal motivation studies.* New York: Columbia Univer. Press, 1931. *[379–380]*

Warden, C. J., and Aylesworth, M. The relative value of reward and punishment in the formation of a visual discrimination habit in the white rat. *J. comp. Psychol.*, 1927, **7**, 117–127. *[429]*

Watson, J. B. Psychology as the behaviorist views it. *Psychol. Rev.*, 1913, **20**, 158–177. *[13]*

Watson, J. B. *Behavior, an introduction to comparative psychology.* New York: Holt, 1914. *[282]*

Watson, J. B. Is thinking merely the action of language mechanisms? *Brit. J. Psychol.*, 1920, **11**, 87–104. *[282]*

Watson, J. B. *Behaviorism.* (rev. ed.) Chicago: Univer. of Chicago Press, 1930. *[439]*

Wechsler, D. *The measurement and appraisal of adult intelligence,* Baltimore: Williams and Wilkins, 1958. *[345]*

Weeks, J. R. Experimental narcotics addiction. *Sci. Amer.*, Mar. 1964, **210**, 46–52. *[406]*

Weinstock, S. Resistance to extinction of a running response following partial reinforcement under widely spaced trials. *J. comp. physiol. Psychol.*, 1954, **47**, 51–56. *[152–153]*

Weiss, B., and Laties, V. G. Titration behavior on various fractional escape programs. *J. exp. Anal. Behav.*, 1959, **2**, 227–248. *[416]*

Weiss, B., and Laties, V. G. Characteristics of aversive thresholds measured by a titration schedule. *J. exp. Anal. Behav.*, 1963, **6**, 563–572. *[416]*

Weissman, N. W., and Crossman, E. K. A comparison of two types of extinction following fixed-ratio training. *J. exp. Anal. Behav.*, 1966, **9**, 41–46. *[173]*

Weitzman, E. D., Ross, G. S., Hodos, W., and Galambos, R. Behavioral method for study of pain in the monkey. *Science*, 1961, **133**, 37–38. *[417]*

Welch, L. A behaviorist explanation of concept formation. *J. genet. Psychol.*, 1947, **71**, 201–222. *[315]*

Wertheim, G. A. Some sequential aspects of IRTs emitted during Sidman-avoidance behavior in the white rat. *J. exp. Anal. Behav.*, 1965, **8**, 9–15. *[424]*

Whiting, J. W. M., and Mowrer, O. H. Habit progression and regression—a laboratory investigation of some factors relevant to human socialization. *J. comp. Psychol.*, 1943, **36**, 229–253. [*428–429*]

Williams, C. D. The elimination of tantrum behavior by extinction procedures. *J. abnorm. soc. Psychol.*, 1959, **59**, 269. [*105–106*]

Williams, S. B. Resistance to extinction as a function of the number of reinforcements. *J. exp. Psychol.*, 1938, **23**, 506–522. [*95, 109*]

Wilson, M. P., and Keller, F. S. On the selective reinforcement of spaced responses. *J. comp. physiol. Psychol.*, 1953, **46**, 190–193. [*176–177*]

Wolfe, J. B. Effectiveness of token-rewards for chimpanzees. *Comp. psychol. Monogr.*, 1936, **12**, 1–72. [*244*]

Wolfle, H. M. Conditioning as a function of the interval between the conditioned and the original stimulus. *J. gen. Psychol.*, 1932, **7**, 80–103. [*49*]

Wyckoff, L. B., Jr. The role of observing responses in discrimination learning: Part I. *Psychol. Rev.*, 1952, **59**, 431–442. [*247*]

Young, F. A. Studies of pupillary conditioning. *J. exp. Psychol.*, 1958, **55**, 97–110. [*50*]

Young, P. T. *Motivation and emotion*. New York: Wiley, 1961. [*434, 461*]

Young, P. T., and Richey, H. W. Diurnal drinking patterns in the rat. *J. comp. physiol. Psychol.*, 1952, **45**, 80–89 [*369*]

Zeaman, D., and Smith, R. W. Review of some recent findings in human cardiac conditioning. Chap. 19 in W. F. Prokasy (Ed.), *Classical conditioning*. New York: Appleton-Century-Crofts, 1965. [*43*]

Zimmerman, D. W. Durable secondary reinforcement: method and theory. *Psychol. Rev.*, 1957, **64**, 373–383. [*241–244*]

Zimmerman, D. W. Sustained performance in rats based on secondary reinforcement. *J. comp. physiol. Psychol.*, 1959, **52**, 353–358. [*241–244*]

SUBJECT INDEX

Acquired drives, 403–407
Acquired reinforcers, 237 ff.
  strength of, 270
Activity, general, 385–389
  food deprivation on, 386
  operant level of, 385, 388–389
  pattern and food deprivation, 388
  sexual cycles and, 387
  spontaneous, 385–389
  in stabilimeter, 387–388
  wheel, 386
    for study of avoidance, 420
Adaptation, to electric shock, 443
  of emotions, 462–463
Addiction, 405–407
Adrenalin, in emotion, 461–462
Aggression, 446–447
Algorithm, 282, 339–340
Anger, 39, 445–447
  conditioned, 447
Animals, in psychological experiments,
    205–207
  ability to form concepts, 301–307,
    319
Animal spirits, 4, 5
Anthropomorphism, 8
Anxiety paradigm, 441–445
  superimposed on avoidance behavior,
    445
Apparatus, for addiction study, 406
  Columbia obstruction box, 379
  jumping stand, 218
  maze, 264
  mirror-tracing, 176

  pigeon chamber, 101, 115
  puzzle box, 9
  response displacement lever, 166
  running wheel, 179, 386
  runway, 152
  shuttle box, 418
  Skinner's lever-box, 15, 65
  stabilimeter, 387–388
  stomach balloon, 392
  string-pull for monkeys, 220
  T maze for study of escape, 410
  teaching machine, 321
  Wisconsin general test, 290 ff.
Approach-avoidance conflict, 454–455
Asymptote, of a function, defined, 55
  of discrimination process, 216
Arithmetic problem solving, 279–282
Attention, as conditioned reinforcer,
    365
  as covert observing behavior, 248
  as a generalized reinforcer, 246
Autonomic nervous system, 51, 458–
    462
Average value, of set of measurements,
    30, 32–33
Aversive stimuli, 409 ff.
  conditioned, 417–426
  unconditioned, 410
Avoidance behavior, acquisition of,
    419–426
  effects of anxiety paradigm on, 445
  of emotional respondents, 463
  and ulceration, 456–457
  without a warning signal, 424–426

Backward conditioning, 49
Baseline; *see also* Steady states
  for study of emotion, 441
Behavior, aggressive, 446–447
  Aristotle's categories of, 4
  covert, 248
  emotional, 433 ff.
  instrumental, 9
  operant observing, 145
  prediction and control of, 13
  reflex, 5
  suppression of, 426–427, 466
  topography of, 73–74
Behavioral baselines, 154–155
Behavioral process, 41
  definition of, 56
Behavioral repertoire, of language re-
    sponses, 318
Behavioral stream, the, 157
Brain (diagram), 394
Brain lesions, and conditioned sup-
    pression, 445
  and food drive, 382
Brain stimulation reinforcer, 395–396,
    449

Cause of behavior, 3
  anecdotal, 8–9
  deprivation variables, 366
  emotion as, 433–437, 455
  extinction as, 107
  fictional, 362
  future as, 419
  medieval conceptions of, 4
  motives, 365
  past conditioning histories, 363–364,
    465
  in pathological cases, 465
Cause and effect, in science, 359–360
  sequence of in emotion, 435
Chains of behavior
  branching, 278
  breakdown due to delayed S^D's, 276
  breaking, 446
  covert, 282–284
  elements of, 257
  grammatical utterances as, 277–278
  heterogeneous (defined), 265
  homogeneous (defined), 269
  language, 274–278
  links (defined), 257
  in mazes, 264–265
  members (defined), 257
  performance of musical passages as,
    273
  in problem solving, 332–343
  processes in development of, 259–260

resolution in, 258–259
  adding response members to, 260–
    262
  and satiation, 370
  selective extinction applied to, 265–
    267
  and sentence development, 277
  of vocal responses, 262, 274–278
  and walking, 271–272
Chained schedules, 268–271
Clasp reflex, 400
Classical conditioning; *see* Pavlovian
    conditioning
Coefficient of correlation, 352
Complex human behavior, 289 ff.
Computer flow chart notation, 280–
    281
Computer simulation of human prob-
    lem solving, 342–343
Concept, acquisition, 289 ff.
  conjunctive, 311
  of conjunctive properties, 312–313
  as control by stimulus relationships,
    299
  of counterclockwise rotation, 306
  and discrimination acquisition, 300–
    301
  disjunctive, 307–310
  drive, 366–367, 383
  hierarchical structure of, 315
  of person, 307
  of reinforcer strength, 383
  relational, 296 ff.
  of "threeness" in chimpanzees, 303
Concept formation; *see* Concept acqui-
    sition
Concepts, of drive, 383
  interdisciplinary, 391
  in scientific laws, 21–22, 27
  simple *vs.* compound, 317
  taught in schools, 320
  transformational, 326
Conditioned aversive stimuli, 417–419
Conditioned fear, 441–445
Conditioned negative reinforcer, 417–
    419
Conditioned reflexes; *see* reflexes, con-
    ditioned
Conditioned reinforcement, "in main-
    taining chains, 266
Conditioned suppression, 443–445
  retention of, 443
Conditioned avoidance, 419–426
Conditioning
  comparison between Pavlovian and
    operant, 85
  escape, 410–415

Pavlovian, of emotions, 438–439
  in experimental anxiety, 441–443
  in mixed emotions, 454–455
  using S⁻, 417–419
  time, 49–50
Conflict, approach-avoidance, 454–455
  of motives, 390
Constancies, perceptual, 326–329
Contingencies, behavioral, 122 ff.; see
      also Schedules, reinforcement
  in acquiring meaning, 315
  aversive in society, 464
  branching, 278–282
  as causes of behavior, 363–364
  in chains, 257 ff.
  discrimination, 135, 217 ff.
    in learning sets, 291
  duration of, 128–129
  escape, 412
  functional, 135–136
  imitative, 252–253
  matching to sample, 305
  multiple, 125–127
  negative, 133–134
  nested, 136–137
  null, 127–128
  phylogenetic, 329, 389, 434, 450–
      451
  probabilistic, 134–135
  punishment, 426–430
  repetitive, 130–132
Contingency, continuous reinforcement
      (crf), 66
  superstitious, 83
Continuity of behavior, 157, 179
Contrast, brightness, 190–191
Control, of behavior, see Causes of be-
      havior; Environmental control
Control, of emotions, 462–465
  experimental, 53
  Sᴰ; see Discrimination
Controlled experiment, 52–53
Correlation, degree vs. form of, 350–
      351
  coefficient of, 352
Covariance, of motivational measures,
      383
Curiosity behavior, 398
Cumulative recorder, 67–70
Cumulative response curves
  construction of, 67 t.
  stacking of, 141

Definition, as a meaning structure, 316–
      317
Delay conditioning, 49–50
Delayed auditory feedback, 276

Dependent variable, definition of, 53
  rate of response as, 15
Deprivation operations, 365–367
Deprivation, of visual exploration, 399
Differential reinforcement of high rates
      (drh), 178
Differential reinforcement of low rates
      (drl), 176–178
Differentiation, 163–181
  of force of responding, 163–165, 169
  progressive; see Successive approxi-
      mation
Discrimination, classified by complexity,
      212
  based on conditioned reinforcement,
      245
  based on intrinsic reinforcers, 398
  contingencies, 217 ff.
  errorless, 226–228
  of forms, 304
  index, 215
  light-dark underwater, 377–378
  odor, 216–217
  process in learning set formation,
      291–294
  social, 253
  as a test operation, 280
Discriminative operant, 229
Discriminative reaction time, 228–229
Dispersion of measurements; see Vari-
      ability in measurements
Drinking, periodicities in, 369
Drives, activity, 397
  acquired, 402–407
  comparison of strengths of, 379–380
  concept of, 366–367, 383
  as director of behavior, 389–390
  as energizer, 385–389
  measurement of, 372–383
  and physiological factors, 391–396
Drive operations, adrenalectomy, 382–
      383
  deprivation, 365–367
    of air, 377
    of food, 375, 380
    of water, 373
  and liquid reinforcers, 367
  prefeeding, 374–375
  satiation, 367
drl, and elation paradigm, 448–449
Drugs, addiction to, 405–407
  effects on behavior, 155
  and emotional behavior, 461–462
  and shock-tolerance level, 416–417
Dualism, 4
Durability of secondary reinforcers,
      239–244

Early experience, 401–402
  on later emotional development, 464
Eating, periodicities in, 368
  physiological mechanisms in, 392–393
Elation, 447–450
Electric shock; see Shock, electric
Electroconvulsive shock (ECS), 445
Electrode implantation in brain, 393
Elicitor, 20
Emotions, 433 ff.
  mixed, 453–455
  primary, 452 t.
Environment, 120–121
Environmental control, of operants, 187–188
  by unrelated stimuli, 310
Escape, from conditioned S$^-$, 423–424
  training, 410–415
Executive monkey experiment, 357, 456–457
Experiment, defined, 55
Experimental method, 52–56
Explanation; see also Causes of behavior
  causal, 24–25
  empty, 24
  Pavlov's conception of, 7
  purposive, 419–420
  teleological, 419–420
Exploratory reinforcers, 397
Expression of emotions, 434
Extinction, 147
  applied to elements of chains, 265–268
  as a cause of behavior, 363–364
  of child's crying, 105–106
  definition of, 104
  emotional effects in, 89
  and forgetting, 100–104
  generalization of, 201–203
  latency, 267–268
  one-trial, 99
  of pathological emotional responses, 465
  process of, 89 ff.
  punishment during, 426–427
  resistance to, 93–97, 109–112
    amount of reinforcement and, 95
    effort of response and, 95
  response rate changes during, 90–91
  in secondary reinforcement tests, 239
  spontaneous recovery from, 97–98
  in testing power of conditioned aversive stimuli, 419
  in testing stimulus generalization, 196
  topographical changes in, 91–93
  variability of behavior in, 92–93

Eye, compared to camera, 189, 191

Fading elements of discriminative stimuli, 273
Fear, 438 t., 460
Feedback, 276
Feelings, as private events, 436–437
Flow chart notation, 280–281
Food deprivation, and general activity, 386
Forgetting, 100–104
Frequency distribution, 32–36
Frequency polygon, 33–34
Frustration, adaptation to, 463
  paradigm, 446
Functional relationships, 359–362

Generalized reinforcers, 245–246
General Problem Solver, 342–343
General activity; see Activity
Generalization; see also Stimulus generalization
  of conditioned suppression, 443–444
  of extinction, 201–203
  gradient, 195–200, 227
Graphical representation, three-dimensional, 110
Group design, 95–97
Guilt, 454

Habituation; see Adaptation
Hallucinations, 465
Heuristic search strategies, 341–343
Histogram, 33–34
  of S^D and S$^\Delta$ response rates, 232
Hue matching in animals, 306
Hunger, 367, 392
Hypothalamus, role in eating behavior, 393
Hypothetical construct, of reflex strength, 26–27

Illusion, Müller-Lyer, 190–191
Imitation, 252–253
  limitations of, 275
Imprinting, 403–405
Incentive, 390–391
Individual differences, 259
  in human problem solving, 346–347
Index, of discrimination performance, 215
  of emotional disruption, 466
Independent variable, definition of, 53
Induction; see Response induction
Information, in concept identification, 343

provided by discriminative stimuli, 246–250
Insight, in problem solving, 335
Instrumental behavior, 9–10, 64
Intelligence, 345–349, 352–353
  and age, 346–47
  measurement of, 353
  quotient, 347–348
Intervening variables; *see* Variable, compound
Intracranial stimulation, 395–396, 449

Joy, 438 t.; *see also* Elation paradigm

Language, as chains, 275–278
  in concept interrelationships, 316
  general problems for psychology and, 274
Latency, of conditioned responses, 46
  of reflex respondents, 20, 23
Latent extinction, 267–268
Laws, concepts in, 21–22
  as functional relationships, 359–362
  generality of scientific, 22
  limitations of scientific, 364
  reflex, 23
  scientific usage, 359–360
  stimulus-response, 6
Law of effect, 10, 16, 75
Law of least effort, 168, 428
Law of the threshold, 23
Learning sets, 290–297
  oddity, 296
  relation to human concept formation experiments, 300
  variables affecting acquisition of, 294–295
Lesions; *see* Brain lesions
Lie detector, 463
Light, as an aversive stimulus, 414
Light reinforcement, 398
Liquid deprivation, and resistance to satiation, 373–374

Masochism, 430
Matching to sample, 305–307
Maze, escape behavior in, 410
  exploratory reinforcers in, 397
Mean, of a frequency distribution, 33
Meaning, as conceptual interbehavior, 310–318
  of response rates, 372–373
Measurements, of behavioral suppression, 466
  of drive, 373–383
  reliability of, 353
  validity of, 353–354

Median of a frequency distribution, 33
Mental processes, 11–13
Mixed emotions, 453–455
Mode, of a frequency distribution, 32–33
Model, Descartes' hydraulic, 4
  of emotional phenomena, 451
Morphine, effect on shock-tolerance level of, 416–417
  experimental addiction to, 405–407
Mother, surrogate, 400–402
Motives of behavior, 364–365
Motivation, 359 ff.
  distinguished from emotion, 441
  physiological factors in, 391–396
Muscle potential in imagery, 283–284

Need, 375–376
Negative reinforcers, 409 ff.
  termination of, 452
Neurosis, 464
Noise, as an aversive stimulus, 414
Nonsense syllables, 101–103
Normal curve, 35–36, 232–233

Observing behavior, 145
Observing responses, 246–248
Oddity problems, 296
Operant; *see also* Response
  behavior, 64
  conditioning, 84–85; *see also* Operant strengthening
  disruption in emotion, 439 ff.
  fixed ratio (*FR*), 170–173, 177, 241–243
  generic definition of, 160–161
  higher order, 170–173, 177
  methods for creating, 170
  relation to computer operations, 280
  small scale, 173–175
  stimulus control, 229–231
  strengthening, 61–87
    behavior stereotypy in; *see* Variability changes
    by conditioned reinforcement, 239 ff.
    as cause of behavior, 363–364
    laws of, 75
    paradigm, 77
    process, 78
    with S⁻, 411
    variability changes in, 73–74
Operant-level measurements, 65–66
Option, to produce discriminative stimuli, 247

Parasympathetic system of ANS, 460

Parameters, defined, 112
of negative reinforcement, 412
Pathological emotional phenomena, 464–465
Pause after reinforcement, *FI*, 141–143
FR, 171–172
Pavlov's law of conditioning, 6
Pavlovian conditioning, 37–59
of emotions, 51–52, 438–439
in experimental anxiety, 441–445
in mixed emotions, 454–455
optimum S_1—S_2 interval in, 49
pairing procedures in, 47–50
in secondary reinforcement training, 250
stimulus substitution in, 42, 50–52
temporal relations in, 47–50
Perceptual constancies, 326–329
neutral color, 327
shape, 326–327
size, 327–329
Periodicities in reinforcement value, 367–369
Phoneme, 78, 85–86
Phylogenetic contingencies, 329, 389, 434, 450–451
Physiological factors, in eating, 392–394
in drinking, 394
Physiological psychology, 391
and emotion study, 458
techniques in, 394–395
Physiological states, of emotion, 435
Pitch, 192
Play, as reinforcer, 399
Prefeeding, as a drive operation, 374–375
Preference experiment, 382–383
Primary emotions, 452 t.
Probability, 56–59
of reinforcement, 147–151
Problem, definition of, 304, 331–332
as a set of discrimination contingencies, 291
Problem solving, as branching chains, 279–282
definition of solutions in, 338–339
tests of, 345–346
Programmed instruction, 67–70 t., 320–326
frames in, 320
teaching machines in, 321
as a vehicle for teaching concepts, 322–326
Programmed text, 322
Progressive ratio procedure, 380–381
Prompts, verbal, 273

Proprioceptors, 193
in chaining, 272
Psychic secretions; *see* Salivary conditioning
Psychosis, 465
Psychology, definition of, 372
Psychophysics, 12
Psychosomatic medicine, 455–458
Psychotherapy, 465–466
Punishment, 426–430
as aid in acquiring alternative behaviors, 429
in educational institutions, 429
as an S^D, 431
Purposive behavior, 62–64
Puzzles, 335–339
as reinforcers for monkeys, 399
Puzzle box, 9–10

Quantity of reinforcement, compared with shock-off time, 415
Quinine adulteration of food, 382

Reaction time, asymptotic, 228–229
to onset of negative reinforcers, 412
in maze experiments, 264
in runway, 152
Receptors, 188
Rectangular coordinate system, 53–54
Reflex, clasp, 400
conditioned, 6–7, 40
compared with unconditioned reflex, 45–47
as explanatory principle, 19
second order, 46–47
fatigue, 24
patterns, in emotion, 437–438
Pavlov's contribution to, 6
relationships, 20
unconditioned, 19–28
compared with conditioned, 45–47
Reinforcement; *see also* Differentiation
circularity of, 76–77
conditioned, and electric shock, 431
contingency; *see* Contingency, behavioral
of continuous behavior, 179
crf, 139, 147
definition of, 76
generalization of, 203
of human and animal sounds, 78–80
intermittent, 139 ff.
non-contingent, 448–449
of rates of responding, 150, 175–178, 448–449
social, 251–254

Reinforcers, activity, 397
  acquired, 237 ff.
  body contact, 464
  brain stimulation, 395–396
  conditioned, 237 ff. 248–250
    negative, 417–419
  definition of, 76
  exploration, 397
  food, and stomach contractions, 392
    and blood glucose, 393
    and hypothalamic centers, 393
  generalized, 245–246, 365
  by imprinted object, 403–405
  intrinsic, 397–400
  lack of normal, 465
  light and dark, 398
  morphine, 406–407
  negative, 409 ff.
    termination of, 452 t.
    as elicitors, 417
  physical contact, 400–402
  primary, 237, 365, 367–368
  quality and quantity, 390–391
  secondary, 237 ff.
  strength of, 364, 372–383
    in emotion, 440
    periodicities in, 367–369
    sexual and general activity, 387
  termination of, 452 t.
  unconditioned, 237
  value; see Reinforcer, strength of
  water, and state of mouth, 394
    and cellular factors, 394
    and hypothalamic centers, 394
Relative frequency distribution, calcu-
    lation of, 36
Repertoire, behavioral, initial, 333
  as skills in problem solving, 279–280
Resistance to extinction, of FR oper-
    ants, 173
  after uniform probability reinforce-
    ment, 153–154
  after VI, 151
Resistance to satiation, 373–374
Respondent behavior, generic definition
    of, 158
  elicitation of, 23–25
Respondent conditioning; see Pavlovian
    conditioning
Respondents, autonomic, 435–458
  in emotion, 434–435
  masked by operants, 463
Response, classes, definition of, 157–
    163
  color-naming, 189
  conditioned, 41–43

differentiation, 163–181
dimensions, 159–160
emitted, 65
induction, 175
observing, 246–248
operant, 16, 75, 118–120
probability, 16, 107–108
rate of, 15
  changes in relative, 71–72
reflex, 5
respondent, 20
strength, 213, 268–269, 373
variability, after VI schedule, 153
  after uniform probability schedule,
    154
variants, distribution of reinforced,
    166
Retention, of conditioned suppression,
    443
of verbal behaviors, see Forgetting
Rage, 438 t.
Runway, 152

S^D, 212
S$^\Delta$, 212
Sadism, 426
Salivary conditioning, 37–40
Salt solution, as reinforcer for adre-
    nalectomized rat, 383
Satiation, 367
  curves of, 371
  of intrinsic reinforcers, 400
  resistance to, 373–374
Schedules, reinforcement
  chained, 268–271
  conditioned, 244
  in discrimination training, 213
  fixed-interval (FI), 140–144
  fixed-ratio (FR); see Operant, fixed-
    ratio
  random-interval (RI), 144
  and response variability, 153–154
  theoretical descriptions of, 181
  uniform probability, 147–149
    in establishing powerful con-
      ditioned reinforcers, 241–242
    of FR operants, 172–173
  variable-interval (VI), 145
    as baseline for emotion study,
      441–442
    with S$^-$, 413
Selective reinforcement; see Differen-
    tiation
Self-stimulation of brain, 396
Sensitization of emotional responses,
    462
Sentences, as chains of behavior, 277

Set, in problem solving, 336–339
Set theory, 162–163, 181–184, 311
Shock, electric
   S⁻ in escape training, 411 ff.
   intensity and escape rate, 413–414
   partial reduction of, 415–417
Shock-tolerance level, 416
Shuttle box, 418
Sidman procedure, 425–426
Similarity; see Stimulus similarity
Simultaneous pairing of stimuli, 48
Skills, in problem solving, 279–280
Sleep, periodicities in, 369–370
   effect on forgetting, 103
Small scale operant, 173–175
Social behavior, 251–254
Soul, 4–6, 8
Sound stimuli, 190–193
Spontaneous activity; see Activity
Spontaneous recovery from extinc-
   tion, 97–98
Stabilimeter, 387–388
Standard deviation, 233
Starvation in rats, 375–376
Statistical tests, of differences between
   two means, 231–235
Statistical significance, 235
Steady states, 154–155; see also Base-
   lines
   of shock intensity, 416–417
Stimulus, 188
   aversive, 409 ff.
      conditioned, 417–426
      unconditioned, 410
   control, in concepts, 300–301
   definition of, 121
   Descartes' conception of, 5
   dimensions, 188–194
   discriminative, 211 ff.
      ability to reinforce, 238–239
      private, 436–437
   eliciting, 23–25
   generalization, 194–205
      gradient, 195–200; see also Gen-
      eralization of extinction
   intensity, in emotions, 451–453
   light, 188–190
   neutral, 44
   novel, as reinforcer, 397–398
   redundancy, 250
   reinforcing; see Reinforcers; Rein-
      forcement
   similarity, 194, 204–205
   sound, 190–193
   substitution, 42–43
   Whytt's rediscovery of, 5

Stomach contractions, role in eating,
   392
Strength of behavior, 107
Successive conditioning and extinction,
   98–99
Successive approximation, 168–170,
   262
   in discrimination training, 227
   of fixed ratio (FR) behavior, 171
Superstition, 83–84
Suppression index, 466
Sympathetic system of autonomic nervous system, 460

Teaching process, as social interaction,
   254
Temporal conditioning, 49–50
Temporal summation, 25
Theories, of emotion, 433–436
Theory of evolution, 8
Thinking, as covert problem solving,
   282–284
Thirst, 367, 394
Threshold, 217
   of reflex respondents, 20, 23
Time-out, from aversive stimulation,
   415
   as punishment, 430
Titration procedure; see Shock, electric
Token rewards, 244–245
Topography of behavior, 159
Trace conditioning, 48
Tracking, 224–226
Transformations of disjunctive concepts,
   309
Trial and error responding, 332–333

Understanding; see Meaning

Value of reinforcement; see Reinforcer,
   strength
Variable, compound, 215
Variability, in measurements, 29–36
   in extinction, 92
   after operant strengthening, 73–74
Verbal conditioning, 81–82

Waiting behavior, 176–178, 254
Wave properties of light, 188–189
Weakening of behavior; see Extinction
White noise, 193
Wisconsin general test apparatus, 222,
   290 ff.

Yoked experiment, 456

Zeitgeist, the, 10–11

Table of Behavioral Paradigms

CHAPTER AND NAME	GIVEN	PROCEDURE	PROCESS	RESULT
[2] Reflex adaptation	An elicitor, S_2	Repeatedly present S_2	R_2, the elicited response, declines in magnitude, increases in latency, etc.	Reflex strength is temporarily lowered
[3] Pavlovian conditioning	Two elicitors, S_1 and S_2	Repeatedly pair S_1 with S_2	S_1 comes to control a new response (CR), which may resemble R_2	S_1 reliably evokes CR
[4] Operant strengthening	1. An operant R at >0 frequency 2. A suitable reinforcer	$R \rightarrow S^+$	1. Increase in rate of R to new stable value 2. R becomes incorporated into a loop of behavior 3. The variability of R topography decreases	
[5] Operant extinction	A previously strengthened R	$R \nrightarrow$	1. Decline in rate of R 2. Disintegration of loop of behavior 3. Increase in variability of form and magnitude of R	Behavior processes approach operant level states
[8] Differentiation	A class of behavior at >0 strength	Reinforcement is applied to one set of variants within	1. Strengthening of reinforced variants	The reinforced variants are at high strength